READER'S DIGEST

IS IT HARMFUL IS IT HEALTHY?

A Complete
Guide to What's
Good For You...
and What Isn't

Reader's
Digest

THE READER'S DIGEST ASSOCIATION, INC.
Pleasantville, New York/Montreal

IS IT HARMFUL IS IT HEALTHY?

A Complete Guide to
What's Good For You…
and What Isn't

Books and Home Entertainment

VICE PRESIDENT
Deirdre Gilbert

MANAGING EDITOR
Philomena Rutherford

ART DIRECTOR
John McGuffie

DIRECTOR OF PUBLISHING
Loraine Taylor

Editorial

PROJECT EDITOR
Anita Winterberg

SENIOR EDITORS
Andrew Byers
Andrew Jones

ASSOCIATE EDITOR
Enza Micheletti

COPY EDITOR
Gilles Humbert

Art

DESIGNER
Andrée Payette

Production

PRODUCTION MANAGER
Holger Lorenzen

PRODUCTION COORDINATOR
Susan Wong

U.S. Staff

EDITOR
Marianne Wait

DESIGNER
Andrew Ploski

ASSOCIATE EDITORS
David Egner
Mary Lyn Maiscott

ASSOCIATE DESIGNERS
Patrizia Bove
Jason Peterson

RESEARCH EDITORS
Deirdre van Dyk
Maymay Quey Lin

EDITORIAL/RESEARCH ASSISTANT
Claudia Kaplan

STAFF CONTRIBUTORS
Susan Howard Biederman
David Diefendorf
Alexis Lipsitz
Bruce R. McKillip
Marisa Gentile Raffio
Thomas A. Ranieri
Susan Welt

EDITORIAL DIRECTOR
Wayne Kalyn

DESIGN DIRECTOR
Barbara Rietschel

Contributors

PRINCIPAL CONSULTANTS
New York Presbyterian Hospital–Cornell
University Medical College

WRITERS
Robert A. Barnett, Jeanine Barone,
Elizabeth Barrett, Colette Bouchez,
Royce Flippin, Eric Oatman, Rita Rubin,
Richard L. Scheffel, James Thornton,
Carol Weeg, Donna Wilkinson

CONTRIBUTING EDITOR
Cinda Siler

CONTRIBUTING DESIGNERS
Dana Terwilliger, Todd Victor

COPY EDITORS
Gina Grant, Joseph Marchetti, Judy Yelon

INDEXERS
Jane Broderick
Northwind Editorial Services

RESEARCHERS
Kathleen Derzipilski, Karen Evoy,
Pamela Kladzyk, Denise Lynch, Paula Phelps,
Martha Plaine, Barbara Rusko, Cathy Sears

ILLUSTRATORS
Phil Bliss, Charlene Rendeiro

COMMISSIONED PHOTOGRAPHY
Nicholas Eveleigh

PICTURE EDITOR
Laurie Platt Winfrey, Carousel Research, Inc.

PICTURE RESEARCHER
J. Christopher Deegan, Carousel Research, Inc.

PICTURE RESEARCH ASSISTANT
Van Bucher, Carousel Research, Inc.

Note to Readers:
The information in this book should not be substituted for, or used to alter, medical therapy without your doctor's advice.
For a specific health problem, consult your physician for guidance.

Address any comments about *Is It Harmful, Is It Healthy?* to Editor, Books and Home Entertainment,
c/o Customer Service, Reader's Digest, 1125 Stanley Street, Montreal, Quebec H3B 5H5.

For information on this and other Reader's Digest products or to request a catalogue,
please call our 24-hour Customer Service hotline at 1-800-465-0780.

You can also visit us on the World Wide Web at http://www.readersdigest.ca

The acknowledgments and credits that appear on pages 382–384 are hereby made a part of this copyright page.

Copyright © 1999 The Reader's Digest Association, Inc.
Copyright © 1999 The Reader's Digest Association (Canada) Ltd.
Copyright © 1999 Reader's Digest Association Far East Ltd.
Philippine Copyright 1999 Reader's Digest Association Far East Ltd.
All rights reserved. Unauthorized reproduction, in any manner, is prohibited.

Reader's Digest and the Pegasus logo are registered trademarks of The Reader's Digest Association, Inc.

Printed in Canada
99 00 01 / 5 4 3 2 1

Canadian Cataloguing in Publication Data

Main entry under title:
        Is it harmful, is it healthy: a complete guide to what's
good for you—and what isn't
Includes index.
ISBN 0-88850-667-8
        1. Health—Popular works.   2. Toxicology—Popular works.
3. Environmental health—Popular works.

RA776.I76 1999   613   C98-901077-5

about this book

Is it harmful? Is it healthy? Whether you're talking about herbal supplements, insect repellents, or house paint, the answer can be hard to come by. Conflicting news reports often add to the confusion, leaving people at a loss when trying to make decisions that affect their health.

Reader's Digest has solved the problem. With the help of more than a hundred experts in dozens of fields, we've written the book that sets the record straight on the issues you wonder about most. *Is It Harmful, Is It Healthy?* also examines products we use every day without giving a thought to their safety—nail polish, carpet cleaners, underarm deodorants, and almost everything in between. From the drugs we take to the food we eat right down to the shoes we wear, if it affects our health, it's probably here.

Amazingly, many concerns vanish once you know the facts (there is little reason, for instance, to live in fear of aluminum pans or electric blankets). On the other hand, dangers lurk where you may not have thought to look. Did you know that antilock brakes are worse than regular brakes on soft snow? Or that talcum powder may cause ovarian cancer? And some things that seem good for you actually aren't. A case in point: taking beta-carotene supplements if you smoke may actually increase your risk of lung cancer.

The information in this book is designed to be used. When there are risks, you'll find out how to minimize them. You'll also pick up countless tips you can act on, such as how to avoid back pain, choose a toothbrush, and eat fewer trans fats (they aren't listed on the label, but we'll tell you how to sniff them out). The entries are organized alphabetically, so it's easy to turn right to the subject you want to read about. (And be sure to use the index, since some topics, such as pain relievers, are covered in more than one place.) Within the entries are special features that offer preventive measures, natural alternatives, health cautions, and sneak peeks at drugs and other medical and technological advances that may soon turn the issue at hand on its ear.

If you'd like to learn more about a topic, turn to the Resource Guide on pages 362–364. It lists organizations you can contact for information on a wide range of subjects.

We hope reading this book leads to small changes in your life that make a big difference in your well-being. Many of them are surprisingly simple—installing a carbon monoxide detector in your home, getting rid of your baby walker, buying a meat thermometer. At the same time, the information you learn will put your needless worries to rest.

—*The Editors*

Contents

Acid Rain

Many people think that acid rain is one of those environmental issues whose dangers are exaggerated by the news media. It may affect a few trees, the thinking goes, but it can't really hurt people, right? The fact is that much still remains unknown about acid rain, but this much is for sure: it is a serious threat to the environment, and there is evidence that it can directly endanger human health.

The problem is not invisible, either. The next time you visit one of our national parks to enjoy the vistas, your view may be tainted somewhat by damaged trees and a haze of acidic particles in the air.

Higher levels of acidic particles in the air are associated with increased rates of respiratory illness and death.

An insidious threat to nature

Acid rain—any form of precipitation, including snow and fog, that contains some amount of sulfuric and nitric acids—wreaks havoc on the environment. It strips the soil of vital nutrients that support the growth of vegetation and contaminates thousands of American and Canadian waterways and lakes. This results in forest damage, such as that in Canada's eastern provinces, and the decimation of many aquatic species. Could acid rain ruin your garden? Not likely. Most cultivated plants can tolerate changes in acidity if they are fertilized with basic nutrients.

What causes acid rain?

It begins with air pollution generated from industrial processes such as pulp and paper, smelting, and natural gas plants, as well as the burning of fossil fuels by power plants, factories, and automobiles. Sulfur dioxide and nitrogen dioxide are released into the air, where they react with sunlight, water, and oxygen to form acids and salts. As "normal" rain falls through the atmosphere, it mixes with these pollutants and turns into acid rain.

Acid rain accounts for about half of the "acid deposition" that falls to Earth. The rest is dry acid deposition, which is comprised of gases and solid particles. Since both forms of acid deposition are easily blown by the wind over long distances, they can cause damage to the environment far from their original source.

Is acid rain harmful to humans?

Studies report that the acidic particles that make up dry acid deposition can exacerbate such respiratory conditions as asthma and bronchitis. Higher levels of these particles in the air are also associated with increased rates of respiratory illness and death.

Acid rain is unlikely to taint your city tap water by seeping into groundwater and corroding pipes. However, the quality of well water in some rural areas of Canada has been adversely affected by acid rain deposition. It is a good idea to have a private lab test your well water for potability.

Structures made of galvanized steel, copper, marble, limestone, sandstone, and granite can be gradually eaten away by acid rain. The damage is seen on the exteriors of buildings, statues, and bridges—even on such beloved monuments as the Parthenon in Greece and the Taj Mahal in India.

Acupuncture

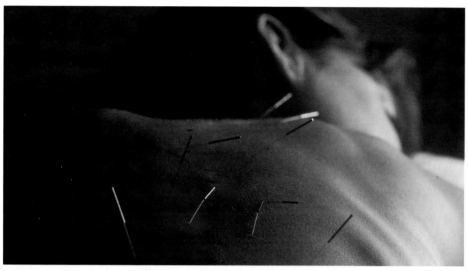

When used correctly, acupuncture needles, inserted at specific points, may cause a slight tingling or a sensation of heaviness, but no significant pain.

How would you like to have needles stuck into your skin to relieve pain or illness? Well, consider this: each year more than a million North Americans turn to acupuncture to treat a variety of ailments, and its benefits continue to be recognized by many in the medical community. In 1978, acupuncture needles were officially classified as medical devices by Health Canada. In 1997 the National Institutes of Health in the U.S. concluded that acupuncture is an effective treatment for nausea and postoperative pain—with potentially fewer side effects than more conventional options.

How acupuncture works
According to the age-old tenets of Chinese medicine, health is determined by the flow of energy, or qi (pronounced "chee"), along specific bodily pathways. Inserting needles at precise points along these pathways restores the flow of qi and aids recovery.

Some experts suspect that the needles stimulate the central and peripheral nervous systems and then trigger the release of various neurotransmitters that block pain and may promote healing. However it works, acupuncture often gets results: it can relieve chronic and acute pain, nausea, asthma, and withdrawal symptoms associated with drug and alcohol addiction.

What happens during a visit?
A typical session begins with a general examination. This is followed by the insertion of 5-centimeter (2-inch) -long needles that are as thin as hair and usually made of surgical steel. Needles may be placed far from the site of the ailment (in the earlobes and ankles, for example, to treat asthma). Despite the unsettling appearance of the needles, the technique causes no significant pain. Most people report feeling relaxed during the treatment, which can last up to an hour. The practitioner may twirl the needles or run a mild electric current through them. It may take as many as 10 treatments to determine if the therapy is working. Some private health insurance companies cover the cost of acupuncture treatment. Check your policy.

Acupuncture is not risk-free, but mishaps (such as broken needles and tissue damage) are extremely rare.

Choosing a practitioner
You may be required by law to consult with a doctor before you try acupuncture. Health Canada recommends that your practitioner uses sterile, single-use disposable needles. Practitioners are licensed in Quebec and B.C., and may be registered in Alberta. Most provinces allow physicians with acupuncture training to perform the procedure.

Acupuncture May Help Ease:
- Postoperative pain, especially after dental surgery
- Nausea (including that caused by chemotherapy)
- Headaches, especially migraines
- Neck and lower-back pain, menstrual cramps, and general chronic pain
- Arthritis pain
- Asthma and bronchitis
- Withdrawal symptoms associated with addiction to alcohol, tobacco, and other substances
- Rehabilitation from stroke

Aerobic Exercise

Most people think that any kind of vigorous exercise qualifies as aerobic. Think again. To be truly aerobic, an exercise must work large groups of muscles for a prolonged period lasting at least 15 to 20 minutes. During that time substantial amounts of oxygen must be delivered to and used by the muscles. Typical examples of aerobic exercise are swimming, fast walking, running, bicycling, cross-country skiing, and some of the livelier forms of dance.

You can't beat the benefits

Like all the other muscles in the body, the heart needs exercise to stay healthy. Because aerobic activity forces the heart to pump large quantities of oxygen-rich blood to the muscles for a sustained period of time, it gradually strengthens the heart muscle. As a result, the heart works more efficiently and can better meet the body's daily demands for oxygen without undue stress. In practical terms, this translates into being able to race up the stairs or run for the bus without becoming short of breath.

Aerobic exercise offers an astonishing array of other health benefits as well. As little as 20 to 40 minutes of aerobics three to four times a week can do the following: burn excess fat, combat stress and fatigue, build stronger bones, lower blood pressure (particularly in women following menopause), increase HDL cholesterol (the "good" kind), improve sleep, quell anxiety, spark creativity, and add years to your life.

And there's more: aerobic exercise can even help people find solutions to perplexing personal or professional dilemmas. Studies have shown that, for reasons still not clearly understood by researchers, aerobic workouts seem to improve clarity of thought along with mood.

Jolts to the joints

When aerobics first became popular almost three decades ago, the trend was toward high-impact exercises—aerobic dancing, jogging, and jumping rope. And although these heart-revving activities produced excellent aerobic results, they put inordinate stress on the joints and bones, particularly the knees, ankles, feet, and lower back. Shin splints, a painful inflammation of the tendons and muscles of the lower leg, is one common injury that often results from too much high-impact activity.

The key to avoiding joint injury is twofold: choosing the right exercises and monitoring and controlling the intensity with which you perform them. These days, many experts recommend low-impact workouts like swimming and cycling, which cause much less wear and tear on joints. Both offer

> Aerobic exercise offers an astonishing array of health benefits. It burns fat, combats stress and fatigue, builds stronger bones, lowers blood pressure, increases HDL cholesterol (the "good" kind), improves sleep, quells anxiety, sparks creativity, and adds years to your life.

Putting Your Heart Into It

To benefit aerobically, you need to exercise hard enough to make your heart beat within an aerobic range (provided your doctor approves). Here's how to calculate the range: Subtract your age from 220; the result is your maximum heart rate. Multiply that number by .60 and .90 (.75 instead of .90 if you're over 65). These two numbers are the lower and upper limits for your exercising heart rate. Take your pulse periodically as you work out to check the rate per minute. Stick to the low end of the range for three to four months.

Age	Lower heart rate	Upper heart rate
20	120	180
30	114	171
40	108	162
50	102	153
60	96	144
70	90	112

substantial aerobic benefits while reducing the risk of injury.

It is important, however, that some weight-bearing activities continue to be part of an exercise regimen, especially for women, because they help deter osteoporosis. Try alternating, say, between swimming and race walking to cut down on hard blows to the joints while still strengthening the bones.

An optimal aerobics schedule is four sessions a week, each lasting about 40 minutes. If you are out of shape, start with three 20-minute sessions a week on alternate days.

Must you do aerobics to stay healthy?

Perhaps not. The new thinking among physiologists is that engaging in even small amounts of physical activity several times a day can have a surprisingly beneficial effect on your health. Many experts say that accumulating a total of 30 minutes of routine physical activity over the course of a day will provide your body with some of the healthful bonuses of aerobics. A likely scenario might include walking for 10 minutes at lunchtime, climbing a flight or two of stairs in the afternoon, doing a little light housework toward the end of the day, and taking a brisk stroll after dinner.

an ounce of Prevention

Train Without Pain

No pain, no gain, right? Wrong. Exercise should help, not hurt. To protect yourself from injury, alternate high-impact activities like running and step aerobics with gentler ones like swimming, and take the following additional precautions.

- Look at what's under your feet. Studies show that the harder the surface, the greater the toll on feet and joints. Cushion the impact whenever possible; jog on level grass instead of pavement, for example, or dance on a wooden floor instead of a concrete surface.

- Choose appropriate footwear. Shoes should have ample cushioning and stability.

- Limit high-impact activities to three times a week, with at least a day of rest between sessions.

- Never try to "work through the pain," say the experts. Exercise doesn't have to be painful in order to be effective—if it hurts, stop.

- Be sure to warm up and cool down before and after each exercise session. Warm-ups prepare your body for exercise by gradually increasing your heart rate and blood flow and by loosening up your muscles. Cooldowns prevent a sharp drop in blood pressure and slow circulation in the muscles so that they won't stiffen up later. You can warm up by gently jogging in place or riding a stationary bike for 5 or 10 minutes. To cool down, simply slacken the pace of your exercise bit by bit.

Aerosol Sprays

Simply said, aerosol sprays have an image problem. The rap against them goes like this: aerosols harm the environment; they contain CFCs, which destroy the ozone layer; and you should avoid them at all costs. Is all this true? In the past, yes. Today, no.

Phasing out CFCs

For years aerosol products contained chlorofluorocarbons, or CFCs, which were used as spray propellants. In the 1970s CFCs were found to damage the ozone layer, and in 1978 the United States banned their use in commercial products; Canada, Norway, and Sweden shortly followed suit. By 1996, CFCs were almost entirely phased out.

They are currently used only in certain industrial machines (recycled in refrigerators and air conditioners) and medical products (inhalers), where their use is exempt from the Canadian Environmental Protection Act (CEPA) ban.

Are today's aerosols safe?

Even the new generation of aerosols presents potential health hazards. Many of them contain volatile organic compounds (VOCs), a group of propellants and solvents that are highly flammable and contribute to smog. The most common VOCs are combinations of propane and butane. VOCs are found not only in aerosols but also in many fast-drying products, including pump sprays, perfumes, and hair gels.

The risks of inhaling aerosol spray

The biggest danger of using an aerosol is inhaling the chemical spray. The spray's fine particles can penetrate deep into the lungs and are easily absorbed by the bloodstream, possibly causing a variety of health problems.

A growing number of teenagers inhale vapors from aerosol cans in search of a cheap high. The practice, called "huffing," deprives the lungs and brain of oxygen and can cause brain damage or death. Parents should be aware of the signs of aerosol abuse: changes in a child's appetite or sleep patterns, a rash or blisters around the mouth, mood swings, and a chemical smell on the breath.

Safer substitutes

When shopping for household cleaners and polishes, hair sprays, and insect repellents, look for products sold as pump sprays, not aerosols. Although pumps may contain VOCs, they do not contain propellants, and the droplets they emit are larger and less likely to be inhaled. To avoid VOCs, use sprays with carbon dioxide propellants or compressed air and stay away from fast-drying products. Finally, if you must use an aerosol spray, be sure to read—and heed—the label.

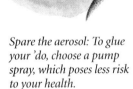

Spare the aerosol: To glue your 'do, choose a pump spray, which poses less risk to your health.

an ounce of **Prevention**

Using Aerosols Properly

- Always use aerosols in a well-ventilated area and do not inhale the vapors. The chemicals in the vapor can be absorbed by the lungs and the bloodstream, potentially causing headaches, dizziness, nausea, and respiratory problems.

- Avoid misdirected spray; it can harm the eyes and skin.

- Keep aerosol cans away from heat and flame. Even the heat of a nearby furnace can cause a can's pressurized contents to expand and explode.

- Dispose of the cans in your regular trash. Even though many of them are now made of recyclable materials, recycling centers do not usually accept them because they may explode. Never disassemble, puncture, or incinerate an aerosol can.

There is no doubt that air bags save lives in automobile collisions. It is estimated that air bags have prevented 150 accident deaths in Canada since they were first introduced. However, they also carry risks. Their explosive force has caused numerous injuries and the deaths of five people. Even as carmakers try to make air bags safer, drivers and passengers should look to minimize their risks.

How air bags work

Upon impact, the bags are signaled to inflate. The bags burst into the car at about 300 kilometers per hour (185 miles per hour). In a split second they have protected anyone in the front seat from life-threatening impact with the steering wheel, dashboard, or windshield.

However, air bags can cause serious injury. Braking before a crash can throw an unbelted person forward into the bag's zone of deployment, where the inflating bag can deliver a severe and potentially fatal blow to the person's head, neck, or chest. The danger is also considerable for children, short adults, and anyone sitting forward. (Side-impact air bags are considered safer since they inflate parallel to the car occupant.)

Reducing the risks

Legislation in Canada requires that you wear a seat belt, no matter where you sit in a car. Air bags are more effective and less dangerous when you are buckled up. Furthermore, seat belts protect people in all kinds of crashes, while front-impact air bags do not.

Avoid leaning forward, and stay out of the bag's deployment zone—keep 25 centimeters/10 inches (excluding bulky clothing) between the center of the sternum and the center of the steering wheel for drivers and as far back as possible for front-seat passengers.

Children under the age of 12 should wear appropriate restraints and always be seated in the backseat. Statistically, air bags do more harm than good to young children. Always strap infants into an appropriate, approved car seat and place them in the back (see page 77, Child Safety Seats).

Can you disconnect an air bag?

In 1998 the federal, provincial, and territorial governments and vehicle manufacturers reached an agreement on a national program enabling certain Canadians to have air-bag switches installed in their vehicles.

You can have the passenger's-side air bag switched off if you must carry children aged 12 or under or infants in rear-facing infant seats in the front seat of your car—for example, if your vehicle does not have a backseat. You can have the driver's-side air bag switched off if you cannot keep at least 25 centimeters (10 inches) between the center of the steering wheel and the center of the sternum or have a special medical problem. To have the switch installed, apply for permission from Transport Canada at 800-333-0371 or in Quebec from La Société de l'assurance automobile du Québec at 514-873-7620.

As demonstrated by these test dummies, adults wearing seat belts face minimal risk of air-bag injury.

On the Horizon

To reduce air-bag casualties, manufacturers are seeking safer alternatives. Within the next few years we may see so-called "smart" air bags. This new generation of air bags will adjust their deployment force based on crash severity, occupant size and position, or seat-belt use. Most manufacturers are now installing "depowered" air bags which deploy with less force than current air bags.

Air Conditioners

Not just a heat beater: air conditioners remove moisture from the air and also filter allergens nearly as well as most air purifiers.

Air conditioners take the sizzle out of hot, humid days by blowing warm air over metal coils filled with a refrigerant. This not only lowers the air temperature but also condenses the water vapor in the air, producing a cooler, drier indoor climate.

The benefits of staying cool

Aside from added comfort, air conditioners provide protection from several health threats, especially heatstroke. A life-threatening condition, heatstroke usually develops over the course of several scorching, humid days and causes the body to lose its ability to release heat. Sweating stops, and the body's temperature soars. However, spending just a few hours a day in an air-conditioned room can short-circuit this dangerous process. People who suffer from diabetes or heart disease and those who take such medications as antihistamines, diuretics, beta-blockers, and vasoconstrictors are at the greatest risk of developing heatstroke.

Air conditioners are also a boon for people who suffer from allergies or asthma. As the units cool the air, they also filter pollen, mold spores, and dust, all of which can trigger allergic and asthmatic reactions.

Hidden hazards

If air conditioners aren't well maintained, they can cause some of the very problems they otherwise prevent. A dirty air filter can harbor pollen, fungi, and bacteria and allow millions of microorganisms into the room, possibly triggering an asthma attack, irritation of the eyes, nose, and throat—even a flulike illness. Proper maintenance will minimize these risks. About every two to four weeks, vacuum the air filter, then wash it in soapy water. Be sure to let the filter dry completely before reinstalling it. You may also want to spray it with a disinfectant to keep it free of mildew. If the air conditioner uses disposable filters, remember to replace them at the recommended intervals.

Air conditioners in large buildings can pose a more serious threat because they use reservoirs of water that can harbor harmful bacteria. When Legionnaires' disease struck at an American Legion convention in Philadelphia in 1976, epidemiologists found colonies of the deadly *Legionella pneumophila* bacterium in the air circulated by the hotel's air-conditioning system. Other organisms that grow in large air-conditioning units can trigger hypersensitivity pneumonitis, also called allergic alveolitis. The condition is caused by inhaling microscopic organic dusts, which inflame the air sacs of the lungs and can eventually interfere with normal breathing.

On the road

The air conditioners in our cars can pose problems of their own. The interior of the units are hot, moist, and dark—an ideal breeding ground for fungi and mold spores. If you are allergic to mold, opt for the fresh-air rather than the recirculated-air setting, aim the air vents away from your face, and crack open the car windows for several minutes after you turn on the air conditioner to allow any microorganisms to escape. If the problem persists, you may want to have a qualified mechanic treat the air conditioner with a disinfectant which will keep it mold-free for about three months.

Air Purifiers

The air pollution outside our homes may be cause for worry, but the air inside may not always be quite as pure as we'd like to believe it is. Enter air purifiers. These units are designed to remove a variety of pollutants—including smoke, dust, pollen, mold, animal dander, and some chemical odors and gases—from the air. Do they work? Yes and no. Studies show that *some* types of air purifiers are effective against *some* types of pollutants. The key to buying one is knowing which pollutants you want to target and how much money you want to spend; prices and maintenance costs vary greatly.

Choosing the right unit

To rid your home of noxious odors—particularly those that emanate from formaldehyde, pesticides, perfume, and tobacco smoke—the best choice is a unit that uses an activated carbon filter. (Note: Air cleaners that do not contain special media, such as activated carbon, will not remove gaseous pollutants, including radon, or reduce their associated health effects.)

Electronic air purifiers may also reduce cigarette smoke, but they may not eliminate the odor. Different varieties, called electrostatic cleaners, electret cleaners, and negative-ionizing cleaners, charge particles in the air so that they can be collected, either by a special filter or by your walls, floors, and furniture. These units neutralize some offensive odors but won't remove odorless gases like carbon monoxide. Neither will they alleviate your allergy to cats, pollen, or dust.

If allergies to dust, pollen, and mold are your biggest complaint, look for a mechanical filtration system that traps large particles. A so-called HEPA filter (high-efficiency particulate air filter) is a good bet. But there's a catch: these units filter only particles that are airborne; most allergens quickly settle on surfaces, where air purifiers can't touch them. (In fact, you may not even need an air purifier to filter allergens from the air; at least one study showed that air conditioners do the job almost as well.)

To remove gases and odors in addition to pollen and dust, you'll need a hybrid unit that uses more than one type of filtration system. If you have central heating or air-conditioning, you may not need to buy an air purifier at all: you can have an electronic or mechanical filter installed in the ducts.

Recognize the drawbacks

Electronic air purifiers and negative-ionizing cleaners may produce ozone, a lung irritant, especially if they are not properly installed and maintained. And negative-ionizing cleaners, especially those that lack a collection system, may eventually create an ugly black film on your walls and furniture. Also, many—even most—units designed to remove gases may actually send the gases right back into the air over time. And some devices fool you into thinking that they work better than they do by releasing scents in order to mask odors.

> Studies show that *some* types of air purifiers are effective against *some* types of pollutants. The key to buying one is knowing which pollutants you want to target.

Shopping Tips

- Know which pollutants you want to remove.
- Match the purifier to the room size. Look for the CADR (clean air delivery rate) to learn how many cubic feet of air per minute the unit can clean.
- Tabletop units are relatively ineffective, unless used in small areas.
- No air purifier is 100 percent effective on its own. You must also control the source of pollution.

For people with allergies, an air purifier with a HEPA system is a fair bet but not a surefire solution.

Imagine a pill that cuts your risk of dying from a heart attack by 30 to 50 percent. But there's a catch: take three a day instead of one or two and you increase your odds of having a stroke, getting cancer or high blood pressure or liver disease, killing someone, taking your own life, or crashing a car—in short, of dying prematurely. What's more, the pills make you feel good—so good, in fact, that you may not be able to control how many you take.

That's the dilemma facing public health officials when it comes to alcohol: a strong showing of both benefits and risks. Studies show that in 1992 alcohol consumption prevented the deaths due to heart disease, stroke, heart failure, and various other causes of some 7,400 Canadians. In the same year however, alcohol-related deaths claimed an estimated 6,700 people. And approximately 5 percent of the population is drinking at levels that may lead to more serious problems.

So, it won't do to encourage people to drink moderately, because some can't. And, after all, there are safer ways, such as diet and exercise, to cut the risk of heart disease.

A toast to longer life

If you already drink in moderation, however, you may live longer as a result. Moderate drinking cuts the number of deaths from heart disease sharply. For example, a major study involving more than 22,000 healthy men found that those who had one alcoholic drink a day were less likely to die in a given time period than nondrinkers. Heavier drinkers were most likely to die. Another study, involving 490,000 men and women, confirmed the benefits of a drink a day.

Alcohol may be of particular benefit to women after menopause, when the risk of heart disease rises rapidly. In a study of 86,000 nurses, women over 50 who drank between 1 and 20 drinks a week had a lower risk of death than the nondrinkers. Why? A whopping 40 percent drop in heart disease.

Yet another study, involving 12,000 doctors, found that moderate drinkers were less likely than nondrinkers to die not only of heart disease but of respiratory illnesses, stroke, and even certain types of cancer. (On the flip side, heavy drinking may *cause* certain cancers, including mouth, throat, and lung cancer.)

Moderate drinking has also been found to lower the incidence of adult-onset diabetes. What's more, moderate drinkers who don't smoke are reported to suffer fewer colds than teetotalers.

A major study involving more than 22,000 healthy men found that those who had one alcoholic drink a day were less likely to die in a given time period than nondrinkers. Heavier drinkers were most likely to die.

How drinking helps the heart

Alcohol protects against cardiovascular disease by raising blood levels of HDL (high-density lipoprotein) cholesterol. This "good" cholesterol carries plaque produced by LDL (low-density lipoprotein, or "bad") cholesterol from the artery walls to the liver to be broken down. The more HDL in your blood, the lower your risk of heart disease. Alcohol

raises HDL significantly: two drinks a day boosts it by 17 percent. Alcohol's ability to boost HDL is responsible for about half of its power to prevent fatal heart attacks.

The other half? No one is certain. One probable factor relates to blood clots. Most heart attacks are caused by blood clots that

Moderate drinking appears to prevent a host of ills—but some people can't control their appetite for alcohol.

Alcohol (continued)

A substance in red wine called resveratrol (found in grape skin and also in peanuts) inhibits the development of cancer in laboratory tests. Studies have yet to confirm its benefits in humans.

block arteries already narrowed by heart disease. Alcohol inhibits clot formation and also enhances the body's ability to break up clots soon after they form. Drinking an alcoholic beverage reduces clotting within a matter of hours, greatly decreasing the short-term risk of a heart attack.

A recent study indicates that alcohol may also curb the formation of arterial muscle cells, which occurs after eating a fatty meal and contributes to atherosclerosis, or narrowing of the coronary arteries.

A fourth factor may be the antioxidants found in certain alcoholic beverages. LDL cholesterol, it turns out, does not contribute to heart disease until it is damaged by free radicals—unstable oxygen molecules that react with it. Antioxidants may help prevent this damage by neutralizing the free radicals. Flavonoids, one type of antioxidant, are found in red wine and dark beer, as well as in onions, broccoli, and apples. So far, however, there is no evidence that red wine is any more effective in preventing heart disease than other alcoholic beverages are. In fact, when it comes to alcohol and the prevention of heart disease, it seems that what matters is not what you drink but how much and how often.

Easy does it

Moderation maximizes alcohol's beneficial effects while minimizing its risks. If you drink too much, you will raise some of the very risks that moderate consumption reduces.

For example, a woman who drinks one alcoholic beverage a day is less likely to develop high blood pressure than one who doesn't drink at all. Increase consumption to two drinks, and her risk of high blood pressure skyrockets. What's more, studies have indicated that people who have two drinks a day may be at increased risk for colon cancer. Scientists now believe this may be because alcohol interferes with the body's absorption of folic acid. Among drinkers whose diets are high in folic acid, colon cancer risk is normal.

Moderate drinking is considered to be up to one drink a day for women, two for men. (A drink is defined as 15 milliliters/¹/₂ ounce of alcohol; that's equal to a 355-milliliter/12-ounce bottle of beer, a 120- to 150-milli-liter/4- to 5-ounce glass of wine, or a 45-milliliter/1.5-ounce shot of 80-proof spirits.) Why the gender difference? Women tend to be smaller and have less blood volume than men. Women also produce lower levels of an enzyme that breaks down alcohol.

Breaking bread: Wine (or any other alcohol) is best consumed with meals, since food slows the absorption of alcohol into the bloodstream.

Pay attention not just to your average alcohol consumption but also to your drinking pattern. Drinking small amounts with meals every day or two is much healthier than consuming 7 to 14 drinks on Friday and Saturday nights. One reason is that food slows the body's absorption of alcohol, so that blood-alcohol levels don't rise as quickly; a meal complete with carbohydrates, protein, and fat slows the absorption threefold.

The other reason is that binge drinking—no matter what your weekly average—is acutely dangerous, and not only because of the obvious dangers of drinking and driving or otherwise inviting an accident. A Finnish study found that middle-aged men who typically drank six or more bottles of beer at one sitting were six times more likely to have a fatal heart attack. They were also seven times more likely to die violently.

A warning to women

Alcohol protects a woman's heart just as well as it protects a man's, but that benefit is most significant after menopause, when a woman's risk of heart disease rises rapidly. Unlike men, though, women face additional health risks when it comes to drinking.

Although alcoholism is more common in men, it is deadlier in women. Women who drink heavily develop cirrhosis of the liver more quickly and die from it sooner than men. In one study, female alcoholics developed enlarged hearts (a common result of alcoholism) just as frequently as men, even though they consumed 40 percent less alcohol in their lifetimes.

Even for women who drink moderately, alcohol may pose certain problems. One relates to pregnancy. Although it is heavy drinking that causes the physical and mental abnormalities known as fetal alcohol syndrome, some studies suggest that even moderate drinking—one or two drinks a day—can cause subtle neurological and behavioral problems in infants. It may be that the women in these studies tended to underestimate their drinking because they felt

Symptom Sorter

Do You Have a Drinking Problem?

According to a survey conducted by The Canadian Center on Substance Abuse 9.2 percent of the overall population has alcohol-related problems. Men are at a greater risk than women. At the greatest risk are young people ages 18 to 24. After age 65, the risk declines somewhat, but remains significant.

A major stress can spark dormant tendencies. Young adults who drink often cut down when they marry and have children, for example, but a divorce can send them back to the bottle. In older people, the loss of a spouse—even retirement—can trigger a problem.

Symptoms of alcohol dependency:

- Do you feel guilty about your drinking or annoyed by criticism of it? Have you tried—and failed—to cut down in the past?

- Do you often start your day with a drink?

- Have you consumed five or more drinks on at least five occasions in the past 30 days?

- Do you have a family history of alcoholism? Children of alcoholics are much more likely to become alcoholics themselves.

- Can you hold your liquor? The ability to drink alcohol without feeling its effects is a major predictor of alcoholism.

If you think you have a problem:

- Get medical help. Your doctor may prescribe naltrexone, a drug that blocks alcohol's opiatelike addictive effects.

- Join a program. They include Alcoholics Anonymous, cognitive-behavioral therapy (to help you manage your desire to drink), and motivational enhancement (to boost your sense of responsibility).

- Quit smoking. Smoking and drinking go hand in hand. Moreover, among recovering alcoholics, about half the deaths are due to smoking.

guilty. But until more definitive research is done, most health experts advise pregnant women—as well as women attempting to become pregnant—to avoid alcohol altogether. Another reason women should consider abstaining, especially during the two weeks before menstruation, is that, for some individuals, alcohol may provoke premenstrual syndrome. *(continued)*

Alcohol (continued)

The breast cancer connection

The other major concern for women who drink is breast cancer. Consuming more than three drinks a week appears to increase a woman's odds of developing the disease; how high the odds rise depends on whom you ask. According to a widely publicized study, the risk of breast cancer rises by 30 percent with one drink a day, by 70 percent with two drinks. According to other research, the link is less dramatic. At any rate, breast cancer kills far fewer women than does heart disease, which is why, on average, moderate drinking boosts longevity in women over the age of 50.

For certain people, however—especially those with a family history of breast cancer—the scales may tip in favor of abstention. Among postmenopausal women undergoing hormone replacement therapy, for instance, alcohol can substantially increase blood levels of estradiol, a form of estrogen. High estrogen levels are linked with increased risk of breast cancer as well as gallstones. But since alcohol raises estradiol levels for only a few hours, occasional drinkers have little to fear.

If you are concerned about breast cancer, you may want to avoid alcohol entirely. Or you may choose to limit yourself to three drinks a week—a level that poses little or no increased risk of breast cancer and still offers cardiovascular protection.

A delicate balance

Alcohol is a classic example of the need to weigh the risks and benefits when making decisions that affect your health. For most people who can drink in moderation and don't have a specific reason to avoid drinking (such as being pregnant or taking a medication), alcoholic beverages can be both enjoyable and healthful. For others, abstinence is clearly the best policy.

Most beer contains less alcohol (3 to 8 percent) than wine (12 percent) and hard liquor (40 to 50 percent), but it has more calories. A 355-milliliter (12-ounce) bottle of regular beer contains about 150 calories.

Dangerous Combinations

Alcohol alters the effects of many common medications, both prescription and over-the-counter—sometimes with serious consequences. Make sure you read the label or check with your pharmacist before you imbibe.

Medication Type	Example	Possible Interaction
Angina drugs	Nitroglycerin	Dizziness or fainting
Antibiotics	Metronidazole, griseofulvin isoniazid, rifampin	Decreased effectiveness and increased side effects (nausea, headache)
Anticoagulants	Warfarin	Increased "thinning" of the blood
Antidiabetics	Tolbutamide (Orinase)	Increased potency; nausea and headache
Antidepressants	Amitriptyline Monoamine oxidase inhibitors	Increased sedative effect Dangerous rise in blood pressure
Antihistamines	Most	Drowsiness, dizziness
Beta-blockers	Propranolol (Inderal), atenolol	Decreased effectiveness
Painkillers (nonprescription)	Aspirin, ibuprofen, naproxen Acetaminophen	Stomach bleeding Liver damage
Painkillers (prescription)	Morphine, codeine, meperidine (Demerol)	Increased effects of the drug and the alcohol and increased risk of death from overdose
Sleeping pills	Benzodiazepines like Valium lorazepam (Ativan)	Severe drowsiness Depressed heart and breathing functions

Aluminum

It's in the water we drink, the antiperspirants we use, the pots we cook in, the pickles we munch on, and the foil that keeps foods fresh. It is even found in over-the-counter medications, including some antacids and many pain relievers, such as buffered aspirin. It's aluminum, and although the metal is toxic in large amounts, only a tiny fraction of what we take in is absorbed by the body, and most of that is excreted.

Aluminum and Alzheimer's

Aluminum hit the headlines when several studies linked it to Alzheimer's disease. One study found that the brains of some patients who had died of the disease contained higher than normal amounts of aluminum. Concerns mounted when another report revealed that people whose water supply contained high levels of the metal were at greater risk of developing the disease. A third study showed that kidney patients who were given aluminum-rich fluid during dialysis developed a form of dementia similar to Alzheimer's. When the metal was removed from the fluid, the dementia passed.

Other studies, however, failed to turn up any evidence that aluminum is harmful, and certainly not at the levels most of us are exposed to daily. As a result, scientists began to question the earlier findings—they postulated, for instance, that the aluminum found in the brain tissues of Alzheimer's patients might have come from laboratory substances used to study the brain. Scientists also wondered whether it was Alzheimer's that caused the body to absorb or retain the metal, rather than aluminum triggering the disease.

No definitive answers have been found. Meanwhile, if you are concerned about the health effects of aluminum, there are some relatively simple precautions you can take.

How to protect yourself

If you must take medications that contain aluminum, avoid washing them down with acidic fruit drinks, particularly orange juice. The acid can cause the aluminum to dissolve, making it easier for the body to absorb.

Although they probably pose little threat, a host of edibles contain aluminum, including relishes, beer, cream of tartar, some grated cheeses, table salts, and most baking powders

Don't wrap acidic foods, such as tomatoes or apples, in aluminum foil. The acids can cause the metal to leach into the food. Also, substitute stainless-steel utensils, pots, and bowls for aluminum ones when cooking acidic dishes.

and self-rising flours (some are available that don't contain aluminum—check the label). Aluminum is also found in some processed foods (it makes them creamy and easy to pour) and most infant formulas. (Formulas with additives, such as calcium salts and soy protein, usually contain the most aluminum.) If you take calcium citrate supplements, be aware that citrate increases the body's absorption of the metal.

Finally, you may want to avoid antiperspirants that contain aluminum—especially aerosol varieties, which release aluminum into the air, where it can be inhaled. In addition, the aluminum found in most antiperspirants can cause an allergic reaction in some people. To be safe, avoid applying antiperspirant directly after shaving, when the skin is the most sensitive.

If you must take medications that contain aluminum, avoid washing them down with acidic fruit drinks, particularly orange juice.

Amniocentesis

I t's been called "the window on pregnancy," and amniocentesis does allow doctors to "peek" inside an expectant mother's body to check the health of her developing baby. The test involves analysis of a sample of the amniotic fluid, the liquid that surrounds the baby in the womb. Because the fluid contains fetal cells, the test can provide important clues about its health. Amniocentesis does have its limits, however: it can predict only some—not all—possible birth defects, and it carries risks that, though slight, need to be weighed.

What the test can tell you

Amniocentesis is nearly 100 percent accurate in detecting chromosomal abnormalities, including Down's syndrome, which causes mental retardation. It can also indicate certain genetic disorders in the fetus, such as a missing enzyme and any neural-tube defects, which impede the development of the fetus's brain or spinal cord.

Amniocentesis is sometimes used late in a pregnancy to gauge the development of the baby's lungs, in case an early delivery is necessary. It may also be used to monitor a fetus afflicted with RH disease, a blood disorder.

Thanks to amniocentesis, treatments for RH disease may be initiated while the baby is still in the womb. If there are other problems, plans for special procedures at the time of delivery may help the baby survive. The test results might also assist parents in making important decisions about the future of the pregnancy or enable them to be better prepared when the baby arrives.

Reviewing the risks

Amniocentesis is usually performed between the 14th and the 18th week of pregnancy. This 15-minute procedure involves inserting an ultrathin needle through the mother's abdomen into the uterus and withdrawing a sample of amniotic fluid. To reduce risks, the doctor is guided by ultrasound, an image showing the position of the needle within the uterus that is projected onto a computer screen. Some patients report mild cramping during or after the procedure. Analysis of the fluid takes two to four weeks.

Problems are rare, and the more experienced the doctor, the less likely they are to occur. Even so, the test does slightly increase the mother's risk of infection, vaginal bleeding, and leakage of amniotic fluid. There is also a slight risk of miscarriage. Before the test physicians usually counsel couples about the risks involved and about the implications of any of the possible results.

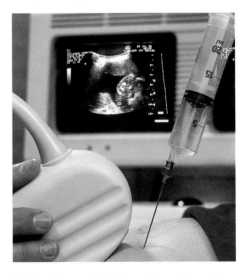

Pairing ultrasound with amniocentesis enables doctors to see the baby's position and better direct the needle.

On the Horizon Currently under development are sophisticated blood tests and advanced forms of ultrasound, both of which may offer some of the same information that amniocentesis does—with fewer risks. They may also be performed at an earlier stage of pregnancy, making crucial information available even sooner.

Anesthesia

Try to imagine having to endure a simple dental procedure without anesthesia, to say nothing of complex cardiac surgery. It's not a pleasant thought. Thanks to anesthesia, which encompasses a wide range of medications, the sensation of pain is magically blocked during medical procedures.

The different types of anesthesia

Although many drugs (and combinations of drugs) are used for anesthetic purposes, they are generally used in four ways:

- For local anesthesia, to numb a small area around the site of the surgery or for dental procedures.
- For regional anesthesia, to block the pain in entire groups, or "regions," of nerves, which is particularly useful during childbirth.
- For monitored anesthesia, to ease the discomfort of nonsurgical medical procedures or to supplement local anesthesia by means of painkillers combined with drugs that make the patient drowsy.
- For general anesthesia, recommended for long or complex surgery to render the patient unconscious and block pain responses throughout the body.

When most people think of anesthesia, they think of general anesthesia. But as medical procedures become simpler to do—and as more procedures are performed on an outpatient basis—general anesthesia is gradually being replaced by the other anesthetic techniques, which are not as risky.

If you are planning to undergo a medical procedure, you may have some choice about the anesthesia. However, in many cases the type of anesthesia and the specific drugs that are used will be determined by the procedure itself. Your doctor will also take into account your general health and other factors, including your tolerance for pain.

How safe is it?

These days, very safe. U.S. statistics show that over the past few decades, the risk of death from all forms of anesthesia has dropped from 1 in 4,500 in 1970 to 1 in 400,000 today.

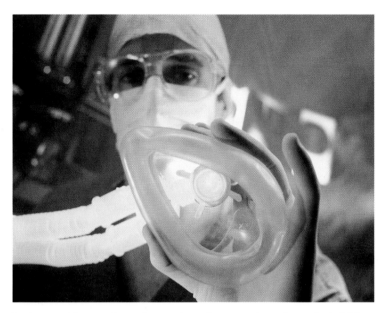

General anesthesia frightens many patients, but it is in fact quite safe. Talking to the anesthesiologist beforehand and following all presurgical instructions helps ensure safety.

In the past 10 years alone, the number of deaths from general anesthesia has fallen by more than 95 percent.

This improvement can be chalked up to the development of safer, faster-acting drugs and more sophisticated monitoring equipment that gauges the breathing rates, blood-oxygen levels, and even brain waves of sedated patients. By carefully measuring your vital functions while you are anesthetized, doctors can almost invariably avoid serious problems.

Preparing to "go under"

To reduce the risk of complications, before surgery your anesthesiologist will discuss your medical history, including the prescription and nonprescription medications you take, your allergies (particularly to medications), any previous experience you or your relatives have had with anesthesia, medical problems (especially asthma), and such lifestyle habits as smoking, drinking, or using recreational drugs. After the evaluation, it is crucial that you follow all presurgical instructions your anesthesiologist gives you to the letter.

> By carefully measuring your vital functions while you are anesthetized, doctors can almost invariably avoid serious problems.

Antacids

Many Canadians have at one time turned to antacids to douse the fiery chest pain of heartburn or to relieve the chronic bitter taste in the mouth or burning sensation in the throat they experience when waking up in the morning. For some people this is a daily trial. Although generally effective and safe for occasional use, antacids do have side effects that you need to know about.

How antacids work

Antacids are sold over the counter under many brand names and are available in chewable, liquid, and tablet form. All of them work by neutralizing gastro-esophageal reflux disease (commonly known as GERD), which occurs when stomach acid backs up into the esophagus and causes that burning sensation in the chest. For the fastest relief, liquid products are probably the best choice, although all forms work relatively quickly, quelling symptoms in a matter of minutes.

When used only occasionally or on a short-term basis, antacids usually pose no

Traditional antacids like these dissolving tablets bind with the acid in your stomach to form neutral compounds and put out the fire.

risk, but sometimes they cause more problems than they solve. Because they contain different active ingredients, each type may affect you differently. If, for instance, you find that relief is only temporary and that your heartburn returns with a vengeance in an hour or so, you may be suffering from acid rebound. This condition sometimes occurs when your antacid contains large amounts of calcium carbonate or sodium bicarbonate. The solution may be as simple as switching to a different antacid (refer to chart, opposite page).

The lowdown on new heartburn drugs

Departing from traditional antacids is a new group of medicines known as H_2 blockers, which include the products Pepcid AC and Zantac 75. Available for many years in prescription form, these medications are now available over the counter. They work by blocking the action of the acid-producing cells that line the stomach.

Although H_2 blockers alleviate most cases of heartburn, you must know which foods cause the condition because you need to take these medicines at least an hour before you intend to eat a problem dish. This means that you not only have to know ahead of time whether you are going to dine on spicy meatballs but also how your stomach is likely to react to them so that you can take the blocker ahead of time.

The H_2 blockers are generally considered safe, but prolonged use can cause some nasty side effects, including headaches, fatigue, dizziness, mild diarrhea, reduced sex drive, and even temporary impotence. Some H_2

an ounce of Prevention

Ways to Avert Heartburn

- Avoid tight clothes, especially belts—and *lose weight*.
- Try not to overeat.
- Don't lie down for at least two hours after meals.
- Elevate the head of your bed 15 centimeters/6 inches (just adding an extra pillow won't work).
- Forgo cigarettes, fatty or spicy foods, citrus juices, peppermint, chocolate, tea, coffee, colas, and alcohol. Limit dietary fiber.

blockers carry warnings for people with kidney or liver problems.

Taking traditional antacids with H_2 blockers reduces the effectiveness of the blockers. To take both, separate the doses by three hours.

Heartburn or heart attack?

People often end up in the emergency room because they are convinced they are having a heart attack when simple heartburn is to blame. Then again, there are also instances of people who have shrugged off the early signs of a heart attack, thinking that all they needed was an antacid.

In fact, though the pain of both heartburn and heart attack strikes in the area of the heart, the symptoms differ. The chest pain of a heart attack is described as a crushing ache, while heartburn really burns. During a heart attack, pain can radiate to the neck and to one arm or both; heartburn pain tends to stay in the chest and sometimes the throat.

Feeling a serious burn

Severe or chronic heartburn can have dangerous consequences. See your doctor if you have one or more of the following symptoms:

- Heartburn that occurs more than twice a week, often for no reason.
- Little relief from antacids or H_2 blockers.
- Regurgitation of food or liquids.
- Difficulty swallowing or food sticking in the throat.
- Bloody vomit and/or stools that look black or tarry.

Chronic heartburn is caused by a malfunction of the lower esophageal sphincter (LES) muscles, the gateway between the esophagus and the stomach. Normally, when we eat, this muscle relaxes just long enough to let food pass from the esophagus into the stomach, and then clamps shut again. This action keeps stomach acid and other digestive juices from splashing back up the passageway and causing heartburn. If the LES muscle relaxes at the wrong time or becomes loose, stomach acid continually backs up, causing chronic burn.

Do not take antacids or H_2 blockers if you have chronic, severe heartburn. You may mask a condition that should be treated by a doctor. When left untreated, chronic heartburn can eventually lead to ulceration and bleeding of the esophagus, breathing difficulties, and even esophageal cancer.

CAUTION!
See your doctor before using antacids if you are pregnant, if you suffer from heart, liver, or kidney disease, or if you are taking other medications (some antacids affect the rate at which certain drugs are absorbed by the body).

Side Effects of Common Antacids

Type of Antacid		Action	Problems
Sodium bicarbonate	Alka Seltzer Bromo Seltzer Rolaids	Main ingredient: baking soda. Provides quick relief, but should be limited to short-term use.	Taken too often, these antacids may cause kidney and heart malfunction, an increase in urinary tract infections, and disruption of the body's mineral balance. Their high sodium content may also make them dangerous for those who have high blood pressure or who are on a sodium-restricted diet.
Aluminum compounds	Amphojel Rolaids	Effective at providing relief, though slower-acting than some other antacids.	Frequent use often causes constipation. Long-term use may also promote mineral deficiencies, particularly of calcium. There is some evidence that increased aluminum intake may increase the risk of Alzheimer's disease.
Calcium carbonate	Calcium-Rich Rolaids Titralac Tums	Quick relief is provided by high calcium content. Can be taken daily.	For some people, daily use may cause severe constipation. Also may cause acid rebound. There is some evidence that excess calcium may promote the formation of kidney stones or impair kidney function.
Magnesium compounds	Gaviscon Maalox Mylanta Riopan	Provide quick relief. May have a laxative effect, except when mixed with other ingredients.	Products often include aluminum or calcium to offset the laxative effect of the magnesium, but these minerals may also cause adverse effects. This group of antacids is not recommended for people with kidney disease. Use among elderly people, particularly those with diabetes, may result in hypertension and/or cardiac problems.

Antibiotics

If you've ever suffered through the pain of strep throat or the hacking cough of pneumonia, then you know what a blessing antibiotics can be. A medication category consisting of some 100 different drugs, antibiotics help save millions of lives each year. But they have limits: they kill only bacteria, not viruses. What's more, overuse of antibiotics has led to the emergence of a host of drug-resistant bacteria that pose an increasing threat to public health. To guard against this threat, everyone must learn to use these drugs wisely.

Only bacterial infections can be cured by antibiotics. Viral infections, such as colds and flu, don't respond to them.

How we get sick

Did you ever wonder why two people can be exposed to the same germs, but only one becomes ill? The answer in large part lies in the strength of an individual's immune system, which enables the body to fight harmful microorganisms. When the immune system doesn't function at peak capacity (the result of anything from lack of sleep to poor diet), bacteria that would normally be destroyed pass into the body's tissues and multiply, causing inflammation and the release of toxins. These, in turn, cause symptoms of bacterial illness, which include fever, sore throat, and coughing.

How the drugs kill bacteria

When you take an antibiotic—in the form of a pill, a liquid, or an injection—it circulates in the bloodstream throughout the body. When the antibiotic encounters invading bacteria, it becomes like a key fitting into a lock: the medication instantly identifies the germ and goes to work destroying it. In some cases, the antibiotic kills the bacteria on contact. In others, it damages either the cell wall or some other part of the microorganism, and this prevents it from reproducing. Whatever the process, the result is that the germ no longer threatens your health. After a few days, your infection and its symptoms disappear.

The antibiotic arsenal

Although there are many antibiotics, all of them fall into one of two categories. The first, narrow-spectrum antibiotics, includes such drugs as penicillin. Each of these medications targets specific strains of bacteria. Because of this, a doctor is able to prescribe the precise medication that will help you get well.

The second category consists of broad-spectrum antibiotics, such as Augmentin and Biaxin. These drugs are capable of killing a wide range of different bacteria that cause ailments ranging from acne to sinusitis to Rocky Mountain spotted fever.

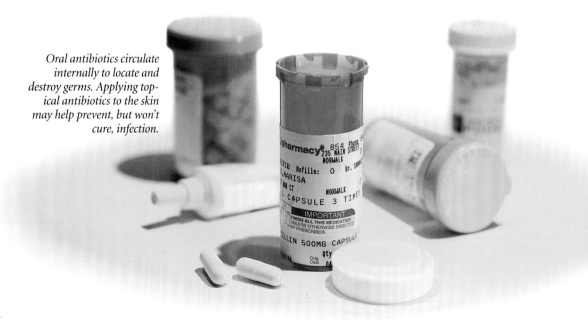

Oral antibiotics circulate internally to locate and destroy germs. Applying topical antibiotics to the skin may help prevent, but won't cure, infection.

Both categories of antibiotics are widely used and are vital in helping us combat such life-threatening illnesses as pneumonia, *E. coli* infection, strep throat, and blood poisoning.

Make the most of antibiotics

Antibiotics are sensitive to what you eat and drink. They won't work as well as they should, or may even cause uncomfortable side effects, if not taken exactly as your doctor prescribes. Here are some precautions:

- Ask your doctor whether your antibiotic should be taken with or without food. An empty stomach ensures that certain antibiotics are absorbed properly, while others need the presence of food to help them enter the bloodstream faster.
- Drink 240 milliliters (8 ounces) of water with antibiotics; otherwise, they may upset your stomach. Don't substitute fruit juice, wine, or soft drinks; the acid they contain prevents some antibiotics from working. Milk also poses a problem; the calcium in it renders several types of antibiotics inert.
- Never take antibiotics with alcohol; doing so can cause dangerous side effects.

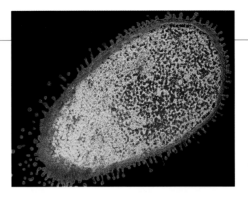

- Avoid using laxatives, antacids, and nutritional supplements while you are taking antibiotics. They all contain minerals that may disrupt the action of some antibiotics.

Too much of a good thing

Why not take antibiotics for every ailment? Because the more you take them, the more often bacteria may mutate into forms that are impervious to the medications. To deter the formation of such antibiotic-resistant bacteria, don't overuse antibiotics (see box, below). Reserving them to knock out ailments that can't be cured otherwise helps to ensure that the medications will be effective when they are truly needed.

Above left: *The antibiotic polymyxin B attacks the cell wall of a salmonella bacterium.* Right: *The antibiotic penicillin is derived from this mold.*

CAUTION!

If you've been prescribed an antibiotic, be sure to take all of it, at the intervals your doctor specified, even if you feel better. Stopping too soon allows the stronger bacteria to survive and reproduce.

an ounce of Prevention

How to Protect Against the Overuse of Antibiotics

- Remember, only bacterial infections can be cured by antibiotics. Viral infections, such as colds and flu, don't respond to them.

- Beware of any doctor who prescribes a drug without firsthand knowledge of what is ailing you. If necessary, ask for tests that will justify the prescription.

- When your doctor prescribes an antibiotic, ask for a narrow-spectrum rather than a broad-spectrum drug, if it will be as effective in curing your ailment.

- When taking antibiotics, be sure to follow all the doctor's directions to the letter.

- Never take antibiotics that have been prescribed for someone else.

- Never take antibiotics that are left over from a former illness.

- If your symptoms don't begin to clear up after several days of antibiotic therapy, contact your doctor immediately.

- Don't routinely take antibiotics to help prevent infection. (There are exceptions: antibiotics are often administered to individuals who are susceptible to bacterial infections, including patients who have undergone certain types of surgery and people who suffer from a chronic health condition, such as pulmonary illness or heart-valve disease.)

- If your child is prone to ear infections, your doctor should prescribe antibiotics sparingly. This problem is one that is commonly linked to the overuse of antibiotics. Research has shown that in most cases ear infections, given time, tend to clear up without medication.

Antidepressants

It is estimated that 80 percent of all cases of depression are treated successfully with the help of a doctor's initial prescription for antidepressants.

People who have been depressed most of their lives may at long last, with the help of these medications, experience a substantial degree of relief.

Ever feel moody? It's perfectly normal. Everybody gets the blues from time to time, especially after a big disappointment, the loss of a loved one, or a major life change. For some, however, depression is an ongoing state of mind or one that comes and goes with excruciating regularity. An estimated three million Canadians suffer from serious depression (more than half of them women.) Only in recent decades have a majority of these cases been treatable, thanks in large part to a variety of medications that have been developed and in part to psychotherapy treatments that are carefully targeted to the needs of depressed individuals.

How antidepressants help the brain

The brain is powered by electrical impulses from neurons, or nerve cells. These impulses release hundreds of chemicals into the gaps between the cells. These chemicals, called neurotransmitters, convey the impulses to adjoining cells.

No one knows for sure what causes depression, but it may be that an imbalance of the neurotransmitters affects how we think and feel. Two of the neurotransmitters, serotonin and norepinephrine, are thought to have a particular connection with the emotions. Antidepressant medications may help to restore the brain's normal balance of such chemicals. (Note: If you suspect you have a depressive disorder, don't rely on your doctor to detect your condition. Some studies have suggested that primary-care clinicians fail to diagnose the disorder 50 percent of the time. *You* may have to request a diagnostic evaluation.)

Antidepressants often enable people with short-term depression to quickly return to thinking and feeling much the way they did before the illness took hold. People who have been depressed longer—sometimes most of their lives—may at long last, with the help of these medications, experience a substantial degree of relief.

These days antidepressants are also prescribed for a host of other ailments: premenstrual syndrome, anxiety disorders (excessive worry and fear), obsessive-compulsive disorder (uncontrollable repetitive behavior), and panic syndrome (extreme feelings of dread, heart palpitations, and shortness of breath).

The chemical options

There are three principal classes of antidepressant medications. Some have been around for years; others are relatively new.

- The oldest class of antidepressants is the monoamine oxidase inhibitors, or MAOs. These drugs, among them Parnate and Nardil, affect the release of serotonin and other neurotransmitters.
- Another category of antidepressants is the tricyclics, which include Tofranil and Elavil. These target a range of neurotransmitters, including serotonin.
- More recently developed, the selective serotonin reuptake inhibitors (SSRIs)—including Prozac, Zoloft, and Paxil—work specifically on serotonin, helping the brain

use it more efficiently and keeping it in circulation among nerve synapses longer than the body can on its own. Close cousins of these drugs are the newer serotonin nonselective reuptake inhibitors (SNRIs), such as Effexor. SNRIs act on the neurotransmitter norepinephrine as well as on serotonin.

Because each person's chemical makeup is different, the doctor may need to prescribe more than one of these medications for a depressed patient before the most effective treatment that causes the fewest number of side effects can be found.

Safety and side effects

Antidepressant drugs are generally safe. Most of the side effects they cause are temporary. They vary according to the drug and the person taking it. Common side effects are dry mouth, dizziness, constipation, skin rash, sleep problems, nervousness, sexual dysfunction, and weight gain or loss. Often the side effects subside after the first weeks of treatment. If not, they can frequently be eliminated by changing the dosage or the time of day the medication is taken.

One caution specifically associated with MAO inhibitors is that they can interact with tyramine, an amino acid found in some foods, leading to a dangerous rise in blood pressure. Consequently, a physician may ask patients who take these drugs to observe a few dietary restrictions. Some over-the-counter drugs may also cause reactions when taken along with these medications.

Antidepressants can, in rare cases, cause mania. This is a state in which the patient has an abnormal degree of energy or euphoria that may lead to inappropriate or even dangerous behavior.

When any antidepressant is prescribed, it is important to have the physician explain what benefits and side effects to expect and outline how long the course of medication is likely to last. Follow-up with careful monitoring is also crucial when taking an antidepressant

so that the prescription can be adjusted or even changed if necessary.

Starting and stopping

Although the chemistry of the brain is affected within a matter of hours after the first dose of an antidepressant, there may be some delay before a patient experiences the full benefits. A patient can usually expect to start feeling better after having taken an antidepressant for about four weeks. The average course of treatment lasts from 6 to 12 months, plus a period of

Can an Herbal Drug Beat the Blues?

St. Johnswort is an herb that may someday offer a measure of relief to those suffering from depression. Its key ingredient is hypericin, which seems to act much as antidepressants do on the brain. Like all drugs, hypericin has side effects. Sensitivity to sunlight, and mild gastrointestinal disturbances are the most common.

Today St. Johnswort has become Germany's leading antidepressant, outselling even Prozac.

The major concern about the herb is the lack of precise studies on its effectiveness or the consequences of its long-term use. For this reason, the drug cannot yet be

safely recommended for treatment of depression.

In Canada, manufacturers who apply for permission to market St. Johnswort as a traditional herbal remedy and as a mild sedative for occasional use may receive authorization from Health Canada. St. Johnswort is not allowed for sale as an antidepressant however.

If you are already on antidepressants, don't add St. Johnswort to your regimen or abandon the prescribed drug in its favor. When combined with other serotonin-enhancing drugs, the herb may result in serotonin overload. St. Johnswort may provide some relief from very mild depression, but it is always wise to talk with your doctor first before taking it. If your doctor gives you the okay to take St. Johnswort, look for brands containing 300 milligrams of the raw herb, standardized to 0.3 percent hypericin.

Antidepressants (continued)

weeks or months at the beginning and end of treatment while the dosage is being adjusted. If the depression recurs after the treatment has ended, the physician may prescribe the same antidepressant again or decide a different medication may be called for. If the recurring condition becomes a chronic one, antidepressants may be prescribed over the long term.

Antidepressants are not addictive, but stopping them suddenly can cause withdrawal symptoms, including upset stomach, sleep disorders, mood changes, or tremors. Gradual withdrawal can often prevent such symptoms.

If you have sexual problems while on antidepressants, see your doctor about a new dosage or a new medication.

Is sex different?

For most patients, overcoming depression leads to a happier sex life. A few, however, aren't so lucky: they experience sexual dysfunction while taking antidepressants, primarily the SSRIs. In men this can include such difficulties as impotence and ejaculatory problems, and both men and women may notice an inability to achieve orgasm or a decrease in libido. The effects on sexual function vary with the medication and with the individual. If you experience difficulties, talk to your doctor; changing the dosage or switching to a different medication can alleviate the problem. Difficulties disappear once the medication is discontinued.

What about psychotherapy and ECT?

Psychotherapy is often combined with a drug regimen to treat certain types of depression. The antidepressant tends to lift despondent feelings, enabling the patient to concentrate on the psychotherapy and to benefit from the self-awareness it engenders. Cognitive behavior therapy helps to change habits that are self-defeating. Interpersonal psychotherapy rebuilds social skills in patients, something medications can't do. Research shows that several months of psychotherapy may cure depression even without medication.

Electroconvulsive therapy, or ECT, is sometimes recommended for cases of severe depression. Fear and misconceptions about this treatment, particularly those stemming from the movie *One Flew Over the Cuckoo's Nest*, have given it a bad name. It is, however, safe and effective, particularly for older patients, for those who are delusional, and for those who are initially unresponsive to antidepressant medication. ECT is usually administered in a hospital and is almost always followed up with a regimen of antidepressant drugs. The most common side effect is a short-term loss of memory.

Symptom Sorter

What are the Signs of Clinical Depression?

Depressed people seldom recognize their own illness. If five of the symptoms below, including one of the first two, appear in someone close to you and last for at least two weeks, arrange for that person to see a doctor, despite any objections he or she may have.

- Persistent feelings of sadness, hopelessness, or pessimism
- Loss of interest or pleasure in ordinary activities
- Inappropriate feelings of guilt, worthlessness, or helplessness
- Difficulty concentrating, remembering, or making everyday decisions
- Reduced interest in sex

- Changes in appetite or weight
- Restlessness or irritability
- Thoughts of death or suicide
- Sleep disturbances (sleeping too much or too little)
- Frequent headaches, backaches, digestive troubles, or chronic pains that don't respond to treatment or have no obvious cause

Antihistamines

If you're among the millions of North Americans plagued by allergies, you probably already know about antihistamines—medicines that block the effects of histamine, a chemical produced by the body when it comes into contact with irritating substances. When taken before exposure to these substances, antihistamines help control sneezing, runny nose, itchy eyes and throat, hives, and more. They should be taken before exposure; they won't soothe reactions you are already suffering from.

Older versus newer drugs

Antihistamines fall into one of two categories. The older, "first generation" brands include Benadryl and Dimetapp. Newer drugs include Allegra, Hismanal, and Claritin. The newer medications are less likely to cause drowsiness or dryness of the mouth, and many of them need only be taken once a day.

Side effects and safety

Children and the elderly are the most susceptible to side effects or adverse reactions; a newer antihistamine that causes fewer side effects than the first generation types may be better for them. The most common side effects of the older drugs are drowsiness and dryness of the mouth, nose, and throat. A few may cause nausea.

Some antihistamines are combined with decongestants, which may make you feel jittery or anxious. People with high blood pressure should check with their doctor before taking them.

Antihistamines are safe if you follow the dosage recommendations and heed the label warnings, but it is always a good idea to check with your physician before using these drugs. They may cause adverse effects when taken with other drugs, particularly certain antidepressants, protease inhibitors, and medications for high blood pressure. Antihistamines may also bring on gastrointestinal distress or affect such medical conditions as enlarged prostate, urinary tract problems, glaucoma, and liver disease. Hismanal has been associated with arrhythmias. (Life-threatening arrhythmias were linked with the antihistamine Seldane, which resulted in its withdrawal in the U.S. by the FDA. It has been withdrawn from the market in Canada by the manufacturer.)

Ragweed, a nemesis of allergy sufferers, releases its windblown pollen—and the misery that goes with it—in late summer.

What to try instead

To combat teary, itchy eyes, try over-the-counter eyedrops containing naphazoline and pheniramine. If your nose is particularly affected by the allergy, over-the-counter nasal sprays may give you relief. Sprays containing decongestants should be used no more than three days at a time; they can be habit-forming. If these aren't effective, ask your doctor about a prescription steroid spray.

Some people claim that a daily superdose of vitamin C—500-milligrams—acts as an antihistamine. Since this amount exceeds the recommended dosage of 40 milligrams a day, you should check with your physician before starting such a regimen.

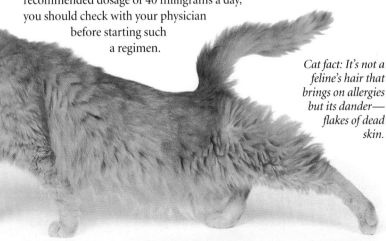

Cat fact: It's not a feline's hair that brings on allergies but its dander—flakes of dead skin.

Antilock Brakes

When antilock brake systems (ABS) were introduced in the 1980s, they were hailed as a major safety feature because of their ability to help drivers avoid crashes that result from skidding on wet roads. Today the brakes are standard equipment on most new vehicles—but at a cost of up to $1,000.

Are you getting your money's worth? Maybe not. When antilock brakes are needed the most—during emergency stops—many drivers do not use them correctly.

To pump or not to pump

Antilock brakes are activated when the system senses that one or more wheels are about to lock up—usually, as you apply firm and continuous pressure to the brake pedal. If your car has ABS, you should not pump your brakes when stopping suddenly.

Pumping antilock brakes is a dangerous proposition because it deactivates the very technology you want to engage. Unlike regular braking systems, antilock brakes will not lock up the wheels or cause the car to skid out of control when you slam on them. That's because the system reduces brake pressure and pumps the brakes automatically (up to 15 times a second) until the wheels rotate correctly. This maximizes road grip, prevents skidding, enables you to steer while braking, and may allow you to stop more quickly.

Do antilock brakes reduce crashes?

Although antilock brakes continue to work very effectively on the test track, they've produced mixed results on the road. U.S. government and insurance-industry studies found that they don't significantly reduce crashes. Even more alarming are two surveys that concluded that cars with ABS are more likely to be involved in fatal single-vehicle crashes. Auto-industry studies, on the other hand, showed that ABS reduced accidents on wet roads by up to 19 percent—and that they prevented nonfatal crashes but not fatal ones.

Some experts blame these inconsistencies on drivers. While ABS is engaged, a driver may hear grinding sounds, feel the vibration from the brake pedal (both of which are normal), and then ease up, deactivating the system. Other drivers may feel overconfident with antilock brakes because they mistakenly believe that they can stop safely at any time.

The bottom line? ABS makes little difference on dry roads and will actually lengthen stopping distances on gravel or soft snow. It is, however, effective in wet conditions.

Mastering ABS

Consumer and traffic-safety groups endorse antilock brakes, provided they are used correctly. To practice, take your car to an empty parking lot or other safe, open space on a wet day and drive up to 50 kilometers per hour (30 miles per hour). Slam on the brakes and maintain the pressure until you stop or can make a turn under control.

CAUTION!
Despite their safety benefits, antilock brakes don't enable you to drive more aggressively or negotiate curves faster. Nor do they shorten the recommended distance you should maintain between your car and the one in front of you.

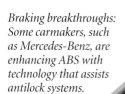

Braking breakthroughs: Some carmakers, such as Mercedes-Benz, are enhancing ABS with technology that assists antilock systems.

In 1513 Juan Ponce de León arrived in Florida, in search of the Fountain of Youth. Even though he never found it, he may have been looking in the right place. Today the oranges that grow in the Sunshine State and elsewhere are themselves a kind of fountain of youth because they are loaded with vitamin C, a prominent antioxidant. The term *antioxidant* refers to a group of vitamins, minerals, and chemical compounds that seem to help ward off disease and, perhaps, some aspects of aging itself. Among the extended family of antioxidants are vitamins C and E, beta carotene, the mineral selenium, and a variety of other compounds found in fruits and vegetables.

Providing our bodies with a generous supply of antioxidants (either from foods or from supplements) may help to prevent disease.

Arresting the free radicals

Free radicals—highly reactive molecules that contain an unpaired electron—are natural by-products of such processes as breathing and metabolizing food. They are also generated outside the body by air pollution, cigarette smoke, the sun's ultraviolet rays, and pesticides. Because unpaired electrons are highly reactive, free radicals can react with many cellular components, potentially damaging the body's cells. This cell damage may help pave the way for such ailments as cancer, cardiovascular disease, diabetes, cataracts, arthritis, and Alzheimer's disease.

Antioxidants protect the body by combining with free radicals before they can damage our cells. While more research is needed, some experts believe that providing our bodies with a generous supply of antioxidants (either from foods or supplements) may enable us to prevent disease.

Antioxidant-rich foods

Vitamins C and E, beta carotene, and the mineral selenium are the most celebrated antioxidants. Below is a list of foods that contain them in high concentrations:

- **Vitamin C:** citrus fruits (chiefly oranges, lemons, and grapefruit), broccoli, peppers, strawberries, potatoes, cauliflower, kale.
- **Vitamin E:** Nuts, vegetable oils, seeds, fish, broccoli, spinach, asparagus, wheat germ.
- **Beta carotene and other carotenoids:** yellow, orange, and red vegetables and fruits (carrots, squash, melons, mangoes, papayas, apricots, sweet potatoes, tomatoes), broccoli, spinach, kale.
- **Selenium:** fish, shellfish, red meat, grains, eggs, chicken, garlic, liver.

Mighty phytochemicals

Lesser known but very important are antioxidant plant compounds called phytochemicals. These compounds may have specialized functions, such as stimulating protective enzymes or inhibiting hormones, and, like other nutrients, they work as a group. Among them are allylic sulfides (found in garlic), tannins (found in berries and green tea), lycopene (found in pink grapefruit, tomatoes, and watermelons), and resveratrol (found in red wine, grapes, and peanuts).

One of the most potent phytochemicals is thought to be epigallo-catechin gallate (EGCG), a tannin found in green tea. This plant compound is estimated to be more than 100 times more effective at combating harmful free radicals than vitamin C and about 25 times more effective than vitamin E.*(continued)*

(continued)

The Top 10 Foods That Fight Free Radicals

One study found the following foods (ounce for ounce and in descending order) to have the greatest antioxidant effects:

1. Blueberries
2. Kale
3. Strawberries
4. Spinach
5. Brussels sprouts
6. Plums
7. Broccoli
8. Beets
9. Oranges
10. Red grapes

Leafy green vegetables, such as kale (below), as well as strawberries and citrus fruits, are packed with healthful antioxidants.

Foods or supplements?

So far, the evidence suggests that, whenever possible, antioxidants are best obtained from foods rather than from the supplements you buy in stores. For example, diets that contain lots of fruits and vegetables are associated with a greatly reduced risk of heart disease and cancer, and such diets may help slow the progression of arthritis. In addition, damage by free radicals and low levels of antioxidants in the blood—conditions that a healthy lifestyle and an antioxidant-rich diet may be able to correct—have been linked with dementia and Alzheimer's disease. Why foods seem to be more beneficial than supplements is still open to question, but the answer may lie in the fact that foods contain phytochemicals and supplements do not.

Solid evidence in support of supplements has been uneven. Scientists of the World Health Organization no longer endorse beta carotene supplements as a preventive measure against cancer. Nor is there conclusive medical evidence to support claims that 200 micrograms (mcg) of selenium daily may lower the risk of cancer. Doses of more than 150 micrograms of this trace element should not be taken without your doctor's advice. Excessive intake has serious side effects and a massive overdose can be fatal.

The bottom line: pills are not a substitute for a healthful diet, but they can be a valuable supplement to a healthful one. Because vitamins C and E in particular may help prevent disease and prolong life, many nutrition experts recommend daily supplements of 250 to 1,000 milligrams (mg) of C and 130 to 530 milligrams of E.

How safe are supplements?

Very safe, for the most part. However, supplements may be harmful under certain circumstances. Consult your doctor to determine a safe dosage, and heed these warnings:

• If you smoke, taking a supplement will most likely not prevent you from getting cancer or heart disease. Quitting smoking is simply the best way to reduce the risk of cancer and heart disease. Furthermore, smokers who take beta carotene pills may actually increase their risk of lung cancer.

• Cancer patients who take high doses of antioxidant supplements may reduce the effectiveness of radiation therapy.

• For those with high iron absorption, excess vitamin C may be harmful.

• Too much vitamin E may cause headaches or diarrhea and may interfere with some medications, such as blood thinners.

• In large doses, selenium can cause nausea, diarrhea, fatigue, and hair loss.

Taking Vitamin E Supplements: Advice You Can Swallow

Health Canada's Recommended Nutrient Intake (RNI) of vitamin E ranges from 7 mg a day for women ages 25 to 74, to 9 to 7 mg daily for men in those age groups. Because, in several studies, vitamin E has shown a variety of potential health benefits, some nutritionists recommend a daily supplement of 130 to 530 mg.

• Two large-scale studies suggest that a daily intake of more than 65 mg of vitamin E (more than you can get from diet alone), taken for two years, may have protected participants against heart disease.

• Studies have shown that 270 mg of synthetic vitamin E taken daily may help prevent heart disease as well as natural vitamin E and that daily doses of 270 to 530 mg may lower the risk of heart attack.

• A study has shown that 50 mg of vitamin E taken daily for five to eight years may reduce the risk of prostate cancer and the incidence of death from the disease.

• Vitamin E supplements may help prevent cataracts and reduce skin damage, including melanoma, caused by exposure to the sun.

• Treatment with vitamin E may also slow the progression of Alzheimer's disease.

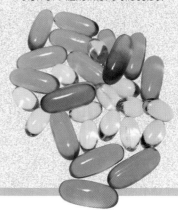

Art Supplies

Suffering for one's art is one thing; getting sick from the materials is quite another. The fact is, even everyday arts and crafts supplies, from permanent markers to rubber cement, can threaten your health and safety, especially if they are not used properly. Fortunately, thanks in part to federal legislation, art material labels must warn of any hazards, identify any hazardous ingredients, and give instructions for using the product safely.

Read the label

Toxic or flammable substances are found in countless materials used in many arts, crafts, and hobbies. The litany of potentially hazardous items includes paint thinners, aerosols, solders, solutions used in etching and photo processing, oil paints that contain cadmium or lead, and most dry clay. But, generally, these products pose problems only if they are used improperly, so always follow the instructions on the label.

How can art supplies hurt you? Toxins enter the body through the skin, through the digestive tract, or through the lungs when fumes, dust, or fibers are inhaled. An acute, or immediate, reaction can cause nausea, dizziness, headache, fatigue, coughing, and even death. Chemicals used in photo processing can decompose and give off sulfur dioxide gas, which damages lung tissue and causes severe asthma. Often,

Shades of safety: Few art materials are entirely risk-free. Many that are safe for short-term use may pose a health threat with long-term exposure.

however, the adverse effects occur only after months or years of frequent exposure. Ailments linked to art materials include rashes, burns, lead and carbon monoxide poisoning, silicosis, respiratory disease, cancer, and damage to the heart, liver, kidneys, nerves, or reproductive system. Especially vulnerable are children, who tend to put things in their mouths and metabolize toxins faster than adults. Others at increased risk are the elderly, pregnant or nursing women, people with allergies or respiratory ailments, as well as heavy smokers and drinkers.

Nontoxic seals

If you work with young children, use only nontoxic materials, or use the least toxic materials you can find—water-based rather than solvent-based paints, prepared clay and premixed dyes and glazes instead of the powdered forms. Keep in mind that even products labeled *nontoxic* can pose health problems in the long term if improperly used. Try to keep your work area apart from everyday living areas. Even then, store materials out of children's reach, and never store toxic substances in pop bottles or other containers where someone might drink them by mistake.

Create with caution

- Keep all art materials away from food, beverages, and cigarettes.
- When possible, work outdoors, upwind of fumes or vapors. If you work indoors, make sure the room is well ventilated.
- When appropriate, wear protective gear, such as a dust mask, goggles, or gloves.
- When working with children, avoid using epoxy, rubber cement, instant glue, or other solvent-based adhesives. Opt, instead, for white paste, glue sticks, or double-sided tape. Also, use only water-based marking pens, paints, and inks.

Artificial Sweeteners

Products of modern research laboratories, artificial sweeteners are chemicals that are intensely sweet but have few or no calories. Compared to sugar, sucralose (found in Splenda and approved for use in all foods and beverages) is 600 times sweeter; saccharin (which may be sold only in pharmacies and is approved only for tabletop use) is about 400 times sweeter; aspartame (used in NutraSweet) is 180 to 200 times sweeter; and acesulfame-K or acesulfame-potassium (found in Sunette) is some 200 times sweeter. Aspartame and acesulfame-K may be used in a variety of foods. Cyclamate, another noncaloric sweetener (found in Sweet 'n' Low), is not permitted in processed foods, but may be used as a tabletop sweetener.

In regard to taste and versatility, each sweetener has its strengths and weaknesses. Saccharin is inexpensive but has a bitter aftertaste. Aspartame has no aftertaste, but it loses its sweetness when heated or exposed to certain acids. Acesulfame-K, which is used to sweeten many different products, can also be used in cooking.

The benefits: real or artificial?

Artificial sweeteners let diabetics enjoy pop, candy, and even ice cream, without consuming sugar. This is a plus but not a necessity, since most diabetics are allowed some sugar in their diets. Even for weight control, sugar substitutes do not work magic; although their use has soared in the past 15 years, North Americans are becoming increasingly obese. Most studies show that dieters experience no greater weight loss with the use of artificial sweeteners, possibly because artificially sweetened foods may still be high in fat. On the plus side, however, unlike sugar, artificial sweeteners do not promote tooth decay.

The cancer connection

According to more than 90 studies, acesulfame-K has been found to be safe. Aspartame, once suspected of causing brain cancer, has also been given a clean bill of health, since numerous studies found no basis for that concern. Although high doses of saccharin were associated with cancer in rats, more recent studies suggest it is unlikely to be a risk factor for cancer in humans, and is not considered a strong risk factor for bladder cancer, as was once feared.

Be savvy about sweeteners

Artificial sweeteners—especially aspartame—aren't for everyone. Aspartame is unsafe for people with the genetic disorder PKU (phenylketonuria) because they cannot metabolize its main ingredient, an amino acid called phenylalanine. Some studies have found that aspartame may also adversely affect children with epilepsy. And some otherwise healthy people may experience headaches from aspartame; if you suspect that you are one of them, try avoiding the sweetener for two weeks to see whether your headaches subside.

Aside from the cautions mentioned above, artificial sweeteners appear to be quite safe when consumed in moderate quantities. According to Health Canada, 40 milligrams of aspartame per kilogram (2.2 pounds) of body weight is an acceptable daily intake. (Most diet pops have 35 to 40 milligrams of aspartame per 100 milliliter serving.)

CAUTION!

Aspartame should be avoided by people with PKU (phenylketonuria), children with epilepsy, and anyone susceptible to aspartame-induced headaches.

On the Horizon Although Health Canada has not yet moved to permit the use of Alitame, a substance 2,000 times sweeter than sugar, approval for this new artificial sweetener is pending in the United States. There Alitame is awaiting one additional animal study requested by the U.S. Food and Drug Administration.

Asbestos

Is Your Child At Risk?

A Harvard University study estimated that for every 100,000 premature deaths, only one is caused by exposure to asbestos in school buildings. Compare that to:

Smoking 21,900

Car accidents. 1,600

Diagnostic X rays 75

Lightning 3

It was common in the Toronto area about a decade ago and is still happening in the U.S.: a school suspected of containing asbestos is shut down. Fear grips the community. Politicians, health officials, and school administrators come under fire. Parents are outraged. Children are kept home until the school is deemed safe. Is the scare justified? The current expert opinion is that occupants of buildings containing asbestos are at little risk. Nevertheless, billions of dollars have been spent removing asbestos from homes and schools to protect the occupants. Often removal may be more harmful than leaving it alone.

Who is at risk?

Although any exposure to asbestos may be harmful, casual exposure is not thought to produce adverse effects. All of us inhale small amounts of the fibers throughout our lives without suffering any harm. Those really at risk are miners, construction, demolition, and building maintenance workers, and anyone who has been regularly exposed to the mineral.

Hazards in the workplace

Asbestos is a generic term for a group of minerals that can be separated into tiny fibers. Because certain kinds—among them chrysotile (white), crocidolite (blue), and amosite (brown)—are durable, resist heat, and possess fire-retar-

dant properties, they were once widely used for insulation and fireproofing. Chrysotile asbestos, considered the least hazardous, is the type found in Quebec.

When inhaled, asbestos fibers may become lodged in the lungs and lead to lung cancer, mesothelioma (tumors in the lining of the lung or abdominal cavity), and asbestosis

Despite the scares of recent years, there has never been a reported case of illness caused solely by exposure to asbestos in the home.

(painful scarring of the lungs). The time between exposure and onset of disease is 10 to 15 years for lung cancer and as long as 20 to 45 years for mesothelioma and asbestosis. Severity of the illness depends on the duration of exposure and the amount of asbestos inhaled.

In Canada, work-related exposure prior to 1980 claims about 10 asbestosis sufferers and many times that number of mesothelioma and lung cancer victims each year. Some experts estimate that thousands more will die in the years to come.

Exposed workers who smoke are more likely to die of lung cancer than exposed nonsmokers. Also, workers' families are at risk because fibers can be carried home on clothing and hair.

On the home front

Many Canadian homes, especially those with hot water heating, schools, and commercial and public buildings built before 1980 contain friable (soft and crumbly) asbestos insulation or other materials. Health experts agree that most of this material poses no threat, since the asbestos fibers are embedded and cannot become airborne. Despite the scares of recent years, there has never been a reported case of illness caused solely by expo-

The pros know: Cleaning up microscopic asbestos fibers requires a high-efficiency particulate aerosol respirator, gloves, protective clothing, and a special vacuum.

sure to asbestos in the home. Furthermore, some doctors now believe that the fluffier chrysotile fibers, which make up almost 95 percent of the asbestos used in homes, are less likely to remain lodged in lung tissue than the needlelike fibers of crocidolite and amosite.

Asbestos use in Canada is governed by provincial and federal labor legislation. Friable asbestos, no longer legal, has not been used since 1980. Nonfriable asbestos is legal, however, but although considered safe, it is not widely used. Some 2,000 Canadians still work mining asbestos.

Managing the danger

Asbestos in older homes presents some degree of risk. If the material deteriorates or is damaged, fibers may be released into the air. So do not disturb undamaged asbestos, avoid any construction that might release fibers, and check the area periodically.

If the asbestos has begun to deteriorate or flake or frequently gets wet, have it examined by an asbestos inspector. If containment or removal is necessary, hire an asbestos contractor. Such contractors are certified only in Newfoundland and Prince Edward Island. Pinchin Environmental, an asbestos consultancy firm, advises consumers elsewhere to choose only contractors who can prove they are trained and experienced in asbestos removal. Usually it is easier and less expensive to contain the asbestos by enclosure (covering it with drywall, vinyl, plywood, or special pipe covers) or encapsulation (application of a protective sealant) than to remove it altogether.

Spot-check: If your heating-pipe insulation looks like this, call in an asbestos professional to have it tested.

Asbestos at Home: Where Does It Live?

If your home was built or remodeled before 1980, there is a good chance that it contains asbestos in some form. Check the following places and items:

• Insulation for heating systems and pipes. Look for a plasterlike coating on your boiler or furnace and chalky, corrugated material around your pipes and air ducts.

• Patching compounds and textured paints on walls and ceilings.

• Wall and ceiling insulation. Installed behind plaster walls, this usually poses no risk unless a wall is cut or torn down during remodeling or demolition.

• Vinyl sheet flooring and tiles. If your flooring was installed before the mid-80s, and is now well worn, it is best removed professionally or simply covered over. Vinyl sheets may have asbestos backing paper and, while safe in place, removal can cause high levels of asbestos dust. Vinyl floor tiles and their underlying adhesive may also contain asbestos.

• Roofing, shingles, and siding. The asbestos fibers in these items are very stable.

• Electrical-wire insulation and fire blankets.

• The walls and floors around wood-burning stoves.

If you suspect that you have found asbestos, do not touch it. If it is worn or water-damaged, or if you plan to remove, sand, drill, or cut the material, have it tested professionally.

Aspirin

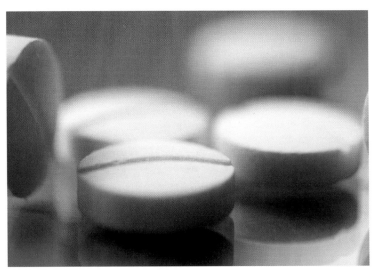

Aspirin is the main ingredient in more than 60 over-the-counter medicines. Taken every day, it may help prevent a second heart attack.

This trusted medicine-chest staple, now more than a century old, is no longer just a pain reliever. It's also a frontline weapon against heart attacks.

Aspirin is part of a family of drugs called salicylates. Its ancestry dates to around 400 B.C., when Hippocrates, known as the father of medicine, eased his patients' pain and fever with salicin, a powder derived from willow bark. In 1897 a German chemist discovered an efficient way to make a related compound called acetylsalicylic acid, and his employer, Friedrich Bayer & Company, gave it the trade name aspirin. Today people around the world take about 58 billion doses a year.

Help for the heart

Although many consumers use aspirin to relieve pain and reduce fever, inflammation, and swelling, some estimates suggest that two of every five doses are taken to prevent heart disease. In fact, in matters of the heart, the humble white pills are proving invaluable. One 325-milligram (mg) tablet a day appears to reduce the risk of a second heart attack by about 20 percent. (Researchers now believe that taking as little as 75 mg or one children's aspirin a day is sufficient.)

Preliminary research suggests that for men in high-risk groups—including those who smoke, are physically inactive, or suffer from hypertension, high cholesterol, or diabetes—even those who haven't suffered a heart attack may benefit from aspirin therapy. Ongoing research may eventually show that aspirin offers similar benefits for women. (Be sure to consult your doctor before taking aspirin for your heart.)

Aspirin can even help while you're having a heart attack. Some doctors and the American Heart Association urge people to take a single tablet (325 mg) at the first sign of a heart attack. Half a tablet taken soon after a heart attack and then for the next 30 days has been shown to cut fatalities by 23 percent.

Of course, aspirin is still used to fight pain and fevers. And although other non-steroidal anti-inflammatory drugs, such as ibuprofen, have edged aspirin out of some medicine cabinets, it still remains popular with arthritis sufferers.

How does it work?

Aspirin works largely by preventing the body's cells from producing prostaglandins, hormonelike substances that regulate many bodily activities. One group of prostaglandins sensitizes pain receptors, another causes redness and fever, and still another dictates the speed at which blood platelets form clots to check bleeding. When cells stop manufactur-

On the Horizon Aspirin's status as a wonder drug seems secure. Strong evidence indicates that aspirin can help some people who have had transient ischemic attacks to ward off a full-blown stroke. Some studies suggest that regular aspirin use can lower the incidence of colorectal cancers and slow cognitive decline in Alzheimer's patients. And ongoing research is testing aspirin's power to do battle with cataracts, gum disease, and preeclampsia, the sudden rise in blood pressure that threatens some pregnant women.

ing prostaglandins, pain and fever fade and platelets are unable to form clots, which can cause a heart attack or stroke.

Prostaglandins can also do damage on their own. Colon cancer tissue contains a suspiciously high level of them, and they may

The American Heart Association urges people to take a single tablet at the first sign of a heart attack.

contribute to the inflammation of blood vessels that causes artery walls to sprout new tissue. This growth could pinch off the blood supply to the heart or brain and raise the risk of heart attack and stroke. High doses of aspirin may help check this inflammation.

Are there dangers?

For all the wonders it works, aspirin is not without unwanted side effects. Frequent use may lead to ulcers. As many as 3 out of 50 users suffer stomach irritation and bleeding from taking even small amounts. (And don't assume that buffered aspirin will solve the problem: according to a recent study, it is just as likely as plain aspirin to cause gastrointestinal bleeding. Enteric-coated aspirin provides more protection, but it also takes longer to work.) Some people experience nausea and heartburn, especially at high doses. When mixed with alcohol, aspirin seems to increase gastrointestinal upset and bleeding. It may even increase the risk of hemorrhagic stroke (caused by bleeding from a ruptured blood vessel in or near the brain).

Aspirin can affect liver function and may be unsafe for people with liver or kidney problems or a bleeding disorder. It can dangerously boost the blood-thinning effect of anticoagulants. Even short-term use can speed the loss of valuable nutrients, such as vitamin C and folate. (If you use aspirin regularly, check with your doctor about taking vitamin supplements.) Finally, aspirin bottles come with childproof caps for a reason: there is always the danger of an overdose. Symptoms include ringing in the ears, dizziness, vomiting, and rapid breathing.

Tips on taking aspirin

- Take aspirin for no longer than 10 days for aches and pains, 3 days for fever. Otherwise, you may mask a serious condition that needs medical attention.
- Take aspirin after meals or with food to reduce the risk of gastric upset (unless you use delayed-release or enteric-coated aspirin).
- Because aspirin can injure gum tissues, it should be swallowed before it dissolves in your mouth. This is especially important after a tonsillectomy or dental surgery or if you have a lesion, such as a canker sore, in your mouth. Even chewable tablets should be washed down with water.
- Because aspirin's anticlotting activity prolongs bleeding, avoid the drug for five days before elective surgery or invasive tests.
- Don't lie down for 30 minutes after taking aspirin to prevent injury to the esophagus.
- Check the bottle's expiration date, and throw away aspirin that smells like vinegar; it's a sign that the drug is breaking down.
- Store aspirin in a cool, dry place—not in the bathroom.

Why Do You Use Aspirin?

Results of a worldwide survey (percentages have been rounded):

Heart disease
    prevention 38%
Arthritis 23%
Headaches 14%
Other pains 14%
Body aches 12%

Aspirin Alert: It's Not Kid Stuff

Not long ago, orange-flavored children's aspirin was in every parent's medicine chest. No more. Unless the child has a condition like arthritis, it's the rare physician who will recommend aspirin for a youngster these days. The reason is Reye's syndrome, an acute and sometimes fatal childhood disease triggered by a viral infection, such as the flu or chicken pox. Some studies suggest that aspirin acts as a catalyst. To be safe, use acetaminophen or ibuprofen to lower fevers in children under the age of 16.

Reye's syndrome typically strikes as the infection begins to lift. A brief recovery period is followed by intense vomiting, lethargy, confusion, coma, and sometimes death. Call a doctor at the first sign of these symptoms.

Automobile Exhaust

In an ideal world, your car's gasoline engine would produce only energy, carbon dioxide, and water. However, cars just don't work this efficiently. Instead, they often produce a toxic cloud of carbon monoxide, nitrogen oxides, and other harmful pollutants, which foul the air and pose a very real danger to public health.

The impact on human health

When exposed to auto exhaust, healthy people can suffer from lowered immunity, impaired cognitive function, and difficulty breathing. Infants, the elderly, and those with heart and lung ailments are particularly vulnerable. Here's a list of these pollutants and their effects:

New cars will emit 80 to 97 percent less pollution over their lifetimes than those built before 1970. . . . The problem now is too many cars—one for nearly every two Canadians!

- **Carbon monoxide (CO).** CO poisoning is debilitating and potentially fatal (see box, below). Smokers, those with anemia, and patients with congestive heart failure are at risk.
- **Nitrogen oxides (NO_3).** These pollutants give smog its brownish hue. They can irritate the eyes and lungs; lower immunity to such respiratory ills as colds and bronchitis; and worsen asthma and allergy symptoms.
- **Ozone (O_3).** A major component of smog, ground-level ozone (not that of the upper atmosphere's ozone layer) is produced in abundance on hot, sunny days. It can make breathing difficult, irritate the respiratory tract, and produce coughing and chest pain.
- **Particulate matter.** These microscopic particles (a fraction of the width of a human

an ounce of Prevention

Carbon Monoxide Poisoning

Here's how to guard against the dangers of this deadly gas:

- Have your car's exhaust system regularly inspected for leaks by a reliable mechanic.
- Never let the car's engine run in a closed garage. Before starting your car in an attached garage, shut the door to the house.
- Even when outside, open a window when sitting in a parked car with the engine running.
- When driving in traffic, crack open your car windows even if you're running the air conditioner.
- When starting your car after a snowstorm, make sure the tailpipe is not blocked by snow.
- Become familiar with the symptoms of carbon monoxide poisoning. They include dizziness, severe headache, fatigue, agitation, stupor, pale skin, and coma.
- If severe poisoning occurs, get the victim into fresh air immediately. Call 911 (or have someone else call) to ask for emergency medical help. If the person has no pulse and is not breathing, perform CPR (but only if you are properly trained). If the person does have a pulse but is not breathing, perform mouth-to-mouth resuscitation.

Even with stricter emission controls in place, the average car's exhaust contains harmful toxins and particles, many of which cannot be seen.

The bad news

Despite all of these good intentions, many major North American cities continue to be inundated by noxious clouds of smog. The problem, in a nutshell, is too many cars—one for nearly every two Canadians at last count!

To complicate matters, light trucks, minivans, and sport utility vehicles have grown in popularity. These vehicles are allowed higher emissions because they are designed to carry heavier loads—even though few soccer moms haul heavy cargo. Nonautomotive vehicles, such as lawn mowers and motorboats, also generate city smog. Research shows that mowing your lawn for an hour with a gas-powered mower creates as much pollution as driving 80 kilometers (50 miles) in your car.

hair) can penetrate the lungs and build up over time, causing lung infections, asthma, and chronic lung disease. The degree of danger is still being debated, but data suggest it may be a potential carcinogen.

The good news

Today's cars emit 80 to 97 percent less pollution than those built before 1970. Since 1971, when vehicle emissions were first regulated under the Motor Vehicle Safety Act, controls have grown progressively stringent. Furthermore, cars have become more fuel efficient: today's cars consume 50 percent less fuel than in 1973. Fuels are also less polluting. For instance, since 1974, lead has been gradually phased out of gasoline, resulting in a 97 percent reduction of lead concentrations in air. Recently, regulations include the reductions of sulfur content in diesel starting in 1998, and benzene—a known carcinogen—in gasoline starting in 1999. Carmakers, which may one day turn out zero-emission vehicles, are developing electric and alternative-fuel cars and more efficient catalytic converters.

How you can help

Here are a few ways to cut down on automobile exhaust:

- Keep your car well tuned. Under-inflated tires can raise fuel consumption by 8 percent.
- Instead of driving to work, join a car pool, take public transportation, walk, or ride a bike.
- If your engine idles for longer than a minute, turn it off.
- Don't tamper with your car's emission controls—this may increase exhaust.
- Never "top off" your car's gas tank—this releases vapors into the air that contribute to the formation of ground-level ozone.
- Buy an energy-efficient car. Most new cars sold in Canada have a fuel consumption label you can check.

Carpooling saves you money spent on gas, helps reduce traffic, and cuts down on emissions. It also provides a break from the maddening task of driving during rush hour.

Baby Equipment

There is perhaps nothing more exciting than welcoming a new baby into the family. And whether you are the parent, a grandparent, or a close friend, you probably can't wait to celebrate the birth with the purchase of any one of dozens of baby-care gifts.

But did you know that some of the very items used to protect and care for a baby can be dangerous? Each year many furnishings cause serious—sometimes fatal—injury to Canadian children. Fortunately, by following a few guidelines, you can help ensure that this won't happen and that the articles you buy will be both helpful and safe.

Shopping for safety: what to look for

During the past 20 years, and particularly within the past decade, the baby-equipment industry has undergone major changes. Most important has been the development of mandatory government safety standards for the manufacture of many items. As a result, much of the baby equipment you purchase today is safer than what was on the market when you were a child. Still, statistics show that injuries related to nursery equipment are common enough to warrant caution. Many accidents occur when parents leave an infant unattended, or when the child is not properly restrained in the equipment.

Recently, two products have received negative attention. Soft-sided playpens with fold-down sides have caused injuries and suffocation when they unexpectedly collapsed, trapping an infant between the mattress and the mesh side. Bath seats have led to drownings, often because the parents overestimated the device's ability to keep an infant upright in the water. These items should pose no problems if used properly with supervision.

A good source of information on safety standards for baby equipment is the Product Safety Bureau of Health Canada. By gathering information and learning which design features have true safety value, you can help guarantee that your selection will be the best and safest you can get for your money. What follows is a quick round-up of the features you should look for—and the ones to avoid—when buying baby gear.

Playpens and portable playpens

Because Baby may want to explore and try to wiggle all the moving parts, any playpen or

Safe and comfortable, this portable playpen has tightly woven mesh sides, vinyl-cushioned top rails, and padding underfoot.

an ounce of Prevention

Protecting Kids From SIDS

Every week in Canada, six infants die of sudden infant death syndrome (SIDS). Many experts believe SIDS may be linked to certain types of sleeping gear. Experts suspect that when a sleeping infant rolls onto his or her stomach, facedown in the soft bedding, the position may force the child to rebreathe exhaled air and possibly suffocate. Reduce risks: buy a firm, flat crib mattress, remove any soft, fluffy items from the crib, and make Baby sleep on his or her back in a smoke-free room.

What to Do When You Can't Afford to Buy New

With the sky-high cost of baby gear, it may seem like good financial and common sense to look to family and friends for used equipment. But remember that the older the item is, the less likely it is to live up to current safety standards. So think twice before you put your pocketbook before your child's safety. Don't overlook these important precautions:

- Check paint for chipping and peeling. If the item was painted before 1976, it may have been coated with lead-based paint.

- Look for any strangulation hazards: end panels with cutouts, in which Baby's head might get caught or corner posts with protruding finials that may snag clothing. Accordion-style, diamond- or V-shaped barrier gates can trap Baby's head.

- Check frames for stability; legs must touch the floor evenly. Examine hinges, brackets, corners, and safety belts to make sure they work and are secure. Replace broken or missing screws or bolts.

- Do not buy or attempt to upgrade cribs built before September 1986. They have a mattress support, suspended by hooks, that collapses easily. Crib slats are often wider than 6 centimeters (2³⁄₈ inches).

- Replace any seat cushion or mattress that has even a small tear or exposed padding.

- Make sure that a stroller does not easily tip. In the locked position, the wheels should resist attempts to push the stroller.

portable playpen must have well-protected hinges and multistep locking actions for assembly and disassembly. There should also be sturdy floor supports, with a fifth leg under the center of the playpen. Top rails of thickly padded vinyl are essential. Mesh sides should be tightly woven, with mosquito-type netting that does not allow baby fingers or little buttons to get through.

Avoid: Sharp edges or protrusions, flimsy legs, and drop sides. The draft guards on the bottom of the playpen must be permanently attached, not stapled or glued. Stay away from fold-down sides that use supports with a scissor-action mechanism. Never leave Baby in a drop-sided playpen with the side down. Baby can roll into the space between the mattress and the drop side and suffocate.

To prevent the playpen from moving, regulations prohibit the use of more than two castors or wheels. Don't add extra padding to the playpen or toys big enough for Baby to step on to climb out. Also check for torn vinyl and foam; children have bitten off pieces and choked, or have crawled inside the torn vinyl cover of a floor pad and suffocated.

Cribs and portable cribs

An easy way to confirm the safety of a crib is to look for a label stating the date of manufacture. A crib built before September 1986 does not meet the Product Safety Bureau's regulations. Also verify that slats are secure and tightly spaced. (You should not be able to slip a cola can between slats.) When lowered, the drop side should be at least 23 centimeters (9 inches) above the mattress at its highest setting. It should also fasten securely enough so that Baby cannot release it. Paint and other crib finishes must be nontoxic.

The mattress must fit snugly inside the crib, with gaps no more than 3 centimeters (1 inch) wide. It should also be firm and not more than 15 centimeters (6 inches) thick. A mattress that is too soft or worn could form a hollow where Baby's head might get trapped.

Remove all toys, mobiles, and crib gyms suspended over the crib when Baby begins to push up on hands and knees. Once Baby can sit up, set the mattress at its lowest position and take out bumper pads and large toys.

Avoid: Elaborate cutouts on end panels or slats; pointed or rough edges; wheels that

Baby Equipment (continued)

CAUTION!

Studies show that children who use baby walkers may take longer to learn to walk on their own. This fact, combined with the poor safety record of baby walkers, suggests that parents should perhaps avoid them altogether.

don't lock; single-motion locks for drop sides; and decorative knobs or corners. Keep the crib away from blinds or drapery cords, which Baby may reach and strangle on.

You may also want to avoid cribs and other baby furniture made of pressed wood or other manufactured wood products; these items often release toxic chemicals, such as formaldehyde, into the air for several years.

Baby swings

Head injuries are most commonly reported with baby swings. The swing should have well-secured safety straps to keep the child from slipping out. Baby should sit, not lie down, in the swing. The seat should be sturdy and needs to be compatible with the child's weight.

Avoid: Sharp edges, rough surfaces, or pieces that can be broken off. Make sure that the ends of supporting tubes are closed and smooth. If the baby swing comes with small toys attached, be certain that they cannot be pulled off and don't have small parts. Never leave your child unsupervised in a swing; place it where you and your infant can see each other.

Baby walkers

There are serious concerns these days about the overall safety of baby walkers because more children

Baby swings are great for soothing and entertaining little ones. This swing has sturdy legs, a secure safety belt, and a well-padded seat. The toys amuse Baby, but can't be pulled or broken off.

have been hurt while using them than with any other nursery product. Most of the injuries occur when Baby falls down stairs, tips over on thresholds or the edges of rugs, or gets burned by reaching for hot objects or liquids. Falls down stairs in walkers are the largest cause of head injuries in Canadian children under the age of two. Experts suggest buying an activity center for Baby instead; he or she will be less mobile but better protected.

If you decide to buy a walker, make sure it meets the voluntary safety standards of the Canadian Juvenile Products Association. It should be stable and too wide to fit through a standard home doorway of 81 centimeters (32 inches). You should double-check that it is wider than the widest opening in your home.

The seat must be secure, and the springs should be covered. It should have a gripping device or other mechanism that stops the walker if one wheel accidentally slips over a step. Safety devices that keep the walker from folding or collapsing while in use are essential.

Avoid: X-shaped frames, since they can pinch and cut Baby's fingers. Also be on the lookout for small parts that could loosen or break off and leg openings wide enough for the child's body to slip through. Never leave Baby in the walker unattended.

Strollers and carriages

Choose a stroller recommended for your child's weight and height. For stability, a wide wheel base is desirable, as is a low-mounted seat and a chassis that resists tipping. Make sure that the wheels are fixed tightly and aligned, with all wheels touching the ground at the same time. Sprocket-style rear wheel locks are safer than the kind that uses levers to press against the tires. There should also be two safety latches that require two releases to close the stroller.

To prevent Baby from sliding out of a stroller, look for leg openings that are restricted or closable. Be sure there is a sturdy restraint belt, one that fastens around the child's waist as well as the crotch, to help prevent the child from slipping. Make sure that the lap belt is solidly attached to the seat or frame. The seat should not pull away from the frame, even if you tug on the belt.

Avoid: Buckles that are difficult to fasten and snaps that are sewn on instead of being molded onto the material. Inspect restraint belts carefully and avoid those that fasten across the stroller rather than across the child. Be on the lookout for any sharp edges or protrusions, as well as X-shaped joints that could pinch Baby's fingers. Strollers built before 1985 may not meet current safety standards. Also never use a stroller on an escalator.

The lowdown on high chairs

Secure restraint belts, including a crotch strap that loops into the waist belt, are a must. Buckles should be sturdy and easy to fasten. The chair itself must have wide legs for stability (to avoid tipping) and a locking device that prevents the chair from accidentally folding while the child is in it. The tray bottom should have no exposed or rough edges. Seat seams should be smoothly sealed, without rough or crimped edges.

Avoid: Crotch straps that attach to the front of the seat and restraint belts that are not adjustable or that have D-ring-style buckles. Also watch out for small parts and easily removed end caps.

Infant seats

To avert accidents caused by the seat collapsing or falling off an elevated surface, look for a wide, sturdy base. If the seat is held erect primarily by a flip-back handle, press down while the handle is in the rear support position to be sure that the locking mechanism holds. Check the base for rubber tips or other nonskid surfacing that might prevent it from "walking" with Baby's motions. A sturdy, easy-to-operate safety belt is essential. Place crossed straps low enough to avoid the neck if Baby slides down in the seat.

Avoid: Any seat that seems flimsy or that is easily tipped over. Test by pressing down on it from different positions to check its stability. Even the sturdiest seat with a nonskid bottom should never be placed on a smooth, elevated surface, or a soft (water bed) or vibrating surface (top of a washing machine). If you set the seat on any high surface, keep an eye on Baby at all times. Never use an infant seat to transport Baby in a car; it is not a substitute for a child safety seat.

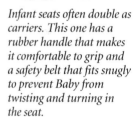

Infant seats often double as carriers. This one has a rubber handle that makes it comfortable to grip and a safety belt that fits snugly to prevent Baby from twisting and turning in the seat.

Readings on New Thermometers

Taking a baby's or a child's temperature doesn't have to be the ordeal that it used to be. Several new choices are available in addition to the traditional glass, mercury-filled oral and rectal thermometers.

The ear, or tympanic, thermometer (shown) takes the temperature of the eardrum in seconds. If used properly, it is a good choice for most children and adults. However, pediatricians do not recommend it for babies under three months or for children who have very small ear canals.

The pacifier thermometer features a temperature-sensing device in the nipple that measures the heat in a child's mouth. In most of these models, it takes about five minutes to provide a reading.

Digital thermometers include those that take underarm, oral, or rectal readings in less than a minute. The number in the window is your child's temperature.

Back Treatments

The familiar twinge or some lingering stiffness—maybe even a debilitating spasm or a pulled muscle. Like death and taxes, sore backs seem to be inescapable. Eight out of 10 Canadians will endure an episode of back pain at some point in their lives. After the common cold, back pain is the second most common reason Canadians visit the doctor.

That's the bad news. The good news is that nearly 90 percent of back problems clear up in two to six weeks without any special treatment. (If back pain does persist beyond a few weeks, see your doctor; it could be a sign of a serious health problem.) Many cases of back pain can also be prevented by following regular stretching and exercise routines.

Bed rest and more

Several treatments come to mind when you think "aching back"—bed rest, ice and heat, painkillers, and chiropractic. Although these options can provide relief, they should be used judiciously. Follow these guidelines:

- Bed rest—two days at most—is advised only after an episode of severe back pain. Be sure to lie flat (not sit up), with a pillow under your knees, and get out of bed as soon as you are comfortable, even if some soreness remains. Too much rest can weaken back muscles and lead to further injury. Once you are up, gentle stretching and exercise is also recommended. For minor back pain, all you may need to do is avoid strenuous activity—you can forgo bed rest altogether.

- Applying ice to a back immediately and during the 48 hours following a sudden, wrenching injury may reduce spasms and swelling. Hot baths, showers, or heating pads may relieve chronic backache.

- Over-the-counter painkillers, such as ibuprofen or aspirin, relieve mild to moderate pain. Muscle relaxants may be prescribed for more severe pain, but be aware that they can have more side effects.

- Chiropractic spinal manipulation can safely and effectively relieve low-back pain but should be used only in the first four weeks after an injury. Yoga, acupuncture, massage, and the Feldenkrais method (a series of gentle exercises that makes you aware of the right and the wrong ways to

an ounce of Prevention

Avoiding Back Problems

- Sit upright. Slouching while you sit puts 10 to 15 times more pressure on your lower back than standing does. For extra support, use a lumbar roll or a molded backrest.

- When sitting for long periods at work or home, take frequent short walks to prevent muscle stiffness.

- When lifting anything, heavy or light, bend at the knees, not the waist, and lift with your leg muscles.

- Avoid sports that involve twisting motions, such as golf and tennis.

- Strengthen your abdominal muscles. Example: Lie on your back with your knees bent and feet flat on the floor. Bring both knees to your chest. Try to raise your forehead to your knees while counting to 6. Repeat 6 times.

- Strengthen your trunk muscles. Example: Rest on your hands and knees. Raise your right arm and left leg; hold for several seconds. Repeat with the opposite leg. Do this 8 to 20 times.

- Do simple stretches. Example: Lie on your back with your legs bent. Grasp one knee with both hands and pull it gently to your chest. Hold for 30 seconds. Repeat with the other leg, then with both legs together.

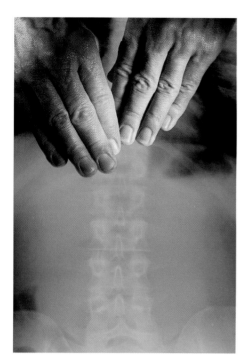

Chiropractic spinal manipulation involves a hands-on realignment of specific vertebrae in order to relieve pressure on nearby nerves.

sit, walk, and exercise) may provide temporary relief, but these methods are as yet unproven in treating chronic back pain.

Is surgery wise?

Surgical procedures, such as a laminectomy to treat a herniated disk, should be done only as a last resort. If your doctor recommends an operation, get a second opinion. Surgery is necessary in only 1 percent of cases of low-back pain, and it is not guaranteed to work. Also, do not let a magnetic resonance imaging (MRI) scan push you into having surgery. MRIs can detect spinal abnormalities that may be completely unrelated to the pain.

Products that pamper your back?

Back care has become a big business. Back stores now offer a wide variety of treatment devices, ranging from handheld massagers to spine-stretching contraptions. These prod-ucts often do not undergo scientific trials, and while they may provide temporary relief, they are not likely to prevent a recurrence of pain. Fortunately, they are also not likely to harm you, either. If you are interested in purchasing a product to relieve chronic back pain, consult your doctor. At the very least, you will become a more informed consumer.

In addition, be wary of two older back products. Back corsets, which may be prescribed for support during acute episodes, have not been proven to work. Canvas or leather back belts, which are worn by some weight lifters and laborers to prevent low-back injuries, have shown no preventive benefits and may even increase the risk of injury.

Back-friendly furniture

The furniture in your home or office could be contributing to your back pain. Consider where you sleep and sit:
- **Mattress.** Choose one that is comfortable. "Firm" is usually recommended. However, a mattress can be too hard; it should have some flexibility to provide support for the contours of the body. The best sleeping position? On your side, with your knees slightly bent. The worst? On your stomach.
- **Sofa.** A soft, oversize sofa that you sink into can put stress on the back. The best are firmer and allow you to sit straighter. Use throw pillows for additional support.
- **Recliner.** Fully extended, with foot- and armrests, recliners provide support for the back. Rocking chairs, which increase the flow of blood to the spine, are therapeutic.
- **Dining room chair.** Use a chair that enables you to sit with your buttocks comfortably against the back of the seat, your feet resting on the floor, and your knees slightly higher than your hips and about a hand's width beyond the edge of the chair.
- **Office chair.** Choose a desk chair with an adjustable seat, a backrest, and a five-wheeled base. Adjust its height so that your knees are slightly higher than your hips and your feet rest flat on the floor. Use a platform under your feet if needed.

Causes of Back Strains and Spasms

Most back pain is limited to a strain or spasm, a condition that is usually minor but can reoccur often. Spasms and strains commonly result from one—or a combination—of the following:

- Injury brought on by a sudden twist or movement
- Bending and lifting a weight
- Poor posture
- Extra abdominal weight, including pregnancy
- Muscle fatigue
- Inactivity or poor muscle tone
- Stress and general tension
- Spinal misalignment, such as lordosis (swayback)
- High-heeled shoes

Bacteria in Food

Many of the bacteria in food are benign. They turn milk into yogurt or cheese. But a number of bacteria are also the main cause of food-borne illness. Outbreaks of food poisoning are not limited to consumption of undercooked burgers and chicken. Recent incidents have been traced to such items as apple cider, cantaloupe, alfalfa sprouts, chocolate milk, eggs, hummus, ice cream, lettuce, and hard salami.

The Canadian Food Inspection Agency monitors processed food and domestic and imported produce for safety. The duties of agency inspectors include checkups on slaughterhouses, meat processing plants, and retail stores. However, it is difficult to gauge sanitation conditions where foreign produce is grown. When outbreaks of food poisoning do occur, public health warnings are issued and dangerous products are recalled.

Other safeguards may soon be in place. For example, a vaccine is in the works to protect cattle against *E. coli*. Also, food irradiation may someday become more common. Approved for use on certain foods (potatoes, onions, wheat, flour, spices, dehydrated seasonings), the process substantially reduces or eliminates many of the bacteria that make people sick.

Ground beef is prone to contamination by E. coli *because the grinding process allows the bacteria —usually found on the surface of meat—to spread.*

Food that harms

Every year an estimated 35 million North Americans suffer a foodborne illness. Usually mild enough to be mistaken for a "24-hour flu," these bouts can be fatal in the very young, the very old, and those already sick; more than 9,000 North Americans die annually from food poisoning. *Campylobacter*, a bacterium that infects 70 to 90 percent of raw chickens, causes flulike symptoms and bloody diarrhea and in rare cases may lead to the potentially fatal nerve disorder Guillain-Barré syndrome. *Listeria monocytogenes*, which sometimes grows in refrigerated foods, may lead to meningitis.

Among healthy people the vast majority of food-borne illnesses are mild, short-lived, and without serious consequences, but even a day or two of cramping and diarrhea is an inconvenience worth preventing. Proper precautions can minimize your risk.

Shopping for and storing foods

- When shopping, buy perishable foods last; when you get home, refrigerate or freeze them first. Make sure meats, poultry, and seafood are double-wrapped at the market.
- Avoid prestuffed, fresh whole birds.
- Don't expect "organic" protection. Organic foods are grown or fed without synthetic pesticides or fertilizers, but they are not safeguarded against bacteria.
- Keep eggs in their original carton on a refrigerator shelf. Never store them in the warmer door compartment, especially in the door's uncovered egg holders.
- Store meat, poultry, and fish in the coldest part of the refrigerator (usually at the back of the middle shelves).
- Put a thermometer in your refrigerator. Make sure it is at 4°C (40°F) or lower; the freezer should be –18°C (0°F). Keep your freezer fairly full.
- When freezing foods, wrap tightly with heavy-duty aluminum foil or freezer wrap.
- Only defrost food in the refrigerator, the microwave, or cold water, changing the water every 30 minutes. Never defrost food at room temperature.
- Refrigerate foods preserved in sugar or acid (jams, jellies, pickles) after opening.
- Toss unused foods. In the refrigerator, raw poultry, seafood, ground meat and poultry, sausage, and variety meats last only a day or two. Uncooked beef, veal, pork, or lamb

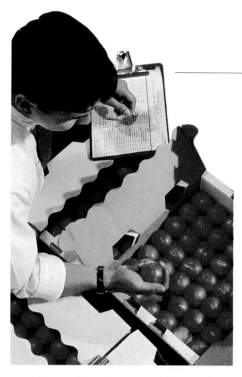

and opened luncheon meats: three to five days. Opened bacon and hot dogs: a week. Eggs: three to five weeks. Cooked poultry lasts three to four days. Cut mold off hard cheeses (plus 2.5 cm/1 in below it), but discard moldy soft cheeses and spreads.

• If the power fails, keep the refrigerator and freezer doors closed as much as possible and follow these guidelines: If food has been kept above 4°C (40°F) for two hours or more, discard anything made with milk, cream, or eggs. However, it is still safe to thoroughly heat and serve (or refreeze) cooked vegetables, casseroles, stews, meats, and poultry for up to eight hours. After eight hours, discard those foods, along with mayonnaise, soft cheese, cartons of milk, and hot dogs.

Preparing and cooking food

• Wash produce before cutting or peeling it. Cold water and a vegetable brush do the job (discard outer leaves on lettuce). Wash rinds of melons and citrus fruits; cutting them can transfer bacteria to the inside.

• Wash your hands before and after preparing food—perhaps the single most effective way to prevent spread of infection. Wash with soap and warm running water for at least 20 seconds, using a nailbrush on fingernails. Repeat each time you handle raw foods, touch your pet, use the bathroom, change a diaper, or blow your nose. Dry your hands with a freshly laundered towel or clean paper towel. If you have a cut, wear rubber gloves to prepare food.

• Marinate food in the refrigerator. To make a sauce from a marinade, boil it first.

• Buy a meat thermometer and use it. Cook ground meats (beef, veal, lamb, pork) to 71°C (160°F), steaks and roasts to at least 63°C (145°F) (medium rare), ground poultry to 74°C (165°F), poultry breast meat to 77°C (170°F), whole birds to 82°C (180°F). Hamburger juices should run yellow or clear, not pink.

• Roast meat or poultry at temperatures no lower than 163°C (325°F).

• Prepare and serve food with temperature in mind. Most bacteria multiply at between 4°C (40°F) and 60°C (140°F), so keep cold foods cold and hot foods hot. Refrigerate any remaining leftovers without delay.

• Reheat leftovers until steaming hot.

• Don't partially cook and then refrigerate

Food inspectors like the one at far left are part of the Canadian Food Inspection Agency's federal program to monitor processed food and domestic and imported produce.

an ounce of **Prevention**

How Fresh Is Your Food? Read the Label

You've seen freshness labels on milk, baked goods, and other foods. The terms are standardized. Here's what they mean:

• **"Best before"** is a date required on all highly perishable foods (such as wieners, milk, and baked goods) to indicate the timespan of optimum quality. After the date expires, the food may be unpalatable, but not unsafe to consume.

• **"Packaged on"** refers to the date on which the perishable product was processed at the retail level. On the label, this date must be accompanied by the product's "durable life"—a date that indicates the number of days for quality and freshness.

• If a food label says **"Keep refrigerated"** or something similar, do so immediately. Freezing food preserves it past the labeled dates.

Bacteria in Food (continued)

foods. If you finish a food on the grill or in the oven, do so immediately.

- Cook eggs well, not runny; avoid foods made with raw eggs. Also don't sample cookie dough or other batters containing eggs. Uncooked eggs can carry salmonella.
- To microwave, cover and rotate foods. Let them stand afterwards to finish cooking.
- Don't try to kill germs by heating food that has been left at room temperature for more than eight hours. Cooking it won't necessarily make it safe. If there is any doubt whatsoever, throw the food out. Never taste it; even if the flavor is good, the food can still make you sick.

A food thermometer measures the internal temperature of meat and poultry during cooking. It indicates when the food has heated up enough to kill any bacteria that are present.

Debugging the kitchen

- Toss dish towels in the laundry every day. Replace sponges frequently; in between, disinfect them in three cups of water with a teaspoon of bleach added.
- Wash dishes promptly in hot, soapy water or in a dishwasher. Let them air dry.

- Wash counters, equipment, utensils, cutting boards, and even salad spinners with soap and hot water after each use.

Eating away from home

On picnics, bring foods in a well-sealed cooler with plenty of ice and store it in the shade. If the temperature exceeds 32°C (90°F), consume foods within an hour. Safest choices: fresh bread, dried fruits, nuts, crackers, and fresh, uncut fruit.

In restaurants, make sure hot foods come to the table steaming. Avoid buffet foods sitting at room temperature if they contain meats, poultry, cheese, or cream sauces.

If you are traveling in less industrialized countries, "cook it, boil it, peel it—or forget it." Before leaving, contact Health Canada's Laboratory Center for Disease Control (by fax at 613-941-3900 or by internet at www.hc-sc.gc.ca/hpb/lcdc) for advisories.

If you do get sick, treat diarrhea first by drinking plenty of fluids. As soon as you feel you are able to eat, follow the BRAT diet (*b*ananas, *r*ice, *a*pplesauce, and dry *t*oast) for 24 to 48 hours. If symptoms persist or become severe—bloody diarrhea; sharp abdominal pain; blurred vision; difficulty speaking, chewing, or breathing—get medical help without delay.

Cutting Boards: Which Ones Make the Cut?

What's better: plastic or wood? Probably plastic because bacteria wash off it more easily. Research has shown that wood does have antimicrobial properties, but bacteria can penetrate it, become dormant, and then reactivate when dampened.

Never cut raw meat, poultry, fish, or dough containing raw eggs on a cutting board and then cut raw salad ingredients on the same board. Bacteria can contaminate the board and spread from one food to another. In fact, Health Canada recommends that you reserve a board for meats, poultry, and fish; you should use another board for other foods.

Wash all boards thoroughly between uses, using hot, soapy water. Rinse thoroughly, and either air dry or pat dry with clean paper towels. Plastic, acrylic, or unlaminated wooden boards can go in the dishwasher. Once a week, sanitize a board by flooding the surface with three cups of water mixed with a teaspoon of bleach. Allow to stand for several minutes, then wash.

If a cutting board gets scarred or deeply grooved, buy a new one. Bacteria become embedded in the grooves and and may contaminate food later on.

Sorting the Symptoms

Bacteria	Sources	Symptoms	Concerns
Salmonella typhimurium	Raw or undercooked chicken, beef, eggs, baked goods; raw fruits, sprouts.	Nausea, fever, abdominal cramps. Onset: 12 to 48 hours. See a doctor if symptoms persist for more than a day.	Common cause of food-borne illness. Dangerous for infants, the elderly, and immuno-compromised individuals.
Campylobacter jejuni	Raw or undercooked poultry, beef, shellfish; unpasteurized milk.	Nausea, cramps, abdominal pain, bloody diarrhea, fever. Onset: two to five days. See a doctor if symptoms persist 24 hours or if neurological symptoms occur.	Common cause of food-borne illness. Rarely may lead to Guillain-Barré syndrome, a potentially fatal nerve disease.
Escherichia coli: 0157:H7 (*E. coli*)	Undercooked beef; unpasteurized apple juice; milk; lettuce and fruits.	Mild to severe abdominal cramps, bloody diarrhea. Onset: three to five days. See a doctor immediately.	Most cases are mild but can lead to hemorrhagic colitis or hemolytic uremic syndrome, which can be fatal. Biggest risk: children under five and elderly or sick people.
Listeria monocytogenes	Soft cheeses and all unpasteurized dairy products; raw or leftover meat, seafood, or vegetables.	Sudden fever, severe headache, vomiting, diarrhea. Onset: 3 to 21 days. See a doctor if symptoms persist for more than a day.	Mild effects in healthy people but in rare instances may cause meningitis, which can be fatal. Frail people and pregnant women should avoid suspect foods.
Clostridium perfringens	Any cooked food left unrefrigerated for more than two hours.	Mild to severe stomach distress, usually lasting around a day. Onset: 6 to 24 hours. See a doctor if symptoms persist for more than a day.	Symptoms can be more severe in the ill and the elderly.
Clostridium botulinum	Home-canned foods; leaky, bulging, or foul-smelling canned foods; any tightly covered food (wrapped or in oil) left out for 24 hours or more.	Progressive weakness; difficulty breathing, swallowing, or speaking; blurred vision. Onset: 8 to 36 hours. See a doctor immediately. Bring suspect food source with you for analysis so that diagnosis can be made quickly.	Can be fatal, especially if not treated immediately.
Staphylococcus aureus	Sandwich spreads; cream-based salad dressings; any foods handled in an unsanitary manner, especially custards, milk, and processed meat and fish.	Severe nausea, vomiting, cramps, diarrhea. Onset: half an hour to six hours. Illness usually lasts for a day or two. See a doctor if symptoms become severe.	Uncomfortable, but usually not serious when symptoms are mild to moderate. Severe symptoms sometimes require hospitalization or even surgery.

Note: Two food contaminants, *Cyclospora cayetanensis* and *Cryptosporidium parvum*, are parasites, not bacteria, that infect untreated water supplies. Lettuce, basil, berries, and other imported produce can carry *cyclospora*. Untreated drinking water can spread *cryptosporidium*. Diarrhea, nausea, vomiting, and cramps occur within a week and recur periodically. Diarrhea may be bloody. Seek medical help if symptoms persist for more than a day.

Listeria *bacteria are rarely found in food but may cause meningitis if ingested.*

Salmonella *bacteria can infect many foods but lead to fatal illness only in babies and frail individuals.*

Baths and Showers

Which is better—a bath or a shower? It depends. A shower is more invigorating (after all, you're standing, not reclining), while a bath is more relaxing and therapeutic, easing sore muscles, circulation problems, arthritis, and stress. Baths, however, are less effective at cleaning away bacteria than showers, and soaking in a bath longer than 15 minutes can exacerbate dry skin.

Bathing hazards

Injuries commonly occur in bathtubs and showers, mostly because of falls and scalding water. Here are some safety tips:

- Never leave a young child alone in the tub; a tot can drown in just 5 centimeters (2 inches) of water.
- When bathing a baby, don't use "support rings"—the suction cups can release, allowing the baby to tip over and drown.
- Use your elbow to test the temperature of babies' and children's bathwater (elbow skin is thinner and more sensitive).
- To reduce the risk of scalding yourself, fill the tub with cold water first, then add hot. You can also lower the setting on your hot-water heater or install an antiscald valve.
- To prevent falls, add grab bars, nonskid mats, and a bath bench in the bathtub area.
- Never use light switches or electrical appliances while in the tub or shower.
- Some bubble baths and bath oils can make the tub slippery and may cause vaginal and urinary tract infections.

Can bathing expose you to pollution?

Studies show that pollutants can be absorbed through the skin. During a 15-minute bath in contaminated water, you can soak up a liter of the stuff. Also, shower steam may contain chloroform. To be safe, use an exhaust fan and install a granulated-carbon filter on the showerhead or on the incoming cold water line.

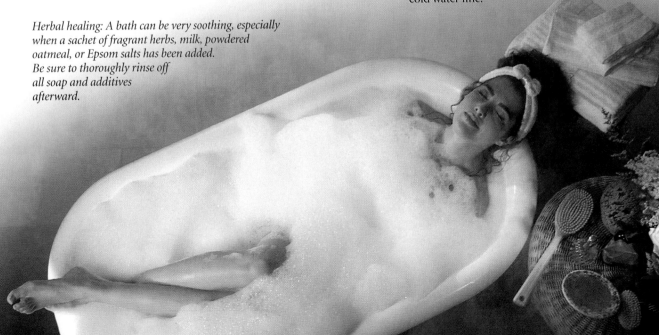

Herbal healing: A bath can be very soothing, especially when a sachet of fragrant herbs, milk, powdered oatmeal, or Epsom salts has been added. Be sure to thoroughly rinse off all soap and additives afterward.

A button cell for the camera, a couple of D cells for the family flashlight, AAA's for the remote—Canadians buy about 220 million dry cell batteries each year. Along with car batteries, it's easy to see how the toxic metals contained in these power packages could pose a threat to the environment and our health.

Safety first

Batteries contain corrosive acids. If they overheat or rupture, they can cause a chemical burn. To avoid this, never combine rundown batteries with fresh ones (this overstresses the weaker batteries), and never use alkaline and carbon-zinc batteries together. Also, before recharging a recently used battery, let it cool to room temperature and always use the correct size recharger.

Each year some 600 tiny button cells are swallowed in North America, many by children. The battery usually passes safely through the body, but it can cause internal burns if it becomes lodged in the intestines. The cells can also get caught in a child's windpipe or nostril. Keep all batteries away from children.

Used batteries account for up to 35 percent of the mercury in landfills.

Battery care

A car battery (known as a wet cell) contains large amounts of lead and sulfuric acid and is inclined to leak. Recycling car batteries is now common, so take your used battery to an automotive shop or auto-parts dealer. Still, those that aren't recycled contribute to the lead found in dumps.

Smaller, dry-cell batteries contain such toxic metals as mercury, lead, and cadmium. Used batteries are estimated to account for up to 35 percent of the mercury and more than one-third of the cadmium—a known carcinogen—in Canadian landfills.

As landfilled batteries corrode, their contents can leach into groundwater. Exposure to these toxic metals has been linked to birth defects and kidney, liver, and brain damage. The good news: industry has responded by changing the formulation of many household batteries. Notably, the use of mercury has dropped by 82 percent from 1992 to 1995—due in large part to the introduction of "no added mercury" alkaline cells. To further reduce risks, follow these tips:

- Switch to rechargeables, which work in place of dozens of disposables; take used rechargeable nickel-cadmium batteries (known as "ni-cads") to retail chains participating in a Canada-wide recycling program.
- Take great care when changing and jump-starting car batteries—they can generate potentially explosive gases.
- Never incinerate a battery: it may release its toxic metals into the air or explode.

When replacing a car battery, wear gloves and goggles, and follow instructions carefully. Fumes inside the battery could explode if a spark is created, causing the battery top to blow off into your face.

Potential Harm from Common Batteries

Type	Possible Hazard	Recycling/Disposal
Alkaline cell	Mercury poses an environmental threat. There are now alkalines with no added mercury on the market.	Municipal waste disposal
Button cell	These dime-size batteries may contain mercury, silver, and cadmium. Small children have been known to accidentally swallow them.	Municipal waste; sometimes collected by hospitals
Nickel-cadmium	The most common rechargeable batteries, these contain nickel and cadmium.	Retail chains; call 1-800-8BATTERY
Lead-acid	The most prevalent type of car batteries, these contain large amounts of lead and sulfuric acid.	Auto-parts dealers, car repair shops

Beds & Pillows

Your bed may be the most important piece of furniture you own. It can determine not only how comfortable you feel during the night but also how well you feel during the day—as anyone who's experienced a sleepless night knows. This is especially true for those who suffer from back pain, an ailment that ranks second only to the common cold in frequency. For 8 out of 10 Canadians who seek medical attention for back pain at some point in their lives, the cure may be simple: another bed.

> For 8 out of 10 Canadians who see the doctor for back pain, the cure may be simple: another bed.

What is the perfect bed? One thing it isn't is rock-hard. In fact, an unyielding mattress can worsen a bad back. The body needs a combination of support *and* comfort. The level of support you require depends on your weight and height. A tall, heavy person, for example, would be better off with a higher-density mattress than someone who is petite and slim.

Decisions, decisions . . .
Today beds come in a dizzying array of types. The most popular is the innerspring—springs, or coils, topped with layers of padding. Available in various degrees of firmness, it will accommodate a spectrum of personal preferences. Nevertheless, a foam mattress also supports the back if you find it more comfortable than an innerspring.

Other, more high-tech possibilities are air beds, water beds, and adjustable beds. An air bed has air chambers, instead of springs, that you pump up as needed. Today's baffled water beds are more stable than earlier, "sloshy" versions. The feeling of weightlessness that these beds create can be therapeutic for arthritis or back-pain sufferers. However, some people may have trouble getting in and out of them. For those who generally have this difficulty with beds, adjustable types, with torso and leg sections that can be raised or lowered, are a great boon. They're also helpful for people with respiratory problems.

Buying a mattress
Experts advise getting a new mattress every 10 years. Shop with these tips in mind:
- Lie down for at least 20 minutes on each mattress you consider. Couples should do this together, making sure that each partner has enough room to shift position.
- Be sure that the mattress provides both firmness for the spine and flexibility for the hips and shoulders when you move or lie on your side.
- When buying an innerspring, ask about coil count. Generally, the more coils, the firmer the bed. A mattress and box-spring set should have at least 300.
- The most supportive innerspring is slightly higher at the center (horizontally).
- If you use a foundation, such as a box spring, invest in a new one when buying a mattress; otherwise, you may shorten the life of the new mattress.
- Be aware that if you buy a firmer mattress, you may experience some discomfort for a few days while your back adjusts.

an ounce of Prevention

Is Your Child Safe in Bed?
Every year in Canada, about 400 babies fall victim to sudden infant death syndrome (SIDS) in their cribs.

Bunk beds can also be dangerous. Injuries have been caused by falls from upper bunks. Some models led Canadian children to become fatally trapped and suffocate in the space between guardrails and the mattress.

To keep such tragedies from happening, do the following:
- Only use a crib built after 1986, when federal safety standards were set. Look for a firm, flat mattress that fits snugly and is no more than 15 centimeters (6 inches) thick.
- Never cover a crib mattress with plastic; instead, use a thin sheet.
- Never let a baby sleep on a water bed, an adult-size mattress, a pillow, or any other soft surface.
- Never let a child less than six use an upper bunk, and don't allow children to play there.
- Check to see that upper-bunk guardrails are sturdy and that they extend on all sides at least 13 centimeters (5 inches) above the mattress, which should fit snugly. Spaces from rail to frame should be less than 9 centimeters (3.5 inches).

Is your bed making you ill?

Many mattresses and pillows are filled with fibers or padding that release potentially irritating odors. For people sensitive to chemicals, this may mean headaches, nausea, or other allergic reactions. Also, permanent-press sheets are treated with a formaldehyde finish that can cause insomnia, coughing, or rashes. To avoid these problems, buy natural materials: cotton mattresses, such as futons, cotton or buckwheat pillows, and combed-cotton or flannel sheets. Wash new mattress pads and bedclothes before using them.

Beds and pillows also harbor allergens—mainly dust mites, which can infest a new mattress in only four months. If you're prone to allergies, wrap mattresses, box springs, and pillows in airtight or allergen-proof casings and use synthetic-fiber pillows instead of feather or cotton, replacing them every two years. Or try antimicrobial bedding, which contains additives that help prevent mites.

Vinyl coverings may not be a good alternative; one study indicates that their emissions may exacerbate asthma in children.

Pillow talk

Like a mattress, a pillow should provide support without rigidity, allowing the curve in the neck to be maintained. Try out a pillow before buying it to make sure it's not too soft or too firm. You may want to consider a buckwheat pillow. Besides being a wise choice for the allergy-prone, it tends to conform to the shape of the head. So does a water-based pillow, because of the fluidity of its inner pouch, which is filled with water.

If you have back pain that is aggravated by sleeping on your stomach, try a body pillow, which may be 1.5 meters (5 feet) long. Place the pillow alongside your body and between bent knees while lying on your side. This takes pressure off the lower back and prevents you from turning onto your stomach.

To maintain an inner-spring mattress, rotate it every other month so that the head and foot are exchanged. Every month, flip the mattress over.

CAUTION!

Mattresses made before 1982, when a federal flammability standard went into effect, are fire hazards. If you have any mattresses that date back to that time, carefully dispose of them.

Beta Carotene

An old wives' tale says, "Eat your carrots; they're good for the eyes." Because carrots are packed with carotenoids, including beta carotene, you can chalk up another one for the wisdom of old wives. Consuming foods rich in carotenoids may help prevent cataracts and age-related macular degeneration (a disease that affects the retina). Beta carotene and other carotenoids may also lower the risk of certain cancers.

However, studies of beta carotene supplements have produced mixed results; for smokers, they may even be harmful.

How it works

Beta carotene is the most plentiful of the carotenoids, a family of more than 500 plant pigments that range in color from red, yellow, and orange to dark green. In the body, some of the beta carotene is converted into vitamin A. Although vitamin A is toxic in high doses, large amounts of dietary beta carotene are nontoxic, since the body converts only as much as it needs.

As an antioxidant, beta carotene protects the body from so-called "free radicals"—unstable molecules that damage cells. Studies are ongoing, but by limiting the development of abnormal cells, it may help prevent cancers of the breast, prostate, lung, and stomach. Consuming beta carotene may also boost the immune system, help lower LDL (or "bad") cholesterol, raise HDL (or "good") cholesterol, and lower the risk of heart disease.

Food first

Experts agree that the best source of beta carotene is food. Because beta carotene is a yellow-orange pigment, its sources are easy to identify. Look for foods that are deep orange, yellow, and red; the more intense the color, the higher the carotenoid level. Carrots and sweet potatoes are excellent examples. Their distinctive hue reflects the large amounts of beta carotene they contain. Other sources are oranges, winter squash, grapefruit (red or pink), cantaloupe, apricots, peaches, pumpkins, and nectarines. In addition, beta carotene is found in dark, leafy greens, such as collards, spinach, broccoli, and kale.

How much is enough?

No Recommended Nutrient Intake (RNI) has been established for beta carotene and the other carotenoids, but according to Health Canada and the Canadian Cancer Society, 5 to 10 daily servings of fruits and vegetables will provide a good amount of beta carotene. The servings add up. Consider this:

- One medium-size raw carrot has more than 5 mg of beta carotene.
- A half cup of mashed, cooked sweet potato has nearly 9 mg of beta carotene.
- One half of a pink grapefruit contains about 1.6 mg of beta carotene and more than 4 mg of lycopene, another prominent carotenoid. Three-quarters of a cup of tomato juice has about 15 mg of lycopene.
- A half cup of cooked kale has about 3 mg of beta carotene and more than 14 mg of the carotenoids lutein and zeaxanthin.

The supplement controversy

Although dietary supplements are thought by some people to be nutritional magic bullets, in the case of beta carotene they have produced alarming results. One 12-year study showed that supplements provided no protection against cancer or heart disease. In two other studies involving heavy smokers, those taking supplements actually showed a small increase in the risk of cancer.

Should you take a beta carotene supplement? If you smoke, no. Otherwise, take it only if you do not eat fruits and vegetables, and limit the dosage to 6 to 15 mg a day. Ultimately, only this is certain: a nutrient isolated in a pill is not a substitute for a healthy diet.

Beta carotene is best consumed through food sources, such as carrots, sweet potatoes, and leafy greens.

CAUTION!
Results from several studies indicate that taking beta carotene supplements may offer no obvious health benefits and may even be potentially harmful, especially to heavy smokers.

Biofeedback

You're stressed! Your heart races, your muscles tense up, your mind blurs, your head pounds. Is it possible to calm yourself down by controlling these physical effects? Using biofeedback, you may be able to. Although doctors disagree on the extent of biofeedback's effectiveness, there is a consensus that it can provide some benefits.

Biofeedback is a treatment that uses simple exercises or counseling in combination with devices that monitor involuntary physical functions, such as brain wave activity, heart rate, or muscle tension. Patients learn to control physical or mental responses in order to help relieve a range of disorders, including asthma, insomnia, and incontinence.

Watch and learn

As a biofeedback patient, you will first be hooked up to a monitoring device. Such devices may include an electromyograph (EMG), which monitors muscle tension, an electroencephalograph (EEG), which monitors brain waves, or a heart monitor. Using the device, you will see how part of your body is functioning—usually by means of a needle moving on a dial or by a flashing light.

Your biofeedback therapist will then guide you through specific exercises that teach you positive physical responses. These responses, which are also monitored, include lowering blood pressure or retraining muscles and may give you a sense of control over your condition. Success comes when you can exert the same control without the use of a monitor.

To find a therapist, ask your doctor. Each session (usually 6 to 10 are necessary) can cost up to $200 per hour but may be covered by private health insurance or Medicare. Note: Biofeedback may be no more beneficial than low-tech relaxation exercises alone and should not be used in place of any medication that you are taking for your condition.

A variety of treatments

Biofeedback employs a variety of therapies, devices, and exercises. Whichever form is used, it works best when the patient is highly motivated. Consider these success stories:

- With the help of an EMG, a patient can retrain specific muscles, relaxing those that are chronically tense or contracting those that are weak or paralyzed. With this method, sufferers of incontinence can learn to retrain their pelvic muscles.
- Using an EEG, a patient can learn to produce more alpha and theta brain waves, the electrical impulses that are associated with calm alertness. This method may also be useful in the treatment of depression and post-traumatic stress disorder.
- Using a heart monitor, a patient can learn to control anxiety by slowing down his heart rate. In one study, people who concentrated on slowing their heart rate for 10 minutes each day had significantly less anxiety after three months.

Biofeedback Can Help Ease:

- Migraine headaches
- Anxiety
- Asthma attacks
- Insomnia
- Incontinence
- Irritable bowel syndrome
- Raynaud's disease
- Musculoskeletal disorders
- Rehabilitation from stroke

Electronic sensors that monitor muscle tension can help patients learn pain-relieving techniques.

Bites & Stings

To avoid stings from such venomous flying insects as these bees, don't wear bright colors, floral prints, or sweet scents, and never go barefoot in the park.

A stinging bee releases a chemical that attracts other bees, so if you are stung, leave the area quickly.

Fangs, stingers, mandibles, tentacles—nature is rife with beastly weapons designed to bite, sting, and poison. Fortunately, most assaults are little more than a painful annoyance, although the very young, the very old, and the allergic need to take special precautions. The stakes increase, however, if you are bitten by an animal that carries a disease.

Common sense goes a long way toward preventing unnecessary encounters. Although some species, such as mosquitoes, actively seek out humans, most animals will attack only if threatened. It pays to know how to treat bites and stings that do occur.

When vacationing, or if moving to a new area, ask the local public health or animal-control department which creatures, if any, pose a threat. If you plan to visit the southern or midwestern United States, for example, bone up on the brown recluse spider, whose venom contains an enzyme that eats away at tissues beneath the skin. If you winter in Florida and swim off the coast, learn to recognize—and give wide berth to—the Portuguese man-of-war, whose burning tentacles can stretch as long as 18 meters (60 feet).

Bee wary

A bee sting is painful indeed. But for people who are allergic to bee venom, it can be deadly. More than 100 North Americans die each year from bee stings. The sting of several other members of the Hymenoptera order, including yellow jackets, hornets, wasps, and red fire ants (see below), can also induce life-threatening reactions.

When confronted by a bee or wasp, stay calm and slowly back away. Stinging bees and wasps release a chemical that attracts others of its kind, so if you are stung, leave the area quickly. If a swarm attacks, lie facedown and cover your head with your hands.

Bees are the only hymenopteras that have barbed stingers that rip away from their bodies, killing the bee. Because the stinger continues to pump venom for several minutes once it is in your skin, it is important to get it out right away. Do so without squeezing the venom sac at the end of the stinger or you'll inject more venom. Scrape it out with your fingernail, or a knife or credit card, then wash the area with soap and water and apply ice to reduce the swelling. Later you may want to apply calamine lotion or a baking-soda paste. If you experience dizziness or difficulty breathing, go to a hospital emergency room.

Among the most painful of the hymenoptera bites is that of the red fire ant, which is

Allergic to Bee Stings?

About 15 percent of North Americans are potentially allergic to bee venom. For many of them, a sting will result in greater-than-usual pain and itching. But for people with severe allergies, bee stings can trigger a life-threatening condition called anaphylactic shock.

Symptoms include hives, breathing difficulties, light-headedness, swelling of the tongue or in the throat, nausea, and severe headache. If you experience any of these reactions, seek emergency medical help immediately; a delay in treatment could be fatal.

People who suspect they are allergic to bee stings should consult an allergist, who will perform a skin test. If the test is positive, the doctor may recommend a series of allergy shots to build resistance to the venom. Doctors also recommend wearing a Medic Alert bracelet and carrying a ready-to-inject syringe of epinephrine (available by prescription). If you are stung, injecting this medication will help you make it to an emergency room for observation and further treatment.

found in the southern U.S. as far north as Virginia. Their beds are found along the borders of sidewalks, driveways, and roads. Anyone who steps on one may be covered with insects in seconds. The ant's venom destroys skin tissue and causes a fluid-filled bump that itches for about a week. Red-fire-ant bites can be deadly. If attacked, get away from the bed and brush the ants from your body. If you have difficulty breathing, go to a hospital.

Mosquitoes, ticks: they want your blood

Humans may rule the food chain, but that doesn't stop some pests from using us as food. Mosquitoes and ticks dine on blood, while chigger mites make a meal of skin (special enzymes allow them to digest skin cells). Itching aside, the main problems these pests pose are the diseases they sometimes carry. Mosquitoes, for example, can on rare occasions transmit encephalitis, an infection of the brain and spinal cord that can cause flu-like symptoms, headaches, seizures, delirium, coma, retardation, and paralysis.

Ticks have also been associated with the spread of serious diseases, from Rocky Mountain spotted fever to Lyme disease. To remove a tick, use fine-tipped tweezers, taking care not to crush the insect. (Forget folk remedies, such as using a hot match or kerosene to shock a tick into letting go. These often traumatize the tick, causing it to regurgitate infectious agents into your blood.) Put the tick in a jar to show to your doctor.

Chigger mites aren't known to spread disease, but because their bites cause intense itching, a person may scratch them so fiercely that the area becomes infected. To reduce the itching, try calamine lotion or a steroid cream.

The best defense against insect-borne diseases is to avoid the insects that carry them.

- Make sure all your doors and windows have adequate screens.
- Stay inside during and after dusk. If you do go out, wear pants and a long-sleeved shirt, and use an insect repellent. *(continued)*

HIV and Mosquitoes

Worried about contracting the AIDS virus from mosquitoes? Don't be. HIV cannot grow inside mosquito cells, which means that mosquitoes can't serve as hosts for the virus. But what if a mosquito bites an infected person, then bites you next? Again, transmission is virtually impossible because the amount of blood transferred is infinitesimal. Experts estimate that you'd have to be bitten by thousands of mosquitoes at the same time before you'd have cause for concern.

Bites & Stings (continued)

The Lowdown on Lyme Disease

Lyme disease is named for an outbreak that occurred in 1982 near Lyme, Connecticut. Every year since some 11,000 cases occur in the U.S. Since 1987 close to 300 cases have been confirmed in Canada, where the highest risk areas are in southern Ontario and southern B.C. The disease is caused by bacteria transmitted by deer ticks that infest birds and various animals, including mice. Signs of infection include flulike symptoms, joint and muscle pain, swollen lymph nodes, and a red circular rash that appears in some patients.

If you think you may be infected, see a doctor. If

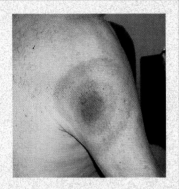

caught early, the disease can be cured with oral antibiotics. If not, intravenous antibiotics may be necessary, although the treatment is controversial. Even with treatment, complications such as arthritis, irregular heartbeat, and disorders such as meningitis and Bell's palsy (a form of facial paralysis) may occur.

A Lyme-disease vaccine may be available soon.

• When hiking, wear long sleeves and pants, tuck your pant legs into your socks, and spray your cuffs and the waist of your pants with insect repellent. Stick to the middle of the trail, away from brush.

• Check your body for ticks—especially your head, armpits, navel, groin, and the backs of the knees—following any potential exposure. Wash the clothes you wore.

• Take a shower. Most ticks do not bite immediately. Showering often washes away those that aren't attached.

Creepy crawlers

Most spiders have venom, but in only a few dozen species is it potent enough to harm humans. Canada has no venomous spiders, but two such species—the black widow and the brown recluse—are found in the U.S.

Ounce for ounce, the black widow is the most poisonous animal in North America. Found in most U.S. states, it lurks under logs and bark and in crevices and garbage heaps. Victims usually don't feel the initial bite, although sharp pain, nausea, vomiting, and sweating may occur within an hour, followed by the appearance of a small red bump. Although death is rare, always get prompt medical attention for a suspected black-widow bite; your doctor may prescribe painkillers and, if necessary, antivenin.

The brown recluse, or fiddleback, found in the southern and central United States, hides in the same spots as the black widow, but also feels right at home indoors, behind drapes or under furniture. Victims rarely die, but many suffer a slow-to-heal ulcer, caused by a skin-destroying enzyme in the spider's venom.

Snakes: don't be rattled

Around the globe, more than 50,000 people die each year from snakebite. In North America the statistics are less dire: about 15 deaths a year, mostly of people who regularly handle venomous snakes. A snakebite doesn't necessarily mean you've been injected with venom; many bites may be "dry strikes." Canada's only poisonous snakes are the massassauga, a small rattlesnake found along lakes Erie and Huron—mostly around Georgian Bay—in Ontario; the Pacific rattlesnake in the B.C. interior; and the prairie rattlesnake in southern Alberta and Saskatchewan. In the U.S. the only snakes that threaten humans are pit vipers, which include rattlesnakes, copperheads, and water moccasins, and coral snakes, members of the cobra family.

Pit vipers are easily recognized by their triangular heads and catlike slit eyes. When they strike, they use their fangs to inject venom deep into their victims. Up to 85 percent of such strikes occur below the knees—a good reason to wear boots in snake country.

Snakes with round eyes, on the other hand, are almost never poisonous, with the exception of the coral snake. It has distinctive red, yellow, and black bands. Coral snakes have small fangs, and the only way they can inject a fatal dose of venom is if they hold on to their victims for several seconds. If one bites you, pull it off immediately.

No matter which kind of snake bites you, immobilize the bitten part and keep it below the level of your heart. Seek medical attention immediately. If someone nearby can safely kill the snake, bring it with you to the hospital for identification. Otherwise, note the snake's size, coloring, and skin pattern. Forget what you've heard about cutting the wound and "sucking out the poison"—this doesn't work and may cause infection. Also avoid tourniquets and ice packs, which might put the limb at risk of having to be amputated.

Rabid encounters

Only some 20 people have died of rabies in Canada since reporting began in 1925, but about 5,000 people receive post-exposure treatment every year. Dogs, cats, farm and wild animals, especially foxes, raccoons, bats, and skunks, are some of the mammals that can transmit rabies and other potentially deadly diseases to humans. To reduce your risk, vaccinate all pets against rabies, and avoid close contact with any wild animal, and with any animal, wild or domestic, that is drooling, foaming at the mouth, or showing signs of nervousness or aggression.

More than half of the reported cases of rabies infection in humans in the U.S. and the most recent Canadian fatalities have been transmitted by bats. You don't even have to be bitten by a bat to become infected. In 1997 two Americans died from rabies after what investigators described as "seemingly insignificant physical contact" with bats. Even a scratch invisible to the naked eye can spell trouble. If you have a close encounter of any kind with a bat, see a doctor promptly.

If a wild animal bites you, do not try to capture the animal; instead, notify your local animal-control department. If your doctor determines that you need rabies shots, don't panic: the old series of painful stomach shots has been replaced by gentler therapy.

Biting the hand that feeds it

Ironically, it's our beloved pets that account for many of the bites people suffer. Every year, some 20 North Americans die from dog bites, and others, many of them children, are seriously mauled. Owners should choose a breed carefully. Male dogs can be neutered to subdue their aggressive tendencies. People, such as mail carriers, who are likely to encounter dogs, may want to carry a dog-repellent spray, sold in many sporting-good stores. If you are bitten, contact the owner to find out if the dog has had a rabies vaccination.

Though dog bites greatly outnumber cat bites, the latter tend to be more serious because of the depth of the wound. If a cat bite punctures the skin, you may need antibiotics as well as a tetanus shot. (If possible, find out if the cat has been vaccinated against rabies.) Cat claws can transmit a dangerous glandular infection called cat scratch fever.

Human bites should also be taken seriously. Infection from bites on the hand can result in finger loss.

Any bite should be seen by a doctor. Apply pressure to a deep wound or a ragged tear to stop blood loss. Don't apply medicine; just wash the area thoroughly with soap and water. If possible, collect any tissue that may have been bitten off in case it can be reattached.

Dogs that attack without provocation are more likely to have rabies. The animals should be vaccinated every one to three years.

Avoiding Dog Bites

- Let a dog see and sniff you before you pet it.
- Don't bother a dog who is eating, sleeping, or nursing.
- If an unfamiliar dog approaches, don't run. Instead, stand still until something else catches his eye, then turn sideways, avoiding eye contact, and slowly move away.
- If a dog knocks you down, curl into a ball and lie still.

Blood Transfusions

After the blood supply scandal of the 1980s, when more than 1,000 Canadians were infected with HIV and some 12,000 more contracted hepatitis C from tainted blood products, many Canadians lost confidence in the safety of their blood supply.

Today, fears of contracting a blood-borne disease through a blood transfusion are still great. However, receiving blood—though not risk-free—has grown safer with the introduction of new laboratory tests and blood screening procedures. Currently, some 600,000 Canadians receive blood each year, the vast majority with no ill effects. By learning about the risks that are involved in a transfusion and the steps you can take to minimize them, you can make this procedure even safer.

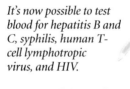

It's now possible to test blood for hepatitis B and C, syphilis, human T-cell lymphotropic virus, and HIV.

Contaminants and mismatches

Potential donors now undergo an extensive screening process meant to ensure that

What Are the Chances?

Though risks of disease and even death exist with blood transfusions, they are very small. Below are the approximate odds for some complications and for fatalities:

Receiving wrong blood	1 in 100,000
Contracting hepatitis B	1 in 200,000
Contracting hepatitis C	1 in 200,000
Contracting HIV	1 in 1,000,000
Contracting malaria	1 in 500,000
Bacterial infection	1 in 1,000,000

their blood doesn't carry disease. Beyond this, all donated blood is tested for a range of contaminants. However, a virus may not be detected if the donor has been recently infected and hasn't produced a measurable level of antibodies. Still, the probability of contracting a disease through a transfusion is extremely slim (see chart, above).

To reduce your risk, consider requesting filtered blood products, from which the white

Giving Blood: Tiny Risks, Big Benefits

The act of giving blood—so important in our society—is very safe. Your chances of getting an infection are virtually nil because the needles used to take blood are sterile and used only once. There is a limit, however, to how much blood you should give: regulations hold a single donation to one unit and require that a minimum of 56 days pass between donations. (If you have recently given birth or had surgery, you should check with your doctor before donating blood.)

If you're a man, giving blood may even benefit your health. In one study, non-smoking men who donated at least one unit of blood in a three-year period reduced their risk of heart attack and stroke by 30 percent. Why? One theory is that donating blood lowers the body's stores of iron, which play a role in hardening of the arteries. Researchers note that women who lose blood through menstruation have a lower rate of heart disease than men and postmenopausal women (menstruating women also produce estrogen, which protects against heart disease). Women in the study who donated blood showed no significant cardiac benefits.

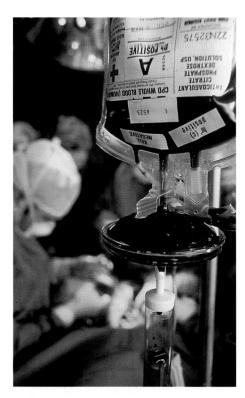

Blood transfusions help save the lives of countless patients undergoing surgery as well as victims of accidents, burns, and an assortment of illnesses.

cells, or leukocytes, have been removed. White cells can carry undetected contaminants, such as viruses that can cause postoperative infection. If filtered blood isn't available, you may be able to obtain "bedside filtration," in which the donor blood is passed through a leukocyte filter before being pumped into your body.

Although you may be tempted to accept blood donations from friends and relatives, think twice before doing so. Studies suggest that those close to the patient aren't as truthful as strangers when asked about behavior relating to disease and blood purity.

The odds of receiving the wrong blood are somewhat greater than those of contracting a disease. Despite safeguards to prevent such occurrences, occasionally a clerical error is made or a harried doctor or health-care worker picks up the wrong blood unit. If the blood chosen is not compatible, a deadly immune-system reaction may occur. One of the most common causes of death from a transfusion is incompatible blood.

Reactions to transfusion

Because a transfusion is in effect a transplant, about 1 in every 30 recipients has a minor allergic or immune-system reaction, even when the blood type has been correctly matched. Characterized by such symptoms as chills and fever, this reaction usually subsides within a couple of hours.

More worrisome is the risk of postoperative infection. Because undergoing a blood transfusion temporarily suppresses the patient's immune system, it's possible that the procedure creates a susceptibility to infection from germs—whether in the donor blood or in the environment—that would otherwise be harmless. In most cases, the duration and severity of an infection depends on the strength of the person's immune system prior to the transfusion.

Drawing on your own resources

If you know that you're going to need blood in the future, you may be able to use your own. Called an autologous donation, this practice can virtually eliminate the threat of rejection and blood-borne disease. However, you need notice of the surgery well in advance to be able to make the donations; you must also be in good health.

If you don't have enough time to store your own blood, ask about another form of autologous transfusion: blood salvaging, which takes place during surgery. In this procedure, blood that is normally lost during an operation is instead suctioned into equipment that washes and filters it and then sends it back into your body.

Because a transfusion is in effect a transplant, about 1 in every 30 recipients has a minor reaction.

On the Horizon New technology may soon virtually eliminate the chance of receiving the wrong blood. Researchers are working on a way to chemically convert other blood types to the universal type O. This would not only rule out mismatches, but it would also increase the supply available for transfusions and reduce the amount of blood that gets "stale" waiting for a patient of the right blood type.

Body Piercing

Pierced earlobes have been in vogue for a long time, but these days some people are going to new extremes, with trendy followers of fashion piercing their eyebrows, navels, tongues, and more.

Getting it done safely

Body piercing involves some pain and can lead to difficulties, particularly with areas other than earlobes. Piercing should be performed by a doctor or other health-care professional or by a trained body piercing professional. The procedure must be done properly to minimize risks (see chart, below), and sterile equipment is essential to prevent infection of the site and the transmission of hepatitis or HIV. If you are undergoing piercing, you may first want to get a tetanus shot and a hepatitis vaccination.

Safe piercing requires a new, sterilized, disposable needle. Don't agree to the use of a "gun," which is difficult to sterilize. Be sure that the practitioner puts on a fresh pair of latex gloves before starting. The jewelry inserted should be nonallergenic (stainless steel or gold, for example), because irritations often occur from a sensitivity to nickel and other metals found in inexpensive jewelry. Also, the jewelry must be the correct size for the particular body part: too thick may cause an abscess; too thin may cause tearing.

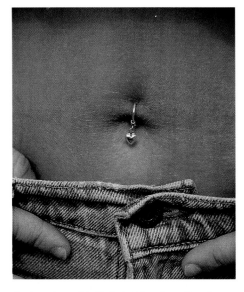

A pierced navel is likely to take a long time to heal, since it may become irritated when rubbing against waistbands or other parts of clothing.

Physicians advise against piercing the ears of babies and young children, who are highly susceptible to infection.

After the piercing

You can speed up the healing process and reduce the risks of complications by taking care of the pierced area. Leave studs in earlobes for the first few weeks, rotating them frequently to keep them from sticking. Clean around the studs twice daily with hydrogen peroxide or alcohol, and then apply antibiotic ointment. After several days, simply wash the area with soap. The care of other external body parts is basically the same, but some areas can take much longer to heal (see chart, left).

Infection and scarring are particular dangers with the upper ear and the nostril because these areas consist primarily of cartilage and have little blood flow. If the area becomes infected, consult a physician immediately; you may require treatment with antibiotic drugs. Signs of infection include unusual discomfort as well as crusting, swelling, redness, and discharge.

Healing Times and Risks

Body Part	General Healing Time	Possible Complications
Earlobe	1 to 2 months	Infection
Eyebrow	1 to 2 months	Black eye
Lip	1 to 2 months	Uncontrollable drooling caused by damage to salivary-gland ducts
Tongue	1 to 2½ months	Swelling, soreness; long-term risks of numbness, loss of taste, speech problems, chipped teeth
Upper ear	1 to 3 months	Serious infection, scarring
Nostril	2 to 3 months	Serious infection, scarring
Navel	3 to 12 months	Infection

Bottled Water

A minimum of four glasses of clean water each day rehydrates, refreshes, and renews our bodies. But how do we ensure that our water is indeed clean? Many people put their faith in bottled water—Canadians consume about 640 million liters of these packaged products every year. But buyer beware: your expensive bottled water may not be any better than what comes out of your faucet for free. To determine the difference, you need to know about both the bottled water labeling and the condition of your tap water.

Deciphering the label

Bottled water is strictly regulated by Health Canada under the Food and Drugs Act. Quality standards, manufacturing practices, and labeling requirements are set. Below are some definitions found on labels:

- **Spring water:** collected from an underground spring that flows naturally to the surface of the earth. If taken from a borehole that taps the underground source, the water must be of the same composition as the naturally occurring surface water. Spring water must contain less than 500 parts per million (ppm) of dissolved solids.
- **Mineral water:** meets the definition of spring water but contains more than 500 ppm of total dissolved solids.
- **Well water:** also the same as spring water except that it does not flow naturally to the surface of the earth. The water is tapped from a bored, drilled, or other type of hole.
- **Artesian water:** also known as artesian well water, it is taken from a well that taps a confined aquifer (a rock or sand layer that holds water) in which the water level starts above the top of the aquifer.
- **Purified or distilled water:** taken from a spring, well, or municipal water supply and treated by distilling or by certain types of filtering. Also may be sold as "deionized" or "reverse osmosis" water.
- **Carbonated bottled water:** bottled water that contains natural or added carbonation. Soda water, seltzer, and club soda are defined as soft drinks, not bottled water.

Choosing your water

Whereas more than 75 percent of bottled water is taken from protected underground sources, municipal drinking water is mostly drawn from surface water such as lakes and rivers. Federal safety and quality standards for tap water are outlined in the *Guidelines for Canadian Drinking Water.* Provincial and territorial governments consult these guidelines to set their water quality measures.

However, because of various contaminants, sometimes tap water fails to satisfy those standards. Besides problems such as accidental toxic chemical spills, mechanical failures at a water treatment plant, or well flooding during a heavy rainfall, tap water may also run the risk of contamination by two infectious parasites, *Cryptosporidium parvum* and *Giardia.* If you are concerned about the quality of your tap water, you should consult your local health authorities.

Bottled water from a spring or other underground source has only a slight risk of containing *C. parvum.* This type of water is also somewhat protected from pesticides, fertilizers, and industrial waste.

People with disorders of the immune system are often advised to opt for distilled water. This type of bottled water is virtually devoid of total dissolved solids. Its taste may be flat, but it should contain no microorganisms.

As for mineral bottled waters (often imported): they have no special nutritional benefit and are often quite high in sodium.

To avoid spoilage, refrigerate bottled water. Health Canada advises a one-year shelf life.

CAUTION!

Unlike many municipal water supplies, bottled water may not contain sufficient fluoride to fight cavities. If your family relies on bottled water, ask your dentist if fluoride supplements are needed.

Breast-feeding

Nursing, the preferred method of feeding a newborn, greatly benefits both the infant and the mother. Indeed, *Nutrition for Healthy Term Infants*, a document issued by Health Canada, the Canadian Pediatric Society, and the Dietitians of Canada, recommends that babies receive only breast milk for the first 4 to 6 months. With additional foods, breast-feeding may continue well into the second year of life.

Mother's milk and infant formula

Breast milk contains the right amount of fatty acids, water, lactose, vitamins, trace minerals, and amino acids for an infant. With at least 100 ingredients that formula does not provide—some impossible to duplicate—the milk helps to support the immune system and protects against diarrhea, rashes, allergies, and infections of the ear, urinary tract, and respiratory system. Nursing can also aid in tooth development, improve response to vaccines, and possibly reduce the chances of future diabetes or obesity. One study suggests that children who are breast-fed even do better in school.

Of course, some women are unable to breast-feed and must rely on infant formula. Though second-best, formula is still an excellent source of nutrition for a baby. Since

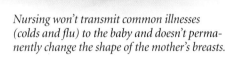

Nursing won't transmit common illnesses (colds and flu) to the baby and doesn't permanently change the shape of the mother's breasts.

homemade formula does not meet a baby's needs and can be dangerous, always opt for commercial brands that are iron-fortified.

What else is in the milk?

Because breast milk contains traces of almost everything a woman eats, a healthy diet is essential if you're nursing. You'll need 1,200 milligrams of calcium daily. (In Canada, vitamin D deficiency is a concern, so breast-fed babies should get a vitamin D supplement; ask your doctor.) Stay away from potentially harmful substances, such as cigarette smoke, artificial sweeteners, and hard liquor. If you have beer or wine, wait at least two hours before nursing. Women who have a disease, carry a virus, or are taking medication should ask their doctor about whether to breast-feed.

It's Good for Mom, Too

Here's what breast-feeding does for the new mother:

- Prompts weight loss
- Helps uterus return to normal size
- Reduces risks of ovarian and breast cancer
- Enhances bond with child

When Breast-feeding Hurts

Nursing can cause discomfort or pain. Here are some tips:

- For a clogged milk duct, massage the area or apply a hot compress. If you also have redness, lumps, or a fever, get medical attention.

- To help prevent sore nipples, position your baby so that the nipple and part of the

  areola are in the mouth. If the baby has trouble latching on, consult your doctor.

- After nursing, let the nipples air-dry to prevent cracking. If the nipples do crack, coat them with breast milk to soothe them.

Breast Implants

Despite the controversy, an estimated 150,000 to 200,000 Canadian women have received breast implants. Used to either augment the size of a breast or replace a breast lost to cancer, implants may be made of silicone gel or saline (salt water). Both types are encased in a thin, silicone-rubber shell.

Saline versus silicone

These days only saline is available for use in Canada. In 1992 the U.S. Food and Drug Administration removed silicone implants from the market because their manufacturers

Whether made of silicone or saline, a breast implant can interfere with a mammogram by obscuring a potential tumor formation.

were unable to prove that they were safe. That same year in Canada, the implants were voluntarily removed from sale. Many women with these implants complained of autoimmune illnesses, including lupus and rheumatoid arthritis, and attributed these diseases to silicone leakage. Some experts also worried that the implants increased the risk of breast cancer. Major studies have not corroborated links with either of these health problems; however, no attempts have been made to remarket silicone implants in Canada.

Known medical disorders

Aside from unproven concerns, there are recognized medical complications. Two difficulties that can stem from the surgery itself involve the scar tissue around the affected breast. In one, called capsular contracture, the tissue becomes tight, causing pain, breast hardening, and altered breast appearance. Calcium deposits, which can form around the implant, may produce similar results. Either problem may require a follow-up operation.

After getting implants, some women experience increased or decreased feeling in the nipples or other parts of the breast. This change may be temporary or permanent. Implants may also shift position, causing discomfort and an uneven appearance.

Because silicone implants gradually deteriorate, most will rupture over time. If the gel spreads after breakage, the immune system may form granules around the pieces of gel to try to isolate them. The resulting nodules, which occur in the hands, abdomen, or other parts of the body, can be painful, and extensive surgery may be necessary to remove the migrating gel.

Saline implants can also rupture— at times suddenly, causing the breast to quickly deflate. The saltwater filling will not harm the body, but a broken implant requires surgery. The rupture rate for saline varies and is somewhat dependent on the standards of the manufacturer. Companies are required to submit safety reports about their products, so a woman considering implants should ask her doctor for copies of the company's information sheet and the product insert sheet.

Implants can interfere with a mammogram by obscuring a potential tumor formation. And because the test places pressure on the breast, it may cause an implant to rupture. A woman who has implants should alert the radiologist in advance so that special techniques can be used.

Nearly 25 percent of breast implants, such as this silicone model, require surgical attention within five years because of complications.

On the Horizon Breast implants filled with soybean oil were tested on a trial basis in Canada in 1996, and are now being tested at medical centers across the United States. Since the oil is translucent, it will probably not obstruct a mammogram. However, long-term effects of oil leakage are not yet known.

Caffeine

It puts the jolt in a morning cup of coffee and sharpens our mental edge. It also boosts the effectiveness of certain medications and even helps fight muscle fatigue. But consume too much caffeine (each person's threshold is different) and you may regret it.

A double-edged sword

Although it occurs naturally in coffee, tea, and chocolate, caffeine is in fact a drug. Even a small amount has a stimulating effect on the central nervous system. Caffeine can increase our alertness and confidence and improve our mood. It boosts our ability to perform monotonous tasks, such as typing, and may even increase endurance in athletes. Too much caffeine, however, can make a person restless and irritable. It may also exacerbate hot flashes and cause increased urination (and, therefore, dehydration) and diarrhea. Moreover, coffee—with or without caffeine—can trigger heartburn.

Most people don't hit caffeine overload until they've had the equivalent of eight cups of coffee or more. But for those who are very sensitive to caffeine or rarely consume it, even two cups can cause the jitters. What's more, smokers who quit find that caffeine suddenly packs more punch. Why? Because smoking speeds the elimination of caffeine from the body.

> Most people don't hit caffeine overload until they've had the equivalent of eight cups of coffee or more.

Coffee with caffeine has the power to speed pain relief—and aggravate PMS.

Headaches: The Caffeine Connection

Give up your morning cup of java and you may end up with one mean headache, a common result of caffeine withdrawal. On the flip side, taking a dose of caffeine along with aspirin, acetaminophen, or ibuprofen for a tension headache or migraine appears to speed relief and make it last longer. Why? Caffeine helps pain relievers work better, which is why it is found in many over-the-counter analgesics. But it also fights headaches on its own. Experts believe that caffeine constricts the blood vessels in the head, reducing the blood flow in the area, which may in turn ease a throbbing headache. But don't go overboard: ingesting too much caffeine (as little as 500 milligrams a day for several days) may trigger a rebound headache that can last for a week.

Grounds for concern?

Caffeine's power to cause long-term health problems has been the subject of considerable debate. A host of studies sought to prove that caffeine increases the risk of heart disease, cancer, and other ills, but no conclusive evidence has been found.

Still, some people might be wise to avoid caffeine, including those with ulcers, hypertension, and heart-rhythm abnormalities and those who suffer from panic attacks. Caffeine is also inadvisable for people taking certain medications, notably antidepressants and tranquilizers. Another caution: coffee prepared in the espresso, French press, or boiled fashion may increase levels of LDL, or low-density lipoprotein—the "bad" cholesterol—which can lead to heart attack. The good news is that instant and filtered coffees do not seem to pose the same threat.

Caffeine may pose additional problems for women. It causes the body to excrete calcium more readily, and if one's calcium intake is already less than ideal, as little as two cups of coffee a day may increase the risk of osteoporosis. There is no increased risk if women consume the Recommended Nutrient Intake (RNI) of 700 milligrams (mg) of calcium per day (800 mg after the age of 50). Caffeine may also decrease a woman's fertility and increase the risk of miscarriage; pregnant women who consume more than 300 mg of it daily run a higher risk of having an underweight baby.

Too much caffeine can also aggravate premenstrual syndrome (PMS) when consumed during the 10 days prior to menstruation. (Ironically, because caffeine helps pain relievers work better, some PMS medications contain a fair amount of it.) On a positive note, new evidence suggests that caffeine may not aggravate symptoms of fibrocystic breast disease, as was once thought.

Kicking the habit

If you're hooked on caffeine and want to cut down, do so gradually. Stopping cold turkey can trigger a monster headache that lasts for days. In some people, caffeine withdrawal can also cause depression, sluggishness, anxiety, and even nausea and vomiting. Symptoms typically begin within 24 hours of your last caffeine "fix" and can last for up to a week or more. You may also experience withdrawal symptoms if you take medication that contains caffeine (such as Anacin, Excedrin Extra Strength, or Midol) for several days and then suddenly stop.

The buzz on decaf

Years ago there was concern about a possible link between cancer and the chemicals used to extract the caffeine from coffee and tea. But scientists have found no justification for these fears. For people who are still worried, water-processed decaffeinated beverages are available—at a price. What about the trace of caffeine that remains in decaffeinated coffee? Since the decaffeination process removes 97 to 99 percent of the caffeine, a cup of decaf poses little threat to a good night's sleep.

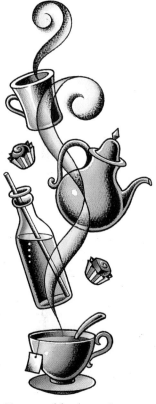

Tea steeped for three minutes contains about half the caffeine of brewed coffee and about as much as most soft drinks. Hot cocoa contains next to none.

Caffeine Counter

Source	Approximate Caffeine Content	(mg)
Coffee	Espresso (60 ml/2 oz)	120
	Espresso, decaf (60 ml/2 oz)	10
	Regular, brewed (180 ml/6 oz)	103
	Brewed decaf (180 ml/6 oz)	2
	Instant, 6 oz (1 rounded tsp)	57
	Instant decaf, 6 oz (1 rounded tsp)	2
Tea	Black (180 ml/6 oz)	53
	Oolong (180 ml/6 oz)	36
	Green (180 ml/6 oz)	32
	Iced tea, instant (360 ml/12 oz)	46
Soft drinks	**(360 ml/12 oz, diet or regular)**	
	RC Cola	48
	Mountain Dew	55
	Coca-Cola Classic	47
	Dr. Pepper	41
	Sunkist Orange	39
	Pepsi	37
Chocolate	Baking chocolate (28 g/1 oz)	58
	Dark-chocolate bar (41 g/1.45 oz)	31
	Milk-chocolate bar (44 g/1.55 oz)	11
	Hot cocoa (180 ml/6 oz)	5

Calcium

We know calcium as the "bone building" mineral—indeed, up to 99 percent of our body's supply resides in our skeleton and teeth. But calcium doesn't just build bones. It also helps maintain healthy cholesterol and blood pressure levels and orchestrate such vital functions as heartbeat and nerve transmissions.

Low levels of calcium in the blood can also lead to osteoporosis, a bone-thinning disorder that dramatically increases the risk of fractures. The incidence of osteoporosis, which affects 1.4 million Canadians, has underscored calcium's importance. In fact, according to some recent dietary recommendations, most of us should increase our daily intake of calcium, no matter what our age.

How much do we need?

The amount of calcium that we should consume, however, does depend on our age. We need it the most when we are young, while the skeleton is forming, and then in our later years to protect us from osteoporosis.

Health Canada set its recommended intakes just high enough to prevent deficiencies. Then in 1997 a panel of Canadian and American nutritional scientists set new calcium guidelines for the U.S. National Academy of Sciences (NAS), which specify a dietary reference intake (DRI) per day for:

- Ages 1 to 3: 500 milligrams (mg)
- Ages 4 to 8: 800 mg
- Ages 9 to 18: 1,300 mg
- Ages 19 to 50: 1,000 mg
- Pregnant and nursing women: 1,000 mg
- Ages 50 and over: 1,200 mg

The DRIs are meant to potentially update and harmonize the U.S. Recommended Dietary Allowances (RDAs) and the Canadian Recommended Nutrient Intakes (RNIs).

Pregnant and nursing women were once advised to take more calcium, but the new evidence reveals that normal intakes are fine. Women in these stages metabolize vitamin D differently and absorb calcium better. But women do need more during menopause, when declining estrogen levels make it more difficult for bones to retain calcium.

Foods before supplements

As with most vitamins and minerals, try to get as much calcium as you can from foods, such as leafy greens and low-fat dairy products (see chart at left). Supplements can provide the balance of your daily intake. When taking a supplement, follow these guidelines:

- To increase absorption, take supplements with meals or one hour to 90 minutes after eating with a glass of water. Taking vitamin D at the same time also helps absorption. The Osteoporosis Society of Canada recommends that Canadian adults get 400 IUs of vitamin D per day.
- Beware of certain foods, such as wheat bran, that inhibit calcium absorption.

Calcium Content in Food

Most nutrition experts recommend that foods, not supplements, be your first choice when trying to meet your daily calcium needs. Here are some of the richest dietary sources of the mineral:

Source		Calcium (mg)
Dairy Products	Ricotta cheese, 1/4 cup	128
	Swiss cheese, 28 grams (1 oz)	260
	Milk (nonfat), 1 cup	296
	Yogurt (plain, nonfat), 1 cup	415
Vegetables	Broccoli (cooked), 1 cup	136
	Beet greens (cooked), 1 cup	164
	Turnip greens (cooked), 1 cup	252
	Collards (cooked), 1 cup	357
Canned Fish	Salmon (sockeye, with bones), 100 grams (3 1/2 oz)	237
	Sardines (in water, with bones), 100 grams (3 1/2 oz)	240
Other sources	Figs, 85 grams (3 oz)	81
	Tofu, 100 grams (3 1/2 oz)	90
	Rhubarb (cooked), 1/2 cup	174

According to some recent dietary recommendations, most of us should increase our daily intake of calcium, no matter what our age.

How Much Calcium Does a Supplement Actually Contain?

Just because your calcium supplement says 500 mg, don't assume that's how much you're getting. The reason: Many products list the total weight of each pill, instead of the actual amount of calcium it contains. Furthermore, the four major types of supplements—carbonate, citrate, lactate, and gluconate—provide different amounts of calcium.

Some labels list the amount of "elemental" calcium. This is how much of the actual mineral is in each pill. If your product lists only the total weight of each pill, calculate the amount of actual calcium using these simple formulas for each type of supplement:

- Calcium carbonate (40 percent calcium). Multiply total weight by 0.4. For example, 500 mg of calcium carbonate (500 x 0.4) equals only 200 mg of calcium.

- Calcium citrate (21 percent calcium). Multiply total weight by 0.21. For example, 500 mg of calcium citrate (500 x 0.21) equals only 105 mg of calcium.

- Calcium lactate (13 percent calcium). Multiply total weight by 0.13. For example, 500 mg of calcium lactate (500 x 0.13) equals only 65 mg of calcium.

- Calcium gluconate (9 percent calcium). Multiply total weight by 0.09. For example, 500 mg of calcium gluconate (500 x 0.09) equals only 45 mg of calcium.

Spinach provides a healthy dose of calcium (240 mg per cup) but also contains oxalic acid, which prevents most of it from being used. However, oxalic acid does *not* interfere with other calcium sources (such as a supplement) consumed at the same meal.

- Only take supplements marked with a DIN or GP number, which indicates Health Canada's approval. "USP" on a label guarantees a high manufacturing standard.
- Take no more than 500 mg at a time. The body processes small doses more efficiently.
- To help retain calcium, engage in some weight-bearing activity, such as walking.

The inside scoop on supplements

In a supplement, calcium is combined with a chemical compound, either carbonate, citrate, gluconate, or lactate. Before choosing one, beware of these potential pitfalls:

- Calcium carbonate, the most common form of calcium supplement, may cause constipation or gas and is difficult to absorb if it is not taken with a meal.
- Calcium citrate, which promotes iron absorption and is the easiest form to digest, does not provide a lot of actual calcium. Calcium lactate and calcium gluconate provide even less (see box, left). It may take several pills to get 500 mg of calcium.
- Higher doses of calcium (1,500 mg or more) may limit zinc and iron absorption.
- Supplements made from bonemeal, dolomite, and oyster shell may contain a very small amount of lead. Experts agree, however, that the benefits of supplements far outweigh the risks of lead exposure.

How much is too much?

The NAS and the Osteoporosis Society of Canada also define an upper limit on tolerable calcium intake—no more than 2,500 mg a day. Regularly surpassing this level can result in an excess of calcium in the blood, a condition that may lead to kidney stones. Although the risk is now disputed, you may wish to check with your doctor before adding supplements to your diet.

Healthy bone is a dense mesh of collagen fibers embedded with calcium and phosphate. Sufficient calcium intake ensures healthy bone density.

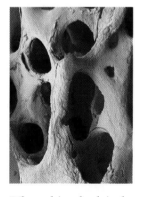

When calcium levels in the blood are low, the body takes calcium from bones, and bone loss may occur. Over time, bone loss leads to osteoporosis.

Canned Foods

Isn't fresh or frozen food better for you than canned? Not necessarily. In many cases canned foods are every bit as nutritious—or even more so. Consider these pantry staples:

- Canned pumpkin and purple plums have more vitamin A than fresh varieties. Why? They're picked at their peak and processed immediately.
- Canned tomatoes contain as much lycopene as fresh ones, although this cancer-protective carotenoid seems to be more readily available in the cooked tomatoes.
- Canned salmon and sardines have edible bones that are rich in calcium.

Foods stored in cans do have drawbacks. The canning process reduces the amount of heat-sensitive nutrients, such as vitamin C and folic acid. Also, canneries often use excess sodium and sugar; for example, chili made with canned tomatoes and beans can contain more than twice as much sodium as chili made with fresh tomatoes and dried beans.

Still, most vitamins, minerals, and the all-important fiber are retained in cans. Judiciously used, canned foods can help you reach your daily quota of vegetables and fruits.

It's safe to refrigerate leftovers in most cans, but they will stay fresher in tightly sealed containers, which limit exposure to air.

To Maximize the Nutrition in a Can:

- Read labels. Look for lowered sodium, fat, and sugar levels, tuna packed in water, and fruits in natural juices.
- Use the vitamin-rich packing liquids. Drink the fruit juice and add vegetable liquids to soups.
- Skim fat from the top of soups and stews. Mix cream soups with skim milk instead of whole milk.
- Resist overcooking; just reheat food to retain more vitamins.
- Store commercially canned foods for no more than two years, except for high-acid foods (tomatoes, sauerkraut), which have a shelf life of only 18 months. Store home-canned foods no longer than a year.

What about botulism and lead?

Nowadays, improperly sealed foods canned at home are the major source of botulism. Commercially canned foods are virtually risk-free, provided they are in good condition. Throw out any can that bulges, leaks, or is dented around the rim or seam. Discard food that is bubbly, odd-smelling, moldy, spongy, or shriveled. Never taste it. If you do accidentally eat bad food and experience difficulty swallowing, blurred vision, headache, muscle weakness, or paralysis, get medical help immediately.

Lead is still a concern; food cans sealed with lead solder are being phased out in Canada, but some canneries still use this method. Imported cans may also be soldered with lead, especially those from China or Taiwan. Avoid cans with a folded seam or with a black smudge on the inner rim.

How about home canning?

Seasonal produce, put up at its flavorful peak, is delicious. But use proper canning methods to avoid botulism. Your best bet: a pressure canner which reaches temperatures high enough (116°C/240°F) to destroy botulin toxins. Meats, vegetables, and other low acid foods are at a higher risk for botulism. Store cans in a dry, dark, cool area.

Carbohydrates

Carbohydrates, or "carbs," are the fuels your body runs on. Whether you eat whole-grain bread or candy, your body turns the carbohydrates in those foods into blood sugar, or glucose. Does that mean both foods are equally good sources of energy? Hardly. Nutritionally speaking, the bread is the better value, supplying fuel to your body over a longer period of time. The candy short-changes your body, providing energy only for a short time.

Categorizing carbs

Nutritionists categorize carbohydrates in two ways: simple or complex. Simple carbs are uncomplicated sugars found in table sugar, honey, fruits, even milk. Complex carbs are long molecular chains of glucose that are broken down slowly by the body. They are found in starchy vegetables (corn and potatoes), legumes (beans and peas), and foods made from grain (bread, cereal, rice, and pasta). The federal government recommends that we get 55 percent of our calories from carbohydrates, with emphasis on cereals, breads, vegetables, fruits and other complex carbs. Sugars should be eaten in moderation.

Unrefined complex carbohydrates are more nutritious than processed ones. Whole complex carbohydrates (whole grains, brown rice, beans) are rich in fiber, vitamins, minerals, and other healthful compounds. Refined carbohydrates (white flour, white rice, most bakery goods) have been processed until few nutrients remain. Worse, refining leaches out precious fiber that lowers cholesterol, prevents constipation, and protects against colon cancer. Eating refined carbs may also increase the risk of diabetes.

Although complex carbohydrates tend be low in fat (like protein, they contain 4 calories per gram compared with fat's 9 calories per gram), you *can* eat too much of them. Excessive amounts of beans, starchy vegetables, pasta, and other grains cause weight gain. The best approach is to mix such foods with plentiful amounts of vegetables, such as cabbage, broccoli, brussels sprouts, cauliflower, peppers, leafy greens, and spinach. They contain complex carbs but relatively few calories.

Eat—and relax

Whole grains, vegetables, and beans are not only nutritious, they may also help you relax. Meals that are rich in carbohydrates boost serotonin levels in the brain, which may produce a calming effect; a little meat protein can block that effect. So to stay alert during the day, eat some protein at breakfast and lunch. Then to relax in the evening, dine on pasta or rice with vegetables.

Say no to carbo loading

The marathoner's tradition of limiting carbs the week before the race and then loading up on them during the last two days has been discounted because it doesn't improve performance and may cause lethargy, weight gain, and cardiac problems. Most marathon runners now eat a normal high-carbohydrate diet during training, and, two days before an event, they add more carbs. Even so, any advantage from the added carbs is slight.

Limit portion sizes of starchy vegetables, beans, and grains. Despite the valuable carbohydrates they contain, their calories can add up.

Carpets & Carpet Cleaners

C arpets give homes and offices a luxuri-
ous look. They also cushion the tumbles
of young children, present a warm, soft surface to walk on, and absorb noise. But can
they make you sick as well? In rare cases, yes.
Old carpets, new carpets, and carpet shampoos all present potential health hazards.

What exactly lies underfoot?

Carpets are a magnet for dust and dust mites,
pollen, and mold spores. Furthermore, as
they wear, they shed minute fibers into the air
and create dust. If you suffer from allergies or
asthma, outfit your vacuum cleaner with a
microfiltration dust bag (which traps small
particles) and vacuum your carpets regularly.
To help reduce mold growth and carpet
odors, keep your carpets dry, particularly those in the bathroom.

New synthetic carpets may
emit toxic volatile
organic compounds
(VOCs). A carpet's latex
backing and foam padding
may also emit noxious fumes. The
risk of exposure to these chemicals
is greatest during the first few
months after installation.

New-carpet precautions

For some people, carpet fumes may
cause respiratory problems, burning
eyes, light-headedness, flulike
symptoms, and nervousness.
Prolonged exposure may lead
to chemical sensitivities. Here's
how to minimize your health risk
when buying a new carpet:
- Ask the dealer about VOCs
  from the carpet, padding, or
  installation adhesives. Know
  that a "green tag" label,

*Carpets come in a variety
of fibers, sizes, shapes,
and colors, but they all
trap allergens and
create dust.*

Safely Cleaning Your Carpet

A professional steam cleaning is
the best and safest choice for
cleaning your carpet. If you'd
rather do it yourself, use a water-
extraction cleaner; it leaves carpets drier than a carpet shampoo,
discouraging the growth of
microbes. Baking-soda-based
cleaners, as well as baking soda
itself (sprinkled on a dry carpet,
left for 15 minutes, and vacuumed), can deodorize your carpet.
If a smaller carpet requires dry
cleaning, ask the cleaner not to
use fragrances or moth-proofers,
and air it out after it is returned.

awarded for passing an indoor air quality
test, does not guarantee safety.
- Have the dealer unroll and air out the carpet for a few days before it is delivered.
- Before removing the old carpet, vacuum it
  and the floor to reduce airborne dust.
- Stay away from the home or the office
  while the new carpet is being installed.
- After installation, open nearby windows
  and doors and use exhaust fans to air out
  the area for at least three days.

Safer alternatives

When deciding what to do with a smelly, old
carpet, here are a few ways to avoid the potential hazards of a synthetic replacement.
- Live without a rug. Choose hardwood,
  ceramic-tile, or sheet-vinyl floors.
- Treat your old carpet with a carpet finish
  to keep water out and seal odors in.
- Select natural-fiber area rugs made from
  cotton, wool, sisal, or sheepskin, and use a
  jute or nylon padding instead of rubber.
  Note: Natural-fiber rugs can also harbor
  allergens and may be chemically treated.

Cellular Phones

Cellular phones are *the* electronic accessory of the '90s, and show no signs of relinquishing their status now that the new millennium has arrived. Cell phones are most helpful in emergencies— if your car breaks down or if you need medical attention. But many people use them simply to keep in touch with the office or the babysitter, or to make social plans.

Are they a health risk? Even though no evidence links cell phones to illness, ongoing studies look into the risks, especially from cell phones with built-in antennas close to the user's head. (The safety of so-called "cordless phones" hasn't been called into question.)

Can they really cause cancer?
When turned on, cell phones emit low-level energy in the form of an electromagnetic field (EMF). As a result, cell phones (as well as other sources of EMFs, such as power lines and household appliances) have raised concerns about possible links to brain cancer and other diseases. At this point, though, there is no proof that cellular phones are harmful. While studies continue, a new type of cell phone has been developed in Germany that significantly reduces the amount of radiation passing into the head.

Potentially harmful interference
A cell phone can interfere with the way a hearing aid or an implanted cardiac pacemaker (or defibrillator) functions. Anyone with a pacemaker should place the phone against the ear that is farther away from the pacemaker, avoid keeping the phone turned on in a chest pocket, and use an analog phone rather than a digital one. Cell phones may also interfere with the electronic devices in an airplane or a hospital. For this reason, their use is often prohibited in these places.

Phones and cars don't mix
A Canadian study found that the risk of having a car accident was four times greater when drivers were talking on the phone, and it was the same whether the drivers used handheld phones or speaker phones. (This accident risk is similar to that of driving with a blood-alcohol level right at the legal limit.) To reduce the danger, limit your car calls to brief and necessary conversations, and pull over if you anticipate a long or emotional call.

People love the convenience of cell phones. The World Health Organization continues to study their health effects.

an ounce of **Prevention**

Reduce Your Exposure to a Cell Phone's EMF
Even though the energy level emitted by a cell phone is considered safe by Health Canada, you can still take some measures to reduce your exposure:

- Limit the number and length of your calls; if possible, switch to a regular phone or car phone. (When it's turned off, the cell phone doesn't emit an EMF.)

- Fully extend the phone's antenna and keep it as far from your head as possible. If you regularly use a cell phone while driving, mount the antenna to the outside of the vehicle.

Cesarean Section

Cesarean Rates Fall in Canada

Since the late 1980s, cesarean rates in Canada have gradually declined as vaginal births after cesarean (VBAC) have increased. These rates indicate the number of cesareans per 100 deliveries:

1979	14.7%
1980	16%
1988	19.6%
1990	19.1%
1993	17.6%

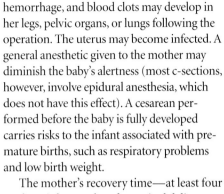

There are roughly 375,000 babies born on average in Canada each year. About 68,000 newborns are delivered by cesarean section. A cesarean section, or c-section, is the surgical removal of a baby from the womb. A doctor may recommend this surgery when certain conditions make vaginal delivery risky. These include such maternal health problems as herpes, HIV, diabetes, heart disease, and high blood pressure; a previous c-section; a prolonged labor; a large baby or multiple babies; an abnormal position of the placenta (when it blocks the cervix, for instance); a breech position; and a slowing fetal heart rate.

Risks and recovery

Though generally considered safe, c-sections may involve complications. The mother may hemorrhage, and blood clots may develop in her legs, pelvic organs, or lungs following the operation. The uterus may become infected. A general anesthetic given to the mother may diminish the baby's alertness (most c-sections, however, involve epidural anesthesia, which does not have this effect). A cesarean performed before the baby is fully developed carries risks to the infant associated with premature births, such as respiratory problems and low birth weight.

The mother's recovery time—at least four weeks—is longer than for vaginal delivery and is initially painful enough to require medication. Hospital stays average four days. Recuperating women may have trouble lifting things, driving a car, and climbing stairs.

Avoiding a c-section

Cesareans save some women and babies from injury and even death. Nevertheless, the operation is controversial because it seems to be performed in Canada far more often than is thought necessary. Although the frequency has gradually declined since 1987, some experts believe that many c-sections are performed unnecessarily. Taking these steps may help you avoid this surgery:

- Get early prenatal care.
- If a cesarean is recommended in advance, get a second opinion.
- If you've already had a c-section, talk to your doctor about vaginal birth after cesarean (VBAC). Most women are able to try a VBAC if they have no other risk factors. (In Canada, VBAC rates increased from 3 out of every 100 deliveries in 1979 to 33 in 100 in 1993.) Rupture of the uterine scar, which was once a major concern, is now rare because the location of the incision has changed in recent years.
- Ask the practitioner if he or she will try, if feasible, manual turning of the baby in the case of a breech position.

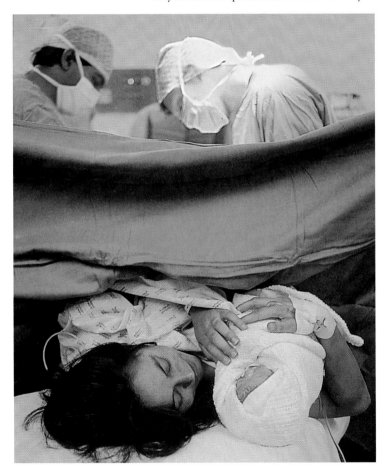

A woman who receives a regional anesthetic that affects only the lower part of her body is likely to be alert enough to hold her newborn after delivery by cesarean section.

Child Safety Seats

Every province requires safety seats for infants and young children riding in motor vehicles. Yet automobile crashes are the leading cause of death among Canadian children over the age of one. If used properly and consistently, an approved safety seat offers protection in most accidents. Unfortunately, studies show that only about 4 percent of Canadian children are properly restrained in their seats.

Seating options

When buying a safety seat, you have to consider your child's age, weight, and height, and the seat's compatibility with your car's seat-belt system. Babies must ride facing rearward until they weigh 9 to 10 kilograms (20 to 22 pounds) *and* are able to sit up or pull to a stand—usually between 9 and 12 months of age. Any child who is not developmentally ready but weighs 9 kilograms (20 pounds) should be switched to a rear-facing convertible (or combination) seat.

A convertible seat can be adjusted from rearward- to forward-facing as the child grows. It may have just a harness or a harness-and-shield combination. The harness type works best for a baby because the shield may come up too high (above the chest); some experts also prefer it for toddlers. They believe that the straps secure the hips and thighs better. However, unlike shields, the straps may become twisted.

Children from 18 to 27 kilograms (40 to 60 pounds) are too big for a convertible seat but too small for a seat belt. They need booster seats. Styles of boosters vary according to cars' seat-belt systems. A high-back, belt-positioning booster (which allows for belt adjustment) used together with a car's lap and shoulder belts offers the best protection.

Car-seat checklist

It is crucial to install and use seats properly:
- Follow instructions in your seat manufacturer manual and car's owner's manual.
- Have all children under 12 sit in the back seat and wear appropriate restraints. The middle seat is the safest.
- Never place a rear-facing infant seat in a passenger-side front seat equipped with an acti-

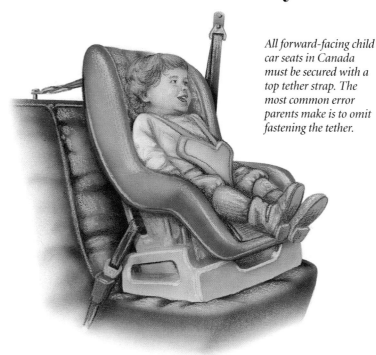

All forward-facing child car seats in Canada must be secured with a top tether strap. The most common error parents make is to omit fastening the tether.

vated air bag. The bag's impact could kill the baby. (See page 11 for air bag deactivation.)
- Test the safety seat's harness to see that it fits snugly. You should be able to fit only one finger between the child and the straps.
- Check the car's seat belt (where it meets the seat) to make sure the seat is held tightly in place. You should not be able to move it more than half a centimeter (quarter inch) from side to side. If your seat belt requires a locking clip, be sure to use it.
- Avoid prolonged use of the seat outside the car.

CAUTION!
Child restraints are sometimes recalled for defects. As soon as you buy a car seat, fill out the registration card and send it to the manufacturer. Keep all receipts and instructions.

Tougher Safety Standards

Don't buy a second-hand seat or use one that's more than 10 years old. Safety restraints have been improved. Seats bought in the U.S. won't do either—Canadian standards are tougher. Check the seat for a label stating conformity to Canada Motor Vehicle Safety Standards (CMVSS). For more advice, call the Canadian Automobile Association (CAA) or Transport Canada's hotline (at 1-800-333-0371).

Chiropractic

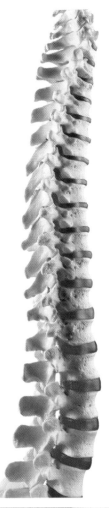

Chiropractic is a therapy that was invented in 1895 by Daniel David Palmer, a self-taught Ontario-born healer who maintained that he had cured a man's deafness by manipulating a displaced vertebra in his spine. Ever since, chiropractors have been criticized by the medical establishment about the lack of scientific evidence for some of their claims—but that hasn't stopped 1 in 10 Canadians from visiting them each year.

What is chiropractic?

Chiropractors believe they can manipulate, or "adjust," a patient's vertebrae by pressing, pulling, and pushing on the shoulders, neck, back, and hips. A typical back problem usually requires 8 to 12 visits of such therapy, which is often combined with exercise, ultrasound, massage, and nutritional counseling.

Today "neofundamentalists" consider manipulation necessary to correct misalignments of the spine they blame for many illnesses. They believe that chiropractic

Although chiropractors can alleviate back pain and muscle spasms and strains, they have little training in general medicine and are not qualified to treat most illnesses.

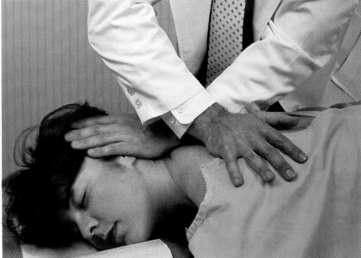

treatments are essential for overall health. "Revisionists" focus primarily on health care involving pain in the back, head, neck, and chest.

Studies show that repeated sessions of spinal manipulation are an effective treatment for acute back pain and are somewhat effective for chronic back pain.

Does it work?

Studies show that repeated sessions of spinal manipulation are an effective treatment for acute back pain and are somewhat effective for chronic back pain. There is a growing acceptance by the medical community for chiropractic treatments intended to relieve back pain and other musculoskeletal problems. Some provincial health care plans partially cover chiropractic treatments; others do not. (Many private health insurance policies also provide coverage. Find out about your burden of the fee before your consultation.)

When it comes to chiropractic's grander claims, however, doctors are less tolerant. Although a chiropractor's education usually consists of four years in a chiropractic college, followed by clinical experience, some medical experts warn against visiting chiropractors for any ailment other than problems like muscle spasms and strains or lower-back pain. In general, see a chiropractor when referred by a medical doctor. The chiropractor should be licensed to practice in your province.

Potential hazards

Avoid rotary neck manipulation (a sudden twist of the neck). The whiplike motion, unlike neck massage, can interrupt the brain's blood supply, causing paralysis or stroke. Spinal manipulation is not recommended if you suffer from herniated disks, severe osteoporosis, rheumatoid arthritis, cancer, spinal infections, fractures, bleeding disorders, and high blood pressure or other risk factors for stroke. Back X rays have no diagnostic value and expose you to unnecessary radiation.

Chlorine Bleach

E ver since a Scottish chemist mixed chlorine gas with limestone back in 1799 to create chlorine bleach (sodium hypochlorite), the world has been a cleaner, less dangerous place. This compound quickly caught on as a whitener for clothing and writing paper and later as a mildew remover for washable surfaces.

Chlorine bleach not only brightens laundry, it also removes mildew from your house's exterior. Always dilute it, using one part bleach to three parts water.

It's everywhere

Chlorine is added to everything from household cleansers, vinyl, plastics, and wood pulp and recycled paper to swimming pools and washing machines. The same chlorine found in bleach is an excellent disinfectant for drinking water. Very small amounts are used to help purify the water supply of many cities in the U.S. and Canada. In the case of chlorinated drinking water, the problem is that chlorine undergoes many changes when added to water, forming small amounts of potentially cancer-causing by-products such as trihalomethanes.

Are these compounds indeed harmful? The question has been under study for two decades and the research at this point indicates that chlorinated drinking water probably doesn't increase cancer risk.

Household hazards

Chlorine bleach leaches out the dyes in fabric that is not colorfast, and if not properly diluted, it eats holes through the fabric. It will not remove rust and can discolor clothing washed in water that has a high iron content.

Even more serious are the health hazards associated with chlorine bleach. Never mix chlorine bleach with products that contain ammonia; the fumes caused by these combinations can be lethal. Also avoid combining chlorine bleach with acids, such as vinegar, or other household products containing acids, such as drain openers, toilet-bowl cleaners, or rust removers; these blends may also emit hazardous gases. To avoid any problems, check the labels on household detergents for ammonia and acids before adding chlorine bleach to them.

Sensitive to chlorine?

Chlorine is not an allergen, but some people may find that fabrics washed in it can be irritating to their skin. Good substitutes for chlorine bleach in your laundry are the non-chlorine bleaches. To help your wash look cleaner, pretreat stains with detergent and presoak clothes that are very dirty. Use the hottest water that your fabrics can stand, and add a little extra detergent to each load.

Chlorine and the environment

Laundry bleach biodegrades harmlessly into oxygen, salt, and water. Unlike some chlorines employed in industry, laundry bleach poses no environmental threat.

CAUTION!
If bleach splashes into your eyes, flush them with water for 15 minutes, then call your doctor. If bleach is swallowed, do not induce vomiting. Immediately drink 180 milliliters (6 ounces) of water, milk, or milk of magnesia. Then call your Poison Control Center.

Chocolate is derived from the cocoa bean, which was used by the early peoples of Mexico and Central America as the basis of a celebrated but bitter drink. Spanish conquerors added cane sugar to the beverage, and the sweet version became popular as an aphrodisiac among European aristocrats. However, it wasn't until the 19th century, when cocoa butter was separated from the bean, that chocolate became the rich food familiar to us.

More than a "sinful" dessert

Chocolate abounds in calories from fat and sugar. Nevertheless, it should not be judged as a total dietary villain. Chocolate (especially dark) contains copper, which aids in iron absorption. It's also a source of the antioxidant alpha-tocopherol, a form of vitamin E.

More intriguing, a recent study revealed the presence of other antioxidants called phenols. These substances are also found in red wine. Researchers believe that the phenols in wine prevent the formation of LDL (low-density lipoprotein) cholesterol, the "bad" cholesterol that can clog arteries. But they are not yet sure that the phenols in chocolate act in the same way. If they do, it's good news for chocoholics: the amount of phenols in a 42-gram (1.5-ounce) milk chocolate bar is about equal to that in a 150-milliliter (5-ounce) glass of red wine.

On the negative side, chocolate can promote heartburn, incontinence, and, for those at risk, kidney stones. It's been widely accepted that chocolate can trigger migraine headaches, but a recent study suggests other reasons for the connection, such as the combination of chocolate with headache-inducing foods like peanuts and alcohol.

The object of desire

Chocolate is not addictive in the way that nicotine and certain drugs are, but one reason so many people crave it may be because of its effect on mood. Researchers have discovered that a compound in chocolate may act on the brain in a manner similar to the active ingredient in marijuana, producing a mild sense of euphoria. This could explain why people often eat chocolate when they feel depressed.

When premenstrual women turn to chocolate, it may be for another reason. Serotonin, a chemical in the brain that possibly helps to maintain a feeling of well-being, decreases at this time in a woman's cycle. Chocolate boosts serotonin levels.

For the weight-conscious

You can indulge and watch your waistline at the same time by doing the following:

A compound in chocolate may act on the brain in a manner similar to the active ingredient in marijuana.

- Use cocoa powder for cooking and flavoring. It has the taste of chocolate, minus the fat and calories.
- When having a candy bar, choose semisweet rather than milk chocolate, which has the highest fat content.
- Eat plain chocolate. Nuts, cream, and coconut add extra fat.
- Drink low-fat chocolate milk. You'll consume less chocolate and more calcium.
- Choose carob as a substitute only if you want less saturated fat. Its total fat content equals that of chocolate.

Myths About Chocolate

Although greatly loved, chocolate has also been much maligned. Below are some of the false beliefs about this delectable delicacy:

- Raises cholesterol. The fat in chocolate is highly saturated, but much of it is a type called stearic acid, which does not elevate blood cholesterol.

- Promotes cavities. Plain chocolate is less harmful than most other candies because it doesn't stick to teeth. In addition, cocoa contains tannins, which inhibit plaque formation.

- Causes acne. Doctors say the development of acne has nothing to do with diet. Studies have failed to prove that chocolate has any adverse effect on the skin.

- High in caffeine. Chocolate has only a tiny amount of caffeine. A cup of cocoa, for example, has about 5 milligrams of caffeine, compared to about 100 milligrams in a cup of coffee.

Cholesterol

Take a look at a typical North American's diet—you'd swear we needed to get a megadose daily allowance of cholesterol. Well we don't. Our liver makes most of the cholesterol we need; the substance is in all of our tissues and is a component of cell membranes and nerves. Raising cholesterol levels through diet increases the risk of heart disease and stroke. With cholesterol, less is better.

Cholesterol works for you, too

Despite its negative rap, cholesterol does perform a few good deeds. It helps the body digest fats, produce hormones, and manufac-

Foods rich in saturated fat—red meat and high-fat dairy products—are the biggest culprits in raising cholesterol levels. If you limit dietary cholesterol intake without also limiting saturated fat, your cholesterol levels will remain high.

ture vitamin D. But cholesterol is waxy and will stick to artery walls. Sometimes it builds up in the form of plaque—a thick, hardened coating that clogs blood vessels and restricts blood flow, reducing the amount of oxygen going to the heart muscle and brain.

During middle age, high cholesterol levels can be so dangerous that men 35 to 65 and women 45 to 65 should have cholesterol screenings at least every five years. Anyone diagnosed with heart disease must be tested more often, as his or her cardiologist advises.

Measured in milligrams per deciliter of blood (mg/dl), the total serum cholesterol level (the amount in the blood) is graded as

follows: less than 200 mg/dl (normal); 200–239 mg/dl (borderline high); 240 mg/dl and over (high). However, recent studies show that even people with normal serum cholesterol levels may still be at risk for vascular problems, so levels as low as 140 mg/dl (but no lower) might be even more beneficial.

"Good" and "bad" cholesterol

As important as your total blood-cholesterol level is, it doesn't tell the whole story. What can also make a difference are the levels of triglycerides (fats that are fuel sources for the body) and two proteins in the blood that transport cholesterol. These transporters are known as high-density lipoprotein (HDL) and low-density lipoprotein (LDL).

HDL has been nicknamed good cholesterol because it carries cholesterol away from body tissues, while LDL has been tagged bad cholesterol because it causes cholesterol to stick more readily to artery walls. The levels of these three components are measured when the blood is tested for overall cholesterol level. Comprehensive treatment involves not only lowering total cholesterol but also increasing HDL and decreasing LDL and triglycerides.

Lowering your cholesterol

The best way to achieve a healthier cholesterol profile is to reduce dietary intake of all fats to no more than 30 percent of daily calories. Saturated fats, found in animal products and in coconut and palm oils, are the most dangerous. No more than a third of your dietary fat should come from saturated fats. The Canadian Consensus Conference on Cholesterol recommends that people with elevated blood cholesterol levels should get less than 300 milligrams a day of dietary cholesterol.

For daily protein, eat small portions of lean meats, skinned chicken, and fish or a bean-grain combination. Cook with polyunsaturated or monounsaturated fats, such as corn or olive oil, which won't elevate cholesterol levels.

Consuming more soluble fiber, found in such foods as oats, beans, peas, fresh fruits,

Cholesterol Medications: A Consumer's Guide

There's a wide array of cholesterol-lowering medications on the market, and they fall into four categories. Listed below are those categories, some individual drugs within them, how they work, their side effects, and special warnings about them.

Category	Medications	How They Work	Side Effects	FYI
HMG-CoA reductase inhibitors, or "statins"	fluvastatin (Lescol); lovastatin (Mevacor); pravastatin (Pravachol); simvastatin (Zocor); atorvastatin (Lipitor); cerivastatin (Baycol)	They block an enzyme in the liver that is needed to produce cholesterol. This causes the body to pull cholesterol out of the blood instead.	A nondangerous and reversible change in liver function.	The only class of cholesterol medications shown to reduce the risk of heart attack and stroke in those with cardiovascular disease. Higher dosages are more likely to control excess triglycerides.
Nicotinic Acid	High potency nicotinic acid (vitamin B_3)	It stops the liver from producing lipid particles, is more effective at raising HDL, and is effective at eliminating excess triglycerides.	Burning sensation in the face after each dosage; loss of appetite; stomach pains; liver toxicity (particularly hepatitis) and, in rare cases, liver failure.	Time-release and fast-acting formulas. The time-release form of niacin generally has more side effects than the fast-acting. An exception: the newer time-release preparation Niaspan, sold only in the U.S., is reportedly easier to tolerate.
Fibric Acid	gemfibrozil (Lopid)	It breaks down triglycerides and raises HDL but is less effective at lowering LDL.	May increase the risk of gallstones and affect liver function. May cause gastrointestinal distress.	Because it doesn't lower LDL efficiently, it is not recommended for treatment of heart disease. This type of medication multiplies the effects of blood-thinning drugs, increasing the risk of hemorrhage. It neutralizes the effects of antidiabetic drugs.
Bile Acid Sequestrants	colestipol (Colestid); cholestyramine (Questran)	They bind to bile, a product of the liver that contains cholesterol, forcing the body to pull its cholesterol supply from the blood.	Slight rise in triglycerides; constipation; heartburn; nausea; belching; gas. Should not be used if you have kidney disease, gastrointestinal problems, or hemorrhoids.	These drugs are not systemically absorbed, but they can decrease the absorption of other medications if taken at the same time.

and vegetables, lowers LDL cholesterol. High-fiber dietary supplements, particularly those containing psyllium, lower cholesterol levels and also improve the ratio of HDL to LDL, but they can interfere with bowel function, so take them only if a doctor recommends them.

Studies show that three daily servings of soy foods, such as soy-protein drinks and tofu, lower cholesterol levels by 9 milligrams. But soy sauce, soy meat substitutes, and tofu cheeses don't offer the same benefit; the heart-protective soy-plant estrogens, called isoflavones, are removed when these foods are processed.

Exercise also helps with cholesterol problems—not only does it promote weight loss, which lowers cholesterol levels, but it raises HDL cholesterol. Smoking, on the other hand, is counterproductive in controlling cholesterol. It lowers the level of HDL in the blood while increasing the level of LDL.

Resorting to medication

If improved diet, more exercise, and no smoking doesn't lower your cholesterol to safe levels, your doctor may prescribe a medication (see chart, above). But cholesterol-lowering drugs are not without side effects, so they should be tried only if other efforts fail.

Now for the good news

A little effort goes a long way. For every 1-milligram drop in cholesterol levels, your risk of heart disease drops by 2 to 3 percent. Lower cholesterol by 10 percent, and reduce the risk of heart disease by a whopping 20 percent.

Circumcision

New parents of a baby boy must decide whether or not to circumcise. Those making the decision for health reasons, not religious ones, should know that it is not clearcut. Although more than a million North American babies undergo the procedure each year, circumcision is no longer considered routine or medically necessary. Even doctors can't agree on whether the possible benefits of the procedure outweigh its risks—chiefly, the potential psychological trauma caused by the painful removal of the foreskin from the tip of the penis. But the Canadian Pediatric Society states there is no valid medical justification for routine circumcision, and a leading Canadian medical ethicist has said doctors should stop doing the procedure.

Even doctors can't agree on whether the possible benefits of circumcision outweigh its risks.

The healthy choice?

Circumcision seems to dramatically reduce the risk of penile cancer. The majority of some 1,000 North American men who develop the disease each year are uncircumcised. However, uncircumcised males can reduce their chances of contracting the rare cancer (it affects about 1 in 100,000 men) by regularly and thoroughly cleaning the genitals. Studies also show that circumcision helps prevent urinary tract infections (UTIs). But since the overall rate of UTIs is low, some physicians recommend circumcision only for high-risk infants, such as those with dilated urinary tracts.

Whether circumcision protects against HIV infection and sexually transmitted diseases (STDs) is debatable. Research in Africa found a "modest but significant" reduction in HIV infection for circumcised as compared with uncircumcised men, but other evidence tends to refute this finding. The results of some studies on herpes and gonorrhea have been conflicting, but a recent U.S. study found that being circumcised made no difference in the risk of contracting STDs.

Easing the baby's pain

Circumcision should be performed only on healthy, stable babies. After surgery, the area remains red and raw for about a week. Minor complications, such as bleeding and infection, are treatable. More severe complications, such as injury to the penis and death from bleeding disorders, are rare.

Much of the controversy about circumcision centers on the suffering that the baby endures. Although researchers haven't found ways to completely block the pain, they at least know now that there is pain, and they have the means to mitigate it. The baby should be lying down on a padded bed. A pacifier dipped in sugar water may reduce distress. More important, experts recommend a local anesthetic and advise parents to have their doctor administer one to the child. There are three main types, but doctors may differ on which one they prefer to use:

- **Topical cream.** An anesthetic is rubbed onto the penis at least two hours before the circumcision.
- **Dorsal penile nerve block.** An anesthetic such as lidocaine is injected into the base of the penis.
- **Ring block.** Lidocaine is injected in a circular pattern midway up the penis shaft.

In the Jewish ritual of the bris, a baby boy is circumcised by a practitioner called a mohel.

Anyone who has needed to wash and quickly dry a favorite blouse or shirt for a last-minute engagement or party doesn't have to be reminded about the convenience of an automatic dryer. Most Canadian families couldn't function well without one. But because these machines are a fact of life for so many of us, it's easy to forget that they are powerful appliances that can pose a health risk if not installed and maintained properly.

The spin on dryers

There are two main types of dryers: those heated by electricity and those fueled by natural gas. Cost comparisons for running the different models are difficult to make since gas and electricity prices vary from utility to utility: what is the cheaper system in one region may be the costliest in another.

Some people favor electric models on the grounds that gas dryers can leak combustion by-products, such as carbon monoxide, into your home. If you have a gas dryer, and are concerned about possible leaks of carbon monoxide, which is odorless and toxic, you can get peace of mind, and assure your general safety, by purchasing a home detector.

But first and foremost, have your dryer (as well as any other fuel-burning appliances) inspected annually by a professional. Gas authorities point out that dryers that are professionally serviced according to the maintenance schedule should not leak gas. Any work related to the appliance, replacing connectors for example, should be done professionally. Never attempt such work yourself.

Current research indicates that people need not be concerned about the electromagnetic field (EMF) surrounding their electric dryer, nor do they need take any special precaution to avoid exposure when the machine is operating. First of all, studies have not proved that EMFs cause diseases or other health problems. Secondly the EMF surrounding the device rapidly decreases as you move away from the source. If you are still unsure, simply minimize your exposure to the electric dryer while it is running.

Dry safely

- Your dryer should be vented outdoors. If the exhaust duct empties indoors, it will spew tiny pieces of lint into the air. These particles may cause breathing problems for some household members.
- Periodically check exhaust ducts for tears, and either repair a damaged area with duct tape or replace it. Metal ducts are preferable to ribbed plastic hose, which can be easily bent and so collect lint.
- Prevent lint buildup (the cause of more than 4,000 fires annually in North America) by cleaning the filter after each use. In the case of electric models, unplug the machine once or twice a year, remove the service panel, and gently vacuum the lint catcher and internal workings, as well as the dryer's base, with a crevice attachment. Apart from cleaning the filter after each use, cleaning or removing lint or dust from the mechanical areas of your gas dryer should be left to the technician who carries out your regular maintenance.
- Never put plastic, rubber, or foam materials in the dryer. They may melt or catch fire. Oil-soaked fabrics may also catch fire.
- Prohibit children from crawling into the clothes dryer. If a youngster pulls the door shut from inside, he or she may suffocate. Lock the laundry-room door when you are not there. Cats also find the inside of dryers appealing, so if you have a feline, remember to check the dryer each time before turning it on.

CAUTION!
Do not pull a gas clothes dryer or any other gas appliance away from the wall unless you are sure that its connector is a flexible type.

Because the heat of a dryer can create a fire hazard under certain conditions, finish drying any clothes before leaving your house.

Cold & Cough Remedies

There is little that is common about the common cold. It can be caused by one of some 200 viruses. And although most colds hit Canadians in the fall and winter, cold weather itself isn't to blame. Rather it's the greater amount of time people spend indoors during those chillier seasons that increases the risk of the virus spreading. No matter what the cause, many people treat their illness with one of the over-the-counter (OTC) medications lining the cold-remedy shelves.

Cold truths

Every over-the-counter product that is approved by Health Canada can have side effects at recommended dosages and can cause serious problems at higher dosages. Know which active ingredients you need, and keep these tips in mind when seeking cold comfort:

- Don't set out to cure the common cold. Whether or not you take medicine, you will get better in about the same amount of time (a week or so). Cold and flu treatments can relieve certain symptoms, but the virus will not be affected. Never pressure a doctor to give you an antibiotic; the drug doesn't kill cold viruses.
- Address your primary symptom and keep medication to a minimum. Many OTC remedies are combination drugs designed to relieve several symptoms at the same time, but you may not have all of those symptoms. Use only a decongestant if you have a stuffy nose; an antitussive if you can't sleep because of a persistent cough; or a pain reliever if you have fever and body aches. And maintain the doses only if they make you feel better.
- Don't forget the basics. Drink plenty of liquids and get lots of rest. Avoid alcohol

Don't rush to give cold medicines to a child. And always choose a children's formula for children and an infant formula for infants.

and dry, indoor air—use a vaporizer if necessary. Finally, wash your hands frequently to prevent a cold from spreading.

The inside dope on cold medicines

Over-the-counter cold medicines designed to treat a single symptom fall into one of the following categories:

- **Decongestants** reduce sinus congestion by opening up nasal passages. Nasal sprays or inhalers work faster and have fewer side effects than those taken orally. Sprays, however, should not be used for more than three to four days—overuse can cause

On the Horizon Two new cold and flu treatments, both of which are currently under study, signal that more relief could be on the way. New from Canadian researchers is a drug known as BIRR-4. Administered as a nasal spray, it appears to reduce cold symptoms by up to 50 percent. The second treatment, also a nasal spray, is a drug called zanamivir. It won't relieve symptoms, but it could help you get well up to three days sooner.

congestion to recur. Decongestants may raise your blood pressure and make you feel jittery. Minimize this risk by using products that contain pseudoephedrine instead of phenylpropanolamine, which is more likely to raise blood pressure.

- **Expectorants** help reduce chest congestion by thinning mucus in the lungs and allowing the mucus to be coughed up more easily. However, a common ingredient, guaifenesin, has not proven reliable. In fact, drinking lots of fluids may be more effective. If you do use an expectorant, don't use it with a cough suppressant.

- **Antihistamines**, which work to relieve allergylike symptoms, such as sneezing and watery eyes, can make you feel worse. Although they may dry up nasal passages, they often cause drowsiness, dry out the eyes and mouth, and impair motor skills. They may also cause mucus to thicken, making it harder to expel from your body.

Natural alternatives

You may not even need an OTC cold remedy. New research has validated the use of several natural remedies, including zinc and echinacea, to fight cold symptoms. There is no proof, however, that vitamin C alleviates cold symptoms. In addition, researchers have gained intriguing insights into the human immune system. It seems that having a broad network of social contacts may actually lower the risk of catching a cold.

Symptom Sorter

Do You Have a Cold, the Flu, or Something Else?

Before you take any medicine, try to determine what ails you. Cold and flu symptoms, listed below, differ slightly, and each illness has certain telltale symptoms, which are marked with an asterisk (*). Typically, a cold comes on slowly and lasts up to one week, whereas the flu comes on suddenly and can last two weeks or longer. In addition, a cold or the flu can lead to other infections, such as sinusitis (marked by severe nasal congestion and painful sinuses) and bronchitis (marked by a deep cough that produces yellow phlegm).

	Cold	Flu
Stuffy nose	Common*	Less common
Sneezing	Common*	Less common
Nasal discharge	Common*	Less common
Sore throat	Common*	Rare
Chest congestion	Common (mild)	Common (can be severe)
Cough	Rare (mild)	Common* (often severe)
Headache	Rare	Common*
Body ache	Common (mild)	Common* (often severe)
Fatigue	Common (mild)	Common* (often severe)
Fever	Rare (mild)	Common* (often high, to 40°C/104°F; lasts a few days)

Clinical studies have shown that such natural remedies as chicken soup, zinc lozenges, and tinctures of echinacea may help relieve cold symptoms.

Caring for a cough

To quiet a dry, nagging cough, use an antitussive (cough suppressant) that contains dextromethorphan. It works like codeine by suppressing the "cough center" in the brain—but with fewer side effects. Note: Although inconclusive, preliminary research has shown that dextromethorphan may cause birth defects. For this reason, pregnant women should avoid remedies that contain this ingredient.

How about cough drops? They may taste and smell like medicine, but they are no more effective than a piece of hard candy. Those that claim to contain a cough suppressant usually provide very little medication. Furthermore, cough drops containing aromatic oils, such as peppermint and eucalyptus, can actually irritate the mucous membranes in the throat or upset your stomach.

Cold Weather

Winter beckons us outside for sledding, skiing, skating, and picturesque walks. However, unless you take certain precautions, prolonged exposure to chilling, wet, and windy conditions (even when the temperature is mild) can endanger life and limb.

The hazards of hypothermia

A chill is a sign that the body is losing heat. Heat loss can occur during a few hours outdoors or a few days in a poorly heated house. If heat loss continues and body temperature falls below 35°C (95°F), hypothermia sets in. Moderate to severe hypothermia is potentially fatal. Particularly vulnerable are older people, who are less sensitive and react more slowly (if at all) to the cold.

Symptoms of hypothermia include excessive shivering, confusion, fatigue, stiffness or numbness of the arms and legs, pallor, slurred speech, and shallow breathing. In extreme cases the shivering eventually stops and the person may lose consciousness.

Hypothermia requires emergency medical attention. To apply first aid, get the person into a warm and dry environment, remove any wet clothes, and slowly rewarm the body using a blanket wrap. Don't rub the skin or force the person to eat or drink, even though a warm, nonalcoholic drink may help.

Jack Frost can bite

Exposure to cold air, water, and wind can lead to frostbite—the freezing of the skin and underlying tissue. The most susceptible areas of the body are the ones most exposed: the hands, feet, nose, and ears. Frostbite initially causes white, gray, or yellow discoloration of the skin. In more severe cases, the skin can look waxy and pale, become numb, and feel cold and hard to the touch. Skin or extremities that are severely frostbitten may have to be amputated.

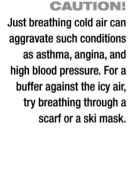

CAUTION!

Just breathing cold air can aggravate such conditions as asthma, angina, and high blood pressure. For a buffer against the icy air, try breathing through a scarf or a ski mask.

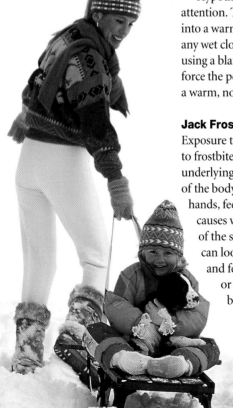

Young kids, especially inactive ones, are more susceptible than adults to the effects of exposure.

To treat frostbite, quickly move the victim to shelter and call for immediate medical attention. Until help arrives, remove any constrictive clothing. Frostbitten hands can be warmed in the victim's own armpits. If possible, avoid walking on frostbitten feet—keep them elevated and covered. If frostbitten skin is partially thawed, place it in warm water (between 39°C/102°F and 41°C/106°F) for 20 to 40 minutes. Do not use direct heat or anything that can burn the skin. Never massage frostbitten skin or rub it with ice or snow.

What to wear? What to do?

To avoid cold-weather problems, prepare yourself and your kids before going out:

- **Choose loose, warm clothing.** Tight garments won't trap the layers of air needed to insulate your body from the cold. Wearing extra thick socks that make boots feel too tight can also impede circulation.
- **Wear layers instead of one thick garment.** Start with socks and long johns; materials that don't retain moisture (polypropylene or wool) are better than those that absorb it (cotton). The middle layer should be wool or cotton. Top it off with a windproof outer layer, gloves, scarf, and hat. Keep your body and clothes dry; trapped moisture will make you chilly.
- **Always put on a hat.** Up to 50 percent of body heat is lost through an uncovered head. This heat loss forces your body to compensate by cutting down the blood supply to your extremities—a good recipe for freezing hands and feet.
- **Prepare for wet weather.** Heat loss speeds up if you are wet, so dig out waterproof boots, coat, and hat (or an umbrella).

While you are outdoors, be sensible. Move around to stimulate circulation—but not to the point of sweating, which can increase heat loss. Eat carbohydrates for extra energy, and drink plenty of fluids. Avoid alcohol, nicotine, and caffeine; they contribute to heat loss. And watch out for kids and older people. If they—or you—get wet or start shivering, it's time to come in out of the cold.

Collagen Injection

It's no secret that the aging process marks our faces with lines, creases, and wrinkles. A recent "remedy" for this unwelcome aspect of aging is a series of collagen injections. In most cases, the procedure is safe and effective, but it does carry a high price tag, and the results are only temporary.

Collagen injections are also being used to treat stress incontinence, the leakage of urine that is caused by weakened pelvic muscles. Placing collagen into tissues around the urethra can help tighten the bladder's closure. Still, as with cosmetic procedures, the results aren't permanent.

Beauty that is fleeting

Collagen is a natural protein that provides structure for your skin and other body tissues. As you age, collagen breaks down, allowing wrinkles to develop in the surface of the skin.

Collagen used for injections is usually a purified form taken from cows. Body fat taken directly from the patient by liposuction has also been used. The material, injected just under the skin's surface, provides a "plumping" effect that can smooth lines, add body to sunken cheeks, fill in scars, and make lips look fuller. The new look usually lasts only 3 to 12 months (enhanced lips may last only a few weeks) because the body eventually absorbs and removes the collagen. To maintain the results, regular injections are needed.

Risks? Costs? Alternatives?

The injections can cause a slight stinging sensation, followed by temporary redness, itching, or swelling. In rare cases, they may cause lumps, bruising, severe swelling, scarring, or allergic reactions (such as hives). Several weeks prior to the first injection, you will be tested for allergies to bovine collagen and lidocaine, an anesthetic that is often mixed with the collagen. Pregnant women and those who suffer from autoimmune disorders, such as rheumatoid arthritis or lupus, should avoid collagen injections.

For the process, patients typically pay per injection—an expense that can

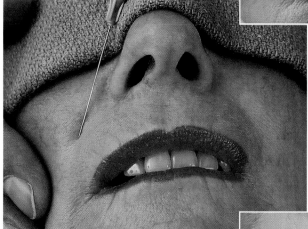

Quick fix? Here, collagen injections "plump out" vertical lines around the mouth. The temporary results (below) can be achieved in less than an hour.

easily multiply over the course of a year. If human body fat is used, the results may last a little longer and the risk of autoimmune reactions is reduced. However, the procedure involves liposuction to remove the fat and can therefore cost more.

Simpler face-saving methods do exist. To help keep your skin smooth, don't smoke, stay out of the sun, and use sunscreen. Apply a moisturizer every day. You may also choose simply to enjoy your natural aging—and wear those wrinkles well.

On the Horizon A new type of injection material called Autologen, which uses the patient's own natural collagen, is being tested. The treatment would eliminate the need for preinjection allergy tests, and its effects could last for a year or more. Even longer-lasting results might come from an injection material called Dermalogen, which is being developed from collagen extracted from human cadaver tissue.

Computers

In less than two decades the desktop computer has revolutionized the workplace, and it now sits in almost half of all North American homes. But with every advance, it seems, comes a setback. While personal computers have shortened the time it takes to do a task, they have contributed a list of complaints we take to our doctors—sore necks, eyes, and wrists, not to mention addictions to the Internet and fantasy games.

There's nothing inherently harmful about desktop computers, experts say. What's unhealthy is the way we use them.

Is the computer the problem?

Experts say there's nothing inherently harmful about desktop computers. What's unhealthy is the way we use them. Preventing computer-related ills begins with understanding how computers have changed the way we work. In the past, typists didn't peck away at keys constantly. They took "microbreaks": returning the carriage, cranking a new sheet of paper into the typewriter, erasing errors, and filing papers. These tasks gave eyes, fingers, and arms a rest. Computers provide no rest for weary body parts. Computer users must make a conscious effort to take microbreaks by stretching, glancing away from the screen, sipping water, or getting up from the desk.

A poorly designed work space compounds the problem. Desks left over from the pre-computer era are often too high; keyboards must be low enough to allow forearms and wrists to be parallel to the floor. Even if you fit a desk with a lower keyboard tray, you can still develop "mouse shoulder" if the tray has no mouse extension because you'll be continually reaching for an out-of-the-way mouse.

What's needed is proper, comfortable posture. Rearrange your chair, desk, computer monitor, keyboard, and pointing device so that your feet are flat on the floor (or on a phone book, if necessary), with your elbows, hip joints, and knees bent at right angles. Position the mouse so that your wrist stays on the same plane as your elbow and your shoulders are relaxed. Shift positions every 15 minutes or so to avoid circulatory problems. Avoid bifocal eyeglasses; tilting your head back to read through them makes your neck sore. Instead, keep handy a pair of computer glasses whose lenses are made from your reading prescription.

Repetitive stress injuries

Any physical labor that entails repeated motions, from carpentry to sewing to violin playing, may cause repetitive stress injuries. Computer work is no different. Using a mouse or keyboard at the wrong height irritates tendons, which connect the muscles to the bones, and the bursas, the fluid-filled sacs

Keyboard tilt: 0–25°

Eye to screen: 18–30 inches; line of sight to screen: 10–20° below the horizontal

Floor to seat: 16–19 inches

Floor to typing surface: 23–26 inches

Feet flat on floor

Sit with elbows, hips, and knees bent at a 90° angle. Elbows should clear the armrests. Place the screen at arm's length directly in front of you, at or below eye level. Keep the mouse close to and level with the keyboard.

that protect tendons as they slide over bones and joints. Repeated motions cause tenosynovitis—inflammation of the sheaths surrounding the tendons.

Carpal tunnel syndrome (CTS) is the most common computer-related repetitive stress injury. Constant typing, especially with the hands arched over the keyboard in a "praying mantis" position, forces tendons within the narrow tunnel formed by the wrist bones (carpals) and transverse ligaments to swell. This swelling squeezes the median nerve, which runs down the arm into the hand, causing pain and numbness in the wrist and palm and tingling in the thumb and forefinger. If symptoms last for more than a day, see your doctor. Without prompt treatment, CTS can progress to shooting pains in the hand and arm and wasting of the hand muscles.

A brace, such as this lace-up model, can support a wrist injured by carpal tunnel syndrome and help it to heal.

Eye problems

Reading from computer screens fosters nearsightedness, but the same is true for reading from a printed page. Eyestrain, however, is another matter. Three-quarters of computer users experience what the Canadian Association of Optometrists calls computer vision syndrome (CVS). Symptoms may include:
• Blurred and sometimes double vision
• Watery, irritated, or dry eyes
• Sensitivity to light
• Aching eyelids or forehead
• Temporary nearsightedness, characterized by an inability to focus on distant objects after a prolonged computer session.
Improper room lighting is one cause of CVS. Minor, uncorrected eye defects can also contribute to the discomfort. Fortunately, proper eyeglasses, adjustments in the work environment, and good work habits can prevent CVS (see box, right).

Compulsive computing

Some people search the Internet less for information than for companionship that may be missing in their lives. In one study hundreds of "Internet-dependent" people displayed addictive profiles similar to those of compulsive gamblers. If nights spent on the Net or other computer work interfere with your career or personal life or impair your physical or mental health, it may be best to seek counseling.

Radiation fears

Anxiety about radiation from computers, scientists maintain, is unfounded. Tests show that monitors give off no more radiation than fluorescent lights and color TVs. Emissions are so slight, scientists say, even a lifetime of daily computer use isn't harmful.

Easy on the Eyes: Avoiding Eyestrain

• Place a computer screen directly in front of you with the top at about eye level, at right angles to windows.

• Incandescent bulbs cause less glare than fluorescents. Diffuse light is better than direct light. If room lighting causes glare, use an antiglare screen.

• Turn the screen as bright as it will go without blurring.

• Blink frequently. Use artificial tears every few hours.

• Every half hour look at something 6 meters (20 feet) away.

• Have an eye exam to find and correct vision flaws.

Contact Lenses

Contact lenses are a godsend for people who hate eyeglasses or play sports. They don't fog up or distort your peripheral vision. And today there is a lens for almost everyone—even people who need bifocals.

But contacts can cause eye damage if you're not careful. The riskiest are extended-wear lenses. These require little maintenance because they can be worn for seven days straight—day and night. Many doctors advise against them, however, because the less often lenses are cleaned, the greater the risk of irritation and infection. Moreover, wearing contact lenses while sleeping is a potential hazard because the eyes are deprived of oxygen. In fact, those who use extended-wear lenses are up to 10 times more likely to develop corneal ulcers than other contact lens wearers.

The eyes have it: Contact lenses can correct poor vision and even improve self-esteem. But problems (among them, allergic reactions to cleaning solutions) are not uncommon.

Daily-wear lenses, which are removed and cleaned at night, are much safer. And people who don't want the bother of cleaning their lenses can buy daily-wear disposable lenses, which are used once and thrown away. Unlike other lenses, disposables never have the chance to accumulate irritating protein deposits. But they don't come cheap.

Yet another type—rigid gas-permeable (RGP) lenses—last longer, offer crisper vision, and correct more vision problems (including severe astigmatism) than soft lenses and may even slow the progression of near-sightedness. But they require a longer break-in period.

A proper fit is crucial when buying contacts. Make sure you see an experienced eye-care specialist who allows unlimited follow-up visits because you may need to try several brands before finding one that is comfortable. Avoid discount stores; they tend to sell poor-quality lenses and seldom offer comprehensive follow-up care. Also inquire about contacts with ultraviolet (UV) protection. They absorb and neutralize UV rays, which can contribute to the formation of cataracts.

Clean up your act

The key to wearing lenses safely is keeping them clean. Follow these precautions:

- Wash your hands before touching lenses.
- Keep the case clean and replace it often.
- Use only the prescribed cleaning solutions.
- Never clean contacts with distilled water, homemade saline solution, tap water, or saliva. Organisms in these media can cause serious infection or even blindness.
- Don't overwear your lenses. Wearing the lenses too long deprives the cornea of oxygen and may impair your vision.
- Unless you have extended-wear lenses, never wear your contacts while sleeping.

If you experience pain, redness, blurry vision, sticky secretions, or light sensitivity, stop wearing the lenses and see your eye-care specialist immediately. Your eyesight may be damaged permanently if you delay.

For Women's Eyes Only

- Hairspray can coat lenses. If you use it, apply it before putting in contacts.
- Put in soft lenses before applying makeup and RGP lenses after; take out both kinds before removing makeup.
- Use water-based liquid foundations and moisturizers and powder-based eye shadow (cream leaves a film on lenses).
- Wear disposable soft lenses during pregnancy, when hormonal fluctuations may cause temporary vision changes.
- Some women on the Pill, which can cause dry eyes, may have trouble wearing contacts. If you do, tell your doctor.

Contraceptives

Preventing pregnancy is the purpose of all contraceptives, but how easily and effectively this is accomplished depends on the method. And not all methods are right for all couples. The best advice: learn all you can about the options, then talk to your doctor.

Surgical solutions

What's the most prevalent form of contraception in North America? Surprisingly, it's tubal ligation, or female sterilization. This means having one's "tubes tied" so that sperm cannot reach the egg. Doctors either use an electric current to seal the Fallopian tubes or bind them with plastic clips. If a woman wants the tubal ligation reversed (this is considered major surgery), the clip method is slightly easier to undo; still, the success rate is low, and insurance companies often won't cover it.

The surgery is usually performed by laparoscopy, which requires one or two tiny incisions in the lower abdomen. Some women report a heavier menstrual flow for several months after surgery. The chance of conception following sterilization is small, but when it does occur, it often takes place in the Fallopian tube. Such a pregnancy, called ectopic, can be fatal.

Slightly more effective is male sterilization, or vasectomy. The procedure blocks the passageway between the testicles, where sperm is made, and the penis, preventing sperm from leaving the body. The surgery takes just 15 minutes, causes only mild discomfort, and does not affect sex drive or performance. Another contraceptive method should be used for at least a month afterward because sperm can live in a man's reproductive tract for weeks following the surgery.

Vasectomy can sometimes be reversed, but it becomes harder to reverse over time. Some men freeze their sperm prior to the surgery to allow for artificial insemination later on.

There's still the Pill

The oral contraceptive for women sparked a sexual revolution when it was introduced in the 1960s. Many women consider it the easi-

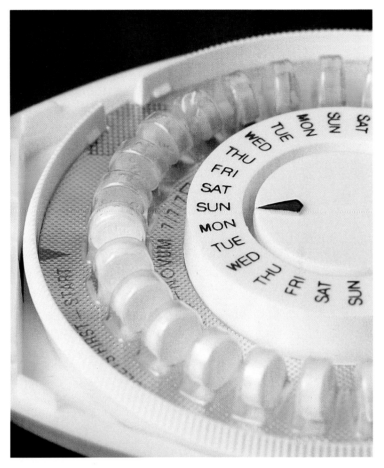

est form of birth control and it remains the method of choice for 25 percent of Canadian women seeking contraceptive protection. Known simply as the Pill, it works by altering levels of estrogen and progesterone hormones so that ovulation doesn't occur. It also thickens the cervical mucus, which decreases the incidence of pelvic inflammatory disease by preventing such bacteria as gonorrhea and chlamydia from entering the uterus.

Although the first pills contained 100 micrograms of synthetic estrogen, most oral contraceptives today are "low dose" pills, containing just 20 to 35 micrograms. They are much safer—but not risk-free. One risk is blood clots in the legs. Women with strong risk factors for blood clots should not use pills that contain estrogen. Since the risk of clotting also rises following pregnancy and major surgery

Oral contraceptives, once off-limits to women over age 35, are now prescribed up until menopause; they may even ease pre-menopausal symptoms.

and during prolonged bed rest, the Pill is not recommended at these times.

Pill users who smoke are more likely than their nonsmoking counterparts to suffer a stroke or pulmonary embolism (blood clot in the lung). Other dangers include a slightly increased risk of benign liver tumors and cardiovascular disease (again, mostly among smokers). In women predisposed to gallstones, the Pill may accelerate the condition.

The incidence of cervical cancer also appears higher among long-term Pill users. This may be because the Pill does not protect against sexually transmitted diseases (STDs), such as the human papillomaviruses, which are linked to cervical cancer. Therefore, Pill users with multiple partners should also use condoms to protect against STDs.

Side effects may include swollen breasts, nausea (for the first three months), spotting, missed periods, weight gain, and water retention. Because water retention sometimes affects the cornea, some Pill users may find contact lenses

Birth-control needs can change over time. Don't be afraid to reevaluate your contraceptive choice.

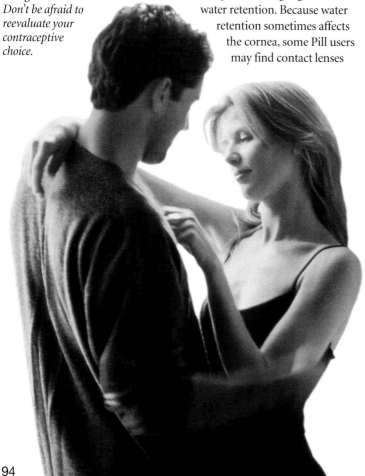

irritating. Nursing mothers may want to avoid oral contraceptives that contain estrogen (they decrease the production of breast milk). So may women who suffer from high blood pressure, diabetes, depression, sickle-cell anemia, or migraines. Pill users taking antibiotics, particularly tetracycline, are advised to use a back-up method of birth control. Finally, women who take pills that contain estrogen should not have more than 500 milligrams of vitamin C per day, since the vitamin increases estrogen levels in Pill users.

Does the Pill cause breast cancer?

Because some malignant breast tumors may be estrogen-sensitive, there has long been concern that oral contraceptives may increase the risk of breast cancer. Although this may have been true of the early, high-dose pills, it is probably not true today.

It is thought, however, that Pill users under age 35 may have a slightly increased risk—not because the Pill causes breast cancer but because it may increase the growth of preexisting tumors. Women with a family history of breast cancer, particularly pre-menopausal breast cancer, may want to consider another form of contraception.

The flip side: health benefits

The Pill offers powerful benefits other than contraception, including protection against endometrial and ovarian cancer. Women who use the Pill for 4 years or less are 30 percent less likely to develop ovarian cancer; 5 to 11 years, 60 percent less likely; 12 or more years, 80 percent less likely. Four or more years of Pill use results in a 60 percent drop in the risk of endometrial cancer. The Pill also reduces menstrual cramps and reduces the risk of cysts in the breasts and ovaries. It is used to treat the early stages of endometriosis (and even acne) and may lower the risk of rheumatoid arthritis and osteoporosis.

Because the early, high-dose oral contraceptives were linked to an increased risk of blood clots, Pill use was once restricted to women under age 35 (after that, a woman's

Safety and Effectiveness

Method	Ideal Effectiveness	Typical Effectiveness	Deaths Per Year
Tubal Ligation	98% plus	98% plus	1 in 67,000
The Pill and the Minipill	99% plus	97%	1 in 63,000 (nonsmokers) 1 in 16,000 (smokers)
Hormone Implants/ Injections	99% plus	99% plus	no data available
Condoms—male and female (without spermicide)	98%	88%	0
Diaphragm or Cervical Cap with spermicide	94%	82%	0
Spermicide alone	97%	79%	0
IUD	Progestasert: 99% plus ParaGard: 98%	97% 97%	1 in 100,000
Natural (or Rhythm) **Method**	94%	80%	0
Vasectomy	99%	99% after the first month	1 in 300,000

This chart is based on U.S. studies. Ideal effectiveness assumes that the product is used exactly as intended; typical effectiveness leaves some margin for common errors in application or use, including occasional nonuse.

risk of heart disease rises). But today's low-dose pills are considered safe for nonsmokers up until menopause. In fact, doctors prescribe them to treat such premenopausal symptoms as hot flashes, insomnia, and mood swings.

The "morning after" pill

This post-coital medication for women is an effective emergency contraceptive when taken within 72 hours of intercourse. Simply a stronger dose of regular birth-control pills, it is usually given with an antinausea medication. Not all contraceptives work equally well for this purpose, however, and the required dosages vary. So don't try to treat yourself, even if you are currently on the Pill. Call your doctor.

Hold the estrogen

For women who want the convenience of hormone-based contraception but who are advised against taking the Pill because of its estrogen content (including nursing women and those with a history of blood clots), three forms of progestin-only birth control are available. They are the "minipill," an oral contraceptive; Norplant, progestin capsules implanted in the upper arm; and Depo-Provera, a progestin injection that is given every three months. All three methods work by suppressing ovulation, thickening cervical mucus (making it more difficult for sperm to get through), and making the uterus less receptive to implantation.

Advantages include a decrease in menstrual flow and pain as well as less discomfort

Norplant capsules, about the size of matchsticks, are surgically implanted in the upper arm; they release progestin for up to five years.

On the Horizon Under development is the "male" Pill. It would work by inhibiting an enzyme in the head of sperm that allows it to penetrate an egg. Also, a new type of IUD known as the Butterfly may soon catch on. It is stringless, and its closed-loop shape allows for easier insertion and less risk of expulsion and infection.

Contraceptives (continued)

during ovulation. But there are drawbacks, including irregular bleeding and weight gain. Less common complaints include headache, mood swings, decreased libido, excessive growth of body hair, and acne. Each method also has additional pluses and minuses.

- **The minipill.** It can be stopped at any time, but missing one pill or taking it late increases your risk of becoming pregnant. Because of its high failure rate and troublesome side effects, the minipill is rarely used in Canada.
- **Norplant.** It works for up to five years, then normal fertility returns. Removal can be difficult and may leave a scar. Preinsertion counseling is key to successful use.
- **Depo-Provera.** It works for three months, but it may cause an erratic menstrual cycle (and often the cessation of menstruation altogether), temporary thinning of the bones, and delayed fertility after the injections are stopped. Widely used in some countries, this drug is not approved for general use as a contraceptive in Canada.

The barrier methods

These contraceptives work by placing a barrier between sperm and egg and are often supplemented by the use of a spermicide. Since barriers don't add anything to the bloodstream, all are relatively safe. In the case of diaphragms, cervical caps, and condoms,

the passage of semen into the cervix is restricted, which protects against STDs. Each method offers further advantages as well:

- **Vaginal spermicides.** These are placed inside the woman's body before intercourse. When combined with other birth-control methods, they are quite effective. Some couples report a contact allergy to the ingredients, but switching brands or types can help. Spermicides containing nonoxynol-9 may help protect against the transmission of chlamydia and gonorrhea.
- **Condoms.** Latex condoms guard against gonorrhea, chlamydia, syphilis, and HIV, as well as sexually transmitted vaginal infections. They also offer some protection against genital warts, herpes, and hepatitis B. Condoms made of animal skin do not offer the same disease protection but are useful for people allergic to latex. Never use oil-based lubricants, such as petroleum jelly and baby oil, with condoms, since they cause the rubber to deteriorate. Lubricated condoms protect against urinary tract infections caused when friction makes small tears in the vaginal lining.
- **Female condoms.** Also called vaginal pouches, these look like male condoms, only larger. The closed end is secured inside the vagina, the plastic ring covering the cervix. In one study, female condoms reduced the risk of STDs by an additional 34 percent over male condoms.

Latex condoms, whether "male" (below left) or "female" (below right), protect against both pregnancy and sexually transmitted diseases.

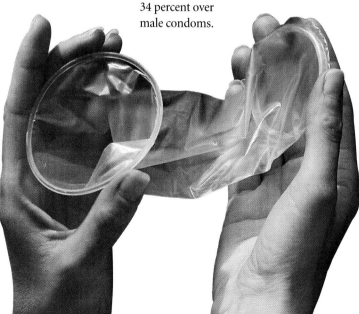

Birth Control the Natural Way

The natural, or "rhythm," method of birth control is based on avoiding intercourse approximately five days before to three days after ovulation.

Among the most popular ways to track ovulation is a simple touch test of cervical mucus. As ovulation nears (about 13 to 15 days into the menstrual cycle), mucus resembles raw egg white and has a slippery consistency.

Immediately following ovulation, mucus production drops and mucus becomes thick and gluelike for several days.

A second method is to chart basal body temperature. A drop in temperature sometimes precedes ovulation by 12 to 24 hours, and a sustained rise in temperature always follows. The fertile period lasts from just before the temperature rise to

three days after sustained higher temperatures are recorded.

For best results, use both methods together, and chart the bodily changes for at least two months before having unprotected sex. Other options include home ovulation tests and computerized methods of tracking body temperature. A home saliva test that detects hormone levels may be widely available soon.

• **Diaphragms and cervical caps.** A diaphragm is a rubber cup that is filled with spermicide and inserted into the vagina up to several hours prior to intercourse. It covers the upper portion of the vagina and the cervix. (Many are made of latex, a problem for women allergic to latex.) The device must remain in the body for six to eight hours after intercourse. Spermicide should be applied again before any additional acts of intercourse. Some women develop frequent urinary tract infections caused by the pressure of the diaphragm against the urethra. A better choice for these women (and for women who have given birth vaginally) is the cervical cap, which is smaller and is held in place by suction against the top walls of the vagina.

Newer, safer IUDs

IUDs, or intrauterine devices, have suffered a bad reputation since the Dalkon Shield was linked to cases of pelvic inflammatory disease in the 1970s. But today's IUDs are designed differently and are considered quite safe. They are made of plastic and release either copper or a synthetic form of progesterone. IUDs create a hostile uterine environment that

makes it difficult for sperm to survive and even harder for a fertilized egg to implant.

An IUD must be inserted by a physician and checked periodically to make sure it has not been expelled. (This is facilitated by a small string that hangs down into the upper vaginal canal.) Once the device has been removed, fertility returns to normal.

IUDs offer protection over the long term: the copper-releasing model can remain in place for up to 10 years; the other model, for one year. Doctors often prescribe antibiotics as a safeguard against infection at the time of insertion.

IUDs may not be the best choice for women who have not yet had children (the risk of expulsion is greater) or women with fibroid tumors. IUDs are not appropriate for women who expect to have more than one sexual partner while the IUD is in place, since the risk of infection is greater.

Unlike a cervical cap, a diaphragm (shown below in its carrying case) must be refitted after any weight gain or loss of 4.5 kg (10 lb) or more.

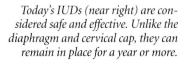

Today's IUDs (near right) are considered safe and effective. Unlike the diaphragm and cervical cap, they can remain in place for a year or more.

97

Cookware

Aluminum pans, nonstick skillets, ceramic pots—each kind of cookware has been the subject of health fears in recent years. Fortunately, few concerns about pots and pans stand up to careful scrutiny. Most cookware sold in Canada is safe provided it is well maintained and used as intended by the manufacturer, and, in fact, some may even be beneficial to your health.

Iron-rich cooking

Cast-iron and stainless-steel cookware add one essential element that can be in short supply in some Canadian diets, especially among women of childbearing age: iron. Cast iron releases the mineral into food, especially when such wet, acidic items as applesauce or tomato sauce are cooked for long periods. For example, spaghetti sauce cooked 25 minutes in a cast-iron skillet contains nearly 10 times more dietary iron per serving than when cooked in an enamel-lined pot.

Foods stir-fried in steel woks also contain more iron. Even stainless steel adds iron to food. Eggs scrambled in a stainless-steel skillet contain 13 percent more iron than when cooked in a glass pan. Foods cooked in stainless steel also absorb trace amounts of another essential nutrient, chromium.

Will that pan cook my goose?

Every kind of cookware releases traces of chemicals into food, but this is rarely a cause for concern. Here's how they stack up:

- **Nonstick.** These allow you to cook with little or no oil, and they are safe except for microwaving. Earlier versions scratched easily, allowing the coating to flake off, but new bonding techniques have essen-

tially eliminated that problem. Never leave an empty nonstick pan on a hot burner—the heat may release fumes that irritate your eyes, nose, and throat. If this happens, turn off the burner, open the windows, and leave the kitchen immediately.

- **Aluminum.** Safe except for microwaving. Past fears about the chance of aluminum intake increasing the risk of Alzheimer's disease have not been confirmed by research. The actual amount released is infinitesimal—hundreds or thousands of times less than the amount contained in many antacids or buffered aspirin.

- **Cast-iron, stainless steel.** Safe except for microwaving. This cookware can add valuable dietary iron to food. However, men and postmenopausal women rarely need the extra iron, and it's not desirable at all for the estimated 0.4 percent of Canadians with hemochromatosis, a genetic predisposition to over-absorb iron. Nickel can also leach from stainless steel, so don't refrigerate foods in these pots; if you're sensitive to nickel, cook with glass or enamelware.

- **Copper.** Safe, except for microwaving, if the cooking surface is lined—usually with tin, but sometimes with stainless steel. Unlined copper

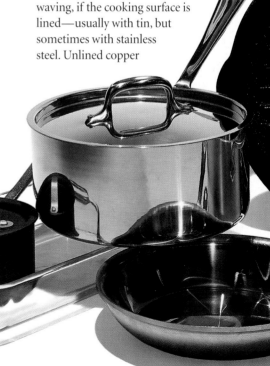

Tiny amounts of metals released from metal cookware during cooking are safe, even beneficial. But refrigeration causes more metal to leach, so place leftovers in plastic or glass containers.

pots and pans, however, can theoretically release enough copper to make you sick, particularly if very acidic foods are cooked for long periods, or left overnight in the pot. Retin worn-out tin-lined cookware right away. (Unlined copper bowls are safe for beating egg whites; not for cooking.)

- **Glass.** Virtually nonreactive. Safe for conventional cooking, storing food in the refrigerator, and, in some cases, microwaving. Glass doesn't react even with highly acidic food. Avoid subjecting glass to sudden extreme temperature contrasts which may cause it to crack. Use only microwave-safe glass in the microwave; other types of glass may get too hot and burn you, or may crack.

- **Enamel-coated metal.** Virtually nonreactive. Safe for cooking, except in the microwave, and also for storing food in the refrigerator.

- **Plastic ware.** Safe for the microwave, but only when labeled "microwavable." To be absolutely safe, use glass or ceramic for long cooking times, reserving microwavable plastic for reheating.

The Hidden Life of Sponges

When you wash a pot with a sponge or dry it with a dish towel, you may think you're getting it cleaner. But you're probably not. Dish towels and sponges are notorious repositories of bacteria, including many of the kinds that cause food-borne illnesses.

In a recent study, 352 sponges and 75 dish towels from households in four major cities were examined. It found that about one in seven contained *Salmonella* and one in five, *Staphylococcus aureus*—bacteria that make millions of people sick each year. Preventive steps can lessen the hazards.

- Disinfect sponges by soaking them in a liter of water mixed with 1 teaspoon chlorine bleach or other disinfectant. Let them air-dry thoroughly before using them again. (Don't rely on antibacterial sponges. They are no safer than conventional sponges.)

- Launder dish towels and hand towels daily to kill bacteria and viruses.

- Use clean paper towels, not sponges or dish towels, to wipe up raw juices from beef, poultry, fish, and shellfish; discard them afterward.

- Minimize the use of towels and sponges by washing dishes, pots, and pans (except cast iron) in a dishwasher whenever possible. If you do wash them by hand, let them air-dry instead of using a towel to dry them.

Never use other plastics, such as old margarine tubs; they can melt and mix with the food. Using plastic wrap as a cover is safe if it does not touch the food, but a plastic cover or dome is preferable, since the wrap may sag enough to touch the food during cooking.

- **Ceramics and clay.** Generally safe for microwaving provided there are no chips or cracks. If the item has a chalky gray residue on the surface after being washed, it should not be used for food. Pots personally imported by Canadians may leach dangerous lead into food (see margin, page 98). If marked "ovenproof," the pots and pans can also be used in a moderate oven.

Cosmetic Surgery

Do you ever wish you could look just a little younger? Or change an unflattering feature? You may want to consider cosmetic surgery. A minor adjustment can smooth away the wrinkles in your brow; more elaborate procedures can "lift" your sagging face or remove excess fat from your thighs or stomach. Properly performed, cosmetic surgery can have a profound effect on how you look and feel. The boost in confidence and self-esteem could affect virtually every aspect of your life.

If you think only grizzled-looking senior citizens seek this kind of enhancement, guess again. Recent figures show that about 40 percent of cosmetic surgeries are performed on people between the ages of 35 and 50, and another 27 percent on those ages 19 to 34. And wanting to look better is not restricted to women; it is estimated that as many as one in four of all cosmetic surgeries may be performed on men.

Surgery always has its risks

Just because an operation is labeled cosmetic doesn't mean it is risk-free. Of course, some procedures are chancier than others, but every operation carries some possibility of complications. Infection, disfigurement, paralysis, and even death can occur as a result of virtually any kind of surgery. Such undesirable consequences of cosmetic procedures are estimated to be no higher than those of other types of surgery.

Even when your cosmetic surgery proceeds without a hitch, you may not be totally delighted with the outcome. Digital photography and computer imaging programs can give you a flattering preview of what your new nose, face, or abdomen may look like, but your appearance after surgery depends to a large extent on the skill of your surgeon—as well as factors unique to you: skin type, bone structure, healing ability, and overall health.

If you find yourself having unrealistically high expectations about what your new look will do for you, it would be wise to mention this to your surgeon. An experienced surgeon should help you prepare for the fact that the outcome of the surgery doesn't always meet the expectations of the patient.

Adding up the cost

Cosmetic surgery is not covered by provincial health insurance plans—and the fees are high. Be sure you understand the fee structure and payment options for all services,

Any type of cosmetic surgery—like all surgery—is a serious procedure. Before having an operation, seek qualified professionals to perform the surgery, and weigh the possible risks against the likely benefits.

including operating room, anesthesia, prescriptions, and follow-up visits. Also be sure you understand the conditions under which additional surgery may be done if the outcome of your operation is not satisfactory.

Focusing on low cost as the sole criterion for choosing where your surgery is performed and by whom may lead to trouble. To boost profits, some cosmetic surgeons skimp on safety: they may use a local anesthetic when a more expensive general anesthetic is called for, or they may perform an operation in their clinic when it should be done in a hospital.

On the other hand, a high fee offers no guarantee that everything will go as planned. Doing your homework—learning what's required for the surgery you are considering and finding out about the surgeon's skills and reputation—helps reduce the risk of potential problems and goes a long way toward ensuring successful results.

Sizing up the surgeon

Here's a bit of news that may shock you: any licensed physician trained in a procedure can perform that surgery. Doctors could have trained in specialties as unrelated as gynecology or dermatology and still perform liposuction, for example, without breaking the law.

One of the best ways to ensure a plastic surgeon's skills is to verify training and credentials. You should contact the Canadian Society of Plastic Surgeons to confirm if the surgeon is fully trained and a member in good standing. Some Canadian plastic surgeons are members of the American Society of Plastic and Reconstructive Surgeons. Also check with your provincial College of Physicians and Surgeons, which is the licensing body for physicians in each province. Always ask what special training and experience the doctor has had.

Once certification is verified, ask for the following information to help ensure that you'll get quality care:
- The names of hospitals at which the surgeon is authorized to perform your operation. (Double-check with the hospitals.)

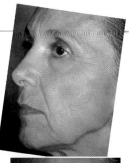

Before-and-after pictures may be misleading because they can be retouched. Even when the pictures are genuine, they may be chosen selectively to show only the best results rather than any average or poor outcomes of surgery.

Reconstruction: When More Than Looks Are at Stake

While most people think of cosmetic surgery as a vanity operation, it can play a much more important role. Reconstructive cosmetic surgery is often used to correct painful or debilitating physical deformities, such as birth defects, or problems resulting from disease or serious accidents.

Burn victims in particular benefit from a reconstructive surgery called skin grafting. The procedure saves lives by protecting tissue that's been exposed by burns.

Microsurgery is used to reattach body parts that have been severed. Precisely and painstakingly performed with the aid of a microscope, it usually must be done soon after the accident to ensure that the reattachment remains viable.

Two free reconstructive cosmetic surgery programs are Operation Smile and Operation Rainbow, which treat children from disadvantaged nations who suffer from serious birth defects, burns, and orthopedic problems. The programs maintain an international roster of surgeons who donate their time to the cause. For instance, the Canadian chapter of Operation Rainbow—based in Vancouver, British Columbia—organizes fund-raisers to fly nurses to various international locations. Its surgeons perform cleft lip and palate surgeries on more than 60 children each year.

Cosmetic Surgery (continued)

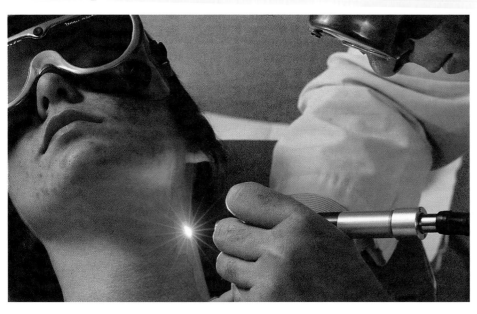

Since some techniques are relatively new—such as argon laser surgery, used here to remove a port-wine stain—find out in advance how much experience your surgeon has had with the procedure.

- The number of times the surgeon has performed the procedure you will undergo and the complications the surgeon's patients have experienced.
- The surgeon's medical school, internship, and duration and type of study in cosmetic surgery. A residency in plastic surgery gives a good foundation for later specialization.
- Recent examples of operations. (Consider before-and-after photos with a grain of salt—particularly digital photos, which can be easily manipulated.)
- Instances when the doctor has been sued for malpractice. (You're more likely to find out the truth if you phrase the question as follows: "I have been told in confidence that you have been sued for malpractice. Can you tell me more about the circumstances of the case?")

Because the field of cosmetic surgery is growing very rapidly, new equipment and surgical techniques are developed every day. But new is not always better, especially when the doctor may have limited experience in these emerging technologies. Ignore advertisements or articles touting the latest techniques. Instead, opt for a surgeon with solid credentials and a good track record.

Ask your family physician for recommendations. Also ask friends, coworkers, and relatives if they've had a procedure like the one you are contemplating, or know someone who has. Good personal experiences can often be reliable sources of information about a cosmetic surgeon's level of competence. Thus ask the surgeon for patient references.

Checking out the clinic

If you are scheduled to have the surgery in a private clinic, ask for proof of the facility's certification with the Canadian Association for the Accreditation of Ambulatory Surgical Facilities (CAAASF). As part of its standards, the CAAASF verifies that the clinic's plastic surgeon has hospital privileges. It also confirms the presence of a CPR-certified head nurse and qualified staff, as well as equipment to monitor blood pressure and other vital signs. If anesthesia will be used in a nonhospital setting, inquire about the training of the anesthesiologist and staff, especially for advanced life-support measures.

Preventing trouble

Beware of misleading pitches made by a prospective surgeon. If, for example, during your discussions surgery is suggested to correct a feature that never bothered you, the doctor might just be trying to generate higher fees. Suppose you seek a consultation about the puffy bags under your eyes and come away convinced that you also need a new nose and a smaller chin; in this case, you would have good reason to question whether the doctor has your best interests in mind.

Be cautious, too, if the surgeon focuses on the benefits of surgery without discussing what might go wrong. All surgery carries risks. If you aren't given a complete explanation of possible problems associated with the surgery along with the benefits, or if risk factors are downplayed, you are not being given fair—or even adequate—treatment.

Cosmetic Surgery Procedures

Below are some of the most common procedures for which patients visit cosmetic surgeons. All of them carry risks, from scarring to facial paralysis and even, in the case of liposuction, death. Choosing a highly skilled surgeon can drastically reduce the odds of a mishap.

Procedure	Purpose	Recovery Time	Risks	Permanence
Face-lift (rhytidectomy)	Improves sagging facial features, including loose jowls and crepey neck, by removing excess fat, tightening muscles, and redraping skin.	10 to 14 days at home; bruising lasts two to three weeks.	Facial paralysis, infection, bleeding, excessive scarring, drastic change in facial appearance.	About 5 to 10 years.
Eyelid Surgery (blepharoplasty)	Corrects puffy bags under eyes and sagging lids above by removing excess fat, skin, and muscle.	7 to 10 days at home, no reading allowed for 2 or 3 days, and no contact-lens use for 14 days or longer; bruising and swelling last for several weeks.	Temporary blurred or double vision, infection, bleeding, swelling, dry eyes; permanent difficulty in closing eyes completely; drooping of lower lids necessitating further surgery; permanent blindness.	Several years; sometimes for life.
Eyebrow Lift	Minimizes brow wrinkles, droopy eyebrows, hooded eyes, and frown lines by removing excess tissue and tightening the skin on the forehead.	7 to 10 days at home (less if performed with an endoscope, which requires fewer incisions); bruising lasts two to three weeks.	Loss of facial motion, muscle weakness, infection, scarring, asymmetrical look.	About 5 to 10 years.
Tummy Tuck (abdominoplasty)	Flattens a sagging stomach by removing excess fat and skin and tightening muscles.	Two to four weeks at home; no strenuous activity for four to six weeks; scars may be highly visible for 3 months to two years.	Blood clots, infection, scarring; may require a second operation.	Lifetime, with sensible diet and exercise.
Liposuction	Changes body shape by removing fatty deposits. Performed by sucking fat out through a tube connected to a vacuum device. In tumescent liposuction the area is first infused with a saline-anesthetic solution to enable fat to be removed with less swelling and bruising. In ultrasound liposuction sound waves are used to liquefy fat before removing it.	One to two weeks at home; swelling and bruising last one to six months or longer.	Rippling or sagging of skin, pigment changes, skin damage, excessive fluid loss leading to shock, infection, burns and cardiac arrest. Complications from liposuction have been the cause of several deaths.	Lifetime, with sensible diet and exercise.
Nose Surgery (rhinoplasty)	Reshapes the nose and may reduce breathing obstructions by cutting or reshaping cartilage or bone or by grafting bone.	One to two weeks at home initially; complete healing may take a year or more.	Infection; damage to tiny blood vessels, causing red blotches on nose. May require repair surgery.	Lifetime.

Cosmetics

Avoid lash-lengthening mascaras, some of which have tiny fibers that can drift into your eyes.

Applying makeup may seem like a thoroughly modern practice, but it actually dates back to prehistoric times. While the earliest cosmetics were made from plant, animal, and mineral substances, many present-day products contain materials created in the lab. Health Canada and the Canadian Cosmetic, Toiletry, and Fragrance Association maintain that these products, particularly those made in Canada, pose no serious health risks—that they are safe for their intended use. But some consumer advocates disagree.

Who's minding the store?

By and large, Canada's cosmetics industry is regulated by Health Canada's Environmental Health Directorate and Product Safety Branch. Manufacturers are not obliged to conduct safety assessments or to report the results when they do. However, it is unlikely that such an

When testing cosmetics in stores, apply them to your hands and wrists only, not to your face.

image-conscious industry would ignore its own safety tests or otherwise damage its image. And unlike the U.S., where the Food and Drugs Directorate needs a court order to remove a potentially dangerous cosmetic from the marketplace, Health Canada can recall, or seize, unsafe products.

Another watchdog group is the Cosmetic Ingredient Review, which is supervised by a panel of scientists and other experts. It submits information to both Health Canada and the cosmetic manufacturers.

What's in the product?

Since there are no long-term test results to rely on, industry critics express concern about new ingredients, and say that some older ingredients may trigger cancer in animals. Among the most controversial are formaldehyde, saccharin, polyvinylpyrrolidone plastic (PVP), and talc (when inhaled, because it may be contaminated with asbestos). Impurities found in some red and yellow dyes may increase cancer risk, and diethanolamine (DEA) and triethanolamine (TEA) can release nitrosamines, compounds that may be carcinogenic, when combined with preservatives called nitrites.

A more immediate problem for some consumers is the possibility of allergic reactions to cosmetics. These may include contact dermatitis, with such symptoms as hives, itching, and inflammation of the skin; eye-related sensitivities, which cause burning and eyelid swelling; respiratory or asthmatic symptoms; and sniffling and sneezing.

Don't assume that "hypoallergenic" or "natural" products will be problem-free. Since there are no specific regulatory standards for hypoallergenic items, the basic ingredients may be the same as those found in regular cosmetics. However, it is generally understood that hypoallergenic products have been submitted to some testing, and any claims made will have to comply with consumer packaging and labeling laws. To prevent allergic reactions, it is best to check labels and stay away from certain ingredients:

- **Dyes:** Generally, the darker the color, the greater the chance of an allergic reaction.
- **Fragrances:** Manufacturers are not required to list what's in a fragrance, and many contain potential irritants. Even

If you think "hypoallergenic" products are safer than regular cosmetics, think again. There are no regulatory standards for such products.

"unscented" products may contain what is called a masking scent.

- **Formaldehyde, gutaraldehyde:** These disinfectants can trigger allergic reactions and may also be carcinogenic.
- **Preservatives:** Under certain circumstances, some preservatives may release formaldehyde into the skin.

Something to keep in mind: in the case of lipsticks and eye shadows, matte types are generally less irritating than frosted or iridescent ones. Also products with no more than 10 ingredients tend to be the least toxic.

Currently, however, cosmetic ingredients are listed at the manufacturer's discretion. Mandatory labeling, now under discussion, will not be in effect before 2000.

Cosmetic hints and tips

Aside from enhancing appearance, cosmetics can offer other, less obvious benefits if you choose your products wisely. Some lipsticks and foundations contain moisturizers that may prevent dry skin and chapped lips. These products may also help protect you against skin cancer, particularly when they include sunscreen among their ingredients.

How you use an item can also make a difference, especially in the case of eye makeup. Wave that mascara wand gently—one of the most common injuries from cosmetics is a scratched cornea caused by careless application of mascara. Never put on mascara while riding in a car or other vehicle. You should also refrain from putting eyeliner along the inner rim of the lower-lash area; the tissue there is delicate. And avoid false eyelashes; the glue can cause inflammation. Remove eye makeup before going to bed to prevent infection.

Don't share makeup—especially for eyes—with anyone, and take proper care of all cosmetics (see box, below).

Lips contain very little of the pigment that helps guard skin from the sun. Lipstick, which acts much like sunscreen, creates a partial barrier between lips and harmful rays.

an ounce of Prevention

Makeup Maintenance

Follow these safety guidelines:

- Replace moisturizers, concealers, foundations, blushes, and lipsticks after 10 to 12 months.
- Replace powders and eye shadows after 12 to 18 months and mascara after 3 months.
- To keep bacteria out, be sure containers are closed tightly when not in use. Store them away from sunlight, which can break down preservatives.
- Never add water, saliva, or any other liquid to a product.
- If you've had a cold or the flu, wipe tops of lipsticks you used with a tissue.
- Throw away any product that has changed in color, texture, or odor.

CPR (Cardiopulmonary Resuscitation)

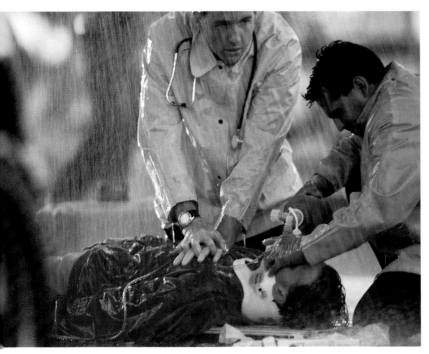

CPR circulates oxygenated blood through the body by chest compression. Done correctly, CPR can achieve 30 percent of the normal cardiac output.

On television, almost every time someone suffers cardiac arrest, a heroic lifeguard, doctor, or rescuer uses CPR to save the day. Unfortunately, that high success rate is a Hollywood illusion. Although reliable statistics are difficult to come by, it is estimated that fewer than a third of the more than 1,000 North Americans who suffer cardiac arrest each day actually receive CPR. Of those who do, only about 15 percent are revived.

Still, that does not diminish the value of learning CPR. This emergency medical technique, also called the ABC method, entails clearing the airway (A), mouth-to-mouth breathing (B), and manually restoring circulation (C) by compressing the chest. Applied properly, CPR may help prolong life for valuable minutes until medical help arrives.

The risk of contracting diseases, including AIDS, from mouth-to-mouth breathing is virtually nonexistent.

The ABCs of giving CPR

CPR should be used only when a person is unresponsive, is not breathing, and has no pulse. Such a condition may occur as a result of choking, drowning, or heart attack. (In the case of choking, remove any blockage first using the Heimlich maneuver or back blows.) If you are trained in CPR, call 911, then perform the technique until help arrives; with children, start chest compressions before calling 911. If you are not trained, call 911 and ask for instructions over the phone. However, if you are the only person available to help in an emergency, try CPR even if you aren't trained—it's better than doing nothing.

When cardiac arrest is caused by respiratory failure (as it often is with children), CPR alone may revive the victim. When cardiac arrest is caused by ventricular fibrillation (often the case with adults), CPR may help prolong life for several minutes. However, survival ultimately depends on the use of a defibrillator—an electrical device that shocks the heart into beating normally. Defibrillators are carried by some ambulance and emergency rescue teams.

The potential hazards

Fear of contracting a disease through mouth-to-mouth breathing may keep some people from giving CPR to a stranger. Studies suggest that, in cases of ventricular fibrillation, correct chest compression alone may be as effective as mouth-to-mouth and compression combined. However, the various agencies that teach CPR still recommend the use of mouth-to-mouth breathing as part of CPR. In more than 80 percent of cases, it is administered by a friend or loved one. Furthermore, the risk of contracting diseases, including AIDS, from mouth-to-mouth breathing is virtually nonexistent.

There are risks for those who receive CPR. Chest compressions can crack ribs, bruise or tear internal organs, or force stomach contents into the lungs. Vomiting may occur, possibly as a result of air being forced into the stomach. In such cases, the airway must be cleared by the person doing the CPR.

To perform CPR effectively, you must be trained by a qualified instructor. Check with your local fire department, Heart and Stroke Foundation, or St. John Ambulance chapter.

Do you feel ambivalent about dairy foods? No wonder. They're the main dietary source of calcium, a nutrient essential to maintaining good health. That's great. On the other hand, dairy foods—whole milk, butter, cream, and certain cheeses—also contain large amounts of saturated fat, which raise cholesterol levels and increase the risk of heart disease. That's bad. Luckily, reduced-fat versions are abundant and allow dairy foods to be consumed as part of a healthful diet.

The importance of calcium

Calcium, the body's most abundant mineral, helps form and maintain teeth and bones, and has a role in nerve and muscle function and blood clotting. As a result, calcium-rich dairy foods promote strong bones and teeth and help prevent osteoporosis. Health Canada recommends that women, 50 years and older, and men, 19 years and older,

consume 800 milligrams (mg) of calcium a day. For women 19 to 49 years of age, it recommends 700 mg daily.

Calcium may also help control blood pressure. In 1997 a major study showed that adults with mild hypertension who ate 3 servings of low-fat dairy foods a day (plus 8 to 10 servings of fruits and vegetables) had significantly lower blood pressure. Another study found that middle-aged men who never drank milk doubled their risk of stroke compared with men who downed 475 milliliters (16 ounces) a day.

How much dairy food do you need?

Health Canada recommends that adult Canadians consume 2 to 4 servings of dairy products daily. One serving might be 235 milliliters (8 ounces) of milk, 175 milliliters (6 ounces) of yogurt, or 43 grams (1½ ounces) of cheese. Whenever possible, choose low-fat

CAUTION!
Dairy foods can aggravate ulcers by stimulating the production of irritating stomach acid. Aged cheeses can trigger migraines and interact adversely with certain medications. Cheeses made with molds may trigger penicillin allergies.

Lactose Intolerant? Don't Have a Cow

Milk doesn't agree with everyone, but some experts believe that the case for lactose intolerance—difficulty digesting milk sugar (lactose) because of diminished levels of the stomach enzyme lactase—has been overblown. Symptoms include flatulence, cramps, and diarrhea. If you think you are lactose intolerant, try these tips to relieve the problem:

- First try eating high-lactose foods (milk, sour cream, fresh cheeses, and ice cream) in small amounts as part of meals. Also try spreading dairy-food servings several hours apart.

- Eat more dairy foods that are low in lactose, such as lactose-reduced milk, aged cheeses, and yogurts made with active live cultures.

- If problems persist, consult your physician. A simple test can verify whether you are lactose intolerant or whether your symptoms stem from other causes. You may be placed on a regimen of lactase supplements.

You don't have to eliminate milk and milk products when you have a cold or the flu. Dairy foods don't promote mucous buildup, as many people once thought.

products. Apart from calcium, dairy foods contain other important nutrients. Milk, for example, is fortified with vitamins A and D and is a good source of riboflavin, phosphorus, and magnesium as well as high-quality protein. Just 235 milliliters (8 ounces) of whole milk provides almost 20 percent of the body's daily protein and calcium needs.

Losing some of the fat

Using low-fat products is one way to cut your intake of fat without losing the healthful nutrients of dairy foods. Milk is a good example. Its fat content ranges from a minimum 3.25 percent in whole milk to 0.5 percent in skim milk. Accordingly, a single serving of whole milk contains 8.2 grams of fat. That's already more than 10 percent of most people's daily fat allowance. Compare that with other forms of milk: low-fat (2%) at 4.7 grams of fat per serving; low-fat (1 %) at 2.6 grams of fat; and buttermilk at 2.2 grams of fat, whereas skim milk provides virtually no fat. Condensed milk contains almost three times as much calcium as whole milk, but also more than three times the fat.

Cutting fat cuts calories as well: 235 milliliters (8 ounces) of whole milk has 150 calories; the same quantity of skim has only 86. The exception is low-fat yogurts that are high in sugary fruit flavorings.

Many people want to cut down on fatty dairy foods but can't get used to the taste of low-fat products. A gradual transition from high-fat to lower-fat usually does the trick. For instance, work your way from whole milk to 2 percent to 1 percent to skim. You can still occasionally indulge in high-fat dairy foods: just stick to small portions.

When milk makes you sick

All milk sold in Canada must be pasteurized. Sale of some raw milk cheeses is permitted but Health Canada urges pregnant women and anyone with weakened immune systems to avoid them. On farm visits, do not drink raw, unpasteurized milk.

Pasteurized milk may contain very small amounts of antibiotics and other drugs. In most milk, the levels are undetectable or so low that they are not deemed harmful. Health Canada specifies the time period for a drug to clear from an animal before its milk can be sold, and provincial agencies monitor these residues. But even pasteurized milk will spoil unless it is refrigerated properly; the perfect temperature is just above freezing. Cardboard containers are ideal as they block out light, which can cause vitamin A and riboflavin to break down.

Be careful when giving milk to children. Do not give cow's milk to infants under one year of age—it is too high in protein and sodium. Most bottle-fed babies don't need anything but infant formula for the first six months of life. Low-fat milk is not suitable for children under two years of age. What's more, some young children may be allergic to the protein in cow's milk. Even formula-fed infants may have allergic reactions since many commercial formulas are modified cow's milk. If chronic diarrhea, vomiting, and colic appear, see your doctor for diagnosis and suggestions for milk alternatives.

Cheese, please?

Although cheese is nutritious, it is very high in saturated fat. Just 28 grams (1 ounce) of Cheddar has 200 mg of calcium but 9 grams of fat. Even reduced-fat cheeses contain about 5 grams of fat per ounce and may be high in sodium. Those with heart disease, high cholesterol levels, or high blood pressure should avoid cheese altogether, or stick to skim-milk cottage, nonfat ricotta, or farmer cheese.

Ice-cream makers usually use 113 grams or 4 ounces (½ cup) as a standard serving size. Some, however, reduce the serving size to 85 grams (3 ounces) so they can lower fat and calories.

Eating Cheddar and other aged cheeses after a meal may offer a measure of protection from tooth decay.

Dental Procedures

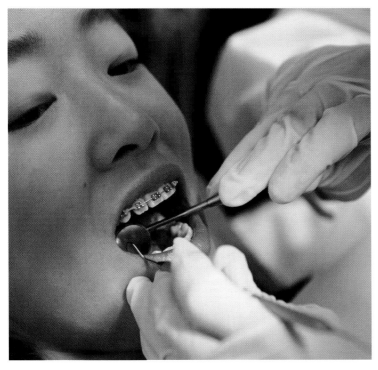

For people with braces, thorough dental cleaning between visits is crucial, since the appliances can trap food and plaque. Use a floss threader to help you floss around the wires.

Whether it's for a cleaning, a filling, or a more complex procedure, you probably find yourself—or should find yourself—in a dentist's chair at least once a year. By becoming aware of the many facets of both familiar and more advanced procedures, you may be able to improve the results.

Saving teeth from decay

Left alone, a decayed tooth can become infected, causing pain and eventually the loss of the tooth. Modern dentistry can prevent this from happening with:

- **Dental amalgams.** For moderately decayed teeth, dentists drill the cavity and fill it with a strong material—usually a dental amalgam made of silver, tin, copper, and mercury. In the past decade, concerns have been raised over the mercury in amalgams. When fillings break down, as they all eventually do, small particles of mercury enter the bloodstream, and some people feared that this

Studies indicate no link between medical disorders, such as Alzheimer's disease, and fillings that contain mercury.

might increase the risk of arthritis, multiple sclerosis, and Alzheimer's disease. But studies have found no link between medical disorders and amalgam fillings that contain mercury. It appears that the amount of mercury released by the amalgam is so minute that it doesn't do any damage. For most Canadians, dental amalgam is the single largest source of mercury exposure. Health Canada says that amalgam is safe for all but a small number of people who are specifically sensitive or allergic to mercury and who may suffer severe health problems even from low exposure.

- **Crowns.** Also called caps, these fit over a badly decayed or damaged tooth. Most are made of porcelain fused to metal, but some people opt for stronger gold for back teeth. The positioning of a crown may leave a small space between it and the remaining part of the tooth, providing a place for plaque to collect. Be sure to brush thoroughly—but gently—around the gum line of a cap and to floss daily. Ask your dentist if you should do anything extra, such as using an antiplaque mouthwash, an electric toothbrush, or a dental-irrigation system (a Water Pik, for example).

- **Sealants.** These plastic films, which bond to the chewing surfaces of teeth and act as a barrier to bacteria, prevent decay. They have been used primarily among children, but many adults could also benefit from sealants. However, the resin does not adhere to metal fillings.

Lose a tooth, gain a bridge

If you lose a tooth, your dentist will replace it, because leaving gaps in your mouth can cause the teeth to shift and crowd one another, increasing the possibility of cavities and gum disease. Teeth that have greatly shifted may also change your bite; this can affect the jaw joints and muscles and may lead to pain and difficulty chewing. Without a full set of teeth, your cheek and other facial muscles may sag. Here are the options for replacing teeth:

- **A fixed bridge.** This consists of one or more artificial teeth attached to crowns or other devices placed on adjacent teeth. When you have a fixed bridge, it's very important to floss regularly around the supporting teeth to keep them healthy enough to retain the bridge. Try a floss threader for reaching between the bottom of the bridge and your gums, and ask your dentist about special brushes that can fit between the replacement tooth and the supporting teeth.

- **A removable bridge.** If any adjacent teeth are missing or unable to serve as a support, your dentist may use a removable bridge, or partial denture. This rests on the gum and attaches to one or more teeth with clasps. Since the pressure of these clasps can loosen supporting teeth, the appliance should be checked periodically. Also, be sure to take it out and brush it daily.

- **Full dentures.** These are plastic devices with a set of false teeth for one or both jaws and secured by the suction between them and the gums. "Immediate" dentures are inserted as soon as teeth have been removed. They help reduce swelling and control bleeding, and they allow for normal functioning while the tissues heal. Once the tissues have healed and shrunk, "conventional" dentures are made and fitted. Expect any new dentures to cause a little soreness at first. Consult your dentist if the irritation persists, especially if your dentures are unstable, because a poor fit can lead to bone loss. Unless advised otherwise, apply an adhesive only as a temporary measure.

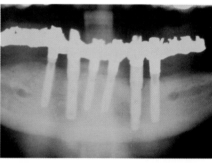

An X ray shows dental implants, consisting of titanium anchors, in the jawbone. The upper posts will support the artificial teeth.

- **Dental implants.** These titanium anchors, which are inserted into the jawbone, are expensive, but they are taking the place of traditional bridges and dentures for many people. Several months after your dentist inserts them—this allows time for bone to grow around the anchors—posts are screwed into the anchors to hold the artificial teeth. When the procedure is successful, the bone attaches to the anchors, allowing gum tissue to form a seal around the posts. The teeth, now permanently secured, function as though they were natural. Studies show that implants are successful for the vast majority of people. However, for some, new bone may fail to grow around the implant base, causing tooth instability and increasing the risk of infection. There is also a very slight chance of serious complications, including nerve damage to the face and mouth, from the surgery. A person undertaking this operation needs healthy gums and adequate bone in the jaw to anchor the implants securely. People with a disorder that may slow healing or increase the chances of infection are not good candidates. If you are thinking of getting implants, know that this decision requires careful diagnosis and treatment planning. Discuss the matter with your dentist.

Amazing braces

Among the most popular of the newer dental procedures are those that alter the surface of the teeth to make them more cosmetically appealing. New braces straighten teeth unobtrusively, and new techniques restore the appearance of chipped, cracked, or discolored teeth:

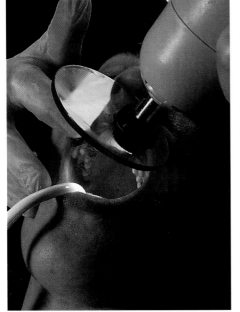

High-intensity light hardens the materials used in bonding, a procedure that evens out chipped or otherwise damaged teeth.

• **Bleaching.** Various substances can be used to whiten teeth. Your dentist may perform this procedure in one to three visits. (You'll also need your dentist's guidance if you want to use a cheaper do-it-yourself home kit.) The process may temporarily irritate gums, mouth, and sensitive teeth. If your teeth are already sensitive to hot and cold, bleaching may not be right for you. Some dentists are experimenting with a new laser process that is speedier, but its safety has not yet been fully evaluated.

• **Tooth bonding.** This not only whitens stained teeth but also fixes chipped and cracked ones. In composite bonding, plastic resin is used to restore the shape of the tooth. This dental procedure can last five years or more before needing to be repaired. In veneer bonding, the tooth's surface is completely covered with a thin, shell-like veneer of plastic or porcelain. Veneers can last a very long time, but they're affected by bite pressure and such habits as grinding the teeth. Compared to crowns, the conventional method for repairing chipped and cracked teeth, bonding is faster, easier, and less expensive. Although some of the enamel of the natural tooth is lost with veneers (and occasionally with composite bonding), the tooth is not reduced in size as significantly as with a crown. But there are some drawbacks. Bonded teeth can be damaged by biting into hard foods, and they're susceptible to staining from berries, coffee, tea, and wine.

• **Braces.** These bands or brackets aren't just for kids anymore. Although the ideal age to get braces is between 10 and 14 years, adults can also benefit from orthodontics. Misaligned teeth not only affect appearance but may pull away from the gum and be difficult to clean, increasing the risk of decay and gum disease. Many types of braces today are scarcely noticeable (the lingual type—attached to the backs of teeth—is completely hidden). Full braces are usually worn for 18 to 30 months, followed by a retainer for a few months. During this period, it's essential to stay away from sugary foods and to maintain good oral hygiene. Periodically, your orthodontist will tighten the braces' wires, which may cause discomfort for a day or two.

On the Horizon What if you could have a cavity filled without needing anesthesia? That's just one of the promises of two high-tech dental systems for treating decay. In one, a laser replaces the drill and allows for more precision, so the dentist can avoid harming healthy parts of teeth. In the other, air abrasion uses a silent blast of air to wear down the decayed area. These systems are on the market but not yet in general use.

Dental Products

Once upon a time, all you needed was a toothbrush and a tube of toothpaste. That was before drugstores stocked their shelves with new products to whiten teeth, prevent tartar, and treat gum disease. Yet while some of these dental products work well, others don't, and a few may even be dangerous.

The perils of home bleaching

For whitening and brightening teeth, bleaching kits are available. Most contain the active ingredient carbamide peroxide, and virtually all are versions of products long used by dentists for this purpose—but at a fraction of the price to the consumer. Unfortunately, without professional guidance, many of these kits can prove harmful, damaging tooth enamel, gums, and other areas of the mouth. Furthermore, evidence suggests that when used incorrectly, some of the products may cause cellular changes that make it easier for cancer-causing agents to attack tissue.

If, despite these risks, you're interested in finding a teeth-whitening agent to apply at home, use the product only after consulting your dentist. Also, be aware that not all teeth respond to this process. The process works best on yellowish teeth, less well on those with a brownish cast, and least well on grayish teeth.

Beyond cleaning

Can toothpaste do more than clean your teeth? These days, it often has a therapeutic as well as a cleansing effect. Always choose a

Any kind of toothpaste will fulfill its original purpose: to act as an abrasive on tooth surfaces.

toothpaste that contains fluoride, which fights decay. Now you can find one that has not only fluoride but also antibacterial triclosan. Together, these ingredients help prevent the development of plaque and tartar and, therefore, both tooth decay and gum disease. If you're prone to canker sores, look for a fluoride toothpaste that does *not* contain sodium lauryl sulfate (SLS), which can increase your risk of developing the painful ulcers.

Many people prefer baking-soda toothpastes. Baking soda has not been proven to fight gum disease or clean teeth in any special way, but if you like it as a flavoring, it may help you to brush longer.

Desensitizing toothpastes, with the active ingredients strontium chloride and potassium nitrate, reduce the nerves' ability to transmit pain and so are helpful to those whose teeth are sensitive to hot and cold. Be aware, however, that it takes four to six weeks of regular use to notice a difference.

"Whitening toothpastes" that contain hydrogen peroxide are similar to home bleaching products and are best avoided.

The best brush

Short-term studies indicate that powered toothbrushes can be more effective than manual ones, but the evidence is not conclusive. Some dentists recommend electric or electronic (sonic) brushes for patients who have trouble removing plaque.

If you take the time to clean your teeth carefully and you rarely have dental problems, a manual brush (soft bristles are best) should be sufficient. Be careful not to brush too hard, since this may cause gum inflammation.

If a physical disability prevents you from holding the toothbrush long enough or from moving it around effectively, you may want to buy a powered toothbrush. A possible alternative is to attach the manual brush to your hand with an elastic band or to extend the

Children should floss, but watch to make sure they're not hurting their gums.

Tooth tools: A gum stimulator can massage gums and also clean between teeth, complementing the toothbrush.

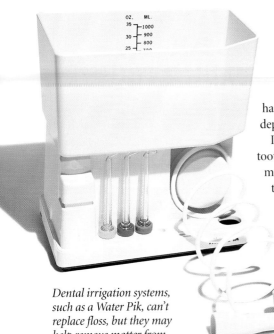

Dental irrigation systems, such as a Water Pik, can't replace floss, but they may help remove matter from around crowns, bridges, and braces.

handle with a taped-on tongue depressor.

It's best to replace manual toothbrushes every three months. Consider buying a toothbrush with indicator bristles whose color fades, usually after two or three months, alerting you that it's time to replace your worn toothbrush.

Weapons in the war on plaque

Studies show that dental floss is still the best way to remove plaque, and nothing is better for getting between teeth and under the gum line, where most dental problems start. While all types of floss are effective, some have particular advantages. Tripart floss has three kinds of filaments in each strand to help remove debris from around bridges and other devices. Shredproof floss may move more easily between your teeth.

Other "interdental" cleaners include toothpicks and stimulators, such as the rubber tips on some toothbrushes. Use a toothpick only in a pinch, when you have to remove food. Stimulators can be helpful for cleaning the gum area around crowns; so can dental-irrigation systems.

At least one electric interdental plaque remover is now on the market. Studies indicate that this powered type works well, but no more so than floss does when it's used correctly.

Antiplaque mouthwashes have been shown to be only about 25 percent effective in studies. However, those that contain fluoride may help fight cavities. Be careful when choosing mouthwashes if you have a sensitivity to alcohol; many contain varying amounts of it. (Choose, instead, rinses without alcohol, now also on the market.) Although research has linked long-term use of rinses that contain alcohol with an increased risk of oral cancer, current evidence indicates these rinses are safe when used according to the instructions. Be sure to pay attention to warning labels about swallowing mouthwash, and keep the bottles away from children. Choose rinses (as well as any other dental products) that carry the Canadian Dental Association seal, which means that their safety and effectiveness have been evaluated.

How to Keep Your Friends: Solutions for Bad Breath

Halitosis, or bad breath, may indicate a medical disorder, such as an oral infection or a kidney ailment. Anyone with a chronic problem should consult a dentist or a physician. If, however, you simply have occasional less-than-fresh breath, here are some possible remedies or quick fixes:

- **Mouthwashes.** Oral rinses may improve breath for up to a half hour.

- **Breath mints and gum.** These have short-term effects similar to those of mouthwashes.

- **Foods.** Fresh parsley, mint, or coriander or anise seeds can sweeten breath after a meal. If you have an important, up-close meeting, skip the garlic and onions.

- **Tongue cleaners.** These devices scrape bacteria off the tongue, thus eliminating sources of odor. You can also clean your tongue with your toothbrush or an inverted spoon, which should be thoroughly cleaned and rinsed in very hot water after each use.

Deodorants & Antiperspirants

Perspiration and other bodily secretions are a natural part of life, and so are the odors they produce. But what's natural isn't necessarily pleasant.

When sweat is first released from the eccrine and apocrine glands, located in the armpits and other parts of the human body, it has no odor. However, it does contain chemicals that provide a feast for bacteria, which flourish in warm, wet places. In the process, pungent by-products are created.

The primary step in controlling body odor is to wash the affected areas daily with lukewarm water and mild soap. But most North Americans want to do more than this. So they spend millions on deodorants and antiperspirants, products designed to cover up, change, or prevent body odor. Most are safe, but some cause reactions in certain people, and a few are best avoided by everyone.

Sweet smells and blocked ducts

Deodorants and antiperspirants work in different ways. Deodorants attempt to eliminate the odor; antiperspirants, the perspiration itself. Both types are generally safe.

Deodorants either mask or neutralize smells. Some have scents that mingle with underarm odor to produce a more pleasing aroma. Others incorporate a sodium bicarbonate base to neutralize odor-causing acids created by bacteria. Still others fight the root cause itself with antibacterial ingredients; herbal preparations use natural antibiotics, such as coriander seeds, to do this.

Antiperspirants are classified by Health Canada as over-the-counter drugs because they contain chemicals that interrupt a biological process—namely, penetrating and blocking the sweat-gland ducts to prevent perspiration from reaching the skin's surface. Because of this, never apply one before exercising, when you need to sweat to cool the body.

In addition to roll-ons and sticks, there are "deodorant" crystals or stones, found in health-food stores, which leave residues of potassium salts that actually work as antiperspirants rather than deodorants.

Roll it, don't spray it

Some people are allergic to ingredients in deodorants or antiperspirants. If a product causes a rash, switch brands or types—a person sensitive to deodorants may be able to tolerate antiperspirants, and vice versa. If that doesn't work, consider such alternatives as a medicated powder or baking soda, used either alone or combined with cornstarch or white clay. Be aware that shaving makes the skin more sensitive, so applying a product soon after shaving may cause a reaction.

The principal ingredient of most antiperspirants is aluminum chlorhydrate. Although it has been suspected, along with other aluminum sources, of promoting Alzheimer's disease, scientists have not found evidence to support this link, and many now question it. However, if you're concerned about this, avoid products that contain aluminum, especially aerosol sprays, which emit fine particles that can be inhaled.

Indeed, since chemicals used in deodorants and antiperspirants are not meant to be inhaled into the lungs, never use aerosols.

Don't use an underarm product before having a mammogram. It can cause confusing spots on the image.

Diets & Dict Aids

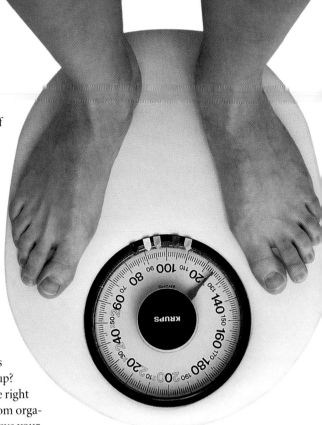

Losing weight is easy. Millions of North Americans do it every day. What's tough is keeping it off. Restrictive diets may work in the short term. So may some diet aids. But soon the weight returns.

There is only one proven way to lose weight and keep it off: make basic, simple changes in what you eat, how much you eat, and how much you exercise. These changes should become part of your everyday life, so think ahead: Could you take a walk and eat an apple daily for the next year? Yes? Now, what about downing diet pills and eating nothing but cabbage soup?

Some people can lose weight the right way on their own; others benefit from organized programs. However you achieve your goals, you'll want to learn the principles of sustainable weight loss and skip programs and products that don't work or are unsafe.

A dreaded sight? Stepping on the scale too often can hinder dieting efforts by provoking anxiety.

Are you really overweight?
Your body-mass index (BMI) indicates the approximate amount of body fat you have, a more accurate gauge of health risk than the bathroom scale. To find your BMI, divide your weight in kilograms by your height in meters squared.

If your BMI falls between 20 and 25, you're at a healthy weight. If it's above 25, you're overweight and should strive at least not to gain any more. A BMI over 27 qualifies you at an increased risk to develop health problems such as diabetes, stroke, and heart attack. If your weight is concentrated in your middle (belly fat) or you have at least two health risk factors, such as high blood pressure or high cholesterol, you ought to lose weight.

How to lose weight and keep it off
If you consume more calories than you burn, your body stores the excess as fat, causing you to gain weight. If you take in only as much as you use, your weight stays the same. But to lose body fat and weight, you'll need to burn more calories than you consume.

If you want to slim down, a reasonable goal is to reduce your weight by 10 percent over six months. Most healthy individuals should aim to lose up to about 500 grams ($\frac{1}{2}$ to 1 pound) a week. To lose weight at this rate, you'll have to burn about 200 to 300 more calories each day than you take in. The best way to do that is to limit calorie intake while increasing exercise.

It's easy to overconsume calories. While fruits and vegetables, which contain plenty of water and fiber, are naturally filling and low in calories, many processed foods, fast foods, and desserts cram loads of calories into small packages. Fat is particularly calorie-dense, and portion sizes in restaurants are often huge. By choosing more lower-calorie,

If you want to slim down, a reasonable goal is to reduce your weight by 10 percent over six months. That's about ½ to 1 pound a week.

Diet Programs: What to Look For

If dieting on your own proves too difficult, you may want to join the millions of North Americans who sign up for weight-loss programs each year. The best ones offer:

- **Proof of effectiveness.** You can review long-term data on all clients who joined the program—not just the success stories.

- **Qualifications.** The program is run by a professional educated in nutrition and weight loss, with the help of a registered dietitian and experts in behavior modification and exercise physiology.

- **Emphasis on slow weight loss.** The program's central aim is to change long-term eating habits.

- **Nutritional balance.** The list of allowed foods is drawn from the basic food groups. Instruction for preparing healthful meals is part of the program.

- **Easy access to foods.** All foods in the plan can be purchased at the supermarket.

- **Exercise instruction.** Basic information about healthy, safe exercises is discussed.

- **Behavior modification.** The program provides written materials or, better yet, counseling on how to change your eating habits.

- **Follow-up programs.** Ongoing support after your goal weight is reached is available for a reasonable fee.

high-fiber foods and limiting portion sizes, you can cut out several hundred calories from your daily diet. But do leave room for your favorite foods—even chocolate—as long as you enjoy them in small amounts.

Equally crucial is the role that exercise plays, not only in losing weight but in keeping it off. Start with 30 minutes of walking three times a week, work up to 45 minutes five days a week, and you'll burn an additional 100 to 200 calories daily.

Once you've lost that first 10 percent of your weight, strive to maintain your weight for several months before contemplating further weight loss. Here is where exercise really helps—it's been proven effective in preventing weight regain. One reason is that it revs up your metabolism, so you burn body fat more efficiently. By developing muscle, which burns more calories than body fat does, you'll also increase the number of calories you burn, even at rest. Of course, regular exercise offers other health benefits, too.

How many calories do you need?
How many calories do you need each day? To maintain your current weight, you need enough to sustain such basic bodily functions as heart rate, breathing, and metabolism at rest, plus the calories needed for activity.

Although each of us is different, the energy intake of at least 1,800 calories per day has been recommended by Health Canada and the National Institute of Nutrition for weight maintenance. That caloric intake is the basic daily energy requirement of a 50-year-old woman who weighs *(Continued)*

CAUTION!

Don't cut calorie consumption to below 1,200 per day without medical supervision; doing so impairs reaction time (which makes driving dangerous) for weeks after dieting and can lead to bingeing. Also, avoid high-protein no-carbohydrate diets, which produce nausea, bad breath, constipation, even gout.

Measure for measure: Good diet programs calculate progress not only by pounds lost but also by inches lost.

Diets & Diet Aids (continued)

62 kilograms (135 pounds). However, a moderately active 35-year-old man who weighs 72 kilograms (160 pounds) needs to consume more to maintain his weight—about 2,700 calories per day. For healthy weight loss, he can cut calories and add exercise, which will boost daily caloric needs. When he does lose weight, his caloric needs for basic bodily functions will actually fall but exercise will allow him to eat more without regaining.

For a healthy day's diet, here's a trim formula: Fill up on veggies like these, then add two pieces of fruit, six servings of breads or grains, two to three servings of lean meat, poultry, fish, or beans, and two servings of low-fat dairy foods.

Fad diets are bad diets

We've heard it a thousand times—fad diets are bad for you. The fact is, they don't even work; they rarely, if ever, yield a weight loss that lasts for long. What's worse, they can wreck your health.

The most common error is simply cutting calories too drastically. Diets that provide fewer calories than needed for basic bodily functions not only make you feel bad, and are usually inadequate nutritionally, but can backfire. They slow down your metabolism, so your body has a hard time burning fat. Diets that are too low in calories also train your body to ignore natural hunger signals. Consequently, when you go off your diet, you are likely to get your mealtime cues from external sources—food ads and emotional highs or lows—which will put you back on the fast track to poor eating habits and weight regain. Here are some warning signs of unhealthy, ineffective fad diets:

- Sales promotions that use such words as *effortless, easy, guaranteed, breakthrough,* and *natural* or make promises to *burn, block,* or *destroy* fat.
- Unsubstantiated testimonials or before-and-after photos. If the diet really worked, its claims would be backed up by scientific studies published in medical journals.
- A focus on consuming large quantities of a single food or food group (such as grapefruit, cabbage soup, protein foods, carbohydrates, and so on).
- A strict menu limited to just a few choices.
- Requirements for combining or separating foods (such as an all-protein meal followed by an all-carbohydrate meal).
- Products that claim to have "secret," "all-natural," or "fat-fighting" components.
- Claims that you can lose weight without having to exercise.

A place for meal replacements

Steady sellers in the weight-loss industry are meal-replacement drinks. They come in liquid form or in powders that you mix with milk, water, or fruit juice. Their low-fat protein sources (such as soy) combined with high-fiber ingredients, vitamins, and minerals give you a balanced meal with a controlled number of calories. The drinks may help you control caloric intake, but experts advise that they be used for no more than one meal a day.

When buying these products, check the label for the following :

- Nutritious protein sources like grains, legumes, whey, or hydrolyzed protein.
- No casein (milk protein). It can be hard to digest and may cause an allergic reaction.
- A minimum of 5 grams of fiber, both soluble and insoluble. A good mix might be oat bran with wheat bran.
- Adequate vitamins, minerals, and essential fatty acids (EFAs).
- A low-fat formula with little added sugar and no artificial flavors or food additives.

Oh, for a pill that melts away fat...

In 1997, two obesity drugs, fenfluramine and dexfenfluramine, promised to revolutionize weight loss when either was prescribed with another drug, phentermine. Instead, the combination, known as Fen-Phen, ended up terrifying thousands of users when their potential for causing serious, even life-threatening, heart defects was revealed. Approximately 30 percent of users were shown to have abnormal echocardiograms. In response, the products were removed from the market in 1997 in both Canada and the United States.

According to many experts, few diet aids are worth the money, and some are positively dangerous. Most health experts discourage the use of weight loss products, emphasizing instead the need for lasting lifestyle changes. Here's the rundown on some diet aids:

- **Chromium picolinate.** Chromium has recently been touted as a muscle builder and weight-loss aid, but there is little scientific evidence for the claims. In fact, large doses may cause cell damage. Health Canada has not approved it for sale.
- **L-carnitine.** This amino acid is thought by some to increase the rate at which stored fat burns. It also has not been approved for sale in Canada.
- **Herbal teas, diuretics, and laxatives.** Laxatives are purported to promote weight loss by "cleaning out" the bowels. But since they work on the large intestine, and caloric absorption takes place in the small intestine, they serve no weight-loss purpose. Diuretics merely cause you to lose water weight. Both can result in serious health problems. Never use any diet aid that makes you visit the bathroom frequently.
- **Pectin, psyllium, and high-fiber pills.** When taken with large amounts of water, these products swell in your stomach and make you feel full. But eating more beans, oats, fruits, and vegetables is just as effective, cheaper, and more nutritious.
- **Appetite-suppressant drugs.** These products are said to inhibit appetite and boost the metabolic rate. Instead, they can cause a dangerous rise in blood pressure, along with nutrient deprivation, dehydration, and a high-risk dependency as ever-stronger doses are needed to achieve the same effect.

- **Hydroxycitric acid (HCA).** This derivative of the brindall berry diminished appetite in animal tests, but it has not yet been tested thoroughly in humans and could cause dangerous side effects.
- **Herbal "fen-phen."** This combination of St. Johnswort and ma huang (Chinese ephedra) has yet to be fully tested, but in the United States, the Food and Drug Administration (FDA) warns of possible cardiovascular side effects. The Canadian government has not authorized herbal "fen-phen" for sale as a diet aid. Also, in the controversial case of ephedra, Health Canada warned consumers in 1997 not to purchase or ingest products containing ephedrine (the most active of the herb's alkaloids) unless the label carries an eight-digit Drug Identification Number (DIN).

Meal-replacement drinks (left) are sold across North America. They shouldn't be confused with dubious diet aids. Balanced drinks can safely replace one meal a day.

Is Fasting Faster?

Not really. In truth, it doesn't even work. Your body can tolerate going without food for two to three days, but much of the weight you lose is water and will be replaced once you start eating again. Fasting may even be counterproductive because it can bring on nausea, weakness, and depression, all of which can sap motivation and lead to overeating.

- Fasting can be dangerous to your health. During a fast, some muscle is always lost. This can trigger gout and, in some people, may cause potentially fatal heart rhythm disturbances.
- Fasting does not detoxify the body. The liver and kidneys detoxify the body, and they function whether you are fasting or not.

- If you are fasting as a spiritual observance, it's advisable to follow a few guidelines. First, never fast for more than 24 hours. During that time, drink lots of liquids to flush away uric acid formed by muscle breakdown. Also, consult your doctor; fasting can alter the effect of any medications you are taking.

Diuretics

If you've ever heard the term *water pill*, then you already know about diuretics, drugs that eliminate excess water from the body. They work by encouraging the kidneys to excrete greater amounts of salt and urine. This means less water in the bloodstream, which in turn helps lower blood pressure and reduces the heart's workload. That's why diuretics are an excellent treatment for hypertension, congestive heart failure, and pulmonary edema (excess fluid in the lungs).

Are diuretics safe?

When taken as directed by a doctor, diuretics are one of the safest medications now available. A U.S. national committee studying high blood pressure indicated diuretics are one of the first-line drug defenses in the treatment of this condition. Many studies show that diuretics, taken alone or in combination with other medications, are effective in preventing stroke and other cardiovascular events.

This doesn't mean that diuretics are problem-free. Because certain diuretics can cause the body to lose potassium as well as salt, they

Such herbs as parsley and uva ursi (often made into teas), foods like asparagus, and herbal "water pills" have some diuretic effect, but not as much as prescription diuretics do.

may cause fatigue and muscle weakness. Doctors often suggest that people taking such drugs increase their intake of potassium-rich foods, including bananas, orange juice, and prunes. Some diuretics, however, cause the body to retain potassium, so speak to your doctor before adding anything to your diet.

Certain types of diuretics can cause still other problems. Some can affect hearing and balance, and they may cause dizziness or lightheadedness, particularly upon rising. Others may affect sexual function. Changing the dosage or the type of diuretic can help.

If you are taking diuretics, don't stop taking them suddenly. Indeed, never take yourself off a prescribed diuretic without first checking with your doctor. Abrupt withdrawal, particularly among the elderly, may cause serious problems, including a dramatic increase in blood pressure and increased risk of heart failure. Diuretics are best decreased over a period of four weeks or more.

Do they speed weight loss or ease PMS?

Diuretics should never be used as a diet aid. Although they can temporarily remove excess water, making you look slimmer for a few hours, they have no effect on fat. And, when used inappropriately, they can lead to a life-threatening form of dehydration.

On the other hand, diuretics may be useful for reducing menstrual water retention, which can help to relieve symptoms of premenstrual syndrome, particularly breast pain. A herbal diuretic may also provide relief. In tea or pill form, these herbal preparations include burdock, buchu, cleavers, and horsetail. Be aware that these unregulated preparations vary in potency and effect.

Some foods, such as asparagus, and beverages containing caffeine, such as coffee and black tea, may have some diuretic effect. If you are already taking a prescription diuretic, do not add these foods or herbs to your diet without your doctor's okay.

Is douching necessary? According to Health Canada, there is no evidence that healthy women need to use douches, except perhaps on medical grounds. Yet the companies that make douches promote the idea that douching is an essential part of a woman's hygiene routine—and many women seem to agree.

Douching involves "cleaning" the vagina by rinsing it with water or a mixture of water and other substances. Doctors maintain that douching is unnecessary, because the vagina naturally cleans itself. Furthermore, some research shows that douching offers no health benefits and may be harmful. Still, Health Canada says it is unaware of any concerns about douches that are significant enough to change its policy about their present availability on the market.

Drawbacks of douching

Most store-bought douches contain water, along with vinegar, baking soda, or a fragrance. A few include a mild medicinal ingredient, such as iodine, intended to relieve minor vaginal infections or irritations.

Although the fragrances and chemicals in some douches can cause irritation, the main problem with douching is the procedure itself. Douching—even with plain water—alters the normal acidic environment of the vagina that checks the growth of harmful bacteria. Changing this environment encourages the development of unwanted microorganisms, including those that cause vaginitis (a general term for vaginal inflammation) and yeast infections. What's more, douching can push harmful bacteria deeper into the reproductive tract, increasing the risk of pelvic inflammatory disease (PID), an infection that can cause infertility. PID can also raise the risk of ectopic pregnancy by damaging the Fallopian tubes.

Douching after sexual intercourse can drive sperm toward the uterus, increasing the likelihood of pregnancy and also infection.

The practice of douching after sexual intercourse also presents problems. Douching can drive semen—and any bacteria it may carry, including those responsible for sexually transmitted diseases—toward the uterus, increasing the likelihood of both pregnancy and infection. In addition, postcoital douching can prematurely wash away any spermicides that were used. One study has even suggested that douching may reduce a woman's fertility overall.

Women should know that some vaginal discharge is normal and that any mild odors can usually be eliminated by washing externally with soap and water. If you experience any unusual odor, discharge, or itching, see your doctor right away.

an ounce of **Prevention**

Douching Dos and Don'ts

Doctors agree that there's no need to douche. If you feel otherwise, follow these precautions.

- Do not douche more than once a month.

- Medicated douches should not be used more than once; if your symptoms persist, see a doctor.

- Avoid douching for six to eight hours after sexual intercourse.

- Never use douches as a form of contraception—they don't work.

- Never douche during pregnancy; doing so can cause a miscarriage.

- Refrain from douching for several days prior to a gynecological appointment; it can affect the accuracy of Pap and other tests.

- If you make a vinegar-and-water douche, use only white vinegar.

- Unless you are using a disposable douche, make sure to clean the nozzle and bag thoroughly before and after each use.

Drain Cleaners

You're taking a shower, and before you know it, you're standing in ankle-deep water. The problem? The drain is clogged from soap residue, hair, and countless other things that build up in pipes. What to do? Before you reach for a chemical drain cleaner, read on. There are less toxic solutions—and ways to prevent clogs in the first place.

Caustic chemical cleaners

Most drain cleaners on the supermarket shelf are likely to contain a corrosive chemical, such as lye or sulfuric acid, which literally burns through the clog. Even though these cleaners are somewhat reliable, they are among the most dangerous of all household products and should be handled with extreme care. Use rubber gloves and goggles, wear long sleeves, and make sure the room is well ventilated.

If the liquid comes into contact with your skin or eyes, flush the affected area with water for at least 15 minutes. Note that using a chemical cleaner when a drain is completely stopped up can be risky; if it doesn't work, the chemical will remain in the standing water and may damage your pipes.

Keep young children away from chemical drain cleaners; even better, store the products in a locked cabinet. Ingesting a cleaner can cause severe internal

When water has backed up in a tub or sink, using a liquid drain cleaner may be no more effective than an old-fashioned plunger.

burns. Symptoms include sharp pain in the mouth, throat, and abdomen; restricted breathing because of a swollen throat; and diarrhea. If you suspect accidental poisoning, give the person milk or water, then call a poison control center immediately. Don't induce vomiting: caustic chemicals can do harm coming up as well as going down.

Safer clog busters

Avoid the dangers of chemical cleaners by using one of these safer methods:

- **Plunger.** Plunging the drain helps work the clog back and forth until it breaks free. Don't use a plunger after using a chemical cleaner; splashes may cause burns.
- **Homemade mixture.** Mix one cup baking soda and one cup white vinegar. (Add salt for extra abrasive power.) Pour the fizzing mixture down the drain, cover the drain, and wait 15 minutes. Flush thoroughly with 2 liters boiling water.
- **Plumber's snake.** Rent or purchase one of these flexible metal cables, which can usually cut through any clog.
- **Enzyme-based cleaners.** These products contain harmless bacteria that eat through soap, grease, hair, and other organic matter. (They won't work in standing water; use only if there is some drainage.) Enzyme cleaners may require several applications.
- **Less caustic chemicals.** Flush the drain with one quarter cup 3 percent hydrogen peroxide. Keep it away from your eyes.

an ounce of Prevention

Keeping Clogs at Bay

If your drains are prone to clogs, try these preventive measures:

- Flush your drains once a week with the mixture of baking soda and white vinegar mentioned above. A pot of boiling water or an enzyme-based cleaner may also work. Do not use chemical cleaners to prevent clogs. Used often, they may harm your pipes.
- Don't pour leftover cooking grease down the drain—collect it in cans.
- Use strainers in all of your drains to catch hair and food.

Dry Cleaning

Taking clothes to the dry cleaner has its advantages: your suits, woolens, and fragile silks usually come back clean and pressed, without having faded or shrunk. On the downside, however, the dry-cleaning process uses toxic chemicals that can pose a health risk not only for customers and employees but even for people who live above or adjacent to dry-cleaning shops.

The dirt on dry cleaning

The process isn't really "dry," except in the sense that very little water is used. Clothes are submerged in a liquid chemical solution that dissolves stains without being absorbed into the fabric. Common dry-cleaning chemicals include trichloroethylene, benzene, and formaldehyde, but the most notorious is perchloroethylene, a hydrocarbon solvent known as perc. According to Health Canada and Environment Canada, perc is a suspected carcinogen. It has been listed as a toxic substance under the Canadian Environmental Protection Act (CEPA). It may irritate the skin, eyes, and sinuses and cause headaches, dizziness, and nausea. Chronic inhalation may depress the central nervous system and damage the liver and kidneys.

To minimize your exposure to these chemicals, remove the plastic covering from your newly dry-cleaned clothes and hang them outdoors or in a well-ventilated room (not in a cramped closet or a child's room) for a few hours. If your clothes frequently come back from the shop with a particularly harsh chemical odor, look for a new dry cleaner.

Perc is hardly a perk

According to the most recent estimate, the Canadian dry-cleaning sector uses about 5,500 tonnes of perc each year. Those who live near or work in dry-cleaning shops face a heightened risk of exposure to toxic chemicals. For example, perc levels in the air may

be high in some apartment buildings with dry-cleaning shops. The federal government is currently working with the dry-cleaning industry to reduce perc exposure, but perc will likely be used for years to come.

Downsize your dry cleaning

Cut down on dry cleaning—and its health hazards—with these helpful tips:

- Dry-clean only those clothes that need it. Some clothes labeled "dry-clean only" (even silk, rayon) may be hand-washed.
- Extend the time between cleaning suits by regularly brushing and ironing them.
- Buy clothes that can be washed the old-fashioned way—with soap and water.

Clean, pressed, and toxic? Potentially dangerous mothproofing chemicals are sometimes routinely added to wool clothes— unless you ask the dry cleaner not to use them.

On the Horizon Consumers may soon have several new cleaning choices that are nontoxic. "Wet cleaning" franchises, which employ water, steam, and biodegradable soaps, are already in business. According to Environment Canada, up to 80 percent of garments can be wet cleaned successfully. Professional cleaners may also one day use environmentally friendly chemicals, such as liquid carbon dioxide, to get the job done.

Dust

If vacuuming and dusting aren't top priorities at your house, you may be endangering your health. Household dust breeds a broad spectrum of harmful microorganisms. Since Canadians spend up to 90 percent of their day indoors, these contaminants create significant health risks by harboring bacteria, causing allergic reactions, and aggravating those who suffer from asthma.

Asthma alert

House dust typically contains minute particles of human skin, hair, and saliva; animal hair and dander; insect parts and feces; and fibers from upholstery, carpets, and clothing. This mixture plays host to molds, viruses, and bacteria, but the worst health threat for many people comes from microscopic insects called dust mites—or, more specifically, from their droppings.

The dust mite (above, magnified about 600 times) lives in such places as carpeting, mattresses, and pillows.

These mites (a single pinch of dust contains thousands) feed on the skin flakes shed by humans. Found even in spotless homes, they're especially dangerous for asthma sufferers because breathing in their droppings contributes to the development of the disease and can trigger attacks.

Allergic reactions to dust occur commonly in both adults and children. Symptoms include a blocked or runny nose and sneezing (especially in the morning), coughing and wheezing, headache, watery eyes, fatigue, and an itchy rash. Symptoms may occur alone or in combination, often making the allergy difficult to identify. A doctor should be consulted for a correct diagnosis.

Getting out the bugs

If someone in your household is being affected by dust, take steps to control your home environment. If the problem is animal hair or dander, either find a new home for any pets or restrict them to certain rooms and bathe them regularly. As for dust mites, taking these measures may keep them at safe levels:

- Wash sheets, blankets, and bed covers weekly in hot (at least 54°C/130°F) water. Or to kill mites while lengthening the life of your linens, place bedclothes in the dryer for 20 minutes on medium and then wash in warm water. (Be aware, however, that dryer heat can set stains in certain fabrics.)
- Use comforters and pillows made of synthetic fiber, such as Dacron or Orlon—instead of down, feathers, or cotton—and wash these in hot water regularly. Replace your synthetic pillows every two years. People with severe allergies should also enclose their mattress, box spring, and pillows in airtight or allergenproof covers.
- Remove carpeting wherever possible, especially in the bedroom.
- Keep your home uncluttered to minimize dust buildup. Store knickknacks, books, and CDs in drawers or closed cabinets.
- Also keep an allergic child's stuffed animals in a cabinet, and clean them regularly. Don't let the child sleep with the toys, especially if they're placed near the face.
- Vacuum weekly and wipe surfaces with a damp cloth—a dry cloth will just release the dust back into the air. (If you're allergic, wear a dust mask.)
- If possible, buy leather or vinyl furniture instead of upholstered.
- Install a humidistat to measure indoor humidity; dust mites thrive in moist conditions. Use central air conditioning and, if necessary, a dehumidifier to keep humidity below 50 percent.
- Clean and ventilate your kitchen, bathrooms, and basement frequently.
- Install high-efficiency particulate air (HEPA) filters in your vacuum cleaner, air purifier, and heating system. They remove dust particles from circulating air.

Fruits, vitamins, toothpaste, mascara, contact lenses, and toilet paper—these are just a few of the items you buy every day that may contain dyes to enhance the products' visual appeal. Dyes have been used since at least 5000 B.C., when colorants derived from plants, animals, and minerals were used as ingredients in cosmetics. Sources over the centuries have included arsenic and lead salts, which proved to be poisonous. Today's dyes, often synthetic rather than natural, are safer, but some carry risks.

Drawbacks of dyes

Barring some exemptions, including natural dyes, Health Canada certifies dyes added to cosmetics, foods, drugs, and other medical items. Synthetic dyes, which are often petroleum-based, may contain carcinogenic impurities. This worries some consumer advocates, but Health Canada contends that it verifies batches of dyes to ensure that impurity limitations are met.

The dye FD&C Red No. 3 (erythrosine) has been suspected as carcinogenic. In the United States, the Food and Drug Administration has banned its use in externally applied drugs and cosmetics and has proposed a total prohibition. In Canada, the dye was reviewed by Health Canada's staff toxicologists in 1994 and found to be safe for use. Thus in Canada it is permitted as an ingredient in such products as jams, concentrated fruit juices, ice cream, catsup, and pickles.

Some dyes can cause allergic reactions. FD&C Yellow No. 5 (tartrazine)—used in such products as foods and

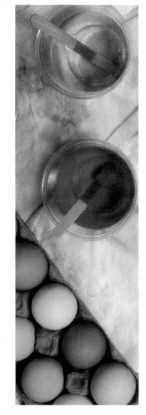

Choose vegetable dyes for Easter eggs if you're going to eat them later. Dyes can pass through the shell and into the egg.

cosmetics—produces itching and hives in a small number of people. (Although this allergy has been associated with sensitivity to aspirin, studies have failed to prove any link.) Yellow No. 5 and other color additives have been suspected of causing hyperactivity in children; however, studies have not confirmed this. Other dyes that have been reported to provoke allergic reactions include D&C Yellow No. 10; FD&C Blue No. 1; and FD&C Blue No. 2. Dyes found in shoe materials, textiles, and paints and inks can also cause rashes.

Dyes in some hair-coloring products may present a more serious problem. The use of dark hair dyes over a period of many years has been linked to an increased risk of certain cancers. Do-it-yourself fabric dyes are also worrisome: A few contain a potential carcinogen, called dichlorobenzidene, that can be absorbed through the skin, especially if dyed fabric is not rinsed thoroughly. When doing the dying, be sure to wear rubber gloves.

Become a discriminating shopper

Read labels carefully to avoid troubling dyes. Besides checking for specific dyes, look for such terms as *artificial color.*

When possible, buy additive-free vitamins and other products. Eat fresh rather than processed foods. Try health-food stores for products that don't contain dye (though the word *organic* does not ensure this). Since you're bound to eat some foods with additives, choose a wide variety instead of sticking to old favorites. This way, you're less likely to be ingesting large amounts of something harmful over an indefinite period.

Pick items with natural rather than artificial dyes, such as cereal with annatto (an orange colorant obtained from a tropical fruit), children's art supplies made with plant or food dyes, and hair coloring made with pure henna. Other natural dyes are caramel, carotene, and saffron. Check labels to be sure that cosmetics advertised as "natural" are. Or make your own from foods and pantry items; articles and books can tell you how.

To avoid artificial dyes, buy white—not colored—paper products.

Eardrops

Ordinarily our ears clean themselves. The outer part of the ear canal secretes earwax, officially called cerumen, in order to trap water, dust, and bacteria. The earwax gradually migrates to the ear's opening, where it falls out or is washed away, carrying foreign particles with it. This self-cleaning process works fine for most everybody, but some people produce excess earwax that builds up and eventually hardens, resulting in discomfort and hearing impairment. Hardened wax can also irritate the fragile tissues of the ear canal.

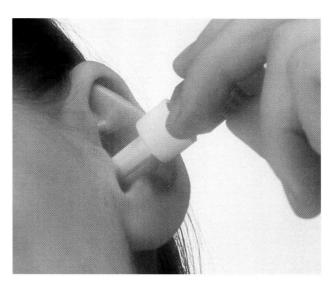

For greater comfort when using eardrops, first warm the container in a bowl of tepid water (but not if the drops contain antibiotics).

Do-it-yourself ear cleaning

To remove hardened earwax, start with a few drops of mineral oil or over-the-counter eardrops. Tilt your head sideways and tug the earlobe gently to open the canal wider as you put in the drops. Place a cotton ball in the ear opening and keep the ear facing up for five minutes. Then remove the cotton and tip your head to allow for drainage. Repeat with the other ear if necessary. Apply the drops twice a day for several days until the wax softens and is released.

For stubborn wax, use a commercial earwax-removal system, available at pharmacies. Follow the directions on the package carefully, applying the eardrops for several days, then flushing the ear with water, using the enclosed syringe.

If your ears still feel full, it's time to seek medical help. Your doctor may prescribe stronger drops to soften the wax, or he may remove it himself with special instruments or a suction device.

Can eardrops ever hurt you?

Anyone who has had a perforated (torn or punctured) eardrum or any type of ear surgery should avoid eardrops unless they have been prescribed by a doctor. Otherwise, it is possible that the drops will seep into the middle ear and cause a serious infection. The same goes for children who have had special tubes implanted in their ears to prevent chronic ear infections.

Some people have an allergic reaction to over-the-counter eardrops or even to prescription products. If the drops you use ever cause pain, burning, redness, or swelling in the ear, discontinue use and call your doctor without delay.

an ounce of Prevention

Drying Up Swimmer's Ear

To prevent recurrences of swimmer's ear, place a few drops of dilute acetic acid or a mixture of equal parts rubbing alcohol and white vinegar in each ear after a swim. Tip your head to let your ears drain. The drops will dry your ears and restore their correct pH balance.

See your doctor if you have any subsequent discharge from either ear or soreness in the ear canals. Severe cases of swimmer's ear are usually treated with prescription eardrops containing antibiotics. Corticosteroids may also be prescribed to reduce swelling.

Echinacea (pronounced *eck-in-AY-sha*), also known as purple coneflower, is a native plant long used by native North Americans to treat everything from measles to colds to snakebite. From the 1870s to the 1920s, some North American physicians prescribed it for a variety of illnesses, including colds. Although its use waned, research continued in Europe, and echinacea is now making a big comeback as an herbal remedy in the U.S. and Canada.

Does it really work?

Medicinal herbs have garnered much interest in recent years in North America. However, the debate about the efficacy of such products—echinacea among them—rages on. In Germany, a government organization known as Commission E—the world's leading authority on the safety and efficacy of herbs—has approved the use of echinacea, taken orally, in the treatment of colds, the flu, and urinary tract and respiratory infections.

Additionally, an article in the *Journal of the American Pharmaceutical Association* states, "Echinacea may be recommended by pharmacists for prevention of colds and influenza or amelioration of their symptoms."

Several compounds in echinacea appear to boost the immune system temporarily by stimulating the body to make more white blood cells to fight off bacteria and viruses. These act as the first line of defense against colds and the flu.

In human studies, the right dose appears to help prevent colds and the flu, or at least helps people recover faster. One 1992 German study of 180 otherwise healthy volunteers revealed that those who took one tablespoon (180 drops) a day of echinacea tincture had fewer and less severe symptoms, and they got over their illnesses about two days earlier than those who took a placebo. Half that dose provided no benefit. Another 1992 German study of 108 people prone to respiratory infections found that 36 percent more of those taking echinacea were healthier over the next eight weeks and that the infections they did get were shorter and less severe than those suffered by people taking placebos.

How to use it

Echinacea appears to be safe for short-term use. Since little is known about its effects over the long term, it's advisable to take it for no more than eight weeks at a time.

Commercial preparations vary widely in the amount of active ingredient they contain (some have up to three times more than others do). If you decide to try it, look for "standardized," fresh-pressed juice in 22 percent alcohol. Take 1½ teaspoons twice a day. Hold the dose on your tongue as long as possible.

Immunity usually increases within three to five days and declines about two weeks after you stop. Take echinacea for no longer than eight weeks, then wait at least two weeks before taking it again.

Tinctures (plant juices preserved in alcohol) and lozenges may be more effective than capsules because echinacea's stimulation of tissues in the mouth is thought to trigger the body's immune response.

Tested solutions are derived from the roots of Echinacea angustifolia *and the flowers, leaves, and roots of* Echinacea purpurea.

When to Avoid Echinacea

- If you are pregnant or nursing.

- If you have an autoimmune disorder, such as HIV, lupus, or rheumatoid arthritis.

- If you have a chronic infectious disease, such as tuberculosis.

- If you have diabetes, multiple sclerosis, or other serious illness.

Eggs are nutritious, delicious, and inexpensive. Yet they are also high in cholesterol and, if eaten raw or undercooked, can make you sick. No wonder many people are confused about whether to indulge.

One whole egg has only 70 calories on average, but it provides about 10 percent of your daily protein needs plus liberal helpings of other nutrients. Its yolk also contains about 215 milligrams of cholesterol. Since dietary cholesterol is thought by some to raise blood cholesterol, and thus the risk of heart disease, the Heart and Stroke Foundation of Canada advises eating egg yolks in moderation as part of a well-balanced, low-fat diet.

The antiegg dogma is beginning to crack, however. A recent analysis of more than 200 studies confirmed that saturated fat, not dietary cholesterol, is the culprit in high cholesterol levels. (A large egg contains only 2 grams of saturated fat.) Other studies found that for young people, eating three or four eggs *a day* had virtually no effect on their blood cholesterol.

Some experts now advise that if your blood cholesterol is in the normal range, it's okay to eat more than four eggs a week; others disagree. But if your blood cholesterol is high, you should limit egg consumption while concentrating on lowering saturated fat in your diet and losing excess weight.

Keeping eggs safe

Salmonella, a common bacterium that causes food-borne illness, can be found inside some clean, uncracked eggs, so it's never safe to eat them raw or undercooked. Scramble eggs and cook omelets until no longer runny. Fry eggs three minutes on one side, one on the other (or four minutes sunny-side up, covered). Soft-boil eggs until the yolk is thick. Avoid raw eggs in such homemade preparations as mayonnaise or ice cream. Keep eggs up to three weeks refrigerated in their carton on a cold inside shelf (not in the door). After handling raw eggs, wash your hands, utensils, and work surfaces.

Supersafe eggs

Many restaurants prepare soft omelets, Caesar salad, and other egg dishes that are not cooked until firm by using pasteurized eggs that eliminate the risk of salmonella. These commercial products come in liquid form (pasteurizing eggs in the shells is not practical). Liquid, pasteurized egg products—free of cholesterol and salmonella—can now be found in some supermarkets.

Dealing with egg allergies

Eggs may cause allergic reactions in children under the age of three. Itchy hives on the skin, usually around the mouth, are a common symptom. If the child has trouble breathing, call for medical help immediately.

For most children, egg allergies disappear within a year. To prevent them, avoid giving eggs to an infant before the age of one. If you are breast-feeding a baby and allergies run in your family, avoid eating eggs for the duration.

> **Some experts now advise that if your blood cholesterol is in the normal range, it's okay to eat more than four eggs a week; others disagree.**

The Shell Game

Do you splurge on brown-shelled eggs, thinking that they are more nutritious than white-shelled ones? Well, save your pennies. Shell color indicates only the laying hen's breed, not health benefits. Also, pricier eggs laid by "free range" or "organically fed" hens aren't necessarily more healthful than regular varieties.

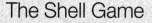

If an egg yolk's color differs a shade from others you crack, don't worry— it's still safe to eat.

Electric Blankets

Electric Blankets

Who Should Be Wary of Using an Electric Blanket?

Pregnant women (because the excess heat may harm the fetus) should be very careful. So should anyone who has decreased temperature sensation, such as:

• Infants and elderly people

• Diabetics

• Victims of stroke or spinal-cord injury

• People who have been drinking alcohol

• People taking medication for pain or insomnia

An electric blanket may help you get cozy, but don't fall asleep without first turning it off.

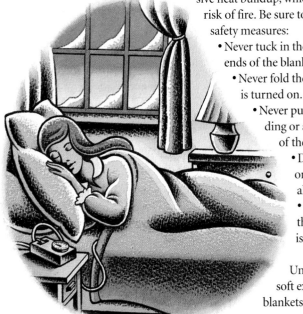

People who have cooled on electric blankets can cozy up to them again. The reported linked between the blankets' electromagnetic fields (EMFs) and an increased risk of cancer has not been conclusively proven. Even more reassuring is the fact that today's electric blankets emit lower EMFs. But some things haven't changed about electric blankets: safety issues about burns, fires, and electric shocks when using them.

The hot issues

Always remember that an electric blanket is a heating appliance and, as such, must be used with care. Here are some suggestions for ensuring that you can sleep worry-free.

Burns. An electric blanket can burn the skin of people who are susceptible, even at a low temperature setting. Those who may experience decreased temperature sensation (see column at left) are at the greatest risk. Even if you are not susceptible, you may still get a nasty burn if you do not use the blanket correctly. To reduce the risk, never lie on the blanket or allow pets to lie on it.

Fire. Electric blankets, like all heating appliances, can start a fire if they are used improperly. It is important to prevent excessive heat buildup, which increases the risk of fire. Be sure to follow these safety measures:

• Never tuck in the cord, sides, or ends of the blanket.

• Never fold the blanket while it is turned on.

• Never put additional bedding or a coverlet on top of the blanket.

• Don't sit or lie on the blanket or allow pets to.

• Always turn off the blanket when it is not in use.

Electric shock. Underneath their soft exteriors, electric blankets contain wires

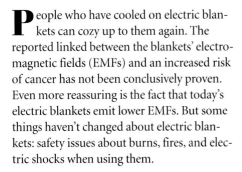

Heating-Pad Don'ts

Heating pads—whether they create dry or moist warmth—can soothe muscle and joint pain. However, they carry all the same risks—and should be used with the same restrictions—as electric blankets. Follow these safety tips in particular:

• Don't use a heating pad for more than 20 minutes at a time.

• Don't apply a pad to bare skin.

• Never fall asleep with a heating pad on (be extra cautious if you're taking medication that makes you drowsy).

• Don't lie on, sit on, or fold a heating pad when it is in use.

• Never use arthritis cream with a heating pad. Heat can cause the skin to absorb toxic amounts of the medication.

that can be damaged to the point at which they become shock hazards. A few precautions can reduce the risk:

• Before using an electric blanket, inspect it carefully and discard it if any area appears worn or damaged or if the cord is frayed.

• Do not use pins to attach the blanket to anything else; they may damage the wiring.

• Wash the blanket gently (unplugged, of course) and don't use bleach.

• Never dry-clean an electric blanket.

• Don't store an electric blanket with anything heavy on top of it or jam it into a space so that it becomes crushed or use moth repellents with it.

• Avoid spilling liquids onto the blanket while it is turned on.

• Never jerk the cord from the socket.

One of the luxuries of using an electric blanket is being able to warm the sheets with it before bedtime. Just don't forget it and leave it unattended for more than a few minutes.

Electromagnetic Fields

They can't be seen, heard, or felt. Still, electromagnetic fields (EMFs) are an almost constant and possibly menacing presence in our home and workplace—wherever electric current runs. During the past 20 years, researchers have closely studied EMFs as a potential threat to human health.

The buzz about EMFs
When you turn on any electric device, the current running through it produces a magnetic field that surrounds the device. The field can't be blocked and, if you stand close

> A 1998 report from the National Institutes of Health determined that electromagnetic fields should be viewed as a possible human carcinogen, although even the panel itself was divided.

enough, passes right through your body. Power lines, power plants, and substations produce the same type of EMFs.

Researchers have focused on EMFs that are produced by alternating current, such as those from power lines, home appliances, and office equipment. Even though some EMFs in the home and workplace are surprisingly strong close to the source, these fields rapidly decrease in strength as you move away from their sources. When people are exposed to these fields, weak electric currents are generated in their bodies.

EMFs: good or bad?
Early research indicated a possible relationship between exposure to EMFs and disease (including leukemia). As of yet, there is no adequate scientific explanation of how these fields might cause disease. Moreover, many studies of EMFs have revealed no links whatsoever to disease. One of the largest was a 20-year-long study of 383,700 people in Finland. It found that living near power lines did not increase cancer risk.

In 1996, the National Academy of Sciences in the U.S. reviewed some 500 studies on EMFs spanning 17 years. No conclusive proof of any health risks, such as cancer, reproductive and developmental abnormalities, or learning and behavioral disorders, was found to be related to EMF exposure in the home.

However, the debate rages on; many experts are still concerned. A 1998 report from the National Institutes of Health in the U.S. determined that electromagnetic fields should indeed be viewed as a possible human carcinogen (although even the panel itself was divided). They concluded that there is a slightly increased risk of leukemia for children living near power lines and for adults working in industries where they are exposed to strong EMFs. But the panel also found that there is insufficient evidence to link household exposure to EMFs to adult cancer, Alzheimer's disease, birth defects, or other ills. Obviously, more research needs to be done before the case can be closed. At present in Canada there are no safety guidelines for exposure to low-frequency EMFs. Health Canada along with electric utilities and other organizations actively continue to carry out research in this area.

What you can do
Here's how to reduce your exposure to EMFs:
- Minimize the use of devices that do emit high levels of EMFs, such as shavers, hair dryers, microwave ovens, sewing machines, fans, blenders, vacuum cleaners, power tools, and copiers.
- When possible, use a laptop computer instead of a desktop model that uses a monitor. When you do use a monitor, sit as far away from it as possible.
- Move electrical devices, such as the bedside clock radio, at least an arm's length away from your head.

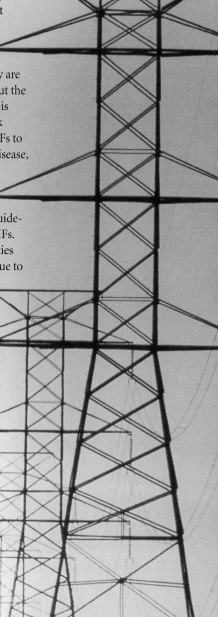

Some scientists believe that the EMFs produced by power lines may lower melatonin levels in the body. Studies have been inconclusive.

Endoscopy

Imagine discovering an intestinal polyp long before it turns cancerous. That's one of the miracles of endoscopy, a nonsurgical procedure that allows doctors to examine the gastrointestinal tract. Since the early 1970s, endoscopy has enabled doctors to diagnose a wide array of gastrointestinal problems. Although endoscopy carries some risk, it is slight compared to that associated with exploratory surgery of the abdomen.

Lights, camera, action!

An endoscope typically contains a miniature video camera or a bundle of fiber-optic strands that allows the doctor to look in one end and see what is at the other. The slender tube of the endoscope is inserted through a

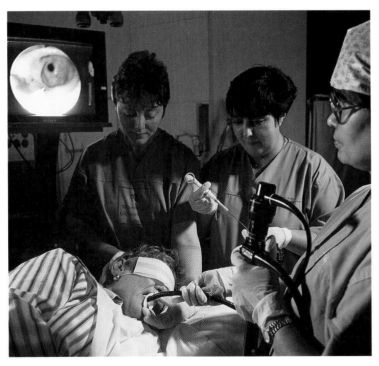

If not disinfected, endoscopes may transmit such viruses as hepatitis C, but such occurrences are rare.

natural opening in the body to view, or take pictures of, the insides of hollow organs. If the esophagus or stomach is to be viewed, the tube is inserted into the throat—a procedure called a gastroscopy. If the intestines are the target, the endoscope is inserted into the rectum—a procedure called either a sigmoidoscopy or a colonoscopy, depending on the

length of the tube. Air is pumped through the tube to open the folds of these internal organs; a small light at the tube's end illuminates the area. A conduit through which tiny instruments can be passed allows the doctor to snip tissue samples for biopsies. Because the procedure is minimally invasive, only mild sedatives are used, and recovery takes just an hour or two. For some procedures, such as a gastroscopy, a local anesthetic eliminates any discomfort. Rarely is a general anesthetic required.

Biopsies taken with the help of endoscopes have dramatically reduced the pain and the mortality rate of many diseases that were scourges no more than two decades ago. Stomach ulcers and cancers of the colon, stomach, and esophagus are commonly diagnosed by endoscopy.

The future of illumination

Although using endoscopy for the gastrointestinal tract is well established, newer uses for other organs are also proving beneficial. An endoscopic procedure called a bronchoscopy allows a doctor to explore the bronchial tubes of the lungs in search of tumors. Without the procedure, these tumors are difficult to locate, much less to biopsy, without debilitating chest surgery. Other organs that endoscopy can now illuminate are the uterus and the bladder.

Doctors are also experimenting with endoscopes enhanced by computers to create three-dimensional views of internal organs—virtual-reality images that may improve a doctor's ability to diagnose gastrointestinal disorders. An endoscopic version of ultrasound is already being developed to diagnose abnormalities more accurately.

Endoscopy doesn't just observe this inner world, it can also change it. New laser-equipped devices are now able to eliminate small abnormalities and remove obstructions that once required surgery. A light-sensitive agent that is readily absorbed by tumor cells can also be injected; when exposed to a laser, the cells die.

Epidurals

Can childbirth be painless? Not entirely. But for women delivering babies, one of the most popular forms of analgesia is the epidural—a way of administering pain-blocking medication directly to the nerves. Because it doesn't enter the mother's bloodstream, it has little or no effect on the infant. And it prevents pain without sedating the mother, so she stays awake and alert.

Recent research shows that an epidural does not increase the risk of cesarean birth.

How it works

A pain medication, injected into the lower back, reaches the epidural space between the vertebrae and the spinal cord, where it bathes the nerves. It takes effect in about 15 to 20 minutes, blocking pain in the lower half of the body. (An epidural may be preceded by a dose of a narcotic drug delivered directly into the sac containing the spinal cord, which gives relief from pain in one to two minutes.) A thin catheter is inserted into the epidural space as the injection is given, allowing additional medication to be given as needed.

In certain instances, some hospitals now offer women in labor a "walking" epidural. In this procedure, a pump is used to deliver continuous low-dosages of medication. The patient experiences little pain and does not lose feeling in her legs, so she is able to move around during labor, which may ultimately speed delivery.

If a surgical procedure, such as a cesarean section, becomes necessary, an anesthetic can be administered through the catheter. Since only the lower body is affected, the expectant mother remains conscious, and can see her newborn right after birth.

Possible side effects

Most women in labor receive an epidural with few complications. Some experts believe that an epidural may prolong labor, but others contend that it doesn't. Recent research shows that an epidural does not increase the risk of cesarean birth, as was once thought.

Still, this procedure is not considered risk-free. Epidural medication may cause a drop in the mother's blood pressure that could affect the baby's heartbeat. To help prevent this, intravenous fluids are given before the epidural is administered. Also, if large doses of the local anesthetic are inadvertently injected into a blood vessel, the mother may experience drowsiness, breathing difficulties, slurred speech, blurred vision, heart-rhythm abnormalities, and possibly even convulsions. To reduce these risks, the anesthesiologist administers a small dose first to test the placement of the medication.

Postpartum problems, such as headache or difficulty urinating, sometimes occur. To head them off, the anesthesiologist will ask the patient to hold as still as possible while the injection is given so that the medication is inserted into exactly the right spot.

Long-term risks are quite rare. They include a possible epidural hematoma (an accumulation of blood under the tissues) or an abscess, which, if left untreated, can result in paralysis.

Beyond birthing: Safer pain relief for many surgeries

Although epidurals are most commonly used in childbirth, they are also proving useful during and after various types of surgery. They are often used in conjunction with general anesthesia to reduce the amount of sedatives needed. Given before limb amputation, for example, an epidural reduces postsurgical pain. For severe postoperative pain, it can even be self-administered by the patient at the push of a button through a catheter and pump. This controls pain better than oral or injected painkillers do and, unlike them, does not affect the liver, gastrointestinal system, or kidneys. Built-in safety measures guard against overdosing.

CAUTION!
If you take blood-thinning medication (particularly heparin) or nonsteroidal anti-inflammatory drugs, epidurals are risky. Be sure to tell your anesthesiologist prior to surgery.

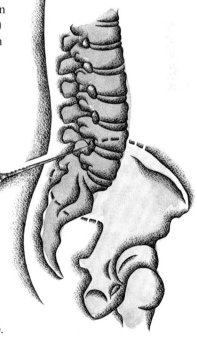

Medications injected into the space between the vertebrae and the spinal cord range from mild analgesics to strong anesthetics.

Exercise Equipment

Did Methuselah exercise? We can't be sure. But Canadians are waking up to the fact that regular, moderate exercise helps them achieve a longer, healthier life. As a result, sales of exercise machines are booming.

Exercise machines fall into two main categories. Aerobic machines help you build cardiovascular strength by working the lungs, heart, and muscles for an extended time period. They include treadmills (for walking or jogging), cross-country-ski machines, stair climbers, rowing machines, stationary bikes, and the "air gliders" advertised on late-night television.

Weight-lifting machines tone and strengthen your muscles, without the dangers of free weights (dropping a dumbbell on yourself, for example). Effective strength training requires you to lift a fairly heavy weight 8 to 12 times with the same muscle group. Doing this twice a week builds strength and endurance and helps maintain flexibility.

Most health clubs and gyms have a variety of aerobic and weight-lifting machines, but you can also bring fitness home by buying some of these machines yourself.

Any sustained moderate physical activity, done for 30 minutes a day, will add to your life expectancy and lower your risk of heart disease and cancer.

The rundown on aerobic machines

The first thing you should know about treadmills, stationary bikes, and the other gleaming devices lining the walls of your health club is that you don't need them to stay reasonably healthy. Any sustained moderate physical activity, done for 30 minutes a day—whether it's walking or bicycling in the park, raking the leaves, or swimming in a pool—will add to your life expectancy and lower your risk of heart disease and cancer.

That said, benefits can be increased up to a point by exercising more, and aerobic-exercise machines offer a convenient way to work out in a comfortable indoor environment. When choosing which machine to use, keep these criteria in mind:

- Is the machine well made? A poorly constructed machine is less likely to provide a good, consistent workout, more likely to cause injuries, and unlikely to stand up to regular use. Be prepared to spend a premium for one of the better brands; with exercise devices, you tend to get what you pay for. Even so, it's a good idea to try out the machine in the store.
- Is it adjustable? Adjustable seats and handlebars are essential to avoid injury and to get the best possible workout.
- Does it have variable resistance? Such a feature allows you to adjust the resistance of the machine in order to increase or decrease the intensity of your workout.
- Do you know how to use it? Exercise equipment can cause serious injuries if it's used incorrectly. Never try equipment without first having a thorough instruction session with a certified

Inclining a treadmill by 15° will triple the number of calories burned. To avoid strain, start flat and increase the incline gradually.

physical therapist or personal trainer. You need to learn not only how to operate it safely but also how to continue to derive benefits from it as you get fitter.

• Do you enjoy the activity? If you buy a machine for doing something you hate or if it makes you feel uncomfortable, you may be better off trying another activity. Since exercising for long periods—even on a machine you like—can be tedious, many people who go to a health club "mix and match" their workouts with different machines. For example, you might combine 10 minutes on a stationary bike with 10 minutes on a treadmill and finish up with 10 minutes on a stair climber.

Aerobic machines: a buyer's guide

Treadmills. These motorized wonders have become a favorite of exercisers in recent years, and today millions of North Americans walk or jog in place on their moving rubber belts. Although expensive and a bit noisy, a well-made treadmill provides you with a very natural walking or running workout (low-impact at lower speeds). If you're buying one:

• Consider motorized treadmills first. Non-motorized models are harder to use and don't allow for a natural gait.
• Look for a belt at least 45 centimeters (18 inches) wide and about 1.5 meters (5 feet) long, with a walking surface that is supportive but has a slight amount of give as you plant your foot.
• Be sure the speed controls and emergency shutoff switch are easy to use.
• Extras: Some experts favor treadmills that can be tilted slightly, since walking "uphill" burns more calories. Digital models may offer computerized workouts and built-in heart monitors.

Safety hints for when you get it home:

• Turn down the belt speed before starting the treadmill, then increase it gradually.
• Hold on to the handrails for balance when you first turn on the machine until you are walking or jogging at the desired speed.
• Walk, jog, or run with a steady gait.

• When you finish, don't stop walking abruptly. Let the machine slow down, then step off to the side.

Stationary bikes. These devices are available in upright and recumbent models (which are easier on the back). Some also have handles you can push and pull on, to increase your aerobic output. At the right level of resistance, stationary bikes provide an excellent aerobic workout. They also break down less often than other machines. What's more, stationary cycling is a low-impact activity, good (even beneficial) for people who have knee and ankle problems. The downside: since cycling isn't a weight-bearing exercise, it won't benefit your bones as much as other aerobic activ-

Two for one: Exercising on a rowing machine provides not only an aerobic workout but also strength training for your whole body.

Calories Burned on Aerobic Machines

Device	Intensity	Calories/hour (120-lb woman)	Calories/hour (150-lb man)
Treadmill	3 mph (20-minute mile)	215	300
	7 mph (8.5-minute mile)	590	700
Stationary bike	5 mph (12-minute mile)	200	245
Cross-country-ski machine	5 mph (11.5-minute mile)	585	700
	9 mph (6.5-minute mile)	830	1,000
Stair climber	slow	380	450
	fast	755	900

Adapted with permission from Consumers Digest.

Exercise Equipment (continued)

Is Your Exercise Equipment Sturdy Enough?

This is a major concern when it comes to home equipment, which may be less expensive than health-club machines and therefore not as well built.

- Look for machines with wide bases that can be shoved without tipping.

- Shake the equipment to make sure it is very sturdy.

- Check to see that joints are welded, not bolted.

- Before buying, try out the model you want in the store for at least 10 minutes to find out whether it squeaks or wobbles or shows any other signs of being flimsy.

Find out how to use these strength-training devices properly to avoid injuries.

ities will. If you are buying a stationary bike:

- Look for the type of bike that has a flywheel, to increase the pedal resistance without changing your speed.

- Find one with an adjustable seat that is comfortable. It is vital to sit at the right height, so that your leg is almost completely straight when the pedal is all the way down.

- Opt for a recumbent bike, which allows you to lean back in a wide, supportive chair, if you have high blood pressure or back, neck, knee, or shoulder problems or if you plan to become pregnant.

Safety hint:

- Lower or raise the resistance level so that you can pedal at a rate of 70 to 80 revolutions per minute (rpm). Adjust the level so you can keep the rpm in that range for at least 10 minutes of pedaling. As you grow stronger over weeks of exercise, you can increase the resistance gradually.

Cross-country-ski machines. These more complex machines come with two movable foot pads or skis and a pair of hand poles or ropes. By moving your arms and legs in a skiing movement, you get a low-impact aerobic workout and burn more calories than with other machines. If you are buying one:

- Check to see whether the foot pads move independently of each other if you want to maintain a more fluid, authentic skiing motion. If this is too difficult for you, you may find the machines that restrict the movement easier to use.

Stair climbers. These machines deliver the benefits of walking up stairs, but add variable resistance to the activity. The best models are expensive, but they give you a better workout (especially if you don't hold on to the rails) and last longer. If you are buying one:

- Find a model with independent steps (the steps move separately), rather than linked steps (one step goes up when the other goes down). Independent steps offer a smoother, more challenging workout.

Increasing the resistance of a stair climber will help build more muscle. Decreasing the resistance will deliver a better aerobic workout.

- Check to see whether the level of resistance is easy to adjust.

- Be sure that the pedals remain horizontal to the floor. If they don't, your knee joints may be seriously injured.

Other aerobic devices. If you belong to a health club, you may already have seen the newest exercise machine on the block. Known as a cross-trainer, it's a hybrid that blends features of the stair climber, stationary bike, and treadmill. Its pedals follow an elliptical path, allowing you to "run" in midair without impact on your joints. Home models provide an excellent workout. But don't confuse the device with the "air gliders" sold on television; the effectiveness of the latter products can vary, and most don't offer enough resistance to give you a sustained aerobic workout.

Rowing machines provide a very good full-body aerobic workout. The best ones, which simulate the feeling of rowing in water, are very expensive. Check with your doctor before buying one; they can exacerbate certain types of back problems.

Machines that build muscle

Such companies as Nautilus and Cybex have revolutionized strength training by making it possible to lift weights safely and easily. There are two types of machines: individual machines that work only one or a handful of muscle groups and multipurpose machines that allow you to work virtually your whole body one exercise at a time. Increasing or decreasing the weight usually requires nothing more complicated than inserting a pin in a stack of weighted plates.

For the best strength workout, and to balance muscle development, join a health club where you can benefit from their wide range of weight-lifting machines. Exercise both the lower and the upper body, front and back. A well-rounded workout should utilize a number of different machines, including the leg-extension machine, leg-curl machine, chest-press machine, and lateral-pulldown machine. Experts recommend doing a dozen different exercises, six for the lower body and six for the upper body.

Home gyms designed for multi-exercise strength training are available with weighted plates or rubber bands, which provide resistance. If you are shopping for one:

- Check to be sure that resistance can be adjusted easily.
- Carefully test each exercise at sev-eral different levels of resistance, making sure the movement feels comfortable and the weight increments are small enough to make gradual increases.
- Avoid machines that have key parts made of plastic.
- Make sure the bench is well padded and has a sturdy cover.

Children beware

Many children are injured each year by home exercise equipment. Little fingers poke into spokes and machinery, and hair can get caught in gears. Until the kids are older, it might be wise to join a health club or buy equipment that can be stored in a closet.

Strength-Training Guidelines

- For each exercise, repeat the movement 8 to 12 times in a row with enough resistance to make the last repetitions feel difficult. Rest for one or two minutes before beginning the next "set," or series of repetitions, and do up to three sets.

- Perform each repetition slowly and smoothly, taking about two seconds to lift the weight and four seconds to lower it.

- Don't hold your breath; instead, breath out when you lift the weight and breath in when you lower it.

- Rest for one to two seconds between muscle contractions to allow oxygen-rich blood to reach the muscles.

- Allow 48 hours between weight-lifting sessions, to let your muscles recuperate, or exercise the upper body one day and the lower body the next day.

- When 12 repetitions feel easy, increase the resistance by adding more weight.

- If you feel pain during an exercise, stop immediately.

Eyedrops

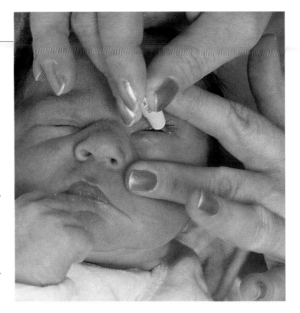

To keep an eyedrop dispenser sterile, avoid touching eyes, lashes, or anything else with it. Cover it when not in use.

Anyone who has stared at a computer all day or suffered through the height of allergy season has resorted to eyedrops to get out the red and the itch. Eyedrops are a staple in medicine cabinets, but unless you know which drops are best for which condition, they may cause more problems than they cure.

Tough on the eyes

Every day the eyes are besieged by any number of irritants. Eyedrops are often beneficial in treating symptoms caused by:

- Overuse of contact lenses.
- Working too long at a computer terminal.
- Swimming in chlorinated water.
- Allergens, such as pollen, dust, and the dander of animals.
- Environmental factors, such as air conditioning, dry heat, wind, sun, and pollution (particularly smoke).
- Medications, such as antidepressants, decongestants, antihistamines, blood pressure drugs, hormones, birth-control pills, diuretics, ulcer drugs, tranquilizers, and beta-blockers. (Talk to your doctor about changes you can safely make.)
- Medical conditions, such as Sjögren's syndrome, rheumatoid arthritis, lupus, thyroid disorders, diabetes, asthma, and Crohn's disease. (Seek medical help for any persistent eye symptoms, since they may signal these or other serious afflictions.)

Differences in drops

Before you buy eyedrops, acquaint yourself with their properties. Most over-the-counter eyedrops fall into one of three categories:

- Decongestant: eliminates redness.
- Decongestant-antihistamine combination: relieves redness and itching.
- Lubricant or "artificial tears": rehydrates dry eyes.

All three provide relief, but their specific drawbacks must be considered.

If you use a decongestant or a decongestant-antihistamine combination for more than a week, you are likely to suffer a "rebound" effect: Not only will the redness and itching return, but they may become chronic. In addition, decongestant drops that contain tetrahydrozoline, naphazoline, or phenylephrine may cause conjunctivitis—an eye inflammation marked by redness, itching, a gritty feeling in the eye, and a sticky discharge, particularly upon waking. If redness and itching develop before the end of a week, or problems persist after you've used the drops for seven days, see your doctor.

Eye lubricants are the safest drops for long-term use, but many contain preservatives that over time cause a superficial erosion of the cornea—a reversible but troubling form of inflammation. In rare cases a reaction to the preservatives may develop into a severe allergic response. Seek medical attention if either problem arises.

For chronic eye problems, including itchy allergy eyes, your doctor may recommend one of several types of prescription eyedrops that contain antihistamines, nonsteroidal anti-inflammatory drugs, histamine blockers, or steroids. Prescription eyedrops are also available for the treatment of glaucoma.

The Natural Way

First try relieving eyes with remedies other than drops:

- Blink as often as you can when doing close work.
- Apply wet paper towels to your eyelids for 10 minutes, four times a day (especially if you work at a computer).
- Wear sunglasses when you are outdoors.
- When using a handheld hair dryer, point it away from your face.
- Aim heating and cooling ducts and vents away from your eyes.

Fabric Treatments

Fabric treatments make many modern wonders possible: pants that resist wrinkling, no-iron sheets, and rain jackets that repel water. There are also fabrics that resist stains, insects, and mildew. But you may have to pay a price for the convenience: formaldehyde and other toxic chemicals used to treat such products may be harmful to people who wear or use them.

The wrinkle in permanent press

A fabric becomes "permanently pressed" by means of a finishing process in which it is treated with formaldehyde resins. Formaldehyde is defined as a possible human carcinogen by Health Canada under the Canadian Environmental Protection Act (CEPA). Formaldehyde resins, which tend to be broken down by body heat and perspiration, can cause allergic reactions in some people. Since the 1980s, scientists have been working to modify these resins so that they release considerably less formaldehyde than before, but they are not yet emission-free.

Product labels aren't required to list formaldehyde, but you can assume it's on fabrics advertised as permanent-press, no-iron, shrinkproof, water-repellent, or easy-care. Most polyester/cotton blends are treated with formaldehyde; poly/cotton sheets are heavily coated with it so they will withstand frequent laundering. Fabrics used to make draperies usually have permanent-press and antifungal finishes. The problem is, whenever the sun shines on curtains made with these types of finishes, they emit formaldehyde.

Hot new flame retardants

Children's and adult apparel, hospital gowns, industrial uniforms, mattresses, and some household furnishings are required by law to meet flammability standards. At one time, they were treated with flame-retardant chemicals that contained possible carcinogens or formaldehyde. Today, these flame retardants meet toxicological standards set for children's sleepwear. Many of these clothes are now made from synthetic fabrics (nylon, polyester, acrylic) that naturally resist burning.

Reducing your exposure

In place of treated fabrics, choose cotton (preferably organically grown), silk, ramie, linen, rayon, wool, down, kapok, and natural-fiber blends without finishes. When it's time to replace your old mattress, look for a cotton futon or order a mattress made of natural fabrics that aren't chemically treated. Shop for natural-fabric clothing that's inherently flame-resistant, such as silk and wool.

To reduce the amount of formaldehyde resin in permanent-press fabrics, wash them before you use them. If your home contains many treated fabrics, take steps to keep it well ventilated and to lower the humidity level.

It helps to air out permanent-press draperies outdoors before hanging them. Better yet, choose drapes or curtains made from untreated cotton, cotton canvas, linen, or a linen/cotton blend. They may have to be replaced more often because they wear out faster, but they are less hazardous. Other safe choices for window coverings are wood, bamboo, or metal blinds and wooden shutters.

The higher the temperature and humidity in your house, the worse the emissions from treated fabrics.

On the Horizon Formaldehyde-free resins that make apparel and bedding easy-care may be available soon. Other safe fabric treatments are under development, including finishes made from silicone or silicone/fluoropolymer blends.

Fast Food

On average, Canadians spend about $7 billion annually on purchases like these at the country's fast-food restaurants.

C ould you eat fast food five times a week and actually keep your fat intake under the recommended limit of 30 percent of total calories? Yes, according to a study sponsored by McDonald's, but it wouldn't be easy. You would have to order only the leanest items—and make the rest of your meals extremely low in fat. Another study found that it's even possible to lower blood-cholesterol levels while consuming a few fast-food meals—but it's nowhere near as effective as sensible meal planning at home.

Why? Fast foods tend to be exorbitantly high in calories, cholesterol-raising saturated fat, and sodium. For example, a Burger King Whopper with cheese has 730 calories, 16 grams of saturated fat, and 1,300 milligrams of sodium. Add fries and a shake, and you

Safer Burgers?

Although fast-food burgers contaminated with a dangerous strain of E. coli bacteria made headlines several years ago, many fast-food chains now do some microbial testing, so their burgers may be safer than those served at home.

could exceed the recommended daily limit for fat and put a big dent in your calorie and sodium allotment. (For those consuming about 2,200 calories per day, saturated fat should be kept to 22 grams. Sodium should be consumed in moderation.)

Another problem is what you're *not* getting. Most fast-food dishes tend to be short on fiber and antioxidants, which help protect against cancer and heart disease. An occasional fast-food meal won't undermine a healthy, well-balanced diet, but it's best not to indulge often, especially when it comes to kids. Obesity is a growing epidemic among children, and fast-food consumption ranks as one of the major contributors.

Slimmer strategies

Here's how to order a relatively healthful fast-food meal:
- **Don't supersize it.** Save calories by resisting (or sharing) large sizes of burgers and fries. Order one piece of fried chicken instead of three.
- **Keep it simple.** Avoid heavy sauces and cheese toppings. Use very small amounts of butter or sour cream on baked potatoes, and low-fat or fat-free dressing on sandwiches and salads. When ordering pizza, choose vegetable rather than meat toppings and skip the extra cheese.

A slice of this 12-inch mushroom-pepperoni pizza contains 200 calories and 7 grams of fat. Remove the pepperoni and you've cut 60 calories and 3.8 grams of fat.

- **Salad days.** A tossed salad makes an excellent side dish. For an entrée, a garden salad with low-fat or fat-free dressing is nutritionally sound. But don't buy something just because it's *called* a salad: high-fat dressings pack on calories and fat.
- **Forget fried.** Fried items, especially if breaded, are loaded with fat. And "extra crispy" means extra fatty. Fried fast foods are usually cooked in partially hydrogenated vegetable oils—high in trans fats, which increase heart-disease risk. Choose baked, broiled, or grilled instead.
- **Know the numbers.** If nutrition information is not in plain view, ask if you may see it, especially if you need to watch your cholesterol or sodium intake. Some restaurant chains also list this kind of data on their Web sites.
- **Think about the drink.** Water, juice, or skim or low-fat milk beats sodas or shakes.
- **Just desserts.** Low-fat ice cream or frozen yogurt is a good alternative to pie or cake.
- **On the road.** A majority of North Americans eat fast foods when traveling. On road trips, supplement drive-through meals with a stash of carrots, grapes, strawberries, apples, and juice. (It's also a good idea when eating fast food at home.)

Wrap it up?

Fast-food wraps—vegetables, beef, chicken, or fish encased in tortillas, pitas, or other flat-breads—are perceived as being lower in calories and saturated fat than standard fare. But not all of them are. Fat and calorie counts vary widely, depending on the ingredients used. For example, the McDonald's Turkey and Ham Club McWrap has 675 calories and 32 grams of total fat (of which 9 grams are saturated fat) whereas the Chicken Caesar McWrap has 471 calories and 20 grams of total fat (but only 4 grams are saturated fat). If you are in doubt, ask to see the nutritional breakdown.

> Fast-food wraps are perceived as being lower in calories and saturated fat than standard fare—but not all of them are.

Fast Foods: How They Stack Up

The data given below on common fast foods were compiled in the United States by the National Heart, Lung, and Blood Institute. Since saturated fats are especially harmful to the heart, the institute has ranked foods according to increasing saturated-fat content and advises consumers to choose items in the top end of each group. Unless a size is given, portions are those usually served; however, be aware that numbers may vary from restaurant to restaurant.

Product	Saturated Fat (grams)	Cholesterol (milligrams)	Total Fat* (grams)	Calories
Entrées				
Grilled chicken breast sandwich, plain	1.0	60	7.0	288
Cheese pizza (one slice)	1.5	9	3.2	140
Roast beef sandwich, plain	3.6	52	13.8	346
Hamburger, plain	4.1	36	11.8	275
Hot dog, plain	5.1	44	14.5	242
Fish sandwich with tartar sauce	5.2	55	22.8	431
Chicken, boneless pieces, breaded and fried (six)	5.5	62	17.7	290
Cheeseburger, plain	6.5	50	15.2	320
Burritos with beans and cheese (two)	6.8	27	11.7	377
Sub sandwich with cold cuts	6.8	35	18.6	456
Chicken fillet sandwich, plain	8.5	60	29.5	515
Baked potato, with cheese sauce and chili	13.0	31	21.9	481
Sides				
Tossed salad, no dressing (one cup)	0.0	0	0.2	32
French fries, regular	3.8	0	12.0	235
Breakfasts				
English muffin with butter	2.4	13	5.8	189
Scrambled eggs (two)	5.8	400	15.2	200
Pancakes with butter and syrup (three)	5.9	57	14	519
Egg, bacon, and cheese biscuit	11.4	261	31.4	477

A fat gram equals nine calories; a gram of carbohydrate or protein equals four.

Fats & Oils

Most of us love fat, and with good reason: it gives a smooth, creamy "mouth feel" and greatly enhances flavor. Our bodies also need fat in order to absorb certain vitamins and to function normally. But consuming too much fat can cause such serious problems as obesity, heart disease, and cancer.

Have Canadians heeded warnings about these dangers? The percentage of fat in the typical diet has dropped from 40 percent (in the 1970s) to 38 percent today—still too high compared to the limit of 30 percent recommended by Health Canada and the Heart and Stroke Foundation of Canada. Total fat intake is perhaps especially a concern for older people. For example, a recent study of women over 60 suggests that a fatty meal, regardless of the type of fats involved, causes levels of a clotting factor in the blood to rise. This may heighten the risk of stroke or heart attack.

But reducing total fat is only part of the picture, for other studies have made it clear that not all fats are created equal.

The "bad" fats

Saturated fats contribute to heart disease and have been associated with cancers of the lung, colon, and prostate. They are found in beef, pork, lamb, processed meats (hot dogs and bologna), tropical oils (palm and coconut), whole milk, butter, lard, cream, and ice cream. Saturated fats raise harmful LDL (low-density lipoprotein) cholesterol levels, clogging arteries and increasing the probability of a heart attack.

Based on a 14-year Harvard University study of more than 80,000 middle-aged female nurses, researchers have estimated that switching a mere 5 percent of one's total calories from saturated to unsaturated fats (such as vegetable oils) may decrease the risk of having a fatal heart attack by a whopping 42 percent. Studies involving men have yielded similar results.

Health Canada recommends that saturated fat should normally account for no more than 10 percent of your total caloric intake; some health experts set an upper limit of 7 percent for those with heart disease. Check food labels for saturated-fat content. In a diet of 2,000 calories a day, 22 grams of saturated fat is about 10 percent of calories; 15 grams about 7 percent. (A gram of fat contains 9 calories.)

Trans fats: worse than saturated?

To increase the shelf life of certain foods, manufacturers often replace saturated fats with artificially hardened

Used in moderation, polyunsaturated oils, such as sunflower, safflower, and corn, are "heart-healthy."

Monounsaturated oils, among them canola and olive, are probably the healthiest of all.

vegetable oils. These "partially hydrogenated" oils usually contain an unnatural configuration of fats called trans fats. They appear in many processed foods: hard margarines, vegetable shortenings, commercial baked goods, and deep-fried foods prepared in restaurants.

Trans fats have turned out to be as bad for the heart as saturated fats—maybe even worse. They not only raise levels of harmful LDL cholesterol but may also lower levels of beneficial HDL (high-density lipoprotein) cholesterol. In the Harvard study of women, researchers figured that for every 2 percent of calories switched from trans-rich hydrogenated oils to natural unsaturated oils, the risk of having a fatal heart attack goes down by an astounding 53 percent. Other studies of trans fats indicate similar risk levels for men.

Trans fats may pose other problems as well. A study of 700 postmenopausal European women found that those who ate the most trans fats had a 40 percent higher risk of breast cancer than did those who ate the least.

To reduce your intake of trans fats, choose liquid rather than solid cooking fats (oils instead of shortening) and soft rather than hard margarines. You may also estimate the trans-fat content by studying the product label (see box on page 144).

The large amounts of trans fat in vegetable shortening and saturated fat in butter predispose the body to heart disease.

The "good" fats

Fats aren't all bad. In fact, some of them can actually be good for you. Natural, unhydrogenated vegetable oils are primarily unsaturated, and unsaturated fats lower LDL ("bad") cholesterol levels. That's true of both monounsaturated fats (the kind in olive and canola oils) and polyunsaturated fats (the kind in corn, sunflower, and safflower oils).

Monounsaturated fats may be preferable because they are more stable and less likely to form free radicals, unstable oxygen molecules that may increase the risk of cancer. Studies conducted in Greece, Spain, and Italy linked olive oil and other sources of monounsaturates with a decreased risk of breast cancer. A study of more than 60,000 Swedish women produced the same results and, in addition,

Switching 5 percent of your calorie intake from saturated to unsaturated fats may decrease the risk of fatal heart attack by 42 percent.

Fat in Your Diet: How Low to Go?

Health Canada recommends that fats make up no more than 30 percent of our daily caloric intake, while some nutritionists advise that the upper limit be 20 percent or even lower. So, what to do? That depends.

A study of men with elevated cholesterol readings showed that for those with simple high cholesterol, 26 percent was the ideal, but for those who also had high amounts of triglycerides (blood fats that raise the risk of heart disease), 30 percent was best. (At lower levels of fat, beneficial HDL went down and triglycerides rose.) A diet with too little fat can also be a problem for people with diabetes or low HDL levels.

For people without these special health considerations, a goal of 25 percent is safe and may even reverse heart disease—but only if fats are replaced with complex carbohydrates from whole grains, fruits, and vegetables rather than with refined starches and sugars.

indicated that polyunsaturated oils slightly raise breast-cancer risk. This doesn't mean that women should guzzle olive oil, especially at about 120 calories per tablespoon. Some experts advise that in a diet in which 30 percent of calories come from fat, about 15 percent should come from monounsaturates. With a lower intake of total fat, about half should come from monounsaturates.

An alternative to olive oil is canola oil, which is versatile in cooking and contains the plant form of the omega-3 fats found in fish oil. (Omega-3 fats inhibit blood clotting, further reducing the risk of heart attack.) Foods that contain monounsaturated fats include avocados, nuts, and seeds.

Fat "impersonators"

To cut the fat yet keep the taste in such foods as salad dressing and ice cream, manufacturers rely on a variety of ingredients to provide the texture and flavor of fat: gums, emulsifiers, soluble fiber, and protein-sugar combinations.

In the United States, a product called olestra has been approved for sale and is used in some fried snack foods, such as potato chips. Olestra's fat-sugar molecules are so large that they pass out of the body unabsorbed. Unfortunately, they take with them carotenoids, beneficial plant compounds that may help prevent cancer. As well, olestra-laced snacks may cause abdominal cramps and diarrhea.

Moreover, there's no evidence that lower-fat products help in weight loss. Low-fat and fat-free foods aid in weight control only if they contain fewer calories than their higher-fat cousins—and only if you consume them with a similar eye toward moderation.

Trans fats, found in virtually all packaged baked goods, may increase the risk of heart attack.

Decoding Food Labels

The federal government has created strict definitions for terms relating to fat content:

Term on Label	Fat Content
Fat-free, free of fat, contains no fat, very low fat, ultra low fat	Less than $\frac{1}{2}$ gram per serving
Low-fat, low in fat, light in fat, lite in fat	No more than 3 grams per serving *and* less than 15 grams per 100 grams of dry matter
Reduced in fat, lower in fat than, % less fat than	At least 25 percent less per serving than regular product *and* at least $1\frac{1}{2}$ grams less per serving *and* no additional calories
Light or lite	Any of the above definitions for fat-free, low-fat, or reduced in fat
Lean	Ground meat: less than 17 percent; other meats: less than 10 percent
Extra-lean	Ground meat: less than 10 percent; other meats: less than $7\frac{1}{2}$ percent

Adding Up the Trans Fats

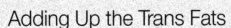

The amount of trans fat a product contains is not shown on the label, but you can figure it out if the amounts of saturated fat, unsaturated fat, and total fat are given. If a label lists 1 gram of saturated fat, 2 grams of monounsaturated fat, 1 gram of polyunsaturated fat, and 6 grams of total fat, the missing 2 grams are probably trans fat. Many people eat 8 to 12 grams of trans fat a day. One study suggests that cutting 4 grams of trans fat out of one's daily diet may reduce heart-attack risk by 50 percent.

Your geraniums, like yourself, need food to survive, and their meals consist of chemical nutrients. A few—carbon, hydrogen, and oxygen—are derived from air and water. The rest—nitrogen, phosphorus, potassium, and some trace elements—are absorbed from the soil or supplied by fertilizers.

Two kinds of fertilizers are used to help plants grow: organic types, which are derived mainly from plant and animal sources, and inorganic types, which are manufactured commercially—mainly from petrochemicals.

Inorganic fertilizers: the drawbacks

Potent and fast-acting, inorganic fertilizers can also be problematic. Used to excess, they may burn and even kill plants. Overuse may also kill earthworms and millions of "good" microorganisms that thrive in healthy soil.

Inorganic fertilizers can be dangerous to humans as well. Some contain nitrates, which in excess can contaminate groundwater that is used for drinking. In rare cases, infants who consume such tainted water may develop blue-baby syndrome, an impairment of the blood's ability to transport oxygen. And some manufactured fertilizers, especially those containing recycled wastes, may be fouled with lead and other heavy-metal residues. Since these residues can be absorbed by growing plants, they can end up in the food we eat.

When excessively or carelessly applied fertilizers (and this applies to organic fertilizers as well) are carried by rain into lakes and rivers, they pollute the waters and cause explosive bursts in the growth of aquatic plants. This growth depletes the water's oxygen supply, causing fish to die, which adds to the pollution.

What's a gardener to do?

Contact a nursery, soil testing laboratory, or your local office of Agriculture and Agri-Food Canada about having your soil tested. Some garden centers sell home soil testing kits. When you have the test results, buy only the types and amounts of nutrients you need. Commercially blended fertilizers list the per-

centages of nitrogen, phosphorus, and potassium. Follow the package directions carefully, and never leave fertilizer on sidewalks or driveways to be washed away or eaten by birds or other wildlife.

Organic fertilizers: the benefits

To avoid the problems that chemical fertilizers can cause, stick with organic ones. You can make your own by creating a compost heap from fallen leaves, grass clippings, and other garden waste. When these materials decay, they may supply all the nutrients your plants need. (At the very least, they will supplement other fertilizers.) Compost will also improve the soil's structure, or tilth, making it a better growing medium for the plants.

Manure is another soil additive that improves both fertility and tilth. It must be well rotted, however, because fresh manure can burn plants. Dehydrated cow manure is sold at garden centers, as are other types of manure. You can also use fish emulsion, earthworm castings, dried blood (rich in nitrogen), bonemeal (rich in phosphorus), and seaweed extract (rich in potassium).

To work fertilizer into the soil, water the area after applying, but not so much that you cause runoff.

Safety Basics

- Wear gloves when using fertilizers, and wash your hands afterward.
- Keep fertilizers in clearly labeled containers.
- Store fertilizers away from children and pets.

Fiber

Anyone who has polished off a bran muffin is well acquainted with fiber's most advertised benefit—it keeps you "regular." By doing so, fiber helps prevent constipation, hemorrhoids, and diverticulitis, a painful inflammation of small pouches along the colon wall. What's not as well known is fiber's increasing role in preventing chronic disease.

Unfortunately, most Canadians don't get enough fiber. To increase your daily intake, eat a variety of fiber-rich foods, always opting for fresh over processed and whole grains over refined grains.

Preventing disease

There are two kinds of fiber: insoluble (found in many grains, cereals, seeds, and vegetables) and soluble (found in beans, lentils, pears, apples, oats, and barley). Insoluble fiber speeds food through the colon and improves bowel health. Soluble fiber helps to lower blood cholesterol and to stabilize blood sugar. Both can help prevent such diseases as:

- **Colon cancer.** A large study suggests that a high-fiber, low-fat diet may help reduce the risk of developing precancerous polyps in the colon.
- **Heart disease.** A diet that includes at least 25 grams of fiber a day (compared to a diet with fewer than 15 grams) has been linked to a lower risk of heart disease.
- **Diabetes.** A study of 65,000 women showed that those who regularly ate cereal fiber as part of a healthy diet had a lower risk of developing adult-onset diabetes.

How to get more fiber

Fiber is abundant in many foods (see box, above right). Increasing your intake can be as easy as replacing your morning bagel with a

High-fiber foods leave less room for high-fat, high-calorie ones, and they're usually rich in vitamins and minerals to boot.

Founts of Fiber

A good source of fiber has at least 2.5 grams per serving. For packaged foods, check the labels.

Food	Fiber (grams)
Grains	
Shredded wheat (one biscuit)	2.5
Brown rice (¾ cup, cooked)	3
Oatmeal (¾ cup)	3
Whole wheat bread (two slices)	4
Raisin bran (¾ cup)	5
100% wheat bran breakfast cereal (⅓ cup)	8
Legumes	
Baked beans (½ cup)	3
Kidney beans (½ cup)	3
Lentils (½ cup)	4
Fruits	
Strawberries (½ cup)	2
Apple with skin (1 medium)	3
Orange (1 medium)	3
Pear with skin (1 medium)	4
Vegetables	
Brussels sprouts (½ cup)	2
Carrot (1 medium)	3
Potato with skin (1 medium, baked)	4

bowl of whole-grain cereal, which can provide an extra 4 grams. Health Canada's *Guidelines to Healthy Eating* recommends you aim for 20 to 35 grams of dietary fiber daily—achieved by eating the recommended servings of grains, vegetables, and fruits (leave the skins on). Excellent sources of fiber include whole-wheat bread, bran cereal, brown rice, legumes, vegetables (cooked or raw), or fresh, unpeeled fruit. Note: Gas, bloating, and abdominal cramps may result if you increase your fiber intake too quickly. Also, drink lots of liquids when consuming more fiber or the extra bulk may slow or block bowel function.

Fiber supplements can help, but, unlike high-fiber foods, they contain no nutrients and can be expensive. Take them only if a fiber-rich diet causes stomach distress. Avoid them if you have a serious intestinal disorder.

Fire Extinguishers

A lightweight fire extinguisher belongs in every home. But unless you know how and when to use it, you will be in trouble during an emergency. Extinguishers are designed to put out small, contained fires. Anything bigger is a job for the fire department.

Fire-extinguisher basics

Choosing the right fire extinguisher requires reading labels and considering the following:

- **Class.** In Canada, extinguishers are classified by the Underwriters' Laboratory of Canada (ULC) for different types of fires: A for basic fires (wood, cloth, and trash); B for kitchen and garage fires (gasoline, oil, grease, and painting supplies); and C for electrical fires (wiring and appliances). Using the wrong extinguisher can be very dangerous. A multipurpose ABC extinguisher is best for use in the home.
- **Size.** An extinguisher should be easy to handle. Small, 2.25-kilogram (5-pound) models are sufficient for most needs. A smaller ABC model should have a rating of at least 2–A:10–B:C. (The higher the numbers, the more chemicals the extinguisher contains and the better chance you'll have of putting out a fire.) A larger model should have a rating of at least 3–A:40–B:C. Smaller models empty in 10 seconds; larger ones, in 25 seconds.
- **Contents.** Most models contain ammonium phosphate, a dry chemical which is hard to clean up and can ruin electronic devices, such as computers. Kitchen extinguishers often contain sodium bicarbonate for fighting grease fires. (Note that an extinguisher isn't always the best way to put out a grease fire.) Some models are rechargeable, but disposable types are lighter and less expensive.

Don't wait until a fire starts to learn how to use a fire extinguisher.

Are you ready for a fire?

Install the extinguishers correctly in your home. Put one fire extinguisher in the kitchen and at least one on every floor, including the basement. (The rule of thumb is to have enough extinguishers so that you don't have to travel more than 12 meters/ 40 feet to get one.) All should be mounted out of the reach of small children, near an escape route, and far from any heat sources.

Every month check the pressure gauges and recharge or replace extinguishers if their pressure has dropped. (Nonrechargeable fire extinguishers should not be kept longer than 12 years.) Remember that an adequate home fire-safety system does not rely on fire extinguishers alone—it also includes operational smoke detectors and planned escape routes familiar to all family members.

How to use an extinguisher correctly

Every adult in your home should know how to use each fire extinguisher. In an emergency, there is no time to read instructions. The PASS method makes them easy to remember:

- **P**ull the safety pin and stand 1.8 to 3 meters (6 to 10 feet) from the flame.
- **A**im low, at the base of the fire.
- **S**queeze the handle or lever.
- **S**weep the extinguisher from side to side in order to blanket the fire. Most important: Never turn your back on a fire, even if it seems to be out. It can flare up again.

Using a fire extinguisher on a grease fire can cause the grease to splash and spread the fire. Instead, wear an oven mitt and smother the fire with a tight-fitting lid.

Fighting Fire:

- Get everyone out of the building.
- Call the fire department.
- Keep near a door which can be used as an escape route.
- Avoid inhaling smoke, vapors, and fumes.
- If you fail to put out the fire immediately, get out of the building without delay.

Fireworks

What is more spectacular than a fireworks display? Left in the hands of experts, the large pyrotechnic displays (which are controlled electronically) are surprisingly safe. The backyard fireworks, some of them legal and some not, are those that lead to emergency room visits—many for children with burns or severe eye injuries. So if you decide to celebrate on your own, keep safety uppermost in your mind.

"Legal" doesn't always mean "safe"

As would be expected, the most serious fireworks injuries—lost fingers and eyes, severe burns, deafness—are caused by powerful, illegal fireworks, such as M-80s, cherry bombs, and ash cans. Bottle rockets are also illegal culprits. If the rocket explodes prematurely in the bottle, it can send shards of glass and metal flying at high speed toward bystanders. Eye injuries are a common result and often necessitate removal of the eye.

Countless other injuries are caused by fireworks that are legal in many areas. Ground spinners and sparklers pose a special risk because they appear to be safer than they really are. Do not throw sparklers or touch the burning tip, which can reach 538°C (1000°F). The best way to dispose of sparklers is in a bucket of water; they can easily start fires when carelessly tossed away. Remember: only adults should set off fireworks.

Pyrotechnic precautions

Before using fireworks of any kind, find out if they are legal in your area. (In Canada, fireworks can only be sold to buyers 18 or older. Some cities restrict their sale and use to special holidays.) To be safe:

- Only buy fireworks that bear the name of the manufacturer and bilingual instructions for the product's safe use.
- Plan ahead and always follow the instructions to the letter.
- Don't hold fireworks in your hand while you are lighting them. Instead, place them on the ground or on another flat surface. Aerial fireworks, such as Roman candles, must be buried to at least half their length.
- Store fireworks in a cool, dry, secured place, away from kids and any possible ignition source.
- Never carry fireworks in your pocket.
- Always use them outdoors in an open space away from dry grass or leaves.
- Make sure that spectators and passersby remain at a safe distance.
- Light only one device at a time.
- When setting off fireworks, wear safety glasses (available at hardware stores), and never place your face or any other part of your body directly over the device.
- Keep a bucket of water or a garden hose on hand for emergencies.
- If the device doesn't seem to ignite, don't stand over it or try to relight it, because it could go off at any time. Instead, douse it thoroughly with water.
- Never explode fireworks inside a container.
- If you think you see someone using illegal fireworks, call the police.

As a result of injuries to children in the early 1970s, firecrackers were restricted in Canada solely for sale and use in traditional ethnic celebrations.

For Pets' Sake

Animals hate fireworks—especially cats and dogs, whose ears are four times more sensitive than ours. Dogs particularly dislike low banging noises and may react by racing away or becoming aggressive. A few tips for humane humans:

- Leave your pets at home (with plenty of water) when you go to see the fireworks. Close the curtains and leave a radio or TV playing to muffle the noise.
- Put a cloth cover over bird, rabbit, and hamster cages, or move them to a quiet part of the house.
- If you have an especially sensitive pet, try putting a drop of mineral oil in the animal's ears to muffle the sound, or ask your vet to prescribe a pet tranquilizer.

Fish

Whole fish should be displayed so that the bellies are lower than the head, allowing seepage to drain away from the fish. Fillets should rest on plastic wrap or in a metal pan instead of directly on ice.

What's for supper: fish or hamburger? If your entrée once lived in water, it will deliver high-quality protein as rich in B vitamins as landlubber protein is. It will also contain hardly any of the saturated fat that elevates cholesterol levels. Those two facts alone make fish a heart-healthy choice. But seafood also happens to be the best dietary source of omega-3 fatty acids, a special type of polyunsaturated fat that protects you from heart disease in many ways.

Preventing heart attacks

Omega-3 fatty acids have a long list of beneficial effects on the heart. For example:

- **Blood clotting**. The tendency of blood to readily form clots increases heart attack risk. The omega-3 fatty acids in fish inhibit this action—especially when the fish is eaten as part of a low-fat diet.
- **Triglycerides**. The risk of heart disease rises when triglyceride levels of the blood are elevated. Omega-3s lower those levels.
- **Endothelial damage.** Studies are beginning to suggest that damage to the arteries increases cardiovascular risk. Omega-3s are thought to lessen that risk.
- **LDL cholesterol.** This harmful type of cholesterol is linked to an increased risk of

heart attack. A recent study found that a diet high in fish lowers levels by as much as 40 percent.

- **Blood pressure.** People with elevated levels are at great risk for stroke and heart disease. Omega-3s tend to lower blood pressure, at least temporarily.

All told, the benefits of eating fish can account for a dramatic reduction in the risk of serious heart problems. Several studies found that eating as little as one or two servings of fish a week significantly lowers risk. One study of nearly 2,000 men reported that those who ate an average of just two servings of fish a week—that adds up to about 200 grams (7 ounces) of fish—cut their risk of dying from a heart attack almost in half.

Catching more benefits from fish

Recent studies indicate that the fatty acids found in fish seem to have a positive effect on medical problems other than cardiovascular disease. Future studies may show that these conditions could be alleviated or even prevented by a diet rich in omega-3s.

- **Inflammatory diseases.** Rheumatoid arthritis, unlike osteoarthritis, is an autoimmune disease marked by inflammation of the joints. Studies show that the fat from fish may decrease morning stiffness and swelling associated with the ailment. People with Crohn's disease, an intermittent inflammation of the bowels, and psoriasis, a skin disease, may possibly benefit as well.
- **Breast cancer.** In animal studies, omega-3s have inhibited similar tumors. Scientists agree that it's too early to recommend eating fish to prevent breast cancer, but in a small-scale human study, intake of omega-3s appears to have increased the amount of beneficial fatty acids in breast tissue.
- **Abnormal fetal development.** In the last trimester of pregnancy, an omega-3 fatty acid that is essential to brain and eye development is laid down in the brain membranes of a fetus. Infants born prematurely don't receive an adequate supply of this crucial fatty acid. The United States Food

and Drug Administration (FDA) is considering adding it to formulas for such infants, to see if their bodies are able to make use of it after birth.

Is fish safe to eat?

You are more likely to get sick after eating chicken or hamburger than fish. Still, fish is a highly perishable food that is vulnerable to pollution, so take precautions, whether eating at home or dining out.

Buy fish from reputable retailers. Whole fish can rest on a thick bed of ice; fillets should be placed on a metal pan or plastic wrap, not in direct contact with ice. Fish should smell mild and clean—never fishy or like ammonia. Whole fish should have clear eyes, shiny skin, and bright red gills. Fillets should be free of bruises. Frozen fish can be very fresh, especially if flash-frozen when caught. It should be solid, with no ice crystals.

To minimize your exposure to industrial pollutants, eat a wide variety of fish. Fish grown on farms are generally safe, although the water they are bred in isn't always pure; check with your fish dealer about the source. As for wild varieties, limit your consumption

of fish caught in habitats near land, such as lake and sport fish and shellfish; their flesh is more likely to contain industrial pollutants.

Deep-water ocean fish are the safest wild fish, although toxic metals like mercury can become concentrated in the flesh of ocean predators, such as sharks and swordfish. Some experts suggest that adults eat no more than 200 grams (7 ounces) a week of these fish. Women of childbearing age, especially if pregnant, should eat them only once a month.

The 10 most popular seafood species sold are relatively low in mercury: canned tuna, shrimp, pollock, salmon, cod, catfish, clams, flatfish, crabs, and scallops. Fish with slightly higher levels are still relatively safe: bass, crappie, pike, mahimahi, mackerel, snapper, and tuna. (Canned tuna is likely to have lower levels than the tuna sold for steaks or sushi because it comes from smaller species, such as albacore or skipjack, that absorb less of the pollutant in their flesh.)

Raw fish (sashimi, sushi, ceviche) can harbor bacteria along with various intestinal parasites. Generally, sushi bars freeze fish before serving it to kill any microbes.

Before cooking fish, trim off fatty areas (in the back and belly). Broiling fish tends to reduce any toxic residues it may contain.

The Omega-3 Report: Good Fats in Fish

Lean fish is low in calories and saturated fat, but even the fattiest fish contains less fat than the very leanest beef, and none of the dangerous saturated kind. Most important, fatty fish is the major dietary source of the valuable omega-3 fatty acids. (A source of a fatty acid similar to that of deepwater fish is flaxseed oil.)

High in omega-3s More than 0.9 gram*	Moderate in omega-3s 0.5 to 0.9 gram*	Low in omega-3s Less than 0.5 gram*
Anchovies	Bass	Catfish
Atlantic halibut	Bluefish	Cod
Carp	Halibut	Flounder
Herring	Pompano	Grouper
Mackerel	Rockfish	Haddock
Salmon (Atlantic, Chinook, Coho, King, Pink, Sockeye)	Salmon (Chum)	Mahimahi
Sardines	Shark	Perch
Sturgeon	Smelt	Pike
Trout (Lake, Rainbow)	Striped sea bass	Pollock
Tuna (Albacore, Bluefin)	Swordfish	Snapper
Whitefish	Turbot	Sole
	Yellowfin tuna	Trout (Brook, Sea)

* per 100-gram (3 ½-ounce) serving

Floor Coverings

Ripping out old, dusty wall-to-wall carpeting—a major source of allergens—and replacing it with brand-new vinyl flooring seems like a sound, healthy strategy. Not necessarily. As it turns out, vinyl and other types of flooring may also make you sick. At particular risk are children, who often play on the floor for hours.

The risks underfoot

Here's the lowdown on the problems associated with the most common flooring options:

- **Hardwood floors** are one of the safest types of flooring. The wood emits few fumes, and the installation usually requires no toxic adhesives or glues.

- **Laminated-wood flooring** is composed of a thin layer of hardwood glued to a plywood or wood-product base. Less expensive than a hardwood floor, it can emit noxious chemicals, from both the glues used in lamination and the adhesives used to keep the flooring in place.

- **Linoleum** is a natural product made of powdered wood, linseed oil, and pine resins with a jute backing, but it may still irritate sensitive people.

- **Vinyl**, easier than linoleum to install, is made of a synthetic resin, usually thermoplastic polyvinyl chloride (PVC) combined with compounds that make it malleable. Vinyl is impenetrable to dust particles, pollen, and mold spores and is easy to keep clean, but it can also emit noxious chemical odors that irritate some people. Warning: Old vinyl tiles may contain asbestos, which is harmless unless the tiles are damaged. If possible, leave them in place and install new flooring over them. If you must replace them, have them removed only by an asbestos contractor.

- **Ceramic tile** is not only one of the oldest flooring choices but also one of the healthiest. Made of baked clay and sometimes finished with a glaze, ceramic tiles are an attractive and easy-to-maintain floor for any room. Other natural choices are cork tiles, marble, brick, slate, and terrazzo.

Ceramic tiles, especially those that are glazed, are a healthy choice.

What's under the floor?

Most flooring materials go on top of a subfloor that is often made of particleboard, composed of wood shavings held together with urea-formaldehyde glue. This glue can emit low levels of formaldehyde fumes for many years, causing throat and eye irritation, headaches, and nausea in susceptible people.

Hardwood floors are one of the safest types of flooring. They usually require no toxic adhesives or glues.

If formaldehyde bothers you, seal the particleboard with three coats of polyurethane or oil-based paint. (Air out the room until it dries.) Or simply use solid wood—or particleboard that is not made with formaldehyde.

Adhesives used to attach flooring materials to subfloors are another potential hazard. Most contain a number of toxic chemicals, including formaldehyde and acrylic plastics.

Taking the fumes out of your floor

If emissions from adhesives and finishes irritate you, choose prefinished solid-wood flooring. Planks are best; they can be nailed into place, eliminating the need for glues. For subflooring, choose plywood or pine boards. For flooring requiring adhesives, look for less toxic types, such as carpenter's glue for laminated wood, water-based adhesives for vinyl, and thinset mortars for ceramic tiles. Self-sticking vinyl tiles, which require no additional adhesives, are also available. Finally, air out any type of flooring before you install it.

Marble, wood parquet, and vinyl tiles are generally safe, but the adhesives used to install them may not be.

Fluoride

In the early 1930s researchers found that people living in areas where drinking water contained high levels of fluoride (a naturally occurring mineral) had fewer cavities than other people. Today, 40 percent of Canadians drink water that has been fluoridated. Now it's also a common ingredient in toothpastes, mouthwashes, and dental treatments.

Fluoride additives have helped to significantly reduce what was one of the most serious dental problems in North America just a few decades ago—multiple cavities among children. Still, adding the mineral to a community's tap water remains controversial because some experts worry that consuming large amounts of fluoride could be dangerous.

Protection for the ivories

When used topically in toothpastes, mouthwashes, and dental treatments, fluoride protects and strengthens the outside of the tooth, making it more resistant to decay. Ingesting it—fluoride is a natural ingredient in many foods and can be taken in supplement form—provides benefits, too. It can strengthen teeth that are forming (in young children) and help protect against cavities in all age groups. Studies also indicate that fluoride ingested in the proper amounts may be useful in treating osteoporosis.

Flaws of fluoride

Consuming too much fluoride may cause dental fluorosis, a largely cosmetic condition that is characterized by mottled, discolored teeth. In addition, fluoride may adversely affect people with kidney disease who are on dialysis. For this reason, patients may be cautioned not to drink fluoridated water.

Ingesting a large amount of fluoride (a rare occurrence) may cause nausea, vomiting, diarrhea, and abdominal pain. Research continues on its potential long-term effects, but the possibility that fluoride in drinking water contributes to cancer or other major diseases has not been proven in tests. Health Canada and other health organizations consider fluoridated drinking water safe.

Monitoring your intake

Although the public is relatively safe from toxic amounts, Health Canada has stated—in the *Guidelines for Canadian Drinking Water Quality*—that the maximum acceptable level of fluoride in tapwater is 1.5 milligrams per liter, or 1.5 parts per million. Most Canadians over the age of five consume fluoride within safe levels—between 17 and 78 micrograms of fluoride per kilogram of body weight each day. Children under the age of five are apt to consume more because they tend to swallow toothpaste while brushing their teeth. Even though it may be difficult to calculate exactly how much fluoride you consume, there are ways to keep fluoride consumption within the range considered safe by Health Canada:

- Ask your municipal water supplier how

much fluoride is in your tap water. Consider taking fluoride supplements only if your drinking water is not fluoridated.
- Never give fluoridated mouthwash to children under age six—they may swallow it.
- If your job involves industrial processes that emit hydrogen fluoride, be aware that exposure to it and other airborne fluorides may severely irritate the respiratory tract, skin, and eyes. Talk with your physician.

CAUTION!

Most brands of bottled water do not contain fluoride. If you drink only nonfluoridated bottled water, you may put yourself at high risk of tooth decay.

Supervise your children's fluoride intake: They should use only a pea-size dollop of toothpaste per brushing; they shouldn't swallow any toothpaste (always have them rinse their mouth); and they shouldn't take fluoride supplements if their water is fluoridated.

Flying

Although accident statistics indicate that flying is twice as safe as taking a train or bus and 30 times safer than driving on a highway, air travel involves a number of health hazards, most of which can be avoided by taking precautions.

Flight jitters? You're not alone. Although air travel is the safest mode of transportation, 90 percent of people admit to having some fear of flying.

The not-so-healthy skies

Spending hours on a cramped, crowded plane isn't conducive to good health. However, you can buffer yourself from a long flight, whether you're a frequent flier or a first timer:

• **Stale air.** Planes built since the 1980s are equipped with air systems that supply half fresh, half recycled air into the cabin. For the best air, avoid flying at peak times (when planes are crowded). If you feel dizzy or faint, ask a flight attendant if the pilot can increase the amount of fresh air.

• **Plugged ears.** Changes in air pressure can make your ears feel plugged. To relieve this discomfort, chew gum or yawn until your ears "pop." Feeding babies during the plane's descent helps allay their ear problems.

• **Dehydration.** To counter the effects of dry cabin air, drink plenty of fluids. Avoid alcohol and beverages that are carbonated or caffeinated: both types of drinks can dehydrate you further.

• **Nasal congestion.** If you have a cold or allergies, be aware that the change in air pressure can cause acute sinus pain. Take an oral decongestant an hour before your flight lands, and use a decongestant nasal spray a half hour before landing.

• **Colds and other viruses.** The air filters on planes can prevent bacteria and clumps of viruses from circulating in the cabin but do nothing about individual cold and flu viruses. If you're seated next to someone who's coughing and sneezing, move to a different seat if you can. Wash your hands often and keep them away from your nose and eyes. Also moisten nasal passages with a saline nasal spray.

• **Air sickness.** Travelers may suffer from motion sickness when the plane encounters turbulence. If you are prone to motion sickness, request a seat near the wing, where the ride is steadier. Take a motion-sickness medication before and during the flight, or try ginger in fresh or pill form.

• **Plane food.** Often tasteless, high in fat, and low in nutrients, plane food deserves its less-than-stellar reputation. Special meals—vegetarian, low-fat, kosher—can be ordered when you make your reservation. Better yet, avoid unsavory plane food altogether by bringing your own healthy snacks on board.

• **"Economy-class syndrome."** Caused by changes in air pressure and sitting in a cramped space for long periods, this condition is marked by stiff joints and swollen ankles and feet. (A blood clot can even form in the lower leg.) To combat this, don't cross your legs and, when permitted, walk around the cabin and stretch. Wear lace-up shoes to accommodate swelling.

• **Jet lag.** This condition, characterized by disorientation and restlessness or fatigue during adjustment to a new time zone, can occur when traveling east or west, but typically it is more pronounced when traveling east. To minimize its effects, adjust your sleeping and eating times closer to those of your destination during the week before you travel. Avoid alcohol and caffeine while flying, and expose yourself to sun-

Flying is twice as safe as taking a train or bus and 30 times safer than driving on a highway.

154

an ounce of **Prevention**

Be Prepared—Just in Case

- Wear clothing made of natural fibers. Avoid panty hose and other synthetic fabrics; fire may make them melt and stick to your skin. Wear flat or low-heeled shoes made of canvas or leather, and keep them on during takeoff and landing.

- Use a child safety seat when traveling with a child under two years of age. Check with the airline for its policy regarding these seats when making flight reservations.

- Always find out where the nearest exit is, and count the rows between you and at least two exits so you'll know how far to go in case the cabin fills with smoke.

- There's no "safest" seat on a plane, but sitting near an exit will make it easier to get out quickly.

---

light and engage in some mild exercise once you arrive. Whatever you do, your goal should be to sleep at night when you arrive at your destination.

- **Fear of flying.** It is estimated that 9 out of 10 people have some fear of flying. Many of us fly anyway and do so with only mild anxiety. For others the fear of flying can lead to panic attacks or may be a symptom of an anxiety disorder. Most cases can be overcome with counseling. A course of medication may also be prescribed.

Have a safe, smooth flight

Follow these tips to make any flight safer:

- Stow carry-on luggage securely in the overhead bins or under the seat in front of you. Luggage, especially a heavy or sharp-cornered bag, may injure you or a fellow passenger if it falls from overhead.

- If you spot snow or ice on the wings and

there's been no announcement about de-icing, notify a flight attendant to alert the pilot. Passengers have a better view of the wings than the pilot does.

- Keep your seat belt fastened when seated; unexpected turbulence can cause injuries.

- Follow the attendants' directions regarding in-flight use of electronic devices, which may interfere with the plane's electronics, especially during takeoff and landing.

What to do in an emergency

Eighty percent of airplane crashes are survivable. Most occur during takeoff and landing, when the plane overshoots the runway or when its landing gear fails, for example. The biggest danger in such crashes is fire or fumes, which can race through the cabin within 90 seconds. In fact, most casualties of survivable crashes result from the inhalation of smoke or toxic fumes.

In an emergency, stay calm and listen to the flight attendants' instructions. If the plane is on the ground and there is fire or smoke in the cabin, cover your nose and mouth and walk crouching down or crawl to the exit. Don't take anything with you. Before you open an exit door, check for fire outside; go to another exit if you see flames. Once you do exit, get away from the plane quickly.

Listen to the flight attendant. Although you've heard it before, you may improve your chances of surviving an accident by noting safety instructions and reviewing the emergency procedures.

Food Additives

Being a savvy shopper isn't easy these days. The ingredients in many packaged foods can read like hieroglyphics. After stumbling through a list of unpronounceable chemicals, you've probably wondered, "Where's the food?" Today most processed foods contain additives, both natural and man-made. Although consumers have a right to be wary of them, the good news is that most additives are safe and, in some cases, can even be beneficial. In fact, more worrisome may be the so-called accidental additives (including pesticides, hormones, and antibiotics) that often wind up on our plates.

Processed and preserved: The foods above contain (left to right) BHT, FD&C Red No. 40, and nitrates —not likely to make you sick but probably best consumed in moderation.

Why food additives?

Over the past century, as more people moved from farms to cities, the demand increased for a year-round supply of many foods. As a result, food manufacturers stepped up the use of additives to extend shelf life, ensure the safety and heighten the appeal of their products. By the late 1990s, some 3,000 food additives had been approved by Health Canada. (A revised version of Health Canada's tables of food additives, now being prepared, will list some 407 additives.) Here are some common categories:

- **Preservatives.** Retard deterioration and spoilage by preventing the growth of bacteria and molds. Examples: antioxidants (vitamin C, vitamin E, BHA, BHT) and antimicrobials (calcium propionate or sodium benzoate).
- **Fortifiers.** Boost nutritional value. Examples: vitamins A, C, and D; calcium; folic acid; iron; riboflavin.
- **Color enhancers.** Improve esthetic appeal. Examples: beta-carotene, FD&C Blue Nos. 1 and 2, Red Nos. 3 and 40, and Yellow Nos. 5 and 6.
- **Flavor enhancers.** Heighten taste. Examples: hydrolyzed vegetable protein, monosodium glutamate, disodium guanylate.
- **Emulsifiers or thickeners.** Add texture and consistency. Examples: gum arabic, lecithin, guar gum.
- **Humectants.** Maintain moisture in foods. Examples: dextrose, glycerin, invert sugar.

The safety issue

Canada has one of the safest food supplies in the world. Federal authorities strictly regulate food additives. Before being approved, new additives undergo long-term testing. Food additives, like other chemicals, may produce adverse effects if consumed in large amounts. However, the quantities in food products are regulated to avert this possibility. Except for a very few people, who may be sensitive to certain additives, such as sulfites, adverse reactions are rare. For the general public, the benefits of additives far outweigh the risks.

Ironically, the food additives that pose the greatest health risk may be natural, not synthetic: sodium and sugar (often in the form

On the Horizon Several synthetic fat substitutes, which pass through the body without being absorbed, are under development. One substitute, olestra (Olean), is awaiting approval in Canada. It reduces one's fat intake but also lowers the absorption rates of cancer-fighting carotenes and phytochemicals found in fruits and vegetables, and it may cause abdominal cramps and diarrhea. The long-term effects of olestra are not known.

Common Food Additives

Most food additives are perfectly harmless, but some may cause adverse effects in susceptible individuals. All of the additives listed below have been approved by Health Canada. Nevertheless, some experts suggest that you may want to limit your intake of these substances.

Additive	Function	Found In	Possible Side Effects
Aspartame	Artificial sweetener	Soft drinks, chewing gum; also used as an additive in drugs, especially in children's medications	May trigger headaches and migraines in some people.
BHA or BHT	Preservative/ antioxidant	High-fat foods, such as bakery items, potato chips, oils, cereals	May cause allergic reactions.
FD&C Yellow No. 5 (tartrazine)	Artificial color enhancer	Candy, ice cream, beverages, custards	May cause allergic reactions, such as hives.
MSG (monosodium glutamate)	Considered to be a food ingredient	Restaurant food, bouillon cubes, soups	May cause headaches, drowsiness, nausea, rapid heartbeat, tingling in face or arms.
Sodium Nitrate/ Sodium Nitrite	Preservative/ antimicrobial	Hot dogs, sausages, ham, processed lunch meats, smoked fish	May increase the risk of cancer; nitrates are converted by the body to nitrosamines, which are carcinogens; may interact with some drugs.
Sorbic Acid (potassium sorbate, calcium sorbate)	Preservative	Yogurts, processed cheeses, pickles and sauces, juices, jams, jellies	No adverse effects
Sulfites (sodium sulfite, sulfur dioxide, sodium or potassium bisulfate, sodium or potassium metabisulfite)	Preservative/ antioxidant	Dried, canned, or frozen fruit; wine; beer; maraschino cherries; bakery items; canned shrimp; precut potatoes; olives; bottled lemon juice	May cause asthma attacks, hives, diarrhea, nausea, and, in some cases, anaphylactic shock.

of dextrose, corn syrup, sucrose, or fructose). The average North American is said to consume up to 68 kilograms (150 pounds) of sugar and as much as 7 kilograms (15 pounds) of salt a year, mostly from processed foods. To limit your consumption, avoid convenience foods and eat a variety of fresh foods.

Another area of concern is the effect of food additives on children. Certain brands of commercial baby food contain added sugar, salt, and modified food starch, which is why some health experts recommend organic baby-food products. Some research has linked food additives (particularly artificial flavoring, artificial coloring, and sugar) with hyperactivity in children, although there is no solid evidence to support this.

Finally, some food additives may interact with certain drugs. Possible culprits include nitrites (found in processed meats), cyclamates (artificial sweeteners), and methyl polysiloxane (found in cooking oil). More research on the problem is needed.

Subtracting additives from your diet

If you are concerned about ingesting too many food additives, the solution is fairly simple: eat more fresh meat, poultry, and fish instead of smoked or processed versions; limit your intake of junk food, prepackaged food, and diet sodas and other foods that contain artificial sweeteners; opt for fresh foods rather than canned whenever possible; and buy organic food when feasible.

Don't look at natural additives, such as those derived from corn, beets, or soybeans, as safer alternatives. All foods are composed of chemicals, and identical nutrients can be produced in the laboratory. In the end, natural additives aren't necessarily superior to artificial ones.

Lunch meats contain nitrates and nitrites, which prevent the formation of botulin. Nitrites also bond with compounds called amines to form nitrosamines, which are carcinogenic.

Formaldehyde

When building or renovating, use oriented strand board instead of other pressed-wood products. It releases less formaldehyde.

In the chemistry lab, formaldehyde is known as a VOC, or volatile organic compound, meaning that it becomes a gas at room temperature. This gas—present in a wide variety of items that you use every day—is suspected of triggering a number of health problems, from mild sensitivities to cancer.

Everywhere you look

Formaldehyde is in products all around you: building materials, household goods, office supplies, and toiletries. It is most concentrated in pressed-wood products (including particleboard, hardwood plywood, and fiberboard), which are used to make furniture, kitchen cabinets, wall paneling, and shelving. Levels have been greatly reduced in the past 15 years, but they are still a concern.

An ingredient in coatings and preservatives, formaldehyde is found in many paints and some adhesives for floor tiles and carpets. It is also chemically released by compounds used to treat certain fabrics, especially wrinkle-free types. (Many Canadian homes built in the 1970s were insulated with urea-formaldehyde foam, but the substance was banned in 1980.) Deodorants, shampoos, nail hardeners, and other cosmetics contain formaldehyde in lesser amounts.

You can't see formaldehyde, but when it permeates the air—sometimes with a pungent odor—it can cause fatigue, headache, nausea, rashes, sniffling, coughing, wheezing, and burning in the nose, eyes, and throat. At elevated levels, it can also bring on chest tightness and breathing difficulties. Emissions increase as temperature and humidity rise. Although the emissions generally drop significantly within about six months, a product may release low levels of the gas for years.

Many people are hypersensitive to formaldehyde, and even those who aren't may develop health problems from continuous exposure to it. Children are especially likely to suffer ill effects. Studies have shown the gas to cause nasal tumors in rats. Although its effect on humans is not yet certain, it may increase the risk of several forms of cancer.

If you suspect that formaldehyde levels are high in your home, consult the Canada Mortgage and Housing Corporation's *Clean Air Guide* (available at 1-800-668-CMHC). Testing for indoor air quality is possible, but note that it may be costly—and single formaldehyde readings are not always reliable.

an ounce of Prevention

Minimizing Formaldehyde in the Home

- Paint paneled walls with new interior paints designed to absorb formaldehyde emissions.

- When choosing building materials, look for fiberboard and particleboard that contain no formaldehyde, such as those made from wheat.

- Purchase furniture made of solid wood instead of pressed wood when feasible.

- If you have pressed-wood furniture, coat all exposed surfaces with varnish or polyurethane. Make certain the sealant itself does not contain formaldehyde. Or seal the edges of pressed wood with aluminum tape.

- Keep your house well ventilated (ideally, use a mechanical ventilation system). Maintain a cool temperature and low humidity.

- If you have urea-formaldehyde foam insulation, check for moisture. Have a specialist remove wet or deteriorating foam.

- Wash permanent-press sheets and clothing before using them. Better still, avoid permanent-press fabrics altogether, along with those labeled "shrinkproof" or "water-repellent."

Fried Food

Fried foods are a nutritionist's nightmare. They're high in fat—often the worst kind of fat—and high in calories, and they may create cancer-causing by-products. It's no surprise, then, that many experts strongly recommend cutting down on such foods, using other cooking options, such as baking and broiling, and, when frying, following some basic rules that minimize fat and calories.

The problem with frying . . .

Frying means cooking in fat. The more fat that is absorbed by the food, the more calories that are added. For example, a peeled 200-gram (7-ounce) potato has 220 calories and 0.2 grams of fat when baked, compared with French fries at 632 calories and 33 grams of fat. Breaded foods may soak up even more fat.

Some types of fat are more problematic than others. Fast foods are often made with partially hydrogenated vegetable oils—dubbed "fry oils"—which are high in trans fats. These highly processed fats raise your LDL (low-density lipoprotein) cholesterol levels, increasing the chances of heart disease.

The way cooking oils are handled makes a difference, too. Heating the oil to high temperatures so that it smokes can create compounds that heighten cancer risk. If you fail to filter oils or to replace them frequently, you end up with degraded residues that can cause stomach problems and may be carcinogenic.

. . . and how to get around it

By using fresh vegetable oils, frying at the correct temperature, and replacing oils frequently, cooks in both restaurants and homes can make fried foods that are less harmful.

Start with foods (except meats and fish) at room temperature. Cook with olive, canola, peanut, corn, or safflower oil. Using a frying thermometer, heat the oil to 190°C (375°F).

Place food in small batches in a wire basket, and gently lower it into the oil. The hiss you hear when the food hits the hot oil is the sound of water in the food being released as steam. Fat seeps into the food to replace it. If you keep the oil hot enough to cook the food quickly 185°C to 199°C (365°F to 390°F) and remove the food as soon as it stops hissing, less oil will be absorbed.

When you remove the food from the oil, drain it on a wire rack placed over a cookie sheet. Follow that by shaking it quickly in a brown paper bag or patting it with paper towels to absorb excess fat.

Don't overpack food into a fryer. It lengthens the cooking time, which allows the food to absorb more oil.

CAUTION!

If oil smokes during frying, remove it from the heat to prevent a fire. Since overheating ruins the oil, discard it after it has cooled.

On the Horizon Healthier French fries may be in your future. Researchers at Oxford University have developed potatoes with a higher starch content, which means that they have a lower water content. Because fat replaces water during frying, these modified potatoes should absorb less fat as they cook.

Frozen Food

In 1820 freezing food meant putting it in the icehouse packed with blocks of natural ice carved laboriously from lakes. Today we take for granted the luxuries of June peas in December and raspberries any time of the year. But frozen foods are more than a convenience. Freezing is the best way to preserve the nutrients in fresh foods. Vegetables picked at their peak may be even fresher than "fresh" produce that sits in the supermarket for days or weeks on end.

The big chill: Buying food in bulk and freezing it means fewer trips to the supermarket with little nutritional sacrifice.

How Long Will It Keep?

Food	Months in the freezer
Processed meats (e.g., bacon, hot dogs)	1 to 2
Ground meat or poultry	3 to 4
Cooked ground meat (e.g., meatloaf)	2 to 3
Small cuts of meat, poultry parts	3 to 6
Roasts, whole chickens	Up to 12
Soups and stews	2 to 3
Breads	2 to 4
Egg whites	12

Words to freeze by

Foods that freeze slowly or thaw and then refreeze develop large ice crystals. These crystals rupture the food's cell walls, making the food mushy. They also absorb water-soluble vitamins (such as vitamin C), which end up down the drain when the food is defrosted. To prevent ice crystals from forming, keep your freezer at −18°C/0°F. Also keep it full; a full freezer keeps food colder than an empty one does. At the supermarket, reject packages of frozen foods with ice crystals on them; they have melted and refrozen. Buy frozen foods last and unpack them first.

When freezing food, leave some space around the items to speed the freezing process; once they freeze, you can stack them. Use freezer-safe wraps or bags, heavy-duty aluminum foil, or plastic or glass containers. When using freezer bags or plastic containers, remove as much air as possible before sealing them. The goal is to keep air away from food to prevent freezer burn—dehydration caused by exposure to air. One technique is to wrap foods tightly in plastic wrap, then again in foil. If you freeze meats in their original supermarket wrap, add a second layer of wrap, since supermarket wraps are porous.

When freezing certain vegetables, blanch them first by briefly boiling or steaming them, then cool them quickly in an ice bath. This slows down enzyme activity that can cause color and flavor changes as well as the loss of nutrients. For fruits, a bath in lemon juice or citric acid does the trick.

Defrost without danger

You've probably heard that it is unsafe to defrost food on the counter. Why? Because the inside can stay frozen while the outside gets warm enough (above 4°C/40°F) for bacteria to grow. Here are safer ways to defrost:

- **In the refrigerator.** This method is very safe, but it takes about 24 hours for every 2 kilograms (5 pounds) of food. Once defrosted, the food can be refrozen.
- **Cold-water bath.** Faster. Seal the food in a leakproof bag and immerse it in cold water; change the water every 30 minutes. Cook before refreezing.
- **Microwave.** Fastest. Follow the directions on the package or the microwave, then cook immediately. Cook before refreezing.

CAUTION!

If the power fails and food begins to thaw, cook it right away. If it has been above 4°C/40°F for more than two hours, throw it out.

Fruit

An apple a day: You know it's a wholesome snack, but can it really keep the doctor away? Yes. People who eat apples frequently are less likely to have heart attacks or strokes or to develop any of several kinds of cancer. The apple's pectin, a soluble fiber found just beneath the skin, can take some of the credit because it helps regulate cholesterol. The rest goes to plant chemicals called flavonoids. Fruits are also good sources of flavonoids, as well as fiber and vitamins and minerals. So it's no surprise that eating plenty of fruit is associated with a lower risk of heart disease, high blood pressure, and several cancers.

Take it to heart

Fiber is another plus that fruits provide. In most fruits, some of the fiber is soluble, which lowers blood cholesterol and helps prevent heart disease. Moreover, most fruits are also low in sodium and high in potassium—a winning combination that lowers the risk of high blood pressure. In one study, people who ate four to five servings of fruit each day, four to five servings of vegetables, and three servings of low-fat dairy products, along with grains and lean meat, fish, or poultry, lowered their blood pressure as much as if they had taken prescription drugs—with no side effects. The drop in blood pressure occurred within two weeks of starting the diet.

Medicine bowl: Fruit fiber promotes bowel regularity. And pectin, found in apples, strawberries, and citrus fruits, lowers blood-cholesterol levels.

An answer to cancer?

Exactly what is protective in fruits remains unknown. It may be the complex interaction of many different nutrients and other compounds that has a protective effect. The Canadian Cancer Society recommends eating a variety of fruits (and vegetables), including those fruits which are believed to have protective effects against cancer. Red fruits and some berries may offer an added benefit: lycopene, a carotene pigment that is thought to protect against cancer—especially prostate cancer. In one study, 10 servings a week of foods rich in lycopene led to a 50 percent reduction in the disease.

Orange, yellow, and red fruits tend to be rich in carotenoids, a class of pigments that includes beta-carotene. Carotenoids are believed to guard against cancers of the breast, cervix, colon, esophagus, lung, mouth,

Eating plenty of fruit is associated with a lower risk of heart disease, high blood pressure, and several cancers.

A Guide to Choosing Fruit

The Canadian Cancer Society recommends that every adult eat 5 to 10 servings of fruit (and vegetables) each day. For fiber, choose whole fruit over fruit juice. In general, choose a variety of fruits (and vegetables) to make sure you get a fair share of vitamins, antioxidants, other essential nutrients, and protective compounds.

Nutrient	Sources
Vitamin C	Apricots, cantaloupes, cranberries, grapefruit, honeydew, kiwifruits, mangoes, oranges, papayas, pineapples, plums, strawberries, tangerines, watermelons
Vitamin A (and other carotenoids)	Apples, apricots, bananas, blackberries, blueberries, cantaloupes, cherries, grapes, mangoes, papayas, watermelon
Fiber	Dates, figs, grapefruit, kiwifruits, oranges, pears, prunes, raspberries, strawberries

stomach, and uterus. Many fruits are also high in vitamin C, which is linked to protection against cancers of the breast, cervix, larynx, mouth, pancreas, stomach, and rectum. Folic acid, found in oranges (and orange juice), strawberries, and cantaloupe, protects against cancer, too. (It also helps prevent birth defects when consumed by pregnant women.) And some forms of pectin may inhibit the spread of tumors. It has been shown to stop the spread of prostate cancer in rats.

The power of flavonoids

There's more. Fruits are also rich in plant chemicals, or phytochemicals, compounds that help ward off cancer. For example, red grapes (as well as red wine) contain the antioxidant resveratrol, which may protect against certain cancers. Another type of antioxidant, flavonoids, also protects against cancer. Flavonoids have been shown to inhibit the growth of breast-cancer cells in test tubes. In a long-term study in Finland of nearly 10,000 people, eating foods rich in flavonoids—including apples, other fruits, fruit juices, even jam—was associated with a 20 percent lower overall risk of cancer and a 46 percent lower risk of lung cancer. People who ate apples regularly had a whopping 68 percent lower risk of lung cancer than those who ate them infrequently. Some studies also indicate that flavonoids may lower the risk of heart disease by preventing the oxidation of "bad" cholesterol. Apples, berries, grapes, and citrus fruits are all good sources of flavonoids.

Quantity counts

Federal nutrition guidelines advise us to eat at least five servings of fruits and vegetables every day; studies point to eight or more as a better goal. To get four servings of fruit, you could start the day with a half cup of orange juice, add a banana to your cereal, have a half cup of fruit cocktail with lunch, and eat a half cup of melon balls after dinner. Keep fresh fruit for snacks, and pack it in lunches. Bring dried fruits on trips. Serve baked apples for dessert. And try using pureed applesauce instead of butter.

Papayas and mangoes are packed with vitamin C, beta-carotene, and potassium.

Humans have revered garlic as both food and medicine for thousands of years—and for good reason. Scientists believe that regular consumption of garlic—as little as half a clove a day—may cut the risk of several significant health threats.

The "stinking rose"

When garlic is crushed, chopped, or chewed, an enzyme is released that converts one of garlic's key sulfur compounds, called alliin, into allicin. Allicin gives garlic its unique odor and provides much of its healing properties. Allicin is also the source of other sulfur compounds, including S-allyl-cystein (SAC), which has been shown to protect against cancer in laboratory tests.

Nature's medicine

Garlic has been shown to have numerous beneficial effects. For starters, it kills many disease-causing microorganisms. Although it is only about 1 percent as effective as penicillin, it works against a wide spectrum of bacteria, viruses, and fungi—including some that antibiotics can't destroy. In test tubes, it inhibits the growth of *Helicobacter pylori,* the bacterium that causes most stomach ulcers.

Garlic's numerous sulfur compounds may also protect against certain types of cancer. A major study conducted in Iowa showed garlic to be the single most powerful protector against colon cancer.

It's not only garlic's sulfur compounds that appear to fight cancer. Garlic increases the production of an enzyme known as glutathione peroxidase, which helps detoxify carcinogens. Garlic also provides selenium, a mineral known to fight cancer.

Garlic lowers blood fats, known as triglycerides, a risk factor for heart disease. And laboratory evidence suggests that it reduces the tendency of the blood to clot, which may help stave off heart attacks.

Much of the research surrounding garlic has focused on the ability of different preparations to lower cholesterol. There have been some positive results, but two recent studies have shown no such effect, perhaps suggesting that the cholesterol-lowering ingredient may not be present in all garlic products.

Raw power

Most researchers agree that garlic offers the greatest benefit when eaten raw. Try mincing it in salsas and salad dressings. If you do cook garlic, chop it, wait 15 minutes, then cook it lightly to preserve its disease-fighting powers. Sauté it for a minute or so in a pan, remove it, continue cooking your meal, and then return it to the finished dish.

If you are not a garlic lover, you can probably get many of garlic's benefits from a supplement. Shop carefully; some brands require that you take as many as 17 pills a day to equal the active compounds in one fresh clove. Look for brands that guarantee an allicin yield of 5,000 micrograms.

Enteric-coated pills are available that pass, undigested, into the small intestine, so that stomach acids don't destroy the all-important sulfur compounds. Enteric-coated pills also reduce or eliminate garlic's unsociable odor. Also odorless is aged garlic extract, the form used in many of the clinical studies and generally considered effective.

Evils, away! Garlic not only wards off vampires but also helps guard against bronchial infections and blockage of the arteries.

CAUTION!

Large amounts of garlic may "thin" the blood. If you take a blood-thinning prescription drug or aspirin for your heart, talk to your doctor before greatly increasing your garlic intake.

Gas Ranges

Turn a knob, and the flames leap up. Turn it back, and they're gone. Unlike the heating coils on electric ranges, which warm up and cool down slowly, the burners on gas ranges can produce high heat—or any other intensity you want—instantly. In addition,

Aside from deadly carbon monoxide, gas flames can produce high levels of humidity in the house plus nitrogen dioxide, which is thought to contribute to asthma in children.

power outages don't affect gas supplies and, in most areas, gas ranges cost less to use than electric models do.

The gassy downside

The major problem with gas ranges is the rare but real possibility of explosions. If gas leaks, the accumulated fumes could be ignited by a mere spark, with disastrous results. It is for this reason that a "marker" chemical is added to gas supplies to give gas its distinctive odor.

If you smell gas, check that all the burners are turned off and that the pilot lights haven't gone out. If neither is the problem and the gas odor persists, get everyone out of the house immediately and use a neighbor's phone to call the gas company. (Using your own phone or even flicking an electric switch could produce a spark that ignites the fumes.)

Less dramatic but more likely is the potential for indoor pollution. The improper installation or operation of a gas range can result in a build-up of combustion by-products—carbon dioxide and nitrogen dioxide, among others—that cause headaches, dizzi-

ness, fatigue, chronic bronchitis, and other symptoms. The problem may be worse in a newer house: better insulation limits the entry of fresh air. Lack of fresh air leads to inefficient combustion, which, in turn, can cause higher levels of indoor pollution.

A potentially lethal pollutant resulting from such incomplete combustion is carbon monoxide. Colorless, odorless, and tasteless, it enters the bloodstream and starves the brain of oxygen. Causing flulike symptoms in mild cases, carbon monoxide poisoning can result in unconsciousness and even death in severe cases.

Minimizing pollution dangers

Although gas ranges usually give off only small amounts of indoor pollutants, you can help to reduce those levels even further. Don't turn flames so high that they curl around the sides of the pot; doing so wastes fuel and increases pollution. Be sure fuel is burning efficiently. Ideally, burners should send out steady blue flames. Unsteady or flickering yellow-tipped flames (and sooty buildup on pots) tell you there is too little air in the fuel mix. High, noisy flames signify too much air. If you have an older model of gas range, you may be able to adjust the gas-air mixture yourself. Follow the directions in your owner's manual. If you have a newer model, you'll probably have to call a professional.

A gas range should be equipped with a range hood and exhaust fan, preferably one that vents exhaust gases to the outdoors. Always turn on the fan when cooking and check the vent once a month to make sure it isn't clogged. (Range vents are not as effective as furnace vents, so never use a range as a space heater, even if it is vented to the outdoors.)

Any home equipped with a gas range (or any other gas-fueled appliances) should be protected by carbon monoxide detectors. They look and act similarly to smoke detectors and warn of dangerous carbon monoxide buildup with loud alarms. Relatively inexpensive and easy to install, carbon monoxide detectors can be lifesavers.

CAUTION!

Carbon monoxide fumes have been known to kill people, especially when they are sleeping. Protecting a home with carbon monoxide detectors is the only way to avoid such a disaster.

Northamericans have carried on a love affair with cars and gas-powered machines since the early years of the twentieth century. But the now-ubiquitous liquid that fuels them must be used with caution. Every year thousands of people suffer injuries from mishandling gasoline. Not only is it flammable, but its fumes are highly combustible and can be ignited by a cigarette, the flame of a pilot light, the heat from an engine, the electrical spark created by the flick of a light switch, or just a spark of static electricity.

Keep the lid on when using gas

Gas should be used only outdoors, and strictly as a motor fuel. Don't use it as a charcoal starter or to get out grease spots. Never use gasoline to clean paint or grease from your hands. It contains benzene, ethylene dichloride, and methanol, all of which can be toxic if absorbed through the skin. Siphoning gas with your mouth is also hazardous and can result in chemical pneumonia (pneumonia caused by inhaling a poisonous gas). Avoid inhaling gasoline vapors or the carbon monoxide fumes produced by gas-powered machinery, which can cause headache, dizziness, nausea, and confusion, and may be fatal.

Before refueling a lawn mower or other machinery, move it out of the garage. Make sure it's turned off and the engine is cool to avoid accidentally igniting the gasoline. Use a funnel and soak up any spills promptly with cat litter or sand. Move any machinery at least 3 meters (10 feet) away from the gas can before starting it, and let it cool off outdoors before storing.

Gas should be used outdoors, and strictly as a motor fuel. Don't use it as a charcoal starter or to get out grease spots.

When working under your car, protect your eyes and hands with chemical-resistant goggles and rubber or vinyl gloves. If gas gets on clothing, leave it outside for several days so the fumes can evaporate before you wash it.

Transporting and storing gasoline

Always place a gas container on the ground to fill it; filling it in the back of a pick-up truck or the trunk of a car or on a plastic surface can create a static spark and start a fire. Leave some room at the top for the gas to expand. Transport it in the car trunk, with the trunk lid slightly open, and remove it as soon as possible. In an accident, a can of gasoline in a car's trunk can be transformed into a bomb.

Keep only small amounts of gasoline, and store it away from the house in a cool, well-ventilated area, such as a detached garage or shed. Use only safety cans intended for gasoline storage and screw the lid on tight to keep fumes from escaping. If you have children, store gas out of their reach. Dispose of dirty gasoline as a hazardous waste.

Never smoke in the vicinity of a filling station. Take care not to drip gasoline on your car or clothes or in the station's driveway; the fumes linger and may later be ignited.

Dealing with Gas

- If you feel ill or groggy around gasoline, get fresh air and seek medical help.
- If gasoline is swallowed, never induce vomiting. Call a poison control center or 911 without delay.
- If gasoline gets on your skin, wash it off immediately with soap and water.
- If you get a gasoline burn, see a doctor right away.

Generic Drugs

Some generic drugs are better than others. The difference depends on the manufacturer. Ask your pharmacist to fill your prescriptions with drugs from the most reliable manufacturers.

Generic drugs—the less expensive versions of brand-name medications—can save you a bundle of money, particularly if you suffer from a chronic ailment that requires that your prescription be refilled often. You may wonder, however, if you are getting the same benefits from generics as you are from brand names. For most people the answer is an unequivocal yes. For others, it depends on the nature of the medication and the health profile of the person taking it.

Generics vs. brands: cousins or clones?

When patented, all drugs—whether prescription or over-the-counter—are given a generic name (acetaminophen, for example) that is generally derived from the medication's chemical composition. Once approved for sale by Health Canada, the medication is licensed to a manufacturer (usually the one that developed the drug), which gives it a brand name (such as Tylenol). The patent is good for 20 years, during which time no other company can make the same drug (note, however, that much of that time may have been taken up in developing the medication and getting Health Canada approval). After 20 years, the medication—but not the brand name—becomes public property. That is, other companies can then make the identical compound, as long as they call it something other than the brand name. These versions, often called by the original chemical name, are what we refer to as generic drugs.

Generic drugs must be identical to the original in the way they work. To ensure the effectiveness of generics, Health Canada requires proof of their bioequivalency. In other words, though inactive ingredients may differ, a generic medication must contain exactly the same active chemical as the original. When tested, generic drugs must also prove to have a bioavailability within 20 percent of the original. This means that when you take the generic drug, the amount of active ingredients that enter your bloodstream cannot differ by more than 20 percent—higher or lower—from the amount that would be present if you were taking the brand-name version. (Bioavailability usually differs by less than 5 percent.)

Exceptions to this rule are the so-called critical drugs—prescriptions that require such an exact dosage that even small changes in amounts could be dangerous. Examples include digoxin, for heart problems; immuno-

CAUTION!
Grapefruit juice will heighten the effects of many common medications to the level of a dangerous overdose for as long as 24 hours after you drink it. If the juice is a regular part of your diet, be sure to tell your doctor.

suppressant drugs, for transplant patients, and theophylline, for asthma. In the case of such drugs, Health Canada applies even more stringent requirements for bioequivalence.

Weighing the differences

The big difference between brand-name and generic drugs is price. Generics manufacturers can charge less because in many cases all they do is copy the original formula; in

> Generics manufacturers can charge less because in many cases all they do is copy the original formula; manufacturers of brand names must pay for research, development, and advertising as well.

contrast, manufacturers of brand names must pay for research, development, and advertising as well.

Generic and brand-name drugs often part company on inactive ingredients, such as fillers, colors, flavors, and dyes, that are added during manufacturing. Different inactive ingredients will not matter to most people, but for a few, switching from brand names to generics may introduce problems. For example, the size, shape, or coating of a generic drug may make it more difficult to swallow. A generic may contain a filler or a dye that triggers an allergy or an added ingredient,

such as lactose, that causes an upset stomach. Generics may also vary from the brand names in the amount of sugar or alcohol they contain. The risk of an adverse reaction is greater if you take more than one medication, since the drugs' interaction may play a role in how you tolerate the inactive ingredients.

Opting for generics

Generally, physicians prescribe brand-name drugs, because they may be less familiar with the generic versions. Increasingly, physicians are leaving it up to patients to choose between the two. To get details about both versions, ask your pharmacist, who will know which are paid for or covered by your province's health-care plan. You may opt for the generic drug because of its low cost. Of course, if you don't mind paying more, you may prefer the costly brand-name. In some cases, the doctor may write "Do not substitute" on the prescription form, if it must be filled with the brand-name drug. If you're having an adverse reaction to a generic drug or wish to find one with the most suitable inactive ingredients, talk to your doctor or pharmacist. Most pharmacies stock versions made by several manufacturers.

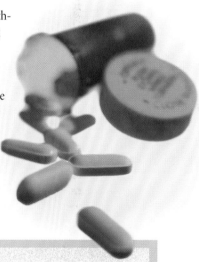

When you travel or move, make sure you know the manufacturer of the generic drug you are taking so you can be sure to find it elsewhere.

Testing and Approving Drugs

Before a new drug is offered to the public, a manufacturer must prove its safety and effectiveness. To initiate research, the manufacturer must first file an Investigational New Drug Submission with the Drug Directorate of Health Canada, which gives information about the latest test data, production methods, and controls, etc. In the case of a brand-name product, tests may include human drug trials. If the tests prove the drug's potential therapeutic value, the manufacturer files a New Drug Submission, which includes details about the drug's proper and chemical names, ingredients, dosage information, etc. If the submission is satisfactory, Health Canada issues a Notice of Compliance, which permits the manufacturer to sell the drug. In the case of a generic drug, safety and effectiveness may be established by comparative studies with the original drug. Some studies involve measuring drug levels in the bloodstream of volunteers who receive the generic and the original brand-name drugs. These studies must show that the generic works in the same way as the original and produces the same therapeutic effects.

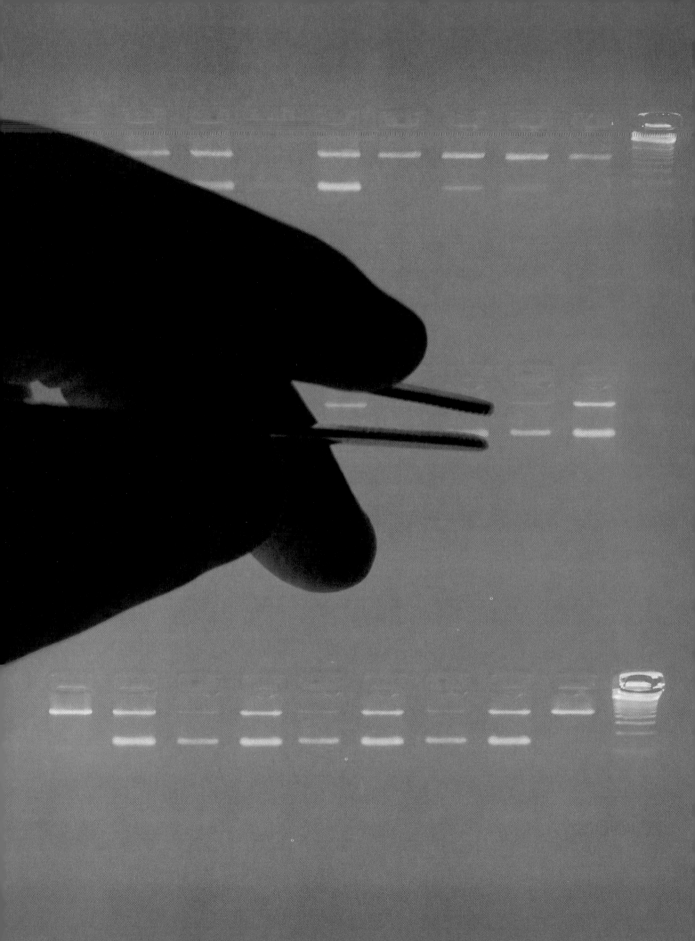

Genetic Testing

The risk of an inherited disease can hang over a family like a black cloud. Fortunately, genetic testing provides an opportunity for you and your physician to obtain information about your genetic makeup and assess your risks for certain diseases. The test results enable you to make informed choices about preventive care, lifestyle changes, and parenthood that may help you or your children to avoid a disease, lessen its effects, or at least prepare for its onset. But genetic testing also has emotional, legal, and social implications.

Detecting genetic clues

Each of your cells contains copies of between 80,000 and 100,000 genes, half of them inherited from your mother and half from your father. The genes play a role in determining everything about you, from the color of your hair to the shape of your foot.

In recent years researchers have discovered that a mutation in a particular gene may signify an increased risk for a specific disease. Scientists can identify such a mutation by testing samples of your blood, tissue, or saliva. Testing is available for dozens of genetic diseases, and more are being added to that list each year as diseases continue to be linked to genetic mutations.

When to test

Some genetic diseases are inherited, and others result from the mutation of a gene during one's lifetime. Prenatal testing can determine some genetic disorders, such as Down's syndrome, before birth. Newborns are routinely screened for a number of diseases, such as sickle-cell anemia and metabolic disorders. If such a disease is identified, the baby can be enrolled right away in a therapeutic program.

If adults have a family history of a disease for which genetic testing is available, they may wish to find out if they are at risk, and what they can do to prevent it or treat the condition. A couple might get information about prenatal genetic testing or learn whether either of them carries a gene that might put their offspring at risk for a disease.

What the results mean

Genetic tests don't always pinpoint who will develop an illness. Everyone is at risk for a number of diseases. In the case of many diseases, a family history increases the risk. If a genetic test shows a mutated gene, the risk increases even more. But even people at high risk of getting certain diseases may never contract the disease. Heart disease and cancer, for instance, are thought to be caused by mutated genes whose effect on risk can be influenced by environmental or lifestyle factors.

There is also the question of degree. Genetic testing of unborn children, for example, may determine whether a certain condition, such as mental retardation, is present, but not how severe the condition will be.

Should you be tested?

If you are considering genetic testing, contact a counselor at the genetics division of a university-affiliated hospital to find out about testing, or ask your pediatrician or family physician to refer you to a clinical geneticist. You will want to discuss the following:

- **Family history.** The counselor will ask if any disease runs in your family, or if you already have a child with birth defects, or if you suffered miscarriages or stillbirths.
- **Treatment options.** Even if you forgo a test because no treatment is available for a particular disease, you may store a genetic sample for your family's use in the future.
- **Emotional factors.** A positive test result may cause anxiety, while a negative result may stir feelings of guilt if another family member suffers from the disease.
- **Family privacy.** Relatives may be unwilling to discuss their medical history or to disclose information from death certificates or postmortem reports, or they may be traumatized by what your tests reveal.

Mutations May Also Be Positive

A genetic mutation that signals a risk for a particular disease may indicate another, protective function as well. The same genetic characteristic for an increased risk of developing cystic fibrosis, for instance, also indicates a greater resistance to cholera. Likewise, if a carrier of the gene for sickle-cell anemia contracts malaria, the effects will be less severe than they would be for others.

On the Horizon Scientists and physicians hope that gene transfer, the process of correcting or replacing mutated genes, can one day be used to treat diseases related to mutation, such as cancer. More than 100 clinical trials are in progress.

Genetically Engineered Foods

Particularly controversial are gene transfers from animals to plants, such as the flounder genes tested in tomatoes in an attempt to make the fruit less likely to freeze.

Are They Labeled?

How Canada will label genetically engineered foods has not yet been decided. In ongoing discussions, government agencies and consumer groups have agreed on mandatory labeling of those that present health or safety risks—if they contain new allergens, for example, or if there is substantial change in their nutritive value or composition.

Breakfast cereals fortified with vitamins and coffee with the caffeine removed are nothing new. But what about growing cereal grains with the extra nutrients built in or coffee beans that are naturally caffeine-free? Both are possible with genetic engineering.

Whether genetically engineered (novel) or produced conventionally, all food sold in Canada is subject to the same rigorous health, safety, and quality reviews by federal regulators. Nevertheless, critics argue for more widespread testing and for mandatory labeling of all foods derived from biotechnology. For consumers who remain wary of such engineered foods, there is only one recourse: Look for industry-certified organic products.

A faster kind of farming

Farmers have traditionally altered the genes of their crops by crossbreeding them over a period of years, to get, say, a delicious tomato that is also hardy. Now scientists can shorten the process by copying genes from one type of plant or animal and transferring them into another, creating "transgenic" plants or animals. This process is being used to boost nutrient content, increase yield, and create pest resistance—a breed of potato has been modified to resist the Colorado beetle, corn has been altered for protection against the European core borer insect. Many soybean growers are using seeds that have been altered so that the crop won't die when sprayed with a weed killer. By 2010, half of our crops may contain at least one "foreign" gene.

Biotechnology also figures in cheese making, a process that requires an enzyme called rennet. Currently most rennet is extracted from the stomach lining of calves. But the rennet gene can now be inserted into bacteria, which produce the rennet more quickly and cheaply.

Are the safeguards strong enough?

Before testing potential agricultural products outside the laboratory, or before selling or importing such products, researchers and manufacturers must convince the Canadian Food Inspection Agency that the modified organism is safe for humans and animals, and that it will not turn into a future pest or weed, affect other plants or organisms, or spread its new characteristics to other related species. Health Canada must approve any transgenic foods that contain toxins, allergens, antibiotic-resistant genes, or any nutrients not in the original food. Take tomatoes, for example. Because the fruit contains a toxin, tomatine, tomatoes which had been genetically modified to ripen slowly could not be sold in Canada until thorough testing showed they were as safe and nutritious as other varieties.

Critics argue that as pest-resistant genes are bred into plants, more pests will adapt to them. Also, they fear that unknown components can pop up in transgenic products. For instance, a genetically engineered bacterium that produced an amino acid in L-tryptophan, a dietary supplement, also secreted another, previously unknown amino acid that may have contributed to 27 deaths.

Global Warming

W hat's hot? Our planet. The last 15 years have seen the 10 warmest years ever recorded on Earth.

This trend called global warming is caused not by forces of nature but by human activity. The good news is that we can help stop the trend we started.

What is global warming?

Worldwide climatic changes are linked to increasing levels of greenhouse gases, so called because they form a shield around the earth like a greenhouse, trapping the sun's heat. Most of these gases occur naturally: evaporation produces water vapor; wetlands and animal digestive processes release carbon monoxide.

But since the Industrial Revolution, humankind has unrelentingly built up the level of greenhouse gases, mostly adding them to the air by burning huge quantities of carbon-based fossil fuels, such as oil, natural gas, and coal, and thus releasing carbon dioxide, methane, and nitrous oxide into the troposphere (the lower atmosphere), but also by activities such as deforestation, which reduce nature's ability to absorb greenhouse gases.

What is it doing to us?

If global warming continues, the earth may heat up another 1 to 3°C (2 to 6°F) over the next century (perhaps even higher thereafter). Such a change could affect:

- **Climate.** Extreme weather events, such as heat waves and hard rainfalls, could intensify and occur more frequently.
- **Land and water.** Melting ice caps might raise sea levels, flooding low-lying coastal areas; the encroaching seawater could contaminate drinking supplies. Heat and drought could expand deserts.
- **Food supply.** Changes in rainfall and temperatures could adversely affect farm productivity, especially in poor countries.
- **Health.** High moisture levels increase the risk of diseases, such as malaria and cholera.
- **Air quality.** Increases in temperature and longer warm seasons could lead to more pollution, such as ground-level ozone.
- **Natural habitats.** Changes in ecosystems, such as forests, wetlands, and coral reefs, could speed up the extinction of wildlife.

How can you slow it down?

The more fossil fuels we burn, the greater the buildup of these gases. To cut consumption:

- Buy fuel-efficient vehicles. A third of Canada's carbon dioxide emissions come from cars, trucks, and buses.
- Drive less. Instead, bicycle, walk, carpool, or use public transportation.
- Plant trees. They absorb carbon dioxide.
- Use energy-efficient lightbulbs.
- Weatherproof houses with added insulation and weather stripping to cut fuel use.
- Turn the thermostat low when you're away.
- When replacing refrigerators and furnaces choose the most energy-efficient models.
- Look for ways to use solar energy.

Canada accounts for less than 2 percent of global greenhouse gases. Most result from energy consumption—burning fuel in cars, heating homes, producing electricity. Across the border, the U.S. produces 23 percent of greenhouse gas emissions, primarily from the country's industries.

On the Horizon Hypercars, which use electric motors and produce the electricity on board from non-fossil fuel, are the new hope in energy-efficient cars. Prototypes have performed better than battery-operated vehicles, which must be recharged frequently, a process that generates a large amount of carbon dioxide.

Glues & Adhesives

Glues and adhesives are indispensable for all kinds of projects, from assembling a model airplane to putting up a wall. Some, like the library paste that generations of children have sampled, are harmless. But others contain toxins that can make you sick.

A sticky situation

Glues and adhesives come in many forms, including white glue, rubber cement, epoxy, plastic adhesives, and instant glue. Solvents are added to thin out naturally thick glues. Problem is, the solvents evaporate after the glue is applied, filling the air with toxic vapors.

When the solvent is water, as in nontoxic glues, the vapor is harmless. But the compounds used in epoxy, instant glue, model glue, rubber cement, and contact cement, among others, are potentially hazardous. They contain chemicals that can irritate the eyes, throat, and lungs if inhaled and can burn the skin on contact: formaldehyde, naphthalene, phenol, ethanol, toluene, acrylonitrile, and vinyl chloride. Toluene has been linked to kidney problems. Even more worrisome are glues that contain phenol, vinyl chloride, and formaldehyde—all suspected carcinogens.

Instant glues contain solvents that evaporate very quickly, making these glues less toxic. (Once solvents are dry, the adhesives pose no risk.) Use instant glue with care, though; it bonds instantly, not just to target surfaces but to skin. If this happens, call a poison control center or doctor immediately. When using this kind of glue, be especially careful not to touch your mouth or eyes with your fingers.

Instant glue (top) is only mildly toxic, whereas model glue may cause kidney problems. Epoxy is irritating to the skin, so use it with care. Contact cement may contain neurotoxins; look for water-based brands.

White glue and glue sticks are nontoxic. They are safe for children to use under supervision.

Handle with care

Before using any glue or adhesive, read (and heed) the manufacturer's instructions. Never use glues near an open flame, and don't use toxic adhesives on items that will come into contact with food, such as plates.

For large projects that require toxic glues, wear long-sleeved shirts and pants, goggles, rubber gloves, and a respirator (available at hardware stores). When using toxic glues, don't wear soft contact lenses; they can absorb solvent fumes. Always use glues in a well-ventilated area, and replace the cap or lid tightly after applying the product, even during frequent applications. You can dispose of nontoxic glues and instant glue in the regular trash, but save spent containers of other adhesives for hazardous-waste collection.

Toxic glues and adhesives are even more dangerous when deliberately inhaled for a high. This is a growing practice among elementary and high-school students. Symptoms include disorientation, headache, and feelings of intoxication followed by drowsiness. Glue sniffing over a long period can damage the liver, kidneys, nervous system, and heart. High concentrations can be deadly.

The strong, harmless type

The safest glues and adhesives are mucilage, white glue, library paste, yellow carpenter's glue, and glue sticks—all low-odor and nontoxic. When starting a project, consider whether one will serve in place of a toxic product. White glue, for example, works surprisingly well for laying hardwood floors.

For jobs that require other types of adhesives, look for less-toxic alternatives. Buy rubber cement with a heptane base instead of the more noxious hexane base. Opt for water-based glues when possible. Water-based adhesives for hanging wallpaper are now available, as are water-based contact cements.

The average North American eats less than one serving of a whole-grain food each day. That's a pity. Eating plenty of whole grains—wheat, rice, corn, oats, barley, rye, and others—is linked with a lower risk of heart disease, diabetes, and several cancers, including colon, stomach, and breast cancer.

Grains consist of three edible parts. At the center is the germ, rich in nutrients and with some fiber. It is surrounded by the endosperm, made mostly of starch and a little protein. Encasing that is the bran, rich in fiber and with some nutrients.

Refining grains to create white flour, white rice, and pearled barley removes nearly all the germ and bran, leaving the nutrient-poor endosperm. By law, some nutrients, such as iron and certain B vitamins, must be added back, making the foods "enriched." Still, white rice has less vitamin E than brown rice. In fact, all refined grains have less fiber than their whole-grain counterparts.

Bountiful benefits

Whole wheat is rich in insoluble fiber, which helps prevent constipation and cuts the risk of colon cancer. Whole oats provide soluble fiber, which can lower blood-cholesterol levels significantly. (Oat bran has the most, but all parts of the oat are rich in soluble fiber.)

But fiber is just the beginning. Grains are a good source of protein when combined with legumes (as in rice and beans) or dairy products. Whole grains are also rich in several B vitamins, including B_6 and folic acid, and many minerals and trace elements, including iron, copper, zinc, magnesium, and selenium. Whole wheat and barley are especially rich in vitamin E, which, in large amounts, prevents cholesterol from oxidizing and building up on artery walls.

The germ and the bran also contain health-protective compounds. For example, whole wheat, rye, and flax seeds supply plant hormones known as lignans, which prevent cellular changes that can lead to cancer, especially of the breast and prostate.

You better shop around

When buying bread, read the ingredients: the word *whole,* as in "whole-grain" or "whole wheat," should be listed first or second. Don't be swayed by labels like "multigrain," "made with whole wheat," "enriched wheat," or "stone-ground"; the bread may still be made mostly with white flour. Most North American rye (and pumpernickel) breads are refined, too. That's too bad, because Finnish studies have found that eating three slices of whole-grain rye a day reduces the risk of death from heart attack by 17 percent.

Look for breakfast cereals that provide at least 3 grams (preferably 5 grams) of fiber; some have as much as 15 grams. Use the same criteria for hot cereals. If you like oatmeal, eat plenty of it: a 1½-cup serving a day contains enough soluble fiber to lower harmful LDL (low-density lipoprotein) cholesterol by about 5 percent.

Also try other whole grains: pot or Scotch barley (as opposed to pearl barley), quinoa, amaranth, bulgur (precooked wheat kernels used to make tabbouleh), millet, and cracked rye. You might also refrigerate a jar of wheat germ and toss some into cereal, pancakes, yogurt, and casseroles to add vitamin E, folic acid, and iron as well as fiber.

The Dish on Pasta

Most pastas are made from refined flour. They provide plenty of complex carbohydrates (our main source of energy) but are not as rich in fiber or trace minerals as whole wheat pastas. Moreover, a recent study found that people who ate a lot of carbohydrates in the form of refined grains (regular pasta, white bread, and white rice) were more prone to type II diabetes than those whose diets were richer in fiber from whole grains.

The whole truth: White flour contains as little as 25 percent of the fiber found in wheat kernels.

Hair Products

Looking like you just stepped out of a salon beats a bad-hair day hands down. For the most part, the products used on hair are safe. However, some can irritate the skin and eyes. Dyes have even been suspected of causing cancer.

The problems with hair products

Some hair products aren't all they're cracked up to be. Consider the following:

• **Shampoos** contain 70 to 80 percent water, plus detergent, perfume, and conditioning oils. Harsh ingredients include formaldehyde, propylene glycol, and quaternarium 15. "Oily," "dry," or "normal" classifications depend on how much detergent and conditioning oils a shampoo contains. A "gentle" shampoo may be a regular shampoo with extra water. Detergents may dry out the hair and skin and irritate the eyes. But the chance of getting cancer from a lifetime of shampoo use is extremely remote.

• **Dandruff shampoos** may keep your scalp from peeling, but they can also contain such irritants as coal tar, selenium sulfide, resorcinol, and cresol; if you are sensitive to them, they may even make dandruff worse. If a shampoo causes itching or burning, switch to another. To prevent the scalp becoming resistant to a dandruff shampoo's active ingredient, users should alternate between sulfur-based and tar-based products.

• **Hair sprays** can irritate the eyes, skin, and respiratory tract and should be used in a well-ventilated area. Pumps are safer than aerosols because they emit larger droplets that are less easily absorbed into the lungs. Styling foams are safer, but they often contain alcohol, which may dry the hair.

• **Permanent-wave solutions** often contain ammonium thioglycolate, which may cause rashes on the hands and scalp. Look for ammonia-free solutions instead. Obstetricians and gynecologists say it's safe to perm or color hair while pregnant.

Do hair dyes cause cancer?

For years dark hair dyes have been suspected of causing cancer. But most experts say there is little to fear, even though some hair dyes contain such potential carcinogens as coal-tar derivatives and paraphenylenediamine (PPD) compounds. But one would have to use them constantly over 20 or more years to even slightly increase the risk of certain rare cancers. Progressive hair dyes for graying men are not carcinogenic, but some products do contain lead, so wash your hands after use. Some dyes may trigger allergic reactions. Before using one, dab a bit behind one ear and leave it on for 48 hours. If you do develop a reaction, consider henna or vegetable dyes.

Temporary hair colors, such as this auburn coloring mousse, can run and irritate the eyes if you get caught in the rain.

Hair Removal

Hair is beautiful—unless it grows where you don't want it. Then the question is, how to get rid of it? Whether you shave it, yank it out, or dissolve it away, each hair removal method has benefits and drawbacks. Moreover, some products that work well for some people may not work as well for others, or may function best only when used on certain areas of the body.

The razor's edge

The most common method of hair removal for both men and women is shaving. It's quick, easy, and inexpensive, and, contrary to popular belief, it will not make hair grow in faster, darker, or thicker. But shaving very closely may cause ingrown hairs. In addition, the results are fleeting—hair usually reappears in only a day or two. If you're not careful, razors can also be rough on the skin. Take the sting out of shaving by following these simple tips:

- To help reduce drag and irritation, wet the skin and hair, apply shaving cream, and use only a sharp, clean razor.
- Use your own razor. Shaving can cause bleeding and transmit infection.
- Shave in the direction in which the hair grows to reduce the likelihood of irritation and ingrown hairs.
- Don't shave right after you get out of bed (the skin is puffier). Wait at least 20 minutes for the skin to tighten a little; you'll be less likely to cut yourself.
- To soothe any dryness after shaving, apply a mild moisturizer. But choose carefully: some lotions (and sunscreens, too) may contain chemicals that can irritate freshly shaved skin.

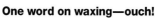

Depilatories leave the skin very smooth, but some may be messy and have a foul odor.

Depilatories: feel the burn?

Usually sold as gels or lotions, depilatories dissolve the protein structure of hair, allowing it to be wiped off like chalk from a slate. Results last longer than with shaving, about three to five days. On the other hand, because skin and hair have similar compositions, what eats away at one can eat away at the other. The result can be mild to severe skin irritation. For your skin's sake, take the following precautions:

- Test your skin for sensitivity. Apply a dab on or near the target area of skin; wait a few minutes and check for any irritation.
- Use the product only where it is intended to be used. Never, for example, use a leg depilatory on the face.
- Don't leave depilatories on too long (usually 4 to 15 minutes is specified). Doing so may result in painful blisters or burns.

One word on waxing—ouch!

Few things, it seems, could be less pleasant than applying strips of wax to your skin and then ripping them off, taking your hair along with them. But that's exactly what waxing involves. Because waxing pulls the entire hair shaft from the follicle, its effects last as long as 2 to 6 weeks.

Warm liquid wax can be messy and irritating. Consider using strips of cloth or paper coated with cold wax instead. When the wax is pulled off, it can hurt and cause skin irritation. If you're still game, try these suggestions to make waxing a little easier:

- Test the skin for sensitivity by using a little wax to remove a few hairs. *(continued)*

Hair Removal (continued)

Removing facial hair — from the upper lip, for example—is better left to a professional than done at home in front of a mirror with an epilator.

The needles used in electrolysis may be (from left to right) insulated, for sensitive patients; plated with 24-karat gold, for patients prone to skin allergies; or stainless steel. The needles are thin enough to slide into a skin pore, along a hair's shaft.

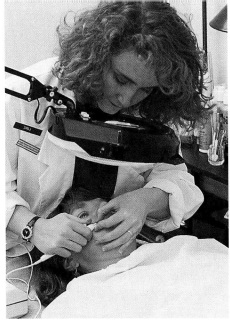

- Clean the skin beforehand and wax only hair that is at least 6 mm (¹/₄ inch) long.
- If you go to a salon, choose one that has a licensed aesthetician and make sure that fresh wax is used. Reused (reheated) wax may transmit infection.
- If you have blond or red hair, be aware that waxing can leave your skin especially sensitive to sunlight.
- To reduce postwaxing irritation, gently rub ice over the skin for a few minutes or apply a soothing antiseptic lotion (such as tea tree oil). Some moisturizers may irritate freshly waxed skin.
- If waxing is too harsh for you, try muslin strips with a thin coat of sugar, lemon juice, and water. Called sugaring, this method may produce the same results as waxing with less pain and irritation.

Electrolysis: hair today, gone tomorrow

One hair at a time, this method sends electric current through a very fine needle or a pair of tweezers, destroying the hair and damaging the hair follicle so that regrowth is difficult. After a series of weekly sessions, the results may be permanent (even though permanence cannot be guaranteed). But you should know a few things before you try electrolysis:

- It can be painful. Each zap may produce a twinge similar to that of tweezing. A topical anesthetic may help reduce the pain.
- For practical purposes, electrolysis is recommended only for small areas, such as the upper lip.
- Health risks, though rare, include electric shock, scarring, and infection. To reduce the risk of disease transmission, including hepatitis and HIV, make sure that your electrologist uses new, disposable needles.
- With the exception of Manitoba, no province in Canada requires a license to practice electrolysis, so make sure your electrologist has been certified by the Federation of Canadian Electrolysis Associations (FCEA) as a Canadian Certified Electrologist (C.C.E.), or by the Association of Professional Electrologists of British Columbia as a Registered Electrologist (R.E.). For a list of provincial associations, contact the FCEA at 1-888-333-2783.
- Electrolysis sessions are time-consuming, may be spread out over several months, and typically cost $40 to $80 per hour.
- Home electrolysis units, called epilators, may be less expensive in the long run, but they may not be as effective as professional electrolysis.

A look at lasers

The latest method of hair removal uses a laser to destroy hair and hair follicles. After three to four sessions over the course of a year, the results may be permanent, although there is no guarantee. The technique is considered less painful than electrolysis but may still produce a stinging sensation, especially in more sensitive areas.

Laser treatments are expensive—removing facial hair over a period of three months, for example, can cost up to $6,000, the hair on both upper legs, around $2,900—and they may cause redness, swelling, scarring, or lightening or darkening of the skin.

Hair Replacement

The average head boasts more than 100,000 hairs. But for millions of people who experience hair loss, half that amount would be something to brag about. Unfortunately, there is no surefire cure for balding. But if you're willing to spend the money, modest gain is possible.

Minoxidil and finasteride

Two drugs are currently used to treat hair loss: minoxidil, a topical solution, and finasteride, a pill.

When minoxidil (sold under brand names such as Rogaine) is applied twice a day, it can slow hair loss in some cases and stimulate new hair growth in a minority of patients. The new hair is often thinner, finer, and lighter in color (read: peach fuzz) and may not fully cover balding areas. Potential side effects include itchy scalp, rashes, and, in rare cases, growth of facial hair, rapid heartbeat, and dizziness.

Finasteride (Propecia) is taken once a day and it has slowed hair loss and promoted new hair growth in some men. However, it is for men only; it has not been proven safe for women; and it may cause abnormal development of a male fetus. So a man using this drug should not father a child and should not expose a pregnant woman to his semen. Common side effects include decreased sex drive and difficulty achieving an erection.

If you choose medication, be aware that:
- It may cost hundreds of dollars a year, and benefits may not be seen for months.
- The younger you are (and the more hair you have), the better it may work. However, the long-term health risks for both drugs have not been firmly established.
- If you stop using either medication, any new hair growth will gradually be lost.

Hairpieces and weaves

Attaching new hair—real, synthetic, or a combination of both—either to the scalp or existing hair may be the hair-replacement option with the fewest side effects. Still, the initial cost can be between $700 and $1,000 and can eventually run to several thousand dollars. For the best results, follow these tips:
- If hair is being woven into existing hair, make certain the strands to which your new hair is being attached are strong and healthy. If they aren't, you may lose them to the weight and pull of the new hair.
- If your hairpiece is attached with glue, test the scalp's sensitivity to the glue at least 48 hours in advance.
- To reduce irritation, keep your scalp and hairpiece clean.

Tricky transplants

Hair-transplant surgery grafts hair, contained in small strips of scalp, from one part of the head to another. Typically, two to six four-hour sessions are required and cost thousands of dollars per session. The results tend to look more natural if you have fine hair that is similar in color to your skin.

Potential problems include scarring and infection. To reduce the risk, use only a specialist in dermatology or in plastic surgery who specializes in hair transplantation and is experienced with your specific procedure. If possible, talk to (and see "before" and "after" photos of) current or former patients.

CAUTION!
Nearly all hair loss is hereditary. Nevertheless, before you spend a cent on hair replacement, make sure that yours isn't being caused by an autoimmune disorder or something temporary, such as trauma, childbirth, medication, chemotherapy, a thyroid problem, or a nutritional deficiency.

A hair-transplant surgeon must not only move hair from place to place but also provide the patient with a natural-looking result.

On the Horizon Researchers at Columbia University have isolated a gene that may be responsible for activating hair growth in humans. This finding may someday lead to the development of medications that directly stimulate hair production. Another possibility (if it is proven safe) is a drug that combines minoxidil with tretinoin (Retin-A), the anti-acne, antiwrinkle cream, which may help minoxidil better penetrate the scalp.

Hearing Aids

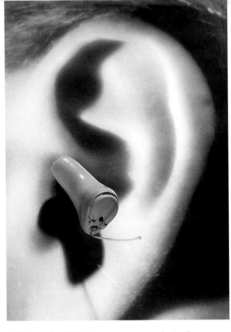

Hearing aids won't bring your hearing back to normal, but they can improve it. And with inconspicuous devices like this one, which is inserted into the ear canal, no one has to know you're wearing one.

"Say what?" It's a common refrain for some 25 million North Americans, including half of all men and a third of all women over age 65. Yet more than three-quarters of people with hearing loss don't wear a hearing aid. Those who go without one are likely to suffer increasing isolation and even depression.

Do you really need a hearing aid?
If you have trouble hearing, don't go straight to a hearing-aid dealer. First see your doctor; you may simply have a buildup of earwax. If it's more than that, you may be referred to a specialist in hearing disorders or perhaps to a certified audiologist for a hearing test. If you need an aid, you may be fitted with one or sent to a reputable dealer.

Take the results of your hearing test with you to make sure you get a device that corrects your specific problem. If the dealer doesn't offer a 30-day trial for the aid, or sells only one brand, shop elsewhere.

One size does not fit all
A hearing aid consists of a microphone that translates sound into electronic signals, an amplifier that augments these signals, a speaker that converts the signals to sound, a battery that powers the device, and a volume control. Aids can be worn in several locations:

- **Behind the ear** (BTE). In this type of hearing aid, most of the components sit in a housing that rests behind the ear. The least expensive choice—and highly reliable—this unit may also provide the loudest, clearest sound. However, it is large and easily noticed if you have short hair. Best for profound hearing loss.
- **In the ear** (ITE). This device sits inside the ear and offers superior reproduction of high-pitched sounds and reduction of annoying "wind" sounds. However, it increases the risk of that screeching electronic "feedback" and the controls are small and can be hard to use. Also, because the unit rests in the ear, it can become clogged with wax and require cleaning. Best for moderate to severe hearing loss.
- **In the canal** (ITC) or completely in the canal (CIC). This aid is virtually invisible to the eye, which accounts for its popularity. Because it sits closer to the eardrum, sound may be clearer. However, controls are hard to reach and good manual dexterity is required to get it into the ear. Best for mild to moderate hearing loss.
- **Pocket devices.** For people who have difficulty tolerating a unit in or around their ear, this unit fits in a pocket or on a belt loop. A thin wire connects it to a tiny ear speaker. Although cumbersome, it is the most powerful aid and provides the best fidelity and excellent reliability. (Do not confuse the professional aids with the low-priced units available at drug stores and through mail-order catalogs.)

Digital hearing devices, the latest development, come in BTE, ITE, and ITC models. They are usually programmable, which allows you to adjust them for different sound environments. Some adapt automatically, letting you hear quiet conversations while muffling louder sounds. Digital aids offer the most "natural" sound, but they are quite costly and are suitable only for moderate hearing loss.

CAUTION!
Try out an aid for 30 days before making up your mind about it. It isn't easy to get used to hearing every sound when your world has been relatively quiet. It also takes time for your brain to adjust to amplified sound.

Heating Systems

Your heating system wards off winter's chill, but it may also create indoor air pollution. Any appliance that burns fuel, whether it's natural gas, oil, propane, coal, kerosene, or wood, discharges exhaust gases, so proper ventilation and maintenance is key.

The right system

Not all heating systems are created equal. If you are building a new home, consider a high-efficiency furnace with sealed combustion chambers, which minimizes your exposure to exhaust gases. The combustion system you choose should be certified to meet the latest safety standards. Also make sure that the furnace is the right size for your home; a unit that is too large is inefficient.

Which fuel is best? Electricity burns with no harmful exhausts, and natural gas is relatively clean-burning. Oil, coal, and wood on the other hand are not as clean, but they are generally cheaper.

Keep it clean

For all systems except electric ones, install a carbon monoxide detector where it can be heard to protect you and your family from leaks of this colorless, odorless gas produced by combustion. At low levels the gas causes headache, dizziness, nausea, fatigue, and shortness of breath. At high levels it can be fatal, especially to children and the elderly.

Make sure your heating contractor inspects your furnace in summer or early fall, before you turn on the heat—especially if your furnace is more than 10 years old. The contractor will see that the furnace is venting exhaust gases properly and has an adequate intake of air, check the flues for leakage or blockage, and inspect the vents to ensure they haven't loosened.

During the winter, clean or replace your furnace's air filter once a month.

Warm air tends to be dry—another reason to set your thermostat low.

Dirty ducts?

Hot-air ducts can circulate pollen, dust, and other contaminants. Some experts recommend having your ducts vacuumed once a year, but others question the practice. If allergies are a problem in your family, replace the furnace's air filter with a high-efficiency model. Ducts that go through your attic can circulate insulation particles if they leak, so make sure your heating contractor checks those each year.

Gas: special concerns

If you have gas heat and you notice an odor, don't touch any electrical switches, don't use the phone, and don't smoke or light any matches. Get everyone out of the house immediately, and call the gas company, or dial 911, from a neighbor's house or a pay phone.

All gas appliances should have a plate showing the Canadian Gas Association logo and the letters CGA—your guarantee of certain safety and service standards. If any of your gas appliances do not have this plate, call your distributor right away. Your gas will be disconnected until your supplier is sure the appliance is safe. Ask your gas company to check out any used appliances you buy.

Finally, never use unvented propane or kerosene heaters indoors; they can release deadly levels of carbon monoxide.

If you have steam-heat radiators, be sure to put covers on them to protect toddlers from burns.

Chimneys for Wood Burners

If you use wood in a fireplace, woodstove, or wood furnace, your chimney needs special attention.

- Before each heating season, call to have your chimney inspected for bird's nests or other blockages and cleaned of creosote buildup, a crusty or powdery residue that can cause chimney fires.

- Burn only seasoned (dry) wood in your fireplace, and never burn treated wood.

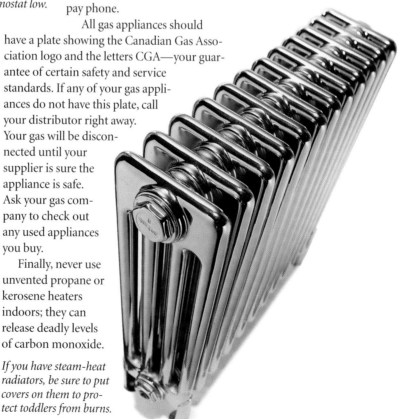

Hemorrhoid Treatments

CAUTION!
Never use preparations containing hydrocortisone for more than a few days, except under a doctor's supervision.

An effective regimen for relieving hemorrhoid inflammation consists of Epsom-salts sitz baths, witch hazel applied with a cotton ball, and a little cream or ointment (several over-the-counter preparations are available).

Ouch! At one time or another, up to 75 percent of all people develop hemorrhoids, a swelling of veins in the lower rectum near the anus. Even though anyone can develop them, older people, pregnant women, and those with low-fiber diets are most susceptible. Fortunately, in most cases self-treatment with over-the-counter preparations or simple home remedies can usually relieve mild discomfort and pain.

A real pain in the —!
Hemorrhoids are caused by excessive pressure on the veins that line the rectum. Such pressure may result from a bout of constipation, being overweight, or sitting or standing for extended periods.

The symptoms of hemorrhoids are anal bleeding or bloody stools, itching, and pain. A hemorrhoid may form inside the rectum or near the anal opening. The latter kind, which may extend outside the anus, typically causes the most pain and discomfort. Generally, symptoms can be eased by the application of topical ointments (surgery is rarely necessary), but if the condition doesn't improve in a few days, see a doctor.

Soothing solutions
Over-the-counter hemorrhoid products typically contain a lubricant, such as petroleum jelly, and a mild anesthetic to temporarily relieve friction, itching, and pain. Nevertheless, you may find relief just as fast with some of these less expensive remedies:

Symptom Sorter

Should You See a Doctor?
Even though hemorrhoids can be extremely uncomfortable, most cases can be successfully treated at home. If the following symptoms persist longer than a few days, see a doctor.

Bleeding The main and often only symptom. Anal bleeding or bloody stools may signal a more serious disorder, such as colitis or cancer of the colon or rectum.

Itching A hemorrhoid that protrudes outside the anus secretes mucus that can seriously irritate surrounding skin.

Pain This can range from mild burning to throbbing pain, especially during and after a bowel movement. Severe pain may result if blood in the hemorrhoid itself has clotted.

- Apply a cold pack for no more than three to five minutes at a time to reduce swelling.
- Sit in a warm bath for 10 minutes, three or four times a day, to soothe the affected area and help keep it clean. Add Epsom salts to the bath to relieve inflammation.
- Use moistened tissues or wipes instead of dry toilet paper after a bowel movement.

To prevent hemorrhoids from getting worse or from recurring, stay active and avoid heavy lifting and straining. Drinking more water, increasing your intake of high-fiber foods (grains, fruits, and vegetables), and cutting down on spicy foods, meat, coffee, and alcohol can also keep hemorrhoids at bay.

On the Horizon In the near future, relief from hemorrhoids may come from a topical preparation made with nitroglycerin, which is currently used to treat chest pain due to blocked arteries. Studies show that it may offer enough pain relief to allow patients to wait out the time it takes for a hemorrhoid to heal on its own.

Herbal Remedies

How can something so old be so new? Herbal remedies have been used throughout the world for thousands of years, yet today they are considered the latest thing. And they are, in the sense that science is beginning to confirm which plants really work medicinally, which ones don't, and which ones are downright dangerous.

The emergence of herbal remedies in health food stores, and even on pharmacy shelves, reflects a growing demand for more natural (and cheaper) alternatives to prescription drugs. But just because a substance is called natural does not mean that it can't be as potentially dangerous as a conventional drug or that it won't interact with any medications you may be taking. So be careful about what you buy, and how much you take.

Nature at its most promising

Herbal medicine is best known for treating minor ills. A cup of chamomile tea may help settle the stomach or relieve menstrual cramps, and a daub of fresh aloe vera gel may soothe a first-degree burn. Some herbs, however, have shown the potential to treat more serious conditions, such as circulatory problems and depression. The following are a few of the most promising herbal remedies. More information on these and other herbs appears in the chart on pages 184 and 185.

- **Ginkgo.** The extract from ginkgo-tree leaves contains compounds that may dilate blood vessels, promote circulation, and inhibit blood clotting. In Europe ginkgo is used to treat certain types of memory loss, vertigo, tinnitus (ringing in the ears), and circulatory problems. Studies indicate that it may improve cognitive function in people who suffer from dementia or are in the early stages of Alzheimer's disease. It should not be taken with other blood thinners except when directed by a physician.
- **St. Johnswort.** This herb, also known as hypericum, is widely used in Europe to treat depression—during 1994, in Germany, 66 million daily doses were prescribed. Exactly how the herb works is not

yet understood, but researchers believe it might indirectly boost levels of serotonin, a chemical in the brain that depressed people may have too little of. It should be used only for mild to moderate depression and only under a doctor's supervision.
- **Echinacea.** This herb may enhance the immune system's ability to ward off or shorten bacterial, viral, and fungal infections—even your next cold. Side effects are rare, but because it may affect the immune system, the herb should not be used by anyone with a severe illness or an autoimmune disorder, such as multiple sclerosis, rheumatoid arthritis, or lupus.
- **Valerian.** The sedative effects of this herb have been known for centuries. It is still used to treat insomnia, in part because it isn't habit-forming, as prescription sleep inducers can be. It may help you nod off

Today's herbal healers often employ the same tools—a mortar and pestle, a scale, perhaps an ancient recipe—that apothecaries used before more exact methods were developed.

181

and even improve the quality of your sleep. Valerian has virtually no side effects but should not be taken along with conventional sedatives.

- **Feverfew.** Its leaves may help lessen the frequency and severity of migraine (a condition that medicine has struggled to treat) and alleviate the nausea and vomiting that can accompany them. However, finding the most effective brand can give you a headache: quality varies, even among commercial products. Consult a doctor first.

Herbs and the law

In Canada, as in most other countries, herbs are not subject to the same level of government scrutiny as pharmaceutical drugs. Manufacturers' premarket research need not include independent guarantees of the purity or potency of their products. However, herbal preparations claiming to treat or mitigate diseases or alter a physiological state are classified as drugs and, as such, must qualify for eight-digit Drug Identification Numbers (DINs). In awarding DINs, Health Canada will accept traditional claims for a medicinal herb as long as these claims are for conditions that you can readily diagnose and treat on your own, and provided the claims are supported by two recognized authoritative herbal references.

Look for "standardized" forms of herbal remedies; in most cases, this indicates that each dose, tablet, teaspoon, or milliliter, will contain a specified amount of the herb's active ingredient. Claims, dosage, cautions, and manner of preparation should appear on the label. The label should also identify the plant part, such as leaf, root, or flower.

Take precautions

If you are considering using an herbal remedy, follow these guidelines:

- Don't use an herbal remedy to treat a serious illness unless your doctor approves.
- If you are pregnant, trying to get pregnant, or nursing, avoid herbal remedies.
- If you take medication, check with your doctor before taking an herb. Herbs can interact with conventional drugs.
- Stick to recommended doses and avoid taking an herb over long periods of time. Some herbs are as potent as prescription drugs.
- Take only one herbal remedy at a time. Never use one that is supposed to have the same effect as a medicine you are already taking.
- Monitor your symptoms closely to determine whether an herbal remedy is providing any relief—or producing unwelcome side effects. If you experience odd symptoms or feel sick, stop taking the herb immediately and call your doctor. *(continued)*

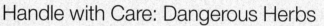

Ginseng, also known as manroot because its root resembles a human shape, has been used as a tonic for more than 2,000 years.

Handle with Care: Dangerous Herbs

While some herbs promise healing remedies for many ailments, some are so toxic that they cannot be safely recommended. Here are a few to avoid:

- **Chaparral.** This herb can cause kidney lesions or liver problems, such as hepatitis.

- **Comfrey.** Ingesting this herb in any form (including tea) or applying it topically over large areas of broken skin can be highly toxic to the liver and kidneys and may even be fatal.

- **Ephedra.** Large amounts, taken to lose weight or achieve a "natural" high, may cause dangerously elevated blood pressure and heart palpitations, even cardiac arrest and stroke.

- **Lobelia.** No safe dosage has been determined. Ingestion can slow breathing and dramatically lower blood pressure.

- **Pennyroyal.** The oil is poisonous, even in small doses. Ingesting it to induce abortion, as was once done in folk practice, can be fatal.

- **Senna.** Although it is used in small amounts in some over-the-counter laxatives, large amounts may cause diarrhea, nausea, and severe abdominal cramps.

- **Yohimbe.** Its extract (yohimbine) is used in prescription drugs for impotence, but yohimbe may cause anxiety, stomach problems, high blood pressure, and heart damage.

Herbal Remedies (continued)

Popular Herbs: How Helpful or Harmful?

Herb	What It Does	How It's Taken	Caution
Chamomile	Its volatile oil has shown antispasmodic and anti-inflammatory properties. The tea may aid digestion and help relieve menstrual cramps, irritable bowel syndrome, and infant colic.	To make a tea, pour boiling water over 1 tablespoon dried chamomile flowers or a chamomile tea bag. Steep 10 to 15 minutes. Drink up to four times a day.	May cause nausea if taken in large doses. Allergic reactions, such as rashes and breathing difficulties, especially among those with hay fever or an allergy to ragweed, are possible.
Chili Peppers	Capsaicin, the active ingredient, temporarily alleviates pain when applied topically. Studies show it helps relieve arthritis pain, diabetic neuropathy, fibromyalgia, and shingles. In a gargle, it relieves a sore throat.	Capsaicin is available in a cream for topical use. To make a gargle, add ⅛ teaspoon cayenne pepper to a cup warm salt water or a lemon-juice gargle. When gargling, don't swallow.	Keep out of the eyes; it will cause a burning sensation and temporary blindness. Topical use may cause burning or stinging, especially on tender skin. Do not ingest tinctures or alcoholic extracts.
Dong Quai	A traditional Chinese herb, it is often added to herbal formulas to regulate menstrual cycles or relieve cramps.	Available as a whole dried root in Chinese herbal pharmacies, in capsules, and as an ingredient in some herbal formulas.	May cause excessive menstrual bleeding, fever, or increased sensitivity to light. Do not take during pregnancy. Some herbalists fear dong quai may be carcinogenic.
Echinacea	It contains compounds that have been shown to stimulate the immune system and help ward off bacterial, viral, and fungal infections. It may help prevent colds and the flu and relieve their symptoms.	Take a dropperful of standardized extract (in tincture form) in water up to four times a day or 1½ teaspoons twice a day. To help fight a cold take at the onset of symptoms. Do not use for more than eight weeks at a time.	Should not be used by young children or anyone with an autoimmune disease, collagen disease, chronic infectious disease, diabetes, multiple sclerosis, or other serious disease, or by pregnant women.
Ephedra	A traditional Chinese herb used to treat asthma, it is the natural source of the synthetic compound ephedrine, found in nonprescription sinus products. It is not appropriate or effective to take ephedra when trying to lose weight.	To make a tea, pour 1 cup boiling water over 1 teaspoon of the herb. Let steep for 10 minutes. Drink only 1 cup per day.	Consult your doctor before taking it. Large amounts may be dangerous, even fatal. Normal doses raise blood pressure and may cause headache, skin irritation, nervousness, dizziness, vomiting, or heart palpitations. Do not take with caffeine. Avoid if you are pregnant or have heart disease, diabetes, or glaucoma.
Feverfew	Feverfew may reduce the frequency and severity of migraines. It contains a compound (parthenolide) that blocks serotonin, a chemical produced by the brain that, in excessive amounts, may help trigger migraine attacks.	Chew two or three leaves, or take a standardized extract that contains parthenolide (250 micrograms), each day to help prevent migraines. (Capsules and tablets may contain little of the active ingredient.)	Consult your doctor before using feverfew to manage migraines. Oral use may cause mouth ulcers and abdominal pain. Not recommended for pregnant women or young children.
Garlic	When ingested, garlic may help lower blood cholesterol and blood pressure and prevent blood clots and perhaps certain types of cancer. Freshly crushed cloves contain the antimicrobial compound allicin, which can help fight both internal and topical infections.	For internal use, freshly crushed cloves of garlic (one per day) or standardized, enteric-coated capsules are most effective. For external use, apply the pulp from a freshly crushed clove.	Large amounts may cause gastrointestinal distress, heartburn, and flatulence. In rare cases it may cause an allergic reaction. If you are taking blood-thinning medications or aspirin, consult your doctor before taking garlic preparations.
Ginger	This popular spice—raw, in real ginger ale, and in supplements—is a proven remedy for indigestion and nausea, including motion sickness and morning sickness.	To prevent nausea, take two 500-milligram capsules of the powdered root 30 minutes before traveling, then one or two more capsules if symptoms begin.	May cause sweating. In recommended amounts, ginger is safe for pregnant women.

Popular Herbs: How Helpful or Harmful?

Herb	What It Does	How It's Taken	Caution
Ginkgo	Studies have shown that leaf extracts can improve blood flow to the brain and extremities. Ginkgo may also help treat circulatory disorders, such as high blood pressure and arteriosclerosis, and slow the progress of cognitive disorders, such as dementia and Alzheimer's disease.	Take 40 milligrams of standardized *Ginkgo biloba* (in extract or tablet form) three times a day, or 60 milligrams twice a day, with food.	May cause mild stomach upset, headache, and restlessness. Consult your doctor first if you are taking any kind of blood-thinning medication, including aspirin or vitamin E.
Ginseng	The root of this Chinese herb contains compounds that may enhance the immune system, counter fatigue, fight stress, and provide a general tonic effect.	Take in the form of the raw root, a tea, or in standardized capsules that contain ginsenosides, the active ingredients, since some ginseng products contain little or none of the active ingredient.	Anyone with high blood pressure, diabetes, heart disease, or pituitary, adrenal, or thyroid problems should consult a doctor before taking ginseng. May cause skin eruptions.
Hawthorn	Extracts have shown some potential to lower blood pressure and cholesterol levels, tone the heart muscle, and help normalize irregular heartbeat.	Available in tea bags, capsules, and extracts.	Don't self-medicate a heart condition with hawthorn or any other substance. Hawthorn may interfere with cardiovascular drugs.
Licorice	This popular flavoring agent has expectorant, anti-inflammatory, and antiulcer properties. The active ingredient, glycyrrhizin, may also help relieve gastric inflammation and stomach spasms.	Available in the following forms: capsules, extract, and as a natural ingredient in candy. (Note: Many licorice candies are flavored artificially, with anise.) Do not consume more than 600 milligrams of glycyrrhizin per day; do not take it for more than four to six weeks.	Anyone with high blood pressure, cardio-vascular disease, or liver or kidney problems should take glycyrrhizin only under a doctor's supervision. Prolonged use may cause high blood pressure, edema, and lowered potassium levels. Never consume large amounts at any one time.
Milk Thistle	The active ingredient, silymarin, may help cleanse the liver of toxins, including those from deadly mushrooms. It shows promise as a treatment for cirrhosis and hepatitis.	Concentrated seed extracts (in capsules) are the most effective form. Forget about teas, since the active ingredient is not soluble in water.	Because it may affect the liver's ability to break down drugs, if you are on any medication, check with your doctor before taking the herb.
St. Johnswort	May be an effective treatment for mild to moderate depression. In nearly two dozen human studies, it helped lift depression for more than half of the patients who took it.	Available in tea bags and capsules. Look for standardized extracts with hypericin, an active ingredient.	Do not self-diagnose or self-medicate depression; see your doctor instead. Your condition may be more severe than you think, or your symptoms may indicate heart or thyroid disorders. Never take the herb with prescription antidepressants. It may also cause sensitivity to sunlight. Pregnant women and nursing mothers should never take it.
Saw Palmetto	Extracts from the berries of saw palmetto have shown the ability to help reduce symptoms of enlarged prostate, also known as benign prostatic hyperplasia (BPH).	Teas are not effective; extracts are.	Consult your doctor before taking saw palmetto to treat a prostate condition. It may interfere with prescription drugs given to treat BPH. In rare cases, it may cause stomachache.
Valerian	Used for more than 1,000 years as a mild sedative, valerian has been proven to help induce sleep without the side effects of some prescription sleeping pills.	To help calm down or induce sleep, make a tea with 1 teaspoon freshly chopped roots per cup of boiling water. Drink two to three times a day, including once before bedtime. Or take in the form of a root tincture or capsule.	Do not take if you are using other sedatives or central nervous system depressants. Avoid long-term use. Not recommended for pregnant women, nursing mothers, or young children.

Herbicides

Potent weapons in the gardener's arsenal, herbicides knock out pesky weeds that compete with cultivated plants for water, sunlight, and nutrients. Each type of herbicide has its own way of working: *contact* herbicides kill only the perennial weeds they touch; *systemics* move through the whole plant right down to the root; *preemergents* are applied to the soil to act on germinating seeds; *post-*

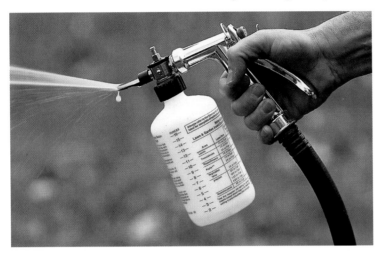

Read the label: Do-it-yourself gardeners often misuse herbicides, and they tend to use too much. With sprays, there is a danger of inhaling toxins.

emergents attack growing plants; and *selective* herbicides kill only certain types of plants.

All of them do the job, but may pose potential health risks if used improperly. Swallowing them, inhaling them, or absorbing them through the skin may induce an array of symptoms, from skin irritation to headaches and dizziness. Long-term exposure has also been linked tenuously to vision loss, neurological disorders, cancer, and other illnesses.

Herbicides can also adversely affect the environment if used improperly: They can foul the water supply, kill tiny water-plant species that provide food for birds and fish, and even kill the birds and fish with which they come into contact.

Some of the older chemicals used on lawns and gardens today may not have been rigorously tested for their effects on humans. The Pest Management Regulatory Agency of Health Canada, established in 1995, is reevaluating some chemicals permitted for use before stricter regulations came into effect.

Tips on spraying safely

When you use a spray herbicide, carefully heed the instructions on the product label. Note the kind of protective clothing you should wear and how to dispose of the empty container. Here are additional suggestions:

- Don't assume that if a given amount of herbicide is good, more is better. It isn't.
- Thoroughly wash skin after exposure.
- Keep people and pets out of treated areas for the recommended period of time.
- Reserve a sprayer and watering can only for herbicide use; store out of reach of children.
- Don't spray excessively on windy days; you could kill the "good" plants and wind up inhaling more of the chemical.
- Don't apply post-emergent herbicides if rain is forecast; they'll be washed away and may end up contaminating streams and leaching into the groundwater.

Natural alternatives to herbicides

An integral part of using herbicides safely is using them sparingly. They may be your best choice for getting rid of poison oak and poison ivy, but for routine lawn and garden purposes, consider these safer options:

- **Hand weeding.** The "old-fashioned way" may be time-consuming, but it works. Be sure to pull weeds before they flower or you'll have more to contend with later.
- **Tilling.** Till the soil between plants with a hoe or hand fork to cut off and dig up weed seedlings. Try to get the entire root; fragments can grow into new plants.
- **Boiling water.** Weeds growing in the cracks between paving stones are easily eradicated by drenching them with boiling water.
- **Mulching.** Mulches suppress weeds by denying them sunlight. Organic mulches—grass clippings, shredded leaves—enrich and improve the soil when they decompose.

Other methods include smothering weeds with "weed mats" made of polypropylene. Perhaps the best defense is to provide good growing conditions for the plants you want to encourage; robust garden plants and a dense lawn leave little room for irksome intruders.

Pity the poor feet. On an average day they take 9,000 steps and absorb hundreds of tons of stress. No surprise, then, that feet are more prone to injury than any other part of the body. In fact, about 75 percent of North Americans—mostly women—have foot problems. Podiatrists say that a major cause of such ailments is constrictive footwear (many women wear shoes that are too small). High heels, which must fit snugly in order to stay on, are often one of the culprits.

The high price of high fashion

Since the 16th century, high heels have been synonymous with fashion. The reason? Sex appeal. High heels make women appear taller and shapelier by defining the calf muscle, arching the lower back, and thrusting out the chest. But looks don't come cheap.

When the toes are squeezed into a narrow toe box, they can overlap or become mis-shapen, leading to all manner of foot prob-lems. Pointy shoes can cause bunions (bony protrusions at the base of the big toe) and hammertoes (toes that are bent into a claw-like position). Wearing them can also lead to a condition known as Morton's neuroma (a growth of nerve and fibrous tissue, often between the third and the fourth toes), which can cause pain, burning, tingling, or numb-ness. Friction from tight shoes can result in painful blisters, corns, calluses, and ingrown toenails. While most of these conditions are treatable, some of them may require surgery.

High heels also wreak havoc on other parts of the body. They shift a person's weight to the ball of the foot, forcing the rear leg ligaments to contract and shortening the calf muscles. They also cause hyperextension of the back and neck, straining those muscles and throwing the body off balance. The higher the heel, the worse the strain.

Preventive stretching

Wearing sneakers or flats will help you avoid these problems. If you do wear heels, try these stretching exercises to help save your back and calf muscles:

- **Lower back.** Lie on your back and bring both knees to your chest. Press the small of your back against the floor. Hold for one minute. Then, keeping your left shoulder on the floor, gently move your knees to the right and hold again. Repeat the stretch on the other side.
- **Calves.** Place your palms against a wall. Bring one foot forward and bend that leg. Keep your back leg straight. Slowly lean forward, keeping the heel of your back foot on the floor, and hold. Repeat on the other side.

Women have four times as many foot problems as men. Wearing high heels can only make them worse.

an ounce of Prevention

Save Your Soles

Most podiatrists frown on wearing high heels regularly. But if you must bow to fashion, follow these tips:

- Wear heels for no more than three hours a day; alternate with flats.
- Choose a "comfort" pump that pro-vides arch support and cushioning.
- Don't wear heels over 5 centimeters (2 inches) high; every 2.5 centime-ters (1 inch) increases the stress on the ball of the foot by 50 percent.
- Buy shoes with square or rounded toes rather than pointed ones.
- Opt for shoes with a wide heel.
- Spring for soft leather; synthetic materials promote perspiration, which can cause blisters.

High-rise Buildings

If a fire breaks out when you're in a high-rise, never use the elevator. A power shortage could occur that might trap you between floors.

Your job just might be making you sick if you work in a high-rise building with air-quality problems. A variety of ailments have been traced to airtight high-rises that have faulty ventilation systems. In addition, high-rise fires are possible, with risk of injury or death. Earthquakes too, though rare, take their toll.

Is your building "sick?"

As buildings have become more airtight to conserve energy, indoor pollution from human respiration, furnishings, and attached garages can build up. If the building's ventilation system is not well maintained, the indoor pollution can give you "sick-building syndrome" (SBS). Symptoms often include headaches, nausea, and allergic reactions. If you suspect that your building is "sick," contact the local office of your provincial Ministry of Labor.

A towering inferno?

Modern skyscrapers are built to prevent fires from spreading beyond a single floor. Stairways are designed to stay smoke-free, and safety is enhanced by ventilation controls, automatic sprinklers, smoke detectors, and fire alarms linked to the fire department.

To find out how well your high-rise stacks up, check with your building managers; they are required to identify and clear all fire exits, distribute emergency escape plans, and conduct fire drills. If they aren't responsive, contact your local fire department. And keep these tips in mind:

- Learn the evacuation plans for your building, and participate in fire drills.
- Count the doors between you and the exits so you can find them in the dark.
- If you're staying in a hotel, make sure your room has a smoke detector and sprinkler before checking in, and locate all exits once you arrive.
- Keep your door key handy; you may need to get back inside if exits are cut off.

Surviving an earthquake

If a quake strikes, your best chance of avoiding injury in a high-rise is to keep a level head. When you feel a tremor, stay away from outside walls and windows. Don't rush for the exit; in fact, most people who try to move more than 1.5 meters (5 feet) are injured. Get under a desk or table and hold on to it with one hand while you cover the back of your head and neck with the other. Repeat for each aftershock. When you're sure it's safe to leave the building, use the stairs—not the elevator.

Fire-Safety Measures That Are Lifesavers

- No matter how small the fire, sound the alarm immediately, and call the fire department.

- Leave the building at once, using the nearest stairway, and close all doors behind you.

- Look for a smoke-free escape route; if there is none, crawl with your face close to the floor, where the air will be cooler and less toxic.

- If you come to a closed door, feel it with the back of your hand. If it's warm, look for another route.

- If escape is cut off, go to a room with an outside window. Shut the door but don't lock it, and stuff a wet towel under the door. Call the fire department to report your location, or wave something out the window to attract the attention of the firefighters. Then stay put until help arrives.

Hip Replacement

The hips are the workhorses of the body's joints. They support your weight and, with assists from your knees, enable you to walk, run, twist, bend, and climb. The wear and tear they endure through the years takes a heavy toll, which is often compounded by injury or by such diseases as arthritis. As a result, later life can be plagued by chronic, debilitating pain and limited mobility.

Fortunately, relief for these aching joints is now available. In Canada more than 17,000 hip-replacement operations are performed each year—about 60 percent on women. The procedure, called total hip arthroplasty, boasts a success rate of 90 to 95 percent.

How does hip replacement work?

The hip, a ball-and-socket joint similar to the shoulder, consists of two parts: the rounded "ball" on the thighbone and the cuplike "socket" on the side of the pelvis. During the operation, both of these parts are cut away. The top of the thighbone is replaced with a metal or ceramic ball attached to a stem, and the pelvic pocket is replaced with a socket made of polyethylene and metal. These prostheses can be implanted into the thigh and pelvic bones and secured with cement, or they may have a porous surface that allows the bone to grow into the implants. (A hybrid type of fixation employs both methods.)

Who should have the operation?

Most candidates for this kind of surgery are between the ages of 60 and 80. Hip replacement is commonly used for those with osteoarthritis, a gradual degeneration of the cartilage that cushions bone joints. As the protective cartilage erodes, the bones eventually rub against each other, causing severe pain and crippling the patient. The surgery can also be used for those suffering from rheumatoid arthritis (an inflammation of tissues around joints that can destroy both cartilage and joints), osteonecrosis (a disruption of blood supply to the bone caused by a serious injury, leading to deterioration of the hip joint), and fractures of the hip.

The benefits usually outweigh the risks

Hip replacement is elective surgery, meaning it's not a matter of life or death. Your doctor may advise it, but ultimately you must weigh the pros and cons of having the operation. A replacement is never the same as a brand-new hip, but it will eliminate pain and restore your ability to walk, bend, and climb stairs.

Most people have uneventful recoveries from hip-replacement surgery. There is a slight chance of complications, including infection in the hip, a blood clot in the leg or lung, a urinary tract infection, or hip dislocation (the ball pops out of the socket). Over time, friction and wear cause material from the implant to break off, which might cause irritation and erosion of the bone. A hip replacement tends to last 15 to 20 years; after that, the implant may loosen.

Hip checks

Although a hip replacement increases mobility, be careful not to stress the new joint. During the first six to eight weeks, use chairs with arms, which can help propel you to a standing position. Avoid low chairs or toilets. Place a pillow between your legs when sleeping on your side. There are also long-term restrictions that can protect your implant:

- Position the repaired leg in front whenever you get up from a sitting position.
- Don't cross your legs.
- Try not to bend all the way over.
- Stick to low-impact exercises—walking, swimming, ballroom dancing, stationary biking, cross-country skiing, and golf.
- Avoid activities that stress the joint—running or lifting heavy weights.

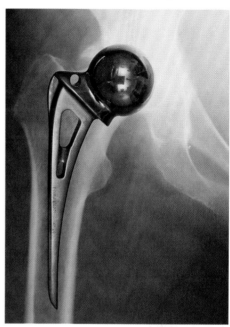

The "ball" part of the hip-replacement prosthesis rests on top of a stem that the surgeon anchors within the thighbone.

CAUTION!

Following a hip replacement, plan to limit physical activity for six months to a year. The operation requires a hospital stay of five to six days. Most patients leave the hospital walking with a cane. Some patients benefit from one or two months of physical therapy.

Home Medical Tests

The verdict? Home medical tests, such as this one for pregnancy, are quick, accurate, and (usually) inexpensive.

Do-it-yourself medical tests, available without a prescription at your local drugstore, can detect and monitor a number of conditions. They enable you to get results quickly, conveniently, and privately—without having to spend the extra time on a visit to the doctor's office. On the other hand, the tests are no substitute for the attention of a professional health-care person.

How well do they work?
Home medical tests are used to diagnose a condition, such as pregnancy, or to monitor a condition, such as diabetes. In order to be approved by Health Canada, a test must be about as accurate as its laboratory counterpart. Like lab tests, home tests are subject to human error, possibly resulting in false positives and false negatives. If your results were negative and your symptoms persist, see your doctor. You may even have a condition that is different from the one for which you tested yourself.

One important benefit of home tests (blood pressure monitors, for example) is that they allow people to take many more readings than would be possible at the doctor's office. But you can overdo it. Taking some tests repeatedly (especially blood-glucose tests, which require new strips each time) can be expensive.

Diligence makes the difference
You can help ensure the accuracy of your home medical test results by following the instructions exactly as given. Note whether you need to avoid certain foods or beverages before taking the test. And keep these points in mind:

- Before purchasing a do-it-yourself test kit, always check the expiration date on the package; outdated products can yield false results.
- Do not use a test kit that has been exposed to heat, either in a store or in your home. (Don't leave the test kit on a sunny windowsill, near a radiator, or in a hot car trunk.)
- Read all instructions on the package before you start. Delays between steps can affect test results.
- Do not skip any steps, even if they seem unnecessary.
- Use a stopwatch or a watch with a second hand when timing is critical.
- Perform the test in a clean area, away from any food or drinks.
- Keep written records of test results. You may need these for follow-up visits with your doctor.
- Call your doctor or look for the toll-free number inside the kit if you don't understand the directions or can't read the results.

On the Horizon A kit may soon be available that allows men to test the quality and quantity of their sperm in about two minutes. This may be helpful for couples having trouble conceiving. Home tests already on the market abroad but not yet available in Canada include one that detects *Helicobacter pylori,* the bacteria that causes some gastrointestinal ulcers, and a PSA test that screens for prostate cancer.

Some Common Home Medical Tests

Test	Tests For	How It's Done	Comments
Pregnancy	Conception	Urine is applied to a stick covered with chemically treated paper.	Delayed reading time of just 10 to 20 minutes can turn a negative result into a false-positive one. The test user who does not have regular periods may find it difficult to determine her missed period and, therefore, could test too early or too late with pregnancy testing kits.
Ovulation	Predicts ovulation within 36 hours	Urine is passed over chemically treated paper.	Sometimes hormone levels are so low that a woman may require twice-daily testing for several days to determine ovulation status.
Blood Pressure	Diastolic and systolic blood pressure levels	A cuff device is wrapped around the upper arm, wrist, or finger, and pressurized air is pumped to the area over the artery. To observe trends properly, take blood pressure regularly at the same time everyday and under the same conditions.	Finger-cuff monitors tend to give less-accurate results and are more sensitive to temperature and to poor blood circulation. Accuracy of all varieties is affected by smoking, caffeine, exercise 30 minutes prior to test, position of arm (cuffed area should be level with heart), and dust or low batteries in electronic units. Mechanical monitors involve the use of a stethoscope to detect the rhythmic beatings of the blood flow, whereas electronic monitors measure changes in the pressure of the cuff. Mechanical monitors are generally more reliable (and less expensive) than electronic types.
Blood Glucose	High or low blood sugar	Drop of blood from a pricked finger or earlobe is placed on chemically treated paper, which is inserted into handheld diagnostic machine for a reading.	Home tests are generally 10 to 15 percent less accurate than lab tests; accuracy is further affected by heat, cold, humidity, altitude, freshness of strips, or large doses of vitamin C or acetaminophen.
Cholesterol	Total blood cholesterol. Test does not differentiate between HDL ("good" cholesterol) and LDL ("bad" cholesterol).	Drop of blood from a pricked finger is placed on chemically treated paper.	Using too little blood, waiting too long or not long enough, taking vitamin C or acetaminophen, can affect results.
Hidden (Occult) Fecal Blood	Colorectal cancer	Chemically treated pad is placed in the toilet bowl after bowel movement. Color change indicates presence of blood. Alternatively, a special wipe is used following bowel movement, and a chemical is then added to the wipe. A color change indicates the result.	Toilet bowel cleaner, large doses of vitamin C, citrus fruits, red meat, broccoli, and artichokes can affect results. Positive test result may also indicate bleeding hemorrhoids or gastrointestinal bleeding from aspirin use. Some test brands are overly sensitive, leading to more false positives. Since cancers do not bleed continuously, test detects only one in three malignancies.
Ear and Throat	Earache examination kit can be used to check for symptoms caused by childhood otitis media, or even earwax impaction; throat examination kit, for detecting conditions such as "strep" infection.	Home versions of ear and throat lights, used by physicians and other health-care professionals. Kits come with guides explaining proper use. The user should be aware the examination kits must not replace or delay proper medical attention.	
Peak Flow Monitors	Airflow in asthma patients	Exhale into mouthpiece connected to meter that measures the amount of air exhaled from lungs.	Not exhaling properly can affect results. Test should be done three times, several minutes apart; take the highest reading.

Homeopathy

Homeopathic remedies, distinguished only by "homeopathic" in small type on the label, are increasingly common on more and more drugstore shelves.

Can 13 million North Americans be wrong about their choice of medical care? That's the number of people, according to one homeopathic organization, who currently subscribe to the controversial practice of homeopathy. Homeopathy originated 200 years ago in protest against the harsh medical practices of the day, such as bloodletting, blistering, and purging. People who depend on homeopathy today tend to object to current practices in conventional medicine as well.

Homeopathy explained

The basis of homeopathic medicine is a philosophy called the "Law of Similars," otherwise known as "like cures like." This means that a substance that produces symptoms in a healthy person can cure a person suffering with the same symptoms. For example, if eating a certain herb causes people to cough, that same herb is used to treat a sick person whose main symptom is a cough. The goal is to stimulate the immune system so that the body heals itself.

The premise is similar to that of conventional vaccines. To fight the flu, for example, a mild form of a flu virus is administered in the form of a vaccine. The vaccine sensitizes your immune system so that it will recognize and destroy real flu germs before they make you sick. Immunotherapy, in which injections of allergy-producing substances are given to patients suffering from allergies, likewise desensitizes people to those allergens.

What's the difference?

One major area where the traditional and the homeopathic medical traditions part company is in the preparation of medications. All conventional medicines are rigorously tested and must contain a specified percentage of their active ingredient, which is printed on the label. Homeopathic medications are under no such constraints. They are highly diluted versions of plant, herb, or animal extracts. The dilution could be as great as one part extract per 1 million parts water.

Most mainstream doctors maintain that the cures are far too weak to produce any results, much less any side effects. Claims of positive results, they suggest, are attributable to the placebo effect. Homeopathic practitioners claim that the mixture, no matter how diluted it is, has been "imprinted" with the memory of the original substance, thereby retaining its beneficial properties.

Testing the effectiveness

Recently, a British medical journal surveyed various homeopathic studies and concluded certain remedies might be effective, especially for seasonal allergies. Until more rigorous testing is completed, one cannot go far wrong in resorting to homeopathic remedies only for self-limiting illnesses such as colds, the flu, headaches and diarrhea. One further caution: many homeopathic extracts are preserved in alcohol, and some doctors believe that the alcohol (like that in some mouthwashes) may increase the risk of oral cancer.

CAUTION!

If you take homeopathic drugs, you run the risk of not getting treatment for serious medical conditions. Never take homeopathic drugs for life-threatening or chronic illnesses.

Hormone Replacement Therapy

Every woman faces a tough decision when she feels the first effects of menopause: "Should I start hormone replacement therapy or not?" Taking a combination of female hormones—estrogen and progesterone—at a time when a woman's own hormone production is dramatically reduced can ease uncomfortable symptoms and provide important health benefits. But this therapy, called HRT, is not without controversy. The reason: a barrage of conflicting studies shows that the treatment has both benefits and risks.

Pros and cons

When HRT first came into use in the 1960s, estrogen was primarily used. The main goal of treatment was elimination of obvious signs of estrogen depletion associated with the "change of life"—hot flashes, vaginal dryness, insomnia, aching joints, fatigue, incontinence, and mood swings.

As time went on, HRT came to play an even more positive role in women's health. Studies indicate that estrogen reduces one's risk of developing heart disease, the major cause of death among older women (estrogen is even being tested in men for this benefit). It also staves off osteoporosis, the bone-thinning disorder so common in older women. Research shows that, alone or in combination with progesterone, estrogen may also reduce colon cancer, speed wound healing, and delay memory loss and Alzheimer's disease.

However, estrogen also has drawbacks. It increases the risk of uterine cancer, unless it is given with progesterone. Even when prescribed with progesterone, links to breast cancer crop up. Unfortunately, the association is not clear-cut. An impressive array of studies has both supported and refuted the breast-cancer links. One of the largest studies, conducted by Harvard University on some 60,000 women, yielded conflicting results. Although HRT was found to cut the overall risk of death by 37 percent—reducing mortality rates from heart disease a whopping 53 percent—death from breast cancer rose 43 percent. But even those findings are ambiguous; the same study revealed that HRT users with a family history of breast cancer actually reduced their chances of dying from it by 35 percent. Clearly, definitive answers are not yet forthcoming.

The Estrogen Effect

Brain: Estrogen relieves hot flashes, mood swings, and depression. It may prevent memory loss and Alzheimer's disease.

Skin: It helps to keep collagen intact, so that wrinkling is less pronounced.

Heart: It lowers bad LDL cholesterol and raises good HDL cholesterol, and is estimated to cut the risk of heart disease by half.

Breast: It may increase the risk of breast cancer. If selective estrogen replacement modulators are substituted for the estrogen in the HRT, the risk is eliminated.

Colon and bladder: It helps prevent incontinence and may lower colon-cancer risk.

Vagina, uterus, and ovaries: It maintains vaginal lubrication often lost after menopause. Although it elevates uterine-cancer risks, they are eliminated if progesterone is taken with it. Cervical- and ovarian-cancer risks are not elevated by HRT.

Bones: It helps build bone, stopping the onset of osteoporosis and rebuilding bone lost to the disease.

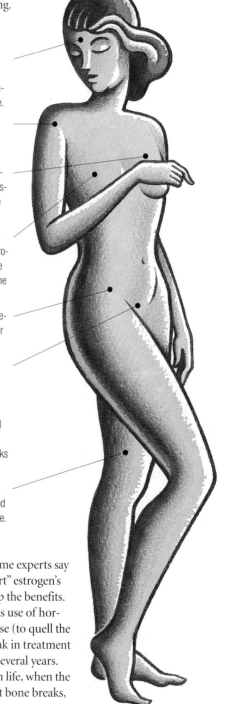

Making the HRT decision

If you are considering HRT, some experts say there may be a way to "outsmart" estrogen's nastier side effects and still reap the benefits. The key may lie in the judicious use of hormones at the start of menopause (to quell the discomfort), followed by a break in treatment anywhere from six months to several years. You might resume HRT later in life, when the risk of heart disease, significant bone breaks, and Alzheimer's disease is greater. In this way, you may benefit from estrogen without risking prolonged exposure to it.

Another way to make your decision is to pay strict attention to your personal health profile (see Is HRT Right for You? at left). If your main reason for taking HRT is bone health, be sure to have a bone-density test first. This will tell you whether you really do have a bone problem.

While considering HRT, you should also be aware that, in addition to possible health risks, it can present some troubling side effects, most notably irregular bleeding. Estrogen can also raise triglyceride levels (blood fats that contribute to heart disease) and increase the risk of developing gallbladder disease, migraines, and deep-vein blood clots that might ultimately lead to pulmonary embolism. The progesterone component of HRT can cause moodiness, depression, and bloating in some women.

One way around some of these side effects is to work with your doctor to customize your HRT treatment. Changing the dose, type, or schedule of progesterone can, for example, reduce vaginal bleeding and alleviate progesterone-related symptoms. Taking a lower dose of estrogen may lessen some of its risks and still deliver its benefits. Switching from pills to a patch can eliminate some threat of gallbladder disease and blood clots, as well as the adverse effects on triglyceride levels. Adding just a touch of testosterone—the male hormone that is also present in women—may ease menopause-related sexual problems, such as a lack of desire. There are numerous treatment options, and your doctor can work with you to find the one that's right for you.

An alternative to estrogen

For women who cannot take HRT for medical reasons, or choose not to, there are other options to consider. A group of medications known as selective estrogen replacement modulators (SERMs) are being studied, particularly the drug raloxifen. So far, they pro-

Is HRT Right for You?

If these factors are present, you may benefit from HRT:

- High blood pressure
- Obesity
- Diabetes
- Early menopause
- Family history of heart disease, colon cancer, or Alzheimer's disease
- Chronic use of medications that accelerate bone loss, such as steroids or coumadin.
- Risk for osteoporosis (Caucasian, thin, lifelong low calcium intake)

If these factors are present, HRT may be risky for you:

- Breast cancer in your mother or sister
- History of blood clots
- Liver disease

"Natural" Remedies

For menopausal discomfort, such as hot flashes and mood swings, some women take herbs like black cohosh, chasteberry, St. Johnswort, and licorice root. These herbs may indeed provide relief, although their long-term effects are unknown, particularly in regard to their ability to relieve more serious aspects of estrogen depletion, such as an increased risk of osteoporosis. In the case of herbal remedies, the quantity and quality of their ingredients can vary widely, even from bottle to bottle of the same brand. Experts warn that this makes it hard to avoid overdosing, which can be dangerous.

Another alternative to HRT is soy, which contains plant estrogens. Some studies indicate that soy protein may alleviate hot flashes and night sweats. You can get soy in tofu, soy milk, soy protein powder (add it to milk shakes) and nutritional supplements.

vide many of the benefits of estrogen, but with fewer risks. They work by providing the positive effects of estrogen in certain parts of the body (for example, building bone and lowering cholesterol levels in the arteries) while acting as an antiestrogen in other areas of the body, such as breast tissue.

Women who are interested only in preserving skeletal health might consider other options, such as Fosamax, a nonhormonal medication, that enhance bone density.

Hospitals

You enter a hospital expecting to exit healthier. And for most people, that is the case. But for some folks, a trip to the hospital becomes a health-care nightmare. The reason? They contract a hospital-based infection, such as bacteria in the urinary tract, pneumonia, staphylococcus, or a variety of gastrointestinal bugs. What's more, sometimes those who enter a hospital die—not from their original problem but from a disease they contracted while there.

In Canadian hospitals, the most common types of medical "misadventure"—that's the term used by the World Health Organization to define accidental harm to patients—are cuts, punctures, perforations, or hemorrhages during medical care. But misadventures, which befall fewer than one percent of Canadian patients, also include failure of sterile precautions. What's a person to do?

Unhealthy health-care

Hospital-based illness is nothing new. When you think about it, catching an infection in a building full of sick people is not so implausible. But experts estimate that one-third of all hospital-based illnesses could be prevented if simple measures were enforced.

One of the most basic ways to control the spread of infection is adequate hand washing by hospital staff, even before they don gloves. Yet studies show that employees involved in patient care typically wash their hands between patients only 40 percent of the time. Another common problem is a scarcity of infection-control specialists on staff. This can affect all aspects of infection control, particularly the sterilization of equipment. Even bed rails and dust bunnies can carry germs, so it's important that the hospital be kept clean.

What the patient can do

Unfortunately, it's the hospital that must take the proper precautions to ensure that you don't contract an infection while you are there. There are also a few steps you can take while you're in the hospital. Request that anyone who cares for you—or enters your room—washes their hands thoroughly. If your room doesn't appear clean, tell a nurse.

Also, make sure that you're protected at those times when you're most susceptible to infection. Ask that your presurgery antibiotic be given two hours before your operation so that its action will peak at the time the incision is made. After surgery, if you haven't developed an infection during the first two days, ask to be taken off your postoperative antibiotic.

If your recuperation requires a urine catheter, ask your doctor how long it should be left in and how frequently it should be drained. If the schedule is not followed, ask why. Make sure all personnel handling your catheter—or performing any other invasive procedure—wear fresh, sterile gloves.

Finally, be an informed patient. This will help guard against other dangers, such as being given the wrong medication or dose. Find out what drugs your doctor has prescribed and when you are supposed to take them, and question the nurse (or have a family member do so) if you notice a deviation.

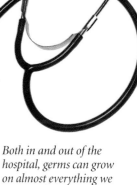

Both in and out of the hospital, germs can grow on almost everything we touch—even a doctor's stethoscope. Doctors should clean all their hand-held instruments regularly.

Surgical teams scrub their hands and arms before donning sterile latex gloves. Only sterile instruments, sheets, and clothing are allowed in the operating area.

Hot Tubs

Relaxing in a hot tub can open and clean the skin's pores, but it may also leave the skin dry and itchy.

After a tough day, soaking in a hot tub, Jacuzzi, or other type of spa may be just the ticket to melt away aches, pains, and stress. Are there health risks? Yes, but not the ones you may think.

Getting in hot water

People once feared that they could contract ailments such as herpes or genital warts in hot tubs. But this isn't the case. These viruses can't survive the hot water and the chlorine in hot tubs. Neither can the virus that causes AIDS. Hot tubs can, however, foster bacteria such as the one that causes folliculitis (itchy red bumps that may contain pus). And some people have developed bronchitis and flu-like symptoms from breathing air contaminated by bacteria growing in the water. A few have even contracted Legionnaires' disease, a form of pneumonia that can be fatal.

To limit bacteria growth, be sure to keep chlorine levels between one and five parts per million and pH levels around 7.5. Change the water and clean the tub and filter often. Remove your bathing suit and take a shower immediately after soaking.

Hot tubs pose other problems, which can be eliminated if you take certain precautions. Drownings in hot tubs have been reported; children under age five are particularly at risk. Always supervise children, and keep a locked cover on the spa when it is not in use. Even adults can drown in a hot tub. If your hair gets sucked into the drain, your head may be pulled underwater. Long hair should be worn up. Make sure your spa has a drain cover, and periodically check to see that it is in place. In older hot tubs, blocking the drain with a body part can increase its suction so much that it may trap you. The risk is lower with newer tubs, which have two drain outlets per pump. Still, know where the tub's cutoff switch is. Finally, keep the water at 40°C (104°F) or below. Water that's too hot may cause you to fall asleep; it can also cause heat stroke.

Who Should Not Soak?

- If you're a man whose partner is trying to conceive, be aware that the water's high heat can temporarily lower sperm count.

- If you're pregnant, check with your doctor before using a hot tub. The heat, especially in the first trimester, is potentially dangerous to a fetus.

- If you are overweight or are on medication, or if you have high blood pressure, heart disease, or diabetes, consult your doctor before using a hot tub or spa.

an ounce of Prevention

How to Enjoy a Healthy Soak

To minimize your health risks, experts recommend the following:

- Limit soaking time to 15 minutes. Get out sooner if your heart is racing, if you are sweating a lot, or if you feel light-headed or nauseated.

- Always wear a bathing suit; use clean, dry towels. One study found that the genital herpes virus can survive for several hours on plastic benches and wet towels near hot tubs.

- Don't drink and soak. Alcohol dilates blood vessels, dehydrates the body, and can cause you to drown.

- Don't soak right after a workout. When you're already hot and sweaty, the heat from a hot tub may place added stress on your heart. Wait at least 30 minutes to cool down.

Hot Weather

For most of us, summer is a special season of barbecues and beach weekends. To enjoy it in good health, protect your skin from the sun and learn how to beat the heat.

I'll follow the sun—carefully

Sunburn can occur even when the temperature is not especially high. It turns the skin red and can cause moderate discomfort. Even though severe cases can blister the skin, sunburn is usually minor. However, repeated sunburn over many years may increase the risk of skin cancer. To help prevent sunburn, use a sunscreen with an SPF (sun protection factor) of at least 15 and avoid prolonged exposure to the sun, especially when it is at its strongest—between 10 A.M. and 3 P.M.

Eat, drink, and stay cool

The body can be overwhelmed by extreme

Symptom Sorter

Sweating and flushed skin are part of the body's natural cooling mechanism. Still, there are signs that the heat is getting the best of you. Be aware of these ills:

- **Heat rash.** Also called prickly heat, this is marked by patches of tingling red bumps. To avoid it, try to keep sweating to a minimum and wear loose, lightweight clothing.

- **Heat cramps.** When the body sweats, the muscles lose minerals and salt and are therefore more susceptible to painful spasms.

- **Heat exhaustion.** Symptoms include heavy sweating, dizziness, headache, nausea, and, occasionally, fainting.

- **Heat stroke.** Body temperature can rise to 40°C (104°F) or more. Sweating may subside or stop entirely, resulting in hot, dry skin. The victim may become disoriented or unconscious. Lay the person down in a cool area, call 911, then cool him or her with wet sponges and fans.

heat and humidity, particularly if you overexert yourself. Take the following precautions:

- **Drink up.** Doing so, even if you don't feel thirsty, will help replace valuable fluids. Water is best. Avoid alcohol and caffeine—both are diuretics, which remove fluids from the body by increasing urination.

- **Eat light.** Cold meals, such as salads, are best; use the oven as little as possible. Replenish the salt and minerals lost to sweating with lightly salted foods and beverages—salt tablets, however, are not recommended.

- **Avoid overexertion.** Take regular breaks during exercise. If you really want to squeeze in your outdoor workout during a hot spell, go out early in the morning or in the evening, and stay in the shade.

- **Wear lightweight, loose-fitting clothing.** Light colors and natural fibers, especially cotton, are the best choice. Baseball caps or sun hats can also help by protecting the eyes from glare and shading the face.

- **Just cool it.** If you have air conditioning, use it. If you don't, make regular visits to air-conditioned public places, such as malls and movie theaters. If nothing else, use a fan. It won't cool the air, but it will encourage the evaporation of sweat.

CAUTION!
Certain drugs can make you more susceptible to heat illness. These include antidepressants (such as Prozac), gastrointestinal drugs containing atropine, and cardiovascular beta-blockers and diuretics.

Older folks, young children, and those who are obese or suffer from diabetes, low blood pressure, or heart disease should be especially careful when the mercury soars.

Household Cleansers

CAUTION!

If a caustic or poisonous substance is swallowed or gets in the eyes, follow first-aid directions on the label, then call the toll-free number listed there or your local poison control center.
Be prepared: display a chart that describes how to handle various emergencies, and make sure family members and babysitters know where it is.

Household cleansers, plus a little elbow grease, make kitchens and bathrooms sparkle, keep floors spotless, and let the sun shine through windows. Regular cleaning also destroys germs on food-preparation areas and rids homes of mold, mildew, dust, and other allergens that can cause asthma and hay fever.

Yet many cleaning products also have the potential to damage the health of people who use them. Some products emit hazardous fumes or are poisonous if swallowed. If misused or spilled by accident, some can burn the skin or present a fire hazard. If poured down a storm sewer or a basement drain, cleansers can pollute local waterways.

What's in that bottle?

Most homes have a collection of cleansers, ranging from scouring powders and glass cleaners to disinfectants and mold and mildew removers. Besides detergents, many of these products contain ammonia, which is excellent for removing grime and grease.

Handle ammonia with care. Its fumes can irritate eyes and lungs. If spilled on the skin, it may cause rashes, redness, or a chemical burn. Although the amount of ammonia in most cleansers poses no acute risk, follow the instructions for use and storage. Never mix ammonia with hypochlorite, the active ingredient in chlorine bleach, because it creates potentially deadly chloramine gas.

Chlorine bleach has drawbacks, too. Some people are highly sensitive to its fumes. If splashed in the eyes, it can cause serious irritation. It can also cause red, itchy skin. If mixed with vinegar or some toilet-bowl cleaners, it will produce toxic chlorine gas, which may be fatal if too much is inhaled.

Another noxious ingredient is lye (listed on the label as sodium hydroxide or potassium hydroxide), found in many oven and toilet cleaners. Lye can burn the skin on contact, irritate the respiratory tract when inhaled, and damage the esophagus and stomach if swallowed. Low levels of formaldehyde, a suspected carcinogen and an irritant to the eyes, skin, and respiratory tract, are also found in a few cleaning products.

Shopping smart

To reduce your exposure to harsh chemicals, shop for less toxic alternatives. How can you tell how dangerous a cleanser is? Check the label. By law, potentially hazardous products that contain chlorine, ammonia, and petroleum distillates must be labeled as follows:

- "Corrosive" means the product can burn your skin or eyes. If swallowed, it will damage your esophagus and stomach.

Most of these products rely on one of three main ingredients: chlorine bleach, ammonia, and lye. If used properly, they pose little risk to your health.

- "Explosive" means the container can explode if heated or punctured. Flying pieces of metal or plastic can cause serious injury, especially to the eyes.
- "Flammable" means the product or its vapors ignites near heat, flames, or sparks.
- "Poison" means if you swallow, lick, or inhale the product, you may become very sick or die.

In addition, symbols on labels are framed by a triangle (for "Caution"); a diamond (for "Warning"); or an octagon (for "Danger").

When stocking up on cleaning supplies,

One way to avoid harsh chemicals is to make some of your own household cleansers with items you may already have in your kitchen.

look for nontoxic alternatives. Some manufacturers participate in industry programs to produce environmentally safe, yet effective cleansers. Even for removing mold and mildew, there are nontoxic alternatives to bleach.

Whenever possible, avoid aerosol sprays: the tiny droplets can easily get into the eyes or be inhaled into the lungs. Aerosol cans can also explode if they are exposed to heat.

Cleaning-product labels are not required to list all the ingredients, except for ammonia, chlorine, and other hazardous chemicals. So you may not know what's in the cleansers you buy. One way to avoid harsh chemicals is to make your own cleansers, using substitutes from your own kitchen (see the chart, right).

Handle with care

When using any cleanser, follow the label's directions. Never mix cleaning products unless the labels state you can; otherwise, you may brew up poisonous fumes. Many products should be used in well-ventilated areas: open the windows and use a fan if necessary. Never eat or drink while using cleansers; you might ingest traces of the chemicals. Keep all flammable products away from heat or flame, and, of course, don't smoke when using them.

Even cleaning products not labeled as poisonous can be toxic if they are swallowed.

Although those that pose the most serious danger must have child-resistant containers, all cleansers should be stored out of the reach of children and pets, preferably in a locked cabinet. To avoid mistaking cleansers for something else, keep them in their original containers and make sure that their labels remain attached.

Dispose of these products properly. If you can't use up a product, give it to a friend, neighbor, or nonprofit organization. If this is not possible, you can pour ammonia, bleach, disinfectants, glass cleaners, and toilet-bowl cleaners into the toilet or the sink's drain and flush them away with plenty of water—unless you have a certain kind of septic system. If you have a septic system, call the wastewater-treatment plant in your area, or the municipal water department, to find out whether you can dispose of cleaning products in this way.

Cleansers can irritate the skin, so protect your hands when using them. If rubber gloves cause an allergic reaction, try vinyl ones, or wear thin cotton gloves underneath.

Homemade Alternatives to Common Cleansers

Product	Active Ingredients	Possible Substitute Ingredients
Scouring powder	Chlorine bleach	Buy nonchlorinated scouring powder. Or scrub with baking soda or borax.
Oven cleaner	Lye, ammonia	Clean up spills promptly, or use a paste of baking soda, salt, and water. Try noncaustic oven cleaners without lye.
Glass cleaner	Ammonia	To remove hard-water spots, wash with $\frac{1}{4}$ cup of white vinegar in 1 liter of water; dry with paper towels or a squeegee.
All-purpose cleaner	Ammonia, chlorine bleach	Use $\frac{1}{2}$ cup of borax mixed in 4 liters of warm water.
Linoleum-floor cleaner	Ammonia	Use $\frac{1}{2}$ cup of vinegar in 4 liters of warm water.
Mold and mildew remover	Chlorine bleach	Wash mildewed area with $\frac{1}{2}$ cup of borax mixed in 2 cups of water.
Basin, tub, and tile cleaner	Ammonia, chlorine bleach	Clean tiles with half a lemon dipped in borax, then rinse with water.
Toilet-bowl cleaner	Lye	Sprinkle on equal parts borax and baking soda, add vinegar, then scrub.

Humidifiers

What could be unhealthy about humidifying dry indoor air? Doing so helps prevent chapped lips, rough skin, scratchy throats, and stuffy noses. But some humidifiers may emit more than water and make your home a haven for bacteria. The bottom line? A clean humidifier is a healthier humidifier.

The breeding ground

If humidifier tanks aren't cleaned regularly, they become breeding grounds for bacteria, fungi, and other microorganisms. When released with the watery mist, these microbes can create their own brand of respiratory problems; eye, nose, and throat irritation; flulike symptoms; and serious infections.

The way they work

If your home has a forced-air heating system, you can humidify your whole house with a central unit mounted in the ductwork (keep in mind that these units, too, require regular maintenance). Otherwise, you can buy a portable model that humidifies one room or more. There are five different types:

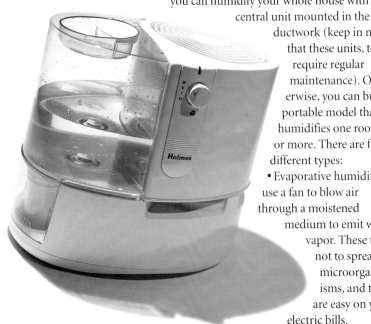

Each type of humidifier, such as this cool-mist unit, works differently, so check the directions before changing filters and cartridges or cleaning one.

- Evaporative humidifiers use a fan to blow air through a moistened medium to emit water vapor. These tend not to spread microorganisms, and they are easy on your electric bills.
- Steam vaporizers create vapor by boiling water. Boiling kills microorganisms in the water but uses more energy than other humidifiers. Also, someone standing nearby may be scalded by the steam, or by the water if the unit tips over.
- Warm-mist humidifiers also work by boiling water, but a fan cools down the air so that the mist won't scald. Boiling the water kills microorganisms, but the water may scald if the unit tips over. This humidifier also uses more energy.
- Cool-mist, or impeller, humidifiers produce a cool, fine mist with a high-speed, rotating disk. They use little energy but are apt to emit microorganisms and, if filled with hard tap water, to release minerals from the water. The minerals settle on surfaces in a room in the form of a fine white dust. (Newer models have filters that trap both the organisms and the minerals.)
- Ultrasonic humidifiers turn water into a fine mist through ultrasonic vibrations. They can disperse microorganisms, including bacteria and molds, as well as the white mineral dust from hard water. Some experts recommend that only deionized, distilled, or demineralized water be used in these models.

The clean humidifier

Regularly cleaning a humidifier helps to cut down on any harmful emissions. Here are some tips to follow:

- Change the water daily. Empty the tank and wipe the surfaces dry before refilling.
- Use distilled water to prevent mineral dispersion and scale (a crusty buildup) in the tank. Use demineralization cartridges or filters if suggested by the manufacturer.
- Clean the humidifier every three days with a brush and a 3 percent solution of hydrogen peroxide, or each week with a bleach solution (1 teaspoon per 4 liters or gallon of water). If you use bleach, let it soak for 20 minutes, then swish it side to side. Rinse thoroughly until the odor is gone. Wipe dry.
- When tank scale builds up, scrub it with a soft brush and a cup of white vinegar, then wipe tank with a vinegar-dampened cloth. Rinse thoroughly with warm water.
- At the season's end, clean the tank and discard the filters and demineralization cartridges. Store the unit in a dry location. Clean the tank again at the start of the next season, and install new filters or cartridges.

Hypnosis

Contrary to what you've seen in old horror movies, when you're hypnotized, you can't be forced to do anything you don't want to do. What hypnosis will do is make you more receptive to suggestion. Studies show that it can even ease some physical conditions. As a result, hypnosis has shed its hocus-pocus image and become an accepted part of mainstream medicine. In fact, hypnosis has developed into a valuable tool to treat pain and anxiety.

How does hypnosis work?

Three out of four adults are receptive to hypnosis to some degree; one in six is highly susceptible. You are a good candidate if you have a vivid imagination, if you like to get absorbed in a project for long stretches, or if you enjoy solitary pursuits. You're less likely to go into a trance easily if *logic* and *rationality* are your bywords.

Hypnosis is a state of relaxed but heightened focus, similar to meditation. A hypnotherapist typically asks you to concentrate by staring at a fixed point or counting slowly to 100 or closing your eyes and visualizing a soothing place. Breathing and heart rate slow as you tune out your surroundings. Your mind becomes extremely receptive to new images and possibilities, and the hypnotherapist can give you a specific healing suggestion. (In some cases you may be taught to reinforce it later with self-hypnosis.) Why you are suggestible in this state is unclear, but hypnotized people appear to have increased blood flow to the frontal cerebral cortex; this tends to block sensory input and a create a surge of theta waves associated with concentrated attention.

Medical uses

Hypnosis is normally used in conjunction with other medical treatments. It has been shown to soothe symptoms of asthma, alleviate nausea, and relieve pain—including cancer pain, post-operative discomfort, chronic back pain, and burn and headache pain.

For instance, a health professional trained in hypnosis might suggest that you are putting on a glove filled with painkillers or that you have a control knob in your mind that allows you to turn off pain. This approach is so effective that some hospitals have tried hypnosis in place of anesthesia for surgery. Hypnosis also shows promise as a treatment for irritable bowel syndrome and clenched-jaw syndrome.

Some psychiatrists employ hypnosis to lessen anxiety and irrational fears. They also find it useful for diagnosing and treating patients with multiple personality disorder. Using hypnosis to recover suppressed memories has yielded uncertain results.

To find a health-care professional trained in hypnosis in your area, you should contact the Canadian Society of Clinical Hypnosis or a professional association of hypnotists in your province.

Depending on your susceptibility, a hypnotic trance can range from mild—like a daydream—to deep—like a trance. Staring at a pendulum or a fixed point can focus your concentration.

What Hypnosis Won't Do

Don't depend on hypnosis to help you quit smoking or lose weight; the evidence is mixed about whether the process works for either one of these problems.

Self-Hypnosis for Stress Reduction

- Seat yourself comfortably in a quiet place. Relax and stare at a fixed point. Breathe slowly and deeply.

- Think of a pleasant experience, phrase, or image.

- Imagine that you are floating in space as you count backward very slowly from five to one. When you've finished, concentrate again on that floating sensation.

- Imagine looking from a distance at your current situation. Think about how simple it looks from so far away. Suggest to yourself that it will still look simple after you "return."

- To come out of your self-hypnosis, imagine yourself coming forward to the present, counting slowly from one to five as you do.

Hysterectomy

Every year, about 55,000 Canadian women undergo hysterectomy—removal of the uterus. It's the most frequently performed major gynecological operation in Canada. Most patients are women aged 35 to 44 years (about 38 percent), followed by those aged 45 to 54 years (about 27 percent).

Although hysterectomy rates in Canada have fallen in the last 10 years, critics still argue that much of this surgery is unnecessary and possibly damaging, since the uterus plays an integral role in the endocrine system, even after menopause. Experts suggest rates may further decline as women learn about effective alternatives and demand less invasive treatments.

Reasons for surgery

Hysterectomy is considered the only option for invasive cancer of the ovary, uterus, or cervix. Yet these cases account for only a percentage of hysterectomies. It is more often performed for non-life-threatening conditions: fibroids, benign uterine growths that can cause pelvic pain and heavy menstrual bleeding; abnormal uterine bleeding; endometriosis, abnormal growth of the uterine tissue; and other problems, such as uterine prolapse (dropped uterus).

Types of hysterectomy

A total hysterectomy is the removal of the entire uterus and cervix; a subtotal, or partial, hysterectomy is the removal of only the top portion of the uterus; and a radical hysterectomy is the removal of the uterus and adjacent tissue, lymph nodes, a portion of the upper vagina, and possibly the Fallopian tubes and ovaries. The surgery can be performed in three ways: through an abdominal incision (abdominal hysterectomy); through an incision in the vaginal

Experts suggest hysterectomies may decline as women gain more knowledge about effective alternatives and demand less invasive treatments.

wall (vaginal hysterectomy); or through one or more incisions below the navel with a laparoscope, a slender, lighted viewing instrument that transmits the image to a video monitor (laparoscopically assisted vaginal hysterectomy).

Healthier choices?

To make an informed decision about a hysterectomy, find a doctor who is aware of new procedures (experts advise choosing one who is affiliated with a teaching hospital). If an operation is advised, get a second and third opinion. Here are possible alternatives:

- **Wait and see.** Women with fibroids who are approaching menopause may want to postpone surgery, since these benign tumors will naturally shrink as estrogen decreases.
- **Myomectomy.** This surgery removes fibroids but leaves the uterus intact and preserves childbearing capacity.
- **Myolysis.** This low-risk surgery shrinks fibroid tumors by destroying blood vessels that feed them.
- **Hysteroscopy.** This ambulatory, transcervical surgery can remove uterine fibroids or polyps, or it can end bleeding by destroying the endometrial lining.
- **Drug/hormone treatment.** Nonsteroidal anti-inflammatories can relieve pain and excessive bleeding caused by fibroids or other conditions. Oral contraceptives or the hormone progesterone can regulate abnormal bleeding. GnRH agonists, which are also hormones, can ease endometriosis by blocking estrogen and reducing endometrial tissue.
- **Kegel exercises.** These simple muscle contractions can prevent uterine prolapse.

The Health Risks

Hysterectomy is major surgery that ends menstruation and the possibility of childbearing. An abdominal operation requires a hospital stay of four to six days and several weeks of recuperation. Most vaginal and laparoscopic operations average a one- to two-day hospital stay and about two weeks for recovery.

Although they are common, hysterectomies do carry risks: infection, bleeding, blood clots, problems with emptying the bowel or bladder, and mortality. Possible long-term complications are loss of sexual desire, pain during intercourse, urinary incontinence, depression, and premature menopause, even if the ovaries are left intact. Removal of the ovaries increases the risk of heart disease and osteoporosis.

Ibuprofen

If you've ever had a toothache, a muscle strain, or a bad headache, chances are you are well acquainted with ibuprofen—one of the mainstays in a category of pain relievers known as nonsteroidal anti-inflammatory drugs. Available over the counter and sold under a variety of brand names, ibuprofen is also considered one of the best medicines for controlling fever, the pain of menstrual cramps, and osteoarthritis. As with all medications, however, there are a few precautions you should take to ensure that you reap the benefits of this powerful medication while reducing the risk of complications.

A capsule summary

Ibuprofen acts on damaged body tissues by reducing pain and inflammation. It works by inhibiting the synthesis of prostaglandins, which are hormonelike chemicals that promote inflammation. One recent study showed that ibuprofen may even lessen the risk of Alzheimer's disease—perhaps because of the drug's ability to reduce inflammation in the brain, which is thought to be part of the disease process. Doctors, however, warn against taking ibuprofen solely for this reason.

That's because the very factor that makes ibuprofen effective at reducing pain and inflammation also contributes to its risks. Inhibiting prostaglandin production too much or too frequently can increase the risk of gastrointestinal bleeding, indigestion, peptic ulcers, and kidney ailments, particularly in the elderly. And because ibuprofen and other anti-inflammatory drugs are compounded with sodium, they may increase fluid retention. This can be especially dangerous for those with congestive heart failure, in whom it can lead to edema (swelling of the ankles) and congestion of the lungs.

Ibuprofen can elevate blood pressure in some elderly people, especially when taken longer than directed. It may also interfere with beta-blocker drugs used to treat hypertension. Ibuprofen has been shown to affect the action of certain diuretics and to raise the blood levels of the medication lithium, which is used to control manic-depressive illness.

Anti-inflammatory drugs, including ibuprofen, may also slow the healing of bone fractures and should be used only after consulting an orthopedist.

Women in their childbearing years should be especially careful with ibuprofen. Those

Ibuprofen and other anti-inflammatory drugs relieve pain and reduce inflammation in a pulled muscle; acetaminophen acts only on the pain.

who take it from the fifth through the eighth week of pregnancy could possibly endanger the health of their baby. Studies show that ibuprofen may increase the risk of gastroschisis—a birth defect that causes a tear in the infant's abdominal wall.

Playing it safe

The good news is that for many people ibuprofen remains among the safest pain medications around if used properly. The most common problem, gastrointestinal bleeding, is confined mainly to people who take the medication while drinking three or more alcoholic beverages a day or who take more than the recommended dosage, particularly for an extended period of time. But to ensure safety, if you have an allergy to aspirin, or if you suffer from peptic ulcers, asthma, kidney or liver problems, diabetes, or heart failure, be sure to consult your doctor before you take any products that contain ibuprofen.

Danger Signs

While taking ibuprofen, watch for the following signs of trouble. Notify your doctor immediately if they occur.

- Persistent nausea
- Stomach discomfort that is not relieved by antacids
- Heartburn with blood reflux
- Bloody or black stools

203

Indoor Air

When someone mentions air pollution, you probably think of smog or ozone—something on the other side of your front door. But do you realize that the air in your home or in the workplace can pose an even bigger danger to your health? Indoor pollutants, ranging from simple molds to high-tech chemical vapors, are potent health threats, especially given the fact that you spend 90 percent of your time indoors.

Indoor pollutants

Indoor pollution is nothing new; in early North American homes the air was so full of soot from open fireplaces that lung disease was a major killer. Closed stoves and heating systems largely solved that problem. (Thankfully, occasional evenings before an open fire aren't hazardous to your health.) Today's pollution became widespread in the 1970s, when, to save energy, North Americans started insulating their homes and offices, cutting down on the fresh air that can "leak" into and out of the house. The result? Pollutants were trapped indoors.

The primary causes of indoor pollution are gases or particles released from sources in the home. Their effects are compounded by humidity levels that are either too high or too low, which can increase the amount of toxins. Common home pollutants include:

- **Combustion by-products.** Invisible gases, such as carbon monoxide and nitrogen dioxide, produced by tobacco smoke and faulty heaters, stoves, or chimneys that burn wood, oil, gas, kerosene, or coal.
- **Biological contaminants.** Mold, mildew, viruses, animal dander, bacteria, dust mites, cockroaches, or pollen.
- **Volatile organic compounds (VOCs).** Carbon-based chemicals used in building materials, furnishings, and many household products. Common VOCs and their sources include formaldehyde (adhesives, man-made wood products, draperies and upholstery, permanent-press clothing), alcohols (carpeting, cosmetics, perfumes), ammonia (cleaning products), and benzene (paints and varnishes).
- **Pesticides.** Toxic chemicals used to control insects and other pests.
- **Radon.** Colorless, odorless radioactive gas that can seep into a home through dirt floors, cracks in concrete walls and floors, floor drains, and sump pumps.
- **Particulates.** Airborne dust particles, such as asbestos (from fire retardants and insulation in older buildings), and lead (from paint and solder).

Dangers to your health

Two illnesses associated with poor indoor air quality are "sick building syndrome"—allergic-type reactions from living or working in inadequately ventilated buildings—and "building-related illness," diseases caused by exposure to specific toxins, such as asbestos or lead. Such pollutants contribute to asthma, allergies, and weakening of the immune system and, possibly, more serious ailments.

If you live in a house with an attached garage, such as this one, install a carbon monoxide detector (above) in the house near the garage. It could save your life.

Keeping Indoor Pollutants at Bay

- Open windows and inside doors as often as possible.

- In damp areas, install exhaust fans vented to the outdoors. Try a dehumidifier if dampness persists.

- Don't smoke indoors.

- Wash or change filters in air conditioners, humidifiers, and dehumidifiers frequently.

- Use an exhaust fan or keep a window open when cooking with gas.

- Have your home tested for radon and lead contamination.

- Buy nontoxic household cleansers, paints, and pesticides.

- Ventilate your home for at least 48 hours after installing carpeting.

- Check the furnace and chimney for cracks or blockages each fall.

- Allow adequate ventilation around laser printers and fax machines, which often emit VOCs.

Common reactions to indoor pollution include sneezing; chronic coughing; nausea; headaches; skin rashes; fatigue; dizziness; and eye, nose, and throat irritations. Some health effects can be grave, even fatal, and may show up years after exposure.

Here are a few sources of pollutants and the illnesses they may cause:

- Tobacco smoke (both firsthand and secondhand): respiratory disorders, lung cancer, and heart disease
- Lead: damage to kidneys and the central nervous system; also, developmental problems in fetuses and young children
- Radon: lung cancer
- Contaminated air conditioning or heating systems: Legionnaires' disease
- Molds: allergies, asthma, and leukemia
- Carbon monoxide: flulike symptoms in low doses, fatal in high concentrations
- Formaldehyde and asbestos: several types of cancer

Who is at highest risk?

Susceptibility runs higher in young children, the elderly, and people with allergic conditions. Babies are especially vulnerable because their lungs are still developing and can be easily damaged. In fact, some experts say that indoor pollution may contribute to sudden infant death syndrome (SIDS), possibly through exposure to tobacco smoke or chemical emissions from synthetic materials in the baby's room, such as new carpeting, crib, mattress, blankets, toys, and clothing. As a precaution, air out or prewash any new synthetic products in the nursery. Never expose children to tobacco smoke.

Check with a building contractor to find out how more ventilation fans, such as this one in an attic, can be installed in your home.

Strategies for breathing easy

If you can't prevent pollutants (see box, left), increasing ventilation in your house is the best way to clear them out. Open doors and windows when weather permits. Make sure the vents in the eaves of the roof (soffits) are clear. Fans of all types—for ceilings and attic, and exhaust fans in kitchens and bathrooms—keep air moving. Running an air conditioner with the vent open can also help.

Air purifiers, available in tabletop or console models, can help keep indoor pollutants under control. They cannot, however, filter out such gases as radon or carbon monoxide. Install carbon monoxide detectors on every floor of the house, including the basement and attic. Also, to test for radon, contact your provincial health department about radon detection kits or hire a certified radon tester.

When to Go to a Pro

If you have an allergy or other problem that you suspect may be related to a pollutant in your home, ask your doctor to help you determine what is causing your symptoms. You might also hire a professional "house doctor" to help you identify the cause. An environmental inspection service or a home inspector (listed in your local Yellow Pages) can assess problems in indoor air quality and recommend solutions for your home.

Indoor Plants

Talking to your houseplants supposedly keeps them healthy. Well, perhaps houseplants return the favor by filtering harmful pollutants from indoor air. Some scientists at the United States National Air and Space Agency (NASA), looking for ways to cleanse the air in hermetically sealed space capsules, have touted houseplants as indoor air cleaners. However, environmental experts advise that more research is needed before you pin your hopes for fresher indoor air on your leafy friends.

The air-cleansing theory

During the photosynthesis process, plants remove carbon dioxide from the air and return all-important oxygen and water vapor to it. In recent years environmental scientists have suggested that many plants may also remove harmful gases from indoor air. Some gases are absorbed through tiny pores in the leaves, called stomata, during the course of the plants' respiration cycle. Others are soaked up by the plants' roots and the moist soil in the pot.

As a result, plants could be valuable in cleansing the air in newer houses and office complexes because modern construction techniques have created tightly sealed, superinsulated structures that can trap pollutants, such as formaldehyde, benzene, trichloroethylene, and ammonia, inside the home or office.

Plants that purify

NASA scientists concluded that some plants work better than others. Areca palms, bamboo palms, lady palms, and dwarf date palms earned high marks. Rubber plants were good at ridding the air of formaldehyde. Spider plants did an excellent job of removing formaldehyde and carbon monoxide. Several dracaenas effectively filtered trichloroethylene from the air. English ivies, Boston ferns, philodendrons, gerbera daisies, pothos, spathiphyllum, Chinese evergreens, and chrysanthemums also stood out as top-notch air purifiers.

Help at home?

Despite NASA's promising results, the U.S. Environmental Protection Agency has called for more tests, ones that better simulate the home environment rather than the conditions inside a hermetically sealed space capsule. Test results so far indicate that a well-functioning ventilation system cleanses indoor air in a modern home or office building more effectively than even a roomful of plants.

Risks posed by indoor plants

Bringing plants indoors means bringing some health risks into your home. The damp soil plants grow in can harbor mold and other microorganisms that may be irritating, particularly to those with allergies. Plant leaves are magnets for dust, a major respiratory irritant. What's more, using a pesticide to control insects contributes to indoor air pollution. And some plants are toxic (see box, below).

Instead of using pesticides indoors for infestations of aphids, mealybugs, mites, and whiteflies, spray plants with a soap solution (3 tablespoons liquid soap to 4 liters/1 gallon of water). To reduce dust buildup, wash or wipe off plant leaves once a week—more often if the leaves are major dust magnets.

To cut down on the irritating dust this date palm's fronds can attract, try placing it in the shower once a week and giving it a thorough dousing.

Please Don't Eat the Plants

Many indoor plants are toxic to humans and pets. Children and small animals are especially vulnerable because of their smaller body mass.

Where possible, keep plants—and cut flowers, too—out of reach of small children and pets. It's a good idea to learn which plants are most dangerous (bulbs and holly or mistletoe berries are leading examples), so you can take extra care with those.

It's true that some indoor plants are harmless. But to be on the safe side, teach kids never to taste, or even bite into, any indoor plants other than the ones on their dinner plates, no matter how tempting they may appear.

Inhalers

Imagine struggling to fill your lungs with air but not being able to get a deep breath. To some people, it sounds like a bad dream. For millions of others who have asthma—a chronic inflammatory disorder of the airways that causes attacks of breathlessness—or other serious respiratory disorders, it's a common reality. For them, medicinal inhalers are literal lifesavers that restore their breathing in 5 or 10 minutes by keeping airways open or opening blocked passages.

Inhaling relief

Asthma medications are grouped into two categories: anti-inflammatories, which reduce the risk of attack and have to be taken regu-

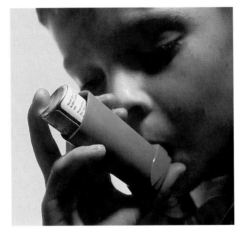

Asthma is a frightening condition for both children and adults. Inhalers deliver medicines that can prevent or stop attacks.

larly, and bronchodilators, which stop or control an attack in progress. Inhalers are an excellent way to deliver both types of medication. They work quickly and have few side effects. However, overusing bronchodilators may make some people's asthma worse.

Inhalers must be used properly to get good results—and that's not always easy. It's crucial to spray the drug just as you begin to inhale, or all of the medication won't make it into the lungs. Using an attachment called a spacer will deliver medication more efficiently and help to ensure that less of it is deposited in the mouth and throat. This plastic tube or chamber also reduces the risk of thrush, an overgrowth of yeast in the throat and mouth that sometimes develops with the use of corticosteroid medications. All patients taking inhaled steroids should use a spacer and clean it after every use.

The less medication that remains in the inhaler canister, the harder it is to get the correct dose. Determine the number of doses in the canister and try to keep count of how many you have used. If a pressurized inhaler has been idle for a few days, you may need to pump it once to prime it. This will ensure that a full dose of medicine will be delivered.

Newspapers have described the dangers of inhalers—in particular, a link to cardiac arrest. But prescription inhalers present little cause for alarm. Most problems stem from over-the-counter inhalers that contain epinephrine, a powerful stimulant that can cause heart problems if used improperly. Fortunately, over-the-counter inhalers are not permitted for sale in Canada.

Here is the correct way to use an inhaler:
- Shake the canister five or six times.
- Test by spraying into the air before using.
- Exhale before pressing.
- Hold the mouthpiece 2.5 to 5 centimeters (1 to 2 inches) away from your mouth (or, if you are using a spacer, close your mouth around it), then squeeze the inhaler and breathe in slowly for five to seven seconds.
- Hold your breath for about 10 seconds, then release slowly.
- Wait one minute before inhaling again.
- After using an inhaler, particularly one containing corticosteroids, brush your teeth or rinse your mouth and spit out the water to prevent overgrowth of yeast.

On the Horizon Inhalers commonly use chlorofluorocarbon gases (CFCs), which have been shown to deplete the ozone layer, to propel the medication into the lungs. Under development are inhalers that use "ozone-friendly" hydrofluoroalkanes (HFAs) instead of CFCs and dry powder inhalers that use no propellants.

Insect Repellents

Pity the poor camper who forgets the bug spray. Shields against pint-size predators, insect repellents work by creating a cloud of scent that keeps pests away. The most common repellent is *N,N*-diethyl-*m*-toluamide, known as DEET. This chemical is found in most major brands for one reason: it works. DEET repels mosquitoes, gnats, fleas, chiggers, and ticks. It also fends off flies. But is it safe?

The dirt on DEET

DEET is relatively harmless unless it is ingested or excessive amounts are absorbed through the skin. Very few people experience side effects from DEET. Skin rash is the most common complaint. Several instances of more serious reactions, including nausea and even convulsions, coma, and death, have been reported, but these have followed repeated heavy applications on small children or other forms of misuse, such as soaking one's clothing in DEET.

Two personal insect-repellent ingredients have had their registrations canceled in Canada—Repellent R-11 (2,3,4,5-bis (butylene) tetrahydro-2-furfural) and ethyl hexanediol (2-ethyl-1,3-hexanediol). Products containing these ingredients should not be used.

Insect repellents keep mosquitoes from making meals of us, and they are quite safe—when used as directed.

If you are worried about the effects of DEET, choose your brand carefully; some contain as little as 5 percent or as much as 100 percent DEET. To stay on the safe side and still ward off insects, choose a repellent with a DEET content of 10 to 30 percent. (Studies indicate that higher amounts may not even boost the product's effectiveness.)

As with any chemical, DEET may cause adverse affects—including neurological damage—among small children. Never use it on children under the age of two. For older

an ounce of Prevention

Attracting Fewer Insects

A few simple precautions will help keep bugs at bay.

- Avoid using perfumes, as well as heavily scented creams, shampoos, hairsprays, and aftershave lotions.
- Cover up with light-colored clothes. Many pests are attracted to bright colors. Mosquitoes are said to be especially drawn to the color blue.
- Keep food tightly covered when eating outdoors.
- Stay inside at dawn and dusk. If you do go outside, try to stay cool; insects are attracted to sweat.
- Eliminate any standing water from your yard, and cover your swimming pool when it's not in use.

children, use a brand made for kids. (Pediatricians recommend children under the age of five use repellents with no more than 10 percent DEET, while children under the age of two not use DEET repellents at all.) Don't spray children's hands, since they are likely to put them in their mouths or rub their eyes. And keep repellents out of the reach of children. As an alternative, cover the child's stroller or playpen with mosquito netting.

DEET may not work well against ticks. More effective are sprays that contain the pesticide permethrin. Never apply permethrin to the skin, only to clothes.

Don't douse yourself

Since it's the scent of the insect repellent that keeps bugs away, you can limit the amount you apply to your skin by lightly spraying the outside of your clothes. When you do apply repellent to your skin, avoid the eyes and mouth. Never use repellent on broken or sunburned skin. One trick for minimizing the amount of DEET your skin absorbs is to apply moisturizer before you apply repellent. Sunscreen will also do the trick, but the repellent may make the sunscreen less effective.

Repellents are effective for about 1 to 12 hours (less if it is washed off by sweat or water), so there's no need to constantly reapply them. Also, be selective. If you are hiking along a trail with low-lying vegetation, guard against ticks by tucking your pants in your socks and spraying your pants and socks. Once you return indoors, wash your skin thoroughly with soap and water. It's also a good idea to change your clothes and wash any clothes that you sprayed; always separate them from the rest of your laundry.

If you have asthma or another respiratory problem, be wary of using insect-repellent sprays; they may trigger a reaction. Always choose a lotion or roll-on repellent instead of a spray.

Citronella candles are a natural way to ward off insects, but you may be less than impressed with how well they work, especially on windy days.

Natural alternatives

There are a host of natural insect repellents, although none is nearly as effective as DEET. Plant oils thought to repel insects include camphor, peppermint, eucalyptus, rosemary, and pennyroyal. Never apply undiluted oils to the skin; they can be toxic. Mix them with spring water or mineral oil instead.

Insect-repellent claims have also been made for garlic, garlic capsules, cream-of-tartar tablets, and brewer's yeast; their odor is emitted through the skin and is said to repel insects. Taking vitamin B_1 tablets is also said to have some effect.

The old standby, citronella, a lemon-scented grass native to Southeast Asia, is believed to suppress an insect's appetite. Formulas containing the oil can be rubbed on the skin. Candles are also available. Overall, citronella is so safe that the U.S. Food and Drug Administration (FDA) has approved it for use in candy and drinks. However, according to some tests, bug sprays that contain citronella oil may be only minimally effective.

Finally, rumors that certain skin moisturizers repel insects have circulated for years. But tests have found that the repellent properties of this product are quite weak and last for as little as 10 minutes.

Debunking bug zappers

What about those electric bug "zappers" that still snap and crackle in backyards across the nation? Don't waste your money. Studies have shown that they destroy "good" bugs, such as ladybugs—ones that birds feed on or that prey on garden pests—but not mosquitoes or flies. Experts also warn against investing in ultrasonic repellents, which supposedly repel insects with electronic vibrations that people can't hear. Most independent studies show that such devices are completely ineffective.

Insulation

A well-insulated house provides healthy savings on winter heating and summer air-conditioning costs. In fact, new insulation generally pays for itself in three to five years. But some insulation materials can pose a health hazard, especially if they're installed or handled incorrectly.

Types of insulation

Glass fiber, known as fiberglass or glass wool, is used more than any other insulation material: it's cheap, easy to install, and resists fire and moisture. Most modern wood-frame houses are insulated with fiberglass. Loose-fill insulation made of fiberglass, cellulose (recycled paper), mineral wool (or rock wool), or cotton fiber is often blown or poured into areas where insulation is lacking. Foam insulation, which must be installed professionally, is injected from a pressurized tank into wall cavities. Rigid boards of pressed fiberglass, polystyrene, or polyurethane (which emits cyanide gas when ignited) are used to insulate exterior walls and wood floors.

Insulation ills

Glass fibers can cause adverse reactions, such as irritated skin and eyes, stuffy nose, and scratchy throat, when touched or inhaled. Although some questions remain about their potential health effects, according to Health Canada it is unlikely that fiberglass (and other man-made vitreous fibers) are a significant risk to the general population.

Cellulose is popular and inexpensive but has several drawbacks: it is treated with a fire retardant, such as boric acid; it can be damaged by moisture, insects, and rodents; and it tends to settle. Some people may be sensitive to boric acid or the dyes, inks, and other chemicals contained in cellulose.

Asbestos, widely used to insulate water pipes, furnaces, and boilers before 1980, can cause respiratory illness or lung cancer if its fibers are inhaled. Urea-formaldehyde, a type of foam insulation popular in the 1970s, can emit formaldehyde gas if it is improperly installed. This causes eye and lung irritation, headaches, and dizziness in some individuals. Both materials are no longer installed.

Smart strategies

- Wear a particle-filter dust mask when installing any type of insulation. When handling fiberglass, also wear clothes that cover the entire body, gloves, and protective goggles.
- Make sure all fiberglass insulation is sealed off around electrical outlets and windows.
- When insulating a room, seal off the area from the rest of the house; a new house should not be occupied until the insulation has been installed.
- Opt for encapsulated (plastic-covered) fiberglass that, except when cut, prevents any contact with the insulation. One brand is made of specially twisted fibers that are less likely to break off into the air when cut.
- Consider an alternative to fiberglass, including natural cork (which is very expensive), or Air Krete, a nontoxic, formaldehyde-free foam.

CAUTION!
If you think your home has asbestos or urea-formaldehyde insulation, get a professional evaluation. Don't try to remove it yourself.

When installing attic insulation, be careful not to block vents that provide proper airflow.

Iron

Consume too little of this essential mineral and you'll feel tired and get sick more often. Consume too much—especially in the form of supplements—and other problems may arise. That's why it's important to eat a balanced diet and have your iron level checked before you take a supplement.

The dangers of deficiency

One in 10 North American women and children is deficient in iron. Diets low in iron are a major cause. In women, heavy menstrual periods are another. Adolescent girls, who tend to eat poorly and diet excessively, are at particular risk. So are some women athletes, women who are pregnant or breastfeeding (they need extra iron), strict vegetarians, and the elderly (who often don't eat enough iron-rich foods). Iron deficiency is uncommon in men and postmenopausal women.

When you don't get enough iron, the body draws on its stores of the mineral. When those stores run out, iron-deficiency anemia results—a condition that requires medical treatment. People who are anemic can't make

Cooking in cast-iron pans increases iron levels in food. In addition to red meat, beans and fortified grains are good sources of iron if they are eaten with foods rich in vitamin C.

enough hemoglobin, a component of red blood cells that supplies oxygen to the tissues.

Even subtle iron deficiency may cause problems. Recent studies have shown that in children and adolescents, mild deficits lessen their ability to learn and solve problems. In adults, small deficiencies have been linked to lethargy, weakness, and fatigue.

Too much of a good thing

Too much iron is just as dangerous as too little. If you have hemochromatosis, a genetic disorder that causes you to absorb too much iron, taking an iron supplement can be deadly. Iron overload may lead to liver damage. And some scientists believe that too much iron may increase the risk of heart disease and possibly cancer. Excess iron may also contribute to joint pain experienced by some women following menopause.

Never take an iron supplement except under the advice of your doctor. He or she should check your iron level with a transferrin saturation test or a ferritin test. If you are deficient, the doctor will need to rule out such causes as internal bleeding due to arthritis drugs or gastrointestinal cancer.

Symptom Sorter

Are You Getting Enough Iron—Or Too Much?

See a doctor if you suspect you have an iron deficiency or overload. Here is a list of the most common symptoms.

Problem	Symptoms
Iron deficiency	Often none, although maximum physical performance may be somewhat impaired.
Anemia	Fatigue, weakness, paleness, breathlessness, irregular or fast heartbeat.
Excess iron	Early symptoms: fatigue, joint pain. Advanced symptoms: diabetes, heart disease, cirrhosis of the liver.
Iron-supplement poisoning	Diarrhea (possibly bloody), nausea, stomach pain, sharp cramping, and severe vomiting. (This is the most common cause of accidental overdose in children under six. Keep all supplements that contain iron away from children. If you suspect an overdose, don't wait for symptoms; call a poison control center right away.)

Irradiated Foods

Wouldn't it be a coup if we could wave a magic wand over the nation's food supply to make it safe to eat? Since we can't, the next best thing could be food irradiation, which cuts down on illnesses caused by bacteria, such as salmonella and *E. coli*.

Food irradiation explained

Irradiation is the process of exposing food to low doses of gamma rays, electron beams, or X rays. It inactivates harmful microorganisms, either by killing or sterilizing them, without making the food radioactive.

The process dates back to the 1940s, when tests showed that irradiated raw ground beef stayed fresh longer than nonirradiated meat. In the 1960s the federal government approved the process for use on potatoes, onions, wheat, and flour. That list was later extended to include herbs and dehydrated seasonings.

Astronauts eat irradiated foods, as do some hospital patients who are at increased risk of infection. Yet irradiation hasn't really caught on in the Canadian marketplace, mostly because of public fear about it. In Canada, all packages of irradiated foods must carry the international food irradiation symbol (right) and a statement ("Irradiated").

Is it safe?

Debate rages on about the safety of food irradiation. More than 30 years of studies have failed to find any direct risk associated with eating irradiated food. For that reason, many health agencies—including Health Canada, the Science Council of Canada, Agriculture and Agri-Food Canada, the World Health Organization, and the American Medical Association—have endorsed the technology.

On the opposition side, however, rank such notables as the Canadian Medical Association, the Consumer Health Organization of Canada, and the British Medical Association. Also, companies such as Heinz, Quaker Oats, and McDonald's have said they will not use or sell irradiated products. The distrust stems from studies, as yet inconclusive, about health risks incurred when irradiated food is ingested. Proponents argue that the process does create microscopic changes in food, but they are similar to those caused by cooking. In U.S. army studies, animals fed irradiated foods over several generations proved no more likely to develop cancer or inherited diseases than those fed nonirradiated food. English studies of 60 generations of mice confirmed those results. In China, 400 people who ate irradiated foods for 7 to 15 weeks had no increase in chromosomal damage, a precursor of cancer.

Some vitamins are lost in the irradiation process. Vitamin C levels may drop 5 to 10 percent, but that's no more than is lost in canning or letting fresh produce sit in the produce aisle for a few days. Possibly more disturbing are environmental concerns raised by the prospect of transporting dangerous radioactive materials to food-irradiation centers.

No hamburger heaven

Irradiation makes meat far safer—but not totally safe. It inactivates up to 99.9 percent of the microorganisms present, but if the food is then handled improperly the remaining bacteria can multiply. And even irradiated hamburgers may not be safe enough to eat rare.

Whether food irradiation ever takes off depends largely on consumer attitudes. A major outbreak of food poisoning might finally tip the scales in its favor. Meanwhile, other methods of making food safer, including the use of steam, light, and ozone, are currently being developed.

Foods that have been irradiated must bear this international symbol. Irradiation is approved for use on spices (above) to reduce microbial content.

Juices

Juices are excellent sources of nutrients and may help put the squeeze on various ailments: one 125-milliliter (4-ounce) glass of juice provides a full serving of fruits or vegetables and can therefore be part of a healthy diet. On the downside, juices lack the fiber of fresh fruits and vegetables and may contain heaping helpings of calories and natural sugars. Giving infants too much juice may increase their risk of tooth decay and even hamper normal development. Of course, downing juice is infinitely preferable to drinking soda or coffee. But be sure to leave room for whole fruits and vegetables, too.

Fresh-squeezed grapefruit juice is high in potassium and vitamin C but low in cholesterol-reducing fiber.

Juicy benefits

Most fruit and vegetable juices are good sources of potassium, which helps regulate blood pressure. Many are also excellent sources of cancer-fighting antioxidants, including vitamin C. One 235-milliliter (8-ounce) glass of orange or grapefruit juice, fresh or from concentrate, supplies between 100 and 200 percent of the vitamin C recommended for all adults. Even juices that don't naturally contain much vitamin C are often fortified with it. Apricot and mango juice are rich in both vitamin C and beta-carotene.

Citrus juices are also great sources of folic acid, a B vitamin that may help prevent heart disease and birth defects. Researchers also believe that folic acid—plentiful in orange juice—may help prevent breast cancer; studies are ongoing. You can now buy orange juice fortified with calcium—an option for adults who don't get enough calcium from other sources.

Researchers believe that folic acid—plentiful in orange juice—may help prevent breast cancer.

Although some people choose to make their own juices, store-bought juices can be quite nutritious, too. Citrus juices are processed for shipment and brought to market so quickly that they retain most of their vitamins and minerals. However, as juice in a carton sits on the shelf, it loses nutrients as a result of oxidation. If the carton is near its "best before" date, pass it up.

Three unique nectars

Certain juices have unique properties that play specific roles in improving health—or, possibly, in harming it. Here are three noteworthy examples:

- **Purple grape juice.** This childhood favorite may help prevent cancer and heart attacks. The pigment in grape skin is rich in flavonoids—the same compounds that give red wine (made from grapes with the skins on) some of its health benefits. In a study at the University of Wisconsin Medical School, 295 to 350 milliliters (10 to 12 ounces) of purple grape juice daily reduced blood clotting by 40 percent—about the same as aspirin therapy.

- **Cranberry juice.** This juice's reputation for preventing urinary tract infections appears to be rooted in truth. Researchers have found that cranberry juice prevents bacteria from adhering to the bladder walls. In one study, 153 older women (with an average age of 79) who drank a 295-milliliter (10-ounce) glass of cranberry-juice cocktail daily for six months had 58 percent lower levels of infection-causing bacteria in their urine than women who drank a noncranberry drink. But cranberry juice is no cure for recurring infections. If you think you have an infection, see a doctor.

- **Grapefruit juice.** Although relatively low in calories and rich in vitamin C and potassium, scientists have discovered that grapefruit juice can increase blood levels

Unlike fruit juices, vegetable juices, such as carrot, are low in sugar and calories. Eating tomatoes with carrot juice will enhance the absorption of the juice's beta-carotene.

of certain drugs. It does so by reducing levels of an enzyme in the small intestine that breaks down drugs. Grapefruit juice affects antihistamines, sedatives, protease inhibitors, calcium-channel blockers, and immunosuppressants. If you drink grapefruit juice regularly and are taking medication with no side effects, don't worry. But if you take medication and want to increase your intake of grapefruit juice, talk to your doctor first.

The downside of juice?

If you're watching your weight, remember that while vegetable juices tend to be fairly low in calories—a 235-milliliter (8-ounce) glass of tomato juice has only 43—many popular fruit juices pack between 100 and 180. Drink several glasses a day, and the calories can add up. If you drink a lot of juice, consider diluting it with seltzer or water. And don't forget to balance your juice intake with whole fruits and vegetables, which often have fewer calories. A glass of orange juice has 100 to 120 calories; a whole orange has only 60.

What's more, unlike juices, whole fruits also supply fiber, which helps keep bowel movements regular, protect against cancer of the bowel, and prevent diabetes and heart disease. (One exception: prune juice contains much of the fiber, and the iron, found in prunes.) Fiber also helps you feel full.

Take precautions when giving fruit juice to children. Nutritionists often recommend that parents not give fruit juice to children under age one, and to limit children ages two to three to 125 to 235 milliliters (4 to 8 ounces) a day, preferably with meals. Drinking a lot of fruit juice may mean drinking less milk and even eating less food. In one study, small children who drank 350 to 890 milliliters (12 to 30 ounces) of fruit juice a day (25 to 60 percent of their total calorie intake) failed to grow and develop normally. Too much fruit juice, particularly apple juice, can also cause diarrhea. And never let your toddler fall asleep while drinking a juice (or milk) bottle: juice and milk sugars can cause cavities.

Buy pasteurized

In one celebrated case, unpasteurized apple cider was contaminated with *E. coli,* a bacterium commonly found in undercooked ground beef; one child died. Health experts now recommend that consumers buy only pasteurized juice. The Canadian government is in the process of preparing a code of practice for manufacturers of unpasteurized juice. If you make juice at home, wash the produce under running water using a vegetable scrub brush. And clean juicers regularly.

Home juicers extract the liquid from fruits and vegetables, leaving behind the fiber-rich pulp.

Juice vs. Juice Drinks

Juices labeled "pure" or "100 percent pure" often cost more than juice "drinks," which might be only 10 percent juice—the rest is added water, sugar, and various other ingredients. But are they worth the expense?

That depends. Juices made from 100 percent juice are usually more nutritious than juice drinks because they contain a full helping of the fruit's healthful plant chemicals. But some juice "blends" are made mostly with apple, pear, or white grape juice—inexpensive juices that lack nutritional punch. Some also have added sugar (although the body can't tell the difference between natural fruit sugars and other sugars, such as high-fructose corn syrup).

To choose the most nutritious juice, look for 100 percent pure juice with no added sugar and such ingredients as orange, berry, and apricot near the top of the list.

Knee Replacement

Creaky knees, damaged by injury or arthritis, can be so painful that they interfere with daily life. When conservative treatments fail, knee replacement may be the answer. While not risk-free, an artificial knee can effectively relieve pain and improve mobility for 10 years or longer.

Do you need a new knee?

If you are experiencing chronic knee pain, knee replacement is not the only option. First try painkillers or anti-inflammatory medication, physical therapy, and knee braces. Avoid strenuous activities. If you need to lose weight, doing so may lessen the pressure. But if these measures don't work, and less invasive arthroscopic surgery isn't appropriate, it may be time to consider total knee replacement.

You may be a good candidate for knee replacement if you suffer daily from knee pain, particularly if it restricts work and other everyday activities. It may also be an option if you have significant knee stiffness, instability, or joint deformity. Often, people who opt for knee replacement have severe osteoarthritis, in which the cartilage of the knee deteriorates so much that bone rubs up against bone.

Knee replacement generally lasts longer in older individuals. Because a younger person's lifestyle is typically more active, the artificial knee experiences more stress and will most likely have to be replaced. The procedure should be cautiously considered if you: cannot avoid strenuous activity (for example, your job requires it), have poor circulation in the legs, are significantly overweight, or have had a previous infection in the leg bones (femur or tibia). It is not recommended at all if you are suffering from an active infection somewhere in your body.

Will you require a second operation?

About one in four knee-replacement patients develops at least one complication. The chief concerns immediately following the operation are infection (in the knee or urinary tract) and blood-clotting. For this reason, antibiotics and anticoagulants are often prescribed after the surgery. An infected artificial knee may require reoperation and, perhaps, removal. Other complications, which may also prompt another surgery, include knee pain, stiffness, and loosening of the new joint.

Over time, the artificial joint's connection to your real bone may loosen, and the knee may once again become painful. Because of loosening, pain, or infection, as many as 10 to 20 percent of knee replacements may require reoperation within 10 years.

Knee-replacement patients may also be susceptible to pain and infection following dental surgery, which can release bacteria into the blood. Because an artificial knee lacks the ability to fight off bacteria, an infection can easily develop. Taking antibiotics before and after dental surgery helps reduce that risk.

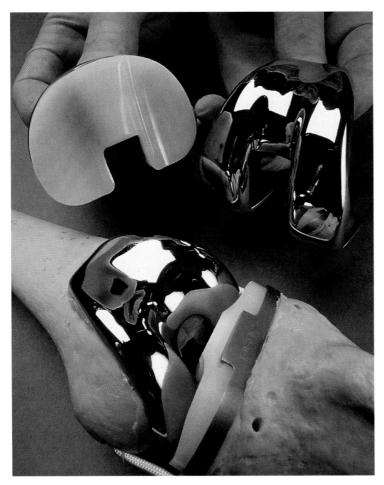

The two major parts of an artificial knee joint are commonly made of cobalt chrome. The tibia (shinbone) component, held on the left, is covered with a polyethylene liner.

asers can shape diamonds, cut through steel, read bar codes at the supermarket checkout counter, and let Ol' Blue Eyes croon on your CD player. But that's all child's play.

Now they can repair knees and bust kidney stones, too. Surgeons, using specialized lasers rather than other surgical tools, such as scalpels, can now perform a variety of medical procedures with less trauma and postoperative pain, a lower risk of infection, and a shorter hospital stay.

Yet laser surgery is expensive, and not always the best option for many conditions. Like any technique, it's only as good as the surgeon who uses it, and relatively few surgeons are experienced with the technology.

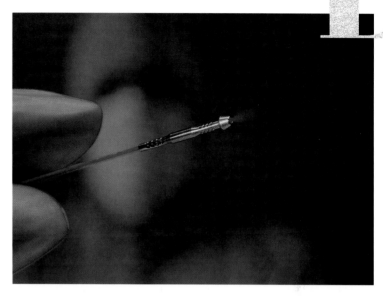

Lasers that heal

Medicine makes use of many different types of surgical lasers—each one tailored to a specific procedure. While these can't slice steel, they can make delicate incisions (often more precisely than a scalpel), excise unwanted tissue (from warts to tumors), correct vision problems (see box, below), and seal blood vessels (to reduce bleeding). Cosmetic surgeons can also use lasers to remove wrinkles, tattoos, and such birthmarks as port-wine stains.

Zapping rather than slicing

Using a laser has potential advantages over a scalpel. Because a laser is more precise, it can more effectively target a specific area with little or no damage to the surrounding tissue. In

The term laser *is an acronym that stands for* light *amplification by* stimulated *emission of* radiation—*which simply means a source of light energy produced in a particular way.*

Can You See a Future Without Eyeglasses or Contact Lenses?

Lasers have been at the cutting edge of eye surgery since the 1960s. Today one of the most popular uses of lasers is to correct nearsightedness, which affects 33 percent of all Canadians. (Lasers can also correct farsightedness.)

In 98 percent of patients, the surgery results in normal sight in one to four weeks. About 2 to 3 percent of patients develop in front of their eye a haze that generally disappears in a few months. There is a minor risk of infection immediately following the treatment. Side effects include eye pain and irritation, and sensitivity to light. In rare cases, the cornea may be damaged and vision worsened permanently. Fewer than 1 percent of patients have poorer vision than they had with their glasses (or contacts) before the treatment.

The surgery costs about $2,000 per eye, an expense that is not covered by provincial health-insurance plans. There are two variations of the procedure: photorefractive keratectomy (PRK) and, the latest, laser in-situ keratomileusis (LASIK). LASIK, which provides quicker results and requires a shorter recovery, was pioneered in Canada. Both are thought to be safer than radial keratotomy (RK), a non-laser procedure that weakens the cornea and leaves it more susceptible to injury.

To qualify for the surgery, your vision cannot be changing rapidly —it's not for anyone younger than age 21. Beforehand, make sure that your surgeon is experienced and uses equipment made by Visx, Summit, or Nidek.

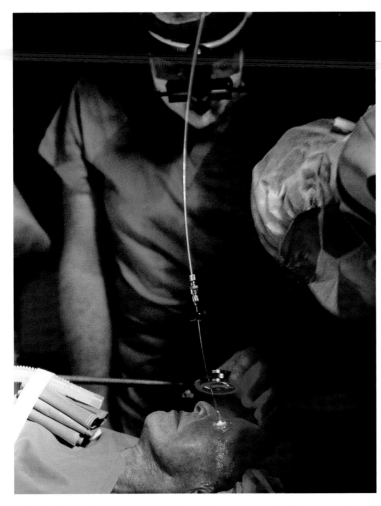

Killer light: In photo-dynamic therapy, a laser activates a photosensitive agent and can selectively vaporize tumor cells—even those in and around the eye—with relatively mild side effects.

- Certain polyps and malignant tumors, including those affecting the skin, head and neck, breast, cervix, and colon
- Skin conditions, including spider veins, pigmented areas, and stretch marks
- Eye problems, including astigmatism, detached retina, and glaucoma
- Gynecological problems, including genital warts, endometriosis, and ovarian cysts
- Other conditions, such as kidney stones, enlarged prostate, tooth decay, and snoring

Lasers are not perfect

Despite the many potential benefits of laser surgery, don't automatically assume it's the best option—and take these precautions:

- Before undergoing any type of laser procedure, find out about the surgeon's qualifications and experience—some may have taken only a short course to become familiar with the equipment. If you are undergoing eye surgery, avoid surgeons who offer large discounts; look for one who performs at least five procedures a week.
- Know your options. Many laser surgeries are not covered by insurance, and your condition may be treated just as effectively with a procedure that costs much less.
- Make sure that your doctor's equipment is approved for treating your specific condition. Call the Health Protection Branch of Health Canada at (613) 957-2991.
- Be aware of the potential risks—even if the doctor and the equipment are up to standard. There is a slim chance of burns or scarring, particularly with dermatological procedures, and permanent vision damage or other complications during eye surgery.

addition, its heat can seal off blood vessels and nerve endings, reducing the amount of trauma, scarring, and postoperative pain. As a result, a surgeon can often make smaller incisions and use less anesthetic. For patients, laser surgery can mean shorter hospital stays and recovery periods.

A surgical revolution unfolds

Thanks to lasers, many conditions can now be treated faster and easier. These include:

On the Horizon Lasers may soon be used to operate on the heart, specifically to alleviate angina pain. The experimental procedure, called transmyocardial revascularization (TMR), punches up to 50 toothpick-size holes in the heart's left ventricle. The increased flow of blood (and oxygen) to the heart prevents pain. Another experimental procedure, called percutaneous TMR (PMR), sends a laser through a tube that is inserted in a leg artery and travels all the way to the heart. The laser then makes the holes from the inside out.

Be honest: Is there anyone reading this who *hasn't* been constipated at one time or another? Symptoms can range from feeling bloated to stomach cramps, but for many people the solution is the same: laxatives. The next time you reach for one, however, bear in mind that laxatives aren't without risks, and overusing them can make your bowels "lazy" and cause rebound constipation. In many cases, all you may need to become "regular" again is more water and fiber.

Do you need a laxative?

If you're constipated, a laxative isn't necessarily the best medicine. To help decide whether you need one, answer these questions:

- **Are you "regular"?** Regularity means having bowel movements that are regular—for you. For some, that's once a day; for others, it's not. Doctors agree that as few as three bowel movements per week is still regular. However, if you have two per week or fewer, or if your stools are dry, hard, and difficult to pass, you're constipated. A laxative may provide temporary relief, but consistent regularity and better long-term bowel health depend on permanent lifestyle changes (see box, below right).
- **Are you eating any differently?** Changes in diet and exercise can cause constipation. Simply reestablishing healthy routines may bring relief. Be aware that normal changes associated with aging can cause temporary or even permanent changes in bowel movements.
- **Are you taking any new medications?** Constipation may be a side effect of many medications—particularly antidepressants, cough syrups, sedatives, antacids, calcium channel blockers, and iron supplements. Your doctor may be able to alter your dosage or prescribe another drug that is less likely to affect bowel function.

A quick fix with potential risks

If you need a laxative in the short term, some over-the-counter types are much safer than others (see chart, page 220). However, using

Some laxatives are gentler than others. Ingredients that can be extremely harsh include phenolphthalein, bisacodyl, castor oil, senna, and cascara sagrada.

any laxative—except fiber supplements—long term can pose a variety of health problems. Laxatives can cause a dangerous upset of body fluids and electrolytes (minerals that help maintain body chemistry), muscle weakness, and heart-rhythm abnormalities. Chronic use can even damage your colon. And once you stop using laxatives, rebound constipation can occur, creating long-term bowel difficulties. *(continued)*

How to Be a "Regular" Joe: Take These Steps Before Using a Laxative

- Drink more water—at least six to eight glasses a day.
- Eat fiber-rich foods, including whole grains, vegetables, salads, beans, and fresh and dried fruits.
- Add a high-fiber cereal to your diet, particularly one that contains bran.
- Exercise regularly, even if only stretching and walking.

- Don't resist the urge to go to the bathroom.
- Set aside time each day to relax, followed by a set bathroom time.
- See your doctor if your bowels do not normalize within two weeks; you have more cramps, nausea, or acute stomach pain; or your bowel habits change suddenly.

Laxatives (continued)

Many laxatives contain magnesium, a mineral often found in antacids and pain relievers as well. If you use large amounts of all three products at once, you risk developing a potentially fatal magnesium overload. You are particularly at risk if you have a kidney disorder or a chronic illness that affects the kidneys, such as diabetes or hypertension.

You should also exercise caution when using herbal laxatives, particularly those containing aloe, senna, rhubarb root, buckthorn, cascara sagrada, or castor oil. Problems, including cramps, diarrhea, nausea, and vomiting, are most likely to occur if a laxative tea is steeped too long or drunk too frequently. Rare but possible complications may include fainting, dehydration, and a dangerous change in blood chemistry.

Finally, never use a laxative to facilitate weight loss. Laxatives do not stop calories from being absorbed, and they can cause physical dependence and serious or even deadly changes in metabolism.

Not All Laxatives Are Created Equal

Type	How They Work	Brand Names	Speed	Possible Side Effects	FYI	Dosage
Fiber products, bulk-forming agents	Make stool larger, which helps the intestines contract and provoke a bowel movement.	Fibrepur, Fibyrax, Metamucil, Mylanta, Prodiem	From 12 hours up to three days.	Bloating, abdominal pain, and gas; intestinal blockage; rare allergic reactions; breathing and swallowing difficulty; skin rash or itching	Slow-acting; best to build up gradually over 7 to 10 days; must drink lots of fluids, particularly water or fruit juice.	Daily. As a fiber supplement, may be used long term, if necessary.
Osmotic agents and saline laxatives	Pull water into the large intestine, creating bulk and pressure to stimulate contractions.	Lactulose: Chronulac, Duphalac, Epsom Salts, Milk of Magnesia	Lactulose: 24 to 48 hours; saline: ½ hour to 3 hours.	Dizziness, confusion, fatigue, muscle cramps, irregular heartbeat can indicate an electrolyte imbalance	Osmotics can cause dehydration and the buildup of magnesium and phosphate, which is dangerous for anyone with kidney problems. To avoid problems, take each dose with 235 to 470 milliliters (8 to 16 ounces) of water.	Short-term use; no more than three consecutive days.
Stool softeners and lubricants	Allow fluids to mix into the stool, making it easier to pass. Lubricants also coat the stool and bowel wall with a water-resistant film.	Colace, Correctol Stool Softener Soft Gels, Regulex, Silace, Soflax. Lubricants include Fleet Mineral Oil, Lansoyl	Average: one to two days; can take as long as five days.	Skin rash, risk of cramping, throat irritation (liquid form only). Mineral oil can also build up in the body, causing health problems, and may cause leakage from the rectum	Liquid stool softeners may be mixed with milk or fruit juices; mineral oil should not be taken within two hours of a meal. Stool softeners do not cause a bowel movement, but they may help prevent constipation.	Softeners: short-term use only unless prescribed. Mineral oil: occasional use only.
Stimulant laxatives	Contain an irritant, such as bisacodyl, that stimulates the lining of the bowel, causing increased contractions.	Correctol, Dulcolax, Ex-Lax, Nature's Remedy, Senokot	Liquid or pill yields semi-solid bowel movement in 6 to 8 hours; suppositories work in 15 to 60 minutes.	Muscle cramps, discolored urine or stools (red, violet, or pink), allergic reactions (such as skin rash), fatigue, and irregular heartbeat can indicate an electrolyte imbalance	Overuse can cause serious intestinal damage and "lazy bowel syndrome," in which the bowel can't function without a laxative. Bisacodyl tablets should not be crushed or chewed or taken with milk or antacids.	Short-term use only; no more than three consecutive days.

Note: Combination laxatives include (osmotic and lubricant) Lagnolax; (stimulant and stool softener) Doxidan Liqui-Gels, Peri-Colace, Regulex-D, Senokot-S; (bulk and stimulant) Prodiem Plus. Because the potential for health problems increases with each ingredient you add, combination products should not be used more than three consecutive days.

In 1975, the Canadian government began the phaseout of lead in gasoline. The next year, the Hazardous Products Act limited the amount of lead in interior house paint. These regulations were intended to lessen the dangerous presence of lead in our environment.

A menacing metal

Lead is a toxic metal that can be harmful when ingested or inhaled. In the body, lead competes with calcium for storage space, interferes with nerve transmissions in the brain, and can damage blood cells.

Children are particularly at risk because of their immature digestive systems. They absorb more of the lead they ingest than adults do. Chronic exposure to low levels of lead can result in learning or behavioral problems in children. An increase of 10 micrograms of lead per deciliter of blood can lower a child's IQ by up to 3 points, scientists estimate. Higher exposures can lead to more serious problems, including kidney and neurological damage, and may even be fatal.

Getting the lead out

One of the best ways to reduce your risk of lead poisoning is to drink milk. A healthy daily intake of calcium helps minimize the body's absorption of lead. You can also help reduce your family's risk of exposure by considering these potential sources in the home:

- **Old (pre-1976) interior house paint.** Wash any areas of old paint weekly, never sand, scrape, or remove with a heat gun, and sweep up paint chips immediately. Whenever possible, cover paint with wallpaper, wallboard, or special sealants. To have paint tested for lead, you should use a laboratory certified by the Standards Council of Canada or the Canadian Association for Environmental Analytical Laboratories. Some contractors with X-ray fluorescence (XRF) equipment can also be hired. Never try to remove lead paint yourself; it should be done by a specialist.
- **Pipes.** The lead pipes or solder in some older plumbing systems can leach lead into tap water, especially water that has been sitting overnight. You may wish to have your tap water tested. Other tips: Use cold water for drinking and cooking, and run the tap for a minute first.
- **Ceramic ware,** especially pieces that are hand-made, may have a lead-based glaze, which can leach lead into foods. Do not use ceramic containers for storing juice, vinegar, or other acidic foods. Children and pregnant women should not use crystal glassware and should use only commercially made mugs for hot beverages. Do not store liquor in a crystal decanter.
- **Mini blinds.** Health Canada has warned against the use of some horizontal mini blinds imported from China, Taiwan, Indonesia, Hong Kong, and Mexico that contain lead.
- **Soil.** Don't let children play in soil that's near a highway. If they do, wash their hands; the soil may contain residue from the leaded-gas era. And wipe your shoes on a doormat before entering the house.

Exposure to pre-1976 interior house paint is a cause of lead poisoning in young children. Keep kids away from old paint and do not let them chew on any painted surfaces.

Symptom Sorter

Lead poisoning can be very hard to detect. Nevertheless, be on the lookout for these symptoms:

- **Children.** Mild cases may cause headache, stomachache, and irritability or no physical symptoms at all. Severe exposure may cause anemia. If your child (particularly an infant under one year of age) may have been exposed to lead, contact your pediatrician. Medication can reduce blood-lead levels.

- **Adults.** If you suspect exposure, get tested. By the time such symptoms as lethargy, high blood pressure, abdominal pain, vomiting, and damage to reproductive organs show up, damage may be irreversible.

Lighting

Even as they illuminate our lives, electric lights go unnoticed. The flick of a switch lets you navigate safely through a room at night or read into the wee hours. But the lighting in your home and office can affect your health more than you might imagine.

Which bulbs are best?

Incandescent lightbulbs—the ones Thomas Edison invented—use electricity to heat a tungsten filament that glows with soft light. The light is appealing to the eye because its warm hue mimics afternoon sunlight. However, the bulbs are energy-inefficient; most of the electricity gets turned into heat, not light.

Much more efficient and longer-lasting are fluorescent lights, which use ultraviolet radiation to make a phosphor coating inside the bulb glow. But there are trade-offs. Traditional fluorescent bulbs emit a harsh, bluish light and cause glare, which may lead to eyestrain. Also, these lights flicker about 120 times per second. Although not noticeable to the eye, this flickering may nevertheless cause headaches or migraines in some people. Erratic flickering of defective bulbs can trigger epileptic seizures in people who are susceptible.

Filters that fit over fluorescent bulbs can reduce glare and add the warm colors of the spectrum that white fluorescent bulbs lack, creating light similar to sunlight. Even better (although expensive) are full-spectrum bulbs, which give off light that resembles natural sunlight. Installed in a room where you spend a lot of time (such as an office or a kitchen), these bulbs enable you to stay alert longer and work more productively. They may even improve your mood.

Halogen hazards

Halogen lamps work the same way as incandescent bulbs do, but they are filled with halogen gas, which prolongs the filament's life. They provide a blazing white light that brightens an entire room. But their intense light comes at a cost: extreme heat. They can reach temperatures above 538°C (1,000°F). Clothing, drapes, or other combustibles that touch the bulbs can quickly catch fire.

Fortunately, newer lamps come equipped with safety guards, and guards for older lamps are available free from manufacturers. Still, don't leave a halogen lamp burning when you leave a room, and place floor lamps where they are least likely to be tipped over by children or pets.

The right light for reading

Forget the old idea that reading in dim light ruins the eyesight—it doesn't. But it is easier to read and work in brighter light. The brightness causes the pupils to constrict, which helps the eyes focus better. A better focus prevents eye muscles from tiring, allowing you to work or read longer. As you age, the eye focuses less easily, so you need more light by which to read. At age 10, it's easy to read with 40 watts of light; by 60, most people need 100 watts.

Too much contrast between bright and not-so-bright areas is hard on the eyes, too. Optimally, reading and task lights should be about three times brighter than the general room lighting. Choose a translucent lamp shade, such as those made of silk, parchment, or linen, which diffuse some light upward and sideways while directing most of it downward. A lamp should be placed so that it lights your work or your book, but doesn't cast your shadow on it. The best way to do this is to place the lamp in front of you, with the bottom of the shade at eye level or slightly lower.

Working at a computer is a different matter because the screen itself is a source of light. Adjust the screen so that it is slightly brighter than the surrounding room. If there is a window nearby, place the computer screen at a right angle to it so that the screen doesn't reflect sunlight. And be sure that the keyboard is well-lit.

Some new halogen lamps have heat-sensitive switches that turn the lamps off automatically before they can start a fire.

Light rooms for safety

Proper lighting is a key factor in making your home safe. Follow these tips:

- Install night-lights in children's rooms, stairways, halls, kitchens, and bathrooms.
- If you need to cross a dark room to turn on a light, have an electrician install a switch near the door.
- Attach lights to timers when you're away from home to discourage intruders.

Eliminate fire hazards

- Replace worn or damaged wires and plugs on lamps immediately.
- When disconnecting a lamp from a wall outlet, pull on the plug, not on the wire.
- Don't connect too many lamps or other devices to a single extension cord; it can overheat, creating a fire hazard.
- Don't use bulbs with a wattage that exceeds the recommended maximum for the lamp; it could cause the lamp wiring to overheat.
- Don't use floor or table lamps that can easily tip over in children's rooms. The bulbs can heat up enough to burn small hands, start a fire if paper or fabric falls on them,

or break and scatter shards of glass.

- When shopping for lighting fixtures, look for the seal of the Canadian Standards Association (CSA) or the Underwriters' Laboratories of Canada (ULC).
- Buy vapor-resistant fixtures for kitchens and bathrooms; moisture is less likely to short out their wiring.

In offices with bright overhead lighting, such as this one, turn your computer screen as bright as it will go to decrease eyestrain.

The Good News About SAD

Do you suffer each year from the winter blahs? Feel depressed, achy, and fatigued despite extra sleep? Do you lose interest in sex and socializing while gaining unwanted pounds thanks to an insatiable yen for starchy foods? If you experience any—though not necessarily all—of these symptoms, you may be one of millions of people afflicted with SAD (seasonal affective disorder).

It is generally thought that this seasonal form of depression is related to the shorter days and reduced exposure to light in fall and winter. Remedies as simple as getting out for a brisk midday walk can be helpful. But in severe cases, the most effective cure is light therapy—regular and frequent exposure to high-intensity light.

Treatment should always be under the supervision of a doctor or a SAD clinic. Special light boxes and other devices, usually equipped with full-spectrum or cool-white fluorescent lights, are used for the therapy. Sessions as short as 30 minutes once or twice a day can relieve symptoms within about a week. Continued throughout the winter months, these "enlightening" experiences can help restore the sunshine to your life.

CAUTION!

Handle all fluorescent tubes with care; they contain mercury. Some older rapid-start fluorescent fixtures may leak hazardous PCBs. To check, turn off the light and remove the cover; if there are black, oily smudges on the metal box, replace the fixture.

Liquid Nutritional Supplements

They were originally developed to help the sick and the elderly—those who, for a variety of reasons, were not able to eat regular meals. However, over the past several years, liquid nutritional supplements have been increasingly promoted as sound meal replacements for healthy people of all ages. In some busy households, they have sometimes shown up at the breakfast, lunch, or dinner table.

Is that where liquid supplements belong? Although these products do offer some benefits, nutritional experts advise most of us to proceed with caution; otherwise we may get much more (in the way of calories) than we bargained for.

Supplement drinks vary in taste from medicinal to sweet. Some leave an aftertaste.

Energy elixirs?

Liquid supplements are composed primarily of water, sugars, oils, milk and/or soy protein, and added vitamins and minerals. Among the most enticing promises made by their manufacturers is that these products supply energy, particularly to those over 50 years of age. However, the only source of nutritional energy in the drinks is calories—200 to 360 of them, depending on the brand—which you are already getting from food. And when we take in more calories than we need we gain weight. Add one of these drinks to your three square meals a day, and you are likely to put on pounds, especially if you choose a brand that's high in fat.

Another claim is that these supplements offer complete nutrition in a can. Although some contain the recommended daily

Add one of these calorie-laden supplementary drinks to your three square meals a day, and you're likely to put on pounds.

amounts of vitamins and minerals, many offer less than half that. In addition, most liquid supplements don't contain fiber; none have the antioxidant plant compounds called phytochemicals that work both alone and together to confer such benefits as neutralizing harmful free radicals in the body. Indeed, as far as most liquid nutritional supplements go, you'd do just as well to take a multivitamin and wash it down with a milk shake.

These products are also often touted as being high in protein and therefore helpful in building muscle. But the typical Canadian diet is already high in protein.

While physicians frequently prescribe liquid supplements, they nearly always do so for people who have difficulty consuming enough nutrients, such as some AIDS patients and cancer patients undergoing chemotherapy. The products may also be helpful to people who need to gain weight and have trouble doing so.

When to pop one open

Nutritionists and dietitians agree that liquid supplements, even with their shortcomings, can occasionally be used as a substitute for a meal—for example, when you are traveling and can't stop to eat or when you are in too much of a hurry even to make a sandwich. Low-fat varieties also make better snacks than high-fat foods, such as doughnuts and potato chips. But remember that healthful foods—a piece of fruit, a bagel, low-fat yogurt, whole-grain crackers—can also be eaten on the run and provide fiber or other nutrients as well.

If you do decide to use a liquid nutritional supplement, be aware that instant breakfast drinks are made of essentially the same ingredients and usually cost less. Under no circumstance should you try to live on these supplements if you can eat regular meals.

If you are ill and can't chew, swallow, or tolerate regular food, or if you are unable to eat more than a limited amount, liquid supplements can provide nutritional upkeep and energy. In short, these products are excellent when used for their original purpose.

Magnet Therapy

Perhaps you've heard testimonials by athletes about the healing power of magnets for pain. Or you may have seen ads for magnets wrapped in belts and cloths that have been applied to aching body parts. Is there any basis for this type of alternative therapy?

The belief that magnets can affect our health goes back thousands of years, but most doctors put little stock in their power. In fact, Health Canada prohibits manufacturers from making health claims for magnetic products. Although some scientific research on magnet therapy has been conducted, only more rigorous investigation will tell whether this type of treatment really has any benefits.

What's the attraction?

Some people think that magnet therapy can be used not only for pain but also for depression and the healing of wounds and fractures. The process involves magnetic fields, which are created and used in various ways.

In transcranial magnetic stimulation (TMS), an electromagnetic coil is placed against the head to produce a mild electric current and a strong magnetic field. This procedure has been used to diagnose abnormalities in the brain, and now some researchers hope that it will prove to be a valid treatment for depression—stimulating the brain in a manner similar to electroconvulsive, or shock, therapy. Minor studies to see whether TMS can improve some symptoms of Parkinson's disease, such as problems with coordination and reaction time, have been conflicting and inconclusive.

Other research indicates that magnetic fields can affect levels of the body's parahormones (substances that act like hormones but are not) and can stimulate bone regeneration, shortening healing times for both wounds and fractures.

Another form of the therapy involves placing small, powerful magnetic disks on different areas of the body. The goal is to magnetize the iron in red blood cells, thereby increasing blood flow and the amount of oxygen and heat delivered to cells. Proponents believe that this increased circulation is a healing force, particularly for chronic pain. In a study conducted at a Texas rehabilitation clinic, small magnets helped to relieve muscle and joint pain in patients who had once had polio. However, other investigations, including one involving heel pain, indicate that magnets have virtually no beneficial effect.

Where are we now?

Most experts remain unconvinced about magnet therapy. Even if it is eventually shown to produce positive results, they may be only short-term, and there is a possibility of long-term side effects. This type of treatment may also interfere with some medications.

Keep in mind Health Canada's warning to be skeptical of electromagnetic devices that misleadingly claim to treat a range of ailments. The Health Protection Branch has received complaints from Canadians who purchased such products and then found them to be ineffective. However, if you still want to try the therapy, speak with your doctor, particularly if you have a pacemaker or are pregnant.

Magnet-therapy products—whether a simple "wrap" containing magnets (above) or an elaborate machine creating magnetic fields—have not been proven to work.

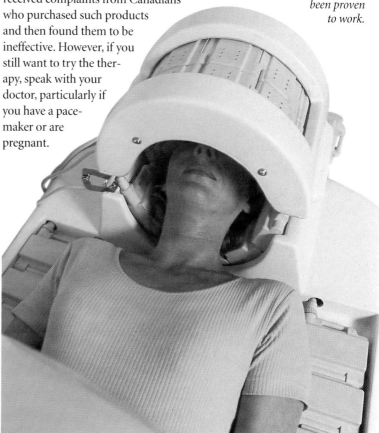

Mammograms

To ensure an accurate reading, the breast needs to be compressed during a mammogram—a discomfort lasting a few seconds.

Perhaps no other proven medical technology is the subject of more controversy than mammography. A type of X ray used to visualize the inside of the breast, it helps a doctor spot malignant tumors with up to 95 percent accuracy, often in their earliest, most easily treated stages. No one argues the value of this screening; the controversy centers on when a woman should begin having the test.

No safety problem

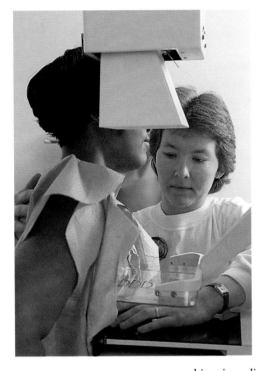

Like other forms of X ray, a mammogram relies on radiation to take pictures of the inside of the body. One of the more advanced forms being tested—called digital mammography—relays pictures directly to a computer screen, where they can be enhanced for what some believe are more accurate pictures.

Once, annual testing was controversial because of a possible cancer risk from the radiation. However, exposure from modern machines is so slight that mammograms are no longer considered even a minor risk.

How early should you start?

Experts recommend annual mammograms for all women over 50. Some doctors recommend tests for those in the 40-to-49 age group as well, although it is not certain how valuable mammograms are for younger women. Critics contend that because younger women's breasts are generally dense, results are more difficult to interpret, making the test itself less reliable. One U.S. study claims that younger women who have annual mammograms for 10 years have a fifty-fifty chance of at least one false positive (that is, what

appears to be a tumor isn't) and a 15 percent chance of having a cancer that goes undetected. Still, for those younger women who have survived breast cancer because of regular mammograms, their value is clear.

The Canadian Cancer Society, in conjunction with Health Canada, recommends that, every two years, all women between the ages of 50 and 69 should have a mammogram, in combination with a physical examination of the breasts by a trained health professional. These two procedures lead to earlier diagnosis of breast cancer and a significant improvement in survival. Medicare will pay for the tests. Experts agree that women of all ages should seek medical advice and consider being tested regularly if:

- She has a family history of premenopausal breast cancer.
- A DNA test shows she has a gene defect related to breast cancer.
- Her breasts are large, making them more difficult to examine.
- She has another breast disease or condition, such as cysts.

How to get the best screening

In the United States, the Quality Standard Act ensures that all mammogram facilities comply with safety standards for training and equipment. Canada has no similar national standards for screening. Some provinces have guidelines, and the Canadian Association of Radiologists has a voluntary accreditation program for mammography facilities.

To increase the accuracy of the image when you have a mammogram:

- If you menstruate, schedule your test during the two weeks following your period. Abnormalities are easier to spot then.
- Don't wear deodorant, powder, creams, or lotions of any kind on your underarms or torso on the day you are tested.
- Always confirm the results of your test with your doctor.
- If you change mammogram facilities, ask to take films of previous mammograms with you (preferably originals, not copies).

CAUTION!

Because some tumors don't show up on mammograms, women should ask their doctor to show them how to examine their breasts manually. Monthly self-exams are recommended.

Beautifully manicured nails are a hallmark of elegant grooming. But polishing your act can cause allergic reactions and infections. And a manicure in a salon may pose added health risks.

Nailing down the hazards

Virtually all nail products—polishes, polish removers, the glues used to apply artificial nails—contain toxic chemicals, including acetone, phenol, xylene, benzene, toluene, acrylic monomers, formaldehyde, and acetonitrile (cyanide). Toluene, found in many nail polishes and polish removers, can damage the liver, kidney, and lungs, and may even harm fetuses if enough is inhaled. Many nail polishes also emit formaldehyde, which may cause an allergic reaction; it is also a suspected carcinogen. Allergic reactions can occur on the neck, face, and eyelids, since women are likely to touch these areas when using nail products. Reactions can even result in the loss of a nail.

Keep all these dangers in perspective, however. Adding or removing nail polish is a speedy task and if you use the product as intended and with proper ventilation, you should not be at undue risk. For extra safety, choose toluene- and formaldehyde-free polishes, but realistically you may not always be able to tell from the label. "Hypoallergenic" products may contain less irritating chemicals. Avoid any product that caused you an allergic reaction or respiratory distress.

Taking polish off may be as hazardous as putting it on: polish remover can cause dizziness and lung irritation. One water-based peel-off polish can be removed without solvents, but this may not be widely available.

Many nail products are also highly flammable. Never smoke or go near an open flame until your nails are dry. Most are also poisonous if ingested, so keep them away from children.

Dermatologists warn that pushing back your cuticles can expose the area to infection. More worrisome is the use of unsterilized implements in salons, which can transmit candida (a yeast infection), staph infections, and warts. Fortunately, there has been no record of the instruments spreading blood-borne disease such as hepatitis or HIV.

Leave nails bare several days a month so that polishes and removers won't make them brittle. Avoid nail-polish removers that contain acetone, which dries the nails, and use remover no more than once a week.

an ounce of Prevention

Applying Artificial Nails Safely

- Never apply artificial nails if the natural nail is irritated or infected.

- Select nail extensions or tips instead of whole nails.

- Wear nails up to three months, then give natural nails a month's rest. Otherwise, moisture may accumulate under the nail and cause a fungal or bacterial infection.

- If an artificial nail comes off, immerse the fingertip in rubbing alcohol before reattaching the nail.

Choosing a reputable salon

Choose your salon carefully.

- If it smells strongly of fumes, it lacks proper ventilation. Go elsewhere.
- Be sure the tools are sterilized (with high heat or germicidal chemicals) before use.
- Bring your own emery board, since these cannot be sterilized.
- You and the technician should thoroughly wash your hands with soap and water before any procedure.
- Never allow a wooden orange stick to be used to push back cuticles; the sticks are breeding grounds for bacteria.
- All materials with blood on them should be discarded promptly.

Margarine

Which is better for you, margarine or butter? Until recently, many experts said margarine. But now it has been implicated as a possible risk factor for heart disease. However, you should know that not all margarines are created equal, and some are actually a healthy choice.

The hard truth

Stick margarine is the type that researchers believe may increase the risk of heart disease. To keep margarine solid at room temperature, prolong its shelf life, and improve the texture of many baked goods that are made with it, manufacturers force hydrogen into the unsaturated vegetable oil. The resulting "partially hydrogenated" vegetable oil contains two ingredients known to be harmful to the heart: saturated fat, which constitutes almost 25 percent of the margarine, and trans fats, which make up another 25 percent.

Both saturated fat and trans fats elevate LDL cholesterol, the kind that clogs arteries. Trans fats also lower levels of so-called good cholesterol (HDL) and raise the level of harmful blood fats called triglycerides. Preliminary evidence suggests that trans fats may also increase the risk of breast cancer; further research is needed to confirm this.

In large-scale studies at Harvard University, participants who consumed as little as 1 teaspoon of stick margarine a day for more than a decade raised their risk of a heart attack by 10 percent. Trans fats are believed to have been the main culprit.

A softer, kinder margarine

Soft (tub) or liquid margarines are better than either stick margarines or butter. Less hydrogen is added, so they don't contain as much satu-rated fat or trans fats, and contain more unsaturated fat, which actually lowers blood levels of LDL cholesterol. Margarine spreads labeled "low in saturated fat" and "non-hydrogenated" are good choices.

Back to butter?

Not on your life. A review of 20 studies comparing butter and stick margarine showed that both raise the risk of heart disease. Although butter has only one-eighth of the trans fats of stick margarine, it contains more than 50 percent saturated fat—more than twice as much as any margarine. If you can't conquer your craving for butter, at least use it sparingly whenever possible; it's easy enough to replace it with jam, for instance, on toast.

The healthiest fats of all—one step better than liquid margarines—are natural, unhydrogenated vegetable oils, particularly canola oil and olive oil (wonderful for dipping bread into). Still, all fat—even the unsaturated kind—should be consumed in moderation; experts advise that it should make up no more than 30 percent of your calories per day.

A rule of thumb for a healthful margarine: The softer it is, the better. As a result, tubs are healthier than sticks—and liquids are better than both.

On the Horizon Sitostanol, a plant compound that lowers blood-cholesterol levels (and the key ingredient in a Finnish margarine named Benecol), is currently being added to some soft margarines sold in Europe. It has no taste, so it doesn't affect the flavor of a spread. It may one day be available in North American markets.

Marijuana

Many people associate the illegal drug marijuana (*Cannabis sativa*) with the hippie movement of the 1960s. But the plant has been used for medicinal purposes since the 15th century B.C. During the 1800s marijuana was advocated for ailments ranging from constipation to earaches. Today doctors are weighing its potential medical benefits against its known hazards.

Marijuana as medicine?

Smoking dried marijuana leaves, whether for medicinal or recreational purposes, induces a "high," or feeling of mild euphoria. But marijuana has also been shown to stimulate the appetite in AIDS patients and help relieve the nausea and vomiting associated with chemotherapy. In addition, it has been found to lower pressure in the eye caused by glaucoma (though only if used throughout the day) and relieve muscle spasms associated with multiple sclerosis.

There has never been a documented incident of lethal marijuana overdose (which is not the case with many legal drugs). Still, marijuana is not without drawbacks. For instance, while marijuana offers the benefits of rapid relief, its effects on patients vary widely. That is one reason why researchers have developed a synthetic form of its active compound, known as THC. Unfortunately, the drug, Marinol (dronabinol), does not provide as much therapeutic relief as marijuana does, probably because it lacks the mix of plant compounds that contributes to marijuana's effects.

Scary side effects

A variety of side effects linked to marijuana argue against using it for any purpose other than short-term medical therapy. They include cognitive impairment (such as problems with attention and memory), increased risk of respiratory illnesses (particularly chronic bronchitis), impairment of the immune system (although research in this area is conflicting), and a general feeling of apathy. Marijuana contains potential carcinogens, and one recent study indicates that smoking it may pose the same risk of cancer as smoking cigarettes. The drug may cause impotence in men and infertility in both sexes. In some people, it may be habit-forming.

Short-term reactions include drowsiness, impaired memory, inability to keep track of time, and poor coordination. (Never drive a car or operate machinery while under the influence of marijuana.) Unlike those of alcohol, the psychological effects of marijuana may linger for days. For people with anxiety disorder or other psychiatric problems, marijuana may turn feelings of distress into panic, paranoia, or even hallucinations.

It's still illegal

In Canada it is against the law for doctors to prescribe marijuana. If marijuana has been suggested to you for medical reasons, remember that, under law, possession and use are illegal. Finally, people who smoked marijuana in the 1960s and '70s should realize that today's form may be as much as four to six times more potent than what they used then.

The high obtained from marijuana interferes with memory, speech, reading comprehension, arithmetic problem solving, and other basic intellectual skills.

CAUTION!
A rare mold that sometimes contaminates marijuana leaves may be fatal if it is inhaled. Heating leaves to 149°C (300°F) for 15 minutes kills the mold.

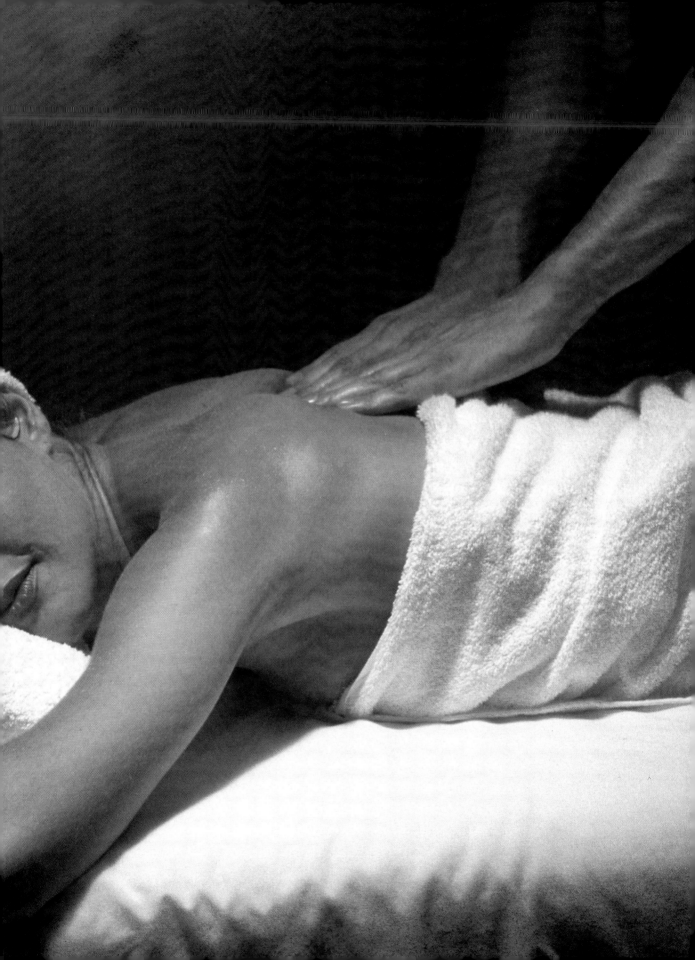

The ancient Chinese did it. Egypt's pharaohs did it. And we do it. Massage has been integral to the healing arts for some 3,000 years, and although it is currently categorized as an alternative therapy, its benefits are being acknowledged by a growing number of mainstream health professionals. A standard treatment in sports medicine and physical therapy, massage is now used to help treat everything from depression and stress to migraines and juvenile diabetes.

Hands-on healing

Massage therapists use their hands—and in some cases their elbows, forearms, knees, and feet—to manipulate muscles and soft tissues. The techniques, such as stroking, kneading, tapping, shaking, and pressing, are rather simple, but they may effectively promote relaxation, relieve aching muscles, and facilitate the healing of some conditions. Studies of its benefits indicate that massage may:

- Reduce muscle tension, temporarily lower blood pressure, and relieve stress.
- Improve circulation, reduce swelling, and speed the healing of muscle tissues.
- Improve joint flexibility and posture.
- Ease pain and fatigue and promote a sense of general well-being.
- Aid the growth and development of premature infants.

Is massage for you?

Before you consider getting a massage, note that it is not recommended in certain situations. If you have been recently injured, check with your doctor before having one, and do not massage an open wound, a skin infection, or an area affected by phlebitis or cancer.

What can you expect when you visit a massage therapist? Before she begins, the therapist will ask you questions about your health and your reason for seeking the treatment (to treat an injury, to simply relax, for example). For some types of massage, you will be asked to remove any clothing or jewelry that may get in the way. In fact, you may be left wearing nothing more than a towel or a sheet.

The massage itself takes place on a padded table in a relaxing environment. The experience should be pleasant and pain-free (if it isn't, speak up). The pressure may be uncomfortable at first but should become tolerable. Massage oil may be used to reduce friction.

Therapy costs vary, but a typical session usually lasts 30 to 60 minutes. A seated massage, which may be performed in a specially designed massage chair and allows you to remain clothed, takes only 10 to 30 minutes.

Aside from its other benefits, massage may be used to help treat:

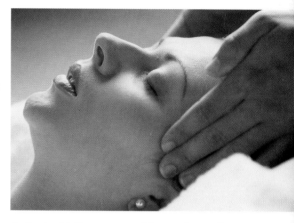

A circular friction massage of the temples can be relaxing and may help relieve a tension headache.

- Muscle spasms
- Lower-back pain
- Migraine headaches
- Depression
- Job-related stress
- Morning sickness
- Premenstrual syndrome
- Arthritis and tendinitis
- Muscle and ligament injuries
- Pain and discomfort after surgery
- Childhood ailments, such as asthma, juvenile diabetes, skin rashes, and insomnia
- Some respiratory and circulatory disorders

Finding the best massage therapist

Ask your doctor, local sports-medicine center, or health club for referrals. Additionally, you should consider calling the massage therapist association in your province for further information and a list of its members.

Therapists in nine provinces (Quebec is the exception) belong to the Canadian Massage Therapist Alliance. However, only Ontario and British Columbia have provincial legislation regulating the profession of massage therapy; in those two provinces, look for a registered massage therapist. In any case, before you get your massage, it's important to confirm that the therapist has graduated from an accredited massage therapy school.

Common Types of Massage

- Swedish massage consists of long strokes and mild pressure with the hands and fingers. It is used to relieve muscle tension and promote relaxation.

- Shiatsu gently works specific pressure points in order to rebalance the body's flow of energy and promote general health.

- Sports massage focuses on specific muscles and is used for rehabilitation and before and after a workout or competition.

Meat

Beef boasts a variety of nutrients. But the more meat you eat, the greater your risk of heart attack and certain cancers.

The simple pleasure of a big, juicy hamburger is getting more complicated all the time. Hamburger, like most red meat, can be high in saturated fat and cholesterol—both bad for the heart. A high intake of red meat can also increase the risk of advanced prostate cancer. And if meat is undercooked,

it can cause mild to severe food poisoning. Despite all this, however, meat can be part of a healthful, low-fat diet. Just choose lean cuts, cook them properly, and make sure to balance your diet with five to 10 servings of fruits and vegetables a day and plenty of whole grains.

The healthy side

A nutritious, balanced diet includes two to three daily servings from the meat food group, which is made up not only of red meat and poultry but also fish, eggs, legumes, tofu, and peanut butter. Small servings of lean meat deliver a solid amount of nutrients without too much fat. Red meat, such as steaks, burgers, and pork, is loaded with protein, B vitamins, iron, and zinc. Chicken and turkey don't contain as much iron and zinc, but they have considerably less saturated fat. Examples of a leaner, 100-gram (3½-ounce) serving include a roasted, skinless chicken breast (4 grams of fat) or turkey breast (1 gram of fat). Look for "lean" or "extra lean" cuts when you shop.

Wild game, such as ostrich, emu, pheasant, venison, and buffalo, is also a lean meat choice. A 100-gram (3½-ounce) serving of bison steak has only 2 grams of fat. Wild birds (some of which may be farm-raised) often have as little as 3 grams of fat per serving.

The harmful side

Although Canadians have become more vigilant about the amount of meat they consume, and the meat sold today is 50 percent leaner than it was 20 years ago, there are still concerns about overconsumption: the fact is, meat is high in both fat and cholesterol. Red meat and some types of poultry contain the most saturated fat and cholesterol. Some of the fattiest meats include brisket, ribs, ground beef, bacon, duck, and goose. Studies have shown that diets high in meat, especially red meat, increase the risk of heart disease and heart attack and are associated with a higher risk of colon, rectal, and prostate cancers.

Bacterial contamination is also a problem. Most raw meat carries some form of bacteria, and when it is not handled or cooked properly it can make you sick. Hamburger may carry a dangerous strain of *E. coli* bacteria, which can cause bloody diarrhea, abdominal cramps, and, in rare cases, kidney failure. Chicken is also prone to contamination—from campylobacter and salmonella bacteria. Symptoms caused by eating tainted chicken include severe diarrhea, abdominal cramps, and nausea and can last a week or longer.

How safe is the beef?

In recent years, the way beef is produced has raised concerns about its safety:

CAUTION!

Don't char meat; high heat causes potentially carcinogenic compounds to form. To avoid this, partially cook meats in the microwave or a slow oven first, and finish them up on a cooler part of the grill. Marinating also cuts down on carcinogens. Remove any charred sections before eating.

- **Bovine growth hormones.** In the U.S., the Food and Drug Administration (FDA) considers beef from hormone-treated cows to be safe. However, individual cases of hormones being misused on particular cows can yield beef with higher, unsafe levels of the chemicals. The hormones have not been approved for use in Canada.
- **Irradiation.** This little-used practice, which uses radiation to kill most bacteria and other microorganisms in meat, has also been approved by the FDA. It doesn't contaminate meat or make it radioactive; on the contrary, proponents say it may prove to be a big step in safeguarding meat from *E. coli*. In Canada, the meat supply is not allowed to be irradiated.
- **Mad cow disease.** This disease, which affected the brains of cows in Great Britain in the 1980s and '90s, may cause a similar (but extremely rare) condition in humans. However, the disease has been traced to feeding practices in Great Britain that are now outlawed, and the chance of eating tainted meat is very slim.

Safer storage, handling, and cooking

Here are tips to safeguard meat at home:
- Store uncooked meat in a freezer at −18°C (0°F) or below, or in a refrigerator below 4°C (40°F), and separate it from other foods. Don't refrigerate fresh poultry or ground beef for more than two days—use it or freeze it.
- Thaw meat in the refrigerator or microwave and cook it as soon as it is thawed. Thawing meat at room temperature (for example, in the sink or on the kitchen counter) promotes bacterial growth.
- Don't allow raw meat or any trimmings to touch any other food that you plan to serve raw or lightly cooked. The bacteria on uncooked meat can spread to other foods.
- Don't let raw chicken sit out—it can spoil in a few hours. If you want to marinate it, do so in the refrigerator.
- Before cooking, trim all visible fat from steak, veal, lamb, or pork.

Where's the Beef? No, Where's the Fat?

When choosing meats, emphasize leaner types (poultry instead of beef and pork) and leaner cuts (sirloin over ground beef, pork loin over bacon). Here's how different meats stack up:

Meat	Fattiest	Leanest
Beef	Brisket, prime rib roast, short ribs, regular ground beef (hamburger).	Sirloin steak, rump roast, eye of round roast. Inside round steak is the leanest cut of all.
Poultry	Dark meat, anything with the skin on, self-basting whole turkey, duck, goose.	Skinless turkey and chicken breast.
Pork	Bacon, sausage, side ribs.	Tenderloin, center cut roast, pork leg, lean ham.
Veal	Veal tends to be lower in fat than beef, lamb, or pork.	Leg cutlet, blade steak, rib roast, shoulder steak, loin chop.
Lamb	Shoulder, blade chop, spareribs, ground lamb.	Leg (sirloin and shank), loin chop, arm chop, foreshanks.
Wild game	Bear. Most wild game is low in fat.	Deer, elk, bison, quail, pheasant, ostrich, emu.
Processed meat	Prepackaged cold cuts, hot dogs. Even "lean" franks may have about 10 grams of fat each.	Cold cuts with less than 1 gram of fat per 30 grams (1 ounce). That's 4 grams or less in a 120-gram (4-ounce) serving.

- After handling meat, clean utensils, countertops, cutting boards, and hands with hot soapy water.
- Cook ground beef above 71°C (160°F), steaks and roasts above 63°C (145°F), poultry breast meat above 77°C (170°F), and whole birds above 82°C (180°F) to kill any bacteria in the meat. For the internal temperature, insert an instant-read meat thermometer for at least 15 seconds near the end of cooking.
- Juices should run clear or yellow, not pink. But don't rely on looks to tell whether meat is done. One study found that even brown meat can be insufficiently cooked.

Look before you buy: Steak that is marbleized—with interior streaks of fat—has a high fat content and should be passed over for a leaner cut.

Meditation

It's been acclaimed as the antidote to most of life's stresses. Indeed, meditation does reduce the body's response to stress and, in the process, may affect our health in perhaps myriad ways. It's also inexpensive to learn, and it can be performed almost anywhere.

Considering that modern medicine draws a link between chronic stress and a host of physical and psychological problems, meditation may certainly be a habit worth forming.

Meditating quiets the mind, providing a sense of detachment from thoughts that normally cause stress.

How do you do it?

Technically speaking, *meditation* can refer to almost any activity that brings about inner calm. One popular form is transcendental meditation (TM), which centers on the repetition of a sound or word—the *mantra* (Sanskrit for "formula"). To perform TM, you sit in a comfortable position with your eyes closed. Then, concentrating on your breathing, you slowly inhale and exhale. On each exhalation, you continually repeat (aloud or to yourself) your mantra, chosen for its personal significance or simply for its sound. Alternatively, you can just focus on your breathing without using a mantra.

Meditation ideally leads to a state of elevated awareness and serenity.

In another form of meditation, called visualization or guided imagery, you bring to mind a peaceful scene, either remembered or imaginary, and concentrate on every aspect of it— sights, sounds, and smells. Such exercises quiet the mind, providing a sense of detachment from thoughts that normally cause stress. Many experts believe that regular meditation— even if only for 20 minutes once or twice a day—can eventually result in not only psychological but also physiological benefits.

The mind-body connection

As a stress-management technique, meditation may make it easier for some people to stick with weight-loss and exercise programs that contribute to the prevention or reduction of high blood pressure. And several studies suggest that regular meditation may benefit people with heart disease when used as part of a larger treatment approach (one that addresses such risk factors as smoking, high blood pressure, and elevated cholesterol levels). It may even help reduce the risk of a second heart attack.

Research indicates that meditation may reduce chronic pain, especially that associated with cancer. It can also take the edge off pain during childbirth; relieve headaches, particularly migraines; ease mild depression; alleviate hot flashes; and help control some symptoms of anxiety, such as rapid heartbeat. (Of course, it should be used in conjunction with appropriate medical care.)

Not everyone agrees that meditation qualifies as medical therapy. Critics believe that much of what seems to be accomplished by meditation may instead be caused by the placebo effect, in which health improves because people have faith in the treatment. They are also concerned about the possibility of misuse of the practice, believing that meditating can cause a sort of trance that makes a person overly susceptible to the suggestions of a group or therapist.

Nevertheless, many people are convinced that meditation leads to better emotional and physical health—and, at the very least, increases your sense of serenity and control. If you want to join a meditation program, call a teaching hospital or adult-education school, check the phone book for meditation classes, or buy a book on the subject.

Melatonin

Some frequent fliers factor in direction flown and time zones traveled to figure out when to take melatonin for jet lag.

In the United States, melatonin has emerged as a "wonder drug," associated with the treatment of insomnia, jet lag, and other disorders. However, there is limited scientific evidence on its use in humans available to support any of these claims.

Your body produces its own melatonin, but less so as you age. The hormone is secreted by the brain's pineal gland primarily during the dark of night, making you drowsy; light diminishes its production. In this way, melatonin helps set your "body clock."

The sleep tablet

Evidence suggests that melatonin supplements can help people fall asleep; the tablets work best when taken 20 to 60 minutes before bedtime. The most convincing studies have focused on individuals whose natural production of melatonin is deficient.

Small-scale studies have concluded that melatonin can also ease the symptoms of jet lag—insomnia, fatigue, and irritability. However, not all travelers are helped by melatonin and taking it at the wrong time can make jet lag worse. If you want to try it, the simplest way to use melatonin for jet lag is to start with a dose of 0.3 to 1.0 milligram to induce sleep for one or two nights after arrival.

There have been claims made that melatonin also helps winter depression, or seasonal affective disorder (SAD), which researchers liken to jet lag. Sufferers in the northern latitudes find it increasingly difficult to get up in the morning as winter goes on. Their body clock no longer meshes with clock time. Studies have shown that taking small doses of melatonin in the afternoon seems to set their body clock ahead so they can get up and also helps to ease their winter blues. In addition, melatonin may act as an antioxidant, neutralizing harmful free radicals in the body. It has also benefited some people who have seizure disorders; in others, the drug has caused an increase in the number of seizures.

Is melatonin safe?

The safety of this drug, especially its long-term effects, is not yet known. This is true even of low doses, but there is particular concern about high-dosage tablets, since risks increase along with the amount. Reported side effects include depression, headaches, daytime drowsiness, nausea, and decreased sex drive. Be sure to check with your doctor before taking melatonin.

Although it is illegal to import melatonin into Canada for marketing and sale, it is not a banned substance; Canadians can purchase it for personal use, which Health Canada defines as a three-month supply of the drug.

A high-intensity, full-spectrum light box used in the morning can inhibit melatonin production naturally, but these boxes are expensive and can produce side effects, so consult your doctor first.

CAUTION!
Melatonin should not be taken by children (unless medically advised), women who are pregnant or trying to conceive, or people who have coronary artery disease or an autoimmune illness.

Microwave Ovens

Health Benefits

Microwaves are not only safe, they can actually be good for you.

- Food retains its water-soluble vitamins and minerals since little, if any, added water is used in cooking.

- Quick cooking helps retain heat-sensitive vitamins.

- By defrosting food quickly, microwaves allow less time for bacteria to grow.

- Dishes cooked in the microwave often require less use of fats, such as butter and oil.

- Because foods aren't charred, there is no buildup of cancer-causing agents.

People with pacemakers were once advised to steer clear of microwave ovens, but today's pacemakers are shielded against electrical interference.

Microwave ovens cook foods at space-age speeds. They work by means of a magnetron, a vacuum tube that creates microwaves, a form of electromagnetic radiation similar to radio waves. The microwaves cause the water molecules in food to spin millions of times a second. The resulting friction creates heat. Have no fear, though: microwaves do not make food radioactive.

Are microwaves safe?

High levels of microwave radiation will burn body tissue just as surely as they will cook food. But the Canadian government has established exposure limits far below the level that can harm humans. In addition, the ovens are designed so that radiation production stops when the door is opened.

Never use a damaged microwave (including one with a bent door or a door latch that doesn't work). Always keep the oven door and seal clean; do not use abrasives for their cleaning. If you feel the need for further precautions, step back from the oven while it's in use; the level of radiation decreases dramatically as you move away from the source.

The Health Protection Branch of Health Canada has established standards governing the design, construction, and functioning of microwave ovens sold in Canada. These regulations, incorporated into the Radiation Emitting Devices Act, are intended to reduce any possible radiation hazard involved in the operation of

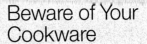

Beware of Your Cookware

Glass is safest for microwave cooking, followed by ceramic containers and pottery. Any items made of metal, including aluminum foil and even gold-trimmed plates, can cause sparks to fly.

Plastic, which is heated not by the microwaves but by the food it touches, can cause contamination when hot because some of the chemicals it contains can pass into the food. Don't use a plastic container that isn't labeled "microwave safe." If you cover a dish with plastic wrap, don't let it touch the food.

microwave ovens. If you suspect that your oven is defective, contact the manufacturer or have it checked by a reputable service person.

If a fire starts in the microwave, don't open the door. Unplug the oven and wait for the fire to go out. If it doesn't, call the fire department.

Hot spots, cold spots

Microwaves sometimes cook food unevenly, and this can present a health problem. If one portion of the food isn't heated to at least 71°C/160°F (82°C/180°F for poultry), harmful microorganisms will not be destroyed. Stirring and standing times are added to the directions in order to give the whole product a chance to heat. To ensure even heating, cook food in small portions in round containers, and completely defrost food before cooking. Some experts advise against heating baby bottles in the microwave; if you do, shake the bottle and let it cool slightly to eliminate hot spots.

Never cook an egg in its shell; it may explode. Pierce microwavable food pouches and foods with thick skins, such as baking potatoes, before cooking to prevent them from exploding.

Minerals

The North American diet, rich in calories and fat, is often poor in minerals, the inorganic elements our bodies need. Minerals perform an amazing number of functions, helping to build bones, regulate metabolism, fire nerves, and maintain overall health. But many women do not get enough calcium and iron, and most people get too little magnesium and zinc. Most of us also consume too much sodium and not enough potassium (together, these electrolytes help maintain fluid balance and regulate muscle and heart function).

Too much can be as harmful as too little. For instance, if you are diagnosed with iron deficiency, your doctor may recommend an iron supplement; however, if you take one when you don't need one, you may increase your risk of heart disease and cancer. Some minerals, such as selenium, are toxic in large amounts. And too much of certain minerals can affect levels of another. Just 18 to 25 milligrams (mg) of zinc—a tad over the recommended 9 mg for women and 12 mg for men—may lower blood levels of copper, another essential mineral. One study of postmenopausal women found that increasing daily calcium intake from 750 mg to 1,400 mg reduced the absorption of zinc. The solution is not to skip calcium supplements if you need them but to add a multivitamin/mineral supplement. Choose one with no more than 100 percent of the recommended nutrient intake.

The best strategy is to eat a balanced diet centered on fruits, vegetables, beans, and whole grains. Doing this will provide most people with all the minerals the body needs.

CAUTION!
If you drink a lot of soda, you may be getting too much phosphorus, which inhibits the body's absorption of iron.

Minding Your Minerals: Seven You Need

Below are some key minerals that many of us don't get enough of. Their benefits are still being studied.

Mineral	Food Sources	Benefits	Caution
Calcium	Low-fat milk and dairy, broccoli, fish with soft bones, tofu	Builds strong teeth and bones; prevents and treats some cases of high blood pressure.	Large doses can interfere with the absorption of iron and zinc.
Chromium	Brewer's yeast, wheat germ, whole grains, meat, cheese	Allows insulin to metabolize sugar; also needed for metabolizing carbohydrates and fats.	Little evidence that supplements, such as chromium picolinate, help people lose weight or gain muscle.
Iron	Red meat, liver, eggs, peas, beans, nuts, leafy green vegetables, fortified grains	Needed for the production of red blood cells; deficiency can cause weakness, fatigue, pallor, and dizziness.	Iron overload can cause liver damage. Don't take a supplement unless one is prescribed by your doctor. Iron supplements can poison children.
Magnesium	Leafy green vegetables, grains, beans, fish, eggs, bananas, nuts, apricots	Maintains strong bones, regulates blood pressure; may help balance insulin and blood-sugar levels.	Supplements can be dangerous to people with kidney disease and may cause severe diarrhea.
Potassium	Fruits, vegetables, beans, fish, meat, milk	Helps heart and kidneys function; may lower high blood pressure in some people.	Supplements may be dangerous to people with kidney disease and those taking certain medications.
Selenium	Fish, whole grains, Brazil nuts, asparagus, mushrooms, garlic	This trace mineral, needed in only tiny amounts, may help prevent cell damage that leads to cancer.	High doses (above 200 micrograms a day) can be toxic.
Zinc	Liver, eggs, milk, poultry, brewer's yeast, seafood, wheat germ, beans	Needed for cell growth, wound healing, and possibly for proper immune-system function.	Too much can impair absorption of copper. High levels (50 to 75 mg a day) may reduce "good" cholesterol.

Mold & Mildew

The ugly, furry stuff that grows in damp spots around your house can be either mold or mildew. These pernicious plant fungi damage walls, shoes, and fabrics and shed microscopic spores into the air, irritating people who are allergic to them. Mold can also attack food in your refrigerator, contaminating it with dangerous toxins.

Can they make you sick?

Mold and mildew thrive in humid conditions on almost any surface, indoors or out. When they grow on foods stored in the refrigerator, molds can ruin the taste of food and may produce poisonous mycotoxins, which cannot be destroyed by heat or cooking.

When inhaled by a sensitive person, some mold or mildew spores can trigger allergic reactions, such as congestion, breathing difficulty, and itchy, watery eyes. In very rare cases exposure may cause hypersensitivity pneumonitis, which can lead to serious heart and lung problems, or a dangerous condition in infants known as pulmonary hemosiderosis, or bleeding-lung syndrome.

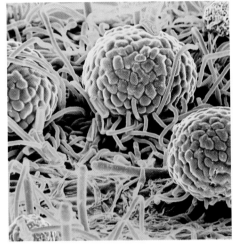

Molds commonly grow on plants and plant fibers. The orange balls contain mold spores.

Mold and mildew in your home

Measure the humidity in your home with an inexpensive hygrometer, sold at most hardware stores. If it's more than 40 percent, mold and mildew may be growing on your furniture, carpets, and bedding. Lower the humidity with air conditioning or dehumidifiers.

Even if your home's air is dry, check damp, poorly ventilated areas: basements, refrigerators, water-damaged wallboard, bathrooms, crawl spaces, attics, closets, leaky pipes, roofs, and trash bins. If you find mold or mildew:

- Discard moldy breads or refrigerated foods. While some foods, such as hard cheeses, may be saved by trimming at least 2.5 centimeters (1 inch) around a small area of mold, molds can leach unseen toxins into food.
- Clean up mold with hydrogen peroxide, white vinegar, or a chlorine-bleach solution. Wear a protective mask and rubber gloves. (If you are allergic, let someone else do it.) For areas larger than .1 square meter (1 square foot), call in an environmental engineer, they're listed in the yellow pages.
- Launder mildewed clothes and bedding in hot water and nonchlorine bleach.
- Air out bathroom area rugs that become damp—or remove them altogether.

an ounce of Prevention

Preventing Mold and Mildew

Following these general rules can help to keep your home clean, dry, and mold-free:

- Check to see that household ventilation fans work and roof soffits are clear.
- Ventilate the kitchen and bathrooms with open windows and exhaust fans ducted to the outdoors.
- Dry out a damp basement with a dehumidifier. Keep it and its filter clean.
- Clean a window-unit air conditioner and its filter regularly. To dry its interior, turn off the cooling function and run the fan for a half hour.
- Vent the exhaust from the clothes dryer outdoors.
- Regularly sponge down shower walls. Use a shower curtain that is mold-resistant or one that can be machine-washed and dried.
- Set the refrigerator below 4°C/40°F; keep it and the condensation tray clean.
- When discarding moldy food, wrap it tightly so that the spores will not spread.
- Wrap your pillow and mattress in moldproof cases.

Mothballs

When it comes to one's wardrobe or furnishings, the moth-eaten look has never been in style. Moths lay eggs that hatch into larvae, which munch on wool or wool blends and soiled fabrics, ruining clothing, blankets and drapes. Enter mothballs—white crystalline pesticides designed to repel moths before they can lay eggs. The problem is that while mothballs do a good job of chasing away the pests, their vapors may cause illness. Fortunately, there are safer alternatives.

Bad for moths, bad for you?

Mothballs are made of either naphthalene or paradichlorobenzene (para-DCB). Exposure to either of these chemicals may irritate the eyes, skin, and respiratory tract and cause headaches, confusion, and liver and kidney damage. Young children are more sensitive, so it's never a good idea to dress infants in clothes that have been in storage for a long time and may be saturated with mothball vapors even after they are washed.

The potential risks don't end there. Naphthalene can help break down red blood cells, causing hemolytic anemia, the symptoms of which range from fatigue to kidney failure. Prolonged exposure may also increase the risk of developing cataracts. Para-DCB may be less toxic, but it is a suspected carcinogen.

In addition, many children have been poisoned when they mistake the tiny white balls for candy and swallow them. Anyone who swallows a mothball, particularly a young child, may experience vomiting, diarrhea, seizures, and liver and kidney damage. Severe poisoning requires immediate emergency medical attention.

Minimizing mothball risks

It's best to avoid using mothballs altogether. However, if you do use them, do so sparingly and follow these directions.

- Keep mothballs in a well-ventilated area away from children and pets—and unused ones in a sealed, childproof container.
- Store clothing in a detached garage or a ventilated attic—not in a bedroom closet, from which mothball vapors can seep out.
- Don't let mothballs touch clothing, since they can damage or discolor fabrics and soften plastic buttons and fasteners.
- Before wearing clothes that have been stored with mothballs, wash and air them out until the pungent odor is gone.
- Discard used mothballs with household hazardous waste.

Safer mothproofing

Moth larvae are drawn to food stains and perspiration, so the first step in safeguarding your clothes is to keep them clean. Dry-clean your clothes or wash them in hot water to remove larvae that may already be on them—something that moth repellents won't do. (Shaking or brushing your clothes or running them through a warm dryer may also do the trick.) Vacuum your storage areas and store clothes in mothproof containers or cloth garment bags.

Once your clothes are put away, you can help protect them with one of these natural moth repellents:

- Products that contain moth-repelling lavandin oil, a nontoxic plant oil.
- Fresh cedar, in the form of blocks, hangers, shavings, or oil. Storing clothes in a sealed, freshly sanded cedar closet also works.
- Old newspapers (moths hate newsprint).
- Moth-repellent herbs, such as lavender, rosemary, mint, sage, lemongrass, and bay leaves. Place a mixture in a muslin bag and hang it in your closet or place it with your clothes in a drawer or a storage container.

Hanging a garment on a cedar hanger may be safer and just as effective as using mothballs.

MRI & CT Scans

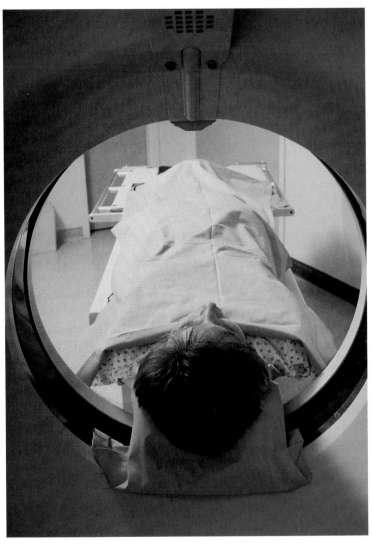

An MRI, like a CT scan, generally takes a half hour or more. If you are claustrophobic or have trouble remaining still, the doctor can give you a sedative.

Medical imaging began with the X ray a little more than 100 years ago, but since then many strides have been made that allow doctors to see under the skin of their patients without the use of invasive exploratory surgery. Two of the most important and fascinating of the new technologies emerged in the early 1970s: magnetic resonance imaging (MRI) scans and computed tomography (CT) scans, which are also referred to as computed axial tomography (CAT) scans.

Each of these methods offers a slightly different advantage in helping physicians to diagnose disorders, including many conditions that are life-threatening. Both often enable doctors to spot diseases in their early, curable stages, and they can also quickly rule out a suspected disorder.

The inside story

The CT scan is actually a kind of computer-enhanced X ray. A scanning machine rotates around the patient, who lies on a movable table, and transmits X-ray beams into the person's body. The device then records the absorption of radiation by tissues in the area being examined. This information is relayed to a computer, which creates two-dimensional cross-sectional views, or "slices," of the area. (Recent advances in computer technology may turn CT scans into three-dimensional, color-coded images.) To enhance the picture, doctors can use dyes, which are swallowed by the patient or injected by the technologist, to provide contrast.

CT scans, which depict blood vessels and organs as well as tumors and other abnormalities, offer a much fuller picture than X rays. They are used to detect not only tumors but also infections, internal bleeding, and structural problems in the heart and other organs.

Magnetic-field magic

Unlike X rays and CTs, MRIs do not involve radiation. As the patient lies within a large device—usually a cylindrical machine—powerful magnetic fields trigger painless vibrations in atoms of the body. These vibrations give off signals that are relayed to a computer and ultimately translated into two- and/or three-dimensional images. The pictures can be made from any direction and in any plane, allowing once-impossible views of multiple angles. The MRI images can be more detailed than those of CTs and show more differentiation within the body's soft tissues.

Currently, MRI tests are most often used to diagnose brain and nervous-system disorders, joint and muscle abnormalities, and tumors of the liver, kidney, bladder, pancreas, reproductive organs, lymph nodes, and vocal cords. Most recently, MRIs have begun to play a role in the diagnosis of heart disease, particularly the type that affects blood vessels, with a procedure known as the MRI angiogram. Continual advances in MRI technology have

Both methods often enable doctors to spot diseases in their early stages, and they can also quickly rule out a suspected disorder.

expanded its possibilities even further. These are some of its newest forms:

- **MRI diffusion imaging.** Documents the motion of fluid within and between brain cells, thus offering important information on how the brain functions. The technique can confirm a stroke within hours after occurrence, thus allowing doctors to administer medication that can help reverse brain damage. Other technologies require from 24 to 48 hours to provide the same information, which may be too late for doctors to help.
- **Functional MRI.** Shows how the brain functions over time and thus can speed up diagnosis of many neurochemical malfunctions, including schizophrenia and bipolar disorder.
- **MRI spectroscopy.** Details the molecular structure of the brain, giving doctors more information about overall brain function.
- **Interventional MRI.** Monitors patients during surgery and therefore helps guide surgeons in performing operations.
- **Magnetic resonance elastography.** May help physicians to electronically "touch" the organs they see to increase diagnostic accuracy.
- **Temperature sensitive imaging.** Monitors the temperature of a tumor. This may eventually allow for the destruction of tumors using very high heat.

Safety precautions

Both MRI and CT scans are relatively safe and painless. During a CT scan you are exposed to only a small amount of radiation. One caution is in order when contrast dyes are used:

Tell your doctor if you have any allergies—particularly to shellfish or iodine—because you might have a reaction to the dyes.

When undergoing an MRI, be sure to let your doctor know if you have a metallic joint replacement or any other type of metallic device. The scanner could adversely affect these appliances. Jewelry, clothing with zippers, and other metallic objects must be removed before an MRI test. Tattoos and MRIs also don't mix. Tattoo inks often contain metals that can interact with the magnetic fields and create an intense heat that results in painful burning and swelling.

Most MRIs require that patients lie virtually motionless in a tunnel-shaped machine that sometimes causes a frightening bout of claustrophobia or a high level of anxiety in many patients. To help patients, doctors sometimes prescribe a tranquilizer prior to the scan. Some doctors also offer patients headphones so that they can listen to music that helps block out the loud clanking noises produced by the machine. Patients are usually provided with a signal button or some other device so they can alert the MRI staff if they begin to feel uneasy during the test.

If you feel a traditional MRI machine will make you uncomfortable, ask your doctor if the new so-called open MRI machines, whose "tunnel" is roomier than those of standard machines, are available in your area. (They are not commonly in use.) Although these newer machines were once considered less effective than the closed ones, advances have made them acceptable for diagnosing many conditions. Halfway between the standard and the open MRIs are those that use smaller tunnels, which encase only the part of the body that is being scanned.

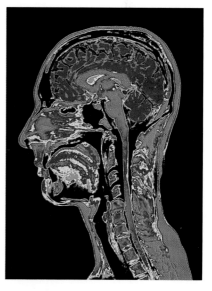

Presenting clear, detailed images of the brain is one of the most important purposes of MRI scans.

Nicotine Gum & Patches

If you want to stop smoking, you may be considering Zyban (bupropion), the newest antismoking medication on the market, or one of the nicotine-replacement products: patches, gum, or a nasal spray. Although these products can increase your chances of quitting, there are issues to consider before deciding which one to use.

Nicotine addiction: The facts

Nicotine works in much the same way that other addictive drugs do—it causes the brain to release large amounts of dopamine, a chemical associated with pleasure. When nicotine levels begin to drop, as they do between cigarettes, the body craves more. That means you want to light up again. If you don't, a variety of symptoms, including anxiety, irritability, insomnia, fatigue, and even depression, may occur. For some people, these feelings can be so overwhelming that it seems impossible to quit smoking.

Children may mistake nicotine replacements, such as patches (above) and gum (right), for adhesive bandages or candy. Keep them locked away; they can make kids seriously ill.

Blow smoking away

The first antismoking medication ever approved in Canada, Zyban must be prescribed by your physician. Together you will decide if you are a suitable candidate for this antidepressant. Zyban, which does not contain nicotine, is thought to help you quit by reducing withdrawal symptoms.

On the other hand, nicotine-replacement products work by supplying your body with just enough nicotine to keep the craving under control, thereby helping you fight the urge to smoke. Of the three types available, the gum and the spray offer a "blast" of nicotine similar to what you experience when you light up a cigarette. The patch works in a slightly different way; it supplies a low but steady stream of nicotine that helps fight cravings around the clock.

The replacement products have side effects worth noting, including headaches, dizziness, blurred vision, itchy skin, muscle weakness, upset stomach, and diarrhea. Sprays may also cause nasal irritation and coughing.

Nicotine-replacement products may satisfy the physical need for nicotine, but they will not affect the psychological cravings associated with smoking. A replacement regimen works best when it lasts a few months and is combined with a behavioral program that addresses smoking's habitual aspects.

Proceed with care

Although the gum, spray, and patch contain less nicotine than cigarettes, there is a small risk of addiction. However, experts contend that the addiction is less harmful than smoking. Still, there is a concern for people with heart disease. One test indicated that if used for an extended time, some of the replacement products may have the same negative impact on the heart as cigarettes have; other studies have shown no ill effects from the products.

To help you decide what to try—and to determine the correct dosage—talk to your doctor about your smoking habits and overall health. Most important, never smoke while using these products. The double dose of nicotine could dangerously overload your system.

On the Horizon New delivery systems for nicotine-replacement medications mimic the delivery of nicotine through smoking. A nicotine tablet (placed under the tongue), a nicotine lollipop, and a nicotine inhaler allow the drug to be absorbed via the mouth and nose.

Night Shifts

These days, many industries and businesses are forced to operate day and night to stay competitive. For consumers and business owners, this 24-hour world is a boon, but if you are among those who must work at night, it can be a nightmare, affecting everything from your mood and social life to your health. Fortunately, there are ways to counter the effects of working the night shift.

Rhythm and blues

The main problem with night work is the interruption of the natural circadian rhythm—the body's internal clock. This complex timing system orchestrates a variety of physiological events, including blood pressure, secretion of stomach acids, and even the degree to which you experience pain. Normally, this rhythm is kept on track by cues from your environment—daylight, social contacts, mealtime, and sleep time. When those cues veer from the norm, as they do if you work nights and sleep days, your body clock may not change to match your new schedule. If it doesn't, your body will long for sleep when you need to be awake and resist sleep when you turn in. Meanwhile, your risk of accidents and health problems will soar.

The night shift nightmare

In the short term, working the night shift makes you feel fatigued and less alert—much the way you would if you were to have a bad night's sleep every single day for weeks. You may have problems making decisions and communicating your thoughts and you are more likely to have accidents, particularly while driving.

Long-term consequences, however, can be more serious. These include gastrointestinal problems (chronic heartburn and indigestion), weight gain, high blood pressure, and a greater risk of cardiovascular disease and heart attack. Emotional problems also occur more frequently. Women working night shifts have increased menstrual difficulties and problems with infertility. Pregnant women are at greater risk of high blood pressure.

When night shifts are also stressful, such as this air traffic controller's, health problems can multiply.

Making day into night

If you can't avoid night shifts, reduce the risks by changing your daily schedule as little as possible. For instance, if you work for several days and then take a few days off, try to keep your sleeping hours the same, even when you aren't working. If it becomes necessary to change shifts, try to move your shift forward; changing the start of your workday from 7 A.M. to 3 P.M. is easier on your body than backing it up from 3 P.M. to 7 A.M.

To sleep better during the day, avoid sunlight for at least an hour prior to bedtime. Keep your bedroom as cool and as dark as possible, and use earplugs, a sleep mask, and a white-noise machine to lessen distractions.

While working at night, adjust your lifestyle so that your schedule runs work-sleep-leisure, rather than the work-leisure-sleep schedule of day workers. Avoid cigarettes and excessive caffeine, and resist using sleeping pills or alcohol to induce drowsiness or stimulant drugs to stay awake.

Finally, be sure to get plenty of exercise, preferably during a break in your night shift. If that isn't possible, exercise before your night shift. Avoid doing any type of strenuous exercise just before you need to go to sleep.

Changing Shifts

To adjust more easily to night work, try taking a three-hour nap prior to starting your shift and going to bed directly after the shift. Then gradually shorten the nap and lengthen your sleep time.

Now hear this: Your environment may be hazardous to your hearing. From thundering jets overhead to the whirring food processor on your kitchen counter, you may be exposed to dangerously high levels of noise every day without even knowing it.

Attending a rock concert carries obvious risks, but sitting too close to the percussion section at the symphony can also cause hearing problems—as can playing a Walkman, cranking up the car stereo, or going to a movie with a state-of-the-art sound system. And noise may disturb more than hearing. One experiment indicates that schoolchildren in quieter classroom environments (away from street noise) perform better on reading tests and have fewer problems with behavior and attention span.

Decibels that damage

Sound is measured in decibels. The scale begins at zero, the threshold of human hearing. It increases logarithmically, meaning that each 10 decibels is perceived as two times louder than the last. For example, at 90 decibels, a food processor is eight times louder than normal conversation at 60 decibels.

Exposure to intense decibel levels for an unsafe period of time can damage the hair cells in the inner ear, eventually causing a loss of auditory range. The process is usually gradual and painless. You may notice ringing in the ears, but more typically a hearing problem manifests itself in the diminished ability to understand what people are saying—particularly the higher-pitched voices of women and children. The Canada Labour Code sets 87 decibels as the maximum permitted exposure level for an 8-hour period of continuous noise.

Sound advice

To protect your hearing, use earplugs when exposed to noises above 85 decibels for an extended period. (If you have to raise your voice to speak with someone 1 meter [3 feet] away, you need earplugs.)

Earplugs work by blocking the outer ear canal with an airtight seal. This reduces noise exposure by 20 to 30 decibels. Various styles (foam, silicone, and wax) are available, but all of them work well as long as the seal stays tight. Dirty or worn earplugs can make for an imperfect seal. Stuffing cotton in your ears reduces noise by about seven decibels at best because sound waves can penetrate the cotton fibers. Workers in extremely noisy environments wear special sound-filtering earmuffs.

In your day-to-day life, be alert to sources of noise, and take steps to minimize them. Vibration mounts (padded feet) can significantly reduce appliance noise. Window caulking and heavy drapes can muffle street sounds. If you experience hearing irregularities, see your doctor. While hearing loss may be the temporary result of a simple ear infection or impacted wax, it may also be a signal of auditory damage.

CAUTION!

Watch the volume when playing your Walkman. One study found the average level to be a dangerous 112 decibels. If you have to raise your voice to hear yourself speak, turn the music down.

A jackhammer's rattle jars the nerves—and, without adequate ear protection, even brief exposure can cause permanent hearing loss.

How Loud Is Too Loud?

Decibels	Source	Safe Exposure
20	Whisper	Unlimited
60	Normal speech Typewriter	Unlimited
80	City traffic Vacuum cleaner Alarm clock	Unlimited
90	Lawn mower	eight hours
100	Power drill Snowmobile Chain saw	two hours
120	Rock concert Subway	15 minutes
130	Jackhammer Drums and cymbals	3.8 minutes
140	Jet engine Gun blast Firecracker	Noise causes instant pain; can injure ears

Nose Sprays

G ot a runny, itchy, sneezy, stuffy nose? This is called rhinitis, and it's symptomatic of a cold or an allergy. An effective weapon against the condition is an over-the-counter vasoconstrictor nose spray, which can provide quick and temporary relief. However, if you use it for more than three days, you may end up even more congested.

There are alternatives. Prescription sprays give long-term relief for allergic rhinitis. Non-medicated over-the-counter saline sprays rehydrate nasal membranes dried out by indoor heat, as do lubricating nasal gels. And a noseful of steam helps ease symptoms.

Breathe easy
Rhinitis, an inflammation of the tissues and blood vessels in the nasal passages, plagues most people either when they have a cold or when pollen and other allergens are plentiful. Vasoconstrictor nose sprays cause the blood vessels to contract, clearing the nasal passages and allowing freer breathing.

However, if you use one of these sprays for more than three days, your nasal tissues become dependent on the medication to keep the blood vessels from dilating. When you stop using the spray, the vessels expand and your nose becomes stuffed up again. Doctors call this reaction "rebound congestion." Nose sprays can also mask symptoms of a sinus infection, which requires treatment with antibiotics.

Finding the right spray
Several effective ingredients to look for in over-the-counter vasoconstrictor sprays are xylometazoline, phenylephrine, or oxymetazoline. All vasoconstrictor sprays ease rhinitis faster than oral decongestants, and they have few of the side effects of the oral medications, which can cause insomnia, dry mouth, high blood pressure, and increased heart rate.

Corticosteroid nasal sprays are currently available by prescription for allergy patients. These sprays are safe when used correctly, but possible side effects include nosebleeds, headache, nausea, burning and stinging in the nose, and light-headedness. The onset of action is not immediate. Several days of treatment are necessary before maximum relief is obtained. Unlike vasoconstrictor sprays, there is no rebound effect when discontinued.

A non-medicinal saline spray rinses and moistens nasal passages parched by dry indoor air.

Relief in the air
If you must fly when you have a cold or allergy symptoms or if you suffer ear pain during air-pressure changes, use a decongestant nose spray 20 minutes before takeoff and again shortly before descent begins (usually 20 minutes to an hour before landing). It can unplug nasal passages and sinuses.

Gentle aids
Over-the-counter saline sprays relieve dried-out nasal passages prone to bleeding. Another gentle way to ease cold and allergy symptoms is to inhale steam for 10 to 15 minutes two or three times a day. Buy a steamer with a plastic mask that fits over your nose and mouth. Or create a steam tent: pour boiling water into a ceramic bowl, then drape a towel over your head and the bowl, and breathe in deeply for at least 10 minutes. (Never place a towel over a boiling pot on the stove; it can catch fire.) Add mint leaves or a few drops of menthol or eucalyptus oil to the water if you wish.

Spray Delivery

Researchers are developing new nasal sprays that transmit medication more effectively and conveniently than pills and injections. The following have gained Health Canada approval or are currently being researched:

- A spray version of a migraine drug that relieves headaches faster than the pill form.
- A nitroglycerine spray used to treat angina.
- A medicine that reduces bed-wetting by suppressing urine production.
- A medicine that lessens a cold's severity.

I t's okay to be nuts about nuts. Although they have long been a forbidden delight, with fat and calorie counts that seemed to far outweigh any nutritional benefit, new research into how the body uses fat indicates that nuts may actually lower the risk of heart attack and cancer while improving overall nutrition.

Even so, nut lovers beware: Prepared nuts and nut butters are often made with cholesterol-raising trans fats and saturated fats that undermine their healthfulness. What's more, nuts are among the most common, potentially dangerous food allergens.

The case for nuts

This popular, tasty food encompasses tree nuts (pecans, almonds), seeds (sunflower, pumpkin), and some legumes (including the misleadingly named peanut). All contain a high percentage of fat calories (50 to 75 percent of total calories). Although some nuts are high in saturated fat (Brazil nuts, macadamias, and pine nuts), the fats in other nuts are mainly monounsaturated and polyunsaturated; they actually improve heart health by reducing LDL (low-density lipoprotein) cholesterol, the "bad" stuff that gums up blood vessels. One study reported that women who ate nuts instead of animal protein more than twice a week had a 60 percent lower risk of heart problems than those who didn't. Eating nuts up

Sunflower seeds are rich in valuable magnesium, thiamine, linolenic acid, and fiber, but they are often heavily salted.

to four times a week can decrease the chance of heart attack by 25 percent. Peanuts also contain resveratrol, an antioxidant compound also found in red wine that protects against heart disease.

Recent research shows that almonds, walnuts, and flaxseeds are good sources of omega-3 fatty acids, which are associated with a decreased risk of blood clots and stroke. Other studies indicate that nuts may be a weapon against cancer-cell growth.

Nutritionally, a handful of nuts or seeds packs a wallop, especially as a source of protein (which protects against cavities). Nuts also provide large amounts of fiber, magnesium, zinc, and the antioxidant vitamin E (which protects against heart disease and cancer). Pumpkin seeds are rich in iron; sesame seeds contain calcium; and sunflower seeds are a great source of energy-enhancing thiamine.

You can increase your intake by adding nuts and seeds, dry-roasted or raw, to stir-frys, salads, yogurt, breads, and muffins and by using sesame, flax, or sunflower oil in dressings.

Preparation problems

Peanuts are one of Canada's favorite "nuts," but they are often among the least healthful. "Roasted" nuts are usually cooked in oils that destroy nutrients while adding saturated fat. Snack peanuts are usually heavily salted.

Peanut butter may contain an artery-clogging partially hydrogenated oil that keeps it creamy. If your peanut butter doesn't separate at room temperature, it contains partially hydrogenated oil.

Of all nuts, almonds have the greatest ratio of nutrients to calories, and the oil is 90 percent unsaturated.

an ounce of Prevention

Allergy Alert

Nuts and peanuts can trigger fatal reactions in people allergic to them. But avoiding them can be tough.

- Read labels carefully. Peanut oils and butters, ground nuts, and other nut products are used by processors to prepare everything from chili and sauces to ice cream and candy bars.

- Stay away from Asian and Middle Eastern cuisines in which nuts are common ingredients.

- If you eat out, review the menu with the chef to make certain the foods are safe for you and the seriousness of your allergy is understood.

Organic Food

Most of our food supply comes to market with the help of chemicals that control insects, stimulate growth, and reduce spoilage. Conventionally grown domestic produce often carries residues from pesticides identified and approved for use by Health Canada's Pest Management Regulatory Agency. Meats, poultry, and dairy products may also bear traces of these pesticides, which the animals ingest with their feed, as well as antibiotics and hormones used to "beef them up."

Through tests of registered pesticides, Health Canada has established safe tolerance levels; it also considers the levels of hormones given to animals (when administered properly) to be safe. But if you want to reduce your exposure to these substances, you can buy foods that are produced organically.

Less is more

Truly organic foods contain virtually no synthetic substances. Growers use such farming techniques as fertilizing with manure and controlling pests biologically. Those who raise cattle and poultry for meat and dairy products do not use hormones or other drugs on healthy livestock, and they provide more healthful environments for their animals.

Because traces of pesticides can remain in the soil for years and can be absorbed from the air and outside water sources, organic foods may contain tiny amounts of synthetic chemicals. However, tests have shown they tend to carry less pesticide residue than conventionally grown food.

New national organic standards

Unfortunately, current criteria for organic foods are made and enforced through a hodgepodge of various associations and

A niche market: Organic foods generate less than one percent of Canada's agricultural revenues.

agencies. Even though you pay from 10 to 75 percent more for foods sold as organic, there's no guarantee that they really are. However, national standards and a certification system are currently being developed to correct this problem. National organic standards may offer an unintentional bonus: more food producers are expected to enter the organic market, which will probably drive down prices. Also, Canadian consumers will likely have more confidence in organic products.

Proposed regulations are currently being developed by the Canadian Organic Advisory Board, assisted by the Canadian General Standards Board (CGSB). The CGSB's Committee on Organic Agriculture is in the process of drafting the standards for sound organic farming. Once consensus is established, the standards will define organic produce (by the number of years land has been free of prohibited pesticides and fertilizers) and organic meats, poultry, and dairy products (drugs given to animals used for such products will be restricted, except in the case of illness). The standards also plan to tighten controls on the use of "organic" on labels.

Baby-food Boom

Food-manufacturing companies are working to accommodate the burgeoning demand for organic baby foods, which now appear on some supermarket shelves.

The surge in interest may be the result of reports in the past few years about pesticides in some baby foods. For example, the Environmental Working Group, a research organization, has calculated that about 84,000 North American infants aged 6 to 12 months ingest unsafe levels of organophosphate pesticides each day because of residues occurring in baby-food pears, peaches, applesauce, and apple juice.

Aching feet are no fun. Neither are hip, knee, and back pain—all of which may be foot-related. If you suffer from any of these problems, therapeutic shoe inserts called orthotics may be just the thing to put the spring back in your step. But they are only one possible remedy. Costly custom-fitted orthotics should be considered only after you and your doctor or podiatrist have determined the cause of your symptoms and explored other options.

A pain in the foot

According to the Canadian Podiatric Medical Association, about 7 million Canadians suffer from foot or foot-related pain. In many of these cases, the pain is a symptom of a structural problem (bones or ligaments), rheumatoid arthritis, diabetes, a bone cyst, or tarsal tunnel syndrome (the foot version of carpal tunnel syndrome). Orthotic devices cannot address the root of these disorders.

What orthotics does best is ease the discomfort of some common complaints, especially heel pain associated with tiny tears in the plantar fascia—the connective tissue in the sole of the foot and sides of the heel—and age-related diminishment of the heel pad, which acts as a natural shock absorber for the foot. (Overweight people, athletes, runners, brisk walkers, and anyone with flat or highly arched feet are especially vulnerable.) An orthotic device works by stabilizing the foot, controlling abnormal movements, and adding arch support to help keep the plantar fascia from being stretched or pulled, and thus becoming irritated or inflamed.

Custom-made or store-bought?

During an orthotic fitting, the practitioner takes a plaster cast of the foot in a relaxed position, then factors in abnormalities, such as uneven leg length, as well as exercise and physical-activity patterns. When the orthotic is intended mainly to stabilize the foot, it will be made of flexible plastic, with cushioning material made of thin, dense foam. Some rigid orthotics are nearly paper-thin; other devices are bulkier. Most orthotics fit inside ordinary shoes.

Some doctors and physical therapists start patients off with inexpensive over-the-counter products to find out whether a shoe insert will help at all. It's probably worth a try: In a University of Southern California study, 80 percent of participants who bought over-the-counter inserts reported relief from heel pain—12 percent more than those who had custom-made orthotics. If problems persist, however, it's wise to consult a specialist.

To make an orthotic, a podiatrist needs to cast a mold of a foot in a non-weight-bearing position.

Alternative Foot Fixes

- To provide arch support: Before physical activity, wrap the foot with an elastic bandage or tape.

- To relieve sole and heel pain or strain: Upon waking, stretch calf muscles by pointing your toes upward and moving your feet in a circular motion.

- To alleviate aching: Gently massage the soles of the feet.

an ounce of Prevention

Foot Problems or Shoe Problems?

Worn or ill-fitting shoes can cause foot pain. Stomp out the problem before it starts:

- Replace running or walking shoes that show wear on the heels and toes or creases and bunching in the midsole, all of which indicate loss of cushioning. If the stitching is frayed or the toes discolored, you may need a larger size.

- When purchasing shoes, be sure that there's a space of about the width of your thumb between your longest toe and the shoe tip.

Outdoor Cooking

When barbecuing, don't get burned: Place the grill a safe distance from the house and any shrubs, use long-handled tools, and have a spray bottle of water handy for flare-ups.

Firing Up the Grill

- Don't start your grill fire with kerosene or gasoline. Both are far more flammable than lighter fluid.

- If your fire needs a boost, resist the urge to squirt more lighter fluid on it. Instead, place a few fresh briquettes in a metal pan, drench them with lighter fluid, then place them on the pile and relight.

- Instead of lighter fluid, try an electric fire starter or a charcoal chimney.

What could be bad about a backyard barbecue? Plenty. Health and safety officials have issued enough warnings about everything from undercooked food to charcoal fires to cast a chill on grilling. However, findings by cancer societies and other groups are the most alarming: grilled food may cause cancer. So is it time to put away the barbecue and move the party back inside? Not if you follow some simple guidelines to minimize the risks.

Where there's smoke, there's cancer risk

Grilling meat, poultry, or fish, whether over wood, charcoal, or gas, exposes the food—and whoever eats it—to two separate carcinogens, or cancer-causing agents. Polycyclic aromatic hydrocarbons (PAHs) are found in the smoke created when fat drips from meat, chicken skin, or fatty fish (such as salmon) onto a heat source. The PAH-filled smoke coats the food, which we then ingest.

The second type of carcinogen, heterocyclic amines (HCAs), develops in meat, poultry, and fish that is cooked over high heat. Extreme temperatures prompt a reaction between the food's natural amino acids and creatine, a substance found in muscle tissue. HCAs are the product of that reaction. HCAs can also form in foods that are fried or broiled, especially in well-done red meat.

Researchers in a 1996 study found that people who eat their beef well done are more than three times as likely to develop stomach cancer as those who prefer their steak medium rare or rare. Other research showed a link between high consumption of well-done, fried, and barbecued meats to increases in colorectal, pancreatic, and breast cancers. Animal studies also associate HCAs with liver and lung cancers.

Safer grilling guidelines

The good news is that if you take a few precautions, you can enjoy the fun and flavor of outdoor cooking and stay healthy, too.

- **Stay clear of burned steer.** This simple change may be the most difficult to make for die-hard fans of charred steaks, burgers, and chicken. At the very least, eat well-done meat sparingly. (While avoiding extremes, you'll still want to cook meat completely, to make sure you eliminate illness-causing bacteria like E. coli.)

- **Keep fat to a minimum.** Cut down on carcinogens by grilling only lean cuts of meat, trimming all visible fat, and removing the skin from chicken.

- **Grill fish instead.** Fish generally contains less fat than meat and poultry do, which makes it less likely to create PAH-carrying smoke. And it

Never use charcoal indoors; it gives off deadly carbon monoxide gas. Outdoors, always let excess lighter fluid burn off before grilling food.

tends to require much less time on the grill, reducing its exposure to carcinogens.

- **Precook your foods.** The higher the temperature at which food cooks and the longer it stays on the grill, the more HCAs develop. Partially cooking meat or poultry in the microwave for two to five minutes draws out most of the potentially harmful chemicals without sacrificing moistness. (Be sure to discard the juices produced.) You can also place it in the oven at a low temperature. An additional benefit to these approaches is that slow-cooking the food and then finishing it on the grill prevents the charred-on-the-outside, raw-on-the-inside result that has embarrassed many an outdoor chef. To prevent bacteria from multiplying, grill the food immediately after precooking.

- **Oil your grill.** A little oil keeps charred material from sticking to the food. (It also helps keep fish and chicken in one piece.)

- **Use aluminum foil.** Make tiny holes in a piece of foil and place it on the grill underneath your meat. The holes let the fat drip down, and the foil reduces the amount of smoke that billows back up. Wrapping the meat completely with perforated foil is an even better idea.

- **Lower the heat.** On charcoal grills, increase the distance between the food and the hot coals by spreading the coals thin or by propping the grill rack on bricks. Simply adjust the heat setting on gas grills.

- **Stick to charcoal and hardwood.** Barbecue briquettes and hardwood products, such as hickory and maple, burn at lower temperatures than softwood and softwood (pine) chips. Mesquite chips are slightly less safe than those made of other hardwoods but are safer than softwoods.

- **Clean your grill.** Scrub your grill thoroughly after every use to avoid a buildup of carcinogens that can be transferred to your food the next time you grill. For tough grease, put the dirty rack into a plastic garbage bag. Add water and dishwashing liquid and leave overnight. Brush off the residue and rinse. You may also want to heat the grill before placing food on it to kill any surviving bacteria. If you have a gas grill with permanent briquettes, turn them greasy side down, light the grill, and with the temperature at high, close the cover. After 20 minutes the briquettes will be as good as new.

Mixed grill: Add vegetables to your barbecue fare to help balance the risks associated with grilled meats.

251

Pain Relievers

Ibuprofen, ASA, and acetaminophen all have advantages and drawbacks. Acetaminophen is the only one that doesn't reduce inflammation or inhibit blood clotting; it's also the only one that won't cause gastrointestinal bleeding.

When your head is pounding or your back is aching, there are dozens of over-the-counter analgesics, or pain relievers, available to make you feel better. But with so many brands, ingredients, indications, and side effects, how do you figure out which one to take? You don't need a pharmacology degree to come up with the answer. A little basic understanding is all that is required to find the most effective—and safest—medication for battling your pain.

The pain relief arsenal

Over-the-counter, or OTC, pain relievers are most people's first line of defense against pain. These analgesics are not addictive and are considered safe enough to use without a prescription. Still, OTC painkillers are not risk-free. They can have serious side effects when used incorrectly or over long periods of time. And self-medicating with OTC analgesics can mask symptoms or delay treatment of problems that require medical attention.

Behind all the brand names and combinations, there are essentially only two types of nonnarcotic pain relievers: nonsteroidal anti-inflammatory drugs (NSAIDs) and acetaminophen. Over-the-counter NSAIDs include ASA (in products like aspirin) and ibuprofen (Advil, Motrin, and others). Prescription NSAIDs include naproxen sodium and ketoprofen.

These drugs block the production of prostaglandins, chemicals responsible for causing inflammation and, with it, pain, fever, and swelling. Acetaminophen is not an anti-inflammatory. Instead, it is believed to work by blocking pain impulses in nerve centers in the brain. Most narcotic analgesics, like morphine, work in a similar way.

For most minor pain relief, the OTC drugs are about equally effective. But you may find that some work better than others in certain situations.

- **ASA.** Acetylsalicylic acid (ASA) is a time-tested drug that remains one of the least expensive, most dependable, and versatile medications. When combined with caffeine (in products like Anacin), it acts faster than any other pain reliever, making it the preferred choice of headache sufferers. Adults can safely use it for headache, fever, aches caused by colds, dental pain, and minor joint pain. Children can use lesser doses but should never take aspirin for fever or a viral illness, such as chicken pox; acetaminophen is safer. Aspirin can put them at risk for Reye's syndrome, a rare but often fatal disorder.

  Because of aspirin's blood-thinning properties, many doctors are recommending small daily doses (81 milligrams, or one-quarter of a standard aspirin tablet) for people at risk of heart attack and stroke. Promising studies also link regular doses with reduced risk of colon cancer.

- **Ibuprofen.** Consider this a stronger version of aspirin. It is recommended for more acute pain, such as arthritis pain (under a doctor's supervision) or sprains. (Don't take it longer than three to five days for swelling without the advice of a doctor.) Ibuprofen is the drug of choice for women with menstrual cramps.

- **Acetaminophen.** Best known as the brand Tylenol, acetaminophen is the only OTC pain reliever that won't irritate the stomach. Recent studies indicate that it may be the most effective fever treatment for both children and adults. Acetaminophen does not thin the blood, so it's a safer choice for pregnant women (they should check with their doctor before taking any medication) and people with postsurgical pain.

If these OTC drugs do not offer enough relief, your doctor may recommend prescription NSAIDs. Among the preparations are:

- **Naproxen sodium.** Sold under the brand name Anaprox, this drug is similar to ibuprofen, but one dose lasts 8 to 12 hours.
- **Ketoprofen.** Sold under brand names including Orudis, ketoprofen is similar to Anaprox. It lasts up to 12 hours.

Choosing your weapon

Although no one knows exactly why, pain relievers affect every person differently. You may need to experiment, following the package (and your doctor's) instructions, to determine which pain reliever works best for you. A woman who doesn't find ibuprofen helpful for menstrual pain might be pleasantly surprised by switching to naproxen sodium.

Side effects are a big factor when selecting a drug. All the NSAIDs—such as aspirin, ibuprofen, naproxen sodium, and ketoprofen—can cause stomach problems, especially in older people. By suppressing prostaglandin production, they rob the stomach lining of the substance that protects it against ulcers. *(continued)*

Creams with capsaicin, which gives hot peppers their heat, deplete the body's stores of a substance that transmits pain signals to the brain. A week of use often relieves arthritis pain.

Fighting Arthritis Pain

Arthritis (specifically osteoarthritis) is the most frequently cited cause of pain among adults. About one in seven Canadians suffer from osteoarthritis.

Osteoarthritis involves joint stiffness and inflammation caused by a loss of cartilage, which acts as a cushion between two bones. Joint deformities are sometimes caused when bones overgrow to fill in for the missing cartilage. Osteoarthritis can result from overuse, injury, or disturbances in cells that help make components of cartilage, such as collagen.

Acetaminophen, which is not an anti-inflammatory, has little effect on arthritis pain. Ibuprofen and ASA offer relief, but using them long term can cause ulcers. New drugs address this problem: A drug called Arthrotec combines an anti-inflammatory with prostaglandin to protect the stomach lining.

If you take over-the-counter (OTC) remedies regularly, tell your doctor and pharmacist. They can warn you of side effects and help coordinate your pain medication with other drugs you take to avoid interactions.

When OTC drugs aren't enough, your doctor may prescribe NSAIDs. Corticosteroid injections or pills may also help, but they can only be used sparingly because of serious side effects.

Creams and liniments, according to most studies, offer only minor, short-term benefits. However, those that contain capsaicin (the "hot" ingredient in chili peppers) may provide real relief.

The nutritional supplements glucosamine and chondroitin sulfate, made from chemical extracts of shellfish and mammal cartilage, are thought to rebuild cartilage in human joints. Research shows promise.

The Arthritis Society encourages patients to look beyond medicinal therapies for pain relief. Options include stretching and strengthening exercises, relaxation techniques, and hot and cold compresses (heat for chronic pain, cold for inflammation).

Experts say the least expensive options can yield results. In one study, people who walked for exercise and lifted light weights for three hour-long sessions weekly reported increased mobility and less pain when climbing stairs or exiting their cars.

Pain Relievers (continued)

Ovarian Cancer Protection

Preliminary findings show that acetaminophen may protect women against ovarian cancer. In one study, women who used the drug at least once a week for six or more months had nearly half the ovarian cancer risk of women who never used it. But more studies are needed, and women should know that, in some people, long-term acetaminophen use can cause liver and kidney damage.

To help avoid stomach trouble, take them with food. Long-term NSAID users, such as those with arthritis, run an increased risk of gastrointestinal problems. Prescription acid blockers may reduce the threat.

Don't think you can necessarily turn to buffered formulas to protect your stomach; research is inconclusive on whether these products make a significant difference in gastrointestinal bleeding. Enteric coated pills go further in solving the problem because they pass through the stomach into the intestine before they are digested; however, they bring slower pain relief. Nausea and heartburn are common symptoms when an analgesic is irritating your stomach. Some people also experience ringing in the ears from painkillers.

Other side effects are less apparent. Since NSAIDs are compounded with sodium, they can cause salt and water retention in the kidneys and have been linked to kidney problems in people with high blood pressure. Elderly people are most susceptible. NSAIDs may also cause bone fractures to heal more slowly. And acetaminophen can cause liver damage if taken in large doses for long periods. Since the liver has no pain receptors, any damage there is silent. Recent evidence suggests that regular use of OTC pain relievers may increase the risk of diverticulosis, a colon disease that can cause abdominal cramping and bloody stools.

There's also the important issue of alcohol interaction. Specifically, anyone who drinks heavily—three or more alcoholic beverages a day—has an increased risk of stomach bleeding when taking any NSAID. Worse, taking acetaminophen and drinking heavily can accelerate liver damage.

A positive side effect of NSAIDs may be the prevention of Alzheimer's disease. Recently, the results of a long-term study indicated that the drugs may reduce risk of the disease by 30 to 60 percent. Why? One explanation is that they reduce swelling in the brain associated with the disease.

The heavy artillery

When other remedies don't work, a doctor may prescribe a narcotic painkiller. Most of these are opiates, or opioid analgesics, and are related to morphine. This is a strong class of medication that requires diligence by the patient and close monitoring to avoid the many possible side effects.

The potency of these drugs demands that you adhere to a strict dosage schedule when using them; taking more than the amount prescribed can cause serious reactions, including dangerously slowed breathing or even coma. Always pay attention to whether the medication is to be taken on a full or an empty stomach. Narcotic pain relievers can cause constipation, nausea, and drowsiness.

Opioid analgesics are usually called on to treat acute or short-term pain. They can be habit forming if used long term. Over time, some people require higher and higher doses to maintain the same level of relief. To minimize withdrawal symptoms, doctors often taper off doses.

Some Pain Relievers at a Glance

Remember that chronic use of NSAIDs (such as aspirin, ibuprofen, naproxen sodium, or ketoprofen) can lead to stomach upset or ulcers. Long-term use should be supervised by your doctor. If NSAIDs bother your stomach, try acetaminophen. Never mix pain relievers and alcohol.

Pain Reliever	Best For	Warnings
ASA (aspirin)	Mild to moderate pain, including headache, backache, toothache, muscle pain, arthritis pain; fever. Inhibits blood clotting.	Can damage stomach lining, so take with food. Avoid if you have asthma; you may be allergic. Do not give to children with fever (to avoid risk of Reye's syndrome).
Ibuprofen	Any intense pain (stronger version of aspirin); menstrual cramps. Causes fewer allergic reactions than aspirin. Inhibits blood clotting.	Can damage stomach lining, so take with food. Can intensify kidney problems. Avoid if you are allergic to aspirin.
Naproxen sodium, Ketoprofen	Similar to ibuprofen but longer-lasting. Inhibits blood clotting.	Same as ibuprofen.
Acetaminophen	Mild to moderate pain. (Does not reduce swelling or inflammation). Best fever fighter. Less likely than aspirin to trigger allergic reaction. Safest choice for pregnant women.	Large doses may cause liver damage, especially when taken with alcohol.

Paint

For do-it-yourselfers, there's nothing a can of paint and a little elbow grease can't fix. But some paints, while they spruce up your surroundings, also threaten your health. So choose carefully, and proceed with caution.

Volatile vapors

Most oil-based paints are made with volatile organic compounds (VOCs), chemicals that transform quickly from liquid to vapor. VOCs make paint easy to spread. Once the paint is applied, the VOCs evaporate into the air we breathe, leaving the binders and pigment in the paint to harden into a coating.

VOCs can be toxic when ingested, inhaled, or absorbed through the skin, either during application or while paint is drying. They can cause headache, eye and nose irritation, nausea, dizziness, throat and chest tightness, fatigue, joint pain, blurred vision, tingling in the extremities, and irregular heartbeat.

Long-term exposure can result in chronic respiratory problems, kidney and liver damage, low sperm counts, menstruation abnormalities, and cancer. Professional painters have been shown to have a cancer rate 40 percent higher than that of the general population. Fortunately, many new paints are safer.

Lingering lead threat

The other major hazard of paints is lead. If your home was built after 1976, when the Canadian government limited lead content in interior paints, lead isn't an issue for you. But Canadian homes built before 1960 likely contain lead paint. When lead from paint enters the bloodstream, it has been shown to cause learning disabilities, hyperactivity, decreased growth, impaired hearing, and brain damage in children. Kids under age eight and fetuses are most vulnerable to its effects, for their nervous systems are still developing.

When it's in good condition or painted over and sealed, lead paint is not a threat, since there are no paint chips for kids to ingest or dust to be inhaled. Problems arise when sanding and scraping release lead-paint dust into the air. The particles can spread all over the house and neighborhood and settle on surfaces. Lead-paint chips that fall from your house into nearby soil can even contaminate the vegetables in your garden. That's why experts recommend that you never try to remove lead paint yourself. Hire a specialist or cover lead paint with wallpaper, wallboard, or special sealants.

If you are concerned, you can test lead levels with reliable home testing kits. However, most experts suggest you use a laboratory certified by the Standards Council of Canada or the Canadian Association for Environmental Analytical Laboratories.

Painting the safe way

If you take the following precautions, there's no reason you can't have the satisfaction—and savings—of doing your own painting.
- Use latex (water-based) and other less toxic paints indoors.
- Ventilate. Open windows and use fans to vent fumes to the outdoors.
- Wear nonpermeable gloves.
- Use a respirator-type mask rather than a dust mask. The respirator should have a HEPA (high-efficiency particulate air) filter to remove particles from the air.
- Never remove lead paint yourself.

Many paints contain any number of suspected carcinogens, and children of painters have increased rates of leukemia. Fortunately, safer paints are now available.

CAUTION!
Extensive renovations to remove lead paint can be hazardous. Health Canada advises pregnant women and children to avoid exposure to the leaded dust. Some experts also recommend that pregnant women avoid paint fumes.

Back to Nature

Some specialty paint manufacturers are producing new "natural" oil-based paints that use ingredients extracted from beeswax, tree resins, plant waxes, and linseed oil in place of petroleum-based solvents that emit volatile organic compounds (VOCs). Some are VOC-free, while others have greatly reduced VOC content.

Paint & Varnish Removers

Buyer Beware

Many of the chemical ingredients in paint and varnish removers are known toxins or carcinogens. Read labels carefully and avoid the following as much as possible:

- benzene
- toluene
- ethyl benzene
- xylene
- chlorobenzene
- methylene chloride
- methyl ethyl ketone
- methanol
- acetone

It's easy to apply paint or varnish; the hard part is removing it. So paint removers, thinners, and strippers often include an arsenal of potent—and potentially dangerous—chemicals. Some manufacturers boast the speed with which their products can strip paint. But solvents that take a little longer to work may also let you breathe easier.

Stripping: a dangerous act?

Most paint and varnish removers are made with a variety of solvents that break down the binders fastening the color to the painted object. As a rule, the faster-acting a solvent is, the more toxic and flammable it is.

Ingesting paint and varnish solvents, or getting them in the eyes, is a serious health threat that requires immediate medical attention. Read the instructions on the label before you start working; if an accident occurs, you won't have time to do so. Always wear protective clothing, including nonpermeable gloves. Direct contact can burn the skin.

Inhaling solvent fumes in large amounts may cause drowsiness, nausea, put you at risk of damaging your central nervous system, and may also increase the risk of cancer. People with respiratory conditions or high blood pressure are most susceptible. Keep children and pets away from the work area.

Using paint and varnish removers requires forethought: Gather all of your safety gear before you begin a project.

Take it slow

Home repair books often recommend that you buy the paint remover with the highest methylene chloride content. However, while methylene chloride is fast and effective, it is also one of the most toxic solvents.

There are several water-based strippers on the market that contain far fewer harmful vapors and flammable materials, but they take longer to work. The typical methylene chloride remover pulls off old paint and varnish in 15 to 20 minutes. Safer water-based brands often take several hours. They may also raise the grain of the wood slightly, so additional sanding may be necessary.

Often you may not even need a stripper. With a power sander, or a heat gun and stripping knife, you can scrape off old paint. Sand the wood lightly before repainting. (Pre-1980 paint may contain lead; and pre-1976 paint almost certainly will, and should be removed by a lead-abatement contractor.)

How to strip safely

Whichever type of solvent you select, it's important to take these safety precautions:

- Protect your eyes with safety goggles, and wear long sleeves.
- Use solvent-resistant, heavy rubber gloves.
- Wear a mask. For more toxic removers, wear a dual-carriage respirator with charcoal filters. Nonorganic filters screen out solid particles only, not noxious vapors.
- Open all windows and doors. Position circulating fans to dissipate fumes. Better still, move your project outdoors if possible.
- Use thick layers of newspapers rather than drop cloths to protect work surfaces.
- Do not smoke or allow others to smoke while working with chemical strippers.
- Keep a bucket of water nearby, so you can quickly rinse off an accidental splash.
- Clean up well. For brushes and tools, use mineral spirits; for skin, wash with soap for removing chemical compounds (available at your hardware store). Dispose of the stripped paint safely.

Palpitations

The heartbeat of Canada doesn't always keep perfect time. Most of us experience some form of palpitations—noticeable irregularities in the heartbeat. The majority are harmless episodes of extra or skipped beats. But some are warnings of heart trouble and require immediate attention. Your doctor can help you tell the difference.

Heartbeat, why do you skip?

A healthy heart beats 60 to 90 times per minute at rest, 100 times or more under conditions of pain, stress, anger, or exertion. An electrical pulse created in the heart's sino-atrial node triggers each beat. When something goes wrong with that current or in the heart's contracting chambers, palpitations—the medical term is arrhythmias—occur.

Extra beats are the most common arrhythmias. Tachycardia, a racing heart, is mostly benign. But not all irregularities are harmless. Atrial fibrillation, which occurs in the heart's upper chambers (atria), can cause the heart to pump 200 times a minute, prompting dizziness, fainting, even a stroke. It's most common in people over 60 and is often linked with high blood pressure, heart defects, or an overactive thyroid. It can be treated with medication. A heart that beats too slowly (bradycardia) may need a pacemaker.

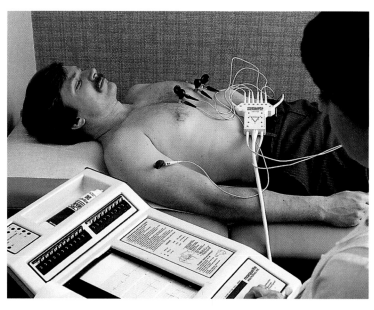

Electrocardiograms, which use painless electrodes to record the heart's electrical activity, help doctors to detect arrhythmias.

Doctors are particularly concerned about arrhythmias in heart-attack survivors. A short episode of tachycardia may be the precursor of a longer episode, which could have serious complications or even be fatal.

Keeping the beat

Simple lifestyle changes often minimize palpitations. Arrhythmias can be triggered by alcohol, smoking, stress, overeating, and even exercise. Some drugs, especially those used in over-the-counter decongestants and diet pills as well as blood-pressure drugs, sometimes cause palpitations. Changing medication or adjusting dosages can reduce or eliminate the problem. Certain foods—aged and soft cheeses, red wine, yogurt, cured and processed meats or fish—can stimulate palpitations even during sleep. Caffeine may trigger them during waking hours.

For serious arrhythmias, treatment is available. Monitoring devices implanted in a patient may slow down a heart that's beating too fast or speed up one that's too slow. Doctors treat supraventricular tachycardia, an arrhythmia that originates in the atria, either with medication or by feeding an electrical wire through a catheter into the heart to cauterize the "excitable" piece of tissue.

Symptom Sorter

Just a Flutter? Or Time to Call the Doctor?

Most people with palpitations need no medical treatment. But see a doctor if:

- Palpitations last for several seconds, minutes, or hours, rather than an occasional skipped beat or pair of beats.

- You feel dizzy during palpitations or have a fainting spell.

- Your personal medical history includes high blood pressure or any type of heart disease.

Panty Hose

If you are one of the millions of women who regularly wear panty hose, avoiding runs may not be your biggest problem. The fabrics that make your stockings fit so snugly also provide a comfortable environment for bacteria and other organisms that can cause infections and discomfort.

Breeding grounds

The number one reason women visit their gynecologists is vaginitis, a vaginal irritation or infection. Vaginitis can usually be cleared up with proper care and, often, short-term medication. But sometimes, it occurs repeatedly. Panty hose may aggravate the problem.

The bacteria and yeast that cause vaginal infections flourish in warm, moist environments. By holding in body heat and water, nylon and spandex, found in most panty hose, encourage the growth of microorganisms. Doctors advise patients to wear hosiery sparingly, if at all, during a bout of vaginitis.

Some panty hose are made with "breathable" cotton panels that create less friendly surroundings for microbes. You can eliminate the risk of panty-hose-related infection entirely by wearing mid-thigh-length stockings instead. And be sure to dry the entrance to the vagina as thoroughly as possible after showers and baths.

Fostering foot fungi

By retaining moisture, panty hose may also promote a fungal infection of the toenails (onychomycosis) that is difficult to eradicate. (Hosiery is not the only culprit; even cotton socks retain perspiration.) The fungi that cause the condition prey on dead tissues of the skin, nails, and hair and thrive in warm, moist environments. The organisms take hold as a result of repeated minor trauma of the toenails, frequently caused by cramming feet into tight or poorly fitting shoes.

CAUTION!

Panty hose and flying don't mix. Spending long hours in flight without moving around can result in phlebitis (inflammation of a vein) or a blood clot. Tight clothing on the legs and midsection raises the risk. Hosiery is also flammable and may be deadly if a fire breaks out.

Panty hose make your legs look sleek, but they can also foster infections.

Onychomycosis can make toenails thick, discolored, and deformed. Prescription creams, liquids, and powders can usually control the infection. For chronic cases, oral anti-fungal medications may be prescribed, but high doses have been linked to disrupted liver function. Older people typically require higher doses because of diminished circulation in the feet. With ongoing treatment, blood tests are needed to check liver function.

A measure of support

Some stockings treat problems. Prescription compression stockings, knee highs, and panty hose (available at most pharmacies) may help discourage blood clots after hip-replacement surgery. They can also provide relief from swollen legs and the leg pain and cramps associated with varicose veins. Patients must be evaluated and fitted for the stockings by a doctor. "Support hose" sold by department and medical-supply stores may help ease very minor leg swelling but are not a substitute for the stronger medical variety.

The Pap test is used to detect cervical cancer in its earliest, most treatable stage. The test, also known as the cervical smear test, was named for its inventor George Papanicolaou. Since the test's introduction in the late 1940s, the death rate from cervical cancer in North America has dropped more than 70 percent.

Some current concerns

Yet, despite this impressive achievement, some 400 Canadian women die each year from a disease that, doctors say, is nearly 100 percent curable if caught early. Why? According to one survey, many Canadian women are not being tested, and the proportion is increasing. In 1990, for example, it was reported that the number of Canadian women between the ages of 25 to 40 that had never been screened had doubled since 1985. Inadequate testing, the misinterpretation of test results, and the failure to follow up on abnormal results are other concerns often cited by medical experts in this field.

When to take the test

All women who are, or ever have been, sexually active need the Pap test. It should be done within six months of first having sexual intercourse, and 6 to 12 months later. Thereafter, a woman may repeat the test at one to three years' intervals depending on the guidelines set by the health department in her province. Tests are performed by general practitioners, most family planning clinics and well woman clinics.

The Pap test is a risk-free procedure, and the cervical smear itself takes only a few seconds. A clinician scrapes away some cervical cells, which are examined for abnormalities by a medical laboratory technologist, who prepares the test result.

Negative vs positive

A negative result indicates that the cells appear normal. A positive result indicates that the cells are abnormal, which may suggest a precancerous or cancerous condition.

To confirm this result, follow-up tests include repeat smears or a colposcopy (the examination of the cervix with a viewing instrument) and a biopsy (the removal of cervical tissue for microscopic analysis).

Aiming for accurate results

In Canada, an average of 16 out of every 1,000 tests come back with positive results. But screening isn't perfect, and the estimated error rate ranges from 5 to more than 20 percent. This means there will be false positives and false negatives. A false positive suggests abnormalities when none exist. Although this can be frightening, additional testing will reverse the result. A false negative suggests that the cells are normal when they are not. Regular testing is essential to avert the potential risk of a false negative result.

To help ensure the accuracy of test results, the Canadian Society of Cytology has set a guideline limiting the number of smears a technologist can handle to 8 to 10 per hour.

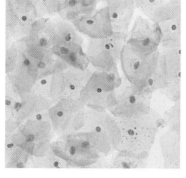

Computer software for screening, ranking, and double-checking also help to reduce human error and improve efficiency.

To boost your chances of receiving an accurate result, schedule a test for 10 to 20 days after your period begins. (Blood and sloughed-off cells make it harder to see abnormalities.) Also, be sure to refrain from sexual intercourse and douching for two days before the test.

For more information about the Pap test or cervical cancer, call the Canadian Cancer Society at 1-888-939-3333.

Worth the Trouble

One reason for the success of Pap tests is that most cervical cancers develop slowly; cells can take several years to become cancerous. Regular screening and pelvic exams lead to detection in plenty of time for treatment and also minimize the long-term risks of a single false-negative result.

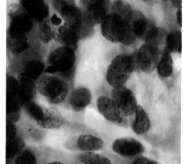

A simple, lifesaving test: Normal squamous epithelial cells, which make up the outer wall of the cervix, are shown in the Pap smear above left. The cells above right are cancerous.

Pesticides

Life is full of trade-offs, and pesticides are a perfect example. You want your house to be free of pests, but sprays can pose a health threat long after they've done their job. You want your family to eat plenty of fruits and vegetables, but not pesticide residues.

It's no secret that exposure to pesticides can be harmful. Prolonged exposure to high levels has been linked to neurological disorders, cancer, immune-system disruptions, hormonal imbalances, and, in children, developmental problems. Fortunately, most of us are exposed to much lower levels, and there are ways to further limit the amounts in your food, air, and water.

Half of all fruits and vegetables contain pesticide residues, and about 40 percent carry residues from more than one pesticide.

The produce paradox

Health Canada recommends eating between 5 to 10 servings of fruits and vegetables every day. Yet some experts estimate that half of all fruits and vegetables contain pesticide residues, and about 40 percent carry residues from more than one pesticide. Should you eat less produce? No. Hundreds of studies have demonstrated that eating more fruits and vegetables dramatically lowers cancer risk. And while produce may have pesticide residues, most of those are well below the maximum residue limits set by Health Canada under the Food and Drugs Act. Still,

many people would like to cut their exposure to pesticide residues even more. How?

The first step is to eat a wide variety of foods to help limit your exposure to any one pesticide. Another might be to buy and eat certified-organic produce, which is grown without the use of synthetic pesticides. A third way to lower your exposure to pesticide residues is to eat domestic, seasonal produce, which—even if it's not organic—typically contains fewer residues than imported, out-of-season produce. You can find it at your local farmers market.

Meat products also contain pesticides: Livestock animals ingest them in their feed, while some fish absorb pesticides from the agricultural and industrial runoff in the waters they inhabit. Because many pesticides accumulate in fat cells, one way to avoid them is to go lean, choosing only low-fat meat, fish, and dairy products. And go easy on liver, in which pesticides can also accumulate.

To peel or not to peel?

Peeling produce often removes most pesticide residue. The trouble is that most of a food's natural fiber and much of its vitamins and minerals are found in and around the edible skin. So unless the skin is waxed, it may be better to leave it on. (Always peel waxed produce. The wax itself is harmless, but it seals in

The Pest Management Regulatory Agency sets the last date that crops can be sprayed with pesticides before they are harvested. This helps ensure that there will be enough time for the pesticides to break down.

pesticides.) Do remove the outer leaves of lettuce and cabbage, where most residues are. Such fruits as bananas, oranges, and melons are always peeled, so you are not likely to ingest much pesticide from them.

Scrubbing your produce will go far to remove pesticides. Wash produce in running water with enough elbow grease to create some friction. Some produce without outer leaves or peels (such as strawberries, mushrooms, and spinach), though, absorbs pesticides at the cellular level, so washing won't help much. These might be good organic choices.

Kill the bugs, protect the kids

Some pesticides arrive with dinner, but others we willingly introduce into our homes. These sprays release volatile compounds that can

If you must use a pesticide, know which pest you want to eradicate and choose the right weapon. Avoid broad-spectrum pesticides, which pose greater risk.

cause headaches, eye irritation, and chest tightness in people who enter the home before 24 hours have passed. If your cabinets are treated by an exterminator, leave them open for 24 hours afterward and ventilate the room. Store-bought sprays are less potent than those used by professional exterminators, but because laymen are untrained, the sprays are more likely to be used unsafely.

Directed sprays introduce less pesticide residue than bug "bombs," which scatter the residue throughout a room or house. Overexposure to chlorpyrifos, a pesticide found in most popular home products, can cause headache, dizziness, muscle spasms, vomiting, and blurred vision. The pesticide can also cling to plastic and foam toys, so remove these from any area to be sprayed.

Lawn pesticides also pose risks if not used properly. Always read the label and follow the directions to the letter. Wear protective clothing, and don't spray on excessively windy days. Steer children and pets away from the lawn until the pesticide has settled or dried. If your lawn is treated by a professional lawn-care company, keep kids and pets off of the grass for at least 24 hours or until the lawn has been watered.

Runoff from pesticides is a challenge for many communities. It can work its way into the water table and contaminate the drinking water. If you are worried about the safety of your tap water, request information from your municipal water provider. Public water utilities are required to provide information on water purity.

an ounce of Prevention

No-Pest, No-Pesticide Gardening

It's possible to keep your garden pest-free without using pesticides. Here are some tricks:

- Wash away bugs (especially aphids on roses) with a strong squirt or spray of water.

- Eliminate slugs with small dishes of beer. Slugs are attracted to the beer, in which they then drown.

- Use biological insecticides such as BT (*Bacillus thuringiensis*). They are slower-acting, but they're effective and chemical-free.

- Create physical barriers by placing clear plastic covers over garden rows, cutworm collars around planters, even panty hose hoods over seedlings.

The Dirtiest Dozen

Each year the Canadian Food Inspection Agency conducts up to 16,000 tests on fresh and processed fruits and vegetables. Here are the 12 foods with the highest levels of pesticide residues, listed from most to least.

1. Sweet peppers (domestic)
2. Oranges (Israel)
3. Blackberries (Guatemala)
4. Cheeses (Switzerland)
5. Oranges (New Zealand)
6. Pears (Colombia)
7. Snow peas (Dominican Republic)
8. Raspberries (Guatemala)
9. Spinach (domestic)
10. Raspberries (domestic)
11. Sweet peppers (Dominican Republic)
12. Spinach (Mexico)

I t's not just a pet theory: Research shows that caring for an animal can improve your health by reducing stress, lowering blood pressure, and slowing the heart rate. Any risks are usually far outweighed by the benefits. Still, pet owners—especially older folks and people with compromised immune systems—should take a few precautions.

A friend indeed

A surprisingly strong body of evidence connects pets to human well-being. Contact with animals, especially dogs and cats, produces a number of different benefits:

- An experiment at England's Cambridge University studied a group of people who didn't own pets. Researchers placed dogs in one-third of the homes, cats in another third, and left the last third pet-free. General health improved in the first two groups, but especially among the dog caretakers, presumably because they got not only companionship but also exercise.
- A University of California at Los Angeles study of 1,000 Medicare patients noted fewer doctor visits among pet owners.
- An Australian study found that people with pets had lower blood pressure and decreased levels of cholesterol and triglycerides (blood fats) in the bloodstream.
- Alzheimer's patients exhibit less isolation when they care for pets, especially dogs.
- A group of doctors reported to the American Heart Association that among people who have had a heart attack, those who own pets have a much better chance of long-term survival. Besides lowering blood pressure and cholesterol, pets also help people feel calmer and less angry.
- Researchers have determined that any pet —bird, fish, snake, turtle, lizard—can counter depression and loneliness by creating a sense of belonging and responsibility. Physical warmth isn't a requirement.
- A study at the State University of New York at Buffalo found that people in wheelchairs who were provided with dogs trained to assist them were less depressed and more

active outside the home. The cost of training the dogs was more than offset by the projected savings in medical costs over the animals' eight-year working life.

Getting your dander up

Of course, everything has its down side. Animal allergies affect up to 40 percent of all the patients who see allergists. The problem generally is not fur or hair, but, rather, saliva and dander—flakes of dead skin that can carry allergens produced by the animals. Dander mixes with household dust and circulates, causing sneezing, watery eyes, and itchy skin. To help remove dander from the air, some allergists suggest buying an air purifier with a HEPA (high-efficiency particulate air) filter.

Cats provoke more allergic reactions than dogs, and unneutered male cats are the worst

Pets heal the heart in more ways than one. It's no wonder that animals are sometimes brought into nursing homes and children's hospitals as therapy.

CAUTION!

If you are pregnant, get someone else to change the cat's litter box. Toxoplasmosis, transmitted through cat feces, can lead to birth defects. In the garden, which cats may use as a litter box, wear gloves.

Pets (continued)

When cleaning a birdcage, try not to shake it. Dust containing bird feces (and bacteria) can become airborne.

offenders. If you are allergic to your pet but can't part with it, a schedule of allergy shots may gradually desensitize your immune system to the allergen. For occasional encounters with cats, an antihistamine relieves symptoms. Bathing your cat weekly helps (good luck), but it doesn't eliminate the problem. At least one pet spray claims to reduce allergens, but one test finds that it's probably no more effective than wiping your pet with a wet cloth.

Flea circus

Cats and dogs that spend time outdoors can bring home ticks, which can then attach themselves to humans. Depending on the kind of tick, this can be a minor nuisance or a cause of Lyme disease or Rocky Mountain spotted fever. Check animals periodically for ticks; if you find one, remove it with tweezers, but be careful not to crush it.

Fleas can also hitch a ride on your pet, and an infested pet quickly becomes an infested house or yard. Flea bites don't usually pose much of a health risk to humans, but they are irritating. Fleas may also contribute to the high incidence of pet allergies. Research indicates that proteins in flea feces, skin, and other debris can trigger allergic reactions. If you are allergic to other dogs or cats but not your own, you may be reacting not to pets but to fleas.

There are several effective flea-and-tick-prevention products on the market. Ask your veterinarian which one is best for your pet.

What the cat dragged in

Cats carry a variety of bacteria that can infect humans with mild to life-threatening illnesses. *Rochalimaea henselae* can prompt chills and fever, and *Bacillary angiomatosis* causes lesions on the bones, skin, and some organs. Both are transmitted through blood or by eating contaminated food. *Toxoplasma gondii*, which causes toxoplasmosis, is a cat-borne parasite that can be passed to humans through contact with cat feces, usually from cleaning a litter box. It may present no symptoms but in pregnant women can cause miscarriage or birth defects.

Cat scratch fever is an infection caused by the bacterium *Bartonella.* Its first symptom is swollen, painful lymph nodes near the site of a cat scratch. Joint pain may also result. Cat scratch fever is treated with antibiotics.

When it comes to salmonella, the bacteria that can cause flulike symptoms (nausea, diarrhea, cramps, fever) in humans, cats aren't the only carriers. Dogs, birds, and, above all, reptiles (including turtles, lizards, iguanas, and snakes) can all carry salmonella. It's particularly risky—even deadly—for young children, the elderly, and people with weakened immune systems.

The bottom line: Wash your hands after handling a pet or changing a litter box, especially before you hold a baby or touch food.

Worse than its bark

Dog bites send hundreds of thousands of people to the emergency room each year—many of them children. If you have a dog (or any other pet), teach your children or grandchildren how to behave around the animal (and vice versa). Children should also be taught never to approach a strange dog.

If you encounter an agitated dog, avert your eyes and back away slowly. Shouting a familiar command, such as "Heel!" or "Sit!" can sometimes stop the dog. If you are attacked, curl into a ball with your arms and hands covering your head. Do not scream; doing so may further excite the dog.

Cat bites, because they are generally deeper, are more likely to cause infection than dog bites. If you are bitten by any animal, wash the wound with soap and water for five minutes, dry it, then see a doctor. You may need rabies shots or treatment with an antibiotic. If you haven't had a tetanus shot in the past five years, you may need a booster.

Photocopiers

Once invented, some things become essential. The photocopier is one. How could a modern office exist without one?

Properly positioned and maintained, copy machines pose no threat to office workers, or to anyone else who uses them regularly, according to safety and health experts. However, if the machine is placed in a poorly ventilated area or not kept in good repair, all bets are off.

Trouble in the air

Some high-speed photocopiers emit ozone gas, an irritating pollutant. Ozone can impair the body's immune system, aggravate asthma, and lead to sore throats and respiratory problems, including shortness of breath, coughing, sneezing, sinus irritation, and headache. (High up in the earth's atmosphere, where it belongs, ozone is actually beneficial, protecting us from ultraviolet radiation.)

Placing photocopiers in high-traffic areas, while convenient, is exactly the wrong approach. To contain the dissipation of ozone, a copier should be set off from the general work area in its own room or space, which should be properly ventilated. See the ventilation requirements that come with the manufacturer's instructions. Ideally, the copier should be placed near a window that can be opened a crack. In many machines, manufacturer-installed charcoal filters help trap the ozone, but the filters need to be replaced regularly. If they aren't, they will have no effect.

Like all electrical equipment, copiers generate an electromagnetic field (EMF). EMFs have received a lot of media attention because of a suspected link with cancer. Although any threat is probably minimal, you can greatly reduce your exposure by standing away from the machine while copying large batches—the field drops off quickly from the source.

A happy copier doesn't pollute

A broken copy machine can be frustrating; it can also be a health hazard. One study showed that regular maintenance can reduce a photocopier's ozone-emission levels from excessive to undetectable. If you smell a sharp odor coming from the copy machine, it is emitting too much ozone.

Another potential hazard is toner, the powdered-ink carrier that fixes a duplicate image onto the paper. If the photocopier is not properly maintained, toner dust can settle on the copies that are made or on surfaces near the machine. These particles may be harmful if inhaled. Toner chemicals can also irritate the eyes, especially of people who wear contact lenses. If you see toner dust on or around the copier, it's time to turn off the machine and call for service.

Finally, never handle the photocopier drum or other parts related to the toner chemicals. If you can't resist adding toner to the machine yourself, at least wear rubber gloves and be sure to keep your hands away from your eyes, nose, and mouth. Immediately afterward, wash your hands thoroughly with soap and water.

CAUTION!
Laser printers and plain-paper fax machines, like photocopiers, can also produce ozone. Read the manufacturer's ventilation, maintenance, and placement instructions before you incorporate one into your work space.

Using a copier with the lid up can strain the eyes after just a few copies. If you can't close the lid, make sure to look away.

Plastics

Be sure your bathroom is well ventilated if you have a plastic shower curtain. It can give off unhealthy volatile organic compounds when heated.

F ew substances are more durable or convenient than plastic, a material that takes all sorts of shapes, forms, and consistencies—from clingy kitchen wrap to superinsulated winter wear, from football players' helmets to foam cheese-wedge hats for the fans.

Plastics are a break-resistant substitute for glass in eyeglass lenses and baby bottles and a lightweight replacement for metal in water pipes and mixing bowls. Despite their safety and convenience, though, plastics may expose you to potentially dangerous chemical by-products.

PVC = SOS

Polyvinyl chloride (PVC) is a plastic commonly used to make raincoats, shower curtains, credit cards, pipes, films, and adhesives. These commodities come at a price, since the vinyl chloride vapor used to create PVC is known to cause cancer. One Swedish study connects high levels of exposure to PVC with a greater incidence of testicular cancer. When PVC burns, it emits hydrochloric acid fumes that are so toxic, NASA has banned any product with vinyl chloride from being used on its spacecraft. Never burn any type of plastic.

At home with vinyls

What's not clear is whether vinyl plastics are harmful if used for everyday purposes. Vinyls contain volatile organic compounds (VOCs) that are sometimes released as vapors under conditions of heat and humidity. Breathing VOCs, or absorbing them through the skin, can lead to headaches, eye and throat irritation, sinus problems, fatigue, dizziness, nausea, chest tightness, tingling in the limbs, loss of balance, and irregular heartbeat. Long-term exposure to higher amounts could cause lung, liver, or kidney damage, infertility, and, possibly, even cancer.

Some people are particularly sensitive to VOCs, and there's no research yet to show what permanent effects long-term low-level exposure can cause. U.S. authorities are currently investigating a controversial illness

Plastic containers used to store leftovers remain inert as long as they don't contain food so hot that it causes them to melt.

called multiple chemical sensitivity, which, some doctors contend, may result from one sizable exposure to VOCs or low-level cumulative exposure.

Hazards in the kitchen

Polystyrene (trademark name, Styrofoam) is made by introducing gas into a plastic substance called styrene. Styrene is another agent that causes cancer in animals and is associated with nerve damage, fatigue, and memory loss. Polystyrene poses the most immediate threat in beverage cups and containers for restaurant leftovers and takeout foods. Some studies indicate that elements of the plastic may leach into heated food and beverages.

Other plastics used for food storage are less harmful. Clingy food wraps and freezer bags are safe—unless they are burned, which can create toxic fumes. Plastic containers used to store leftovers remain inert as long as they don't contain food so hot that it causes them to melt—an important consideration when you microwave leftovers. Never use a plastic container that isn't labeled "microwave safe."

Protection from plastic

People who want to limit their exposure to plastic by-products should drink hot beverages from glass mugs, not Styrofoam cups. Instead of hanging a vinyl shower curtain, use a fabric curtain or install glass doors around the shower. (If you do use a plastic curtain, let it air out first until the plastic smell goes away.) And don't let plastic wrap touch the food when you use it in the microwave.

CAUTION!

If you are worried that plastic wrap on imported foodstuffs might not comply with Canada's stringent food-packaging standards, discard and rewrap with materials manufactured domestically.

Polishes & Waxes

Somewhere in your home stands a reserve of polishes and waxes ready to protect or put a shine on furniture, floors, and silverware. But that stockpile of shine owes its spiffy results to certain volatile substances that may be possible health risks. Next time you're ready to impart a glow to that lovely mahogany sideboard or ceramic floor, consider reaching for a safer alternative.

Chemical warfare

Commercially available furniture and floor polishes usually contain phenol, which reacts with air to form a hard, shiny coating. However, it can emit irritating gases for days after use. Phenol is known to cause severe skin irritation in some people. Other reactions among those who are sensitive to phenol include weakness, sweating, fatigue, headache, and depression. Although rare, high exposure (through the lungs or the skin) can cause damage to the liver, brain, or kidneys. It has caused cancer in some animals.

Shining safely

To avoid such irritation, try refurbishing wood surfaces with one of these homemade mixtures instead of phenol-based polishes:
- Combine ½ teaspoon olive oil with ¼ cup vinegar.
- Mix 2 to 3 parts vegetable oil and 1 part lemon juice.

If you'd rather stick with commercial furniture polish, avoid overusing it. When polishing, wipe on liquid polish with a soft cloth. (Buy polish that comes in a bottle or a pump spray container; both are cheaper and safer for the environment than aerosols.) To limit your exposure, use only a little

Polish and wax are less likely to cause irritation when used in an area that is well ventilated; open the windows before applying them.

polish, and wear nonpermeable rubber gloves as you apply it. A good substitute for non-wood floor cleaners is a mixture of ¼ cup liquid soap, ¼ cup lemon juice, and 7.5 liters (2 gallons) warm water. Buff the surface after cleaning with a bit of mineral oil on a cloth or clean dust mop.

Remove water marks on wood by covering them with equal parts salt and vegetable oil; let sit a minute and wipe off. Or rub in toothpaste, then wipe away with a damp cloth. Treat rust spots with a paste of 2 parts salt and 1 part lemon juice; rub with a dry cloth.

The big brass

Metal polishes contain particularly toxic ingredients—ammonia, ethanol, petroleum distillates, and sulfur. Skin and eyes are at risk when you use them (manufacturers usually recommend wearing gloves). But you can get good results with these substitutes and some vigorous rubbing:
- Aluminum and chrome (also good for stubborn spots on glass): Clean with a soft cloth dipped in vinegar.
- Brass: Apply a paste of equal parts flour, salt, and white vinegar. Leave it on for 15 minutes. Rub well, then rinse and dry.
- Copper: Treat the same as for brass, but omit the flour in the paste.
- Silver and stainless steel: Apply a paste of baking soda and water; rub well. Soak for a few minutes in a saltwater bath, then rinse thoroughly in clear water and dry. Try a little toothpaste on dark spots. Rub it in, then rinse with warm water and dry.

The Truth About Labeling

Product labels on polishes and waxes won't necessarily warn you about toxins or substances that irritate the skin because manufacturers don't have to list their ingredients. A federal warning label is required only if a product is immediately harmful or is fatal when swallowed.

Pollen

People are rarely allergic to the large, heavy pollen grains (right) of flowers, which are carried not by wind but by insects.

In the plant world, pollen may be part of the miracle of reproduction, but it's a thorn in the side of anyone who's allergic to it. A runny nose, sneezing, itchy eyes, and blocked nasal passages are regular symptoms of "seasonal allergic rhinitis"—better known as hay fever. Don't let the *hay* fool you: the most common allergens are actually tree pollens in spring, grass pollens in summer, and ragweed pollens in fall. A series of simple skin tests can pinpoint your allergy triggers.

Almost all common trees are culprits. Grasses that trigger allergies include redtop, timothy, rye, orchard, sweet vernal, and Kentucky bluegrass. Of the weeds, ragweed is the worst offender; others are sagebrush, redroot pigweed, tumbleweed, Russian thistle, and English plantain.

Peak pollen days

Some pollen seasons are worse than others. Summers that follow long, wet springs can be unbearable to people with grass allergies. Mild winters in normally cold climates make for a bumper crop of tree pollen in spring. Pollen counts, often included in local weather reports, tend to be high on warm, dry days and low on wet, cool days. When pollen counts soar, even people who aren't strongly allergic may have a reaction.

Hay-fever medicine

To control the symptoms of mild to moderate pollen allergies, most doctors recommend antihistamines, along with decongestants if necessary. But most over-the-counter antihistamines make you drowsy (non-sedating versions don't), and decongestants can affect blood pressure and cause sleeplessness and edginess. If you take antihistamines, remember that they work best at preventing allergy attacks rather than stopping them once they've started. "Artificial tears" products help soothe itchy, watery eyes by washing away pollen. Other alternatives include prescription corticosteroid nasal sprays, such as Rhinocort and Nasocort, which work topically on the nasal passages. They must be used daily during allergy season. For severe allergies, immunotherapy shots, which gradually desensitize the body to allergens, are an option. But getting shots regularly is inconvenient and, in some cases, may not completely ease allergy symptoms.

Smart strategies

Avoidance is the best policy for people with pollen allergies. Try the following:

- On peak pollen days, limit your exposure by staying indoors with the windows closed and the air conditioning on.
- Consider buying an air cleaner with a HEPA (high-efficiency particulate air) filter.
- Keep the windows up in the car and use the air conditioner, not the fresh-air vent.
- Avoid going outside during early morning, when the pollen count is at its highest. If you do go out, wear a dust mask, available at paint and hardware stores.
- Hire someone to mow the lawn.
- If you wear contact lenses, switch to glasses during peak allergy season.

Pollen on Your Plate?

If you have hay fever, certain foods may worsen your allergy attacks or trigger an itchy tongue, mouth, or throat. The following foods contain proteins similar to those in certain pollens. Keep a food diary to determine if they affect you.

Pollen Trigger	Foods to Avoid
Ragweed	Bananas, cantaloupes, chamomile tea, cucumbers, honeydew melons, watermelons, zucchini
Grass	Apples, carrots, celery, oranges, tomatoes, watermelons
Birch tree	Apples, carrots, celery, cherries, fennel, hazelnuts, oranges, pears, potatoes, walnuts, maple syrup

A salmonella vaccine for chickens is in the works. Recently, a spray for newly hatched chicks was developed that prevents salmonella from growing. Many industry experts, however, have expressed skepticism about its effectiveness.

N orth Americans have birds on the brain. Turkey has made its way to the table year-round, and, for the health-conscious, chicken has replaced beef as the staple of choice. It's no wonder: poultry is rich in protein and can be prepared to suit any palate. Yet it is also a major source of food-borne illness. The federal government is working to improve safety standards, but it's up to you to further minimize your risks.

Poultry positives

Skinless, light-meat poultry is lower in calories, fat, and cholesterol than most red meat. Like red meat, poultry provides iron, zinc, and the vitamins B_6 and B_{12}. Turkey breast is the leanest of all meats, followed closely by chicken breast. Cornish hens are also lean. Duck and goose, which are all dark meat, have the most fat and calories.

Chicken can be lean or fatty, depending on which part you eat. The leanest part is the breast, followed by the drumstick, leg, and wing. Eating it with the skin nearly doubles the amount of fat—most of it saturated. It's okay to cook chicken with the skin on; it adds little or no fat if you remove it before serving.

Of all cooking methods, roasting at low temperatures seems to melt away the most fat from a bird. Prick duck skin with a fork during roasting so that the fat drips into the pan.

In recipes, ground chicken and turkey are tasty substitutes for ground beef. But beware: depending on how much skin and other fat is included in the grinding, they may be just as fatty. Moreover, some "self-basting" turkeys are injected with coconut oil (full of saturated fat) or partially hydrogenated oils.

Bird-borne bacteria

More than any other food, poultry has the potential to put harmful bacteria on your plate. Food poisoning is increasingly caused by *Campylobacter jejuni*, although salmonella remains the leading offender. In one recent study, a Quebec-based consumer magazine found 41 percent of chickens sold in the Montreal region carried salmonella.

For both, early-stage signs of infection are fever, nausea, abdominal pain, and diarrhea. The elderly and anyone with a compromised immune system may suffer serious complications. Salmonella symptoms occur within 6 to 48 hours; campylobacter, within 2 to 5 days.

Poultry is one of many products which may be irradiated by U.S. food processors. Canada, which led the way in developing irradiation technology, irradiates only spices, onions, and potatoes. Many consumers in both countries are leery of the process.

Don't Play Chicken

Follow these guidelines to minimize your risk of food-borne illness:

- Thaw in the refrigerator (or, if you plan to cook right away, in the microwave).

- Don't let raw poultry or its juices touch any other foods, especially those that won't be cooked.

- Wash your hands and any plates, utensils, and cutting boards used during preparation.

- Refrigerate raw poultry no longer than two days.

- Marinate in the refrigerator, then discard the marinade.

- Stuff poultry immediately before cooking. Cook at 325°F or higher.

- Cook whole chickens and dark meat to 180°F, breasts to 170°F, ground poultry to 165°F.

Pregnancy

Creating a child is a miracle. It's also inherently risky. At one time, pregnancy was a major cause of death among young women. But thanks to medical advances and our health care system, maternal mortality in Canada has decreased from 60 per 100,000 births in 1930 to less than 3 per 100,000 today. (This compares with 14 per 100,000 in the U.S., and rates as high as 1 in 100 in rural Africa.) Statistically, the risks are greatest for women younger than 20 and over age 30. But for any woman, proper prenatal care is the key to a healthy pregnancy.

Women who have all their children before age 30 are less likely to develop breast cancer than those who have children after 30. Giving birth at any time may lower your risk of ovarian cancer.

Preconceived notions

Even before a woman gets pregnant, she should visit her obstetrician-gynecologist to discuss any unique risks that pregnancy might pose. The doctor will want to discuss her and her partner's medical and family histories, nutritional habits, any drug or environmental exposures, and other issues that could affect the pregnancy, including medications the woman may be taking. It is especially important to see your doctor before becoming pregnant if you have one of the following conditions: chronic hypertension, a history of ectopic pregnancy, diabetes, lupus, a seizure disorder, liver or kidney disease, a history of blood clots or cancer, a previous cone biopsy of the cervix, asthma, heart disease, thyroid disease, HIV, chronic hepatitis, a congenital abnormality of the uterus, cervix, or vagina, or exposure to diethylstilbestrol (DES). If you or someone in your family has a genetic disorder, such as sickle-cell anemia or Tay-Sach's disease, consult a genetic counselor to find out your chances of having a child affected by the disorder and plan for additional tests before or during pregnancy.

To reduce the risk of neural-tube defects (such as spina bifida) in children, all women of child-bearing age should make sure their diet contains adequate folic acid. A fetus's spine and spinal cord are formed in the first four weeks of pregnancy, and women at risk of becoming pregnant should drink plenty of orange juice and eat ample amounts of dried beans, soybeans, raw broccoli, spinach, and whole-wheat bread (or take folic acid supplements), even if they aren't currently planning a pregnancy; accidents happen, and the neural tube is already developed by the time most women realize they are pregnant. (Health Canada recommends pregnant women, ages 16 to 49, consume almost 400 micrograms of folic acid, as folate, daily, more than double the recommended intake for nonpregnant women of that age group.)

Putting on weight

From the moment of conception, the embryo takes nourishment from the mother. So unless you have a serious weight problem, never diet while pregnant, lest you deprive your baby of vital nutrients. Expect to gain 0 to 1.8 kilograms (0 to 4 pounds) in the first three months, then about 0.5 kilogram (1 pound) a week during the second and third trimesters—a total of 11.3 to 15.8 kilograms (25 to 35 pounds). Gaining substantially less weight puts the mother's fat and nutrient stores in danger of becoming depleted. Gaining too much weight increases the risk of pregnancy-induced hypertension and gestational diabetes.

Bleeding gums and varicose veins: the price we pay?

Along with increased fat stores, a pregnant woman's blood volume naturally increases to provide for the needs of the fetus. This change can contribute to a variety of minor problems, from bleeding gums to varicose veins and hemorrhoids.

Many pregnant women are frightened to encounter bleeding gums when they brush or floss their teeth. This bleeding is typical and shouldn't keep you from maintaining your oral hygiene regimen. Tell your dentist you are pregnant before a cleaning or an exam.

Another result of increased blood volume is varicose veins, which may appear anywhere on the body but typically in the legs. Sometimes the control valves in the veins can't handle the increased workload, so blood pools in the veins, causing them to bulge. Most varicose veins clear up after the baby is born, but they may persist. To minimize your risk, take these precautions:

- Don't stand or sit in the same position for extended periods.
- Elevate the legs regularly to even out blood flow in areas below the heart.
- Support hose may help. Check with your doctor.

Hemorrhoids: another hazard

Hemorrhoids are varicose veins in the rectum and are commonly experienced by pregnant women. They often linger for some time after delivery. Bleeding hemorrhoids can contribute to anemia during pregnancy. Doctors recommend the following to minimize hemorrhoids and their discomfort:

- Drink plenty of fluids to avoid constipation, which aggravates hemorrhoids (your doctor may also recommend an over-the-counter stool softener).
- Don't strain when using the toilet.
- Take warm baths or sitz baths (using a plastic tub).
- An ice pack held against the hemorrhoids may ease the itching.
- Use over-the-counter ointments, but only as recommended by your doctor.

A high-pressure situation

Obstetricians monitor a woman's blood pressure throughout pregnancy to check for pregnancy-induced hypertension (PIH). For some women (about 7 of every 100), PIH can turn into preeclampsia, a more dangerous condi-

Rest for the Weary

Getting enough sleep is essential throughout a pregnancy. But it isn't easy.

Is there a certain position you should sleep in while you are pregnant? No. However, sleeping on your stomach becomes difficult. Sleeping on your back, especially after the fifth month, may be uncomfortable and may also constrict blood flow to the mother's heart.

Sleeping on your side seems to be the best solution. Some doctors may recommend sleeping on your left side (which allows for the best circulation to the heart), but this isn't necessary. Try placing pillows between your knees and under your back to help you get comfortable and relieve backache. Later in the pregnancy, you may want a pillow under your belly, too. Or try using an extra-long "body" pillow for support you can mold to your needs. Finally, sleep on a firm mattress to keep backache to a minimum.

tion, late in the pregnancy. Untreated, preeclampsia can lead to low birth weight or premature delivery or it may result in kidney or liver problems or blood clotting for the mother. Women who are over age 30 or overweight are at greater risk for preeclampsia. A handful of cases escalate into life-threatening eclampsia, which can result in maternal seizures and coma. Preeclampsia sometimes occurs without warning, or it may be signaled by sudden swelling of the face and fingers, blurred vision, headaches, or pain in the upper abdomen during the last three months.

Preeclampsia is extremely dangerous if not controlled, and it is cured only by delivery of the baby. On delivery day, the doctor may

Is Sex Safe?

If your pregnancy is without complications and you are not at high risk of premature labor, there is no reason intercourse can't continue well into the third trimester.

To dispel some myths: It is impossible for a penis to harm the fetus during sex; and it is unlikely that orgasm will cause premature labor, despite the fact that orgasm may be accompanied by contractions during the late stages of pregnancy.

administer magnesium sulfate to guard against seizures. In extreme cases, preeclampsia may dictate a cesarean section.

Not so sweet: gestational diabetes

Gestational diabetes, an inability to store or use glucose properly, develops in 3 to 5 percent of pregnant North American women. It can cause serious problems if left untreated. Babies can be born macrosomic—weighing more than 4 kilograms (8 pounds 13 ounces), with large deposits of body fat that make for a difficult delivery. If the woman's blood sugar is high enough to require insulin, there is a greater risk of preterm labor and stillbirth.

Gestational diabetes can often be controlled by strict adherence to a high-protein, low-carbohydrate diet (less breads and legumes, no fruit juices, and more fish, eggs, and lean meats). However, insulin may be required. Patients are taught how to monitor blood-sugar levels at home, and are usually tested six weeks after delivery. The majority of gestational diabetes cases clear up by then, but there is a slightly elevated chance of developing adult-onset diabetes.

Alcohol, coffee, and other concerns

While protecting your own health, you'll also want to protect the health of your child. Everything you consume finds its way to the baby, so do not eat or drink anything that can harm it. One of the most important things a mother can do for her unborn child is eat well. She should consume a balanced diet

Low-impact exercises are best for pregnant women. Avoid activities that involve hopping or jumping, such as jogging.

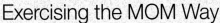

Exercising the MOM Way

Staying in shape while you are pregnant is important; it may even result in a shorter labor. According to one study, expectant mothers who worked out three times a week had 21 percent fewer cesarean sections and faster recoveries.

Of course, use common sense. Avoid any exercise that may cause you to fall (skiing, skating, horseback riding). Skip high-altitude and underwater sports, which divert too much oxygen from the fetus. Avoid exercises that require you to lie on your back (sit-ups, some yoga and aerobics positions), to keep the weight of your uterus from constricting blood flow through the vena cava, which returns blood to the heart. Finally, follow the MOM rules:

- **Moderation.** Exercising too hard diverts blood and nutrients from the baby. You should be able to converse while working out. Drink plenty of water to keep cool; an elevated core temperature can harm the fetus.

- **Orientation.** Consider your physical condition before you became pregnant. Don't radically increase your level of physical activity. If you weren't formerly active, try walking or short, low-impact workouts on a treadmill or other cardiovascular machine.

- **Modify.** Even athletes feel more taxed during pregnancy. Many women dial down their workouts by as much as half. Switching to swimming or water aerobics can reduce stress on the joints. Walk instead of running once you reach the middle of the second trimester.

Prenatal Tests: The Big Four

Over the course of a pregnancy, a number of tests are sometimes used to ensure the health of the unborn child. Here are some of the most common:

Test	Description	Timing	Purpose
Sonogram/ Ultrasound	Painless procedure that uses sound waves to create a visual image of the fetus	At 16 weeks, and sometimes later	To date a pregnancy, confirm multiple fetuses, evaluate fetal well-being, and verify position of the placenta.
Chorionic Villus Sampling (CVS)	Collection (through the vagina or the abdomen) of placental cells	10 to 12 weeks, if required	To screen for a variety of birth defects.
Amniocentesis	Insertion of a needle through the abdominal wall and into the uterus for sampling of amniotic fluid	14 to 18 weeks (and possibly later), if required	To screen for genetic disorders, such as Down's syndrome, and neural-tube defects when risk is indicated (the mother is over 35, there is a family history of genetic defects, birth defects or chromosomal abnormalities, or there was an abnormal triple-screen test).
Triple screen	A simple blood test to measure levels of three hormones whose high levels might indicate problems	16 weeks, if required	To reveal the risk of having a child with either a chromosomal disorder (such as Down's syndrome) or a neural-tube or an abdominal defect.

(increasing her intake of raw vegetables and fresh fruit and cutting down on sugary, salty, and processed foods) and take any vitamin and mineral supplements recommended by her doctor. As well as increased amounts of iron and folic acid, she will need extra protein.

Avoid raw eggs, processed luncheon meats, potato chips, salted nuts, soya sauce and excessive amounts of mustard and ketchup. Buy 100 percent juices; synthetic brands may contain little fruit.

Even a glass of wine daily or a few times weekly might adversely affect your baby, so it is best to avoid all alcohol during pregnancy. Whatever you drink finds its way through the placenta to your baby's bloodstream, and it will have twice the effect on your baby's system as it does on yours.

Excessive drinking or binge drinking puts the fetus at risk of fetal alcohol syndrome (FAS), which causes retarded growth and mental function, small head size, and malformation of the face and heart. Alcohol effects are different for every woman and baby, but approximately 40 percent of babies whose mothers drink heavily during pregnancy are affected with FAS. Babies don't grow out of fetal alcohol syndrome, or any of several other alcohol-related physical and mental birth defects.

Controversial evidence suggests that caffeine (found in coffee, tea, and hot chocolate) may increase the risk of miscarriage. Most doctors recommend no more than one to two cups of caffeinated drinks a day and suggest you try to eliminate them altogether.

Soft drinks, high in sugar and low in essential nutrients, can cause you to gain weight. Trade them in for water, fruit juice, and milk.

Most herbal teas won't harm your baby but check with your doctor first.

Smokers beware

Researchers now know that smoking can harm a developing baby by depriving it of oxygen. Smoking also increases the likelihood of miscarriage, stillbirth, or premature delivery, and the chances of having a malformed baby or one who dies shortly after birth. The baby of a mother who smokes is twice as likely to be too small at birth as the baby of a nonsmoker. However, pregnant women should not resort to the patch or nicotine gum in an effort to quit. Their bodies, and eventually their babies, will absorb too much nicotine. Sudden infant death syndrome (SIDS, or crib death) happens more often in the homes of smokers than nonsmokers so nonsmoking pregnant women should avoid breathing secondhand smoke.

Playing It Safe

- Check with your doctor before taking any medication or herb while you are pregnant. If you do self-medicate, choose acetaminophen over aspirin and ibuprofen, which increase bleeding.

- Forgo hot tubs and saunas, which elevate body temperature to levels that are unsafe for the fetus.

- Avoid flying in your last trimester. Until then, fly only in large commercial jets.

- Do not smoke. If all pregnant women stopped smoking, low birth weights would decrease by 20 percent and there would be 5 percent fewer miscarriages.

- Limit your exposure to paint thinners, varnishes, and other toxic substances.

Prostate Drugs

The bane of existence for more than one third of men over the age of 50 (and most over 80) is benign prostatic hyperplasia (BPH), or enlarged prostate. While the condition isn't life-threatening, the uncomfortable symptoms—strained, urgent and frequent urination that often interrupts sleep, slowing of the urine stream, and incomplete emptying of the bladder—have many men looking for relief.

Surgery is an option that provides several symptom-free years for some men with BPH. For others, prostate drugs provide a solution, although they usually need to be taken daily, over a lifetime, or symptoms may return; in many cases, the medications take months to start working.

Shrinking the prostate

The prostate gland is a walnut-sized gland that surrounds the urethra near the bladder. The goal of some prostate drugs is to shrink the gland, which, for unknown reasons, enlarges with age, so that it doesn't compress the urethra and obstruct urine flow. The most popular prostate-shrinking drug is finasteride (Proscar), which may take six months to a year to show any benefits. Studies suggest that finasteride can reduce the need for surgery by more than 30 percent.

The drug works by suppressing an enzyme that turns testosterone into DHT, a hormone known to cause prostate enlargement—and possibly cancer. But there is a drawback: it also tends to lower concentrations of prostate-specific antigens (PSAs) in the blood. Testing a man's PSA levels is an important means of detecting early prostate cancer, and an artificially low reading can compromise the screening process. Some doctors recommend a baseline PSA screening before starting a finasteride regimen and an initial digital rectal exam.

The other prostate drugs

Alpha blockers work in a different way: by relaxing the gland's smooth muscle tissue. The drugs (Hytrin and Cardura are two pop-

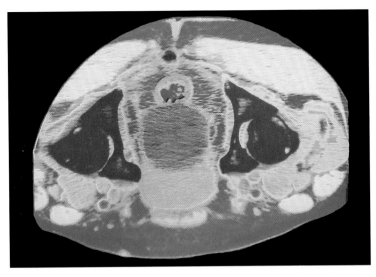

A computer-tomographic image of a pelvic cross section shows the enlarged prostate gland (green) pressing against the bladder (yellow).

Another Prostate Problem

Prostatitis is an inflammation and swelling of the prostate; it does not indicate a likelihood of having either BPH or prostate cancer. If it's caused by a bacterial infection, it can be treated with antibiotics. If you experience any of these symptoms, see your doctor:

- Chills and fever
- Bloody urine
- Lower-back pain and/or perineal discomfort
- Urgent or difficult urination

ular brand names) are also used to reduce blood pressure. Clinical studies suggest that these drugs may be more effective than finasteride, especially for men who suffer urinary problems but don't have a significantly enlarged prostate.

Alpha blockers bring relief to many patients. They work faster than finasteride, but they don't halt further enlargement of the prostate (as finasteride may) or inhibit prostate cancer. They aren't recommended for men with heart disease or sensitivity to the lowered blood pressure the drugs cause.

Screening for prostate cancer

Men with BPH have no greater or lower risk of prostate cancer than men without it. Since prostate cancer often has no noticeable symptoms, all men over the age of 50 (and over 40 if there is a family history of the disease) should have an annual prostate exam to ensure early treatment.

Doctors use combinations of surgery, radiation, and drugs to treat prostate cancer. Hormone medications may slow the cancer's growth by reducing testosterone production. In some clinical studies, the drug Lupron (or a similar drug) in combination with other treatments, such as chemotherapy, reduced the size of the prostate or slowed the growth of cancer.

To hear some people tell it, the blood test for prostate-specific antigens (PSAs) is a valuable tool for spotting prostate cancer in the highly curable early stages. Others say it's an unreliable predictor that doesn't identify enough men with cancer and subjects too many others to unnecessary ultrasound imaging and biopsies. So who's right? What should a man do about screening for prostate cancer?

The best answer is to understand the limitations of the PSA test and then use it as part of a regular monitoring program. Urologists generally recommend annual PSA screenings along with digital rectal exams (in which the physician uses a gloved finger, or digit, to feel the prostate gland and check it for abnormalities). For now, this combination represents the most comprehensive approach for men age 50 and older.

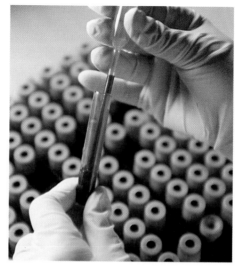

Some urologists take PSA readings every 6 to 12 months. A sudden jump in the numbers may call for a digital rectal exam or a biopsy.

An unreliable indicator of cancer

PSAs are enzymes that the prostate releases into the blood. A PSA reading of 0 to 4 is considered normal, 4 to 10 is borderline or slightly elevated, and above 10 is high. But the test is an indicator of prostate activity, not necessarily prostate cancer. Therefore, it can be misleading. Such common conditions as prostatitis (inflammation and swelling of the prostate) or benign prostatic hyperplasia (BPH), also known as enlarged prostate, can produce elevated counts. Conversely, a normal count does not guarantee prostate health; 10 percent of men with prostate cancer have a low reading.

If a PSA score is high, a biopsy or transrectal ultrasonography (TRUS) test are often recommended; the former is the only definitive test for prostate cancer. Even though these tests are painless, they can cause undue alarm if no trace of cancer is found.

Should you get tested regularly?

Talk to your doctor first. The Canadian Urological Association recommends regular PSA testing for men between the ages of 50 and 70. (Black men—whose incidence of prostate cancer is higher than that of the general population—and men with a family history of prostate cancer are urged to begin PSA screening as early as age 40.) However, the Canadian Cancer Society (CCS) recommends PSA screening only for men who show symptoms that suggest prostate problems, such as difficulty with urination or blood in the urine; or if the test is part of a clinical study to learn more about diagnosing prostate cancer. Instead, as part of a regular prevention program, the CCS recommends annual digital rectal exams for men over the age of 50.

an ounce of Prevention

Truer Readings

Avoiding ejaculation at least 48 hours before a PSA test may reduce the risk of a false high reading. University of Michigan researchers found that ejaculating may produce temporarily elevated PSA serum concentrations among older men.

On the Horizon When the first "Free PSA" blood test was approved for use in the United States in 1998, it ushered in a new era of more accurate PSA screenings. The test, still undergoing clinical trials in Canada, measures the amount of free-floating PSAs, which are more likely to be produced by cancerous prostate cells. As the test predicts cancer more accurately, it may allow some healthy men to avoid undergoing a prostate biopsy.

Radiation

Radiation is a kind of energy that has the properties of both waves and particles. It exists around us all the time. It can be ionizing (able to displace electrons in atoms to create charged ions) or nonionizing. Both types emanate from natural and man-made sources. While all kinds of radiation can have health consequences, it is the ionizing form that is cause for the most concern.

Energy that can damage cells...

Nonionizing radiation has the power to move atoms but not to change their chemistry. Varieties include visible light, infrared waves, ultraviolet waves, radio waves, television waves, microwaves, and the electromagnetic fields emitted by electric blankets, cellular phones, and power lines. While nonionizing radiation doesn't break chemical bonds, it can cause physical changes. For example, ultraviolet and infrared waves from the sun or a tan-

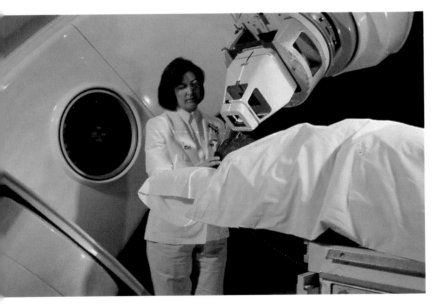

The linear accelerator delivers a highly targeted dose of radiation that destroys cancer cells.

ning or heat lamp can damage the skin and the eyes, increasing the risk over time of skin cancer and even blindness. Microwave radiation can destroy tissues by heating them. And strong electromagnetic fields may cause cancer, although more research is needed.

Ionizing radiation can actually alter the chemistry of biological tissue, without gener-

ating heat. About 80 percent of our exposure to ionizing radiation comes from natural sources, primarily background radiation from radon and its decay products; other radioactive substances in rocks and soil; and even cosmic rays from the sun and the stars. Man-made sources consist primarily of diagnostic X rays and computerized tomography and radiation therapy. Coal-fired power generating stations, nuclear reactors, and improperly stored radioactive waste also release ionizing radiation.

Radiation passes through the body, usually without leaving a trace. But overexposure can affect tissues, causing molecular damage, including mutations in genetic material that, over time, may lead to cancer. If the genetic material of cells in the sex organs is affected, birth defects in the children of exposed individuals may result. That is why the use of radiation must be carefully controlled.

...or save lives

As many cancer survivors can attest, however, radiation also saves lives. High doses can be tolerated by the body if directed at only a small area. That is the fundamental principle behind radiation therapy to treat cancer. Radiation can be delivered by an external beam or by radioactive material placed inside the body, usually in or near the tumor. The radiation targets and eventually kills malignant cells and normally produces minimal damage in healthy cells. Radiation is also being used in the treatment of benign proliferative diseases, such as keloid (thick scar) formation and heterotropic (abnormal) bone formation that can develop after hip surgery.

Dodging the rays

Since overexposure to X rays can have deleterious long-term effects, ask your doctor if an X ray is absolutely necessary before you agree to have one. When using X rays or radiation therapy, technicians protect parts of the body not involved in the procedure by covering them with a lead shield. Pregnant women are advised to avoid having X rays if possible.

Radon is a colorless and odorless radioactive gas released by decaying uranium in soils and rocks. Because uranium is found everywhere, radon is constantly finding its way into the atmosphere. Outdoors, the gas dissipates into the air and is relatively harmless. As such, it poses no health risk: you generally exhale the same quantity as you inhale. However, indoors, radon can reach high concentrations. It seeps through cracks in foundation floors and walls, and through unsealed gaps around drain pipes and sump pumps.

Radon's health risk

Radon undergoes radioactive decay to form radioactive particles, called "radon daughters" or "radon progeny." As you inhale, these particles enter the lungs, where they may stick to lung or bronchial tissues. Once embedded there, they emit radiation that, over time, may lead to lung cancer.

Since the 1970s, Canada has carried out research into radon's health risk. The U.S., Great Britain, and Sweden have also conducted studies in this field. In 1998, the U.S. National Research Council (NRC) issued a report stating that radon is responsible for up to 21,800 lung-cancer deaths a year in America. The report concluded that radon poses a major public-health problem because high levels exist in many homes. It also stated that smoking combined with radon exposure may increase the risk of lung cancer. Experts from Canada and other nations were involved in the preparation of the NRC report.

Guidelines for radon exposure

Radon is present in the air of every house in Canada. The highest levels generally occur in basements. However, there is no certain way of predicting whether any given house will have a high level of radon.

Health Canada has set a guideline of 800 becquerels per cubic meter of air as an average annual concentration of radon in a living area. If this limit is exceeded, householders should reduce radon levels by sealing cracks in basement floors and walls and venting the radon's gas to the outside. Because the guideline represents an upper limit, Health Canada suggests householders take remedial action at lower levels. The United States, Great Britain, and Sweden have set much lower levels, at 150 to 220 becquerels per cubic meter of air.

Measuring radon

The only certain way of finding out the radon level is to measure it. It is essential to detect the average concentration, because levels can change from hour to hour, and from day to day. A test can last for seven days, or up to a year. The longer the test, the more accurate the measurement. Passive devices such as charcoal canisters and alpha track detectors, and active devices as the CAIRS Home Radon Monitor, can be used for home-testing. These devices are exposed to the air for a specified time and sent for analysis.

Do-it-yourself home radon detectors, such as charcoal canisters, are available at home-supply stores for $15 to $30. Testing done by environmental specialists can cost much more.

an ounce of Prevention

Testing Your Home for Radon

Inexpensive home radon test devices are available for both short-term (7 days minimum) and long-term (up to a year) evaluation. The long-term test is more representative of annual average levels because it factors in seasonal changes in home ventilation and radon emission.

For more information about radon testing, call your provincial health department, or the Canadian Institute for Radiation Safety (CAIRS) at 1-800-263-5803.

In Canada, the national average cost of reducing a home's radon level is roughly $1,000.

Raw Foods

The adventurous palate is always looking for new taste sensations, but it may find more than it bargained for when it takes on the delights of uncooked cuisine. Eating raw foods, such as sushi, oysters, and steak tartare, poses an increased risk of food-borne illness.

When uncooked is a raw deal

Many foods, including meat, seafood, fruits, and vegetables, can harbor disease-causing microbes. Yet they become a health threat only when handled or cooked improperly. Cooking food thoroughly and with sufficient heat kills most microbes.

Raw foods, of course, are uncooked. For produce like fruit and salad greens, rinsing thoroughly under running water (use a vegetable brush and discard outer leaves) minimizes exposure to disease-causing microbes. But raw animal foods cannot simply be made safe by washing, and the bacteria they may contain can cause such symptoms as nausea, stomach cramps, and diarrhea. These illnesses are especially dangerous, even fatal, among the young, the old, and anyone with a weakened immune system.

Sushi chefs may be rigorously trained in selecting and preparing fish that is clean and safe, but eating sushi is inherently risky.

Frozen sushi, chilly oysters

Raw fish is a delicacy in many countries and is very popular in the form of Japanese sushi and sashimi. But that doesn't make it safe. Even if the fish has been frozen below −18°C (0°F) to kill potential parasites, freezing will not kill bacteria. Sushi lovers, beware: your health risk may be determined by the reliability and cleanliness of your chef.

Eating raw oysters can send you to the hospital, and, in rare cases, can even be fatal. The culprit is a common saltwater bacterium, *Vibrio vulnificus*, that can cause fever, muscle aches, blackened or reddened skin, and a drop in blood pressure in susceptible people. (For healthy people, the risk is much lower.) *V. vulnificus* breeds best in warmer waters, so oysters from the Gulf of Mexico are potentially more dangerous than those from the colder waters of New England, Nova Scotia,

CAUTION!
Restaurant chefs may intentionally undercook some fish dishes, such as pan-seared tuna, to preserve its fresh flavor. Don't be afraid to ask ahead of time about the rawness of a dish. Order undercooked fish at your own risk.

and the Pacific Northwest. One way to lower risk, even from raw Gulf oysters, is to follow the old rule of thumb: "Eat oysters only in months with an R." They are harvested in colder months: September through April.

Bye-bye, steak tartare

Knowingly eating raw meat, in the form of ground steak tartare or thinly sliced carpaccio, is less common than unknowingly eating undercooked meat. However, the dangers—from *E. coli*, campylobacter, and salmonella bacteria—are the same. To be safe, stick with thoroughly cooked meat dishes.

There is also a risk of salmonella poisoning from raw eggs. To increase food safety, many restaurants have cleared their menus of such items as soft-boiled eggs, custards, and authentic Caesar salad, which includes raw egg in the dressing. At home, take these steps to steer clear of egg-borne salmonella:

- Don't buy or use cracked eggs.
- Use the eggs you buy within five weeks.
- When making eggnog or Caesar salad dressing, use pasteurized egg products.
- When you bake cookies, brownies, or cakes with raw eggs, don't give in to the temptation to taste even a fingerful of raw batter.

Oysters are a treat in any season, but to be safe, eat them only in months with an R in them.

Reflexology

When is a foot massage not just a foot massage? When it's reflexology—an alternative medical therapy in which pressure is applied to specific points on the feet. Studies suggest that by stimulating the body's nervous and circulatory systems, reflexology may provide therapeutic benefits, with only minimal discomfort, side effects, or risk of injury. But can it really improve health?

Pushing the right buttons

Reflexology was brought to the West in the early 1900s, but its principles can be traced to ancient healing practices in Egypt and China. The technique, which mimics acupressure and massage, applies pressure to specific areas, called "reflex areas," on each foot. (In some instances, the hands are worked on, too.) The pressure on the foot is said to cause a healing reflex in a corresponding part of the body.

Every part of the body is represented by an area on the feet. The left foot corresponds to the left side of the body; the right foot, to the right side. In fact, reflexologists see the feet, placed together and seen from their bottoms, as an exact representation of the human body. Examples of reflex areas that correspond to parts of the body include:

- The toes, to parts of the head, including the face, eyes, ears, and sinuses.
- The tips of the toes, to the brain.
- The ball of the left foot, to the heart, which is slightly left of center in the chest.
- The heels, to the hips and pelvis.
- The inside edge of each foot (from the heel to the big toe), to the spine.

A relaxing massage—and maybe more

How reflexology works is not entirely understood, but it may aid healing by stimulating blood flow and triggering the release of endorphins, hormones that help relieve pain. However, the benefits may have less to do with working specific reflex areas than simply the soothing nature of a foot massage.

How well reflexology works for you may depend on the skill of your therapist. There is a chance that you won't respond at all to the therapy, which may last 45 to 60 minutes and cost between $15 to $75 per session, an expense that is not covered by most insurers. Four to six sessions with a qualified therapist (see box, below) are usually necessary to determine whether reflexology is providing any benefit. A minor risk is mild discomfort as the foot is manipulated; the therapy should not be done on an injured foot.

Reflexology is not a cure-all—it should never replace medical attention—and may provide little more than relief of stress. Still, studies show that the therapy may help relieve headaches, chronic constipation, back pain, sinus troubles, premenstrual syndrome, dizziness, and the pain associated with arthritis and diabetes.

Shoulder line
Diaphragm line
Ligament line
Waist line
Pelvic line

Five guidelines divide the foot into sections that mirror the body. For example, the reflex areas for the head are above line 5; for the chest, between lines 5 and 1.

Finding the Right Reflexologist

To find a qualified reflexologist and get the most benefit from the therapy, follow these guidelines:

- Your therapist should be certified. The Reflexology Association of Canada is one association that sets standards for practitioners and provides referrals. Call 1-519-887-9991.

- Don't expect miracles and be wary of any reflexologist who guarantees results. The therapy is not for everyone.

- If you try a session, you should feel no pain and find it relaxing.

- A specialist in reflexology is preferable to a practitioner of multiple therapies.

- If you are seeking help for an injury or illness, a reputable therapist will ask you to get a diagnosis from a doctor beforehand.

Restaurant Food

Clean and efficient service is a good predictor—but not a guarantee—of safe food.

Whether you grab a sandwich between meetings, treat the family to a night out, or enjoy a romantic rendezvous, if you're a typical Canadian, you eat outside the home more than 250 times each year. For most of us, there's nothing more pleasant than letting someone else do the cooking.

Yet dining in restaurants isn't necessarily safe. Many of the reported cases of food-borne illness result from food that has been eaten away from home. A Health Canada report, based on statistics from Ontario, cited 1,348 outbreaks (roughly 340 a year) of food-borne disease for the 1993 to 1996 period in that province. The report also showed restaurants topping the list of risk settings for these outbreaks.

Dining out can also be hard on your waistline. Some restaurant food contains extra fat and calories, as well as sodium. But with a few dietary precautions, you can keep your meals pleasurable, safe, and healthful.

Deciding where to eat

A major culprit in food-borne illness is the *Salmonella* bacterium, which thrives in raw or undercooked meat, poultry, and eggs. Moreover, salmonella can be transmitted to other foods that have been contaminated by raw meats.

Local municipalities enforce provincial regulations that are designed to ensure the safe handling and preparation of food. But those regulations are effective only if restaurant workers adhere to them. Wise consumers must use their judgment and experience when deciding where they can dine safely. Here are commonsense ways you can determine the quality and cleanliness of the restaurants that you frequent:

- **Pay attention to reputation.** A restaurant with a loyal following usually earns it with high-quality food.
- **Look around you.** Are the tables, rest rooms, and other public areas messy or neat? Do surfaces and utensils look clean?
- **Take a peek into the kitchen.** Is it clean and well organized? Understaffed operations breed carelessness, which, in turn, can allow bacteria to breed.
- **Ask questions.** Do servers seem knowledgeable about the food and its preparation? A well-trained wait staff is a good indicator of a well-trained kitchen staff.

Once you're persuaded that a restaurant is safe, turn your attention to the foods you select. Salmonella and most other bacteria can't survive high heat, so thorough cooking eliminates that threat. Stay away from dishes that are raw (steak tartare, carpaccio, oysters on the half shell) or undercooked (pan-seared tuna, rare beef, runny eggs). If you order Caesar salad, make sure it isn't prepared with raw eggs. If food looks undercooked, send it back. Better to wait a few extra minutes than to endure the effects of food poisoning.

Making healthy food choices

Now that you've selected a safe spot and skipped the riskiest items on the menu, you'll want to order foods that aren't overloaded with fat, salt, and calories. More and more restaurants offer some heart-healthy dishes. For the rest of your choices, you'll have to develop smart ordering habits.

Ask for sauces, dressings, and butter on the side to control how much you use. Specify whether you want skim milk in your coffee or chicken served without the fatty skin. Stick to menu items prepared nutritiously: poached, steamed, broiled, or roasted. Go easy on dishes that are creamed, fried, or pan-fried and anything described "buttery," "cheesy," or "crispy." Beware of foods that may seem healthy but aren't, such as fried eggplant (extremely high in fat) and Cobb salad. Finally, ask about preparation methods. Braising in broth is quite healthy; in butter, it's highly fattening.

IN

Retinoic Acid

Are wrinkles as inevitable as birthdays? Perhaps not. For some people, Renova, the best-known prescription skin treatment containing retinoic acid (a derivative of vitamin A), can make many fine wrinkles disap-

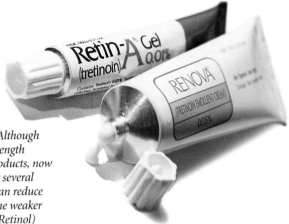

Buyer beware: Although prescription-strength retinoic acid products, now available under several brand names, can reduce fine wrinkles, the weaker version (called Retinol) found in some over-the-counter preparations has not been shown to have the same effect.

pear. It does so only for some people, however; others get minimal benefits, or none at all. Still, if it works for you, retinoic acid might leave the guests at your next birthday party counting the candles in disbelief.

A wrinkle in time

As skin ages, it produces less oil, which can make the outer skin layer (epidermis) dry and rough. At the same time, the under layer (dermis) produces less elastin and collagen—the connective-tissue proteins that keep skin soft and supple. That results in thinner, less elastic skin that tends to develop wrinkles. For some people, the wrinkling is minor. But for others, especially the fair-skinned, smokers, and anyone with heavy exposure to the sun, the wrinkling may be pronounced.

The promise of newer, softer skin

Retin-A, one of the brand names for retinoic acid (also known as prescription medication tretinoin), was introduced in 1971 as an acne remedy and still serves that purpose. But in 1988, a study showed the seemingly magical effects of Retin-A on aging and sun-damaged skin. Since that time, it has been widely used as an antiwrinkle cream. The most common

problems associated with Retin-A include redness and sensitivity to sunlight. Some patients prefer Renova, a retinoic acid mixed with an emollient cream, which they find less irritating.

Whether applied in gels, creams, or liquids, retinoic acid works its magic by speeding up exfoliation—the shedding of dead skin cells on the epidermis. This causes the dermis to regenerate skin cells, which creates a more youthful appearance. There's also evidence that retinoic acid prompts the skin to retain moisture better.

Even at its best, though, retinoic acid is no fountain of youth for the skin. A U.S. review of research showed that, after six months of daily application, only about 30 percent of people showed moderate improvement in fine wrinkles and spotty discoloration. Thirty-five percent experienced minimal improvement; another 35 percent, no improvement at all. About half the users reported less skin roughness. The treatment doesn't affect deep wrinkles.

Retinoic acid takes from weeks to months to deliver a visible effect, with peak results showing in about six months. After that, you can expect little improvement, just maintenance. If you stop using retinoic-acid creams, your skin will gradually return to its previous state, allowing wrinkles to come back.

Moisturizers and sun sense

Ironically, retinoic acid actually slows the production of skin oil, so experts recommend using moisturizers to offset this drying action. Skin irritation, itching, and redness are also problems, but for most users, they subside after a few weeks.

You'll need to take a few precautions when using a retinoic-acid product. Don't apply it to the skin around the eyes or mouth, and avoid getting it in your eyes. Forgo retinoic acid if you have eczema, sunburn or windburn. If it irritates your skin, stop using it and see your doctor. And minimize exposure to sunlight, a good idea in any case, to protect your skin from further damage.

CAUTION!

Retinoic acid skin creams and gels should not be used by pregnant women or any woman trying to conceive. Animal studies have indicated that high doses may delay proper fetal bone formation.

In-line skating is on a roll. The sport, popularly known as Rollerblading (from the brand name of the skates that started the craze), now boasts some 2.5 million enthusiasts across Canada. Since the early 1990s, sales of in-line skates in this country have totaled some 4 million pairs, and the estimated annual sales run to 500,000 pairs. What do Canadians see in this racy kind of skating?

They have fun. They get a vigorous aerobic workout. They go fast. And they fall—it's all part of the thrill of this popular new sport. Unprotected falls can (and often do) result in serious injuries, but with proper training and protective gear, including helmet, wrist guards, and knee and elbow pads, you can greatly lessen the risk of injury.

Wellness on wheels

How did in-line skating get so hot so fast? It may be the speed and maneuverability that in-line skates, with their single row of wheels down the middle, offer over traditional skates. It may also be that a generation of joggers was looking for an aerobic activity that's kinder to the knees.

Whatever the reasons for its popularity, in-line skating can give you a muscle-building, flexibility-enhancing workout that packs a cardiovascular punch. With its vigorous leg-pushing motion, the sport has been likened by some experts to a weight-training workout on wheels. Moreover, in-line skating is a great calorie burner. It can also improve balance and coordination for people of all ages. That could translate into fewer falls later in life.

Ready, set, roll!

Since falls can occur with in-line skating, always protect yourself with the appropriate equipment. To avoid or reduce the severity of hand injuries, use wrist guards. If you're not wearing these guards, the natural impulse to break a fall with your hands can cause wrist sprains and fractures. A helmet is essential to prevent accidents that may result in head trauma. Elbow and knee pads complete the array of recommended safety equipment. Serious elbow injuries are far more likely for skaters who don't wear elbow pads. Knees aren't subject to as many injuries, but wearing knee pads helps you to avoid cuts and bruises.

Since the mid-1990s, skate manufacturers have started selling more protective equipment. Moreover, some Canadian communities have passed bylaws that permit skaters to go anywhere on streets and roads, if they wear safety equipment. Anyone inadequately protected faces fines.

Taking the fall

When you lose your balance, try to land first on your wrist guards (absorb the impact by bending your elbows), then catch the rest of your weight on your knees. If you aren't wearing wrist guards (recommended for skaters of all levels, not just beginners) be prepared to break any fall you might take with your wrists, elbows, and shoulders.

Learning Curve

Like any sport, in-line skating uses skills that have to be learned. Skate manufacturers and health and safety officials recommend that novices get instruction before they first roll out. One important skill to learn is stopping. The heel-mounted brake requires bringing the brake foot forward, a motion that can be awkward for beginners. It's best to practice in rinks rather than on bumpy (and busy) streets or sidewalks.

Get in the habit of keeping your knees bent during in-line skating. The position helps stabilize you, especially when a fall is imminent. And don't go without protective gear—including elbow pads, which this woman has forgotten.

Running

C an you lose weight, improve cardiovascular fitness, and overcome stress and fatigue without spending a lot of time or money? Yes, by running. For the cost of a pair of running shoes, a routine as simple as 20 to 30 minutes a day, three days a week, can provide you with a premier aerobic regimen.

Walk, Don't Run

Some experts recommend slower-paced exercise. While you'll have to walk longer to equal running's calorie burn, you'll strengthen bones and help ward off osteoporosis—without causing the same stress to your muscles and joints.

And walking could add a few years to your life. A 12-year study showed that non-smoking retired men who walked 2 or more miles each day had only about half the death rate of similar men who walked less than a mile.

The ups and downs

Studies show that regular running can reduce cholesterol levels, blood pressure, and body fat. It can also ease your mind and improve sleep. Running, especially over long distances, may trigger the release of hormones called endorphins, which can create a sense of well-being and produce the exhilarating feeling known as a runner's high.

Still, running is an impact sport that puts stress on the bones, joints, and muscles of the legs, feet, and back. The addictive runner's high can also lead to overtraining. Running more than 32 kilometers (20 miles) per week—or more than 8 kilometers (5 miles) at once—can increase the risk of injury, especially if not alternated with days of rest or low-impact activities, such as bicycling or yoga.

Running with a partner strengthens motivation and makes it easier to stick to a weekly routine.

Just do it—the smart way

All runners, from beginners to marathoners, are susceptible to injury. Reduce your risk:

- **Buy a good pair of running shoes.** Look for cushioning to absorb the impact and stability for the arch, heel, and ankle. Shoes will last 480 to 800 kilometers (300 to 500 miles) before they have to be replaced.
- **Be realistic.** Take a modest approach to speed, distance, and frequency. Beginners should alternate running and walking and increase speed and distance gradually. Running only 20 to 30 minutes at a time, three times a week, is a sensible goal.
- **Drink plenty of water.** Don't wait to fill up just before you start or during your run; your body can't process water that quickly, and you'll just feel bloated. Drink throughout the day to avoid dehydration.
- **Warm up and cool down.** Before you run, walk or jog lightly for a few minutes. Then stretch your hamstring, thigh, and calf muscles (use gradual 20-second stretches, not short bounces). Afterward, cool down with a short walk, then stretch again.
- **Pay attention to your body.** After a run, your muscles may ache for hours, even a day or two. If there's pain, stop running for a few days. If it persists, see your doctor.

Symptom Sorter

"No Pain, No Gain" Can Lead to Overuse Injuries

As good as running can be, doing too much can cause significant muscle and joint pain—and the following injuries:

Injury	Symptom	Causes	Remedies
Runner's knee	Pain under the kneecap	Improper form, e.g., pronating feet; running on hills or crowned roads	Rest; proper shoes; improved running form
Shin-splints	Pain in the front of the lower legs	Worn-out shoes; running on hard or uneven surfaces; overtraining	Rest; running on cinder tracks or level surfaces; new shoes
Achilles tendinitis	Extreme pain in the back of the ankle	Insufficient warm-up or stretching; overtraining	Rest; applying ice; some light jogging prior to stretching

What's in your salad-bar salad? Is it a light alternative to a hefty lunch, a boon to weight control, a nourishing cornucopia of fresh greens and vegetables—or a nutritional nightmare? What you put on your plate is entirely your choice. Just be aware: A few tablespoons of this and that, a sprinkle of little bits and tiny chunks, a side trip to the hot entrées, and you've turned a potentially healthy meal into a conglomerate of fat, calories, and sodium. If you're not careful, you might even be serving yourself germs.

Tossing in good health

A salad's nutritional value is up to you. For a healthful salad, keep it simple: greens, vegetables, fruits, beans, small pieces of lean meat, and a modest amount of light dressing (if any at all). Consider these basics:

- **Greens.** All varieties supply some fiber and are low in calories. The darkest greens (such as Romaine lettuce, arugula, and spinach) provide more beta-carotene, vitamin C, and other nutrients than paler varieties (such as iceberg, which is mostly water). One cup of arugula, for instance, provides 150 milligrams (mg) of calcium and only 12 calories. But not all greens are as good as they look. Some establishments, in order to make the leaves appear fresher, soak lettuce in water before placing it on the salad bar. If the greens are soaked for a long time, they may lose some of their nutrients.

- **Vegetables and fruits.** All by itself, a large, well-made salad can provide you with a good portion of the recommended five to 10 servings of fruits and vegetables for the day. Piling on raw vegetables—such as broccoli, red peppers, cauliflower, carrots, peas, mushrooms, zucchini, and onions—loads a salad with fiber, vitamins, and minerals, including antioxidants that may help prevent disease. Fresh fruits, such as apples, oranges, and melons, can add some healthful zip—they're better than syrupy canned fruits, which are high in sugar.

- **Beans, seeds, and meat.** Kidney and garbanzo beans (chickpeas) are rich in soluble fiber and protein, and low in fat. A sprinkle of sunflower seeds, pine nuts, or walnuts will add fat and calories but will also provide some vitamin E, fiber, potassium, calcium, and protein. (Just be sure to stop at a sprinkle.) Small chunks of lean chicken, turkey, or tuna also complement a salad. *(continued)*

CAUTION!

Anyone with severe food allergies or celiac disease should be wary of salad bars. Some options, including certain salad dressings, may contain unseen flour, wheat, or cornstarch.

Dressing Down

You've built the perfectly healthy salad and are about to top it off with some flavorful dressing. Hold on! It's not difficult to add a few hundred calories or more with only a couple of tablespoons. Instead, take your dressing on the side. Then, before each forkful of greens, dip your fork into the dressing. Whatever sticks to the tines will add enough zest and help you avoid calories.

Or skip the typical dressings altogether and add your own low-fat, low-calorie substitute: a squeeze of lemon, a splash of flavored vinegar, or a bit of olive oil mixed with mustard, soy sauce, salsa, or vinegar. On fruit, try yogurt. You may discover that without the rich dressing, the flavors of the salad shine brighter.

With so much to choose from, a salad can easily become large. Maintain a modest portion size, especially of high-fat items, but do pile on the greens.

Salad Bars (continued)

Salad-in-a-bag

Ready-mixed salads are convenient because the greens are already washed. But should you wash them again at home? No need, say health officials. In fact, the salad is probably cleaner than if you'd washed it yourself. Just make sure the package is marked "pre-washed" or "ready to eat."

A see-through "sneeze guard" helps protect the food from germs, but you must take some responsibility, too: Don't touch the food with your hands or use utensils that have dropped to the floor.

Tossing out fat and calories

Surprise: A Mississippi State University study showed that students who ate a salad-bar lunch typically consumed more calories than students eating hot entrées. How could this be? Many items in a salad bar, in addition to the dressings, are high in calories. Consider these sources:

- **Prepared foods.** Unless you know exactly how they were made, their nutritional content is hard to figure. Bean or pasta salad and marinated vegetables may be drenched in fatty oils. Coleslaw, tuna salad, potato salad, and pasta, chicken, or turkey salads will be high in calories and fat if they are swimming in mayonnaise.

- **Bits and sprinkles.** Some of the smallest items in a salad bar, including bacon bits, croutons, cheese, fried noodles, sesame sticks, green olives, salami cubes, ham strips, even raisins, can add a substantial amount of calories. A small portion of any of these items can add flavor and some nutrients, but in combination, or in quantity, they may provide more calories than you need.

- **Hot stuff.** Salad bars often offer such hot items as macaroni and cheese, fried chicken wings, and creamy soups, but these fatty foods aren't any healthier just because they're near the greens and veggies. Even clear-broth soups can be high in sodium.

Who's tending the bar?

Sulfites, preservatives once commonly added to cut fruits and vegetables to keep them looking fresh, were banned (for this use) because of their potential to trigger severe allergic reactions. But salad bars pose other potential health problems. Ask yourself:

- **Is there an attendant?** The safest salad bars are monitored by an employee who keeps food and ice refreshed and whose presence serves to keep customers from touching food with their hands or using utensils that have been dropped.

- **How fresh is it?** Food that was just put out is likely to be fresher than anything that has been sitting for a few hours. Cold foods should be surrounded by plenty of ice; hot food should be very hot. Signs that a salad bar is not so fresh include unappetizing limp greens or dry-looking pasta or fruit.

- **How clean is it?** Many salad bars have "sneeze guards," chest-high covers that shield the food from dust, germs, and other contaminants. The whole area—utensils, tables, floors—should look clean and well-maintained. If you see flies or other insects, look for another place to eat.

How Can a Salad Be Fattening?

A salad bar is a mix of high-fat and low-fat options. Check out the typical fat and calorie counts for these items:

Ingredient	Serving	Fat (g)	Calories
Dressings			
Ranch	2 tbsp	11	109
Low-calorie Ranch	2 tbsp	6	62
Russian	2 tbsp	11	118
French	2 tbsp	18	134
Low-fat French	2 tbsp	2	42
Italian	2 tbsp	18	138
Low-calorie Italian	2 tbsp	2	16
Vinaigrette	2 tbsp	16	144
Blue cheese	2 tbsp	16	152
Toppings			
Egg, chopped	2 tbsp	1	16
Garbanzo beans	2 tbsp	0.5	21
Bacon bits	1 tbsp	2	27
Fried noodles	2 tbsp	1	28
Parmesan cheese	2 tbsp	3	46
Cheddar cheese	2 tbsp	5	56
Ham, lean (chunks)	1/3 cup	5	70
Turkey breast (chunks)	1/3 cup	1	70
Sunflower seeds	2 tbsp	7	97
Sides			
Three-bean salad	1/4 cup	0	60
Potato salad	1/4 cup	5	90
Coleslaw	1/3 cup	7	120

So, is salt bad for you or not? For years, doctors have recommended low-salt diets to combat high blood pressure and heart disease. While reducing salt intake won't lower blood pressure in everyone with elevated levels, the majority of evidence shows that it often helps. And if everyone in our society consumed less sodium, there would be less high blood pressure in the first place.

It's not just a matter of restraining the hand that holds the saltshaker. Salt added during cooking or at the table comprises only a portion of the sodium we consume. The rest comes from processed foods—and not just "salty" ones. So focus on consuming more naturally low-sodium fresh fruits and vegetables, which lower blood pressure even as they provide vitamins, minerals and fiber.

Salt or sodium?

While a half teaspoon of salt contains more than 1,000 milligrams (mg) of sodium, salt and sodium are not the same thing. Table salt (sodium chloride) is about 40 percent sodium, but sodium also shows up in flavor enhancers and preservatives. It's sodium that should concern us most. Here's why:

- **Sodium, not chloride, carries the greater health risk.** Consuming too much sodium is associated with an increased risk of high blood pressure, stroke, and kidney disorders. Chloride carries no such risks.
- **Sodium is more prevalent.** Although "salt" is listed as an ingredient on many food labels, sodium may be present in foods in which salt is not. It may appear as baking soda, MSG, sodium saccharin, sodium benzoate, and sodium propionate.

A fluid balance

The body uses sodium to help maintain fluid balance and regulate blood volume. The kidneys, brain, heart, and glands work in unison to maintain the optimum level of sodium in the body. When sodium levels rise or fall, the body is forced to correct the imbalance. The corrections constitute a dazzling array of causes and effects, which may include thirst, fluid retention, the secretion of hormones, a sudden appetite for salty foods, and changes in blood volume, blood pressure, or the amount of sodium excreted in the urine.

It's rare for sodium levels to be too low. The average Canadian consumes between 3,500 and 5,000 mg of sodium each day. That level of dietary sodium greatly exceeds the needs of the human body. Sodium intake can easily be reduced to between 1,800 and 2,300 mg daily without harm.

The salt we add in cooking or dining comprises only a portion of our sodium intake—most of it comes from processed foods.

Sodium pumps up the pressure

In some people, a high amount of sodium in the blood causes the body to retain fluids, swelling the volume of the blood. The heart has to work harder to pump the extra blood volume around the body. The end result is higher blood pressure.

Can cutting back on sodium lower high blood pressure? For many people, yes. Research clearly shows that people with high blood pressure can significantly improve their overall health by reducing the sodium intake in their diet.

A 1998 study, one of many showing the benefits of a low-sodium diet, looked at people age 60 to 80 who were taking medications for high blood pressure. Over two and a half years, limiting sodium (and losing weight if needed) led to fewer cardiovascular complications and a reduced need for medications. The regimen enabled nearly a third of the subjects taking blood pressure drugs to go off their medication entirely, under the supervision of their doctor.

CAUTION!
Many salt substitutes contain potassium. If you take blood pressure medication or have kidney disease, check with your doctor before using a salt substitute. Your body may retain too much of the potassium, which can cause an irregular heartbeat.

Salt (continued)

Sodium sensitivity

It's estimated that sodium intake affects blood pressure in only 10 to 20 percent of North Americans, but it's difficult to determine if you are "sodium sensitive." (Medical tests may help.) Even if you're not, cutting back on sodium is still a healthy choice. High sodium intake can cause water retention (edema), trigger migraine headaches, and worsen kidney and liver problems and premenstrual syndrome.

As people age, they often become more sensitive to sodium, so cutting back may be even more important. Older bodies tend to be less efficient at excreting sodium. The result, again, is higher blood pressure, which is particularly dangerous to older people, whose blood vessels are less pliable and more likely to rupture or become clotted under stress.

At first, sticking to a low-sodium diet may be hard, but within a few weeks your taste adjusts, so even lightly salted foods taste salty. A low-sodium diet, though, is only part of a strategy to control blood pressure. You'll also need to maintain a healthy body weight, exercise regularly, abstain from smoking, moderate alcohol intake, and learn to handle stress. Eating more vegetables and fruits, plus low-fat dairy foods, may enable you to lower your blood pressure even more. Nevertheless, medication may still be necessary.

Shaking salt

Here's how to cut down on sodium:

- **Eat fresh, unprocessed foods.** Both fresh fruits and vegetables typically have less than 10 mg of sodium per serving. A serving of fresh beef, fish, or poultry may contain less than 100 mg.
- **Cut back on processed foods.** Most of our daily sodium intake comes from the salt added to breads, cereals, processed meats, cheeses, sodas, canned foods, soups, snacks, and restaurant and fast food meals. Here's one tip: Discard the salty liquid in canned vegetables or meats.
- **Taste before shaking.** Sample your food; you may find it's seasoned just fine. Or try using a little less each time.
- **Spice it up.** When cooking, replace salt with herbs, spices, garlic, or onion (garlic or onion powder is fine, but not garlic or onion salt), even lemon juice. Regular soy sauce, steak sauce, some mustards, and salted butter, though, are high in sodium.
- **Expect the unexpected.** Mineral water, vitamins, and such medications as antacids and laxatives may contain sodium; check labels. Water-softening filters can also add substantial amounts to your tap water.

Labels for less

Check food labels carefully. Products with labels stating "salted," "with added salt," "double salted," or "extra salted" are exempt from listing their sodium and potassium content. Here are some other label definitions:

- **"Sodium-free"** or **"salt-free"** has less than 5 mg per 100 gram serving
- **"Low sodium"** or **"low salt"** or **"light in salt/sodium"** contains no added sodium *and* at least 50 percent less than a comparison food *and* no more than 40 mg in a 100 gram serving (except for cheddar cheese, meat, poultry, and fish)
- **"Less sodium than"** or **"lightly salted"** has at least 25 percent less in a serving than a comparison food and at least 100 mg less per serving
- **"Unsalted"** or **"no salt added"** has no added salt or sodium

A bag of microwave popcorn may contain more than 1,000 mg of sodium. So there's absolutely no need to add salt.

Saunas & Steam Rooms

Aaahhhhh, a sauna. Stress just melts away. Muscle kinks dissolve. Sinuses and pores open up. For many people, spending time in a sauna or steam room is both relaxing and invigorating. But it's not safe for everyone, and certain precautions should be followed.

Splashing cold water on hot myths

In the heat of a sauna or steam room, the body cools down by sweating. To make more sweat, the heart beats faster, in order to circulate more blood to the skin. But all that sweating and heart pumping isn't aerobic exercise, and can't replace it. Just sitting there doesn't make your muscles burn more oxygen.

It's not a safe or effective way to lose weight, either. Any weight lost is water weight, which is quickly restored. Excessive use of saunas to lose weight can be very dangerous. Nor can sitting in a sauna "sweat away toxins." In healthy people, the kidneys filter out metabolic waste. People with kidney damage may be helped somewhat by sweating, if their doctors advise it.

So what's the benefit? It's relaxing. It limbers up the muscles, especially if you also stretch. It temporarily makes the skin look better. And after a workout, it just feels good.

Steam savvy

Prolonged exposure to a sauna's dry or steam heat can overtax the body's capacity to regulate its temperature, causing dehydration and fainting. Heat stroke, in which your body's temperature can climb to 42°C (106°F), is also a threat. Look out for reduced sweating, rapid heartbeat, and skin that suddenly becomes hot, flushed, and dry. Symptoms also include feeling faint or disoriented. Heat stroke is an emergency; get out immediately, cool down, and seek medical help.

For healthy men and women, though, a few precautions make saunas safe:

- **Don't stay in longer than 10 to 15 minutes.** If you start to feel at all uncomfortable, flushed, or hot, leave.
- **Keep the sauna temperature low.** For a "dry" sauna, set no higher than 82°C (180°F); for a "wet" sauna or steam room, no higher than 49°C (120°F). Beware that the saunas at some health clubs may be set higher.
- **Turn down the humidity.** Higher humidity impairs your ability to sweat. Plus, wet heat is more apt to burn the skin than dry heat.
- **Sit on a towel.** Unclean surfaces in a sauna can harbor bacteria and transmit infection.
- **Drink some water.** Hydrate before, during, and after steaming to restore fluids.
- **Don't steam right after a workout.** Cool down for 20 to 30 minutes first.
- **Don't eat or drink alcohol beforehand.** Digesting food and alcohol steals blood from the skin, where it helps cool you down. Alcohol can also make you sleepy and unaware of overheating.

Not for Everyone

Saunas and steam rooms are off-limits for pregnant women. The extreme heat can damage a young fetus' brain or spinal cord and may significantly increase the risk of birth defects.

Young children, older adults, and people with diabetes are also susceptible to extreme heat. In addition, a sauna's heat may aggravate a heart condition or circulatory problem, high or low blood pressure, arthritis, and some skin conditions.

CAUTION!
The popular sauna technique, which originated in Finland, of jumping directly from a hot sauna into ice-cold water is not recommended. It can be very dangerous for anyone with cardiovascular problems.

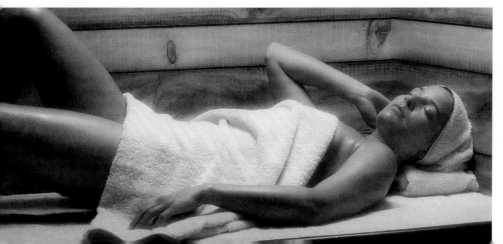

It feels good, relaxes muscles, and makes the skin glow, but a sauna is no substitute for working out.

Seat Belts

Don't Bag the Belt

Air bags are not a substitute for seat belts. Seat belts protect you from all sorts of collisions while most air bags are deployed only during front-end impact. Even then, lap and shoulder harnesses can hold passengers clear of the air bag deployment zone, protecting them from serious injury by the bag itself.

Lap and shoulder belts should lie flat against the body; a twisted belt can injure you in an accident. Seats should not be tilted back very far, as your body might be jolted forward in a collision, causing the seat belt to harm organs and the abdomen.

Wearing a seat belt isn't just obeying the laws of the road; it's also defying the laws of physics. When a car is in a head-on collision, it comes to an immediate stop, but the passengers continue moving forward at the vehicle's precrash speed. If the passengers are not restrained by a seat belt (preferably a three-point shoulder-strap/lap-belt combination), they will be propelled forward and will slam into the dashboard or the steering wheel.

In Canada, most people understand the use of seat belts is essential for passenger safety. Since 1988, there has been a 20 percent increase in the number of Canadians using seat belts. A 1997 Transport Canada report states that more than 90 percent of car occupants now wear seat belts.

Transport Canada and the provinces have initiated the National Occupant Restraint Program (NORP) to promote seat-belt safety and to increase the percentage of those using seat belts. It is estimated that an increase of only one percent can save 500 lives a year.

Playing it safe

How you wear your seat belt can impact its effectiveness and safety. When you put your lap belt on, make sure it's strapped as low as it can go. In an accident at 48 kilometers per hour (30 miles per hour), the belt restrains

Jet Sot

Some airlines are now encouraging passengers to wear seat belts at all times during flights. They say that passengers who stay buckled up can avoid injuries from sudden jolts during unexpected turbulence, while unsecured passengers may be thrown from their seats and injured. Airplane seat belts should be fastened snugly across your lap any time you are seated.

your body with a force that can reach 20 times your body weight. As speed increases, so does the restraining impulse. Not surprisingly, your abdomen and organs can't withstand that degree of force. Wearing the belt low, across the stronger hip area, can prevent internal injuries.

If the shoulder harness doesn't fit you comfortably, don't slip it under your arm. That will place the belt across your abdomen, diaphragm, and lungs, all of which are more likely to be damaged by the jolt of an accident than the collarbone and sternum are. Many newer-model cars have adjustable shoulder harnesses that eliminate this problem.

Babies on board

If you're pregnant, you must wear a seat belt. A three-point restraint is safest for mother and fetus, even during an accident. Place the shoulder strap between the breasts and the lap belt under the abdomen as low as possible.

For babies, rear-facing infant seats are the safest. Properly strapped in, they decrease an infant's chances of serious crash-related injuries or fatalities by an average 70 percent. Toddlers who weigh 9 to 18 kilograms (20 to 40 pounds) need a convertible (or combination) forward-facing seat. (Check the car's owner's manual to see whether you need a special locking clip to secure the seat with the seat belts.) Children weighing 18 to 27 kilograms (40 to 60 pounds) can use a booster seat. Larger kids should use regular seat belts. (See page 77 for child safety seats.)

Secondhand Smoke

Where there's smoke, there's fire. And where there's secondhand smoke, there's a firestorm of controversy. Actually, there's not much to argue about when it comes to the dangers of secondhand smoke; study after study makes the case that they are real. The controversy has more to do with the extent and the nature of the harm nonsmokers suffer when exposed to such smoke. And recent research indicates that nonsmokers have more reason than ever to avoid it.

More risk, more ways

Secondhand, or "sidestream," smoke may be even more dangerous than mainstream smoke inhaled by a smoker. Cigarettes are designed to draw smoke through a cooling and filtering mechanism on its way into the lungs. About two-thirds of this smoke is not inhaled by the smoker, but may find its way into the surrounding air where it enters a nonsmoker's lungs. Such unfiltered smoke may contain as many as 50 chemicals identified as cancer-causing agents.

Scientific studies have convincingly linked sidestream smoke with lung cancer. More than 300 lung-cancer deaths per year in Canada may be attributed to secondhand smoke. What's worse is that its damaging impact is not restricted to the lungs. The heart and the arteries may also be harmed.

Research shows that heart disease may pose even more of a threat than lung cancer to exposed nonsmokers, or "passive smokers." A U.S. study tracked the health of 32,000 nurses who never smoked over the course of 10 years. It found that regular exposure to secondhand smoke at home or work doubled the risk of heart disease. Another U.S. study found that nonsmokers exposed to passive smoke for 20 hours per week experienced 20 percent more hardening of the arteries than a nonsmoking control group.

Along with lung cancer and heart disease, some research has indicated that passive smoke exacerbates symptoms in people suffering from asthma, bronchitis, and middle ear infections. Secondhand smoke has also been linked to cancers of the sinuses, brain, breast, uterus, and cervix, and to leukemia.

Children are at particular risk from secondhand smoke, because their bodies are still developing. Parents who smoke are offering their offspring what Health Canada terms "a lethal legacy." Children exposed to smoke at home are high-risk candidates for respiratory illnesses, such as asthma, bronchitis, and heart disease.

What about secondhand smoke from cigars? Is it equally damaging? Some cigar smokers mistakenly believe their habit is less harmful than cigarette smoking because they don't inhale. Evidence has shown that a cigar contains more carcinogens than a cigarette and emits far more carbon monoxide—all of which can be inhaled secondhand by the smoker or anyone else in the same room.

Breathing free

With so many reasons to avoid secondhand smoke, your best course of action may be to persuade your family, friends, or co-workers to quit. If this doesn't work, the next best thing is to steer clear of smoke-filled rooms.

But what if that smoke-filled room is not a bar or restaurant that you can choose not to frequent but your own home, in which family members or visitors smoke? First, don't depend on air filters or so-called smokeless ashtrays. Neither will filter out the toxins in smoke. Instead, set aside a smoke-free zone, preferably a room with ventilation and windows, and persuade household smokers to respect it. Or send smokers outside, where they can light up without harming others.

CAUTION!
One study has shown that passive smokers had very low blood levels of vitamin C, an antioxidant that fights cancer and heart disease. You may be able to offset some of the harmful effects of secondhand smoke by taking additional vitamin C.

Cigarette smoke is rife with dangerous free radicals, which can cause cellular damage that is linked with chronic disease.

Sex

A sign of a loving commitment, a bout of physical pleasure, a moral and emotional minefield—sex is a lot of things to a lot of people. And although humans have played the game of love throughout the ages, the rules keep changing. On the one hand, an enlightened understanding of this instinctive act—which, after all, ensures the survival of our species—has eroded the stigma that was once attached to it. On the other hand, social shifts have meant an increase in the incidence of sexually transmitted diseases (STDs). To enjoy the benefits of sex, you need not only the right relationship but also the right information.

Research suggests that oxytocin, a hormone released during sexual contact, helps a couple to bond emotionally.

The pleasure principle

Consider the myriad ways sex can improve your life and health. Regular, loving sexual activity typically characterizes successful long-term relationships. Besides enhancing the connection with your mate, sex has the power to relieve stress. (This assumes that both partners are satisfied with their sex lives. If sexual issues are creating problems, they should seek counseling.)

Beyond the emotional and psychological aspects, there are significant physical benefits (aside from the obvious) to be derived from sexual activity. Sex increases certain hormone levels in both men and women. Men manufacture more testosterone, which sustains the sex drive and helps maintain bone and muscle. Women experience a rise in estrogen, which researchers associate with protection of the heart and respiratory system.

Other chemicals released in the body during arousal and orgasm can provide natural pain relief. Researchers believe that the analgesic effects can mitigate a variety of ailments, including arthritis and headaches.

Because sexual intercourse empties fluids held in the prostate gland, experts also credit regular sex with helping to protect the health of a man's prostate.

Playing it safe

For all the positive factors associated with sex, there are negatives that everyone needs to know. Intimate contact usually entails the exchange not only of affection but also of bodily fluids. These may contain viruses and bacteria that carry STDs, which can have long-term effects varying from inconvenient to fatal. Some of the most common STDs are syphilis, gonorrhea, and chlamydia (bacterial infections); genital herpes and genital warts (viral infections); and hepatitis B and AIDS (potentially fatal, blood-borne viral diseases).

The only surefire way to avoid these diseases is to abstain from sex or to have a mutually monogamous, long-term relationship

Viagra and More: Help for Men and Women

There are some potent treatments for impotence these days. Men have several options. They can inject a prescribed drug directly into their penis to produce an erection moments later. More recent oral alternatives—most notably the breakthrough drug Viagra, which became available in the United States in 1998—affect neurochemicals that help maintain blood flow in the penis. (Be aware that it is dangerous to combine Viagra with certain heart-disease medications, notably nitroglycerin.)

Pharmaceutical firms are also testing drugs, including Viagra, to help women with sexual dysfunction. About 10 percent of women never have orgasms. By increasing blood flow to the genitals, new treatments may make this experience possible for them.

with a disease-free partner. Outside of these situations, the safest way to have sex is to limit the transmission of bodily fluids: use a latex condom that contains a spermicide, preferably nonoxynol-9, during intercourse. Because it's possible that HIV, the AIDS virus, can be transmitted during oral sex, a condom should also be used for this activity; for a woman, a dental dam—a square piece of latex available in some drugstores as well as dental- and medical-supply stores—serves the same purpose. Watch for signs of STDs on a partner's mouth and genitalia, including warts, rashes, and sores. But don't rely on visual cues: STDs often do not exhibit symptoms until they are relatively advanced, and sometimes not at all.

If there is any possibility that you have acquired an STD, have medical tests performed. Remember that all of these diseases can be treated, at least to some extent, and the sooner the better. Untreated STDs can cause such disorders as infertility, childbirth complications, chronic pain, even certain kinds of cancer. See a doctor and inform your partner so he or she can do the same. Do not resume sexual activity until your doctor confirms that it's safe. There is a vaccine for the liver infection hepatitis B, and people who have multiple sex partners are advised to get one.

It's never too late

As the population grays, the concept of "too old for sex" has taken its rightful place on the sidelines. Nevertheless, sexual activity into middle and old age can entail physical challenges. An American study showed that 52 percent of men between 40 and 70 had some erectile dysfunction. Some experts claim as many as one in 10 men go through total erectile dysfuntion by age 60. However, recent medical breakthroughs may alleviate such problems (see box, opposite).

Women can also experience sexual difficulties. Age-related vaginal dryness and thinning of the vaginal walls may cause discomfort during sex, but they can often be helped with hormone-replacement therapy

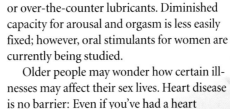

Symptom Sorter

The STD Lineup

If you notice any of the symptoms below and suspect a sexually transmitted disease (STD), consult your doctor immediately.

Syphilis	Painless chancre, or open sore; enlarged lymph nodes; recurring fever and/or rash
Gonorrhea	Painful urination; discharge from penis or vagina; spotty vaginal bleeding; pelvic pain
Chlamydia	Painful urination; discharge from penis or vagina; abdominal pain; itching in the urethra
Genital herpes	Flulike symptoms; painful, recurring genital blisters and sores
Genital warts	Irritation and itching in the genitals; soft, flat growths (warts) on the penis or vagina
Hepatitis B	Flulike symptoms; jaundice; nausea and vomiting
AIDS	Various infections, including thrush, pneumonia, toxoplasmosis; swollen lymph glands; recurrent yeast infections

or over-the-counter lubricants. Diminished capacity for arousal and orgasm is less easily fixed; however, oral stimulants for women are currently being studied.

Older people may wonder how certain illnesses may affect their sex lives. Heart disease is no barrier: Even if you've had a heart attack, the act of sex rarely causes a second heart attack; most patients resume normal relations after three to four months. Stroke rarely impairs sexual function. But diabetes can lead to vaginal dryness or impotence. Some medications, such as blood-pressure drugs, can reduce vaginal lubrication; antidepressants can lower desire or block orgasm.

Your doctor can help you identify the causes of any dysfunction and work with you to try to eliminate barriers to sexual enjoyment.

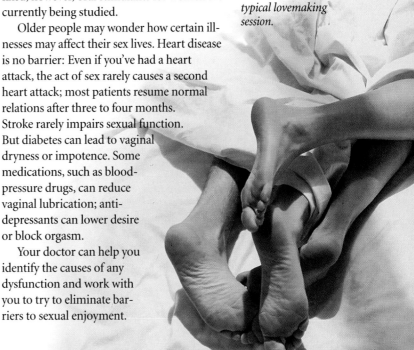

Sex is exercise: You burn about 50 calories in a typical lovemaking session.

Shellfish

Shucked or peeled, sautéed or skewered, shellfish has always had a special place at the dinner table. Wrongly branded a dietary villain for years, it is making a comeback as a heart-healthy food.

Along with your lobster, however, you may be reeling in some risks, including bacteria, viruses, and pollutants. Learning to cook smart can reduce the dangers and keep deep-sea delights on your menu.

CAUTION!

Anyone at risk for gout should always avoid foods high in uric acid, such as shellfish.

A good catch

Shellfish was long thought to contain dangerously high levels of cholesterol, but the levels are actually comparable to those in lean cuts of beef and chicken. Your daily cholesterol intake should not exceed 300 milligrams and saturated fat should be no more than 10 percent of daily calories. So an 85-gram (3-ounce) serving of shrimp (15 shrimp), for example, with 166 milligrams of cholesterol and almost no saturated fat, gets the thumbs-up.

Your heart will love shellfish, too. Studies have shown a significantly reduced risk of sudden cardiac death among men who ate shellfish at least once a week. Further, a joint Rockefeller University/Harvard University study showed that subjects who ate 280 grams (10 ounces) of shrimp daily for three weeks had reduced levels of triglycerides, blood fats that can clog arteries. One reason is that crustaceans (such as lobsters and shrimp) and mollusks (oysters, clams, and mussels) contain omega-3 fatty acids, which may control blood pressure and cholesterol levels. Among shellfish, oysters, mussels, and crabs contain the most. Shellfish is also rich in protein and bone-friendly calcium, as well as zinc (linked with prostate health), iron, and B vitamins. And it is relatively low in sodium and calories.

Bounty from the sea: A steaming pot of shellfish makes a delicious, heart-healthy meal.

Deep-sea dangers

Shellfish are quick to absorb contaminants from the sea, including bacteria, such as salmonella, and viruses, such as hepatitis A. Uncooked oysters may also contain a bacterium called *Vibrio vulnificus,* which can cause serious illness, mainly in people with liver disease, diabetes, gastrointestinal disorders, or compromised immune systems.

Thoroughly cooking oysters and other shellfish usually kills bacteria, although steamed oysters may still contain *V. vulnificus.* Because bacteria thrive in warm water, eat oysters only in the colder months—those with an R in their name—and steam clams at least six minutes to eliminate any bacteria.

If you're careful in preparing your shellfish, the odds are in your favor: studies show that fewer than one-quarter of 1 percent of all food-borne illnesses can be attributed to seafood.

There is one additional worry: Shellfish absorb pollutants if they live in contaminated water. Don't eat the green tomalley, or liver, in lobsters or the "mustard" in blue crabs; they may contain high levels of harmful chemicals known as PCBs or other toxins.

Precautionary measures

Raw shellfish is highly perishable. Keep it from spoiling with these techniques:

- Raw mussels and clams should be alive, with their shells tightly closed, before cooking. Discard those with open shells.
- Store fresh shellfish in the coldest part of the refrigerator as soon as you get home.
- Live shellfish need ventilation. Store in open containers; cover with a damp cloth.
- Eat fresh shellfish within one or two days of purchase.

Skin Ointments & Treatments

Skin isn't just the wrapper we come in. It's a vital organ—our largest one—that regulates body temperature, guards the internal organs, and turns away infectious organisms. It also provides nourishment by converting sunlight into vitamin D. And if we treat it right, skin can be a healthy, attractive reflection of the person inside.

It is also big business. From creams and lotions to chemical peels, an array of products and procedures aims to smooth wrinkles and otherwise restore the glow of youth to aging skin. Some of the most expensive concoctions are harmless but offer few real benefits; others may do more harm than good, especially for people who have sensitive skin. The trick to finding effective treatments for the skin is to learn a little bit about what you're buying.

Moisturizers: daily defense

No matter how careful we are about protecting our skin from the sun, it will still dry and wrinkle over time. Dermatologists recommend using a moisturizer every day to discourage the aging of skin. Moisturizers don't actually add moisture to the skin; rather, they help seal in the moisture that's already there. (That's one reason it's important to drink plenty of water—six to eight glasses a day.) For best results, apply lotion after a shower or bath, when the skin is still damp.

How to choose a moisturizer? Lotions that contain lanolin or petrolatum last longest and are best for extremely dry skin, but they may cause allergic reactions. Some people also find them too thick. For normal to dry skin,

While Retin-A and Renova can improve the overall texture and appearance of skin, imparting a smoother, rosier complexion, they are not proven to remove deeper lines and grooves.

use a lighter lotion with an oil base. People with oily skin should still use a moisturizer, as long as it's water-based (look for "oil-free" on the label). If you have acne, choose one that's "noncomedogenic," which means it won't

clog pores. Finally, remember that more expensive doesn't always mean better. Often price has more to do with packaging and marketing than with the effectiveness of the product. On the other hand, the more expensive brands may contain a finer grade, or density, of ingredients. Base your selection on what works best for your skin.

Feel-good facials

Facial treatments are more luxury than science. Whether made from avocado oil or volcanic mud, a face mask basically cleanses pores and may temporarily increase blood flow to the area, imparting a youthful, albeit short-term, glow. Facials have no lasting impact on wrinkles or dryness.

Abrasive masks, even the so-called natural types, can actually harm the skin by removing too many skin cells too rapidly. The skin already sheds millions of cells daily. Overdoing it can lead to sensitivity, scaly patches, and gray skin tones.

Facial masks can be soothing and relaxing, but they offer few tangible long-term benefits for the skin.

The Retin-A revolution

Retin-A and Renova are brand names for the prescription medication tretinoin, also known as retinoic acid, made from a naturally occurring vitamin A derivative. First used as an acne treatment in 1971, tretinoin was discovered to remove fine lines and wrinkles and was hailed as a miracle antiaging drug. It works by peeling away the dead skin cells of the epidermis (the skin's outer layer) and boosting collagen production in the dermis (the skin that lies below the epidermis). Of course, these products won't give you the

Spotting Age Spots

Age spots, or "liver" spots, have nothing to do with the liver and little to do with age. These harmless changes in skin pigment are caused by sun exposure and occur most often in fair-skinned people. Bleaching creams can lighten the spots, although laser treatment is more effective. A blemish is probably an age spot if:

- It appears on your forehead or the back of your hand.

- It is yellowish, tan, or light brown in color.

- Its color is homogeneous, not variegated. (Age spots come in shapes from round to irregular, and may be the size of a freckle or an overcoat button.)

- There is no growth, soreness, or color change associated with the spot. (If you see any such changes, have the spot evaluated by your physician.)

skin you were born with. While Retin-A and Renova can improve the overall texture and appearance of skin, imparting a smoother, rosier complexion, they are not proven to remove deeper lines and grooves. Moreover, they may dry the skin and cause temporary burning or stinging. Redness, flakiness, and sometimes skin inflammation may occur with overuse. (Renova, which combines tretinoin and an emollient cream, may be less drying.) Tretinoin also makes the skin more sensitive to the sun, so be sure to apply sunblock before going outside when using this medication.

Alpha hydroxy acids

If you've been anywhere near a cosmetics counter or have picked up a women's magazine lately, you've no doubt heard of alpha hydroxy acids (AHAs), acids derived from fruits or milk sugars that claim to make the skin look younger. Do they work? Yes. Like retinoic acid, AHAs strip away dead skin cells and increase the speed at which they are replaced. Unlike retinoic acid, they aren't proven to boost collagen production.

Not all AHA lotions and creams are created equal: some contain much higher concentrations of the acids than others. Under the cosmetics' industry guidelines, AHA concentrations in all over-the-counter products will be limited to 10 percent or less. Some of the creams sold in stores contain no more than 2 or 3 percent. They may cause old cells to be sloughed off, but they won't penetrate as deeply as higher concentrations do.

When buying an over-the-counter alpha hydroxy lotion, look for products with AHA concentrations of 5 to 10 percent. (If the percentage is not listed, make sure the AHA is among the first three ingredients. AHAs go by many names, including glycolic acid, lactic acid, malic acid, citric acid, alpha-hydroxyoctanoic acid, alpha-hydroxycaprylic acid, and fruit acid.)

Some creams prescribed by dermatologists may contain higher concentrations of AHAs (and have a higher pH balance, to offset irritation). AHAs in higher concentrations should be used with care and only under a physician's supervision. Since cosmetic AHAs have

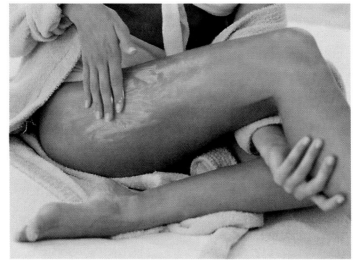

So-called cellulite creams have proved to be of little use in burning off the fatty deposits that show up on hips and thighs. The best defense against cellulite: regular exercise.

Using Alpha Hydroxy Acids

The cosmetic industry offers these guidelines for anyone using alpha hydroxy acids:

- Protect your skin when outdoors. Apply sunscreens with a sun protection factor (SPF) of at least 15 and wear a wide-brimmed hat.

- Buy products with adequate labeling. There should be a list of ingredients, including which AHA or other chemical acids are present and the manufacturer's name and address. Also look for the AHA concentration and pH level (this information is not mandatory). Industry safety recommendations dictate concentrations of 10 percent or less and pH levels of 3.5 or greater.

- Test the product on a small patch of skin when first using it.

Stop using it if you have any adverse reactions at any time; cosmetics should never burn, sting, or cause redness.

- Follow the label instructions, don't exceed recommended amounts, and keep the products away from children.

---

been widely available only since 1992, their long-term effects are not known. Adverse reactions such as severe redness, swelling (especially in the eye region), burning, blistering, bleeding, rashes, itching, and skin discoloration have been reported. Like retinoic acid, AHAs increase the skin's sensitivity to sunlight.

For people content with mild exfoliation, the simplest solution may be a loofah, rough sponge, or granular scrub. All are effective if used gently and with enough water to avoid too much friction. Generally, the fine, smooth grains in synthetic scrubs are actually safer than many natural scrubs, whose jagged-edged grit can cause irritation.

Chemical peels

Chemicals peels, performed by dermatologists and plastic surgeons, involve the application of high-concentration (up to 70 percent) AHAs, which allow the peels to penetrate to the dermis. Chemical peels may be more effective than AHA creams at removing deep wrinkles, but not without considerable side effects: they can cause pain, swelling, and burns, as well as infection and scarring. The skin takes up to two weeks to heal and up to three months to return to a normal color.

Two other procedures, dermabrasion and laser resurfacing, remove the entire epidermis and various portions of the dermis through a process called microsanding. They are commonly used to remove acne scars or fine lines around the mouth. Recently, laser resurfacing has replaced dermabrasion as the safer and more effective method. With dermabrasion, skin may stay pink for about three months, and the patient is often advised to use sunscreen and nonallergenic makeup in the first six months to one year after the procedure. Neither dermabrasion nor laser resurfacing is guaranteed to work, and more than one treatment may be necessary to rid the skin of deep acne scars.

A stitch in time

Skin ointments and treatments can do only so much to renew the skin; preventing skin damage in the first place is easier than reversing it. Experts believe that up to 90 percent of skin damage is due to prolonged sun exposure. Sunscreens that block both UVA and UVB rays are still your best defense. Wear a hat with a wide brim and avoid the sun's rays at their strongest—generally, between 10 A.M. and 3 P.M. Take care of your skin in other ways, too: eat a balanced diet, stay active, get enough rest, shun tobacco, drink alcohol in moderation, and keep weight fluctuations to a minimum.

Alpha hydroxy creams sold over the counter may be weaker in strength than those available from your dermatologist, but some are still modestly effective.

Sleeping Pills

If you've ever spent a night trying in vain to get some sleep, you know how a lack of shut-eye can affect your energy, performance, and mood the next day. That's why many North Americans turn to over-the-counter (OTC) sleeping pills for relief, or to prescription drugs if the problem persists.

Insomnia, whether it lasts for a few days, weeks, or years, affects about one-third of all adults. Stress, depression, and the use of alcohol or certain drugs are common causes. Sleeping pills—even relatively safe OTC types—aren't necessarily the best answer. They do offer short-term relief to help you break a pattern of sleeplessness, but in the end, altering your behavior is a more reliable way to cure insomnia.

Stopgap remedies

The active ingredient in OTC sleeping pills are antihistamines (for example, diphenhydramine hydrochloride or diphenhydramine citrate may be found on the product label). These are the same ingredients found in many cold and allergy pills that make you drowsy. OTC sleeping pills can be helpful on the occasional sleepless night. They may work in part simply by boosting your confidence in your ability to fall asleep.

But sleeping pills can cause unpleasant side effects, such as dry mouth, constipation, blurred vision, and ringing in the ears. Worse, they tend to suppress neurotransmitters in the brain that control breathing, so people with breathing problems should avoid the products, as should anyone with angina, glaucoma, or an enlarged prostate. Pregnant and nursing women are advised to consult with their doctors before taking sleeping pills, and children under 12 should never use them.

Older people have trouble metabolizing sleeping pills; a single dose can remain in their system more than 96 hours. This compromises their alertness the next day and can lead to bone-breaking falls. No one should take sleeping pills with alcohol or antidepressant drugs; the combination could leave you drowsy the next day and lead to accidents.

Prescription drugs: the last resort

If your insomnia lasts a month or more, a prescription drug could kick-start an improved pattern of rest while you begin a behavior-modification program. The widely prescribed medications are benzodiazepines, known as the brand names Valium, Librium, and Ativan, among others. Although they are relatively safe, do not take them for long periods. The drugs can be habit-forming and are ineffective once a person's system becomes accustomed to them. Withdrawal can cause "rebound" insomnia. As with their over-the-counter cousins, the drugs should never be mixed with alcohol or antidepressants. The elderly may experience daytime drowsiness while taking these drugs.

Sleep Soundly Without Pills

Here are several ways, based on sleep-laboratory research, to overcome insomnia without drugs:

- Get up at the same time every day, including weekends, no matter what time you go to bed or fall asleep.

- Avoid alcohol before bedtime. It disrupts the second half of a night's sleep.

- Limit naps during the day.

- Exercise half an hour or more a day, at least three hours before bedtime.

- Relax near bedtime. Try a warm bath, a small snack, or a spray of lavender oil in your bedroom.

- Don't stay in bed if you can't sleep. Get up and read or listen to quiet music until you're drowsy.

- Try not to fret if you can't sleep. One sleepless night will affect you less than too much worrying will.

A darkened room can help you get to sleep. Put up window shades that block out light.

Smoked & Cured Foods

Smoked and cured foods are highly prized for their flavor, but they won't win any prizes for their effects on your health. Stomach cancer deaths in Japan outnumber all other cancer deaths combined; according to scientific surveys, this high rate may be caused in part by the Japanese diet, which is rich in smoked, salted, pickled, and barbecued foods. Research has suggested that there may be possible links with other cancers as well.

The problems with preserving

Foods were once cured by various methods—smoking (slow drying over fire at low temperatures), air drying (dehydrating), and salt curing (using salt or a brine solution to kill bacteria)—as a way to preserve them. Today, however, most curing is done with additives.

Some scientists are concerned that curing methods may jeopardize your health. Smoked foods contain cancer-causing substances called polycyclic aromatic hydrocarbons (PAHs). The more smoke used, the greater the buildup of PAHs. Yet recent studies by the Health Protection Branch of Health Canada examined PAHs in smoked fish, shellfish, charbroiled meats and cured meats sold in Canada, and the results revealed very low levels that do not pose any long-term health risk.

Another ingredient added to such foods as bologna, bacon, hot dogs, sausages, ham, and salami are nitrites. These preservatives keep meat from turning gray; they also prevent contamination by such bacteria as *Clostridium botulinum* (which causes botulism). While nitrates have been linked to the formation of carcinogenic nitrosamines in some laboratory animals, they have never actually posed a serious threat

Ripened cheeses are cured by aging. Since they have less lactose than fresh cheeses, they are easier to digest for people who are lactose intolerant.

to our health—indeed, 80 percent of the average per capita intake of nitrates comes from our own saliva.

Cured foods like pickles, sauerkraut, and olives pose yet another problem: they are extremely high in sodium, which can be bad for people with high blood pressure and others who need to limit the amount of salt in their diet.

Must smoking end?

North Americans are eating fewer smoked and cured foods. Researchers credit the trend to increased consumption of fresh produce and less reliance on preserved foods. In Canada, the use of nitrates and nitrites in cured meat products has become strictly regulated and manufacturers may only use up to the maximum permitted levels stipulated in the Canada Food and Drugs Act and Regulations. Most manufacturers now replace the smoking process with the addition of "liquid smoke," which provides flavor without nitrates. And many home smokers now use a cold- or liquid-curing process that is smoke-free.

In the end, an occasional serving of bacon or smoked trout won't harm you. But don't overdo it. And counter the effects of any smoked and cured foods you do indulge in by eating a diet high in fiber, fruits and vegetables, and antioxidants, such as vitamins A, E, and C.

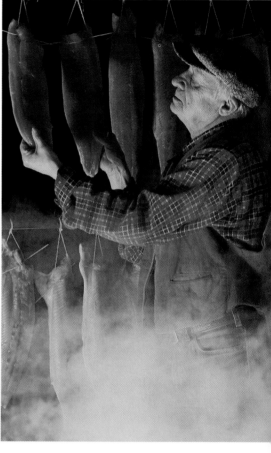

Some smoked food, such as this fish, is eaten without reheating. However, cold-smoked meats may need further cooking; follow the package directions. Home-smoked food should reach an internal temperature of 68°C (155°F).

CAUTION!

Tyramine, a substance found in aged and fermented foods, can trigger migraines in people who are susceptible.

Snoring

Wives may be tortured by it more than husbands, but the noisy, nerve-racking reality is that almost half of all adults snore at least occasionally. A quarter of all adults snore habitually. Most of them are men or over age 50 or overweight.

Snoring is an annoyance: some couples are forced to sleep in separate bedrooms; some friends who travel together have to rent two rooms. But it can also be an alarm call. Severe snoring may indicate sleep apnea, a condition in which breathing often stops between snores for 10 seconds to two minutes at a time.

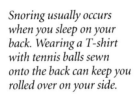

Snoring usually occurs when you sleep on your back. Wearing a T-shirt with tennis balls sewn onto the back can keep you rolled over on your side.

What's that racket?

Snoring is caused by disruption of the airflow through the back of the mouth and nose, where the tongue and upper throat meet the soft palate and uvula (the soft tissue that dangles from the roof of the mouth). There are different reasons someone might snore. The muscles of the upper throat may be weak, allowing the tongue, soft palate, and uvula to sag and block the airway; they then vibrate as air is forced past them. Alcohol, drugs, and deep sleep can further relax the muscles so that they sag even more.

Anything that narrows the airway, including sinus congestion, also makes the problem worse. Your airway may be narrowed if you smoke, have allergies, are overweight, or have large tonsils, a long soft palate or uvula, or a nasal deformity, such as a deviated septum (an irregularity in the wall between the two nostrils).

When snoring is more than annoying

People who snore loudly enough to keep others awake or who snore even when sleeping on their side should see a sleep specialist to rule out sleep apnea. In the short term, this syndrome merely causes fatigue; in the long term, such complications as high blood pressure and an enlarged heart may develop. Other common side effects include loss of energy, drowsiness while driving or watching television, memory loss, irritability, depression, decreased interest in sex, morning headaches, and obesity.

Quieting the nightly storm

Medical remedies for snoring include removing the tonsils or adenoids (a pair of swellings at the back of the nose that normally disappear by puberty) or undergoing a series of laser treatments to tighten throat tissue or pare away excess tissue.

If the diagnosis is sleep apnea, a nasal mask that increases air pressure in the throat can be used each night. If that is not helpful, medication may be prescribed. As a last resort, surgery may be recommended to clear the airways. But if the person is overweight, a rigorous diet and exercise program should be tried before other remedies, since weight reduction sometimes relieves the condition.

---

an ounce of **Prevention**

How to Silence the Snoring

For quieter nights, try these tips:

- Eat a light dinner at least three hours before you turn in.

- Avoid alcohol for at least four hours before bedtime.

- Go to sleep and wake up at the same time every day.

- Raise the head of your bed 8 to 10 centimeters (3 or 4 inches).

- If you're overweight or a smoker, go on a fitness regimen to firm up, lose weight, and stop smoking.

- Try specially designed adhesive strips that lift the nostrils to allow more air to pass through the breathing pathway.

- Avoid other antisnoring devices (some 300 have been patented). They usually work only by keeping you awake.

Soaps & Detergents

We are a well-scrubbed nation, using millions of liters of soaps and detergents annually to wash our laundry and stay clean from head to toe. But our zeal for cleanliness may actually strip the skin of natural oils and cause our clothes to make us itch.

The dope on soap

Soap is a combination of fats and alkalis. Some brands also contain perfumes and deodorizers, but even those that don't still remove dirt. What many soaps also remove is moisture. For no matter what the package says, soaps do not moisturize, although superfatted products such as Dove may deposit fat or cream that helps retain moisture. Of course soaps containing oils, fats, and cold cream may also be less effective at cleaning than regular soaps, since a product cannot simultaneously remove dirt and deposit moisture-retaining cream or fat.

People who have dry or sensitive skin should avoid deodorant and antibacterial soaps, which contain chemicals that may cause an allergic reaction to light. Reducing the skin's normal bacteria may also lead to infections. It is important to rinse well after bathing to remove soap's alkaline residue. This can disrupt the skin's natural acid balance, causing drying and chapping.

Laundry detergents once contained phosphates, which are harmful to the environment; most no longer do.

Ideally you should bathe no more than once a day. One exception to this rule is hand washing. Washing your hands several times a day with soap rids them of germs that transmit colds, the flu, and other ills.

Detergent dangers

Unlike bath soaps, laundry detergents contain strong chemicals and can, in fact, be poisonous if ingested, so store them out of children's reach. Some leave a residue on clothes that may cause rashes or other allergic reactions. If you have sensitive skin, avoid brands containing dyes, and look for "fragrance free" products. ("Unscented" items may have masking fragrances.) Or you may want to choose a laundry soap made for baby clothes (Ivory Snow is one).

Laundry soap is gentler than laundry detergent. However, if you have hard water, soap may leave a scum on clothing. You can eliminate this by adding $\frac{1}{2}$ cup white vinegar to your rinse water (put it in the fabric softener dispenser if your washer has one).

In the dishwasher

Dishwasher detergents often contain chlorine or sodium hydroxide; both chemicals may leave a film on dishes, so make sure your dishwasher rinses well. (One way is to use very hot water.) If you have soft water, try using less than the recommended amount of detergent. Or you can forgo detergent by using a mix of 1 tablespoon each borax and washing soda. If spots are a problem, add 1 cup white vinegar to the rinse compartment.

Glycerine soaps are among the mildest. As facial soaps, they may be a good choice for people with normal or oily skin.

The Antibacterial Bandwagon

Antibacterial soaps are luring more and more consumers by claiming to protect against bacterial infection. Some promise to kill viruses, too. But research shows that these soaps offer little benefit beyond that of ordinary soap unless you have an open cut or are immunocompromised (that's why they are used in hospitals). Experts also worry that the soaps may encourage the growth of resistant bacteria.

What about alcohol wipes and "instant hand sanitizers" (which also contain alcohol)? They won't remove dirt but may be handy for killing germs when you don't have access to soap and water.

Soft Drinks

A cool, refreshing soft drink can really hit the spot. As with most dietary indulgences, downing one now and then won't hurt you. But too much of a good thing can upset your nutritional balance, especially if it keeps you from drinking water and other, more nutritious, beverages.

Check the label: In addition to sugar and caffeine, some soft drinks may contain a fair amount of sodium.

How empty can calories get?

A typical 350-milliliter (12-ounce) soft drink contains 140 calories and the equivalent of about 3 tablespoons of sugar. It has virtually no nutritional value. For those who drink several soft drinks a day, the empty calories can add up.

Switching to a diet soda will help. They are mostly water, and the calories drop to one or two. Just be sure you're not totally replacing more nutritious drinks. Citrus juices are high in vitamin C and folic acid, for instance, while fortified skim milk provides protein, riboflavin, calcium, and vitamins A and D.

Even though they are low in calories, diet soft drinks may not facilitate weight loss. Although Canadians are drinking more of them, weight maintenance remains a problem. Almost 35 percent of Canadian adults are overweight. If you are watching your calories, water may be a better choice. Why? It's better at quenching thirst. Often, "hunger" pains actually signal a mild state of dehydration. Reaching for a cool glass of water rather than a soft drink may be a more effective way to curb your appetite.

Caffeinated soft drinks, regular or diet, are dehydrating. Caffeine acts as a diuretic, so your body loses fluid and you feel thirstier. It also may make you jittery: at 40 to 50 mg of caffeine in 350 milliliters (12 ounces), a soda

Soda Substitutes

- Drink a full glass of water, then wait 20 minutes; you are likely to find your thirst is quenched. (You may also feel less hungry.)

- Fruit juices are rich in nutrients—and calories. They're good for you in moderation.

- Herbal teas, cold or hot, can satisfy your thirst.

- For a bit of fizz, try fruit-flavored sparkling water, but check calories on labels.

has less caffeine than coffee but still enough to overstimulate children, who weigh much less, and some adults, too.

Bad news for bones, bowels, and teeth

While moderate consumption of soft drinks is an innocuous habit, there are reasons to be concerned about excessive intake. Colas are rich in phosphates, which in excess cause calcium to be released from bones into the bloodstream, theoretically weakening bones and increasing the risk of osteoporosis. Moderate consumption appears to be safe: a recent study of women aged 44 to 98 found no loss of bone density from drinking one soda a day or less.

Several of the artificial food colors in soft drinks are considered to be possible carcinogens, which also argues for moderation in your intake of these beverages. And the high-fructose syrups used in them can trigger irritable bowel syndrome in some people.

Sugary soft drinks can also promote tooth decay, especially in children, whose tooth structure is still developing. The problem is not so much the amount of sugar found in soft drinks, but the length of time it stays in contact with the teeth. It encourages the growth of plaque, which produces an acid that eats away at tooth enamel. For this reason, sipping a soft drink over the course of an hour sustains the destructive action on teeth longer than eating a candy bar in five minutes. Even diet soft drinks, which don't contain sugar, still expose teeth to acids that may damage enamel.

A soothing sip for the queasy

There is also an upside to soft drinks. The quick energy derived from a soda's sugar can be beneficial in some cases: doctors may suggest soft drinks, for instance, for people who are temporarily unable to tolerate solid foods. Soft drinks (especially noncaffeinated ones) can also help replace some of the liquids lost from vomiting or diarrhea. And ginger ale and cola, if allowed to go flat, may help quell nausea in some people.

Cultivated around the world, the soybean is a miracle food—an inexpensive and nutrient-packed source of protein. Soy-based foods are a staple in many Asian diets, and researchers believe that is part of the reason why people in these countries often enjoy significantly lower rates of heart disease and breast, prostate, and colon cancer. Soy may also protect against osteoporosis.

With so many health benefits to recommend it, soy deserves a place in your shopping cart. Soybeans (dried, canned, and frozen), sprouts, soy milk, soy protein powder, miso, tofu, tempeh, and soy flour are available at many grocery stores.

The heart-healthy cancer fighter

Soy contains proteins and plant estrogens that benefit the heart and boost resistance to cancer. In a landmark 1995 analysis, researchers culled results from 38 different studies and found that in most studies of people with high cholesterol, adding soy to the diet lowered potentially harmful LDL cholesterol by 13 percent while leaving levels of beneficial HDL unchanged. On average, eating 25 grams of soy protein each day lowered cholesterol by 9 points. Although people with normal or borderline cholesterol (under 200 or so) don't get the same cholesterol reduction from soy, they achieve other health-related benefits when they use it to replace artery-clogging animal protein in meals.

In addition to protein, soy contains plant estrogens (isoflavones). Like human estrogen, isoflavones inhibit bone loss and thus may help prevent osteoporosis. They may also fight cancer. Soy's main isoflavone, genistein, suppresses proteins that protect cancer cells from the immune system. That allows the body to more easily destroy errant cells.

How much is enough?

To benefit from this mostly low-fat, cholesterol-free protein source, eat three to seven servings of soy products a week. To lower elevated cholesterol, you'll need about half a cup of tofu, two to three cups of soy milk, or 28 grams (1 ounce) of soy protein powder a day.

The best sources of soy protein are made by water extraction. Alcohol extraction, used for such products as meat or cheese substitutes, strips the beneficial isoflavones away. Check the labels carefully: If a product says "soy protein concentrate," it is made by alcohol extraction; you'll still get the soy protein but not the protective plant estrogens.

It's easy to use soy in recipes. Toss textured soy protein instead of ground meat into pasta sauces and chili. Tofu (soybean curd) makes a tasty stir-fry and substitutes well in recipes for cream cheese. Miso (fermented soybean paste) makes a good soup base. Grill tempeh (fermented soybean cakes) like burgers, pour soy milk on your cereal, and sprinkle soy powder into smoothies to add richness.

Tofu comes in different levels of firmness; some are great for stir-frys, others for cheesecake. Although the fat in tofu is mostly unsaturated, which won't harm your heart, do be aware of fat grams if you are on a diet.

Fresh or frozen soybeans are good either boiled or steamed as a side dish, or added to soups.

A Replacement for Estrogen?

Nutrients in soy imitate properties of the hormone estrogen and can alleviate the symptoms of menopause, especially night sweats and hot flashes. In fact, soy is being studied as a natural alternative to estrogen replacement therapy, since, unlike estrogen, it does not increase the risk of breast cancer.

Space Heaters

CAUTION!

If the flame of your portable kerosene heater flares uncontrollably, don't try to pick up the heater or move it. You could be burned or splash fuel that may feed the fire. If the heater has a manual shutoff switch, and you can reach it without getting burned, use it. If that doesn't work, clear the area immediately and call the fire department.

The chill of a fall day may put you in the market for a portable space heater, one of the most convenient and inexpensive ways to stay warm. Whether kerosene-burning or electric, space heaters provide an immediate blast of heat where you want it, when you want it.

But if used improperly, space heaters can pose a safety hazard. Space heaters are more likely to cause fires than central heating, according to fire safety experts. Despite an array of warning labels and safety enhancements—from automatic tip-over shutoffs to coil-covering grates—they still pose serious fire risks with careless use. Learn to operate and maintain your heater correctly, to keep your home warm—and safe.

kerosene heater is clean and set to the correct level and that there are no fuel leaks.

- Place the heater about 1 meter (3 feet) from combustible items (curtains, papers). Never drape wet clothes over the heater.
- Don't use flammable products (aerosol sprays, solvents, or lacquers) near the heater.
- Don't leave home or go to sleep with the heater on. Doing so increases the risk of fire or carbon monoxide poisoning.

Electric warmth

Some homes are heated solely by electricity, with central heating units that distribute heat via hot-air ducts, hot-water pipes, or baseboards. But plug-in portable electric space heaters are also very popular. Although electric space heaters don't use flammable fuel, as kerosene ones do, they do use a lot of power, so they can tax old or faulty wiring, creating a fire risk. If other appliances will be on the same circuit, don't buy a heater rated higher than 1,000 watts.

Open the window a crack

Many households use space heaters fueled by wood, kerosene, propane or natural gas. While several of these fuels burn cleanly, without soot, any burning fossil fuel releases potentially deadly gases, particularly carbon monoxide, so proper ventilation is essential. Experts recommend 6 square centimeters (1 square inch) of window opening for every 1,000 BTU your heater puts out. Also install a carbon monoxide detector.

Never leave a space heater on unattended, especially when children and pets are around.

Get cozy, but don't start a fire

Look for the Canadian Standards Association certification when buying a space heater, and give the owner's manual a thorough read once you buy it. After that, your best guide to maintaining safety is plain old common sense. Some guidelines for using space heaters:

- Don't use a space heater as your primary heat source, except in emergencies.
- Check electric models for frayed or loose wires; make sure that the wick of a

Keep your kerosene clear

Fuel your heater with kerosene only. Mixing kerosene with another fuel creates the risk of fire or explosion because the fuel may burn hotter and more rapidly than the heater was designed for. Finally, never replenish fuel indoors or when the heater is hot. Let it cool at least 15 minutes before refueling. Stop at or below the "full" line. Kerosene expands as it heats up; if the heater is too full the fuel can spill over and increase the risk of fire.

Sport Utility Vehicles

North Americans are having a love affair with the sport utility vehicle (SUV), and and their passion has a lot do the vehicle's size and utility, not to mention its stylish, tough-guy exterior. Although the size and strength of this off-road truck masks an underlying vulnerability—increased risk of rollovers—it is still safe for its drivers and passengers. As a class, SUVs have the lowest fatality rates of any type of passenger vehicle, even figuring in their higher rollover rate.

For drivers and passengers of other cars, it's a different story. In a crash involving a passenger car and an SUV, the fatality rate in passenger cars is four times greater than in SUVs. Fortunately, newer models in the works may address this problem.

Fatal encounters

Smaller, lighter cars are naturally more vulnerable in collisions with bigger vehicles. The lighter the car, the heavier the casualties. Studies show that drivers of lighter cars run a 50 percent higher risk of dying than drivers of larger, midsize cars. SUVs, with about a 450-kilogram (1,000-pound) advantage over the average car, are a major force on the road.

It's not just the SUV's weight but its higher front end and stiffer frame design that may account for this. A study by the U.S. Insurance Institute for Highway Safety found that car occupants were 20 times more likely to die when hit broadside by an SUV than the SUV occupants.

Making SUVs safer for everyone

To help level the playing field, automakers are looking at ways to narrow the disparity between SUVs and cars. One consideration is to make small passenger cars heavier. Efforts are being made to fashion lower bumpers and lighter frames for SUVs while retaining their ground clearance and interior space. There's even talk of putting an exterior air bag up front. Manufacturers, of course, want to retain the construction elements that make riding in an SUV safe and practical for its occupants.

On a roll

SUVs are two and a half times more likely than passenger cars to roll over in emergency situations. Experts say the SUV's high center of gravity makes it less stable and harder to maneuver when trying to avoid a crash, resulting in a greater risk of rollover. Still, SUV occupants account for only 14 percent of rollover deaths; passenger-car occupants account for 52 percent. According to one report, 60 percent of SUV rollover deaths occur when someone is ejected from the vehicle—an unlikely event if seat belts are worn.

Rides great, less polluting

Foes claim that SUVs are gas-guzzling, polluting hazards; manufacturers point out that new SUVs run considerably cleaner. Environmentalists also decry off-road abuse: While only 33 percent of SUV owners drive off-road, those who do have been accused of eroding soil and vegetation and damaging wildlife habitats. Enjoy the ride, but not on someone else's home.

Heavy Hitters

Sport utility vehicles and other light trucks make up only one-third of passenger vehicles, but they are involved in more than half of multiple-vehicle crashes that cause fatalities, according to the U.S. National Highway Traffic Safety Administration.

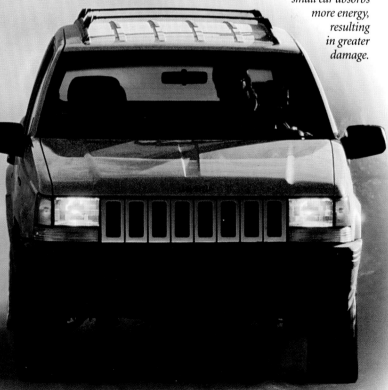

Being struck in the side by an SUV is one of the worst types of collision for a small car. The stiff construction of many light-truck frames allows little "give" in a crash. The small car absorbs more energy, resulting in greater damage.

Sports

CAUTION!

If you are a man over the age of 40 or a woman over the age of 50—or a person of any age who has been sedentary for several years—get an okay from you doctor before beginning a fitness routine.

Is fitness drudgery? Not if you are getting fit playing a sport that you love. For instance, swimming provides a complete balanced workout, stimulating cardiovascular fitness, muscle strength, and flexibility. On the other hand, golf is relaxing but improves circulation only if you walk. All sports entail risk of injury (some more than others), but the benefits usually far outweigh the dangers.

Sore muscles, healthy hearts

Twenty percent of Canadians are involved in competitive sports. Sometimes, the fun and sweat results in sports-related injuries—the most common are sprained ligaments and pulled muscles. To greatly minimize these risks, choose the right sport for your needs, learn it well (including safety precautions), and wear appropriate protective equipment.

The benefits of sports are legion. Regular physical activity lowers the risks of cardiovascular and lung diseases, diabetes, and osteoporosis. It's essential for weight control and eases the pain of osteoarthritis. It also enhances life by reducing stress, increasing energy, elevating mood, bettering self-image, improving appearance, stimulating creativity, and reinforcing such healthy lifestyle changes as eating right and quitting smoking.

Which sport is right for you? Whichever one you like well enough to stick with, although various health concerns may influence your decision (see box, page 309). The key is to design a plan that *(continued)*

After warming up, you can significantly increase your flexibility by stretching: Hold each stretch for 20 to 30 seconds, to the point of tightness but not pain.

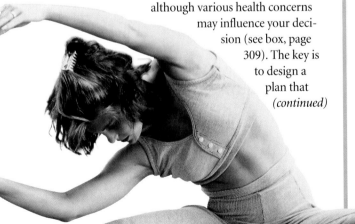

an ounce of Prevention

The Dos and Don'ts of Stretching

Flexibility is an important part of injury prevention, and you're never too old to improve it by stretching regularly. When done right, stretching may help lengthen muscles, increase range of motion, improve speed and agility, and relieve tension. Done improperly, it can do more harm than good. Follow these tips to get the most out of stretching:

• DO warm up before stretching. Five minutes of aerobic activity (brisk walking, jogging, jumping rope, etc.) increases the flow of blood to the muscles before they are stretched. Stretch after exercise, too.

• DO stretch the larger muscle groups first, going through the full range of motion for each group. Match your stretches to the demands of your sport.

• DO hold a stretch for about 20 seconds. Time is essential for muscle tissue to lengthen safely.

• DO stretch every day, if possible, or at least three or four times a week.

• DON'T bounce. Quick, jerky stretching is hard on the joints and can tear muscle fibers, causing scar tissue to develop. Stretch slowly and deliberately.

• DON'T hold your breath while in a stretch. Inhale and exhale naturally.

• DON'T keep stretching if it is painful. Any discomfort you feel should be mild and brief.

Sports (continued)

Are Intense Sports Healthy?

Walking, hiking, golf: Today's popular sports emphasize moderate physical activity. That's good for the heart and for longevity, especially if you've been sedentary. But what if you're already in good shape—are there added benefits to more intense workouts? Probably. The more you run—even up to 50 miles a week—the higher your levels of HDL ("good") cholesterol. To be safe, though, build up your fitness level slowly.

emphasizes your favorite sport while meeting fitness goals. For your heart, try to accumulate at least 30 minutes of moderate physical activity on most days. Building muscular strength and endurance is also important, as is stretching for flexibility.

Let's say you like soccer and play it once a week. You're getting a great cardiovascular workout and good lower-body strength training. If you also swim twice a week to promote cardiovascular health, upper-body strength, and flexibility, your fitness regimen will be more complete. If you add a few brisk walks, including stretches, even better.

Young hearts at play

Kids love to run and play sports. But television and other distractions have made today's children increasingly sedentary. The Canadian Fitness and Lifestyle Research Institute

Wearing a helmet while cycling reduces the risk of head injury by up to 85 percent. To prevent hand cramps and shoulder strain, ride upright, not hunched.

estimates that 66 percent of Canada's youths are not active enough to set a foundation for their future well-being and health.

Playing sports can get kids in shape and provide lasting benefits. For example, young athletes tend to have lower blood-cholesterol and blood-pressure levels than their sedentary peers, reducing heart disease risk later on. By playing sports, girls build not only self-esteem but bone density, which helps prevent osteoporosis decades later. Here's how parents can encourage safe participation in sports:

- **Make sports fun.** Be supportive and don't put pressure on your child to excel. Winning is fun, but pressure isn't.
- **Don't rush it.** A child may not be ready for organized sports like soccer, baseball, or softball until the ages of 8 to 10. Such sports as football and lacrosse demand even more emotional and physical maturity and are better left until the early teens.
- **Don't overdo it.** Children who specialize in a sport early on in life are more likely to drop out in later years. Encourage them to try different sports, both individual and team activities. The variety develops different skills and keeps them eager to play as seasons change.

The sporting life

After high school and college, many adults slow down. Jobs, marriage, and kids take up time that sports once occupied. Yet staying fit not only helps you control your weight and reduce chronic disease risk, it also fights stress and sharpens your mental edge. When the going gets tough, the tough play ball.

It's literally never too late to start. Even people in their nineties benefit from weight-training programs. Many more older people are using low-impact sports and exercise to help fend off frailty and illness. Do take a few extra precautions, though: While older athletes sustain the same types of sprains and strains as younger ones, injuries may be complicated by arthritis and bursitis, and falls can be more damaging. Check with your physician first; if you have heart disease, diabetes, asthma, or osteoporosis, he may recommend certain sports over others.

Dodging damage

Regardless of your age, experience, or the sport you play, reduce your injury risk with these tips:

- **Go easy.** Minimize high-impact sports, such as basketball, running, or tennis—or alternate them with low-impact activities, such as walking, bicycling, or swimming.
- **Mix it up.** Vary your activities. Walk one day, lift weights another, swim or play golf on the third. You'll work different muscles while giving sore muscles and joints an opportunity to recover.
- **Keep at it.** Aim for at least 30 minutes of daily activity. If you're sore or tired, ease up.
- **Follow the 10 percent rule.** No matter how good you may feel, don't increase the intensity or the duration of your activity more than 10 percent in any week.
- **Warm up.** Playing any sport cold invites injury. Get your heart going for five minutes, then stretch (see box, page 306).
- **Think safety.** Wear appropriate safety gear, such as helmets when bicycling or goggles for racquetball. Practice proper technique, especially when using weights.

- **Get in shape and stay in shape.** Weak muscles, tendons, and ligaments can lead to tears or strains. Prepare for sports with strength training and flexibility exercises.
- **Listen to your body.** Sore muscles from a new sport (or an old one played harder) are normal. But if there's pain or swelling in a joint or tendon, try rest, ice, compression, and elevation ("RICE"). Later, add gentle exercise: Resting an injury isn't as healing as regular, pain-free movement. *(continued)*

Tennis elbow, which may stem from poor technique or from overusing the hand, wrist, and elbow, may not cause pain until the next day.

Choosing a Sport Wisely

Sports are not one-size-fits-all. For certain individuals, some sports are not recommended, while others may be particularly beneficial. When deciding which activities to pursue, take into account your fitness level, injury history, and other medical factors. Here are some examples:

- **If you're overweight,** stay away from jarring weight-bearing sports, such as running or high-impact aerobics; they may over-stress joints. Instead, try swimming or cycling, both of which provide cardiovascular benefits.

- **If you are at risk of osteoporosis,** focus on activities that do require you to bear your own weight. Try fast-paced walking, running, tennis, volleyball, or golf (without riding the cart).

- **If you have arthritis,** even golf, with its motion and impact, can be hard on the back, elbows, wrists, and knees. So try swimming or water aerobics. The fluid movements enhance mobility without pounding the joints.

- **If you have back, neck, or knee pain,** discuss cycling and swimming with your doctor. They both offer a solid workout without the bone-jarring impact of running and court sports. Golf's twisting movements may cause back pain, but if your swing is correct, it can be pain-free.

Sports (continued)

Keeping Injuries at Bay

Any sport can strain muscles, but some are more likely to cause fractures or concussions. Always wear appropriate protective equipment. Also, the better you play, the more able you will be to stay in control, so practice your sport often. What follows are some specific risks for individual sports and how best to avoid them. Whichever sport you choose, be sure to warm up for at least five minutes before and cool down afterward, and don't forget to stretch.

Sport and risk level		Common injuries	How to avoid injury
Low risk	Bowling	Back strain	Don't use too heavy a ball or hold the ball too long; work on a smooth delivery.
	Golf	Golfer's elbow, back strain	Swing upright with little sideways twist; take practice swings; don't overswing or overuse your wrists; bend from the knees.
	Hiking, walking	Blisters, sprains	Wear proper footwear.
	Rowing	Back strain	Keep your back straight; work your legs, not back; don't hunch.
	Swimming	Swimmer's ear, neck pain	Remove water from ears quickly; breathe without jerking your head up and back. If your back hurts, skip the butterfly and breast stroke.
Medium risk	Aerobic dance	Shinsplints; calf, lower-back, foot, ankle, and knee problems	Choose low-impact (no jumping) exercises, such as step aerobics. Wear appropriate sneakers and replace them often.
	Baseball, softball	Injuries to the shoulders, elbows, hamstrings, knees, ankles	Don't use too heavy a bat; develop a smooth swing. Wear protective equipment.
	Bicycling	Shoulder problems, back strain; fractures and concussions from crashes	Don't hunch; get a mountain or hybrid bike so you can sit up straighter. Wear a helmet; be aware of terrain and traffic.
	Racquetball, tennis	Tennis elbow, an inflammation of a tendon that bends the wrist backward; back pain	Make sure your racket isn't strung too tight and the grip isn't too large. Work on your backhand; learn to turn with your entire body.
	Running	Runner's knee, shinsplints, Achilles tendinitis	Wear supportive shoes; replace them every 480 to 800 kilometers (300 to 500 miles). Stretch; run on soft surfaces; don't overtrain.
	Soccer	Scrapes, bruises, pulled or strained muscles, ankle sprains, bone fractures, knee injuries, concussions	Stretch; get in condition with interval training and strength training. Balance training—catching a ball with your hands while standing on one leg—has been shown to help prevent ankle sprains.
High risk	Basketball	Ankle sprains, torn hamstrings, back problems, jumper's knee (soreness under the kneecaps)	"High-top" sneakers protect ankles. Try not to jump and twist your body at the same time.
	Football, rugby, hockey	Back strain, fractures, concussions	Wear protective equipment, including proper footwear.
	Skateboarding, in-line skating	Back strain, fractures, concussions	Wear protective equipment; learn how to slow down, stop, and fall safely; keep to manageable speeds.
	Skiing	Rupture of the anterior cruciate ligament (ACL), which attaches the upper leg bone to the lower one; skier's thumb; fractures	Ski within your ability level. Minimize ACL risk with conditioning exercises for the lower leg and hamstring muscles. To reduce the risk of skier's thumb, don't strap your hands into ski-pole straps. Have skis, boots, and bindings checked by a certified technician in a ski shop or resort. And skip that "last run" when you're overtired.
	Snowboarding	Injuries to the upper extremities: wrists, elbows, and shoulders	Wear a helmet and wrist guards; elbow and knee guards are also recommended. As with skiing, stop when you are fatigued.

Since Gatorade was concocted by the University of Florida in 1965, a billion-dollar sports-drink industry has emerged, making many wonder: If you regularly exercise or work up a sweat, isn't water good enough to quench your thirst and replace lost fluids?

The answer is yes. For recreational athletes and anyone who exercises for no more than an hour at a time, water is the perfect quencher. For endurance athletes, however, a sports drink may be the better choice.

Building a better beverage

While you exercise, your body loses fluids through sweating. To avoid dehydration, you need to replace these fluids. Ideally, you should drink at least 500 milliliters (16 ounces) of water (two cups, or a large tumbler) two hours before a workout; then, during exercise, 120 to 240 milliliters (4 to 8 ounces) every 15 minutes. After exercise, drink at least 500 milliliters (16 ounces), more if you're exercising in hot weather.

Sports drinks provide not only water but also potassium, sodium, and sugar. While sweating does cause you to lose a little potassium and sodium, it's likely that you consume more than enough of each mineral in your daily diet to cover the loss. (If you're worried about a lack of potassium, eat a banana.) The sugar provides extra energy—as would a soft drink or fruit juice—but for the first hour of exercise, your body's energy stores give you plenty.

Endurance athletes are a different story. Because they sweat over long periods, they may need the extra salt and potassium. The sugar may help, too. Studies show that the carbohydrates supplied by sports drinks may improve athletic performances that last longer than an hour—more so than plain water. They replenish energy not only while you exercise but also during recovery afterward.

Drink to your health

Whether you choose a sports drink or water when you exercise, follow these health tips:

- Don't wait until you are thirsty to drink. By that time, you are already dehydrated. In severe cases, it could take days to normalize your body's fluid balance.
- Avoid alcohol right after you exercise; it promotes dehydration.
- Dilute sodas or fruit juices that are 10 percent sugar or more; otherwise, they are absorbed slower and may lead to stomach cramps, nausea, or diarrhea.
- A sports drink's sugar content and acidity may increase the risk of tooth decay. To limit contact with the teeth, don't swish it around in your mouth and use a straw or a sports bottle.

Weekend athletes do just fine with water. But if you like the taste of sports drinks—and that encourages you to drink more when you exercise—all the better. For athletes who exercise for more than an hour, a sports drink may provide an energy boost.

Smarter Snacks?

For active people, energy bars provide a quick boost before or during exercise. They are great to take along on a hike or bike ride, but they can be expensive and difficult for some to digest (drinking water helps). Look for bars that are high in carbohydrates and low in fat. And keep in mind that you can get a similar lift simply by eating a piece of fruit, a bagel, fig bars, or a handful of raisins.

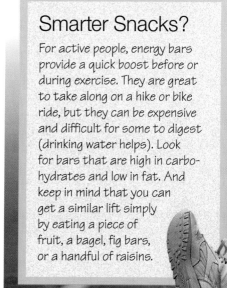

Steroids

There are many sides to the steroid story. On the one hand, corticosteroids are strong, highly effective medicines for pain and inflammation. But doctors are rightfully wary of prescribing them, because if they are used for too long, they can cause damaging and long-lasting side effects. Steroids have an even darker side: anabolic steroids. Used primarily to bulk up muscles, they can lead to aggression, irrational behavior, and harmful physical changes.

A miracle for a moment

Big changes: Anabolic steroids help grow muscles, but they can also shrink the testicles and stunt overall growth.

Steroids are hormones. The body produces them naturally, and they help regulate heart, lung, muscle, and kidney function. During times of stress or injury, the body produces the steroid cortisol to combat inflammation.

So it should be no surprise that synthetic steroids are the active ingredients in many anti-inflammatory medications. Oral corticosteroids may be prescribed to treat severe cases of inflammation, stifle allergic reactions, and stave off asthma attacks. For example, prednisone, a common corticosteroid, is used to treat ulcerative colitis, Crohn's disease, and the inflamed joints and organs associated with rheumatoid arthritis or lupus. Topical hydrocortisone creams—the only steroid medications sold over the counter—relieve itching, pain, and inflammation.

The short-term use of oral corticosteroid drugs often produces near-miraculous results, especially in large doses. But their potency poses problems over the long term. Common side effects of overuse include high blood pressure, elevated blood-sugar levels, thinning of the skin, bruising, osteoporosis, mood changes, and cataracts. That's why physicians tailor dosages and schedules carefully. These drugs require gradual withdrawal; the steroid-producing adrenal glands need time to start working normally on their own.

Anabolic abuse

When most people think of steroids, they think of anabolic steroids, drugs that are used by some athletes to bulk up and enhance performance. Taken as tablets or injected directly into muscle tissue, they promote muscle growth because they mimic testosterone, the male sex hormone. Anabolic steroids are banned by most sporting associations, including the Olympics, because athletes who use them usually gain a distinct advantage over those who do not.

Although anabolics do have legitimate medical uses (for example, to treat serious growth deficiencies), they are used mostly by healthy people who want to get bigger, stronger, and faster in a hurry. Adult male athletes and bodybuilders are the most common abusers, but use is rising among female athletes and teenagers. The largest percentage of first-time users may be boys under age 15.

Anabolic steroids are dangerous drugs. Their many side effects may include acne, mood swings, irrational behavior, increased aggressiveness (sometimes called "steroid rage"), hormonal imbalances, damage to the liver and adrenal glands, impotence, infertility, and heart disease.

A Shot of Relief

An injection of cortisone, a type of corticosteroid, can provide quick and lasting pain relief in a specific area of the body. But these direct hits are so potent that doctors are reluctant to use cortisone shots too often. As few as six injections in a year can do irreparable damage to joints and tendons. Some conditions that might call for a cortisone shot are:

- Joint pain from bursitis or rheumatoid arthritis
- Severe tendinitis, including persistent tennis or golfer's elbow and frozen shoulder
- Plantar fasciitis, a painful inflammation of the sole of the foot
- Carpal tunnel syndrome

How many phones can ring at once? Aarrgh! But you can be busy without stress, especially if you have a chance to make decisions, learn skills, socialize with coworkers, and earn promotions.

S tress! It's as inevitable as death and taxes, and it has more disguises than you can imagine, including frustration, anxiety, fear, job and family pressure, sadness and happiness, and boredom and overactivity. Stress is a normal part of life; it's how you respond to it that affects your health.

Stress is any pressure, good or bad. Negative experiences—work hassles, traffic jams, fights at home, or more serious ones like a death in the family, a divorce, or the loss of a job—are obviously stressful. But even "happy" events—a new job, marriage, buying a house, having a baby—can be challenging. Reacting to these tensions can elevate blood pressure. When that reaction becomes chronic, it can contribute to more serious problems, such as heart disease. That's why it's important to learn how to handle stress.

Fight, flee, or just stand there

The body's response to stress is rooted in the survival instinct that we share with our prehistoric ancestors and many animal species. It's called the "fight or flight" response: Faced with danger, we take it on or we escape. Either way, the body's nervous system *(Continued)*

Symptom Sorter

A Quick Stress Test

If you answer yes to fourteen or more of the following questions, you probably need to reduce stress in your life. A score above twenty is in the "danger zone" and requires a change of lifestyle. Do you:

- Neglect your diet?
- Try to do everything yourself?
- Blow up easily?
- Seek unrealistic goals?
- Fail to laugh at what others find funny?
- Act rude?
- Make a big deal of everything?
- Look to others to make things happen?
- Complain you are disorganized?
- Avoid people whose ideas differ from yours?
- Think there's only one right way of doing something?
- Neglect exercise?
- Get too little rest?
- Use sleeping pills without your doctor's approval?
- Have few supportive relationships?
- Get angry when kept waiting?
- Ignore stress symptoms?
- Put things off until later?
- Fail to build relaxation time into your day?
- Gossip?
- Race through your day?
- Keep emotions bottled up inside?
- Spend a lot of time complaining about the past?
- Fail to get a break from noise and crowds?

Quiz supplied by the Canadian Mental Health Association, Saskatchewan Division.

goes into overdrive. The brain releases the hormones cortisol and epinephrine (also known as adrenaline), which quicken the heart rate, elevate blood pressure, contract muscles, and increase breathing. Then as the body slowly comes down from its tensed state, we feel edgy or fatigued.

People under pressure

A stressful lifestyle, which may include a high-pressure job that involves little decision-making, isolation from family and friends, and lack of regular exercise, can set the stage for illness. In the short term, stress may cause headaches, back-aches, and insomnia. More alarming are studies that reveal that over a longer period, stress can contribute to serious conditions, such as diabetes, memory loss, immune-system dysfunction, and reduced bone density. Maternal stress during pregnancy may adversely affect the child's early development. Consider these other links between stress and illness:

- **Common cold.** Studies have shown that work-related stress can diminish the immune-system function. So you may be more likely to catch a cold (and other infections) when you're under the gun.
- **Heart disease.** After measuring levels of blood pressure, blood sugar, and cholesterol, as well as hormone secretion and abdominal fat, researchers at Rockefeller University concluded that a higher load of daily stress, experienced over time, may compromise physical and mental function and increase the risk of heart disease.
- **Heart attack.** Duke University researchers monitored the blood circulation of heart disease patients after they performed math calculations against the clock and gave speeches in front of experts without adequate time to prepare. Many responded with a temporary drop in blood supply to the heart—and those people were more likely to suffer a heart attack in the future. In addition, researchers from Harvard

> Not all stress is unhealthy. A certain amount of stress in day-to-day life can be motivating and help keep you on your toes.

How Do You Deal With Stress?

Stress can be unhealthy enough, but how you handle it can be even worse. Alcohol, drugs, cigarettes, junk food, and other vices may provide a temporary sense of escape from everyday problems, but they may also lead to addictions that carry dangerous health risks. The best advice is to make stress work for you—for example, use your pent-up energy to exercise.

How Stressful Was Your Year?

The Social Readjustment Rating Scale, originally designed by Holmes and Rahe in 1967, assigns "life-change units" to a variety of events (positive and negative) that can cause stress. Each unit score estimates the intensity and length of recovery time for a specific life change. The higher the score, the greater the stress. If you've experienced one or more of these changes in the past year, you may be at a higher risk for stress-related illness.

Event or Situation	Life-Change Units
Death of a child	123
Death of a spouse	119
Death of a parent	100
Divorce	96
Being fired	79
Significant illness or injury	74
Death of a close friend	70
Being laid off	68
Pregnancy	67
Decreased income	60
Parents getting divorced	59
Foreclosure of a mortgage or loan	58
Retirement	52
Marriage	50
Moving to different town, city, or province	47
Sexual difficulties	44
Birth of a grandchild	43
Loss or damage to personal property	43
Child leaving for college	41
Increased income	38
Major purchase	37
Major personal achievement	36
Change in work hours or conditions	35
Trouble with the boss	29
Major change in eating habits	27
Major dental work	26
Vacation	24

University have found that people with phobias (such as a fear of enclosed spaces) are more likely to die of cardiac arrest.

Ease up and chill out

Not all stress is unhealthy. A certain amount in day-to-day life can be motivating and help keep you on your toes. But if stress is getting to you, learn to reduce it.

Lifestyle, personality, and even genetic makeup influence our emotional and physiological responses to stress. But we can modify those responses by making changes in how we act, think, relate, move, and relax. Although simple, many of these may take sustained work to adopt successfully:

- **Gain a sense of control.** Lack of control at work is a high risk factor for stress-related illness. If you can't gain some measure of control at work, find a sense of control in a nonwork activity, such as a hobby.
- **Downsize your life.** Learn to say no, and avoid taking on more responsibility than you can handle. Cut out unnecessary activities. Be willing to delegate.
- **Be more flexible.** In both your personal and professional lives, remember that mistakes happen, and no one, including yourself, is perfect. Arguing only intensifies the effects of stress.
- **Take things one at a time.** When you feel overwhelmed, make a list and tackle the most important tasks first. Then check off items as you go; the sense of accomplishment can be satisfying and motivating.
- **Rest and rejuvenate.** Your work may suffer if you spend too many hours on the job. Even during busy periods, try to leave work at a reasonable time a few nights a week. Also, every hour take a five-minute break, and walk around. Get a good night's sleep; when times are stressful, you need more rest.

- **Keep in touch.** The more social contacts you have, the less stressed you feel and the lower your risk for many illnesses, including heart disease. If you have difficulty sharing your emotions, try writing them out in a journal.
- **Hug your dog.** Pets provide a sense of normalcy, and they will love you no matter what.
- **Work out, jog, or walk.** Exercise is one of the best antidotes to stress. It takes your mind off your worries, relieves anxiety, helps you think more clearly, and reduces the physical effects of stress by lowering resting heart rate and blood pressure.

Healthy dish: Just hanging out with a close friend helps you unwind and reduce stress.

Busting Stress in 30 Minutes or Less

Here are some quick and easy relaxation techniques that can help relieve daily tension:

- **Breathe deep:** For a sense of calm and control, try this anywhere, even in a traffic jam (as long as you're not distracted by it). Inhale slowly and deeply as you expand first the belly (below the navel), then the diaphragm (between stomach and chest), and finally the chest. Hold for a few seconds, then exhale in a reverse 1-2-3 pattern. Hold again for a few seconds before inhaling. Repeat 10 times.

- **Stretch:** Ten minutes a day of simple stretching or yoga can keep tense or underused muscles loose, help prevent future tension, and recharge your batteries. Just five minutes in the morning and another five in the evening before bed may be all you need.

- **Meditate:** Calm, inward reflection for only 10 to 20 minutes a day may help lower blood pressure. Sit or lie down in a quiet, comfortable place. A nice view, fresh air, soft music, or sweet scents can help clear your mind.

- **Visualize:** Athletes use mental imagery to preview their performance before a game. Ease your mind by envisioning a particularly anxious situation—a big meeting or delicate family talk—unfolding successfully.

- **Set a worry schedule:** Consolidate concerns into a 30-minute worry session. By designating time each day for fretting, you not only eliminate stress from other parts of the day, but you may also realize that on any given day, you don't have 30 minutes' worth of troubles.

Sugar

Sugar is no villain. It doesn't make kids hyperactive. It's not the primary cause of weight gain, nor is it linked with an increased risk of cancer or heart disease. The sweet stuff is only part of the tooth decay story. And if you're physically active enough, you may even benefit from the extra calories that sugary foods provide.

But few of us really need those extra calories. Unlike naturally sweet fruits, pure sugar provides essentially no nutrients. Sugar becomes a dietary problem when it regularly replaces foods that contain vital nutrients and when it is overconsumed by people with lower calorie needs, such as the elderly or the sedentary. A diet high in sugar and low in fiber-rich whole grains may also increase the risk of diabetes.

Cravings for sweets are built into the genes—and may be the body's way of telling babies to drink their milk, which is rich in lactose, a kind of sugar.

Sugar by any other name...

Sugar is much more than the white stuff you stir into your coffee. It is a natural component of fruit, milk, honey, even vegetables (why do you think they call it sweet corn?). But what we think of as sugar is the refined, highly concentrated substance that may appear on ingredient labels as sucrose, glucose, fructose, dextrose, lactose, mannitol, sorghum, or sorbitol. These ingredients show up not only in cookies, cakes, and candies but also in many processed foods, from cereals and canned fruits to ketchup and spaghetti sauce. All sugars are used by the body in much the same way.

Sugars belong to a class of nutrients known as carbohydrates—the body's primary fuel source. Our bodies convert all carbohydrates—whether they come from brown rice or honey-glazed doughnuts—to glucose, which is stored in the muscles and the liver and circulates as blood sugar. However, a diet rich in complex carbohydrates, in the form of whole grains, legumes, vegetables, and fruits, is sufficient for the body to make all the blood sugar it needs. (In a pinch, we can even convert fats and proteins to blood sugar.) There is no need for added sugar in the diet.

If not a villain, an accomplice?

When it comes to your teeth, there is a direct link between sugar and disease: sugar promotes tooth decay and, thus, cavities. But so do many foods. Proper oral hygiene is the most important factor in dental health.

Hyperactivity in children has also been linked to sugar intake. But studies published in *Pediatrics* and the *New England Journal of Medicine* refute this theory. Researchers have observed that both normal children and kids identified as hyperactive had diets high in sugar as well as artificial sweeteners. They found no evidence that sugar increases hyperactivity, attention deficit disorder, or any behavioral problems.

Weight control is a more complex issue. Dieters have long shunned sugar as a source of excess weight. Yet fat is a bigger contributor

CAUTION!

Never feed a baby under one year of age raw honey or use honey in baby foods or to coat a pacifier. Honey occasionally contains bacteria spores that can cause botulism in infants.

Brain Candy

Can sugar improve memory? In young adults, maintaining a steady blood sugar level enhances attention, memory, and learning. In the elderly, something as simple as a sweetened beverage can boost blood sugar enough to improve memory. Studies at the University of Virginia found that elderly subjects—healthy participants, those with Alzheimer's, and head-injury victims—were better able to recall stories, words, and faces after drinking lemonade sweetened with sugar rather than a similar beverage with saccharin.

Healthier Sugars?

Many people bake with molasses, brown sugar, or honey in the belief that they are healthier alternatives to refined white sugar. True or not?

You'll get a little extra nutritional value when you consume molasses, a by-product of cane-sugar production, which contains trace minerals and vitamins. Blackstrap molasses, for example, is the least-refined molasses. It contains moderate amounts of iron and chromium. Brown sugar, on the other hand, is simply white sugar colored with a bit of molasses or caramelized sugar. Nor does raw sugar contain significant nutrients. Honey, which comes from plant nectar and is gathered by honeybees, has only minimal traces of vitamins and minerals and is actually a more concentrated source of calories than table sugar.

to calories: A gram of fat has 9 calories, more than double the 4 calories in a gram of sugar. One study even showed that overweight people prefer foods higher in fat than in sugar. The problem is that many "sweets" are rich in both sugar and fat—and, therefore, calories. Moderation is the key: excess carbohydrates, like all extra calories, are stored in the body as fat.

A diet low in fiber-rich complex carbohydrates and high in sugars (from cola drinks), as well as refined starches (white bread, white rice, pasta, French fries) more than doubles diabetes risk.

Whenever possible, try to tame your sugar cravings by indulging in sweet whole fruits, which are usually low in fat and calories yet rich in vitamins and healthful plant compounds. You'll satisfy your sweet tooth and get some nutrition in the bargain.

Recent research on diabetes, the "sugar disease," has reinforced the idea that more of our carbohydrates should come from whole foods rather than highly refined starches and sugars. In a large study of middle-aged women, a diet low in fiber-rich complex carbohydrates (such as bran cereals and whole-grain breads) and high in sugars (cola drinks), as well as refined starches (white bread, white rice, pasta, French fries) that the body easily converts to sugar, more than doubled the risk of developing adult-onset diabetes.

In a healthful diet, a little sugar is a harmless pleasure. Just don't let it elbow out foods that are better for you.

In the final analysis, the body processes honey, molasses, brown sugar, and even raw, unrefined sugar in much the same way it does table sugar, converting each to glucose.

Sunglasses

For most outdoor activities, sunglasses that block 95 percent of UVB and 60 percent of UVA rays offer adequate protection.

S unglasses are not just for movie stars and Secret Service agents. They're for anyone who spends enough time outdoors to get a suntan or even a sunburn. And they should be worn not only in summertime, but during winter as well.

What you can't see can hurt you

A growing body of evidence suggests that long-term exposure to the sun's visible light and ultraviolet (UV) rays damages the lens, retina, and cornea of the eye. This damage can lead not only to vision deficiencies, such as cataracts (a clouding of the lens) and macular degeneration (a breakdown of the retina), but to cancer of the eyelids and the skin around the eyes. In the short term, overexposure can cause photokeratitis, a painful "sunburn" on the surface of the eye, and may even lead to a temporary inability to see objects in the dark.

People who are most vulnerable are those who spend a great deal of time in the sun, live near the equator or at high altitudes, have had cataract surgery, or take photosensitizing medications (such as psoralen, tetracycline,

doxycycline, or allopurinol). If you're not in a high-risk category, you don't have to buy expensive sunglasses from an optician. Although drugstore or department store shades are of lesser quality, they will do fine.

Any sunglasses are better than none at all, but some types are better suited to certain activities. The goal is to block out the greatest amount of UVA and UVB rays. Here are some guidelines:

- **Rating.** "General purpose" sunglasses, which block 95 percent of UVB rays and 60 percent of UVA rays, are suitable for most outdoor activities. "Special purpose," which block up to 99 percent of UVB rays and 60 percent of UVA rays, are designed for very bright environments. "Cosmetic purpose," which block only 70 percent of UVB rays and 20 percent of UVA rays, offer inadequate protection.
- **Size.** Choose lenses large enough to shield the eyes on all sides. Or buy wraparounds.
- **Lens.** Plastic lenses are lighter and safer than glass are, but are less scratch-resistant. Polarized lenses, which reduce reflected glare, are particularly useful for driving, boating, and fishing. Mirrored lenses, which also reduce glare, are good for skiing and water sports, but they scratch easily and may not offer UV protection. Gradient lenses, darker at the top and lighter at the bottom, are best suited for driving. Photochromic lenses, which darken according to light levels, are good for cycling, golfing, and other activities where conditions vary, but they may not be suitable for driving.
- **Darkness.** Sunglasses should be dark enough that when you look in a mirror you can barely see your eyes—but not so dark that your vision is restricted.
- **Color.** Gray and green lenses are best for drivers and pedestrians, who need to see traffic lights; amber, for skiers, boaters, and pilots, who need to see contrast.
- **Distortion.** When buying nonprescription sunglasses, look at a vertical line and tilt your head from side to side. If the line bends or wiggles, choose another pair.

S lather on plenty of sunscreen and you can have fun in the sun without worrying about skin damage. Right? Not quite. North Americans spend more than $520 million a year on sunscreens and sunblocks. Yet the number of cases of malignant melanoma (a potentially deadly form of skin cancer) has nearly doubled since 1980, raising questions about the effectiveness of such products.

A false sense of security?

Until recently, scientists believed that skin damage was caused only by the sun's UVB rays, which are absorbed by chemicals in sunscreens. But studies now indicate that longer-wavelength UVA rays, previously thought to be harmless, may actually penetrate the skin more deeply and damage cells. Since there is no rating system to indicate the degree of UVA protection, two sunscreens with the same SPF (sun protection factor) may vary in effectiveness. The solution is to use a broad spectrum sunscreen that not only is SPF rated but contains the ingredient avobenzone (also called Parsol 1789), which absorbs UVA rays.

Even these sunscreens may not guarantee blanket protection. According to a 1998 report—highly publicized but controversial

Buy a broad spectrum sunscreen to protect yourself against UVA and UVB rays. Choose one that is waterproof, hypoallergenic, fragrance-free, and PABA-free.

and inconclusive—by a scientific researcher at the esteemed Memorial Sloan-Kettering Cancer Center in New York City, while sunscreens may guard against less serious forms of skin cancer (basal-cell and squamous-cell), they appear to be less effective against malignant melanoma. One reason may be that some people are genetically predisposed to developing melanoma. But it's also possible that, by preventing burning and permitting longer stays in the sun, sunscreens may increase long-term sun exposure for such people, and thus raise their risk.

To get the greatest benefit from sunscreens, follow these guidelines:

About 80 percent of our total lifetime sun exposure comes before we reach age 18. Since severe sunburns during childhood have been linked to malignant melanoma, children need even more protection from the sun than adults do.

- Everybody needs a sunscreen. Even the deepest tan affords limited protection.
- Buy a broad spectrum sunscreen to protect yourself against both UVA and UVB rays. Choose one that's waterproof, hypoallergenic, fragrance-free, and PABA-free.
- Choose an SPF of 15 (higher if your skin is fair or if you are in the tropics or the mountains). To determine how long you can stay outdoors, multiply the SPF by the length of time it takes your unprotected skin to burn.
- For the nose and other highly sensitive areas, use a block that contains titanium dioxide or zinc oxide.
- In summer and winter, apply sunscreen liberally to all exposed body parts (including the lips) at least 30 minutes before going out. Shake the bottle well; reapply every two hours and after swimming.
- Ask your pharmacist if any medications you take, such as antibiotics, birth-control pills, or anti-inflammatories, will make your skin more sensitive to the sun.
- Some ingredients degrade, so discard sunscreens at the end of the season.

Be Sun Savvy

Sunscreens should be part of an overall plan to safeguard yourself against the sun. Here are some tips:

- Avoid direct sunlight between 10 A.M. and 3 P.M., when the sun's rays are most intense.

- Wear opaque, tightly woven clothing and a hat with a wide brim. Also, look into new sun-protective clothing, which can block UVA and UVB rays.

- Always wear sunglasses to protect your eyes.

- Don't use sunscreens on children under six months old. Instead, keep them under wraps.

Swimming Pools

What could be better than a dip in a pool on a hot summer day? Swimming is even good exercise. But do you ever wonder about the germs swimming alongside you? Or the chemicals used to keep the pool clean? If you have small children, an even bigger concern is the risk of drowning.

A delicate balance

Most pools are treated with chlorine to keep them germ-free. Chlorine binds with microorganisms to destroy them. When the disinfectant is doing its job, the water should be clear and have little odor. If a pool smells strongly of chlorine, you may think it's overloaded with the chemical. On the contrary, it may mean the pool doesn't have enough, since a strong odor is released only after all the chlorine has been "used up" by the microorganisms.

A pool should have a pH level of 7.4 to 7.6 to allow the chlorine to function effectively. The pH level may be off if the water is greenish, there is scale on the pool walls, or the water stings your eyes or irritates your skin.

Testing, testing, testing

Health Canada regulates and approves the chemical and sanitizing devices used to clean swimming pools. When using pool chemicals, follow the directions carefully. Also, keep these tips in mind:

- Run the filter long enough—usually 12 hours—so that it processes the entire contents of the pool twice a day.
- If you have a new pool, test the water daily until you become familiar with its demands. Thereafter, how often you test will depend on the number of swimmers, the pool's location (tree leaves can throw the pH balance off), and the temperature (in hot weather chlorine evaporates faster).
- About every month, take a water sample to a pool store for analysis.
- The chlorine level should remain between 1 and 3 parts chlorine per 1 million parts water. To calculate the number of liters in a rectangular pool, multiply the length by the width by the average depth (in feet) by

28.5; for a round pool, multiply the surface (πr^2) by the average depth (in feet) by 22.42; or ask the salesperson to give you the volume of water in your new pool.
- Consider using bromide instead of chlorine. It is gentler and works equally well. If you'd like to greatly reduce the need for chemicals, invest in an ozonator. These devices are expensive, however.

Rules for the pool

If you own a pool, ask everyone to shower before swimming. Why? Because a pool's disinfectant is more effective and lasts longer when it is not hampered by body oils, suntan lotions, and dirt. People should wash well with soap; a quick rinse won't do the trick. Small children should wear watertight plastic pants to reduce the risk of passing along infectious parasites transmitted by fecal matter. More important, have children use the bathroom before entering the pool, and schedule regular bathroom breaks. Ban kids who have had diarrhea within the past two weeks.

an ounce of **Prevention**

Safety Is Everything

Drowning is by far the biggest risk associated with swimming pools. To prevent accidents, be sure to follow these tips:

- Install a 1.2-meter-high (4 feet) fence around the pool and secure it with a self-latching gate. The best kind are chain-link fences, which allow you to see through to the swimming pool.

- Never leave a child, even in a baby pool, unattended or out of your sight.

- Keep toys away from the pool area when you're not there, to avoid luring an unsupervised child.

- Keep such rescue devices as a life ring and hook near the swimming pool.

- Never allow anyone to dive into the shallow end. Check that the diving board is well anchored.

- Make sure there is a cover over the main drain.

- Install a pool cover, and lock up chemicals used to keep the pool clean.

Synthetic Fabrics

These days the word *natural* connotes healthy and the word *synthetic* anything but. When it comes to clothing, that's not the case. With minor exceptions, synthetic fabrics pose no risk to health and, in some cases, may be preferable to natural fabrics.

Man-made marvels

Although some people prefer the softness and drape of natural fibers—cotton, wool, silk, and linen—a new generation of man-made fibers, created from wood pulp or chemicals, has useful properties that even Mother Nature can't match: lightweight yet insulated, waterproof yet breathable, flexible yet durable. Synthetic/natural blends, such as polyester/cotton, combine the best of both worlds.

Fabric chemists are modern alchemists, fashioning humble raw materials into space-age fibers with high-performance properties. In athletic wear and all-weather gear, for example, such fibers as Gore-tex, Hydrofil, and Cool Max not only excel at wicking moisture away from the skin and letting air in but also dry faster and provide superior insulation in cold weather.

Health concerns are few. While formaldehyde, a suspected human carcinogen, is used in the finishes of no-iron bed linens, permanent-press garments, upholstery, and drapes, new technology ensures that little is released. To further reduce exposure, wash a new shirt or no-wrinkle sheet before first using it, air permanent-press draperies outdoors before hanging, and keep your home well ventilated.

Flame-retardant children's sleepwear is also safer these days. Years ago, it was treated with a chemical that was later found to pose a health threat, and was banned. New laws require manufacturers to use special synthetic fibers that are inherently flame-resistant.

Minor wrinkles

In certain highly sensitive people (less than 1 percent of the population), the type of dyes and finishes used on some synthetic fabrics may cause skin irritations, such as a rash or, in even rarer instances, hives. Like all consumers, such people should wash new clothing, but they should also avoid nylon hosiery, fabrics containing polyester, and garments labeled "no-iron," "permanent-press," "durable-press," or "wrinkle-free."

Synthetic fabrics like nylon are not recommended for women's underwear. Even if the garment has a cotton crotch, it prevents moisture from evaporating beneath clothing, raising the risk of vaginal infections.

Spandex, originally developed as a substitute for rubber, exemplifies the virtues of a synthetic fabric. Lightweight, resistant to body oils and perspiration, and capable of being stretched over 500 percent without breaking, it is ideal for workout apparel.

Talcum Powder

For some years doctors have warned mothers against sprinkling talcum powder on their babies' bottoms. The fine airborne particles are a health hazard, especially to immature lungs. But research now suggests that the same advice applies to Mom.

The bottom line

The main ingredient in talcum powder is talc, which is finely ground magnesium silicate. The particles are so tiny that they easily become airborne. Once inhaled, they can settle into even the smallest reaches of the lungs. Pneumonia, inflammation of the airways, and, in extreme cases, even death have been linked to inhalation of talc. The risk to a baby's lungs is the reason pediatricians now advise parents to avoid talc. To prevent diaper rash, simply pat an infant thoroughly dry and, if you want, apply an ointment. Another concern is that talc may potentially be contaminated with asbestos, a carcinogen whose fibers are difficult to distinguish from talc fibers.

A cancer connection?

Although the final word is far from written, there's increasing evidence that women who use talcum powder may significantly increase their risk of developing ovarian cancer. While the incidence of ovarian cancer remains low (about 15 cases for every 100,000 North American women), some experts estimate that 10 percent of those cases may be connected to the use of talc.

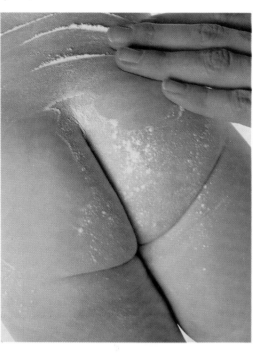

A 1997 study published in the *American Journal of Epidemiology* concluded that women who used powder (either talcum powder or cornstarch) in the genital area had a 60 percent greater chance of developing ovarian cancer. For women who use feminine deodorant sprays—even those that do not contain talc—the figure might be even higher. These findings concur with other studies that point to a link between ovarian cancer and the use of talc near the genitals or the perineum (the area between the vulva and the anus). Surprisingly, another study found traces of talc in the cancerous ovaries of women who didn't even use powder, at least as adults.

If you use talc to dust your diaphragm before storing it, however, there's no need to stop doing so. Researchers have found no increase in the risk of ovarian cancer for women who used talc on such birth-control devices. One reason may be that contact is intermittent. Condoms, which are sometimes packaged with talc, were not studied.

Although the research is far from conclusive, women who prefer to err on the side of caution may want to avoid using talcum powder, as well as feminine hygiene products that contain talc, in the genital area.

Sprinkling talcum powder on baby's bottom to prevent diaper rash may seem harmless, but doctors now agree that ointment is safer.

Foot Note

Talcum powder is still considered safe for use on the feet, especially during summer, when excessive perspiration and fungal infections are most common. Shake some into your hands first so that very little becomes airborne, then rub it onto your feet and sprinkle some inside your shoes. Talcum powders with deodorants work fine, but those with cornstarch are not ideal; cornstarch does absorb moisture, but the bacteria that grow on sweaty feet happen to thrive in its presence.

CAUTION!

If you have diabetes, consult your physician before using any powder—even cornstarch. Cornstarch may encourage fungal skin infections, which are problematic for diabetics.

Tampons

Anyone who read the newspapers in the early 1980s may recall the disturbing headlines: hundreds of women were struck down by a mysterious bacterial infection that was believed to have been brought on by their use of high-absorbency tampons. In the media hysteria and consumer uncertainty that followed, the infection turned out to be toxic shock syndrome (TSS)—and tampons were pulled from store shelves. Today, in the wake of new government regulations and better product labeling, TSS occurrences are rare. Used properly, tampons are a convenient and safe feminine-hygiene product for menstruating women and adolescent girls.

Tampons, used properly, are a convenient and safe feminine-hygiene product for menstruating women.

The tampon-TSS connection

Toxic shock syndrome is a potentially fatal disease caused by infection with a bacterium called *Staphylococcus aureus,* which produces toxins that poison the body. For reasons still unclear, it is most likely to attack women using tampons during their menstrual period. But it can also occur in non-menstruating women and, rarely, in men.

Tampons are not the cause of TSS. Its bacterial source has never been found in packaged tampons. However, the improper use of tampons seems to create conditions that encourage the production of the toxins. Researchers generally agree that the infection is closely associated with the use of high-absorbency tampons. Scientists originally believed synthetic tampon fibers were to blame, but two recent studies proved that idea to be false. However, both studies underscored the fact that super-plus-absorbency tampons provide a fertile breeding ground for bacteria. Scientists theorize that, as the tampon absorbs blood, it expands: the higher the absorbency, the greater the expansion, and the more likely the tampon is to adhere to the vaginal wall. When the tampon is removed, tiny bits of the vaginal-wall lining may be torn away with it, leaving openings for bacteria to enter the bloodstream.

Although TSS is a serious, if rare, disease, it is treatable with early detection and prompt medical attention. The onset is swift and may include the following symptoms: high fever, vomiting, diarrhea, fainting, dizziness, and a rash resembling a sunburn. If TSS is not treated right away, the body can go into kidney failure, shock, or liver shutdown.

Other troubles with tampons

TSS is not the only potential problem related to tampons. Deodorant tampons have been linked with yeast infections and vaginitis. If you have a yeast infection, don't use tampons. Finally, contrary to popular belief, tampons cannot become "lost" inside the vagina. There have been cases, however, in which women have forgotten to remove a tampon, resulting in it being lodged near the top of the vagina. If you have trouble removing a tampon, go to the nearest hospital emergency ward.

an ounce of Prevention

Avoiding TSS

Taking these simple precautions can help minimize your risk of getting TSS:

- Use the lowest-absorbency tampon that works for you. Make adjustments as your flow varies. If the tampon shows some white area after use, switch to one with lower absorbency.

- Replace tampons frequently, every four to six hours.

- Health-care specialists discourage using tampons overnight. Instead, they recommend pads.

- Alternate tampons with sanitary napkins during a menstrual period. When menstrual flow is minimal, be sure to wear minipads instead of tampons.

- Be extremely careful when inserting the tampon to avoid scratching or irritating the vaginal wall. Because of their harder edges, plastic applicators increase the possibility of irritation.

- Wash your hands with soap and water before and after handling the tampon.

- You should never use tampons between periods.

Tanning Salons

Tanning-bed sessions may be brief, but they expose skin to intense light that penetrates deeper than sun. In the short run, itchy, dry skin may result. Long-term dangers include skin cancer and cataracts.

Indoor tanning gets the thumb's down from dermatologists, and for good reason: there is no such thing as a healthy tan. Don't be fooled by claims that these commercial establishments offer "a healthy way to tan."

When you step into a tanning salon, you may as well be walking out into the noonday sun in the Sahara. Either way, you are subjecting yourself to ultraviolet rays that can do irreparable damage to your skin, your eyes, and perhaps your life.

What you can't see may kill you

Tanning is the skin's reaction to overexposure to ultraviolet radiation. Whether the rays come from the sun or from a tanning bed or booth, the result is the same: repeated overexposure causes cumulative damage to the inner connective tissue of the skin, which can lead to, at best, wrinkled and leathery skin (called photo-aging) and, at worst, precancerous cell growth, tumors, and skin cancers.

Tanning salons have long sold themselves as a safe alternative to outdoor sunbathing. Their tanning devices, which bathe the user with ultraviolet light, are designed not to emit the shortwave ultraviolet rays (known as UVB) that cause burning. Instead, they bathe the user in mainly longwave ultraviolet rays (UVA). Scientists concede that UVA rays don't burn. But they may do much worse harm.

There is mounting evidence that UVA rays increase the risk of malignant melanoma, an often fatal skin cancer that is on the rise.

Nor are these the only concerns. Just as natural sun poses risks to people with certain illnesses or who take specific medications, so too do sessions at a tanning salon: People with diabetes or lupus may experience flare-ups, and anyone using birth-control pills, antihistamines, antibiotics, or tranquilizers may suffer accelerated burning or such reactions as hives and blisters.

Finally, tanning booths make it easy to overexpose skin and eyes. Outside, we can't feel ourselves burning, but the sun does make our skin feel hot. That doesn't happen in a tanning salon, so there's no clue you're damaging your skin—or your eyes. In the short term, UVA rays can damage the retina or burn the cornea; over time, they can increase the risk of cataracts. Wearing ordinary sunglasses or closing your eyes won't protect you. Tanning salons are required to direct customers to wear protective eye goggles. It's not smart to step into these salons in the first place, but if you do, at least wear the goggles.

Salon Therapy?

One treatment for people with psoriasis is phototherapy, doctor-supervised exposure to UVB rays. Some patients turn to tanning salons for relief. Not a good idea, say experts. Tanning-salon equipment produces mostly UVA, not UVB, rays, so they're not effective at treating psoriasis.

Tannins

Think tannins and you probably think tea. But this broad class of compounds is also found in red wine, cocoa (and the chocolate that's made from it), coffee, some herb teas (including maté), and persimmons, grapes, and other fruits (especially blackberries and cranberries). They have remarkable properties that are not at all well understood. Many tannins fight cavities and treat diarrhea, while certain ones may also protect against cancer and heart disease.

Tannins disable bacteria in the mouth, inhibiting plaque formation and fighting tooth decay. Unfortunately, they can also stain teeth.

Some prime sources of tannins are red wine, coffee (regular and decaf), and tea, including brews made from raspberry leaves.

Pucker power

The most recognizable characteristic of tannins is astringency. By binding together surface proteins in the mouth, they produce a dry, tightening sensation, which is most evident when you're drinking a strong tea or full-bodied wine. The binding action of tannins also disables bacteria in the mouth, inhibiting plaque formation and fighting tooth decay. But tannins can stain teeth and dental work, so if you're concerned about discoloration, limit your consumption of tea and coffee.

Tannins also have the ability to "trap" some minerals, including iron—especially the iron in plant foods. So if you drink tea with meals, you may absorb less iron. It's not clear how significant this is in people who eat a well-balanced diet. But you can reduce the effect simply by adding milk or lemon to your brew; each binds with tannins. Or drink tea between meals—say, at teatime.

Healing properties?

The term *tannins* can be confusing—even to experts—since individual tannins vary greatly. However, most belong to a group of compounds called polyphenols, many of which are antioxidants. These antioxidants may protect against heart disease and cancer by preventing cellular damage. Polyphenols in grapes and red wine (resveratrol), and different ones in green and black tea (catechins), are currently being examined for their potential health benefits.

Perhaps future studies will also shed light on the possible link between tannins and migraines. Some researchers suspect that tannins can trigger the headaches, but the evidence so far is inconclusive. If you suffer from migraines, you may want to try avoiding foods that contain tannins for a period of time to see if you have fewer attacks.

A Natural Remedy

Because of their astringent properties, tannins form the basis of many traditional herbal treatments, usually taken in tea form.

Here is a sampling of tannin-containing herbs that are recommended for some everyday ailments (to be safe, check with your doctor before trying any of them):

- **Bayberry:** To stop diarrhea.
- **Blackberry:** To check diarrhea and to stop bleeding from minor cuts and scrapes.
- **Raspberry:** To alleviate morning sickness in pregnant women and to stop diarrhea.
- **Sage:** To soothe canker sores, bleeding gums, and sore throats (by gargling with a not-too-hot tea.)

Tap Water

I t has been drummed into us by just about every health authority we've ever read or consulted: For optimum health, drink six to eight glasses of water a day. But is the tap water we're filling our glasses with safe?

The answer is a qualified yes. Canada has one of the safest and best supplies of drinking water in the world. Water quality is a provincial responsibility and most municipal water systems are voluntarily regulated to guidelines set by Health Canada. Alberta and Quebec have legislated standards that are based on the guidelines. Essentially, the guidelines spell out the maximum acceptable concentra-

Tap Water Tips

To make your drinking water as safe as it can be, here's some advice:

- To flush the lead out of tap water, let it run until it gets cold. Use only cold water for drinking or cooking.

- Let the water sit in a clean container in the refrigerator overnight. Chlorine and its by-products are highly volatile and dissipate within hours, along with any unpleasant odor or taste.

- To disinfect tap water, boil it vigorously for one minute. Add a pinch of salt to improve the flat taste.

- If you have doubts about the safety of your water supply, send a sample to a water-testing laboratory. Your regional health authority can refer you to a certified lab. The cost of a standard microbiological test is about $50. A regular physical chemical test runs to about $275, and a test for PCBs can run as high as $350.

tion of any of more than 100 potential contaminants. Most communities chlorinate their drinking water to kill bacteria, parasites, and other harmful organisms, or fluoridate it to prevent tooth decay. (Vancouver, Montreal, and Kitchener, Ont., are exceptions among Canadian cities with fluoridated systems.)

But any water system can be polluted easily by chemical leaks from hazardous waste or nearby farms or septic tanks. Just one gram of 2,4-D, a common herbicide, can contaminate 10 million liters of drinking water. Some water supplies are more vulnerable than others. If you're concerned about yours, ask your local supplier for a safety report or have your water tested by an independent lab.

Potential pollutants

Tap water comes from two main sources: groundwater (wells), which provides 26 percent of the Canadian supply, and surface water (rivers, lakes, and reservoirs), which provides the remainder. About 57 percent of Canadians are served by wastewater treatment plants, considerably less than Americans (74 percent), Germans (86.5 percent), and Swedes (99 percent). Whatever its origin,

Fluoridated water, once hotly debated, poses no significant health risks and protects teeth from decay.

A Hard Choice

Many areas have "hard" water, which contains so much calcium and magnesium that soaps won't lather and a residue remains on pots. Most water softeners replace the calcium and magnesium with sodium. According to a University of Michigan study, each liter of treated water averaged 278 milligrams (mg) of sodium. Such levels should concern the average Canadian who consumes between 3,500 and 5,000 mg of sodium a day, far more than needed.

most water is disinfected with chlorine. Disinfection, however, does not equal purification. Chlorination does not destroy *Cryptosporidium parvum,* a parasite found in small numbers in most surface water. In high concentrations, this parasite can cause intestinal distress and other flulike symptoms for up to three weeks. Most at risk are infants, the elderly, and people with weakened immune systems. If the problem exists in your area, boil your water vigorously for one minute before drinking it. Some home filters can remove this organism.

Some consumers are also concerned about the following:

• **Chlorine.** Ironically, the chlorination process that helps purify water actually creates chemical by-products that can be harmful. Each water system regulates its own use of chlorine. After a heavy rainstorm, your system may add a particularly large dose of chlorine to compensate for contamination from sewage back-ups. When that chlorine interacts with acids from decomposing leaves, twigs, and other plant matter that falls into the water, it forms trihalomethanes (THMs), which in large concentrations can cause bladder and colon cancer over time. However, the overall benefits of chlorination are much greater than the small risk of health being affected by THMs (see box, bottom left).

• **Nitrates.** Generally a problem only in rural areas, nitrates stem primarily from fertilizer runoff, but also come from animal and human waste. Large amounts reduce the amount of oxygen carried by the blood, and are particularly dangerous to infants.

• **Lead.** This toxic mineral damages the kidneys, nerves, and the brain, especially in fetuses, infants, and children. Just one gram in 20,000 liters of water makes it unfit for drinking. Lead pipes are no longer used in plumbing, but since lead can leach into water from pipes, solder fittings, and even alloys in faucets, it might be a problem if you live in an old home or an area where water-service lines have not been replaced in many years. To flush out any lead in your pipes, run your taps for a few minutes first thing every morning, and again before drinking any water.

How well is your well?

If you're one of some 7 million Canadians who get their water from private wells, you are responsible for its safety. Do not use pesticides or fertilizers in areas around your well or those of your neighbors. Regularly check pumps and distribution systems and investigate any changes in water quality. Examine well casings regularly for leaks or breaks. Most provinces recommend that you test well water twice yearly; once after the spring thaw and again in late summer, when water levels are low. Your regional health authority can advise you on sampling and testing. Disinfect it once or twice a year with bleach or hypochlorite granules, or according to the manufacturer's directions.

Home Water Purifiers

Most home water-treatment devices can remove a limited number of impurities, and some are used in conjunction with others. Point of entry units treat the entire house supply as opposed to point of use devices which can be installed on a faucet or under a kitchen sink. The effectiveness of these products can vary widely, however, and if you don't maintain them properly they can actually contaminate your water. Some can only be used on microbiologically safe water.

Before buying a purifier, have your water tested so you know which pollutants need to be removed. Particle filters remove sediment but not microorganisms; oxidizing filters remove pollutants such as iron; activated carbon filters remove several chemical compounds including THMs; reverse osmosis filters stop iron, salt, and calcium; and distillers remove bacteria.

Whoever said "nothing lasts forever" probably didn't have a tattoo. If applied by a qualified technician using sterile equipment under sanitary conditions, tattoos are relatively safe. But remember that they're made to last, with durable pigments injected into the skin. While removal is possible, it comes at a high cost: significant pain, a hefty bill, and cosmetic results that are often unsatisfactory.

Tattooing has other downsides as well. In some people the injected dyes can cause painful immediate or long-term allergic reactions. Worst of all, improperly sterilized needles and unhygienic conditions can introduce dangerous diseases, including hepatitis B and AIDS, into the bloodstream. And if you ever need to have a magnetic resonance imaging (MRI) scan, the metals in some tattoo dyes can cause burning and swelling during the procedure.

Not so easy off

Tattoo inks are applied through a series of tiny needle pricks that penetrate the skin two

After a tattoo is applied, swelling and itching can result, either immediately or some time later.

millimeters deep. The needles leave behind large ink particles that color the skin from the inside. The painfulness of the procedure depends on the site of the tattoo, its size, and the skill of the technician. A healing period of a week to 10 days follows, during which the area may crust and peel. It's important to keep it clean and moisturized.

Tattoos are designed to last as long as you do. But several methods have been developed to remove them, with varying degrees of success. For years, surgery and dermabrasion were the only options. Surgery involves stretching the skin, then cutting away the tattoo and stitching together the surrounding skin over the tattoo site. Dermabrasion, or "sanding" of the skin surface, is very painful and generally leaves unsightly scars.

The newest approach uses lasers to dissolve the large ink particles under the skin, breaking them into tiny pieces that the immune system can attack and purge. But lasers are far from foolproof. They work better on dark colors than light ones and in some cases may actually darken, rather than fade, a design.

Laser removal is also pricey: Insurers consider it cosmetic and don't cover the cost. With as many as 10 treatments required, each costing $100 to $500, you could easily pay several thousand dollars to remove a tattoo that cost you $100 to acquire.

Dyeing words

Tattoo dyes can be made either from metal oxides, such as chromium, or from synthetic pigments. Ask the technician about the content of the dyes and keep a record (down to the manufacturer and lot number) just in case reactions occur later. A dermatologist can treat you much more effectively if he or she can identify the irritant.

Some people complain of sun sensitivity in tattooed skin, but there is no evidence that tattoos have any long-term impact on a person's reaction to UV rays.

Design Without Danger

Tattoos may be relatively safe, but that does not mean they pose no danger. Any procedure that involves puncturing the skin should be considered risky. Many hepatitis B virus transmissions have been traced to tattoo establishments. Some were caused by the use of inadequately sterilized needles. To reduce risks, tattooists should:

• Have an autoclave (heat sterilization device) on the premises.

• Use disposable needles and dispose of them in puncture-resistant receptacles.

• Make sure that all other equipment is disinfected with bleach or other disinfectant between clients, and between procedures on the same client.

• Thoroughly wash and dry hands before the procedure, wear latex gloves throughout, and use a plastic barrier on equipment.

Tea

Green or black, tea leaves spell health. Green-tea leaves should be light yellow or green. If they are brown, they've lost some of their healing powers.

A nice spot of tea is a soothing pick-me-up and a harmless pleasure. But scientific studies have led many experts to ask: might it also help prevent a stroke, a heart attack, or cancer? Tantalizing evidence says yes. Although green tea has the most well established benefits, black tea appears to protect one's health, too.

Green tea: drink to your health

Tea leaves come from an Asian shrub. They are steamed and then dried to produce green tea. Black tea is made from leaves that are partially dried, crushed, then "fermented," or allowed to oxidize for several hours. Oolong tea is fermented for a shorter time.

Green tea is in the spotlight because of its powerful antioxidant compounds called polyphenols. (Since fermentation destroys polyphenols, they are less abundant in black tea.) Lauded above all is a polyphenol called epigallocatechin gallate (EGCG), one of the most potent antioxidants ever discovered. Laboratory tests have shown that it is 25 times stronger than vitamin E at protecting DNA from damage that can cause cancer. It also blocks an enzyme necessary for the growth of tumors.

Human population studies are promising, too. In China, drinking green tea regularly is linked with lower rates of intestinal cancer. Studies in both China and Japan link green tea to lower rates of esophageal cancer. Still another Chinese study found that people who drank green tea frequently had a 29 percent lower risk of stomach cancer.

The beverage may benefit the heart, too. Green tea inhibits blood clotting, which can lead to a heart attack. It also protects LDL (the "bad") cholesterol from free radicals, which make it more harmful, and may also lower LDL levels. Studies indicate that drinking several cups of green tea a day cuts the risk of stroke and heart attack in half.

That's not all. Green tea may also boost the immune system by increasing the activity of certain cells that help fight disease.

What about black tea?

Despite the amazing health benefits of green tea, it's black tea—usually in the form of iced tea—that most North Americans prefer. Are we missing out? Not entirely. Although black tea may not contain any of the EGCG that makes green tea so healthful, it has other antioxidants that may ward off illness.

CAUTION!
Anyone with a gastro-intestinal ailment, such as an ulcer, or a sensitivity to caffeine should avoid drinking black tea. You can reduce tea's acidity—and its caffeine content—by reducing its steeping time.

Studies have shown that black tea helps fight both cancer and heart disease. In a recent study of mice genetically prone to lung cancer, 76 percent of the mice given water developed tumors, compared with 39 percent of those given black tea. In another study, this one involving more than 35,000 post-menopausal American women, those who drank two or more cups of tea daily had a 60 percent lower likelihood of developing kidney and bladder cancer and 32 percent less chance of getting cancer of the digestive tract. A California study also suggests a link to less pancreatic cancer among older tea drinkers.

Black tea may also guard against heart disease and stroke. In a Dutch study, men whose diets were rich in a type of antioxidant called flavonoids—supplied largely by tea—were only half as likely to develop heart disease. And the same men who drank more than 4½ cups of black tea a day were found to have about 70 percent fewer strokes than those who drank less tea. Other research suggests that black tea may protect LDL cholesterol from free radicals, just as green tea does.

So if you like black tea, drink it in good health. And if you prefer it with milk, that's fine, too. Although milk may make the tea's antioxidants less available to the body, adding milk makes tea easier on the stomach and also counteracts tea's tendency to decrease the body's absorption of iron (this matters only if you drink tea with meals). Adding lemon has a similar effect on iron absorption.

A cup of black tea contains three times the caffeine of green tea, but only about half that of coffee.

Tooth protection

Besides polyphenols, tea contains other compounds that affect our health, notably fluoride (especially abundant in green tea), theophylline, and caffeine. Fluoride protects against tooth decay, and black tea's antioxidants fight the bacteria that cause gum disease. (On the other hand, tea can stain the teeth.) Black tea is also an astringent and is useful in treating diarrhea. Caffeine and theophylline are stimulants that can help asthmatics by dilating the bronchial tubes. However, the caffeine in tea can act as a diuretic, potentially dehydrating the body. In higher amounts, caffeine can cause restlessness as well as irritability.

On the rocks? In a pill?

You can now buy green tea in tea bags, iced in bottles, and flavored with spices and fruits. Do all of these provide the same benefits as hot tea? Yes, but be careful of calories: Presweetened iced tea, green or black, may have as much sugar and as many calories as soft drinks. Green tea's unique polyphenols, EGCG, are also available in capsule form. Scientists don't yet know whether the capsules supply the same health benefits as green tea does.

Herbal Alternatives

When is tea not tea at all? When it's herbal. Unlike real tea, almost all herbal "teas," properly called infusions or tisanes, are caffeine-free. Although they don't contain tea's beneficial polyphenols, many have other useful properties. Some, including chamomile and lemon-balm infusions, are mildly relaxing. Many, including infusions of chamomile, fennel, ginger, peppermint, rosemary, spearmint, and thyme, settle the stomach. With no caffeine and no calories, herbal drinks are a pleasant alternative to coffee, tea, or soda.

Still, some herbs can be dangerous. Among those to avoid entirely are comfrey, chaparral, lobelia, woodruff, and sassafras. All herbal teas should be drunk in moderation.

Television

Watching television is safe—for your eyes, at least. Experts have determined that sitting up close to the screen won't harm your vision. Concerns about radiation from TV screens causing cancer have also subsided now that manufacturers have lowered emissions to minimal levels.

But what about violence? And the so-called couch potato syndrome? Unfortunately, these hazards are more serious than ever. When children, in particular, watch too much television, they run a greater risk of experiencing developmental and learning problems and becoming overweight.

North Americans certainly seem to be addicted to TV. Nearly all homes in North America have at least one television set. While a typical Canadian youngster watches less TV than his American cousin (16.8 hours a week compared to 21.7 hours), that still adds up to 875 hours per year. By age 70, he or she will have spent five to seven years of his or her life in front of a television set.

Virtual violence

Of all the statistics compiled on the power of television, none is more alarming than that concerning violence. Some two-thirds of children's programming contains violence—half of it in seemingly innocuous cartoons. By the time a youngster finishes grade school, he or she will have witnessed 8,000 murders, as well as countless graphic, disturbing news reports (particularly from cable news channels and American networks). By high school graduation, the number of violent acts he or she has seen on TV will number about 200,000. Countless studies have come to the same chilling conclusion: Children exposed to long-term violence on television are far more likely to be tense, impatient, fearful, disobedient, aggressive, hostile, and, not surprisingly, violent themselves. Constant exposure to so-called virtual violence, psychologists find, leads to an insensitivity to violence in real life.

A nation of couch potatoes

Television can be detrimental to our physical as well as mental health. A recent U.S. study

TV Guide: How to Set Limits

Here are some recommendations by the Media Awareness Network to keep your child's TV viewing healthy and balanced:

- Limit viewing to two hours per day, after homework.

- Turn off the TV during dinner.

- Make sure your babysitter follows your TV rules.

- View programs with your children so that you can discuss issues as sex, violence, alcohol, drugs, and commercial content.

- For adolescents, use TV as a springboard to discuss issues of concern to them—AIDS, sex, divorce, and peer pressure.

- Encourage your children in sports, hobbies, and reading. Don't let them become couch potatoes.

younger age and more frequently; to suffer from sleeplessness and fatigue; and in rare cases even to commit suicide. They are also less likely to socialize with other children and to develop their imaginations through creative play.

Canadian kids have far more responsible parents when it comes to TV— a 1995 study prepared for the Canadian Radio-television and Telecommunications Commission (CRTC) revealed that 81 percent of Canadian parents "intervened actively" in their children's use of TV, either by limiting the hours their children can watch or by watching shows with their kids.

Children who watch four hours or more per day are significantly more likely to have performance problems in school and on standardized tests, studies show.

Some news is good news

Despite its faults, television remains an undeniable source of entertainment, relaxation, inspiration, and education. For the lonely, the elderly, and shut-ins, TV can provide something even more vital—companionship.

TV can also play a significant role in the development of language, cognitive, and social skills in children. The right programs can expand vocabulary, kindle imagination, and reinforce good behavior, such as sharing and cooperation. In moderation, TV can even enhance academic performance. A study of young people who had watched educational programs as preschoolers found that they were not only better adjusted to school but scored higher on standardized tests and had higher high school grade-point averages in math, science, and English.

by Johns Hopkins Medical Center found that kids who watch more than four hours of TV daily are more likely to become obese—as children and as adults. Not only is watching television a sedentary act, but it provides plenty of time to snack on junk food and view commercials promoting high-calorie, fatty fast foods.

Other U.S. studies have also warned of performance problems in school by children who watch more than four hours of TV daily. These children may also be more likely to experiment with and consume alcohol and tobacco; to engage in sexual activity at a

Tobacco Products

Smokers put themselves at higher risk for everything from asthma to cancer to heart disease. Those who also drink heavily are even more likely to develop cancer of the mouth, throat, and esophagus.

Cigarettes have been deemed one of the greatest health hazards of the 20th century, and are now widely regarded as the chief preventable cause of death. Directly or indirectly, cigarettes are responsible for the deaths of more than 473,000 North Americans each year—more people than are killed by AIDS, alcohol, drug abuse, car crashes, fires, murders, and suicides combined. And that does not even include deaths attributed to other tobacco products: cigars, pipes, and "smokeless" tobacco (snuff and chewing tobacco). If you use tobacco products, quitting now is the single most powerful thing you can do to protect your health.

A heart-breaking habit

Although much of the bad press about cigarettes tends to focus on nicotine, this chemical can be faulted mainly for its addictive qualities. Far more serious is the fact that when tobacco is burned (it reaches 925°C [1700°F] at the glowing tip of a lit cigarette), it is broken down into its chemical elements, from which lethal chemical compounds are created. The period between puffs allows time for ammonia, acetone, formaldehyde, hydrogen cyanide, and some 4,000 other chemical constituents to become irritants, poisons, mutagens, nerve gases, and more than 40 types of carcinogens. And since these chemicals are released into the air, they affect other people present as well.

Among the most devastating effects are those to the heart. Each year, nearly 220,000 North Americans die as a result of tobacco-related heart disease. In addition to increasing blood pressure and heart rate, many of the chemicals in tobacco also raise "bad" (LDL) cholesterol while decreasing "good" (HDL) cholesterol. At the same time, they constrict blood vessels, decreasing blood flow and oxygen to all of the organs, particularly the heart. As if that weren't enough, when tobacco is burned, it yields a chemical residue that damages the lining of the arteries, making the blood more "sticky." This increases the risk of blood clots and dramatically raises the risk of a heart attack or stroke.

If you have high blood pressure or high cholesterol and you smoke, you are putting yourself at very high risk of a heart attack.

Lung cancer and beyond

Smoking is well-established as the leading cause of lung cancer: 87 percent of all lung cancer deaths are attributed to tobacco use. Among women, the rate of lung cancer has increased by 400 percent since 1950. Yet tobacco contributes to many other cancers, too; in fact, as many as 80 percent of all cancer deaths are linked to it. Smokers are at much greater risk for cancers of the mouth, throat, larynx, esophagus, bladder, kidney, pancreas, and cervix, and they are three times more likely to die of cancer than non-smokers.

The hazards of tobacco do not end with heart disease and cancer. Because smoking impairs the body's ability to keep the lungs clear, it contributes to such respiratory illnesses as asthma, bronchitis, pneumonia, and emphysema. Smoking is also thought to increase the risk of hip fractures, peptic ulcers, cataracts, and premature mental decline.

The Myth of "Safer" Cigarettes

Many cigarette manufacturers have introduced "low-tar" and "low-nicotine" versions of their products. But are they really safer? No. Studies show that smokers often take deeper and more frequent puffs of these products and that they smoke the cigarette down lower—thereby actually increasing health risks. Even when smoked correctly, these cigarettes may not be significantly less dangerous than regular ones.

Menthol cigarettes, for instance, are so soothing that smokers inhale more deeply and hold the smoke in their lungs longer. Filtered cigarettes, while they do reduce toxins to a small degree, also encourage smokers to inhale more deeply, increasing the risk of a form of lung cancer called adenocarcinoma. And don't forget that "additive-free" cigarettes still have addictive nicotine and cancer-causing tar.

Ironically, cigarettes made prior to 1950 were so harsh tasting that smokers inhaled less, which actually reduced their risk.

All tobacco products, but particularly cigarettes, increase the risk of infertility in both men and women. Pregnant women who smoke risk miscarriage and increase the likelihood of preterm delivery (putting the infant at risk), stillbirth, and infant death. Moreover, their babies are more likely to be born underweight. Children of smokers are also far more susceptible to asthma and ear infections.

Like pipes, cigars are leading causes of cancer of the lips and tongue.

Pick your poison

There is a notion circulating that such forms of tobacco as pipes, cigars, snuff, and chewing tobacco are safer than cigarettes. Not true. In fact, many of these products may be even more harmful than cigarettes.

A large cigar contains more tobacco than an entire pack of cigarettes. Compared with a cigarette, a cigar has 90 times the amount of nitrosamines, which are potent carcinogens. Even a short "stogie" yields a powerful blast of toxic chemicals, including 7 times as much tar, 4 times as much nicotine, and 11 times as much carbon monoxide as in a cigarette.

Although cigars are generally not smoked as frequently as cigarettes, thereby slightly lowering their likelihood of causing lung cancer and heart disease, their sheer size cancels out that good news, making them just as bad as cigarettes. What's more, if you are a former smoker, you may puff on cigars more deeply than non-smokers.

Although pipe tobacco may be less risky, depending on the blend, it too carries its share of hazards—most notably, oral cancer,

If there is any good news, it is this: quitting a tobacco product, at any time in your life, not only halts further damage to the body but also greatly reduces your risk of future disease.

Tobacco Products (continued)

Chewing tobacco, often held in the mouth for hours, can cause leukoplakia (precancerous white lesions on the lining of the mouth) and gum disease. Dry snuff, which is inhaled, irritates the nasal lining. Both may lead to nicotine addiction and, over time, to coronary heart disease and cancers of the mouth and throat.

which is attributed, in part, to the heat and friction generated by the pipe. Both cigar smoke and pipe smoke are considerably more alkaline than cigarette smoke. Therefore, their cancer-causing chemicals may be absorbed by the lungs more quickly and easily. And nonsmoking patrons of cigar bars, beware: Secondhand cigar smoke is even more dangerous than secondhand cigarette smoke.

When it comes to "smokeless" tobacco—chewing tobacco and snuff—the news is equally grim. Because it contains higher concentrations of nicotine and the body is directly exposed to it for longer periods, it tends to be even more habit-forming than cigarettes. Unfortunately, the habit starts young: More than half of the 10 million North Americans users started by age 13.

Undoing the damage

If there is any good news to be found amid all these smoking guns, it is this: quitting a tobacco product, at any time in your life, not only halts further damage to the body but greatly reduces your risk of future disease. Just 10 years after quitting, for example, an ex-smoker's risk of lung cancer drops by a dramatic 50 percent.

When it comes to heart disease, you can reverse virtually all of the damage if you quit smoking: After 15 years of being tobacco-free, the risk of coronary heart disease is about equal to that of people who never smoked.

Although many people find the "cold turkey" method of quitting works best, you don't have to go it alone. There are plenty of approaches, products, and even drugs that can help you kick the habit for good. If you give up cigarettes for a period of time but return to the pack, don't get discouraged; quitting is a skill, and sometimes it takes practice. Every year, some 1.3 million North Americans join the ranks of those who take great pride in calling themselves quitters.

Tips to Help You Kick the Habit

- The first three or four days of being smoke-free are the toughest. If you can get through the first week without a cigarette, your chances of quitting forever are good. By the time you reach the three-month mark, you'll be more or less home free.

- Smoking is as much an oral fixation as a physical addiction. To distract your mouth in the absence of a cigarette, choose a substitute, such as sugar-free chewing gum or candy, whistling, singing, chewing on carrot sticks, or sucking a lollipop.

- The first blast of nicotine in the morning increases energy and alertness. To achieve this state without the hazards of smoking, try a round of morning exercises to get you going. Then, to help you calmly focus during the day, use such therapies as music, meditation, or yoga.

- Talk to your doctor about nicotine-replacement products, such as gums, skin patches, and nasal sprays. New research shows that certain antidepressants may also help you break the habit. One such antidepressant, Zyban (bupropion), has already been approved as an antismoking medication in Canada.

- Acupuncture may help you overcome the physical addiction, and hypnosis may help some people with the behavioral aspects.

- Don't fret about gaining weight. On average, quitters put on only about 2 kilograms (5 pounds).

When ya gotta go, ya gotta go, even if it means using a public rest room. For many women, at least, the goal is not to touch the dreaded toilet seat, which must be crawling with germs, right?

Actually, a toilet seat is the least of your worries. According to the Centers for Disease Control and Prevention, you can't get syphilis, tuberculosis, or HIV (the virus that causes AIDS) from a toilet seat. And it is nearly impossible to catch genital herpes this way.

The real risk arises after you've flushed and before you've left the washroom. Did you wash your hands? Did the person before you?

A roomful of germs

A number of diseases are spread by fecal-oral contact. Touching a surface—a toilet, toilet seat, flush handle, faucet handle, doorknob—contaminated with stool from an infected person and then touching your mouth or handling food can expose you to the following: E. coli infection, hepatitis A (a liver infection), shigellosis (its symptoms are similar to those of hepatitis A, plus diarrhea), and giardiasis, a parasitic infection that can cause diarrhea, abdominal cramps, and nausea.

So your best protection from rest room germs isn't those disposable toilet-seat covers but good old soap and water. Always wash

an ounce of **Prevention**

Proper Hand-Washing Technique

You don't have to spend all afternoon at the sink to do the job right. According to the Centers for Disease Control and Prevention, just 10 or 15 seconds is all it should take to remove most contaminants from your hands. After soaping up, vigorously rub together all surfaces of your lathered hands, even between fingers. Then rinse under the faucet.

your hands after using the toilet. In addition, minimize contact with rest room surfaces as much as possible. Rest rooms in newer buildings often feature toilets that flush automatically and sink faucets that start flowing as soon as you place your hands under them.

The great unwashed

Unfortunately, people aren't washing their hands as often as they should, concludes a study cosponsored by the American Society for Microbiology. It was conducted in public men's and women's rooms in five major cities: Atlanta, Chicago, New Orleans, New York, and San Francisco. Paper towels and soap were available in all the rest rooms. Researchers counted how many people washed up after using the facilities. Among their findings:

- Nearly a third of the more than 6,000 men and women studied did not wash their hands after using the bathroom.
- The dirtiest hands were in New York's Pennsylvania Station, where only 60 percent of rest room users washed up.
- Overall, 74 percent of women and only 61 percent of men washed up. The gap was greatest in Atlanta, where 89 percent of women at a Brave's baseball game washed their hands, compared to only 46 percent of men.

So wash your hands. And to be safe, protect yourself against the hygienic lapses of other people: Use a paper towel to turn on the faucet, wash up, then use a fresh paper towel to turn off the faucet and to turn the doorknob when leaving.

The fact is, almost any disease you are likely to catch from a public rest room can be avoided simply by carefully washing your hands.

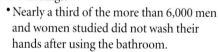

According to the Centers for Disease Control and Prevention, you can't get syphilis, tuberculosis, or HIV (the virus that causes AIDS) from a toilet seat.

Ultrasound

This radiation-free way of looking inside the body was developed in the 1950s, when the U.S. Navy used it to track submarines. By the 1970s doctors recognized its power to safely peer at human organs in a way that X rays cannot. Today ultrasound is used as a diagnostic tool in many areas of medicine, such as obstetrics, gynecology, cardiology, and oncology. The procedure is painless, and there are no known risks or side effects.

What the echoes show

During an ultrasound, the technician uses a wand-shaped device called a transducer to pass high-frequency sound waves through the skin. As the sound bounces off the body part being examined, the transducer tracks it and turns it into a computer image.

Ultrasound was first used as an obstetrical tool to determine the position and sex of an unborn child and help identify any abnormalities. Today doctors use it to diagnose problems in many parts of the body, including the heart, liver, kidney, gallbladder, rectum, colon, prostate, thyroid, breast, and vagina. A saline sonogram, in which the uterus is filled with fluid before imaging, can show abnormal growths. Recently, a high-definition imaging device was developed that differentiates benign breast lumps from malignant ones; often used in conjunction with mammograms, it may eliminate the need for a biopsy. Ultrasound is also now used to test for osteoporosis. A simple one-minute scan of the heel of the foot can estimate bone density in the entire body.

A Doppler ultrasound even shows movement, such as blood flow, on a computer screen so that blood-vessel abnormalities and blockages can be studied. A Doppler image of the brain can locate aneurysms and other blood-vessel problems and monitor the effectiveness of migraine medications.

As good as ultrasound is, it has limitations. It cannot provide images of the interior of bones or lungs. In addition, scar tissue can sometimes obscure the image. And ultrasound may not work well in obese people.

Not just an onlooker

Today ultrasound is being used not just to diagnose but to heal. Techniques include:

- Using sound waves on bone fractures, which speeds healing up to 45 percent. Patients use the ultrasound device at home through a window cut in the cast.
- Pulverizing kidney stones by means of sound waves in order to avoid surgery.
- Using ultrasound for liposuction (to liquefy fat cells so they can be sucked away). This procedure is somewhat controversial and may cause burns.
- Combining ultrasound with magnetic resonance imaging (MRI) to burn tumor cells without damaging surrounding tissue.
- Using sound waves to make cancer cells more vulnerable to drugs.
- Increasing the effectiveness of clot-busting drugs, particularly in the brain.

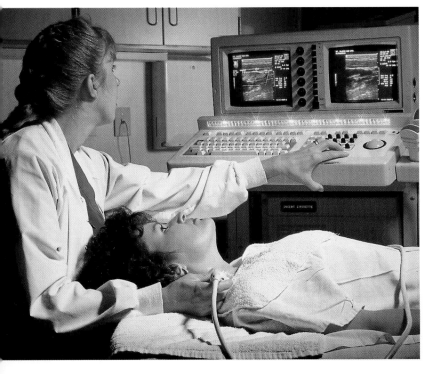

A Doppler ultrasound can diagnose atherosclerosis. The accuracy of the image depends on the technician's skill; seek one who is experienced.

During the past 50 years, vaccines have been hailed as medical miracles and have virtually eliminated such dreaded illnesses as smallpox, polio, and diphtheria. By preparing the immune system to fight off infection, they help the body defend itself against certain diseases. But though vaccines are generally safe, they aren't risk-free, and there are some important cautions to note.

A shot in the arm

When we get sick, our immune system identifies the viruses or bacteria causing the illness as foreign invaders and begins making antibodies to destroy them. It also stores an imprint of the invaders so they can be recognized and destroyed if they enter the body again. That's why once you've had measles, you are immune to the virus.

A vaccine is a highly purified and much weaker version of a disease-causing virus or bacterium. Acting just like the actual virus or bacterium, the vaccine triggers the immune system to make antibodies and store an imprint of the invader.

Vaccines vary in when and how often they are given. For example, the measles vaccine requires only two doses in early childhood, whereas the diphtheria and tetanus vaccine requires several childhood doses and a booster every 10 years throughout adulthood. A yearly flu shot (newly designed for each flu season) is recommended for health-care workers, anyone age 65 and over, and anyone with certain long-term health problems, such as heart, lung, or kidney disease.

What about side effects?

Vaccines can greatly reduce your risk of certain diseases. But they may cause mild side effects, including redness or pain at the site of injection, fatigue, sore muscles, and fever. Tell your doctor if you currently have an illness.

Also inform the doctor if you are allergic to eggs or baker's yeast. In rare cases you may have an allergic reaction to the vaccine itself, the materials in which it was grown, or the chemicals in which it is suspended. For example, if you have an egg allergy, beware of flu shots or the MMR (measles, mumps, and

rubella) vaccine, since both are grown in an egg medium. People who are allergic to the drug neomycin are urged to avoid the chicken pox vaccine, available in the United States but not yet licensed in Canada.

Safer shots

Medical experts agree that vaccines present a far less serious health risk than the diseases they are meant to prevent. They may cause minor temporary side effects such as soreness or fever, but there is little evidence linking vaccination with permanent health problems. Only in the rarest cases does a vaccination cause seizure, shock, coma, or death.

In response to misconceptions about the safety of the DTP (diphtheria, tetanus, and

Beginning at birth, keep a log of which vaccines your child has had, and when. Childhood immunization means lifetime protection against major diseases. Health protection agencies urge parents to see that their children have the recommended vaccines before starting school, and preferably by age two.

On the Horizon In the near future, we may all face more shots. Several new vaccines are being developed to protect against rotavirus, which kills up to 1 million babies a year worldwide; skin and breast cancer; and Lyme disease. Also on the way are flu vaccines that may be administered via nasal spray or skin patch.

Vaccinations (continued)

Commonly Recommended Vaccines

These vaccines are routinely prescribed. People who travel to countries outside Canada may also need protection against diseases that are common there.

Vaccine	Who Needs One	Side Effects	Risks
DTP and DTaP Diphtheria, tetanus (lockjaw), and pertussis (whooping cough)	Infants and preschoolers (five doses are recommended before age six), their parents, and people who care for young children. Td (tetanus and diphtheria) booster is needed every 10 years.	Common: soreness, redness, or swelling at the site of injection; fever; irritability. Rare: nonstop crying, lasting muscle pain, high fever.	Very small chance of seizure, severe allergic reaction, or brain damage. Children who should *not* get pertussis vaccine should get Td vaccine, not DTP or DTaP.
Polio	Infants and preschool children (for oral polio vaccine, four doses are recommended from two months to six years of age)	Oral polio vaccine (OPV): none. Inactivated Polio Vaccine (IPV): mild soreness at the site of injection (it is given as a shot in the arm or leg).	OPV: extremely small risk of getting polio or (for those who are not vaccinated) from close contact (e.g., kissing, changing of diapers) with someone who got OPV in the past 30 days. IPV: no risk.
MMR Measles, mumps, and rubella (German measles)	Young children, their parents, and people who care for young children.	Common: soreness at the site of injection. Less common: rash, high fever, swollen glands, joint pain and stiffness. Rare: ongoing joint pain, seizure.	Could trigger an allergic reaction to eggs or the drug neomycin. May cause drop in blood platelets (extremely rare). Pregnant women are advised to wait until after delivery.
Hepatitis B	Infants, children, and high-risk adults.	Soreness at the site of injection, mild to moderate fever.	Extremely small risk of serious allergic reaction or anaphylactic shock.
Hib *Haemophilus influenzae* type B	Children under the age of five.	Common: soreness at the site of injection. Rare: fever, vomiting, diarrhea.	Extremely small risk of contracting paralytic polio.
Influenza	Anyone whose health could be endangered by getting the flu, particularly people over the age of 65.	Soreness at the site of injection, mild flulike symptoms (fever, muscle aches) for one to two days.	Could trigger an allergic reaction to eggs. There is an extremely small risk of Guillain-Barré syndrome, a severe paralytic illness.

Hepatitis B vaccination, which may be given as early as one month, is not always routine. Teenagers who did not get vaccinated in infancy should check with their doctors.

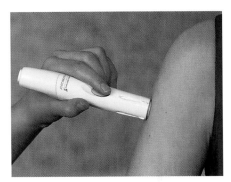

Needle-free injection devices use compressed air to deliver the vaccine.

pertussis) vaccine and concerns about a possible link to sudden infant death syndrome (SIDS) and severe brain damage, a new form of the vaccine has been developed. Called DTaP, it is now used (in combination inoculations) in all provinces and territories.

(Rumors to the contrary, large epidemiologic studies have found no relationship between SIDS and vaccination, and studies regarding DTP vaccines and chronic nervous system dysfunction in children are inconclusive.) Finally, vaccines are not 100 percent fail-safe (though they are often close). One reason is that a person's immune system may not respond to a vac-

cine as it should. For more information on vaccines, and the inoculation schedules recommended by your provincial health ministry, contact your local public health unit.

Canada differs from many countries in that immunization is not mandatory—Canadian courts consider forced immunization a form of battery. Health legislation in Manitoba, Ontario, and New Brunswick makes immunization a prerequisite for school enrollment—inoculation against measles is mandatory in Manitoba; vaccinations against diphtheria, tetanus, polio, mumps, and rubella are required in Ontario and New Brunswick. But even these provinces make exceptions for those who object on religious or medical grounds or for reasons of conscience. In all provinces, unvaccinated children may be absent from school during outbreaks of vaccine-preventable diseases.

Vacuum Cleaners

Most household vacuum cleaners do a fine job of picking up dust and dirt, but the story doesn't end there. Tiny particles of mold spores, pollen, dust-mite droppings, flakes of human skin, and pet dander may easily pass through a vacuum's filters and be blown right back into the air through the exhaust. Small wonder that, in susceptible people, vacuuming may trigger allergy or asthma attacks.

The Best Dust Bags

If you're willing to spend the extra money, you can buy special dust bags that may trap particles more efficiently. For example:

- Bags with multiple linings.
- Ones with specially treated linings that attract dust.
- Bags, for certain vacuums, that close up as you remove them to keep dust from escaping.

Sizing up the problem

Conventional vacuum cleaners trap particles as small as 30 micrometers in diameter, but some components of household dust are even smaller. Pollen can measure 10 micrometers; pet dander, 5 micrometers; and bacteria, 0.3 micrometer—200 to 300 times smaller than the width of a human hair.

Some newer models are specially designed to trap many of these microparticles. One uses a cyclonic system, which filters dirt and dust by way of high-velocity air currents that spin the particles out of the air. Another traps dust in a water reservoir.

Vacuum-cleaner filters also play an important role. The most efficient—and most expensive—is a high-efficiency particulate air (HEPA) filtration system, designed to pick up 99.97 percent of all particles as small as 0.3 micrometer in diameter.

Canister or upright?

The type of vacuum cleaner you choose will affect the air quality in your home. The brushes built into upright vacuums are very good for loosening dirt in carpet pile. But for uncarpeted floors, a full-size canister vacuum picks up dirt and particles better (the rotating brushes on an upright vacuum cleaner may simply push them around and stir them into the air). And most canister vacuums have electric brush attachments that make them effective for cleaning carpets, too.

The location of the fan is another concern. Uprights with the fan in front of the dust bag generally retain more dust than canisters, which have the fan behind the bag.

It's all in the technique

Whichever model you choose, vacuum slowly and carefully to avoid stirring up dust unnecessarily, especially if you have allergies or asthma. Spend at least two minutes going over each square meter (square yard) of floor. If you are likely to pick up fleas, moths, or other pests, seal the dust bag in a plastic bag before discarding.

The future of housework

Another way to clean up your vacuuming act is to install a central vacuum system in your home. Using tubes that are permanently mounted in the walls and vented outside, such a system is so convenient to use that you are very likely to vacuum more often. Although it is more expensive to retrofit the system in an older home than to install it into a newly built one, it provides relief for people with allergies because it totally eliminates the recirculation of airborne particles.

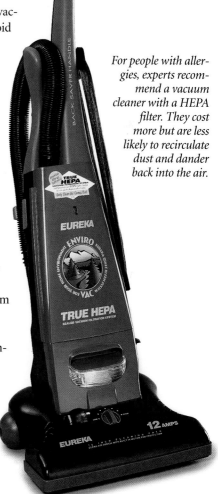

For people with allergies, experts recommend a vacuum cleaner with a HEPA filter. They cost more but are less likely to recirculate dust and dander back into the air.

Varicose Veins

Appearing most often as bulging, bluish, cordlike swellings in the legs, varicose veins usually look more dangerous than they are. Frequently inherited, the condition tends to show up between ages 30 and 60. Women, who are particularly vulnerable during pregnancy, are affected far more often than men. While most varicose veins are not life-threatening, they can cause significant pain and limit mobility. Fortunately, medical treatments can help. Self-help measures also make a difference.

Unsightly blood backup

The arteries are equipped with muscle tissue to help the heart pump blood through the body, but the veins are not. They rely on the surrounding muscles to push blood toward the heart. To encourage blood flow to the heart, the leg veins are equipped with one-way valves that prevent blood from flowing in the other direction.

If the leg veins lose their elasticity because of high blood pressure, obesity, pregnancy, or other reasons, the valves may malfunction. As a result, blood may leak backward, collect in the veins, and create the protrusions we know as varicose veins. Although they can occur anywhere in the body (varicose veins in the rectum are called hemorrhoids), they most often develop in the legs. Accompanying symptoms can include an aching, heavy feeling after standing or sitting too long; dry, itchy skin around the vein; and a brownish discoloration of the skin in the lower leg. Open wounds called skin ulcers may also occur.

Don't Make Varicose Veins Even Worse

If you have varicose veins, avoid the following:

- High-impact aerobics and jogging
- Tight clothes, girdles, and control-top pantyhose
- High heels with narrow, pointed toes
- Standing or sitting (without putting your feet up) for long periods of time
- Crossing the legs
- Direct sun exposure on the affected areas
- Exposure to very hot water
- Constipation
- Obesity

While most varicose veins are harmless, the vein wall may become inflamed and small blood clots may form, causing a painful condition called superficial thrombophlebitis. If clotting occurs in deep-lying veins, deep-vein thrombosis, a potentially life-threatening condition, may develop. Its symptoms can be similar to those of varicose veins, so bring any vascular condition to your doctor's attention.

Getting the bulge out

Only in rare cases is surgery necessary to treat varicose veins. If it is, the vein may be removed from the leg. A varicose vein may also be treated with sclerotherapy, in which a corrosive chemical is injected into the vein, causing it to close up and disintegrate. The blood that once traveled through the vein re-routes itself through healthier ones. There are advantages and drawbacks of each procedure, so discuss your options with your doctor.

Most important in the management of varicose veins is taking self-help measures:

- **Wear elastic support stockings.** Put them on before you get up (elevate your legs for a few minutes first). Make sure they aren't too tight; custom-made stockings are best. They do wear out, so replace them about every three months.
- **Lie or sit with your legs elevated** as often as possible.
- **Exercise your legs** (walking is great) to tone muscles and promote circulation.
- **Massage the legs and feet,** particularly with rosemary oil, to promote circulation.

Vegetables

"Eat your vegetables." What child hasn't been told this by his or her parents? But the truth is, adults don't eat enough vegetables, either. That's too bad, because inviting these foods onto your plate may be the most effective dietary action you can take to protect yourself from high blood pressure, diabetes, stroke, heart disease, and many forms of cancer.

Nature's wonder foods

Vegetables—provided they aren't fried, creamed, or drowned in cheese or butter—are the perfect foil for the typical North American diet, which is high in sodium and low in potassium. (The right balance of potassium and sodium helps regulate blood pressure.) Most are rich in fiber, which helps promote normal bowel function, prevent diverticulosis, and lower high cholesterol levels. Fiber may even help prevent colon cancer. Fresh or slightly cooked, vegetables are also excellent sources of vitamin C.

Folate, or folic acid, a nutrient many North Americans don't get enough of, is also abundant in vegetables. Adequate supplies guard against birth defects, help prevent colon cancer, and lower homocysteine levels in the blood (high levels are a strong risk factor for heart disease). Folic acid is found in many vegetables, but it's especially plentiful in dark, leafy greens, such as spinach. (The word *folic* derives from the Latin for "leaf.")

The various pigments that make vegetables colorful also make them healthful, so paint your plate with as many of them as possible. Dark, leafy greens, such as spinach and kale, are rich in lutein, a pigment linked with cancer protection. Green, yellow, orange, and red vegetables are good sources of carotenoids, pigments that may ward off heart disease and certain cancers. Carotenoids also help prevent blindness by lowering the risk of macular degeneration, the most common cause of sight loss among people over age 65. Tomatoes—especially cooked ones—are rich in lycopene, another carotenoid linked to a reduced risk of cancer and heart disease.

And that's only the beginning. Vegetables in the cabbage family contain compounds called isothiocyanates, which stimulate the body to detoxify potential carcinogens. Onions, scallions, leeks, chives, and garlic are rich in sulfur compounds that protect against both cancer and heart disease. Phthalides, substances found in celery and parsnips, have also shown cancer-protective properties.

Measurable benefits

Think of vegetables as insurance against major diseases. Evidence is mounting that eating more vegetables can significantly reduce your risks of these health threats:

- **Cancer.** More than 200 human studies have linked increased vegetable consumption with reduced risk of many cancers, especially stomach, esophageal, lung, mouth, throat, endometrial, pancreatic, and colon cancer. The best protection is offered by vegetables in the onion and cabbage families, plus carrots, celery, green

A rainbow of resistance: The more colors of vegetables on your table, the more likely you are to fend off disease.

Eating cruciferous vegetables—including cabbage, broccoli, cauliflower and brussels sprouts, above—every day helps prevent cancer. Bok choy and collard greens are also part of the cruciferous family.

vegetables, parsley, peppers, and tomatoes. There is also some evidence that vegetables may help prevent breast cancer. In a study of Greek women, for example, those who ate four to five servings of vegetables a day had a 46 percent lower risk of the disease than those who ate less than two servings a day. A study of American women revealed that those who ate either carrots or spinach more than twice a week were less likely to develop breast cancer compared with women who ate them rarely.

- **High blood pressure.** Several studies show that people who eat plenty of vegetables

(and fruits) tend to have lower blood pressure than people who rarely eat them. In one major study of subjects with high blood pressure, a diet rich in vegetables, fruits, and low-fat dairy foods lowered blood pressure substantially.

- **Stroke.** By lowering blood pressure, vegetables may also help prevent stroke. In one study, men who had the highest intake of fruits and vegetables had a 59 percent lower chance of having a stroke. A study among women suggested similar benefits.

- **Heart disease.** Although the link is not as well established as that between vegetables and cancer prevention, evidence suggests that eating an abundance of vegetables may help reduce the risk of coronary heart disease. The fiber, folic acid, vitamin C, carotenoids, and flavonoids contained in vegetables may all contribute to this effect. Dutch researchers found that elderly men who consumed a diet high in flavonoids—found in red and yellow onions, broccoli, French beans, and kale, as well as some fruits—had a 60 percent lower risk of dying from heart disease than men who consumed few of them. In a separate study of Italian

Raw Versus Cooked Vegetables

Studies consistently show that people who have low rates of cancer regularly enjoy raw and lightly cooked (steamed, for example) vegetables. One possible reason is that nutrients, such as vitamin C, folic acid, and other cancer-fighting antioxidants and phytochemicals, are reduced by cooking. For example, watercress provides a bounty of vitamins A and C and other nutrients, but only when it's served raw or cooked (and served) quickly.

Cooking isn't all bad, however. It can benefit carotenoids, the plant pigments that include beta-carotene (which makes carrots orange) and lycopene (which makes tomatoes red). Cooking breaks down the plants' cell walls, making the nutrients more available to the body. Eating cooked tomatoes with a little dietary fat is even better because it improves lycopene absorption.

One study found that men who ate four servings of cooked

tomatoes a week (even in tomato sauce or pizza) had a much lower risk of developing prostate cancer. (Tomato juice didn't help.) Lycopene intake has also been linked with a significantly lower risk of heart disease.

So enjoy vegetables raw in salads or as snacks. Or you can steam or boil them quickly in a little water. But take time to cook the carrots and tomatoes.

women, those who ate the most carrots and green vegetables were the least likely to have a heart attack.

Garden variety

The number of produce items available in supermarkets has sky-rocketed from about 160 in the mid-1970s to more than 400 today. And farmers markets are booming. To pack the best nutritional punch, your daily intake of vegetables should include lots of variety, more than just potatoes and corn—which are slim in nutrients when compared with other vegetables, especially such heavy hitters as kale, spinach, sweet potatoes, carrots, winter squash, broccoli, and brussels sprouts.

When it comes to salad greens, try to avoid iceberg lettuce, which is all but devoid of nutrients. Another common lettuce, romaine, packs more nutritional punch. Watercress is even more healthful, and, because it is a cruciferous vegetable, it helps guard against cancer. So, in addition to eating your recommended servings of vegetables each day, choose dark greens—the darker, the better—and strive for variety.

Also pay attention to how the vegetables are prepared. Avoid fried vegetables; eggplant, for instance, absorbs oil like a sponge, making a serving of fried eggplant more fatty than an enormous slab of steak. And while a baked potato is high in potassium and low in sodium and fat, French fries are loaded with both sodium and fat.

To avoid sacrificing such water-soluble nutrients as vitamin C, steam or microwave vegetables rather than boil them. If you do boil them, boil them whole or in large pieces; smaller pieces lose more nutrients.

Sprouts: Good Things Come in Small Packages

Vegetable sprouts, shoots from germinating seeds, may be short in stature, but they can be long on nutrition. For example, legume sprouts often have higher concentrations of vitamin C, protein, iron, and B vitamins than some vegetables.

The current stars among sprouts are broccoli sprouts, which are becoming available in more and more stores. While three-day-old shoots have much less vitamins, fiber, and folic acid than the grown-up vegetable, they contain 20 to 50 times more cancer-fighting sulforaphane. As little as 30 to 60 grams (1 to 2 ounces) provides as much of the substance as 900 grams (2 pounds) of mature broccoli. So sprinkle some sprouts on your salads and sandwiches, but eat your fully grown vegetables, too.

The safety issue

In recent years, food-borne illnesses have been traced to vegetables eaten raw, including salad greens and even alfalfa sprouts. To be safe, wash all vegetables thoroughly in cold running water. Tear off the outer leaves of lettuce and cabbage, peel carrots, and scrub other root vegetables.

While pesticides are widely used on both domestic and imported produce, the Canadian Food Inspection Agency (CFIA) conducts tests to ensure that pesticide residues do not exceed regulatory limits. Sometimes, produce is found to contain excessive pesticide residues. Organic produce, of course, has less pesticide residue, but it usually costs more to stock up your refrigerator.

On the Horizon Researchers are hoping to create medications with the same cancer protection found in vegetables. At Johns Hopkins Medical Center in Baltimore, Maryland, mice treated with broccoli extracts containing high concentrations of sulforaphane, a known cancer fighter, developed significantly fewer tumors than untreated mice. The tumors that did occur in the treated mice were smaller and took longer to develop.

Vegetarianism

An increasing number of studies point to the health benefits of a plant-based diet, which may reduce the risk of several chronic diseases. So if you're tempted to give up meat, you're not alone. And as long as you make sure to eat enough of a wide variety of foods, even strict vegetarians—people who exclude not only meat, fish, and poultry but also eggs and dairy products from their diets—can get the nutrients they need. All it takes is a little bit of planning.

The American Institute for Cancer Research found a plant-based diet key in reducing cancer risk.

The good news

Simply eating plenty of vegetables and fruits can cut cancer risk by at least 20 percent. So say the experts at the American Institute for Cancer Research. After recently reviewing more than 4,000 scientific studies on diet and cancer, they found a plant-based diet to be key in reducing cancer risk. That fact is borne out in Mediterranean and Asian populations, where cancer rates are lower than in such countries as the United States, Canada, and Britain, where less plant foods are consumed in the diet.

In the soup: A hearty vegetable stew becomes a complete, nutritious meal when you include such protein sources as chick peas or other legumes.

Research has also shown that vegetarians are less prone to many other illnesses, including heart disease, stroke, type II diabetes, high blood pressure, and possibly kidney stones, gallstones, and osteoporosis. A study of 48 patients with coronary artery disease suggests that a vegetarian diet may even reverse heart disease. There's another bonus: Vegetarians tend to be leaner than meat eaters.

Plants are thought to work their magic by employing such disease fighters as antioxidants (beta-carotene, vitamin C, selenium), fiber, folic acid, potassium, and other plant chemicals. Vegetarian eating also means getting less of the dietary troublemakers: saturated fat, cholesterol, and meat protein. However, even vegetarians must be wary of many high-fat snack foods that qualify as vegetarian fare. The fat found in nuts, seeds, and vegetable oils can add up.

Nutritional concerns

The more restrictive your diet, the more difficult it is to meet nutrient needs. Vegans, who swear off all animal products, may be deficient in certain essential nutrients, such as vitamin B_{12} (available only in animal foods) and vitamin D. The calcium, iron, and zinc in plants are not as easily absorbed as those in animal foods. Even vegetarians who eat eggs and milk (ovo-lacto vegetarians) need a varied diet to avoid nutritional deficiencies.

Fortunately, focusing on a few key foods can help. Vitamin B_{12} (found in dairy products and eggs) is often added to soy milk and fortified cold cereals. Iron is found in fortified cereals, dried beans, and dried fruits; you can increase your absorption by eating foods rich in vitamin C. Nuts and beans are good sources of zinc, and tofu, fortified orange juice, and broccoli will help satisfy calcium needs. With the exception of soy, single plant foods are not sources of complete protein. But vegetarians who eat grains along with nuts or beans should get enough protein; the combinations constitute complete protein. As insurance, vegetarians might consider taking a multivitamin/mineral supplement.

Kids love the cartoonish thrills of video games, whether played in arcades, at home on video consoles, or on small hand-held devices. Computer games are equally popular. Some call this infatuation harmless and point out that playing computer and video games helps children develop computer literacy and hone such skills as spatial visualization, improved hand-eye coordination, and problem solving. But many others worry that hours spent playing these games leave children with a crippled imagination and an inability to focus on schoolwork or friends—or worse, prone to violent behavior. All agree that moderation is the key.

Cyber violence

The theme of many of the most popular video games is "vanquish the enemy," complete with gory visuals—decapitations and the like—and sound effects. The jury is still out on the long-term effects of video-game violence on children. Some experts claim that kids who are given the chance to act out their aggression in a game will be less aggressive in real life. But most researchers assert that media violence has the opposite effect: when kids see violence on television or in a video game, they are more likely to behave aggressively or antisocially.

Other video-game pitfalls

One of the main problems with video games may be the amount of time kids spend playing them. Seventh- and eighth-grade students surveyed in one study played the games an average of 4.2 hours a week, time that could have been spent reading, doing homework, or engaging in creative play. For a few children, game playing becomes an obsession or an escape from real-life problems. It also provides stiff competition for teachers, some of whom find that kids expect all learning to be approached as a "game" and are able to concentrate less on books or educational projects than on electronic entertainment.

The sedentary nature of video games is a cause for concern as well. Some experts warn that video games displace exercise and participation in organized sports at a time when more and more children are obese.

What parents can do

While some parents are tempted to ban electronic games altogether, doing so may make

Video games used to be the favored domain of boys. Now manufacturers also cater to girls, who generally prefer nonviolent fare.

them all the more irresistible to children. Here's a better approach: monitor the games your child plays and limit playing time.

Concerned parents should also screen games for violent content. Although games are rated (E for everyone, KA for "kids to adults", T for teenagers 13 and older, and M for mature players over age 17), that's only a starting point; a game rated E may have little violence, but what it has may be frighteningly realistic. Steer your child toward nonviolent games that involve solving puzzles, fashioning elaborate structures, designing clothing, or using their imagination in some other way. You can also choose among the many video selections that offer an entertaining way to learn geography, history, math, and reading.

Regulating Game Time

- Set time limits for your child's video- or computer-game playing, such as an hour a day after homework. Have your child log time spent playing games.

- Put the computer or video console in a room used by the whole family, not in your child's bedroom. This will give you a better idea of how much time he or she spends playing.

- Come up with alternative activities based on your child's favorite video games. Substitute playing soccer in the park for virtual soccer or a real game of chess for video chess.

Vitamins

Adult men and postmenopausal women should look for a multivitamin supplement that does not contain iron. Unless your doctor determines that you have a deficiency, extra iron could cause health problems.

Looking at the drugstore shelves crowded with vitamin supplements, you'd swear the food supply was devoid of nutrients. Not so: For most people, eating a balanced diet rich in grains, vegetables and fruits, with smaller portions of dairy products and meat, poultry, fish, or beans, provides almost all of the vitamins we need.

So why do we buy supplements? Some people—the elderly, for example—may have trouble eating a diet that supplies enough vitamins. Others take high doses of vitamins in hopes of preventing chronic disease. Many are simply seeking dietary insurance. But are supplements necessary?

All 13 vitamins are, in fact, essential to life (the word actually derives from the Latin *vita*, meaning "life"). However, only small amounts are needed to regulate your metabolic processes and prevent deficiency diseases, such as rickets (vitamin D), scurvy (vitamin C), and beriberi (vitamin B_1). For instance, one glass of orange juice supplies the recommended nutrient intake (RNI) of vitamin C, and even less prevents the scurvy that plagued British sailors centuries ago.

Many nutritionists believe that supplements are necessary only in specific instances. In fact, if you take them when you don't need them, or you take too much of a vitamin, you may do yourself more harm than good.

Make D while the sun shines

Vitamin D makes it easier for the body to absorb calcium. It may also help to prevent osteoporosis and to protect against colon cancer. But many people don't get enough. We need 5 micrograms (mcg) or 200 international units (IU) a day until we're 50, when the requirement goes up to 10 mcg (400 IU); after 70, it's 15 mcg (600 IU). In one test, close to 60 percent of hospitalized patients were deficient. Even among those who said they consumed enough vitamin D, almost 40 percent did not. A cup of fortified milk supplies about 100 IU; a serving of fortified cereal, about 50 IU. In addition, sunshine (except during winter in northern latitudes) helps skin manufacture it. But some people may still need a supplement.

Folic acid takes center stage

Women of childbearing age should consume 400 mcg of folic acid daily. That's easily obtained from a diet rich in fruits and vegetables, but if yours isn't, consider a supplement. This B vitamin, abundant in leafy greens, citrus fruits, and fortified grains, slashes the risk of spina bifida and anencephaly, two common neural-tube birth defects affecting newborns.

Folic acid may also help prevent certain cancers, including cervical cancer. The vitamin is intimately involved in maintaining the integrity of the body's genetic material, DNA. Scientists believe that folic acid deficiency can make chromosomes more likely to break—a prelude to abnormal cell growth.

Folic acid, along with two other B vitamins—B_6 and B_{12}—also shows promise in battling heart disease. The three Bs prevent the accumulation of homocysteine, a by-product of amino acid metabolism, in the blood. Although heart disease researchers once focused solely on blood cholesterol as a cause of heart disease, they now find that excess homocysteine may also be a significant risk factor. High levels encourage the formation of blood clots and may also damage artery walls, resulting in the plaque buildup that can lead to heart attacks and strokes.

The problem is half of all Canadians don't get enough folic acid. Another 20 percent get too little B_6, found in whole wheat, peanuts, bananas, soybeans, fish, chicken and meat. And while most adults get plenty of B_{12}, found in animal foods, some elderly men and women don't absorb it well.

The homocysteine story confirms the importance of a well-balanced diet rich in whole grains, vegetables, and fruits. But supplements may also play an important role. In stroke survivors, B_6, B_{12}, and folic acid supplements reduced blood levels of homocysteine and damage to artery walls. There is not enough evidence yet to say whether supplements directly cut the risk of heart disease.

Antioxidant arsenal

The body is continually doing battle with free radicals, unstable oxygen molecules in the body and in the air we breathe that injure the eyes, blood vessel walls, and even DNA. Such damage can lead to cataracts, heart disease, and cancer. Although the body has built-in defense mechanisms, the antioxidant vitamins C, E, and beta-carotene (along with the mineral selenium) can neutralize free radicals, reducing the risk of these diseases.

Of all the antioxidant vitamins, vitamin E shows the most promise for reducing heart disease risk. Several studies have found that a supplement of at least 100 IU of vitamin E daily (almost 10 times the RNI) can significantly cut the risk of disease. Other research shows that vitamin E guards blood vessels from damage caused by LDL cholesterol that leads to plaque formation.

The link between antioxidant supplements and cancer is not as clear. Although there is some evidence that consuming slightly more than the recommended levels of vitamin C may reduce the risk of certain cancers, other studies that found a connection involved levels that are considered unsafe. Rather than taking large amounts of vitamin C, a better idea might be to combine a modest amount of C with vitamin E. Recently, scientists found that male smokers who took 50 IU of vitamin E daily for up to eight years reduced their risk of prostate cancer. The evidence is

Multicolored salads provide vitamin C, folic acid, and beta-carotene. For vitamin E, add dressing made with virgin or extra-virgin olive oil.

mixed regarding whether or not beta-carotene lowers cancer risk.

Antioxidants may also help prevent cataracts. The eye's lens concentrates vitamin C at levels 60 times greater than those found in the blood. This may be the body's way of protecting the lens from ultraviolet light,

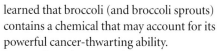

which generates free radicals and increases the risk of cataracts. Studies suggest that diets rich in vitamins C and E lower the risk.

Revving up the immune system

All nutrients are crucial to a healthy immune system, especially vitamins C, E, B_6, and B_{12}. Starting at age 50, the body's immunity declines, increasing one's susceptibility to illnesses from pneumonia to cancer. But the decline is not inevitable. Studies show that older individuals who take multivitamins have a stronger immune response. Vitamin E supplements may also boost defenses.

Food comes first

Supplements don't work miracles, however. If your diet is high in fat, salt, and sugar and lacking in the disease-fighting phytochemicals found in fruits and vegetables, don't expect supplements to save the day. Hundreds of studies have revealed that diets rich in fruits and vegetables combat cancer and heart disease. Antioxidant supplements have shown no such consistent benefits.

That's because fruits and vegetables are complete disease-fighting packages that contain protective agents not found in supplements. Beta-carotene, for example, is only one of hundreds of carotenoids, all of which may contribute to health. Also, scientists recently learned that broccoli (and broccoli sprouts) contains a chemical that may account for its powerful cancer-thwarting ability.

Another advantage of getting vitamins from a plate instead of a pill: it's nearly impossible to overdose on vitamins from food. To get too much vitamin C, you'd have to drink gallons of orange juice. But it's very easy to get too much with a supplement. Vitamins A and D are two of the most toxic vitamins if taken in large doses.

Recently beta-carotene has come under close scrutiny because of possible adverse effects. One research study was stopped almost two years early because lung cancer rates rose among the heavy smokers and drinkers who took supplements. Such results would have been highly unlikely if the subjects had been eating mangoes, apricots, and other beta-carotene-rich foods instead. One reason is that fruits and vegetables are also high in vitamin C, which protects beta-carotene from damage that can actually turn this antioxidant into a health risk. Since smokers are often deficient in vitamin C, taking beta-carotene supplements increased their already high risk of getting lung cancer.

When to pop a pill

Some people should take certain supplements. Talk to your doctor to find out whether you may need the following.

- **Vitamin E.** Anyone who eats a low-fat diet isn't likely to get a lot of this nutrient, found in nuts, margarine, and vegetable oils. Because of its antioxidant properties, many health professionals suggest that people with high LDL cholesterol, a family history of heart disease, or risk factors for prostate cancer take a supplement.
- **Vitamin D.** If you are over 50 or you rarely go outside, live in the northern latitudes, or wear sunscreen to ward off skin cancer (sunscreen dramatically reduces the amount of vitamin D your skin can make), you may need a supplement.
- **Vitamin B_{12}.** The U.S. National Research Council's Institute of Medicine recently

Wheat germ is an excellent source of B vitamins, vitamin E, and fiber. Try it in muffins and pancakes or sprinkle it on your breakfast cereal.

A fortified breakfast cereal provides extra vitamins, but it's no better (and costs more) than a multivitamin. Focus instead on a choosing a cereal that's high in fiber and low in fat, sugar, and salt. For extra vitamins and fiber, add berries or raisins.

recommended that everyone over age 50 eat foods fortified with vitamin B_{12} or take a B_{12} supplement; it's estimated that 15 to 20 percent of people over age 65 are deficient. That's because their stomachs can no longer produce enough acid to adequately absorb B_{12} from food. Mood changes and poor memory, often thought to stem from depression or even dementia, may actually be symptoms of B_{12} deficiency.

- **Vitamin C.** Until they quit, smokers may be helped by supplements that reduce free-radical formation created by tobacco smoke.
- **Multivitamin supplements.** Women of childbearing age, people older than 50, and heavy drinkers should take a supplement that contains about 100 percent of the RNI for each vitamin daily.

Are There Benefits to Larger Doses?

Some research indicates that large doses of certain vitamins—larger than those typically found in a healthy diet—can help ward off certain diseases. In other cases, large doses can be toxic. Remember that vitamins can interfere with some medications. Check with your doctor before taking them.

Vitamin	What It Does	Benefits of Large Doses	Risks of Large Doses
Vitamin D	Builds bones and teeth. Needed for calcium absorption. May reverse or halt osteoporosis and reduce the risk of colon cancer.	None	2,000 IU or more daily may cause fragile bones, diarrhea, and calcium deposits in the heart, kidneys, and blood vessels.
Vitamin E	Acts as an antioxidant.	May help prevent cancer, heart disease, and cataracts and boost immunity.	More than 1,000 IU daily may increase the risk of bleeding in people taking blood thinners. Can cause diarrhea and nausea.
Beta-Carotene	The body converts it to vitamin A. Acts as an antioxidant.	May help prevent heart disease, cataracts, and macular degeneration and boost immunity.	Stains the palms of the hands and soles of the feet orange. Heavy smokers and drinkers may increase their risk of cancer.
Folic Acid	Needed to manufacture DNA and red blood cells. Prevents certain birth defects and may prevent heart disease and cancer.	None	The safe limit is set at 1,000 micrograms per day. Can prevent seizure medication from controlling symptoms and can mask vitamin B_{12} deficiency.
Vitamin B_6	Important for carbohydrate, fat, and protein metabolism; needed for red blood cell formation and for proper functioning of the nervous and immune systems. May reduce risk of heart disease.	None	One study has shown that more than 100 mg a day can cause nerve damage in hands and feet, resulting in numbness and problems with walking; prevents seizure medication from controlling symptoms.
Vitamin B_{12}	Needed for DNA synthesis, red blood cell formation, proper functioning of the nervous system, and carbohydrate and fat metabolism. May reduce the risk of heart disease.	Some experts recommend 25 milligrams (mg) for older adults who often do not absorb the vitamin from food very well.	No known risks in adults
Vitamin C	Forms collagen, a substance that holds cells together; speeds wound healing; needed for proper immune functioning; helps form neurotransmitters; important for the metabolism of iron and folic acid; acts as an antioxidant.	May help prevent heart disease, cancer, and cataracts.	More than 2,000 mg daily (and for some people, 1,000 mg) may cause diarrhea and nausea. May produce false negatives in colon cancer tests and false positives in blood-sugar tests. Reduces the effect of oral blood thinners.

Warts & Wart Removers

No one knows why some people get warts and others don't, but three out of four people develop one sooner or later. The good news is that most warts are benign and usually disappear on their own. If you can't stand the sight of them, there are a number of ways to speed their healing or get rid of them altogether. But some treatment methods can cause serious burns or painful scars—and the wart may simply grow back.

Causes and types

Warts are small growths caused by a mildly contagious organism called the human papillomavirus (HPV). They are most common in children and adolescents but may develop at any age. You get warts not by touching toads but by person-to-person contact or from such public places as shower stalls and swimming pool decks. Typically, the virus enters the skin through a cut or an abrasion. It can take from two to six months to incubate, although sometimes it lies dormant for years. There are dozens of HPV strains, accounting for at least six types of warts. These include:

- **Common warts.** Often found on sites subject to injury, such as the face, hands, knees, and scalp, these are round or irregular with a raised, rough surface.
- **Flat warts.** Smaller and smoother, these grow in clusters of up to 100 on the hands, legs, and face.
- **Plantar warts.** Resembling calluses because they grow from the outside in, these flat warts appear on the sole of the foot and can be extremely painful.
- **Filiform warts.** These long, fingerlike projections are found on the eyelids, armpits, face, and neck of overweight or middle-aged people.
- **Periungual warts.** People who bite their nails or pick their cuticles may find these warts around their fingernails.
- **Genital warts.** Sexually transmitted, these pink, painful cauliflowerlike growths can appear on the genitals of men and women. Unlike other varieties of warts, these require prompt medical treatment. In

women, they may be a precursor of cervical cancer. Since laryngeal (voice box) warts can become malignant, a condom should always be used for oral sex.

Treatment options

For children, the best treatment, unless the wart spreads, is none; 20 percent of all cases clear up on their own within six months, and up to 67 percent disappear within two years. In adults, warts are more persistent. There are several treatment options:

- **Salicylic acid.** An over-the-counter topical preparation for common or plantar warts. Highly concentrated, it can cause serious burns, so protect surrounding skin with petroleum jelly before application.

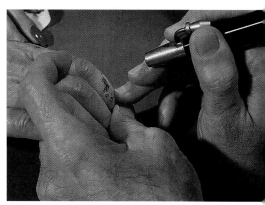

A dermatologist can use a laser to vaporize a wart. This method leaves little scarring.

- **Podophyllum.** This caustic prescription drug must be applied by a physician. It should never touch healthy tissue.
- **Cryotherapy.** Liquid nitrogen is used to freeze warts. This treatment may result in scarring or infection. Since HPV can survive in liquid-nitrogen solutions, make certain your doctor uses a fresh, individual, disposable nitrogen container for each patient and each treatment.
- **Surgical scraping.** This method removes the wart but carries the risk of scarring and pain, particularly for plantar warts.
- **Pulsed-dye laser.** Best therapy for persistent warts. Leaves minimal scarring.

If you are pregnant, nursing, or have diabetes or a vascular disease, check with your doctor before using salicylic acid.

CAUTION!

In rare instances warts may become malignant or may in fact be precancerous skin conditions. Bring any skin growth to your doctor's attention, particularly a wart that appears after age 45. Never attempt to self-treat a wart that is inflamed or bleeding.

Wood-Burning Stoves

The wood-burning stove has made a comeback. Again. When the black, cast-iron stove of days gone by was first revived in the 1960s, many models were inefficient and dangerous, leaking toxic fumes into the house and spewing soot into the sky. Today's wood-burning stoves are not only environmentally friendly and fuel-efficient but safe—as long as they're properly installed and operated.

The new generation of wood burners

The new models come in many designs and colors, and can be installed in just about any room in the house. They can even be set in fireplaces. But the most significant improvement is that they emit minimal air pollution.

A Canadian emission standard for solid-fuel-burning stoves, inserts, and low-burning-rate factory-built fireplaces was developed in 1992. Two technical innovations, catalytic smoke combustors and a catalyst-free design, led to a new generation of stoves. In addition to lowering air pollution, these stoves cut back on creosote, a by-product of incomplete combustion, which builds up in the flue and causes chimney fire.

Even more environmentally friendly are pellet stoves, which burn dried, compacted chips of waste wood. They create a clean and fuel-efficient form of heat and are popular in areas where pellet fuel is cheaper than wood.

The proper setup

Look for a stove certified by the Underwriters' Laboratory of Canada (ULC), then follow your local building code and the manufacturer's instructions. Connect the stove to a lined masonry chimney, built to local regulations, or a ULC-certified factory-built chimney. When installing the stove on a combustible floor, cover the area under the heater with a floor protector of noncombustible material at least 9.5 millimeters (mm) (⅜ inch (in.)) thick, or with sheet metal about 6.5 mm (¼ in.) thick. Extend the protector 46 centimeters (cm) (18 in.) at the front and 20 cm (8 in.) at the sides and rear. Uncertified stoves may need additional protection. To remove a stove that has asbestos insulation, hire an asbestos-removal expert.

A wood-burner needs a fresh supply of oxygen to let smoke drift up the chimney. In a new or airtight house, have the stove tested to ensure that enough fresh air is reaching it. Or buy a stove equipped with special ducts to draw air to the fire and exhaust fumes away.

an ounce of **Prevention**

A Safer Hearth and Home

- For the cleanest, safest burn, use dense hardwood cut a year before and allowed to dry out under cover. During the heating season, try to keep about a week's supply of firewood indoors to dry it further.

- Use a metal container with a tight-fitting lid for ash removal.

- At the start of each heating season, woodstove owners would be well advised to have the connections and flues inspected and, if required, cleaned by a professional chimney sweep.

- Keep any combustible materials at least 1.2 meters (4 feet) from the stove, and an unprotected stovepipe at least 45 cm (18 in.) from the ceiling or wall.

- Install smoke and carbon monoxide detectors. The latter will alert you to the presence of the invisible, odorless, and potentially lethal gas, created when combustion is incomplete.

Wood Preservatives

When exposed to the elements, wooden objects—sundecks, playground structures, and outdoor furniture—are no match for nature. If left unfinished, they can decay

Deck chairs treated with wood preservatives should be sealed with at least two coats of outdoor-grade polyurethane, epoxy, or shellac so that your skin will not come into contact with any of the preservative chemicals. Reseal every two years as necessary.

and rot within a few years. Commercially applied preservatives can greatly increase the life of some woods, but the chemicals in them may be toxic to people and the environment.

Fortifying wood

Wood has four natural enemies: the sun's ultraviolet (UV) rays, which change wood's color; rain, which makes wood warp and split; fungi, which discolor or decay wood; and insects, which dine on wood. Enter pressure-treated wood. Preservatives are forced into the wood under pressure, where they bond with wood fibers and protect against decay and insects.

Creosote and pentachlorophenol are used mainly in industrial applications. Chromated copper arsenate (CCA) is found in lumber sold in most Canadian home-improvement stores. Although CCA is considered to be safe, two of its ingredients, arsenic and chromium, are carcinogens. Repeated exposure, particularly in industrial situations, may cause liver and kidney failure, birth defects, or cancer.

In the United States, the Environmental Protection Agency (EPA) has ruled that wood

treated with CCA doesn't pose "unreasonable risks" to children or adults. (Health Canada, on the other hand, has issued no such ruling.) However, the EPA does require people who work with CCA regularly to wear protective clothing and respirators. Those who occasionally saw, sand, or drill CCA-treated wood would be wise also to wear a dust mask.

Safety measures

Excess chemicals on the surface of wood can be absorbed through the skin. To help prevent this, power wash the wood before using it and wear gloves when working with it. Chemicals can also be transferred to nearby soil. A U.S. study of playgrounds built with CCA-treated wood showed that the sites had much higher, although acceptable, levels of arsenic than the surrounding soils.

Brushing on wood preservatives yourself can also help extend the life of wood, whether it's pressure-treated or not. Choose one that contains a mildewcide, water repellent, and UV blocker, and reapply every few years. Longer-lasting exterior stains that contain a water repellent and mildewcide are also available.

an ounce of Prevention

Handling Pressure-Treated Wood

- Wear protective clothing, such as long pants and a long-sleeved shirt.

- Wear a mask and goggles if sawing, sanding, or drilling it.

- Use a sealant on pressure-treated wood, particularly if you've any concerns about exposure.

- Never use it to build countertops or bird and animal feeders that might touch human or animal food.

- Never burn it; the fumes and ashes are hazardous.

More than a century ago, the German physicist Wilhelm Roentgen discovered the X ray, and in the process revolutionized medicine. Today more than 260 million X rays are performed for medical purposes in North America annually. Although you might worry about reports linking X-ray exposure to cancer, most doctors say there is little to fear if proper precautions are taken.

Shedding light on X-ray radiation

An X ray is a form of electromagnetic radiation. When one is taken, a small amount of radiation passes through the body and is recorded on supersensitive film. Wherever the radiation is blocked—most often by bone— an image is produced on the film. This image can serve a multitude of purposes, from indicating the presence of pneumonia to determining whether metal pins are necessary to stabilize a bone fracture. With the help of a radiation-absorbing enema or injection, X rays can pinpoint a duodenal tumor or a mass of plaque blocking a carotid artery.

The amount of radiation needed for an X-ray image is very small. Indeed, advances over the past 50 years have reduced the average level of exposure by nearly 90 percent. In 1930, for example, a chest X ray yielded about 160 millirads (mrads) of radiation; today it averages less than 20 mrads. Experts say people can get as much as 5,000 mrads in a single dose without risk of adverse effects.

The problem, however, is that radiation exposure is cumulative, and medical X rays aren't the only source of radiation in our lives. You are exposed to an average of 360 mrads per year, most of it from the earth itself, the atmosphere, your own body, and even outer space. Only about 15 to 20 percent comes from man-made sources, including X rays and radioactive drugs used in nuclear medicine. Too much radiation can cause genetic changes in the cells of your body. This

A lead shield should cover parts of your body not involved in an X-ray test. The ovaries and testes are particularly susceptible to radiation damage.

could eventually lead to cancer. Keep a written record of all X-ray exposures, along with where the film is stored.

How to minimize exposure

Fortunately, most physicians are aware of radiation overexposure and won't subject patients to unnecessary tests. Still, talk to your doctor about other imaging options when possible. Computerized tomography (CT) scans and fluoroscopy both employ X rays, but ultrasound and magnetic resonance imaging (MRI) use nonionizing radiation, which cannot alter the chemistry of body tissues. Also, ask about the new digital X-ray systems that may expose you to less radiation because the tests are less likely to be repeated.

One of the most frequent uses of X rays is in dental care. Research indicates that if no problems are evident, youngsters may need just one dental X ray every one to two years; adults, just one every two to three years.

Although X rays should be used conservatively, it is important to put the radiation risk in perspective. Because the threat is relatively small, it is very likely to be outweighed by the health benefits you gain from any medical X rays your doctor or dentist recommends.

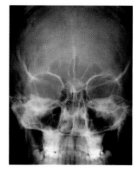

Skull X rays often help to diagnose fractures, congenital abnormalities, and tumors or other diseases that may affect the skull.

CAUTION!

If you are pregnant, avoid any unnecessary X rays, especially during the first trimester. If you do need one, tell the radiologist you are pregnant and make sure your abdomen is covered by a lead shield.

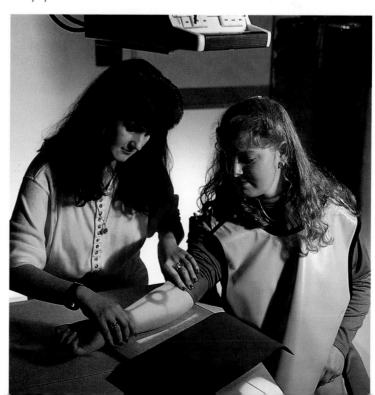

Yeast-Infection Treatments

Hardly a woman alive today is not aware of the troublesome symptoms of a vaginal yeast infection. For evidence, look no further than the $49 million spent each year in Canada on antifungal treatments used to treat vaginal yeast infections. About $27 million is spent on over-the-counter (OTC) treatments, while the remaining $22 million represents the size of the prescription market.

The beast behind yeast
Nearly all yeast infections are caused by a microorganism known as *Candida albicans.* Normally, this organism inhabits the healthy vagina in small numbers. However, owing to a variety of factors—stress, a weakened immune system, hormonal changes, or the use of some antibiotics—Candida can grow out of control, triggering a host of uncomfortable symptoms. These can include an itchy, red vaginal rash, vaginal discharge, pain during intercourse, and swelling.

The good news
You can deter chronic yeast infections by taking some preventive steps (see box, right). Even if you find yourself in the throes of a nasty infection, however, rest easy. Yeast infections are highly treatable. Most OTC medications generally used for these conditions are available in the form of creams, suppositories or ovules. They have been shown to be 85 to 95 percent effective in knocking out infections. To work, though, they must be used for the recommended times (usually from three to seven days) and dosages. If you don't like using OTC products, ask your doctor to prescribe oral fluconazole, available in a single-dose tablet and as effective as most other yeast therapies. Be aware this drug may cause side effects. A doctor will not prescribe it while a woman is pregnant or breastfeeding.

To self-treat or not?
Although OTC treatments are readily available, take caution before treating yourself without a doctor's supervision. Women who have suffered from yeast infections appreciate the convenience of OTC products. But self-treatment with these products can have its drawbacks. For example, if the problem is not a yeast infection, using these products may disrupt the natural vaginal environment, causing irritation and even masking a serious infection. Also, a yeast infection may be confused with more serious bacterial infections or sexually transmitted diseases, which can be aggravated by the use of yeast-infection treatments. For this reason, a first-time sufferer should consult a doctor before undertaking self-treatment. Moreover, if infection recurs, call a doctor before using an OTC treatment.

Repeated OTC treatment may cause resistance to the medication. If you are among the 10 percent of women with a yeast infection caused by a resistant species of the Candida organism, your doctor can prescribe some alternative therapies.

One last caution: Women should not treat infections with homemade douches. Most experts doubt their efficacy; use an approved antifungal treatment instead.

an ounce of **Prevention**

Keeping Yeast Infections at Bay
Deter yeast infections by taking the following measures:

- If you're taking antibiotics, eat yogurt with acidophilus bacteria.

- Avoid synthetic underwear; choose "breathable" cotton instead.

- When using the toilet, always wipe from front to back.

- Avoid dyed or perfumed toilet paper, soaps, and detergents.

- Avoid feminine-hygiene sprays.

- Yeast thrives in damp environments; dry the vaginal area thoroughly after bathing.

CAUTION!
Whether you're using an over-the-counter yeast-infection treatment or a prescription medication, you should seek medical attention immediately if you experience abdominal pain, fever, or a foul-smelling discharge; if your symptoms have not improved in three days; or if your symptoms recur within two months.

Yoga

Steeped in more than 5,000 years of tradi- tion, yoga is a way of life for true-blue followers—a discipline that promotes har- mony of body, mind, and spirit. But many who practice yoga today do so for more prac- tical reasons. Studies show that yoga may have a hand in strengthening the immune system and controlling blood pressure, heart rate, respiratory function, metabolic rate, body temperature, even brain waves. This stress-free, low-impact form of exercise also helps ease anxiety and promotes flexibility, it is even said to aid travelers overcome jet lag. It's no wonder that some 6 million North Ameri- cans use yoga as a conduit to good health.

The power of breathing
Utilizing a series of breathing exercises and postures, or asanas, yoga works to stretch, strengthen, and relax the body. What sepa- rates the practice of yoga from other exercises is not so much how you feel while you are performing yoga postures but how you feel afterward—relaxed and renewed. Indeed, relaxation is one of the main goals of a yoga workout. Because of its gentle approach, yoga is beneficial not only as a fitness program but also as a rehabilitation tool, helping the body recover from injury or illness.

The different types of yoga all rely on a form of slow, meditative breathing that works to relax the mind and body while deepening the stretch of a posture. Experts believe it is this deep breathing that is responsible for many of yoga's reported health benefits, such as reducing hypertension, increasing blood flow to the heart, aiding digestion, and foster- ing deep relaxation.

In addition, yoga's ability to increase flexi- bility without stressing the joints makes it an ideal exercise for those suffering from osteoarthritis. Indeed, a research study conducted at the Veterans Admin- istration Medical Center in Philadelphia found regular yoga practice extremely effective in the relief of pain associated with osteoarthritis of the hands.

Yoga is considered such a safe and effective form of exercise that many hospitals, nursing homes, rehabilitation centers, and wellness programs are not only endorsing the practice but offering classes as well. Learning yoga the right way has never been easier.

A posture a day
It's always wise to check with your doctor before starting any yoga or other exercise pro- gram. Moreover, if you are pregnant or have high blood pressure or glaucoma, tell your yoga instructor as well as consulting with your doctor; some yoga programs feature positions that you would be advised to avoid.

Yoga positions are quite safe, but there are various levels of difficulty, and starting too high up the ladder may cause you to become discouraged and keep you from reaping yoga's benefits. Yoga is not meant to be a competi- tive exercise; indeed, if the practice had a maxim, it would be, Go at your own pace.

Although many who practice yoga regu- larly begin with books or videos, most participants find some form of one-on-one instruction useful. In addition, there are

So-called power yoga uses a series of difficult yoga postures to promote strength and endurance.

357

Yoga

T'ai Chi: The Dance of Health

What can an ancient Chinese method of self-defense do to improve your health? When the method is t'ai chi ch'uan, the answer is, plenty. Although originally developed hundreds of years ago as a way for soldiers to overtake their opponents during battle, today t'ai chi is practiced as a disciplined form of no-impact exercise to strengthen muscles and joints, harmonize breathing, and improve circulation.

Like yoga, t'ai chi involves a number of postures and specific breathing techniques. Unlike yoga, the postures are done in succession, creating dancelike movements that, in the words of a Chinese philosopher, are "as smooth as pulling silk from a cocoon." It is, in fact, the fluidity of the t'ai chi moves, along with the breathing and balance techniques, that contribute to its ability to lower hypertension, reduce the risk of developing cardiovascular disease, alleviate back pain, stomach ulcers, and gastrointestinal problems, and help fight anxiety.

In addition, two studies published in the *Journal of the American Geriatrics Society* revealed that seniors over 70 who had done three months of t'ai chi were able to improve both their balance and their strength. Additional research from Emory University in Atlanta found that seniors over 70 who participated in regular sessions of t'ai chi reduced their risk of falling by more than 47 percent.

As with yoga, however, t'ai chi does require some professional training, so it's wise to start out taking a class with a qualified teacher. If done incorrectly, some of the movements used in t'ai chi can cause injury. When done correctly, however, and under proper guidance, this form of exercise is not only safe but stress-free.

different styles of yoga, some more vigorous than others. The newest form, a "western" version called power yoga, is, for example, best suited for athletes and distance runners looking to help prevent sports injuries. The more gentle hatha yoga is good for those just starting out or for people recuperating from an injury or illness. Classes are often filled with people at all levels; again, with yoga, the individual is there to challenge himself, not try to best his neighbor.

Always be sure that you practice the type of yoga that is most comfortable for you. Each yoga teacher conducts class in a slightly different manner. Some, for example, concentrate on meditation and breathing exercises in a softly lit room, while others use a well-lit gym and focus on physical movements. You should feel free to experiment with different classes to find the approach that suits you best. Remember that the goal of learning yoga is to leave class feeling a little healthier, more flexible, and more relaxed—not stressed, intimidated, or annoyed.

Inhale, exhale

The breathing exercises you practice in yoga are rooted in meditation techniques and can help even the most tightly wound fast-tracker relax. Be sure to concentrate your focus on the breath. Here's an easy breathing exercise, called Double Nasal Breathing, that you can do on your own in your home whenever you're feeling anxious or stressed.

- Using your thumb, press on your right nostril, blocking airflow.
- Breathe in through your left nostril. After inhaling, use the ring finger on your right hand to block this same nostril. Then release your thumb from the right nostril, and let air flow out.
- Inhale through the right nostril; block with the thumb, release the ring finger over the left nostril, and exhale. Repeat the process, from the beginning.
- Continue to alternate breathing on different sides of your nose, concentrating on each breath until you feel your body start to relax.

Yogurt

As nutritious as milk and possibly even more healthful, yogurt is what you get when "good" bacteria feast on fresh milk. These "live active cultures" digest some of the milk's sugar (lactose), converting it into lactic acid, which gives this "spoonable" dairy food a refreshing tang.

Yogurt is not only tasty; it's easily digested and calcium-rich (1 cup supplies a third or more of daily needs). It's a good source of protein, zinc, riboflavin, and vitamin B_{12}, and, if made with fortified milk, vitamins A and D. It's available in low-fat or fat-free varieties. What's more, there's evidence that yogurt with live active cultures may prevent intestinal ills and possibly even colon cancer.

For a nutritious snack, top off a cup of nonfat yogurt with a spoonful of granola and fresh fruit.

Yogurt Versus Yeast

Eating a cup a day of yogurt that contains live *L. acidophilus* cultures may help prevent vaginal yeast infections. In one study, a daily 1-cup serving over six months reduced recurrent yeast infections threefold. Acidophilus not only produces an environment that repels yeast, but also releases hydrogen peroxide, which halts the growth of other microorganisms.

Fit for a king

Yogurt's reputation as a health food is centuries old. In the 1500s the French king Francis I was relieved of intestinal ills when the sultan of Turkey's doctor arrived with a herd of milk-producing sheep—and a recipe for yogurt.

Yogurt, now made more often from cow's milk, is one dairy product that many people with lactose intolerance (who suffer bloating, cramps, and diarrhea from ingesting milk, ice cream, or cheese) can eat, since the bacteria reduce the lactose in the milk by as much as two-thirds.

Two cultures used to make yogurt, *L. bulgaricus* and *S. thermophilus,* die in the stomach. But *L. acidophilus,* also added to some yogurt, survives digestion and may offer definite health benefits. These "friendly" bacteria may help restore proper digestion during a course of antibiotics, helping to head off such gastrointestinal side effects as diarrhea.

There is even heartening evidence that live-culture acidophilus yogurt may help prevent colon cancer. In older men and women with atrophic gastritis, eating acidophilus yogurt inhibits enzymes that can promote colon cancer. In animals, it slows the growth of colon cancer cells. And at least one study found that eating yogurt daily boosts immunity.

The cultural elite

To do its work, though, yogurt may need more acidophilus than commercial brands supply. The yogurt used in some studies contains as much as 1 billion cultures per gram, but an American study found that seven popular brands had no more than 100,000 cultures per gram. Still, yogurt is nutritious, and if it contains live active cultures—look for this information on the label—including acidophilus, it may offer something more.

On the Horizon *Lactobacillus* GG (LGG), a strain of bacteria discovered in 1985 at Tufts University in the United States, treats diarrhea caused by certain viruses and antibiotics. It works against traveler's diarrhea, too. Unfortunately, yogurt made with LGG is currently available only in Finland.

Zinc, an essential mineral, is necessary at every stage of life. It helps children grow, adults function, and older folks stay well. Yet some people—particularly children, women, and the elderly—don't get enough zinc. As with many minerals, though, getting enough is healthy, and a varied and balanced diet usually provides all that we need; but too much can harm.

In the pink with zinc

The recommended nutrient intake (RNI) for zinc is 9 milligrams (mg) for adult women and 12 mg for adult men. We need it to make DNA, the basic genetic material of life, as well as more than 300 enzymes. Even mild zinc deficiency can adversely affect growth, appetite, night vision, and immune response.

Avoiding zinc deficiency may be particularly important as we age. In a study of 118 elderly people, those who took a 25-mg zinc supplement had more of certain immune-system cells and improved immune responses. A few studies also suggest that zinc may help prevent macular degeneration, the most common cause of blindness in people over age 65.

But if adequate zinc is important, too much can cause problems. Taking in just over the RNI—18 to 25 mg a day—may lower blood levels of copper; 50 mg a day may, over time, impair immunity. Larger amounts (50 to 75 mg) can reduce levels of "good" HDL cholesterol, increasing the risk of heart attack.

A reason to eat meat?

The richest sources of zinc are animal foods, such as red meats, organ meats, and eggs. We also assimilate zinc better from animal than from plant sources, absorbing about 25 percent of the zinc in beef, for example, but less than 5 percent from wheat bran.

Although many people limit animal foods in their diets for health reasons, zinc deficiency rarely results. A well-balanced diet, even a vegetarian one, contains more than enough absorbable zinc to meet daily recommended amounts. Eating eggs as well as small lean portions of meat a few times a week certainly won't threaten your health and will provide high levels of zinc. But the mineral is

Can Zinc Cure the Common Cold?

Well, no. But in 5 of 10 studies conducted on adults, zinc reduced cold symptoms. In one U.S. study, conducted in 1996, participants began sucking on lozenges within 24 hours of getting a cold. Those whose lozenges contained zinc got better about three days sooner than those who received a placebo. (Most of the people who took zinc lozenges disliked the taste, though, and about 20 percent experienced nausea.) If you want to try it, look for lozenges that contain zinc gluconate glycine (ZGG), which is absorbed through saliva. Stop when you feel better, or after a week. Pregnant women and anyone with liver or kidney disease should avoid using zinc for colds.

Moreover, it may not work in kids. A 1998 U.S. study of school-age children found that ZGG lozenges had no effect on cold symptoms. Researchers urge that more studies of zinc be performed, using subjects of all ages.

also found in lean turkey and in shellfish (six medium oysters provide 125 mg). Low-fat milk and dairy products also have some. Other sources include whole-grain breads, brown rice, wheat germ, beans, lentils, split peas, and spinach.

If your diet is still low in the mineral or if you are pregnant or breastfeeding, a supplement with 5 to 10 mg of zinc may provide insurance. Talk to your doctor first. A zinc supplement may be especially important if you are taking calcium supplements: One study found that a daily 600-mg calcium supplement taken before eating cut zinc absorption by 50 percent at a meal, but adding 8 mg of zinc to the diet offset the losses.

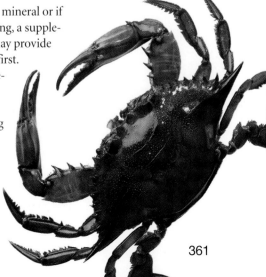

This crab, like all shellfish, is a good source of zinc. But he'll never catch up to the oyster, the zinc king.

Resource Guide

The following is a list of resources that will help you find out more about many of the topics covered in this book. Some offer information through the mail or over the telephone. If you have access to the Internet, you can log on to their Web sites for a wealth of instant information, including the latest developments.

Alternative Medicine

Acupuncture Foundation of Canada
2131 Lawrence Avenue E, Suite 204
Scarborough, ON M1R 5G4
Phone: (416) 752-3988
Fax: (416) 752-4398
http://www.afcinstitute.com
(offers referrals to physicians, dentists, and physiotherapists with AFC certification)

Canadian Association of Herbal Practitioners
#400 - 1228 Kensington Road NW
Calgary, AB T2N 4P9
Phone: (403) 270-0936
Fax: (403) 283-0799
(offers referrals to some 100 professional members)

Canadian Chiropractic Association
1396 Eglinton Avenue W
Toronto, ON M6C 2E4
Phone: (416) 781-5656
Fax: (416) 781-7344
http://www.inforamp.net/~ccachiro
(offers information on chiropractic, or chiropractic education)

Canadian Institute of Hypnotism
110 Greystone Street
Montreal, QC H9R 5T6
Phone: (514) 426-1010
Fax: (514) 426-4680
(provides information on hypnotism; offers national referrals)

Canadian Massage Therapists Alliance (CMTA)
365 Bloor Street E, Suite 1807
Toronto, ON M4W 3L4
Phone: (416) 968-2149
Fax: (416) 968-6818
http://www.collinscan.com/~collins/clientspgs/cmtai.html
(an alliance of the professional associations of massage therapy of Canada)

Reflexology Association of Canada
Box 110, 451 Turnberry Street
Brussels, ON N0G 1M0
Phone: (519) 887-9991
Fax: (519) 887-9792
(provides referrals to its certified reflexologists across Canada)

Animals

Canadian Society for the Prevention of Cruelty to Animals (SPCA)
5215 Jean-Talon Street W
Montreal, QC H4P 1X4
Phone: (514) 735-2711
Fax: (514) 735-7448
http://www.spca.com
(offers pet adoption, pet-care education, investigates complaints of animal abuse)

Consumer Information

Bureau of Microbial Hazards, Health Canada
Address Locator 2204A2,
Tunney's Pasture
Ottawa, ON K1A 0L2
Phone: (613) 957-2991
http://www.hc-sc.gc.ca/
(conducts research into bacterial, viral, and parasitic pathogens that occur in food; reports on foodborne disease outbreaks in Canada, investigates botulism outbreaks, etc.)

Bureau of Pharmaceutical Assessment, Health Canada
Address Locator 0202D1,
Tunney's Pasture
Ottawa, ON K1A 0L2
Phone: (613) 957-2991
http://www.hc-sc.gc.ca/
(reviews all drug submissions to ensure the drugs meet the requirement of the Food and Drugs Act and its Regulations)

Canada Mortgage and Housing Corporation (CMHC)
700 Montreal Road
Ottawa, ON K1A 0P7
Phone: (613) 748-2000
Fax: (613) 748-2098
http://www.cmhc.schl.gc.ca
(information on housing for homeowners, potential buyers, builders, people with special housing needs, or researchers)

Canadian Association of Retired Persons (CARP)
27 Queen Street E, Suite 1304
Toronto, ON M5C 2M6
Phone: (416) 363-8748
Fax: (416) 363-8747
http://www.fifty-plus.net
(protects and promotes the rights and quality of life of mature Canadians)

Canadian Institute of Child Health (CICH)
885 Meadowlands Drive, Suite 512
Ottawa, ON K2C 3N2
Phone: (613) 224-4144
Fax: (613) 224-4145
http://www.cich.ca

Chemical Health Hazard Assessment Division, Health Canada
Address Locator 2201B1, Tunney's Pasture
Ottawa, ON K1A 0L2
Phone: (613) 957-2991
http://www.hc-sc.gc.ca/
(provides information relating to food additives, food irradiation, food packaging; assesses risks associated with chemical contaminants in the food supply)

Eye2Eye
P.O. Box 27014
4190 Finch Avenue E
Toronto, ON M1S 5C2
Phone: 1-888-EYE2EYE
Fax: (416) 221-2585
http://www.eye2eye.com
(provides information about computer vision syndrome [CVS] prevention)

Health Promotion and Programs Branch, Health Canada

Jeanne Mance Building, room 1616A
Postal Locator 1916A, Tunney's Pasture
Ottawa, ON K1A 0K9
Phone: (613) 957-2991
http://www.hc-sc.gc.ca/
(provides national leadership to develop, promote, and support measures such as policy development and health research in order to preserve and promote the health and well-being of Canadians)

Health Protection Branch, Health Canada

Health Protection Building
Postal Locator 0701A1, Tunney's Pasture
Ottawa, ON K1A 0L5
Phone: (613) 957-2991
http://www.hc-sc.gc.ca/
(provides information about the quality and safety of food, the safety and effectiveness of drugs, cosmetics, medical devices, radiation-emitting devices and other consumer products)

Laboratory Centre for Disease Control, Health Canada

Tunney's Pasture
Ottawa, ON K1Z 8R1
Phone: (613) 725-3769
http://www.hwcweb.hwc.ca/hpb/lcdc/hp_eng.html
(national center for the identification, investigation, and prevention of human disease)

La Leche League Canada

P.O. Box 29
18C Industrial Drive
Chesterville, ON K0C 1H0
Phone: (613) 448-1842
(provides information on breast-feeding)

The Natural Health Products Division, Bureau of Pharmaceutical Assessment, Health Canada

Postal Locator 0202C, Tunney's Pasture
Ottawa, ON K1A 0L2
Phone: (613) 957-2991
http://www.hc-sc.gc.ca/
(evaluates submissions made by manufacturers wishing to market herbal drugs, homeopathic drugs, and other natural products)

Office of Food Biotechnology, Health Canada

Address Locator 2204A1, Tunney's Pasture
Ottawa, ON K1A 0L2
Phone: (613) 957-2991
http://www.hc-sc.gc.ca/
(provides information about the human health safety of novel foods)

Planned Parenthood Federation of Canada

1 Nicholas Street, Suite 430
Ottawa, ON K1N 7B7
Phone: (613) 241-4474
Fax: (613) 241-4474
http://www.ppfc.ca
(provides information and services relating to sexual and reproductive health)

Product Safety Bureau, Health Canada

Statistics Canada Main Building
Tunney's Pasture, 031B2
Ottawa, ON K1A 0K9
Phone: (613) 957-2991
http://www.hc-sc.gc.ca/
(provides information pertaining to mechanical, electrical, chemical, and flammable hazards of consumer products)

Transport Canada

330 Sparks Street
Ottawa, ON K1A 0N5
Phone: (613) 990-2309
Road Safety: 1-800-333-0371
Fax: (613) 954-4731
http://www.tc.gc.ca
(offers information on seat belts, air bags, antilock brakes, child-safety seats, vehicle defects and recalls)

Underwriters' Laboratories of Canada

7 Crouse Road
Scarborough, ON M1R 3A9
Phone: (416) 757-3611
Toll-free in Canada and U.S. 1-800-infoULC
Fax: (416) 757-9540
http://www.ulc.ca
(sets safety standards for such products as smoke detectors and life jackets; provides consumer information on safe product use)

Drugs, Smoking & Alcohol

Addiction Research Foundation

33 Russell Street
Toronto, ON M5S 2S1
Phone: (416) 595-6144
Fax: (416) 595-6601
http://www.arf.org
(provides information and resources on alcohol, tobacco, and other drugs)

Canadian Centre on Substance Abuse

75 Albert Street, Suite 300
Ottawa, ON K1P 5E7
Phone: (613) 235-4048
Fax: (613) 235-8101
http://www.ccsa.ca
(disseminates information on the nature and consequences of substance abuse)

Environmental Health

Canadian Centre for Occupational Health and Safety (CCOHS)

250 Main Street E
Hamilton, ON L8N 1H6
Phone: (905) 572-4400
Toll-free 1-800-263-8466
Fax: (905) 572-4500
http://www.ccohs.ca
(provides information on noise and hearing protection, and other workplace issues, as well as ways to prevent disease and injury)

Canadian Household Battery Association

885 Don Mills Road, Suite 301
Don Mills, ON M3C 1V9
Phone: (416) 535-6710
Fax: (416) 536-9892
(offers information on the environmental impact of batteries)

Environment Canada

Enquiry Centre 110 Wellington Street
Ottawa, ON K1A 0H3
Phone: 1-800-668-6767
Envirofax line: (819) 953-0966
http://www.ec.gc.ca
(provides information on pollutants, climate change, clean-air issues, and water quality)

Resource Guide (continued)

Rechargeable Battery Recycling in Canada (RBRC)
P.O. Box 236, Station E
Toronto, ON M6H 4E2
Phone: 1-800-8-BATTERY
Fax: (416) 510-8043
http://www.rbrc.com
(provides information about recycling used nickel cadmium rechargeable batteries)

Food and Nutrition

Canadian Food Inspection Agency (CFIA)
59 Camelot Drive
Nepean, ON K1A 0Y9
Phone: (613) 225-2342
http://www.cfia.acia.agr.ca
(information on food recalls, food safety tips, publications, and related sites)

Dietitians of Canada
480 University Avenue, Suite 604
Toronto, ON M5G 1V2
Phone: (416) 596-0857
Fax: (416) 596-0603
http://www.dietitians.ca

National Institute of Nutrition
265 Carling Avenue, Suite 302
Ottawa, ON K1S 2E1
Phone: (613) 235-3355
http://www.nin.ca
(offers publications and advice on diet, from fat guidelines to salt intake)

Nutrition Research Division, Health Canada
Address Locator 2203C, Tunney's Pasture
Ottawa, ON K1A 0L2
Phone: (613) 957-2991
http://www.hc-sc.gc.ca/
(provides information about nutritional safety, interactions, requirements)

Medical Organizations

The Arthritis Society
393 University Avenue, Suite 1700
Toronto, ON M5G 1E6
Phone: (416) 979-7228
Fax: (416) 979-8366
http://www.arthritis.ca

Canadian Breast Cancer Network
207 Bank Street, Suite 102
Ottawa, ON K2P 2N2
Phone: (613) 788-3311
(a support organization for people affected by breast cancer)

Canadian Cancer Society
10 Alcorn Avenue, Suite 200
Toronto, ON M4V 3B1
Phone: (416) 961-7223
Fax: (416) 961-4189
http://www.cancer.ca
(provides information about all aspects of cancer; Canadians can call a toll-free Cancer Information Service at 1-888-939-3333 from 9 a.m. to 6 p.m. Monday to Friday)

Canadian Dental Association
1815 Alta Vista Drive
Ottawa, ON K1G 3Y6
Phone: (613) 523-1770
Fax: (613) 523-7736
http://www.cda-adc.ca
(provides consumer information)

Canadian Diabetes Association
15 Toronto Street, Suite 800
Toronto, ON M5C 2E3
Phone: (416) 363-3373
or 1-800-BANTING
http://www.diabetes.ca

Canadian Lung Association
1900 City Park Drive, Suite 508
Blair Business Park
Gloucester, ON K1J 1A3
Phone: (613) 747-6776
Fax: (613) 747-7430
http://www.lung.ca

Canadian Medical Association
1867 Alta Vista Drive
Ottawa, ON K1G 3Y6
Phone: (613) 731-9331 or
1-800-267-9703
Fax: (613) 523-0937
http://www.cma.ca

Canadian Paediatric Society
2204 Walkley Road, Suite 100
Ottawa, ON K1G 4G8
Phone: (613) 526-9397
Fax: (613) 526-3332
http://www.cps.ca
(nutrition guidelines for infants)

Canadian Pharmacists Association
1785 Alta Vista Drive
Ottawa, ON K1G 3Y6
Phone: (613) 523-7877 or
1-800-917-9489
Fax: (613) 523-0445
http://www.cpha@cdnpharm.ca

Heart and Stroke Foundation of Canada
222 Queen Street, Suite 1402
Ottawa, ON K1P 5V9
Phone: (613) 569-4361
Fax: (613) 569-3278
http://www.hsf.ca
(provides information on the prevention and reduction of heart disease)

Migraine Association of Canada
365 Bloor Street E, Suite 1912
Toronto, ON M4W 3L4
Phone: (416) 920-4916
Fax: (416) 920-3677
http://www.migraine.ca
(provides up-to-date information and education to the general public)

Osteoporosis Society of Canada
33 Laird Drive
Toronto, ON M4G 3S9
Phone: (416) 696-2663
toll-free English line: 1-800-463-6842
toll-free French line: 1-800-977-1778
(provides medically accurate information to patients, health care professional and the public)

Mental Health

Canadian Mental Health Association
550 Sherbrooke Street W, Suite 310
Montreal, QC H3A 1B9
Phone: (514) 849-3291
http://www.icomm.ca/cmhacan
(provides referrals to therapists, clinics, or counseling services)

Index

Index

Index

Index

Index

H

Index

Index

Index

Acknowledgments & Credits

Contributors

New York Presbyterian Hospital–Cornell University Medical College

Louis Aronne, M.D.
Obesity Treatment

Marc Avram, M.D.
Dermatology

David Bank, M.D.
Pediatric Emergency Medicine

Parrin Barton, M.D.
Obstetrics/Gynecology

Ernst Bartsich, M.D.
Obstetrics/Gynecology

Paul Basuk, M.D.
Gastroenterology

David S. Becker, M.D.
Dermatology

David V. Becker, M.D.
Nuclear Medicine

David Behrman, D.M.D.
Oral Surgery

Sandra Belmont, M.D.
Ophthalmology

Gilbert Botvin, Ph.D.
Public Health

Jessica Davis, M.D.
Genetic Medicine

Joseph Deltito, M.D.
Psychiatry

Andrea Dmitruk-Ronning, R.D.
Food and Nutrition

Lewis Drusin, M.D.
Epidemiology

Teri Edersheim, M.D.
Obstetrics/Gynecology

Thomas Fahey III, M.D.
General Surgery

Neal Flomenbaum, M.D.
Emergency Medicine

Maura Frank, M.D.
Pediatrics

Farida Gadalla, M.D.
Anesthesiology

Bruce Gordon, M.D.
Lipid Metabolism

Robert Guida, M.D.
Otorhinolaryngology

Lloyd Hoffman, M.D.
Plastic Surgery

Jonathan Jacobs, M.D.
Department of Medicine

Elizabeth Leef Jacobson, M.D.
Allergy and Immunology

Jacqueline Jones, M.D.
Otorhinolaryngology

Craig Kent, M.D.
Vascular Surgery

Elisabeth Lachmann, M.D.
Rehabilitation Medicine

William Ledger, M.D.
Obstetrics/Gynecology

Barbara Levine, Ph.D.
Nutrition Information Center

Suzanne Levine, D.P.M.
Podiatry

Patricia McLaughlin, M.D.
Ophthalmology

Louise Merriman, R.D.
Food and Nutrition

Shari Midoneck, M.D.
Center for Women's Healthcare

Robert Millman, M.D.
Psychiatry

Margaret Moline, Ph.D.
Sleep Disorders

Willibald Nagler, M.D.
Rehabilitation Medicine

Dattatreyuda Nori, M.D.
Radiation Oncology

Mary Louise Patterson, M.D.
Pediatrics

Margaret Polaneczky, M.D.
Obstetrics/Gynecology

Dix Poppas, M.D.
Pediatric Urology and
Reconstructive Surgery

Marcus Reidenberg, M.D.
Clinical Pharmacology

Richard Rivlin, M.D.
Nutrition

Calvin Roberts, M.D.
Ophthalmology

Ruth Rosenblatt, M.D.
Mammography

Isadore Rosenfeld, M.D.
Cardiology

Elaine Rosenthal, R.D.
Food and Nutrition

Howard Rosner, M.D.
Anesthesiology

Gail Saltz, M.D.
Psychiatry

Abraham Sanders, M.D.
Pulmonary Medicine

John Savarese, M.D.
Anesthesiology

Stephen Scheidt
Cardiology

Shain Schley, M.D.
Otorhinolaryngology

Rachelle Scott, M.D.
Dermatology

Theodore Shapiro, M.D.
Psychiatry

Gillian Shepherd, M.D.
Allergy and Immunology

Susan Teeger, M.D.
Abdominal Imaging, Radiology

David Valacer, M.D.
Allergy/Immunology/Pulmonary
Medicine

Roger Yurt, M.D.
Burn Center

Hospital for Special Surgery

Steven Haas, M.D.
Orthopedic Surgery

Deborah Saint-Phard, M.D.
Sports and Spine Medicine

Russell Windsor, M.D.
Orthopedic Surgery

Rogosin Institute

Stuart Saal, M.D.
Nephrology

Cornell University

Charlotte W. Coffman
Department of Textiles and Apparel
College of Human Ecology

Joseph Laquatra, Ph.D.
Associate Professor, Department of
Design and Environmental Analysis

Ann T. Lemley, Ph.D.
Water and Household Chemical
Specialist, Cornell Cooperative
Extension

Larry Thompson, D.V.M & Ph.D.
Toxicology, College of Veterinary
Medicine

New York Blood Center

Celso Bianco, M.D.
Vice President for Medical Affairs

Other Consultants

James F. Astarita, M.S.,
D.A.B.M.P
Medical physicist

Mark Blumenthal
Founder and Executive Director,
American Botanical Council
Adjuct Associate Professor of
Medicinal Chemistry,
College of Pharmacy,
University of Texas at Austin

Robert H. Brown, M.D.
Ophthalmology

Finis L. Cavender, Ph.D.
Information Ventures, Inc.
Toxicology

Linda Cook, Ph.D.
Cancer Epidemiology
Department of Community Health
Sciences, University of Calgary

Edward M. Croom, Jr., Ph.D.
National Center for the
Development of Natural
Products School of Pharmacy,
University of Mississippi

**Stanley Darrow, D.D.S., F.A.C.D.,
F.A.G.D.**
General Dentistry

Ralph K. Della Ratta, M.D.
Winthrop University Hospital

Suzanne E. Farkas, L.Ac.
Acupuncture

Arthur W. Feinberg, M.D.
Chief, Geriatric Medicine,
North Shore University Hospital
Professor of Clinical Medicine,
New York University School of
Medicine

Timothy Ford, D.P.M.
American Podiatric Medical
Association

Charles M. Jacobson
Labeling, Consumer Products

Arielle N. B. Kauvar, M.D.
Associate Director, Laser & Skin
Surgery Center of New York
Clinical Assistant Professor of
Dermatology, New York University
Medical Center

Zafar Khan, M.D.
Beth Israel Medical Center
Adjunct Clinical Professor of
Urology, Cornell College of
Medicine

Jacqueline A. MacDonald
Associate Director, Water Science
Technology Board
National Research Council

Gregory May, Ph.D.
Plant Molecular Biology

Lilia Mead, L.M.T.
Certified Jivamukti Yoga Instructor

Marion Nestle, Ph.D., M.P.H.
Department of Nutrition and Food
Studies, New York University

Laura Norman, M.S.
Nationally Certified Reflexologist
Director of Laura Norman
Reflexology Treatment and
Training Center

Robert M. Otto, Ph.D.
Professor and Director, Human
Performance Laboratory
Adelphi University

Michael L. Reed, M.D.
Assistant Professor of Clinical
Dermatology, New York University
Medical Center

Joseph Schwarcz, Ph.D.
Professor, chemistry

Dorothy Singer, Ed.D.
Codirector, Yale University
Family Television Research and
Consultation Center

R. L. Slaughter, D.C.
Executive Director, National Association of Chiropractic Medicine

Stanley H. Smith, Ph.D.
Electronics

**With special thanks to the
following organizations**

Addiction and Mental Health
  Services Corporation
Agriculture and Agri-Food Canada
Canada Mortgage and Housing
  Corporation
Canadian Cancer Society
Canadian Food Inspection Agency
Canadian Medical Association
Dietitians of Canada
Environment Canada
Health Canada
Transport Canada
Underwriters' Laboratories
  of Canada

Illustrations

Phil Bliss 10, 12, 28, 41, 69, 90, 130, 147, 170, 193, 209, 250, 266, 300, 315
John Fraser 77
Charlene Rendeiro 4, 35, 45, 117, 127, 133, 175, 184, 185, 194, 227, 271, 279, 310

Photographs

Cover *top left* PhotoDisc; *top right* PhotoDisc; *middle left* FoodPix; *middle right* Comstock; *bottom left* PhotoDisc; *bottom right* PhotoDisc **Back Cover** Index Stock **1** *top* David Woods/Stock Market **1** *left* Rosenfeld Images/Stock Market **1** *bottom* Nicholas Eveleigh **3** Steven Needham/Envision **4** *left* Peter Cade/Tony Stone **4** *bottom* Nicholas Eveleigh **5** *top* Nicholas Eveleigh **5** *left* Uniphoto **5** *bottom* Nicholas Eveleigh **6** PhotoDisc **7** Kindra Clinefxf/Tony Stone **8** Jurgen Reisch/Tony Stone **9** Bruce Ayres/Tony Stone **11** Donald Johnston/Tony Stone **13, 14** Nicholas Eveleigh **15** Bruce Ayres/Tony Stone **16** Renee Lynn/Photo Researchers **18** Steven Needham/Envision **19** Nicholas Eveleigh **20** Saturn Stills/SPL/Photo Researchers **21** Kaluzny/Thatcher/Tony Stone **22** T.J. Florian/ Rainbow **24** Nicholas Eveleigh **25** *left* Kari Lounatmaa/SPL/Photo Researchers **25** *right* Phil Degginger/Tony Stone **26** Josh Pulman/Tony Stone **27** Colin Cooke **29** *top* Virginia Weinland/Photo Researchers **29** *bottom* Ron Kimball Photography **30** Rick Graves/Tony Stone **31** *all* Steven Needham/Envision

32 David Bishop/Envision **33** PhotoDisc **34** *top* Andy Ploski **34** *bottom* Nicholas Eveleigh **36** Merritt Vincent/PhotoEdit **37** *left* Bob Daemmrich/Image Works **37** *right* Andy Ploski **38** Steve Taylor/Tony Stone **39** Ebby May/Tony Stone **40** PhotoDisc **42** James Levin **44, 45** James Levin **46** Phil Jude/SPL/ Photo Researchers **47** Zigy Kaluzny/Tony Stone **48** Yoav Levy/Phototake **49** Jeff Zaruba/Tony Stone **50** Tony Freeman/PhotoEdit **51** *top* Institut Pasteur/CNRI/Phototake **51** *bottom* Chris Bjornberg/Photo Researchers **52** Rick Rusing/Tony Stone **53** Joe Sohn/Image Works **55** Pellegrini/International Stock **56** Steven Needham/Envision **57** Charles Thatcher/Tony Stone **58** Scott Camazine/Photo Researchers **59** *top* Stephen Dalton/Photo Researchers **59** *bottom* Richard T. Nowitz/Phototake **60** James Marshall/ Image Works **61** Don Mason/Stock Market **62** Charles Thatcher/Tony Stone **63** Ed Eckstein/Phototake **64** Sonda Dawes/Image Works **65** Index Stock **66** Chris Harvey/Tony Stone **67** SIU/Photo Researchers **68** *top* Steven Needham/Envision **68** *bottom* Esbin/Anderson/Omni Photo **70** Phillip Hayson/ Photo Researchers **71** *all* Andrew Syred/Tony Stone **72** Nicholas Eveleigh **73** Ken Karp/Omni Photo **74** Nicholas Eveleigh **75** Bruce Herman/Tony Stone **76** Martin Dohrn **78** *top* Mednet/Phototake **78** *bottom* Art Stein/Science Source/Photo Researchers **79** Debra P. Hershkowitz/Bruce Coleman **80** Nicholas Eveleigh **81** Steven Needham/Envision **82** Michael Pohuski/Envision **84** Bill Aron/PhotoEdit **85** Paul Gerda/Leo de Wys **86** Vincent Oliver/Tony Stone **87** International Stock **88** Uniphoto **89** *all* Yoav Levy/Phototake **91** Will & Deni McIntyre/Photo Researchers **92** Zigy Kaluzny/Tony Stone **93** T.J. Flo-

Acknowledgments & Credits (continued)

rian/Rainbow **94** Steve Prezant/Stock Market **95** Scott Camazine/Photo Researchers **96** *left* Yoav Levy/Phototake **96** *right* Scott Camazine/Photo Researchers **97** Douglas Mason/Woodfin Camp **98** Nicholas Eveleigh **99** PhotoDisc **100** Hank Morgan/Rainbow **101** *all* American Society for Aesthetic Plastic Surgery **102** Andrew Popper/Phototake **104** *top* James Darell/Tony Stone **104** *bottom* Ted Morrison/Still Life Stock **105** Ted Morrison/Still Life Stock **106** Bruce Ayres/Tony Stone **107** Index Stock **108** Peter Cade/Tony Stone **109** *top* Bob Thomas/Tony Stone **109** *bottom* R Maisonneuve/Publiphoto/Photo Researchers **110** PhotoDisc **111** Dr Norman Cranin, Dept of Oral & Dental Surgery, Brookdale University Hospital, Brooklyn, NY **112** Yoav Levy/Phototake **113** *top* Nicholas Eveleigh, *left* Colin Cooke, *right* Colin Cooke **114-115** Nicholas Eveleigh **116** Michael Newman/PhotoEdit **118** Michael Keller/Stock Market **119** Michael Newman/PhotoEdit **120** Nicholas Eveleigh **122** Laurence Dutton/Tony Stone **123** Michael Newman/PhotoEdit **124** Andrew Syed/Tony Stone **125** *top* Jim Corwin/Tony Stone **125** *bottom* Rosanne Olson/Tony Stone **126** CC Studio/SPL/Photo Researchers **127** Michael Newman/PhotoEdit **128** Diana Miller/Tony Stone **129** Steven Needham/Envision **131** Henley & Savage/Stock Market **132** Deep Light Productions/SPL/Photo Researchers **134** PhotoDisc **135** Sanders Nicolson/Tony Stone **136** *left* Steven Needham/Envision **136** *right* David Young-Wolff/PhotoEdit **137** Jurgen Reisch/Tony Stone **138** SIU/Visuals Unlimited **139** James Housel/Tony Stone **140** *left* Nicholas Eveleigh **140-1** *center* Osentoski & Zoda/Envision **142-4** Nicholas Eveleigh **145** Jean Higgins/Envision **146** Steven Needham/Envision **147** Yoav Levy/Phototake **148** Martine Mouchy/Tony Stone **149** Charles D. Winters/Photo Researchers **150** Steve Allen/Image Bank **151** Dan Gair/Gamma-Liaison **152** Nicholas Eveleigh **153** David Sams/Tony Stone **154** Joe Towers/Stock Market **155** Jeff Greenberg/Omni Photo **156** Nicholas Eveleigh **157** Index Stock **158** John Blaustein/Woodfin Camp **159** Chris Everard/Tony Stone **160** Steven Needham/Envision **161** Christel Rosenfeld/Tony Stone **162** *left* Colin Cooke **162** *right* PhotoDisc **163** Steven Needham/Envision **164** Jonathan Selig/Tony Stone **165** Index Stock **166** Bruce Ayres/Tony Stone **167** John Kuczala/Still Life Stock **168** Fernand Ivaldi/Tony Stone **171** Jeremy Walker/Tony Stone **172** Nicholas Eveleigh **173** David Henstock/Tony Stone **174** Jerome Tisne/Tony Stone **176** *right* David Young-Wolff/PhotoEdit **177** *all* Courtesy of Medical Hair Restoration ©1998 **178** Ted Morrison/Still Life Stock **179** *top* Courtesy of Broan Manufacturing Co., Inc., Hartford, WI **179** *bottom* Steve Wisbauer/Still Life Stock **180** Nicholas Eveleigh **181** Kevin Anderson/Tony Stone **182** Donna Day/Tony Stone **183** George Mattei/Envision **186** Richard Hutchings/Photo Researchers **187** Index Stock **188** Jeff Greenberg/Omni Photo **189** S.J Allen/International Stock **190** Yoav Levy/Phototake **191** Yoav Levy/Phototake **192** Nicholas Eveleigh **195** *top* PhotoDisc **195** *bottom* Charles Thatcher/Tony Stone **196** Jonathan Nourok/PhotoEdit **197** David Stewart/Tony Stone **198** Nicholas Eveleigh **199** Steve Strickland/Visuals Unlimited **200** Nicholas Eveleigh **201** PhotoDisc **203** Jon Feingersh/Stock Market **204** *top* First Alert **204** *bottom* Michael Keller/Stock Market **205** Tony Freeman/PhotoEdit **206** Nicholas Eveleigh **207** Phil Starling **208** John Millar/Tony Stone **210** *top* Robert Brons/BPS/Tony Stone **210** *bottom* Grace Davies/Omni Photo **211** Bruce Forster/Tony Stone **212** *left* Steven Needham/Envision **212** *right* Agence Top/Envision **213** *top* PhotoDisc **214** *top* PhotoDisc **214** *bottom* Ted Morrison/Still Life Stock **215** *top* Ted Morrison/Still Life Stock **215** *bottom* PhotoDisc **216** Mark Godfrey/Image Works **217** Rich LaSalle/Tony Stone **218** Chuck O'Rear/Woodfin Camp **219** Michael Newman/ PhotoEdit **221** Tony Freeman/PhotoEdit **222** Nicholas Eveleigh **223** Rick Stiller/Gamma-Liaison **224** Nicholas Eveleigh **225** *top* Courtesy of Magnetherapy, Inc./Tectonic Magnets **225** *bottom* Berg Alistair/Spooner/Gamma-Liaison **226** Will & Deni McIntyre/Photo Researchers **228** Nicholas Eveleigh

229 Vaughan Fleming/SPL/Photo Researchers **230** Rick Rusing/Tony Stone **231** Bruce Ayres/Tony Stone **232** Rita Maas/Image Bank **233** Steven Needham/Envision **234** Claudia Kunin/Tony Stone **235** Bruce Ayres/Tony Stone **236** Nicholas Eveleigh **238** Microfield Scientific Ltd./SPL/Photo Researchers **239** Nicholas Eveleigh **240** Uniphoto **241** Dan McCoy/Rainbow **242** *top* Yoav Levy/Phototake **242** *bottom* Will & Deni McIntyre/Photo Researchers **243** Charlie Westerman/Gamma-Liaison **244** Chris Shinn/Tony Stone **245** Howard Dratch/Image Works **246** Grace Davies/Omni Photo **247** *left* Chuck Szymanski/International Stock **247** *right* Steve Wisbauer/Still Life Stock **248** Felicia Martinez/PhotoEdit **249** D. Wells/Image Works **250** Nicholas Eveleigh **251** McCormick/Stock Market **252** Bob Schatz/Gamma-Liaison **253** Nicholas Eveleigh **255** Rosenfeld Images/Stock Market **256** Nicholas Eveleigh **257** Sepp Seitz/Woodfin Camp **258** Ted Morrison/Still Life Stock **259** *left* SPL/Photo Researchers **259** *right* Spike Walker/Tony Stone **260** Jose Carrillo/PhotoEdit **261** *top* Tony Freeman/PhotoEdit **261** *bottom* PhotoDisc **262** GK & Vikki Hart/Image Bank **263** Pat Rogers/Leo de Wys **264** PhotoDisc **265** Jacques Menasche/Woodfin Camp **267** Nicholas Eveleigh **268** *left* PhotoDisc **268** *right* S. Lowry/University of Ulster/Tony Stone **269** Gary John Norman/Tony Stone **270** P Wysocki/Explorer/Photo Researchers **272** Maratea/International Stock **274** Dept of Clinical Radiology, Salisbury District Hospital/SPL/Photo Researchers **275** Giancarlo de Bellis/Omni Photo **276** Matt Meadows/Peter Arnold **277** Dion Ogust/Image Works **278** *top* Mark Richards/PhotoEdit **278** *bottom* Kenneth Chen/Envision **280** Michael Newman/PhotoEdit **281** Nick Vedros/Gamma-Liaison **282** Nicholas Eveleigh **283** Gary Holscher/Tony Stone **284** Lori Adamski Peek/Tony Stone **285** Kenneth Chen/Envision **286** Kenneth Chen/Envision **287** David Woods/Stock Market **288** George Mattei/Envision **289** David Schultz/Tony Stone **290** David Young-Wolff/PhotoEdit **291** David Young-Wolff/Tony Stone **292** Ebby May/Tony Stone **293** Regine M./Image Bank **294** *top* Davies + Starr/Gamma-Liaison **294** *bottom* Katrina de Leon/Still Life Stock **295** Dennis O'Clair/Tony Stone **296** Gio Barto/Image Bank **297** Nicholas Eveleigh **298** James Darell/Tony Stone **299** *left* Dennis Gottlieb/Stock Market **299** *right* David Neele/Tony Stone **301** *left* Nicholas Eveleigh **301** *right* Ted Morrison/Still Life Stock **302** Jay Hostetler/Still Life Stock **303** *left* Nicholas Eveleigh **303** *right* Victoria Pearson/Tony Stone **304** Nicholas Eveleigh **305** Donald Johnston/Tony Stone **306** Zephyr Images **307** Aldo Torelli/Tony Stone **308** Aaron Strong/Tony Stone **309** Amwell/Tony Stone **311** *top* Bob Winsett/Index Stock **311** *bottom* Michael Newman/PhotoEdit **312** PhotoDisc **313** Steven Weinberg/Tony Stone **316** Steven Needham/Envision **317** Nicholas Eveleigh **319** Peter Cade/Tony Stone **320** Pascal Crapet/Tony Stone **322** John Henley/Stock Market **323** Penny Gentieuz/Tony Stone **325** Index Stock **326** Nicholas Eveleigh **327** Donna Day/Tony Stone **328** Nicholas Eveleigh **329** Michael Newman/PhotoEdit **330** Nicholas Eveleigh **331** Shaun Egan/Tony Stone **332** Donna Day/Tony Stone **334** Roy McMahon/Stock Market **336** *left* Nicholas Eveleigh **336** *right* Ted Morrison/Still Life Stock **338** Matt Meadows/SPL/Photo Researchers **339** Bruce Ayres/Tony Stone **340** Damien Lovegrove/SPL/Photo Researchers **341** The Eureka Company **343** Comnet/Leo de Wys **344** *left* Michael Newman/PhotoEdit **344** *right* Comnet/Leo de Wys **345** Steven Needham/Envision **346** Philip Salaverry/Tony Stone **347** Index Stock **348** Nicholas Eveleigh **349** Rudy Muller/Envision **350** Nicholas Eveleigh **352** *left* Nicholas Eveleigh **352** *right* Russell Curtis/Photo Researchers **353** Abarno/Stock Market **354** Annabelle Breakey/Tony Stone **355** *top* Dept of Clinical Radiology Salisbury District Hospital/SPL/Photo Researchers **355** *bottom* Will & Deni McIntyre/Photo Researchers **357** Robert Randall/International Stock **358** Sally Gall/Gamma-Liaison **360** Dan Templeton/Still Life Stock **361** *left* Nicholas Eveleigh **361** *right* Steven Needham/Envision

Picture Research: Carousel Research, Inc., New York